D0079643

Effect Size (Between-Subjects Design)

$$R^2 = \eta^2 = \frac{SS_{BG}}{SS_T}$$ (Eta-squared estimate for proportion

of variance)

$$\omega^2 = \frac{SS_{BG} - df_{BG}(MS_E)}{SS_T + MS_E}$$ (Omega-squared estimate for proportion of variance)

ONE-WAY WITHIN-SUBJECTS ANALYSIS OF VARIANCE (CHAPTER 11)

Within-Subjects Design

$$F_{obt} = \frac{MS_{BG}}{MS_E}$$ (Test statistic for the one-way within-subjects ANOVA)

Effect Size (Within-Subjects Design)

$$\eta_P^2 = \frac{SS_{BG}}{SS_T - SS_{BP}}$$ (Partial eta-squared for proportion of variance)

$$\omega_P^2 = \frac{SS_{BG} - df_{BG}(MS_E)}{(SS_T - SS_{BP}) + MS_E}$$ (Partial omega-squared for proportion of variance)

TWO FACTOR ANALYSIS OF VARIANCE (CHAPTER 12)

$$F_A = \frac{MS_A}{MS_E}$$ (Test statistic for the main effect on factor A)

$$F_B = \frac{MS_B}{MS_E}$$ (Test statistic for the main effect on factor B)

$$F_{A \times B} = \frac{MS_{A \times B}}{MS_E}$$ (Test statistic for the A × B interaction)

CORRELATION AND REGRESSION (CHAPTER 13)

Correlation Coefficient

$$r = \frac{SS_{XY}}{\sqrt{SS_X SS_Y}}$$ (Pearson correlation coefficient)

Analysis of Regression With One Predictor Variable

$$F_{obt} = \frac{MS_{regression}}{MS_{residual}}$$ (Test statistic for analysis of regression)

CHI-SQUARE TESTS (CHAPTER 14)

Chi-Square Tests

$$\chi_{obt}^2 = \Sigma \frac{(f_o - f_e)^2}{f_e}$$ (Test statistic for the chi-square goodness-of-fit and the chi-square test for independence)

Effect Size (Test for Independence)

$$V = \sqrt{\frac{\chi^2}{n \times df_{smaller}}}$$ (Cramer's V effect size)

Maximize your study time.
Get a better grade.
SAGE edge online tools *help you do both!*

edge.sagepub.com/priviteraess2e

 Get more out of your study time and accomplish your coursework goals with these free, easy-to-use **SAGE edge** study tools, featuring:

- **SPSS® in Focus Screencasts** that accompany relevant sections from the book and show you how to use SPSS® step-by-step

- **eFlashcards** and **eQuizzes** for anywhere, anytime studying

- **Exclusive access to influential SAGE journal content** tying important research to chapter concepts to strengthen learning

ESSENTIAL STATISTICS FOR THE BEHAVIORAL SCIENCES
SECOND EDITION

● ● ● Employing the hallmark pedagogical support of his successful comprehensive text, award-winning author, teacher, and advisor Gregory J. Privitera offers this updated, brief, and engaging introduction to the field. Students will welcome Privitera's clear instruction, conversational voice, and application of statistics to current, real-life research problems.

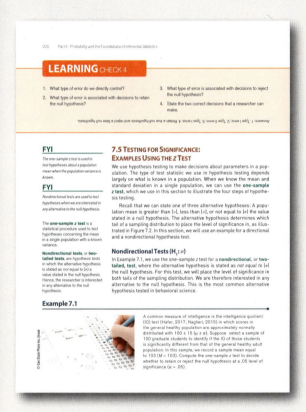

Real-world examples make statistics relevant for students.

"Most impressive is [the book's] relevance to the current state of the field (e.g., introduction to multiple regression)."

–Alexander O. Crenshaw, *University of Utah*

● ● ●

A FOCUS ON CLARITY

SPSS® in Focus sections provide step-by-step, classroom-tested instruction using practical research examples of how chapter concepts can be applied using SPSS®.

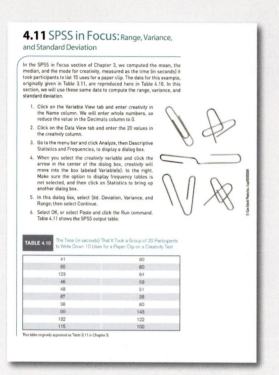

4.11 SPSS in Focus: Range, Variance, and Standard Deviation

In the SPSS in Focus section of Chapter 3, we computed the mean, the median, and the mode for creativity, measured as the time (in seconds) it took participants to list 10 uses for a paper clip. The data for this example, originally given in Table 3.11, are reproduced here in Table 4.10. In this section, we will use these same data to compute the range, variance, and standard deviation.

1. Click on the Variable View tab and enter *creativity* in the Name column. We will enter whole numbers, so reduce the value in the Decimals column to 0.

2. Click on the Data View tab and enter the 20 values in the *creativity* column.

3. Go to the menu bar and click Analyze, then Descriptive Statistics and Frequencies, to display a dialog box.

4. When you select the *creativity* variable and click the arrow in the center of the dialog box, *creativity* will move into the box labeled Variable(s): to the right. Make sure the option to display frequency tables is not selected, and then click on Statistics to bring up another dialog box.

5. In this dialog box, select Std. Deviation, Variance, and Range; then select Continue.

6. Select OK, or select Paste and click the Run command. Table 4.11 shows the SPSS output table.

TABLE 4.10 The Time (in seconds) That It Took a Group of 20 Participants to Write Down 10 Uses for a Paper Clip on a Creativity Test

41	80
65	80
123	64
46	59
48	51
87	36
38	80
90	143
192	122
115	100

This table originally appeared as Table 3.11 in Chapter 3.

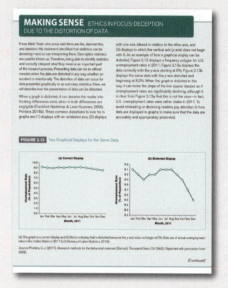

MAKING SENSE ETHICS IN FOCUS: DECEPTION DUE TO THE DISTORTION OF DATA

It was Mark Twain who once said there are lies, damned lies, and statistics. His statement identified that statistics can be deceiving—and so can interpreting them. Descriptive statistics are used to inform us. Therefore, being able to identify statistics and correctly interpret what they mean is an important part of the research process. Presenting data can be an ethical concern when the data are distorted in any way, whether on accident or intentionally. The distortion of data can occur for data presented graphically or as summary statistics. Here, we will describe how the presentation of data can be distorted.

When a graph is distorted, it can deceive the reader into thinking differences exist, when in truth differences are negligible (Frankfort-Nachmias & Leon-Guerrero, 2006; Privitera 2018b). Three common distortions to look for in graphs are (1) displays with an unlabeled axis, (2) displays

with one axis altered in relation to the other axis, and (3) displays in which the vertical axis (y-axis) does not begin with 0. As an example of how a graphical display can be distorted, Figure 2.13 displays a frequency polygon for U.S. unemployment rates in 2011. Figure 2.13a displays the data correctly with the y-axis starting at 0%; Figure 2.13b displays the same data with the y-axis distorted and beginning at 8.2%. When the graph is distorted in this way, it can make the slope of the line appear steeper as if unemployment rates are significantly declining, although it is clear from Figure 2.13a that this is not the case—in fact, U.S. unemployment rates were rather stable in 2011. To avoid misleading or deceiving readers, pay attention to how data are displayed in graphs to make sure that the data are accurately and appropriately presented.

FIGURE 2.13 Two Graphical Displays for the Same Data

(a) This graph is a correct display and (b) this is a display that is distorted because the y-axis does not begin at 0%. Data are of actual unemployment rates in the United States in 2011 (U.S. Bureau of Labor Statistics, 2015).

Source: Privitera, G.J. (2017). Research methods for the behavioral sciences (2nd ed.). Thousand Oaks, CA: SAGE. Reprinted with permission from SAGE.

(Continued)

Making Sense sections break down the statistical concepts students typically find most challenging, review important material, and help students make sense of it.

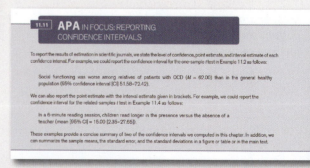

Research in Focus sections provide context by reviewing pertinent, current research that clarifies or illustrates important statistical concepts discussed in the chapter.

1.6 RESEARCH IN FOCUS: EVALUATING DATA AND SCALES OF MEASUREMENT

While qualitative variables are often measured in behavioral research, this book will focus largely on quantitative variables. The reason is twofold: (1) Quantitative measures are more common in behavioral research, and (2) most statistical tests taught in this book are adapted for quantitative measures. Indeed, many researchers who measure qualitative variables will also measure those that are quantitative in the same study.

For example, Jones, Blackey, Fitzgibbon, and Chew (2010) explored the costs and benefits of social networking among college students. The researchers used a qualitative method to interview each student in their sample. In the interview, students could respond openly to questions asked during the interview. These researchers then summarized responses into categories related to learning, studying, and social life. For example, the following student response was categorized as an example of independent learning experience for employability: "I think it [social software] can be beneficial ... in the real working environment" (Jones et al., 2010, p.780).

The limitation for this analysis is that categories are on a nominal scale (the least informative scale). So many researchers who record qualitative data also use some quantitative measures. For example, researchers in this study also asked students to rate their usage of a variety of social software technologies, such as PowerPoint and personal websites, on a scale from 1 (never)

11.11 APA IN FOCUS: REPORTING CONFIDENCE INTERVALS

To report the results of estimation in scientific journals, we state the level of confidence, point estimate, and interval estimate of each confidence interval. For example, we could report the confidence interval for the one-sample t test in Example 11.2 as follows:

Social functioning was worse among relatives of patients with OCD (M = 62.00) than in the general healthy population (95% confidence interval [CI] 51.58–72.42).

We can also report the point estimate with the interval estimate given in brackets. For example, we could report the confidence interval for the related-samples t test in Example 11.4 as follows:

In a 6-minute reading session, children read longer in the presence versus the absence of a teacher (mean [95% CI] = 15.00 [2.35–27.65]).

These examples provide a concise summary of two of the confidence intervals we computed in this chapter. In addition, we can summarize the sample means, the standard error, and the standard deviations in a figure or table or in the main text.

APA in Focus sections explain how to summarize statistical results for each inferential statistic taught and how to read and report statistical results in research journals that follow APA style.

A FOCUS ON PEDAGOGY AND PRACTICE

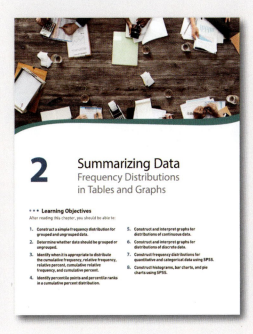

Updated Learning Objectives and Chapter Summaries improve chapter organization and help students retain important information.

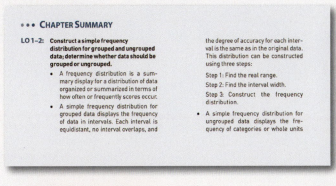

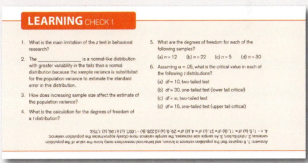

Learning Checks with answers support a deeper understanding of the material.

Chapter-ending review problems, categorized as *Factual Problems, Concept and Application Problems,* and *Problems in Research,* allow instructors to easily identify and specifically test the type of knowledge they want to assess.

New Support for R, SAS®, and Stata® Users:
Essential Statistics for the Behavioral Sciences, Second Edition can be packaged with an alternate, companion guide, **Essentials of Statistical Analysis for the Behavioral Sciences: In Focus 2e,** that aligns coverage of R, SAS®, and Stata® with all SPSS® components within the textbook. These alternate versions of Privitera's "In Focus" coverage plug into each chapter of the text in context to offer helpful replacement coverage for students not using SPSS® software.
ISBN: 9781544325842

Also Available With the Text: WebAssign, a powerful tool for creating online, autograded homework specific to the text.

An updated Student Study Guide also by Privitera provides even more opportunity for review, practice, and mastery of concepts. Bundle the **Second Edition** with the accompanying **Student Study Guide With IBM® SPSS® Workbook for Essentials Statistics for the Behavioral Sciences, Second Edition** for only $5 more!
Use Bundle ISBN: 9781544330440

$SAGE coursepacks

Our Content Tailored to Your LMS

Instructors! SAGE coursepacks makes it easy to import our quality instructor and student resource content into your school's learning management system (LMS). Intuitive and simple to use, SAGE coursepacks allows you to customize course content to meet your students' needs. Learn more at **sagepub.com/coursepacks**.

Sara Miller McCune founded SAGE Publishing in 1965 to support the dissemination of usable knowledge and educate a global community. SAGE publishes more than 1000 journals and over 800 new books each year, spanning a wide range of subject areas. Our growing selection of library products includes archives, data, case studies and video. SAGE remains majority owned by our founder and after her lifetime will become owned by a charitable trust that secures the company's continued independence.

Los Angeles | London | New Delhi | Singapore | Washington DC | Melbourne

Essential

STATISTICS

for the BEHAVIORAL
SCIENCES

SECOND EDITION

Essential STATISTICS for the BEHAVIORAL SCIENCES

SECOND EDITION

GREGORY J. PRIVITERA

St. Bonaventure University

Los Angeles | London | New Delhi
Singapore | Washington DC | Melbourne

FOR INFORMATION:

SAGE Publications, Inc.
2455 Teller Road
Thousand Oaks, California 91320
E-mail: order@sagepub.com

SAGE Publications Ltd.
1 Oliver's Yard
55 City Road
London EC1Y 1SP
United Kingdom

SAGE Publications India Pvt. Ltd.
B 1/I 1 Mohan Cooperative Industrial Area
Mathura Road, New Delhi 110 044
India

SAGE Publications Asia-Pacific Pte. Ltd.
3 Church Street
#10-04 Samsung Hub
Singapore 049483

Acquisitions Editor: Lara Parra
Content Development Editor: Lucy Berbeo
Editorial Assistant: Zachary Valladon
Production Editor: Kelly DeRosa
Copy Editor: Melinda Masson
Typesetter: C&M Digitals (P) Ltd.
Proofreader: Theresa Kay
Indexer: Judy Hunt
Cover Designer: Michael Dubowe
Marketing Manager: Katherine Hepburn

Copyright © 2019 by SAGE Publications, Inc.

All rights reserved. No part of this book may be reproduced or utilized in any form or by any means, electronic or mechanical, including photocopying, recording, or by any information storage and retrieval system, without permission in writing from the publisher.

All trademarks depicted within this book, including trademarks appearing as part of a screenshot, figure, or other image, are included solely for the purpose of illustration and are the property of their respective holders. The use of the trademarks in no way indicates any relationship with, or endorsement by, the holders of said trademarks. SPSS is a registered trademark of International Business Machines Corporation.

Printed in Canada

Library of Congress Cataloging-in-Publication Data

Names: Privitera, Gregory J., author.

Title: Essential statistics for the behavioral sciences / Gregory J. Privitera, St. Bonaventure University.

Description: Second Edition. | Thousand Oaks : SAGE Publications, [2018] | Revised edition of the author's Essential statistics for the behavioral sciences, 2016. | Includes bibliographical references and index.

Identifiers: LCCN 2017039411 | ISBN 9781506386300 (pbk. : alk. paper)

Subjects: LCSH: Social sciences—Statistical methods. | Psychology—Statistical methods.

Classification: LCC HA29.P755 2018 | DDC 519.5—dc23
LC record available at https://lccn.loc.gov/2017039411

This book is printed on acid-free paper.

18 19 20 21 22 10 9 8 7 6 5 4 3 2 1

••• Brief Contents

PART V: MAKING INFERENCES ABOUT PATTERNS, PREDICTION, AND NONPARAMETRIC TESTS   405

••• Detailed Contents

©Can Stock Photo Inc./OG_vision

Chapter 3: Summarizing Data: Central Tendency · 72

© iStockphoto.com/Davizro

PART II: PROBABILITY AND THE FOUNDATIONS OF INFERENTIAL STATISTICS — 131

© iStockphoto.com/Bennewitz

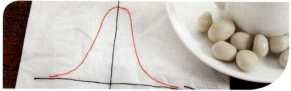

Marek Uliasz/iStock/Thinkstock

cosmin4000/iStock/Thinkstock

Chapter 6: Characteristics of the Sample Mean   162

Chapter 7: Hypothesis Testing: Significance, Effect Size, and Power   190

PART III: MAKING INFERENCES ABOUT ONE OR TWO MEANS 227

© iStockphoto.com/JohnnyGreig

Chapter 8: Testing Means: One-Sample *t* Test With Confidence Intervals 228

©iStockphoto.com/nastinka

Chapter 9: Testing Means: Two-Independent-Sample *t* Test With Confidence Intervals 254

MAKING SENSE—The Pooled Sample Variance 263

© iStockphoto.com/Shaiith

Chapter 10: Testing Means: Related-Samples *t* Test With Confidence Intervals 280

PART IV: MAKING INFERENCES ABOUT THE VARIABILITY OF TWO OR MORE MEANS 309

©iStockphoto.com/PeopleImages

Chapter 11: One-Way Analysis of Variance: Between-Subjects and Within-Subjects (Repeated-Measures) Designs 310

©iStockphoto.com/vvmich

PART V: MAKING INFERENCES ABOUT PATTERNS, PREDICTION, AND NONPARAMETRIC TESTS   405

©iStockphoto.com/Rawpixel Ltd

Chapter 13: Correlation and Linear Regression   406

©iStockphoto.com/diane39

Chapter 14: Chi-Square Tests: Goodness of Fit and the Test for Independence   460

··· About the Author

Gregory J. Privitera is a professor and chair of the Department of Psychology at St. Bonaventure University, where he is a recipient of the school's highest teaching honor, the Award for Professional Excellence in Teaching, and its highest honor for scholarship, the Award for Professional Excellence in Research and Publication. Dr. Privitera received his PhD in behavioral neuroscience in the field of psychology at the State University of New York at Buffalo and continued to complete postdoctoral research at Arizona State University. He is an author of multiple books on statistics, research methods, and health psychology, in addition to authoring more than three dozen peer-reviewed scientific articles aimed at advancing our understanding of health and well-being. He oversees a variety of undergraduate research projects at St. Bonaventure University, where dozens of undergraduate students, many of whom are now earning graduate degrees at various institutions, have coauthored research in his laboratories. For his work with students and fruitful record of academic and research advisement, Dr. Privitera was honored as Advisor of the Year by St. Bonaventure University in 2013. He is also the award-winning author of *Research Methods for the Behavioral Sciences*, for which he received the Most Promising New Textbook Award from the Text and Academic Authors Association in 2014. In addition to his teaching, research, and advisement, Dr. Privitera is a veteran of the U.S. Marine Corps and is married with two children: a daughter, Grace Ann, and a son, Aiden Andrew.

••• Acknowledgments

I want to take a moment to thank all those who have been supportive and endearing throughout my career. To my family, friends, acquaintances, and colleagues—thank you for contributing to my perspective in a way that is indubitably recognized and appreciated. In particular to my son, Aiden Andrew, and daughter, Grace Ann—every moment I am with you I am reminded of what is truly important in life. As a veteran, I also want to thank all those who serve and have served—there is truly no greater honor than to serve something greater than yourself.

To all those at SAGE Publishing, know that I am truly grateful to be able to share in and work with all of you. It is your vital contributions that have made this book possible and so special to me. Thank you.

I especially want to thank the thousands of statistics students across the country who will use this book. It is your pursuit of education that has inspired this contribution. My hope is that you take away as much from reading this book as I have in writing it.

Last, but certainly not least, I'd also like to thank the many reviewers who gave me feedback during the development process.

Alissa Baker-Oglesbee, *Northeastern State University*

Amy R. Pearce, *Arkansas State University, Joneseboro*

Diana L. Young, *Georgia College & State University*

Douglas P. Cooper, *Johnson C. Smith University*

John Pfister, *Dartmouth College*

Mary Jo Carnot, *Chadron State College*

Ray Garza, *Texas A&M International University*

Rochelle Caroon Santiago, *University of the Incarnate Word*

Rowland S. Miller, *Sam Houston State*

Shai Tabib, *Kean University*

Stacy Hughey Surman, *The University of Alabama*

Yukiko Maeda, *Purdue University*

... Preface to the Instructor

PHILOSOPHICAL APPROACH

On the basis of years of experience and student feedback, I was inspired to write a book that professors could truly teach from—one that would relate statistics to science using current, practical research examples and one that would be approachable (and dare I say interesting!) to students. I wrote this book in that spirit to give the reader one clear message: Statistics is not something static or antiquated that we used to do in times past; statistics is an ever-evolving discipline with relevance to our daily lives. This book is designed not only to engage students in using statistics to summarize data and make decisions about behavior but also to emphasize the ongoing spirit of discovery that emerges when using today's technologies to understand the application of statistics to modern-day research problems. How does the text achieve this goal? It exposes students to statistical applications in current research, tests their knowledge using current research examples, gives them step-by-step instruction for using IBM® SPSS® Statistics* with examples, and makes them aware of how statistics is important for their generation—all through the use of the following key themes, features, and pedagogy.

THEMES, FEATURES, AND PEDAGOGY

Emphasis on Student Learning

- **Conversational writing style.** I write in a conversational tone that speaks to the reader as if he or she is the researcher. It empowers students to view statistics as something they are capable of understanding and using. It is a positive psychology approach to writing that involves students in the process of statistical analysis and making decisions using statistics. The goal is to motivate and excite students about the topic by making the book easy to read and follow without "dumbing down" the information they need to be successful.

- **Learning objectives.** Clear learning objectives are provided at the start of each chapter to get students focused on and thinking about the material they will be learning. At the close of each chapter, the chapter summaries reiterate these learning objectives and then summarize the key chapter content related to each objective.

---

*SPSS is a registered trademark of International Business Machines Corporation.

- **Learning Checks** are inserted throughout each chapter (for students to review what they learn, as they learn it), and many figures and tables are provided to illustrate statistical concepts and summarize statistical procedures.

- **Making Sense** sections support critical and difficult material. In many years of teaching statistics, I have found certain areas of statistics where students struggle the most. To address this, I include Making Sense sections in each chapter to break down difficult concepts, review important material, and basically "make sense" of the most difficult material taught in this book. These sections are aimed at easing student stress and making statistics more approachable. Again, this book was written with student learning in mind.

- **Review problems.** At least 32 review problems are included at the end of each chapter. They include *Factual Problems*, *Concept and Application Problems*, and *Problems in Research.* Unlike the questions in most statistics textbooks, these questions are categorized for you so that you can easily identify and specifically test the type of knowledge you want to assess in the classroom. This format tests student knowledge and application of chapter material while also giving students more exposure to how current research applies to the statistics they learn.

- **Additional features.** Additional features in each chapter are aimed at helping students pull out key concepts and recall important material. For example, key terms are bolded, boxed, and defined as they are introduced to make it easier for students to find these terms when reviewing the material and to grab their attention as they read the chapters. At the end of the book, each key term is summarized in a glossary. Also, margin notes are placed throughout each chapter for students to review important material. They provide simple explanations and summaries based on those given in detail in the text.

Focus on Current Research

- **Research in Focus.** To introduce the context for using statistics, Chapters 1 to 5 include Research in Focus sections that review pertinent research that makes sense of or illustrates important statistical concepts discussed in the chapter. Giving students current research examples can help them "see" statistical methods as they are applied today, not as they were done 20 years ago.

- **APA in Focus.** As statistical designs are introduced in Chapters 6 to 14, I present APA in Focus sections that explain how to summarize statistical results for each inferential statistic taught. Together, these sections support student learning by putting statistics into context with research and also explaining how to read and report statistical results in research journals that follow American Psychological Association (APA) style.

- **Current research examples.** Many of the statistics computed in this book are based on or use data from published research. This allows students to see the types of questions that behavioral researchers ask while learning about the statistics researchers use to answer research questions. Students do not need a background in research methods to read through the research examples, which is important because most students have not taken a course in research methods prior to taking a statistics course.

- **Problems in Research.** The end-of-chapter review questions include a section of Problems in Research that come straight from the literature. These classroom-tested problems use the data or conclusions drawn from published research to test knowledge of statistics and are taken from a diverse set of research journals and behavioral disciplines. The problems require students to think critically about published research in a way that reinforces statistical concepts taught in each chapter.

- **Balanced coverage of recent changes in the field of statistics.** I take into account recent developments in the area of statistics. For example, while eta-squared is still the most popular estimate for effect size, there is a great deal of research showing that it overestimates the size of an effect. That being said, a modification to eta-squared, called omega-squared, is considered a better estimate for effect size and is being used more and more in published articles. I teach both, giving students a full appreciation for where statistics currently stands and where it is likely going in the future. Other examples include full coverage of confidence intervals and detailed reviews of factors that influence power (a key requirement for obtaining grant money and conducting an effective program of research).

Integration of SPSS

- **Guide to using SPSS with this book.** For professors who teach statistics and SPSS, it can be difficult to teach from a textbook and a separate SPSS manual. The manual often includes different research examples or language that is inconsistent with what is in the textbook and overall can be difficult for students to follow. This book changes all that by nesting SPSS coverage into the textbook. It begins with the guide at the front of the book, "To the Student—How to Use SPSS With This Book," which provides students with an easy-to-follow, classroom-tested overview of how SPSS is set up, how to read the Data View and Variable View screens, and how to use the SPSS in Focus sections in the book.

- **SPSS in Focus.** Many statistics textbooks for the behavioral sciences omit SPSS, include it in an appendix separate from the main chapters in the book, include it at the end of chapters with no useful examples or context, or include it in ancillary materials that often are not included with course content. In *Essential Statistics for the Behavioral Sciences*, SPSS is included in each chapter as statistical concepts are taught. This instruction is given in the SPSS in Focus sections. These sections provide step-by-step, classroom-tested instruction using practical research examples for how the concepts taught in each chapter can be applied using SPSS. Screenshot figures and explanations provide support for how to read SPSS outputs. In Appendix B, a guide for using SPSS is given for each SPSS in Focus section in the book, with page number references given to make it simple for students to find where those SPSS sections are taught in the book.

In addition, there is one more overarching feature that I refer to as *teachability*. While this book is comprehensive and a great reference for any undergraduate student, it is sometimes too difficult for instructors to cover every topic in this book. For this reason, the chapters are organized into sections, each of which can largely stand alone. This gives professors the ability to more easily manage course content by assigning students particular sections in each chapter when they do not want to teach all topics covered in the entire chapter. So this book was not only written with the student in mind; it was also written with the professor in mind. Here are some brief highlights of what you will find in each chapter:

CHAPTER OVERVIEWS

Chapter 1. Introduction to Statistics

Students are introduced to scientific thinking and basic research design relevant to the statistical methods discussed in this book. In addition, the types of data that researchers measure and observe are introduced in this chapter. The chapter is to the point and provides an introduction to statistics in the context of research.

Chapter 2. Summarizing Data: Frequency Distributions in Tables and Graphs

This chapter provides a comprehensive introduction to frequency distributions and graphing using research examples that give students a practical context for when these tables and graphs are used. In addition, students are exposed to summaries for percent data and percentile points. Throughout the chapter, an emphasis is placed on showing students how to decide between the many tables and graphs used to summarize various data sets.

Chapter 3. Summarizing Data: Central Tendency

This chapter places particular emphasis on what measures of central tendency are, how they are computed, and when they are used. A special emphasis is placed on interpretation and use of the mean, the median, and the mode. Students learn to appropriately use these measures to describe data for many different types of distributions.

Chapter 4. Summarizing Data: Variability

Variability is often difficult to conceptually understand. So I begin immediately with an illustration for how this chapter will show students what variability is actually measuring. I clarify immediately that variability can never be negative, and I give a simple explanation for why. These are difficult obstacles for students, so I begin with this to support student learning from the very beginning of the chapter. The remainder of the chapter introduces various measures of variability to include variance and standard deviation for data in a sample and population.

Chapter 5. Probability, Normal Distributions, and z Scores

At an introductory level, the normal distribution is center stage. It is at least mentioned in almost every chapter of this book. It is the basis for statistical theory and the precursor to most other distributions students will learn about. For this reason, I dedicate an entire chapter to its introduction. This chapter begins by introducing the concept of probability, then uses a variety of research examples to help students identify z scores and work through locating probabilities above the mean, below the mean, and between two scores.

Chapter 6. Characteristics of the Sample Mean

This is a comprehensive chapter for sampling distributions of both the mean and variance. This chapter introduces the sampling distribution and standard error in a way that helps students to see how the sample mean and sample variance can inform us about the characteristics we want to learn about in some otherwise unknown population. In addition, the chapter is organized in a way that allows professors to easily manage reading assignments for students that are consistent with what they want to discuss in class.

Chapter 7. Hypothesis Testing: Significance, Effect Size, and Power

In my experience, shifting from descriptive statistics to inferential statistics is particularly difficult for students. For this reason, this chapter provides a comprehensive introduction to hypothesis testing, significance, effect size, power, and more. In addition, students are introduced to power in the context that emphasizes how essential this concept is for research today. Two sections are devoted to this topic, and this chapter uses data from published research to introduce hypothesis testing.

Chapter 8. Testing Means: One-Sample t Test With Confidence Intervals

This chapter introduces students to t tests for one sample using current research examples. This allows students to apply these tests in context with the situations in which they are used. In addition, students are shown how data for one sample are described using confidence intervals. Two measures for proportion of variance are also introduced: one that is most often used (eta-squared) and one that is less biased and becoming more popular (omega-squared). This gives students a real sense of where statistics is and where it is likely going.

Chapter 9. Testing Means: Two-Independent-Sample *t* Test With Confidence Intervals

This chapter introduces students to *t* tests for two independent samples using current research examples. This allows students to apply these tests in context with the situations in which they are used. In addition, students are shown how data for the difference between two independent samples are described using confidence intervals. Two measures for proportion of variance are again introduced: eta-squared and omega-squared.

Chapter 10. Testing Means: Related-Samples *t* Test With Confidence Intervals

Many textbooks teach the related-samples *t* test and spend almost the entire chapter discussing the repeated-measures design. This is misleading because the matched-pairs design is also analyzed using this *t* test. It unnecessarily leads students to believe that this test is limited to a repeated-measures design, and it is not. For this reason, I teach the related-samples *t* test for both designs, explaining that the assumptions, advantages, and disadvantages vary depending on the design used. Students are clearly introduced to the context for using this test and the research situations that require its use.

Chapter 11. One-Way Analysis of Variance: Between-Subjects and Within-Subjects (Repeated-Measures) Designs

The one-way analysis of variance (ANOVA) is introduced for both the between-subjects and the within-subjects designs. A particular emphasis is placed on distinguishing when it is appropriate to use each test and what should be done following a significant ANOVA (i.e., post hoc tests). Post hoc tests are reviewed in order of how powerful they are at detecting an effect. This gives students a decision-focused introduction by showing them how to choose statistics that are associated with the greatest power to detect an effect. In addition, a full discussion of consistency and power is included to help students see how each design can influence the power of detecting an effect.

Chapter 12. Two-Way Analysis of Variance: Between-Subjects Factorial Design

This chapter provides students with an introduction to the two-way between-subjects factorial design. Students are given illustrations showing exactly how to interpret main effects and interactions, as well as given guidance as to which effects are most informative and how to describe these effects. This is a decision-focused chapter, helping students understand the various effects in a two-way ANOVA design and how they can be analyzed and interpreted to answer a variety of research questions.

Chapter 13. Correlation and Linear Regression

This chapter introduces the Pearson correlation coefficient, effect size, significance, assumptions, and additional considerations up front. In addition, three other common types of correlation coefficients are introduced. A comprehensive review for defining how a straight line is used to predict behavioral outcomes is also included. Many figures and tables are included to illustrate and conceptualize regression and how it describes behavior. Also, an analysis of regression is introduced, and parallels between this test and ANOVA are drawn. This is aimed at helping students see how this analysis relates to other tests taught in previous chapters.

Chapter 14. Chi-Square Tests:
Goodness of Fit and the Test for Independence

One of the most difficult parts of teaching chi-square tests can be explaining their interpretation. Much of the interpretation of the results of a chi-square is intuitive or speculative. These issues and the purposes for using these tests are included. In addition, this chapter is linked with the previous chapter by showing students how measures of effect size for the chi-square test are linked with phi correlations. This gives students an appreciation for how these measures are related.

APPENDICES

Appendix A gives students a basic math review specific to the skills they need for the course. The appendix is specifically written to be unintimidating. From the beginning, students are reassured that the level of math is basic and that they do not need a strong background in mathematics to be successful in statistics. Learning Checks are included throughout this appendix, and more than 100 end-of-chapter review problems are included to give students all the practice they need to feel comfortable.

Appendix B provides a general instruction guide for using SPSS. Throughout this book, these instructions are provided with an example for how to analyze and interpret data. However, it would be difficult for students to thumb through the book to find each test when needing to refer to these tests later. Therefore, this appendix provides a single place where students can go to get directions for any statistical test taught in this chapter. Each instruction also provides the location within the text where readers can find an example of how to compute each test using SPSS.

Appendix C gives the tables needed to find critical values for the test statistics taught in this book.

Appendix D gives the answers for even-numbered problems for the end-of-chapter questions. This allows students to practice additional questions and be able to check their answers in the appendix.

NEW TO THIS EDITION

The second edition provides substantive changes that have improved clarity of content, linkage to learning objectives, and updated scholarship throughout. The changes allow for a stronger presentation of the material, based on years of feedback from colleagues, instructors, and students, that is more illustrative in nature and meaningful for students. Two major overarching themes to the revisions are apparent. A broad summary of changes in the second edition is given briefly here.

One theme that arose was to strengthen the chapter transitions and chapter introductions. Added to the second edition are introductory vignettes for each chapter. The aim of these vignettes are to introduce each chapter using practical, everyday language and sense. These vignettes allow students to realize the value of the content to be taught and how it applies to the behavioral sciences.

Another theme in the writing of the second edition was that the figures, tables, and writing were revised to improve clarity throughout. Many revisions were specifically based on feedback from instructors and students, such as revisions to clarify the different distributions of data as well as to expand on parts of the hypothesis testing chapters. Changes included revising figures and tables, in addition to revising and adding new content throughout to build stronger writing around the content being presented, as per feedback from students and instructors.

Another theme that arose was updating scholarship throughout. As disciplines in the behavioral sciences advance, it is important to link hypothesis testing and statistical analysis to current examples to help students realize the value and real-world application of statistics in the behavioral sciences. Scholarship was updated throughout to provide dozens of new references, while also removing references that are now outdated. The scholarship was updated both in the text and in the end-of-chapter problems to bolster student learning.

In addition, Appendix B was added. This new appendix has two key benefits in the book: (1) It gives readers a step-by-step instructional guide for using SPSS throughout the book, and (2) it links each instruction to the specific chapter and page number in the book where students can locate within the text where to find an example of how to compute each test taught using SPSS. This makes the book easier to navigate when searching for specific types of tests and analyses for practicing SPSS.

Additional changes in the book include learning objectives that were updated throughout and learning objective summaries that were revised with those corresponding changes. Examples were added and revised as needed to further clarify the examples in chapters and make the writing more concise where appropriate. End-of-chapter pedagogy was revised and updated to include new key terms and new content and remove old content no longer in the book. If end-of-chapter materials required an answer key, then the the corresponding answer keys were also updated. Overall, the changes allow for a stronger presentation of the material based on years of feedback from colleagues, instructors, and students.

SUPPLEMENTS

Supplements and digital resources for this book include the following:

- **Student Study Guide:** Contains learning objectives, chapter outlines, key formulas, tips and cautions, self-tests and quizzes, and exercises designed to test students' understanding of APA style and SPSS.
- **SAGE edge Instructor Resources site:** Contains an extensive test bank, chapter-specific PowerPoint presentations, lecture notes, sample syllabi for semester and quarter courses, solutions for the problems in the Student Study Guide, and solutions for all end-of-chapter problems in the text, as well as Excel data sets structured by discipline, SPSS in Focus data sets, and more.
- **SAGE edge Student Resources site:** Contains screencasts for each SPSS in Focus section in the book, eFlashcards, eQuizzes, access to full-text articles from SAGE Journals, multimedia resources, and more.

Visit **edge.sagepub.com/priviteraess2e** to access the resources at SAGE edge.

Thank you for choosing *Essential Statistics for the Behavioral Sciences*, and best wishes for a successful semester!

Gregory J. Privitera
St. Bonaventure, New York

•••To the Student—How to Use SPSS With This Book

SPSS is an innovative statistical computer program used to compute most statistics taught in this book. This preface provides you with an overview to familiarize you with how to open, view, and understand this software. The screenshots in this book show IBM® SPSS® Statistics Version 24.0 for the PC. Still, even if you use a Mac or different version, the figures and instructions should provide a rather effective guide for helping you use this statistical software (with some minor differences, of course). Note that an alternative guide has been created that corresponds to this book for all SPSS in Focus sections: *Statistical Analysis "In Focus": Alternate Guides for R, SAS, and Stata for Statistics for the Behavioral Sciences*. If you prefer instead to use one of those alternative statistical software packages (R, SAS, or Stata), the alternative guide will be a valuable resource. Within this book, SPSS is introduced, so it will be worthwhile to read this preface before moving into future discussions of SPSS. This preface includes a general introduction to familiarize you with this software.

Understanding SPSS is especially important for those interested in research careers because it is the most widely used statistical program in the social and behavioral sciences. That is not to minimize the importance of understanding how to compute a mean or plot a bar graph by hand—but knowing how to enter, analyze, and interpret statistics using SPSS is equally important for no other reason than you will need it. This is an essential complement to your readings in this book. By knowing how and why you compute certain statistics, you will better understand and interpret the output from SPSS software.

OVERVIEW OF SPSS: WHAT ARE YOU LOOKING AT?

When you open SPSS, you will see a window that looks similar to an Excel spreadsheet. (In many ways, you will enter and view the data as you would in Microsoft Excel.) At the bottom of the window, you will see two tabs as shown in Figure P.1. The Data View tab is open by default. The Variable View tab to the right of it is used to view and define the variables being studied.

Data View

The Data View screen includes a menu bar (located at the top of the screen), which displays commands that perform most functions that SPSS provides. These commands include File, Edit, View, Data, Transform, Analyze, Graphs, Utilities, Add-ons, Window, and Help. Each command is introduced as needed in each chapter in the SPSS in Focus sections, although the command of most use to you will be the Analyze command in the menu bar.

Below the menu bar is where you will find the toolbar, which includes a row of icons that perform various functions. We use some of these icons, whereas others are beyond the scope of this book. The purpose and function of each icon are introduced as needed in each chapter in the SPSS in Focus sections.

Within the spreadsheet, there are cells organized in columns and rows. The rows are labeled numerically from 1, whereas each column is labeled

FIGURE P.1   The Data View Default View in SPSS

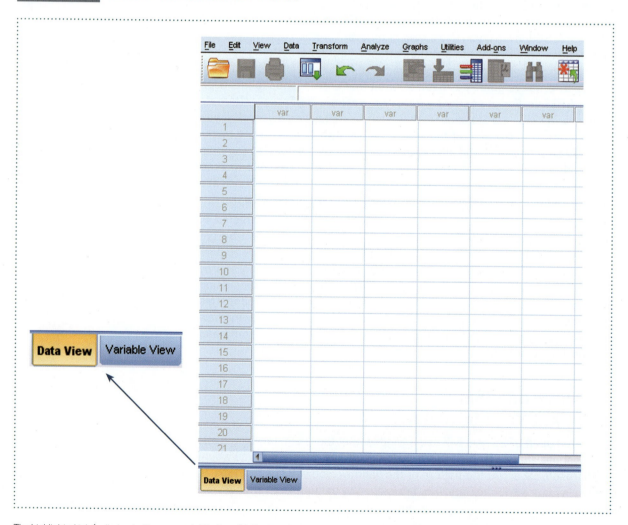

The highlighted tab (pulled out with an arrow in this figure) indicates which view you are looking at. In this figure, the Data View tab is highlighted.

var. Each column will be used to identify your variables, so *var* is short for *variable.* To label your variables with something other than *var*, you need to access the Variable View tab—this is a unique feature to SPSS.

Variable View

When you click the Variable View tab, a new screen appears. Some features remain the same. For example, the menu bar and toolbar remain at the top of your screen. What changes is the spreadsheet. Notice that what changed are the labels across the columns. There are 11 columns in this view, as shown in Figure P.2: Name, Type, Width, Decimals, Label, Values, Missing, Columns, Align, Measure, and Role. We will look at each column.

FIGURE P.2   The Variable View Page With 11 Columns

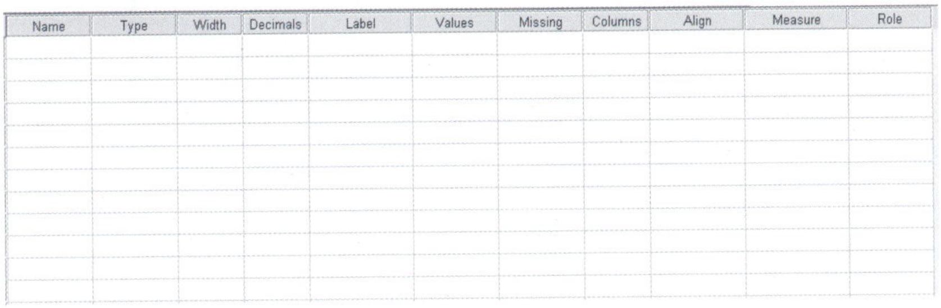

Name	Type	Width	Decimals	Label	Values	Missing	Columns	Align	Measure	Role

Each column allows you to label and characterize variables.

Name

In this column, you enter the names of your variables (but no spaces are allowed). Each row identifies a single variable. Also, once you name your variable, the columns label in the Data View will change. For example, while in Variable View, enter the word *stats* in the first cell of this column. Now click on the Data View tab at the bottom left. Notice that the label for column 1 has now changed from *var* to *stats.* Also, notice that once you enter a name for your variable, the row is suddenly filled in with words and numbers. Do not worry; this is supposed to happen.

Type

This cell identifies the type of variable you are defining. When you click in the box, a small gray box with three dots appears. Click on the gray box and a dialog box appears, as shown in Figure P.3. By default, the variable type selected is numeric. This is because your variable will almost always be numeric, so we usually just leave this cell alone.

Width

The Width column is used to identify the largest number or longest string of your variable. For example, grade point average, or GPA, would have a width of 4: one digit to the left of the decimal, one space for the decimal,

FIGURE P.3 Variable Type Dialog Box

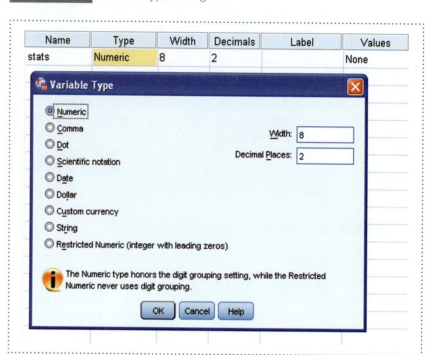

The dialog box shown here appears by clicking the small gray box with three dots in the Type column. This allows you to define the type of variable being measured.

and two digits to the right. The default width is 8. So if none of your variables are longer than eight digits, you can just leave this alone. Otherwise, when you click in the box, you can select the up and down arrows that appear to the right of the cell to change the width.

Decimals

This cell allows you to identify the number of places beyond the decimal point your variables are. As with the Width cell, when you click in the Decimals box, you can select the up and down arrows that appear to the right of the cell to change the decimals. If you want to enter whole numbers, for example, you can simply set this to 0.

Label

The Label column allows you to label any variable whose meaning is not clear. For example, we can label the variable name *stats* as *statistics* in the label column, as shown in Figure P.4. This clarifies the meaning of the *stats* variable name.

Values

This column allows you to identify the levels of your variable. This is especially useful for coded data. Because SPSS recognizes numeric values,

FIGURE P.4 Labeling Variables

Name	Type	Width	Decimals	Label
stats	Numeric	8	2	statistics

In this example, we labeled the variable name *stats* as *statistics* in the Label column.

nominal data are often coded numerically in SPSS. For example, *sex* could be coded as *1 = male* and *2 = female*; *seasons* could be coded as *1 = spring*, *2 = summer*, *3 = fall*, and *4 = winter*.

Click on the small gray box with three dots to display a dialog box where we can label the variable, as shown in Figure P.5. We can label *day class* as *1* and *evening class* as *2* for our *stats* variable. To do this, enter *1* in the Value box and *day class* in the Label box; then click the Add option. Follow these same instructions for the *evening class* label. When both labels have been entered, click OK to finish.

Missing

It is at times the case that some data researchers collect are missing. In these cases, you can enter a value that, when entered in the Data View tab,

FIGURE P.5 Value Labels Dialog Box

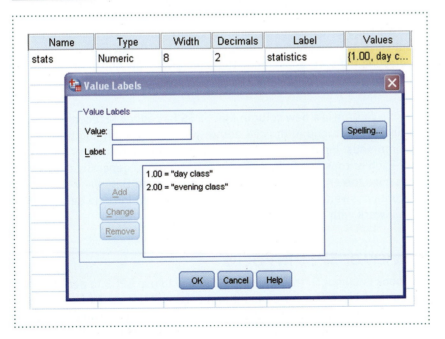

The dialog box shown here appears by clicking the small gray box with three dots in the Values column. This function allows you to code data that are not inherently numeric.

means the data are missing. A common value used to represent missing data is *99*. To enter this value, click on the small gray box with three dots that appears to the right of the cell when you click in it. In the dialog box, it is most common to click on the second open circle and enter a *99* in the first cell. When this has been entered, click OK to finish. Now, whenever you enter *99* for that variable in the Data View spreadsheet, SPSS will recognize it as missing data.

Columns

The Columns column lets you identify how much room to allow for your data and labels. For example, the *stats* label is five letters long. If you go to the Data View spreadsheet, you will see *stats* as the Columns label. If you wrote *statisticscourse* in the Name column, then this would be too long—notice that this name continues on to a second line in the Data View column label, because the Columns default value is only 8. You can click the up and down arrows to increase or decrease how much room to allow for your Columns label.

Align

The Align column allows you to choose where to align the data you enter. You can change this by selecting the drop-down menu that appears by clicking in the cell. The alignment options are Left, Right, and Center. By default, numeric values are aligned to the right, and string values are aligned to the left.

Measure

This column allows you to select the scale of measurement for the variable (scales of measurement are introduced in Chapter 1). By default, all variables are considered scale (i.e., an interval or ratio scale of measurement). If your variable is an ordinal or nominal variable, you can make this change by selecting the drop-down menu that appears by clicking in the cell.

Role

The Role column is a new column that SPSS has added in recent versions. The drop-down menu in the cell allows you to choose among the following commands: Input, Target, Both (Input and Target), None, Partition, and Split. Each of these options in the drop-down menu generally allows you to organize the entry and appearance of data in the Data View tab. While each option is valuable, these are generally needed for data sets that we will not work with in this book.

PREVIEW OF SPSS IN FOCUS

This book is unique in that you will learn how to use SPSS to perform statistical analyses as they are taught in this book. Most statistics textbooks for behavioral science omit such information, include it in an appendix separate from the main chapters in the book, include it at the end of chapters with no useful examples or context, or include it in ancillary materials that often are not included with course content. Instead, this book provides instructions for using SPSS in each chapter as statistical concepts are taught using practical research examples and screenshots to support student learning. You will find this instruction in the SPSS in Focus sections. These sections provide step-by-step instruction for how the concepts taught in each chapter can be applied to research problems using SPSS.

The reason for inclusion of SPSS is simple: Most researchers use some kind of statistical software to analyze statistics; in behavioral science, the most common statistical software used by researchers is SPSS. This textbook brings statistics in research to the 21st century, giving you both the theoretical and computational instruction needed to understand how, when, and why you perform certain statistical analyses under different conditions and the technical instruction you need to succeed in the modern era of data collection, data entry, data analysis, and statistical interpretation using SPSS statistical software. This preface was written to familiarize you with this software. Subsequent SPSS in Focus sections will show you how to use SPSS to perform the applications and statistics taught in this book.

Part I

Introduction and Descriptive Statistics

iStock/thumb

1

Introduction to Statistics

• • • Learning Objectives

After reading this chapter, you should be able to:

1. Distinguish between descriptive and inferential statistics.

2. Explain how samples and populations, as well as a sample statistic and population parameter, differ.

3. Describe three research methods commonly used in behavioral science.

4. State the four scales of measurement and provide an example for each.

5. Distinguish between quantitative and qualitative variables.

6. Distinguish between continuous and discrete variables.

7. Enter data into SPSS by placing each group in a separate column and each group in a single column (coding is required).

Are you curious about the world around you? Do you think that seeing is believing? When something seems too good to be true, are you critical of the claims? If you answered yes to any of these questions, the next step in your quest for knowledge is to learn about the basis upon which we understand events and behaviors—specifically, ways in which scientists acquire knowledge. Much of what you think you know is actually based on the analyses scientists use to answer questions and "crunch the numbers"—such that the numbers themselves make more sense or are more meaningful.

For example, on a typical morning you may eat breakfast because it is "the most important meal of the day." If you drive to school, you may put away your cell phone because "it is unsafe to use cell phones while driving." At school, you may attend an exam review session because "students are twice as likely to do well if they attend the session." In your downtime, you may watch commercials or read articles that make sensational claims like "scientifically tested" and "clinically proven." At night, you may try to get your "recommended eight hours of sleep" so that you have the energy you need to start a new day. All of these decisions and experiences are related in one way or another to the science of behavior.

This book reveals the details of analysis and how scientists crunch the numbers, which will allow you to be a more critical consumer of knowledge in terms of being able to critically evaluate the analyses that lead to the claims you come across each day. Understanding the various strengths and limitations of analysis in science can empower you to make educated decisions and confidently negotiate the many supposed truths in nature. The idea here is that you do not need to be a scientist to appreciate what you learn in this book. *Science* is all around you—for this reason, being a critical consumer of the information you come across each day is useful and necessary across professions.

Master the content.

edge.sagepub.com/priviteraess2e

●●● Chapter Outline

1.1   The Use of Statistics in Science

1.2   Descriptive and Inferential Statistics

1.3   Research Methods and Statistics

1.4   Scales of Measurement

1.5   Types of Variables for Which Data Are Measured

1.6   Research in Focus: Evaluating Data and Scales of Measurement

1.7   SPSS in Focus: Entering and Defining Variables

1.1 THE USE OF STATISTICS IN SCIENCE

Why should you study statistics? The topic can be intimidating, and rarely does anyone tell you, "Oh, that's an easy course . . . take statistics!" **Statistics** is a branch of mathematics used to summarize, analyze, and interpret what we observe—to make sense or meaning of our observations. Really, statistics is used to make sense of the observations we make. For example, we can make sense of how good a soccer player is by observing how many goals he or she scores each season, and we can understand climates by looking at average temperature. We can also understand change by looking at the same statistics over time—such as the number of goals scored by a soccer player in each game, and the average temperature over many decades.

Statistics is commonly applied to evaluate scientific observations. Scientific observations are all around you. Whether you are making decisions about what to eat (based on health statistics) or how much to spend (based on the behavior of global markets), you are making decisions based on the statistical evaluation of scientific observations. Scientists who study human behavior gather information about all sorts of behavior of interest to them, such as information on addiction, happiness, worker productivity, resiliency, faith, child development, love, and more. The information that scientists gather is evaluated in two ways; each way reveals the two types of statistics taught in this book:

- Scientists organize and summarize information such that the information is meaningful to those who read about the observations scientists made in a study. This type of evaluation of information is called *descriptive statistics*.
- Scientists use information to answer a question (e.g., is diet related to obesity?) or make an actionable decision (e.g., should we implement a public policy change that can reduce obesity rates?). This type of evaluation of information is called *inferential statistics*.

This book describes how to apply and interpret both types of statistics in science and in practice to make you a more informed interpreter of the statistical information you encounter inside and outside of the classroom. For a review of statistical notation (e.g., summation notation) and a basic math review, please see Appendix A. The chapter organization of this book is such that descriptive statistics are described in Chapters 2–4 and applications for probability are further introduced in Chapters 5–6, to transition to a discussion of inferential statistics in the remainder of the book in Chapters 7–14.

The reason it is important to study statistics can be described by the words of Mark Twain: *There are lies, damned lies, and statistics.* He meant that statistics could be deceiving, and so can interpreting them. Statistics are all around you—from your college grade point average (GPA) to a *Newsweek* poll predicting which political candidate is likely to win an election. In each case, statistics are used to inform you. The challenge as you move into your careers is to be able to identify statistics and to interpret what they mean. Statistics are part of your everyday life, and they are subject to interpretation. The interpreter, of course, is *you*.

In many ways, statistics allow a story to be told. For example, your GPA may reflect the story of how well you are doing in school; the *Newsweek*

Statistics is a branch of mathematics used to summarize, analyze, and interpret a group of numbers or observations.

poll may tell the story of which candidate is likely to win an election. In storytelling, there are many ways to tell a story. Similarly, in statistics, there are many ways to evaluate the information gathered in a study. For this reason, you will want to be a critical consumer of the information you come across, even information that is scientific. In this book, you will learn the fundamentals of statistical evaluation, which can help you to critically evaluate any information presented to you.

In this chapter, we begin by introducing the two general types of statistics identified here:

- Descriptive statistics: applying statistics to organize and summarize information
- Inferential statistics: applying statistics to interpret the meaning of information

FYI

Two types of statistics are descriptive statistics and inferential statistics.

1.2 DESCRIPTIVE AND INFERENTIAL STATISTICS

The research process typically begins with a question or statement that can only be answered or addressed by making an observation. The observations researchers make are typically recorded as **data** (i.e., numeric values). Figure 1.1 describes the general structure for making scientific observations, using an example to illustrate. As a basic example adapted from studies evaluating healthy food choice, such as increasing intake of fruits (Capaldi & Privitera, 2008; Privitera, 2016), suppose a researcher asks if adding sugar to a sour-tasting fruit juice (a grapefruit juice) can increase intake of this healthy juice. To test this question, the researcher first identifies a group of participants who dislike plain grapefruit juice and sets up a research study to create two groups: Group No Sugar (this group drinks the grapefruit juice without any added sugar), and Group Sugar (this group drinks the grapefruit juice with a small amount of sugar added). In this study, the researcher measures intake (i.e., how much juice is consumed). Suppose she decides to measure amount consumed in milliliters (note: 30 milliliters equals about 1 ounce). The data in this example are the volume of drink consumed in milliliters. If adding sugar increases intake of grapefruit juice, then we expect that participants will consume more of the grapefruit juice when sugar is added (i.e., Group Sugar will consume more milliliters of the juice than Group No Sugar).

In this section, we will introduce how descriptive and inferential statistics allow researchers to assess the data they measure in a research study, using the example given here and in Figure 1.1.

Descriptive Statistics

One way in which researchers can use statistics in research is to use procedures developed to help organize, summarize, and make sense of measurements or data. These procedures, called **descriptive statistics**, are typically used to quantify the behaviors researchers measure. Thus, we measure or record data (e.g., milliliters consumed), then use descriptive statistics to summarize or make sense of those data, which describe

Data (plural) are a set of scores, measurements, or observations that are typically numeric. A **datum** (singular) is a single measurement or observation, usually referred to as a **score** or **raw score**.

Descriptive statistics are procedures used to summarize, organize, and make sense of a set of scores called *data*. Descriptive statistics are typically presented graphically, in tabular form (in tables), or as summary statistics (single values).

FIGURE 1.1   General Structure for Making Scientific Observations

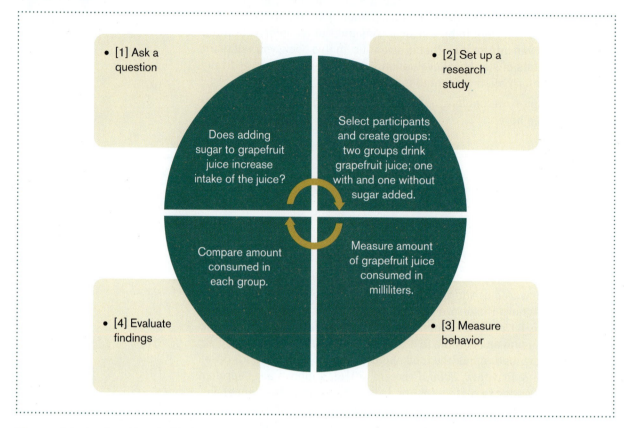

The general structure for making scientific observations, using an example for testing if adding sugar increases intake of a grapefruit juice.

the phenomenon of interest (e.g., intake of a healthy fruit juice). In our example, *intake* could be described simply as amount consumed, which certainly describes intake, but not numerically—or in a way that allows us to record data on intake. Instead, we stated that intake is milliliters consumed of the juice. Here, we define intake as a value that can be measured numerically; hence, intake can now be measured. If we observe hundreds of participants, then the data in a spreadsheet will be overwhelming. Presenting a spreadsheet with the intake for each individual participant is not very clear. For this reason, researchers use descriptive statistics to summarize sets of individual measurements so they can be clearly presented and interpreted.

Data are generally presented in summary. Typically, this means that data are presented graphically, in tabular form (in tables), or as summary statistics (e.g., an average). For example, instead of listing each individual measure of intake, we could summarize the average (mean), middle (median), or most common (mode) amount consumed in milliliters among all participants, which can be more meaningful.

Tables and graphs serve a similar purpose to summarize large and small sets of data. One particular advantage of tables and graphs is that

FYI

Descriptive statistics summarize data to make sense or meaning of a list of numeric values.

FIGURE 1.2   Summary of Expected Findings

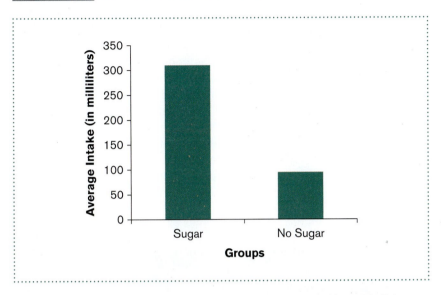

A graphical summary of the expected findings if adding sugar increases intake of a grapefruit juice.

they can clarify findings in a research study. For example, to evaluate the findings for our study, we expect that participants will consume more grapefruit juice in milliliters if sugar is added to the juice. Figure 1.2 displays these expected findings. Notice how summarizing the average intake in each group in a figure can clarify research findings.

Inferential Statistics

Most research studies include only a select group of participants, not all participants who are members of a particular group of interest. In other words, most scientists have limited access to the phenomena they study, especially behavioral phenomena. Hence, researchers select a portion of all members of a group (the *sample*) mostly because they do not have access to all members of a group (the *population*). Imagine, for example, trying to identify every person who has experienced exam anxiety. The same is true for most behaviors—the population of all people who exhibit those behaviors is likely too large. Because it is often not possible to identify all individuals in a population, researchers require statistical procedures, called **inferential statistics**, to infer that observations made with a sample are also likely to be observed in the larger population from which the sample was selected.

To illustrate, we can continue with the grapefruit juice study. If we are interested in all those who have a general dislike for sour-tasting grapefruit juice, then this group would constitute the **population** of interest. Specifically, we want to test if adding sugar increases intake of a grapefruit juice in this population; this characteristic (intake of a grapefruit juice) in the population is called a **population parameter**. Intake, then, is the characteristic we will measure, but not in the population. In practice,

Inferential statistics are procedures used that allow researchers to infer or generalize observations made with samples to the larger population from which they were selected.

A **population** is the set of all individuals, items, or data of interest. This is the group about which scientists will generalize.

A characteristic (usually numeric) that describes a population is called a **population parameter**.

FYI

Inferential statistics are used to help the researcher infer how well statistics in a sample reflect parameters in a population.

A **sample** is a set of individuals, items, or data selected from a population of interest.

A characteristic (usually numeric) that describes a sample is referred to as a **sample statistic**.

researchers will not have access to an entire population. They simply do not have the time, money, or other resources to even consider studying all those who have a general dislike for sour-tasting grapefruit juice.

An alternative to selecting all members of a population is to select a portion or **sample** of individuals in the population. Selecting a sample is more practical, and most scientific research is based upon findings in samples, not populations. In our example, we can select any portion of those who have a general dislike for sour-tasting grapefruit juice from the larger population; the portion of those we select will constitute our sample. A characteristic that describes a sample, such as intake, is called a **sample statistic** and is the value that is measured in a study. A sample statistic is measured to estimate the population parameter. In this way, a sample is selected from a population to learn more about the characteristics in a population of interest.

MAKING SENSE POPULATIONS AND SAMPLES

A population is identified as any group of interest, whether that group is all students worldwide or all students in a professor's class. Think of any group you are interested in. Maybe you want to understand why college students join fraternities and sororities. So students who join fraternities and sororities is the group you are interested in. Hence, to you, this group is a population of interest. You identified a population of interest just as researchers identify populations they are interested in.

Remember that researchers select samples only because they do not have access to all individuals in a population. Imagine having to identify every person who has fallen in love, experienced anxiety, been attracted to someone else, suffered with depression, or taken a college exam. It is ridiculous to consider that

we can identify all individuals in such populations. So researchers use data gathered from samples (a portion of individuals from the population) to make inferences concerning a population.

To make sense of this, suppose you want to get an idea of how people in general feel about a new pair of shoes you just bought. To find out, you put your new shoes on and ask 20 people at random throughout the day whether or not they like the shoes. Now, do you really care about the opinion of only those 20 people you asked? Not really—you actually care more about the opinion of people in general. In other words, you only asked the 20 people (your sample) to get an idea of the opinions of people in general (the population of interest). Sampling from populations follows a similar logic.

Example 1.1 applies the process of sampling to distinguish between a sample and a population.

Example 1.1

On the basis of the following example, we will identify the population, sample, population parameter, and sample statistic: Suppose you read an article in the local college newspaper citing that the average college student plays 2 hours of video games per week. To test whether this is true for your school, you randomly approach 20 fellow students and ask them how long (in hours) they play video games per week. You find that the average student, among those you asked, plays video games for 1 hour per week. Distinguish the population from the sample.

In this example, all college students at your school constitute the population of interest, and the 20 students you approached make up the sample that was selected from this population of interest. Because it is purported that the average college student plays 2 hours of video games per week, this is the population parameter (2 hours). The average number of hours playing video games in the sample is the sample statistic (1 hour).

LEARNING CHECK 1

1. _____ are procedures used to summarize, organize, and make sense of a set of scores, called *data*.

2. _____ describe(s) characteristics in a population, whereas _____ describe(s) characteristics in a sample.

    (a) Statistics; parameters
    (b) Parameters; statistics
    (c) Descriptive; inferential
    (d) Inferential; descriptive

3. A psychologist wants to study a small population of 40 students in a local private school. If the researcher was interested in selecting the entire population of students for this study, then how many students must the psychologist include?

    (a) None, because it is not possible to study an entire population in this case.
    (b) At least half, because this would constitute the majority of the population.
    (c) All 40 students, because all students constitute the population.

4. True or false: Inferential statistics are used to help the researcher *infer* the unknown parameters in a given population.

Answers: 1. Descriptive statistics; 2. b; 3. c; 4. True.

1.3 RESEARCH METHODS AND STATISTICS

This book will describe many ways of measuring and interpreting data. Yet, simply collecting data does not make you a scientist. To engage in science, you must follow specific procedures for collecting data. Think of this as playing a game. Without the rules and procedures for playing, the game itself would be lost. The same is true in science; without the rules and procedures for collecting data, the ability to draw scientific conclusions would be lost. Ultimately, statistics are often used in the context of **science**. In the behavioral sciences, *science* is specifically applied using the **research method**. To use the research method, we make observations using systematic techniques of scientific inquiry. In this section, we introduce three research methods that are commonly applied in the behavioral sciences.

To illustrate the basic premise of engaging in science, suppose you come across the following problem first noted by the famous psychologist Edward Thorndike in 1898:

Dogs get lost hundreds of times and no one ever notices it or sends an account of it to a scientific magazine, but let one find his

Science is the study of phenomena, such as behavior, through strict observation, evaluation, interpretation, and theoretical explanation.

The **research method**, or **scientific method**, is a set of systematic techniques used to acquire, modify, and integrate knowledge concerning observable and measurable phenomena.

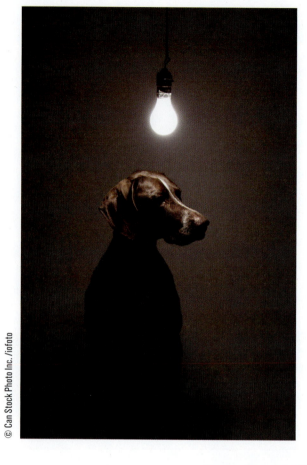

© Can Stock Photo Inc. /iofoto

way from Brooklyn to Yonkers and the fact immediately becomes a circulating anecdote. Thousands of cats on thousands of occasions sit helplessly yowling, and no one takes thought of it or writes to his friend, the professor; but let one cat claw at the knob of a door supposedly as a signal to be let out, and straightway this cat becomes the representative of the cat-mind in all books. . . . In short, the anecdotes give really . . . *supernormal* psychology of animals. (pp. 4–5)

Here the problem was to determine the animal mind. Thorndike posed the question of whether animals were truly smart, based on the many observations he made. This is where the scientific process typically begins: with a question. To answer questions in a scientific manner, researchers need more than just statistics; they need a set of strict procedures for making the observations and measurements. In this section, we introduce three research methods commonly used in behavioral research: experimental, quasi-experimental, and correlational methods. Each method involves examining the relationship between variables, and is introduced here because we will apply these methods throughout the book.

Experimental Method

Often, the aims of a researcher are to demonstrate a causal relationship (i.e., that one variable causes changes in another variable). A study that can demonstrate cause is called an **experiment**. To demonstrate cause, though, an experiment must follow strict procedures to ensure that all other possible causes are eliminated or highly unlikely. Hence, researchers must control the conditions under which observations are made in order to isolate cause-and-effect relationships between variables. Figure 1.3 shows the general structure of an experiment using a basic example adapted from studies evaluating metacognition and memory recall (Diemand-Yauman, Oppenheimer, & Vaughan, 2011; Price, McElroy, & Martin, 2016). In this example, we are evaluating if writing key terms in bold font (just like we do in this book in each chapter) improves recall of those words. A sample of students at a similar reading level was selected from a population of college undergraduates. In one group, students read a short passage with 10 bolded key terms; in the other group, students read the same short passage but with the 10 key terms in regular font. After reading each passage, students were asked to write down as many key terms as they could recall. The number of correct key terms listed was recorded for each group.

For this study to be called an experiment, researchers must satisfy three requirements. These requirements are regarded as the necessary

An **experiment** is the use of methods and procedures to make observations in which a researcher fully controls the conditions and experiences of participants by applying three required elements of control (manipulation, randomization, and comparison/ control) to isolate cause-and-effect relationships between variables.

steps to ensure enough control to allow researchers to draw cause-and-effect conclusions. These requirements are the following:

1. Manipulation (of variables that operate in an experiment)

2. Randomization (of assigning participants to conditions)

3. Comparison/control (a control group)

To meet the requirement of randomization, researchers must use **random assignment** (Requirement 2) to assign participants to groups. To do this, a researcher must be able to manipulate the levels of an **independent variable (IV)** (Requirement 1) to create the groups. Referring back to the key term bolding example shown in Figure 1.3, the independent variable was font type. The researcher first manipulated the levels of this variable (bolded, regular font), meaning that she created the conditions. She then assigned students

Random assignment is a random procedure used to ensure that participants in a study have an equal chance of being assigned to a particular group or condition.

An **independent variable (IV)** is the variable that is manipulated in an experiment. This variable remains unchanged (or "independent") between conditions being observed in an experiment. It is the "presumed cause." The specific conditions of an IV are referred to as the **levels of the independent variable**.

FIGURE 1.3   The Basic Structure of an Experiment

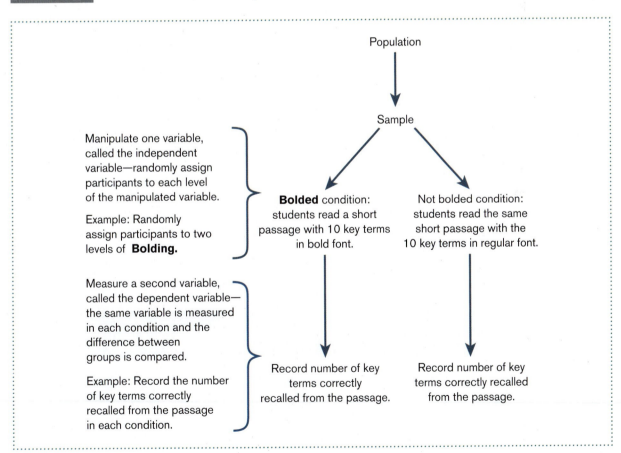

The basic structure of an experiment that meets each basic requirement for demonstrating cause and effect using an example of a study in which a sample of students at a similar reading level was selected at random from a population of college undergraduates to test if bolding key terms in a short passage improves recall. To qualify as an experiment, (1) the researcher created each level of the independent variable, font type (manipulation); (2) students also were randomly assigned to each level of font type (i.e., they read a passage with or without bolded key terms [randomization]); and (3) a control group was present where the manipulation of bolding the key terms was absent (comparison/control).

at a similar reading level at random to experience one of the levels of font type. As an example of random assignment, the researcher could select participant names at random from names written on pieces of paper in a bowl—with every other participant name selected assigned to the experimental (bold font) group, and all others to the control group (regular font group).

Random assignment and manipulation ensure that characteristics of participants in each group (such as their age, intelligence level, or study habits) vary entirely by chance. Because participant characteristics in both groups now occur at random, we can assume that these characteristics are about the same in both groups. This makes it more likely that any differences observed between groups were caused by the manipulation (bolded vs. regular font key terms in a passage) and not participant characteristics.

Notice also that there are two groups in the experiment shown in Figure 1.3. The number of correct key terms listed after reading the passage was recorded and can be compared in each group. By comparing the number of correct key terms listed in each group, we can determine whether bolding the key terms caused better recall of the key terms compared to those who read the same passage without bolded key terms. This satisfies the requirement of comparison (Requirement 3), which requires that at least two groups be observed in an experiment so that scores in one group can be compared to those in at least one other group.

In this example, recall of key terms was recorded in each group. The measured or recorded variable in an experiment is called the **dependent variable (DV)**. Dependent variables can often be measured in many ways, and therefore often require an **operational definition**. An operational definition is a description for how a dependent variable was measured. For example, here we operationally defined *recall* as the number of key terms correctly listed after reading a passage (students could recall 0 to all 10 key terms). Thus, we measured the dependent variable as a number. To summarize the experiment in Figure 1.3, bolding versus not bolding key terms (IV) was presumed to cause an effect or difference in recall (DV) between groups. This is an experiment in which the researcher satisfied the requirements of manipulation, randomization, and comparison/control, thereby allowing her to draw cause-and-effect conclusions, assuming the study was properly conducted.

FYI

An experiment is a study in which researchers satisfy three requirements to ensure enough control to allow them to draw cause-and-effect conclusions. These are manipulation, randomization, and comparison/control.

The **dependent variable (DV)** is the variable that is measured in each group of a study, and is believed to change in the presence of the independent variable. It is the "presumed effect."

An **operational definition** is a description of some observable event in terms of the specific process or manner by which it was observed or measured.

MAKING SENSE EXPERIMENTAL AND CONTROL GROUPS

While a comparison group is sometimes necessary, it is preferred that, when possible, a control group be used. By definition, a control group must be treated exactly the same as an experimental group, except that the members of this group do not actually receive the treatment believed to cause changes in the dependent variable. As an example, suppose we hypothesize that rats will dislike flavors that are associated with becoming ill (see Garcia, Kimeldorf, & Koelling, 1955; Privitera, 2016). To test this hypothesis, the rats in an experimental group receive a vanilla-flavored drink followed by an injection of lithium chloride to make them ill. The rats in a control group must be treated the same, minus the manipulation of administering lithium chloride to make them ill. In a control group, then, rats receive the same vanilla-flavored drink also followed by an injection, but in this group the substance injected is inert, such as a saline solution (called a *placebo*). The next day, we record how much vanilla-flavored solution rats consume during a brief test (in milliliters).

Note that simply omitting the lithium chloride is not sufficient. The control group in our example still receives an injection; otherwise, both being injected and the substance that is injected will differ between groups. Other important factors for experiments like these include some control of the diets rats consume before and during the study, and to ensure that many other environmental factors are the same for all rats, such as their day–night sleep cycles and housing arrangements. These added levels of control ensure that both groups are truly identical, except that one group is made ill and a second group is not. In this way, researchers can isolate all factors in an experiment, such that only the manipulation that is believed to cause an effect is different between groups. This same level of consideration must be made in human experiments to ensure that groups are treated the same, expect for the factor that is believed to cause changes in the dependent variable.

Quasi-Experimental Method

A research study that is structured similar to an experiment but meets one or both of the following two conditions is called a quasi-experiment:

1. The study does not include a manipulated independent variable.

2. The study lacks a comparison/control group.

In a typical quasi-experiment, the variables being studied cannot be manipulated, which makes random assignment impossible. This occurs when variables are preexisting or inherent to the participants themselves. A preexisting variable, or one to which participants cannot be randomly assigned, is called a **quasi-independent variable**. Figure 1.4 shows an

FYI

A quasi-experiment is a study that (1) includes a quasi-independent variable and/or (2) lacks a comparison/control group.

A **quasi-independent variable** is a preexisting variable that is often a characteristic inherent to an individual, which differentiates the groups or conditions being compared in a research study. Because the levels of the variable are preexisting, it is not possible to randomly assign participants to groups.

FIGURE 1.4   The Basic Structure of a Quasi-Experiment

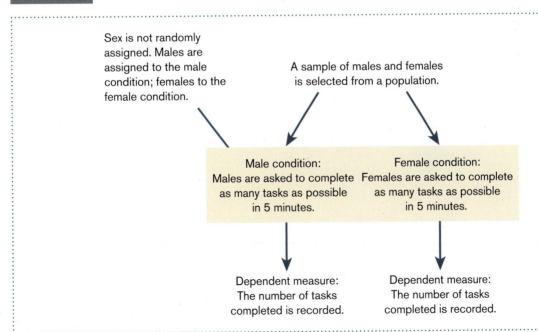

In this example, researchers measured differences in multitasking behavior by sex. The grouping variable (sex) is preexisting. That is, participants were already male or female prior to the study. For this reason, researchers cannot manipulate the variable or randomly assign participants to each level of sex, so this study is regarded as a quasi-experiment.

example of a quasi-experiment that measured differences in multitasking ability by sex. Because participants cannot be randomly assigned to the levels of sex (*male*, *female*), sex is a quasi-independent variable, and this study is therefore regarded as a quasi-experiment.

A study is also regarded as a quasi-experiment when only one group is observed. With only one group, there is no comparison or control group, which means that differences between two levels of an independent variable cannot be compared. In this way, failing to satisfy any of the requirements for an experiment makes the study a quasi-experiment when the study is otherwise structured similar to an experiment.

Correlational Method

Another method for examining the relationship between variables is to measure pairs of scores for each individual. This method can determine whether a relationship exists between variables, but it lacks the appropriate controls needed to demonstrate cause and effect. To illustrate, suppose you test for a relationship between times spent using a computer and exercising per week. The data for such a study appear in tabular form and are plotted as a graph in Figure 1.5. Using the correlational method, we can examine the extent to which two variables change in a related fashion. In the example shown in Figure 1.5, as computer use increases, time spent exercising decreases. This pattern suggests that computer use and time spent exercising are related.

Notice that no variable is manipulated to create different conditions or groups to which participants can be randomly assigned. Instead, two variables are measured for each participant, and the extent to which those variables are related is measured. Thus, the correlational method does

FYI

The correlational method can determine whether a relationship exists between variables, but it lacks the controls needed to demonstrate cause and effect.

FIGURE 1.5   An Example of the Correlational Method

(a)

Participant	Computer Use (Hours per week)	Exercise (Minutes per week)
A	3	80
B	2	83
C	0	96
D	10	60
E	8	78
F	12	46

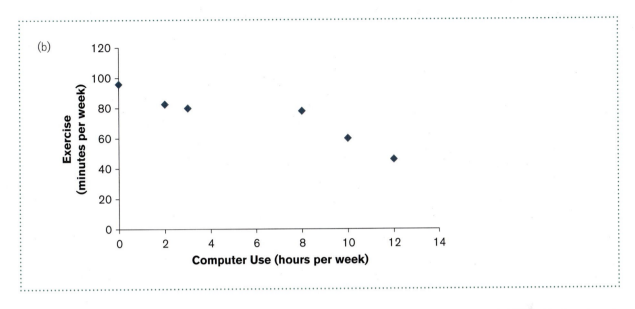

In this example, researchers measured the amount of time students spent using the computer and exercising each week. (a) The table shows two sets of scores for each participant. (b) The graph shows the pattern of the relationship between these scores. From the data, we can see that as computer use increases, time spent exercising decreases. Hence, the two factors change in a related pattern.

not at all control the conditions under which observations are made, and is therefore not able to demonstrate cause-and-effect conclusions. This book describes many statistical procedures used to analyze data using the correlational method (Chapter 13 and 14) and the experimental and quasi-experimental methods (Chapters 7–12).

Example 1.2 applies a research example to identify how a research design can be constructed.

Example 1.2

A researcher conducts the following study: Participants are presented with a list of words written on a white background on a PowerPoint slide. In one group, the words are written in red (Group Color); in a second group, the words are written in black (Group Black). Participants are allowed to study the words for 1 minute. After that time, the slide is removed, and participants are allowed one minute to write down as many words as they can recall. The number of words correctly recalled will be recorded for each group. Explain how this study can be an experiment.

To create an experiment, we must satisfy the three requirements for demonstrating cause and effect: manipulation, randomization, and comparison. To satisfy each requirement, the researcher can

1.   randomly assign participants to experience one of the conditions—this ensures that some participants read colored words and others read black words entirely by chance;

2. create the two conditions that are identical, except for the color manipulation—the researcher can write the same 20 words on two PowerPoint slides, on one slide in red and on the second slide in black; and

3. include a comparison group—in this case, the number of colored (red) words correctly recalled will be compared to the number of black words correctly recalled, so this study has a comparison group.

Remember that each requirement is necessary to demonstrate that the levels of an independent variable are causing changes in the value of a dependent variable. If any one of these requirements is not satisfied, then the study is not an experiment.

LEARNING CHECK 2

1. _____ is the study of phenomena through strict observation, evaluation, interpretation, and theoretical explanation.

2. State whether each of the following describes an experiment, a quasi-experiment, or a correlational method.

    (a) A researcher tests whether dosage level of some drug (low, high) *causes* significant differences in health.

    (b) A researcher tests whether citizens of differing political affiliations (Republican, Democrat) will show differences in attitudes toward morality.

    c) A researcher measures the relationship between annual income and life satisfaction.

3. True or false: An experiment is the only method that can demonstrate cause-and-effect relationships between variables.

Answers: 1. Science; 2. (a) Experiment; (b) Quasi-experiment; (c) Correlational method; 3. True.

1.4 SCALES OF MEASUREMENT

Many statistical tests introduced in this book will require that variables in a study be measured on a certain **scale of measurement**. In the early 1940s, Harvard psychologist S. S. Stevens coined the terms *nominal*, *ordinal*, *interval*, and *ratio* to classify scales of measurement (Stevens, 1946). Scales of measurement are rules that describe the properties of numbers. These rules imply that the extent to which a number is informative depends on how it was used or measured. In this section, we discuss the extent to which data are informative on each scale of measurement. In all, scales of measurement are characterized by three properties: order, difference,

Scales of measurement identify how the properties of numbers can change with different uses. Four scales of measurement are nominal, ordinal, interval, and ratio.

and ratio. Each property can be described by answering the following questions:

1. *Order*: Does a larger number indicate a greater value than a smaller number?
2. *Difference*: Does subtracting two numbers represent some meaningful value?
3. *Ratio*: Does dividing (or taking the ratio of) two numbers represent some meaningful value?

©iStockphoto.com/skvoor

Table 1.1 gives the answers to the questions for each scale of measurement. In this section, we begin with the least informative scale (nominal) and finish with the most informative scale (ratio).

TABLE 1.1 Scales of Measurement

		Scale of Measurement			
		Nominal	**Ordinal**	**Interval**	**Ratio**
Property	**Order**	No	Yes	Yes	Yes
	Difference	No	No	Yes	Yes
	Ratio	No	No	No	Yes

The four scales of measurement and the information they provide concerning the order, difference, and ratio of numbers

Nominal Scales

Numbers on a **nominal scale** identify something or someone; they provide no additional information. Common examples of nominal numbers include ZIP codes, license plate numbers, credit card numbers, country codes, telephone numbers, and Social Security numbers. These numbers simply identify locations, vehicles, or individuals and nothing more. One credit card number, for example, is not greater than another; it is simply different.

FYI

Nominal scales represent something or someone, and are often data that have been coded.

In science, values on a nominal scale are typically categorical variables that have been coded—converted to numeric values. Examples of nominal variables include a person's race, sex, nationality, sexual orientation, hair and eye color, season of birth, marital status, or other demographic or personal information. Researchers, for example, may code men as 1 and women as 2. They may code the seasons of birth as 1, 2, 3, and 4 for spring, summer, fall, and winter, respectively. These numbers are used to identify sex or the seasons and nothing more. **Coding** words with numeric values is useful when entering names of groups for a research study into statistical programs such as SPSS because it can be easier to enter and analyze data when group names are entered as numbers, not words.

Nominal scales are measurements in which a number is assigned to represent something or someone.

Coding is the procedure of converting a nominal or categorical variable to a numeric value.

Ordinal Scales

An **ordinal scale** of measurement is one that conveys only that some value is greater or less than another value (i.e., order). Examples of ordinal scales include finishing order in a competition, education level, and rankings. These scales only indicate that one value is greater than or less than another, so differences between ranks do not have meaning. Consider, for example, the *U.S. News & World Report* rankings for the top psychology graduate school programs in the United States. Table 1.2 shows the rank, college, and actual score for the top 25 programs, including ties, in 2017. Based on ranks alone, can we say that the difference between the psychology graduate programs ranked 3 and 7 is the same as the difference between those ranked 13 and 17? No. In both cases, 7 ranks separate the schools. However, if you look at the actual scores for determining rank, you find that the difference between ranks 3 and 7 is 0.2 points, whereas the difference between ranks 13 and 17 is 0.1 point. Hence, the difference in points is not the same. Ranks alone do not convey this difference. They simply indicate that one rank is greater than or less than another rank.

TABLE 1.2   Ordinal Scale

Rank	College Name	Actual Score
1	Stanford University	4.8
1	University of California, Berkeley	4.8
3	Harvard University	4.7
3	University of California, Los Angeles	4.7
3	University of Michigan, Ann Arbor	4.7
3	Yale University	4.7
7	University of Illinois at Urbana-Champaign	4.5
8	Massachusetts Institute of Technology	4.4
8	Princeton University	4.4
8	University of Minnesota, Twin Cities	4.4
8	University of Pennsylvania	4.4
8	University of Texas at Austin	4.4
13	University of California, San Diego	4.3
13	University of North Carolina at Chapel Hill	4.3
13	University of Wisconsin–Madison	4.3
13	Washington University in St. Louis	4.3
17	Carnegie Mellon University	4.2
17	Columbia University	4.2
17	Duke University	4.2
17	Indiana University Bloomington	4.2
17	Northwestern University	4.2
17	University of Chicago	4.2
17	University of Virginia	4.2
24	Cornell University	4.1
24	The Ohio State University	4.1

A list of the *U.S. News & World Report* rankings for the top 25 psychology graduate school programs in the United States in 2017, including ties (left column) and the actual points used to determine their rank (right column).

Source: https://www.usnews.com/best-graduate-schools/top-humanities-schools/psychology-rankings.

FYI

Ordinal scales convey order alone.

Ordinal scales are measurements that convey order or rank alone.

Interval Scales

An **interval scale** of measurement can be understood readily by two defining principles: equidistant scales and no true zero. A common example for this in behavioral science is the rating scale. Rating scales are taught here as an interval scale because most researchers report these as interval data in published research. This type of scale is a numeric response scale used to indicate a participant's level of agreement or opinion with some statement. An example of a rating scale is given in Figure 1.6. Here we will look at each defining principle.

An **equidistant scale** is a scale with intervals or values distributed in equal units. Many behavioral scientists assume that scores on a rating scale are distributed in equal units. For example, if you are asked to rate your satisfaction with a spouse or job on a 7-point scale from 1 (*completely unsatisfied*) to 7 (*completely satisfied*), then you are using an interval scale, as shown in Figure 1.6. By assuming that the distance between each point (1 to 7) is the same or equal, it is appropriate to compute differences between scores on this scale. So a statement such as "The difference in job satisfaction among men and women was 2 points" is appropriate with interval scale measurements.

However, an interval scale does not have a **true zero**. A common example of a scale without a true zero is temperature. A temperature equal to zero for most measures of temperature does not mean that there is no temperature; it is just an arbitrary zero point. Values on a rating scale also have no true zero. In the example shown in Figure 1.6, 1 was used to indicate no satisfaction, not 0. Each value (including 0) is arbitrary. That is, we could use any number to represent none of something. Measurements of latitude and longitude also fit this criterion. The implication is that without a true zero, there is no outright value to indicate the absence of the phenomenon you are observing (so a zero proportion is not meaningful). For this reason, stating a ratio such as "Satisfaction ratings were three times greater among men compared to women" is not appropriate with interval scale measurements.

Ratio Scales

Ratio scales are similar to interval scales in that scores are distributed in equal units. Yet, unlike interval scales, a distribution of scores on a ratio scale has a true zero. This is an ideal scale in behavioral research because any mathematical operation can be performed on the values that are measured. Common examples of ratio scales include counts and measures of

FYI

An interval scale is equidistant but has no true zero.

Interval scales are measurements that have no true zero and are distributed in equal units.

An **equidistant scale** is a set of numbers distributed in equal units.

A **true zero** is when the value 0 truly indicates nothing on a scale of measurement. Interval scales do *not* have a true zero.

Ratio scales are measurements that have a true zero and are distributed in equal units.

FIGURE 1.6   An Example of a 7-Point Rating Scale for Satisfaction Used for Scientific Investigation

Satisfaction Ratings						
1	2	3	4	5	6	7
Completely Unsatisfied						Completely Satisfied

length, height, weight, and time. For scores on a ratio scale, order is informative. For example, a person who is 30 years old is older than another who is 20. Differences are also informative. For example, the difference between 70 and 60 seconds is the same as the difference between 30 and 20 seconds (the difference is 10 seconds). Ratios are also informative on this scale because a true zero is defined—it truly means nothing. Hence, it is meaningful to state that 60 pounds is twice as heavy as 30 pounds.

In science, researchers often go out of their way to measure variables on a ratio scale. For example, if they measure hunger, they may choose to measure the amount of time between meals or the amount of food consumed (in ounces). If they measure memory, they may choose to measure the amount of time it takes to memorize some list or the number of errors made. If they measure depression, they may choose to measure the dosage (in milligrams) that produces the most beneficial treatment or the number of symptoms reported. In each case, the behaviors are measured using values on a ratio scale, thereby allowing researchers to draw conclusions in terms of order, differences, and ratios—there are no restrictions for variables measured on a ratio scale.

FYI

A ratio scale is equidistant, has a true zero, and is the most informative scale of measurement.

LEARNING CHECK 3

1. _____ are rules for how the properties of numbers can change with different uses.

2. In 2010, *Fortune* magazine ranked Apple as the most admired company in the world. This ranking is on a(n) _____ scale of measurement.

3. What are two characteristics of rating scales that allow researchers to use these values on an interval scale of measurement?

   (a) Values on an interval scale have a true zero but are not equidistant.

   (b) Values on an interval scale have differences and a true zero.

   (c) Values on an interval scale are equidistant and have a true zero.

   (d) Values on an interval scale are assumed to be equidistant but do not have a true zero.

4. A researcher measures four variables: age (in days), speed (in seconds), height (in inches), and movie ratings (from 1 to 4 stars). Which of these variables is *not* an example of a variable measured on a ratio scale?

Answers: 1. Scales of measurement; 2. Ordinal; 3. d; 4. Movie ratings (from 1 to 4 stars).

1.5 TYPES OF VARIABLES FOR WHICH DATA ARE MEASURED

Scales of measurement reflect the informativeness of data. With nominal scales, researchers can conclude little; with ratio scales, researchers can conclude just about anything in terms of order, difference, and ratios. Researchers also distinguish between the types of data they measure. The variables for which researchers measure data fall into two broad categories: (1) continuous or discrete and (2) quantitative or qualitative. Each category is discussed in this section. Many examples to help you delineate these categories are given in Table 1.3.

Continuous and Discrete Variables

Variables can be categorized as continuous or discrete. A **continuous variable** is measured along a continuum. So continuous variables are measured at any place beyond the decimal point. Consider, for example, that Olympic sprinters are timed to the nearest hundredths place (in seconds), but if the Olympic judges wanted to clock them to the nearest millionths place, they could. Time (in seconds), then, is a continuous variable.

A **discrete variable**, on the other hand, is measured in whole units or categories. So discrete variables are not measured along a continuum. For example, the number of brothers and sisters you have makes sense only when given in whole units or numbers. Likewise, categories are also discrete, such as the political affiliation of a family member. Refer to Table 1.3 for more examples of continuous and discrete variables.

Quantitative and Qualitative Variables

Variables can be categorized as quantitative or qualitative. A **quantitative variable** varies by amount, so it is measured in numeric units. Thus, continuous and discrete variables can be quantitative. For example, we can measure food intake in calories (a continuous variable), or we can count the number of pieces of food consumed (a discrete variable). In both cases, the variable, food intake, is measured by amount (in numeric units).

A **qualitative variable**, on the other hand, varies by class. These variables are often labels for the behaviors we observe—so only discrete variables can fall into this category. For example, socioeconomic class (working class, middle class, upper class) is discrete and qualitative; so are many behavioral disorders such as categories of depression (unipolar, bipolar) and drug use (none, experimental, abusive). Refer to Table 1.3 for more examples of quantitative and qualitative variables.

To practice identifying the types of data that researchers measure, let us evaluate a few more variables in Example 1.3.

FYI

Continuous variables are measured along a continuum and thus can be measured in fractional units; discrete variables, however, are measured only in whole units or categories.

A **continuous variable** is measured along a continuum at any place beyond the decimal point. A continuous variable can thus be measured in fractional units.

A **discrete variable** is measured in whole units or categories that are not distributed along a continuum.

A **quantitative variable** varies by amount. This variable is measured numerically and is often collected by measuring or counting.

A **qualitative variable** varies by class. This variable is often represented as a label and describes nonnumeric aspects of phenomena.

TABLE 1.3   A List of 20 Variables Showing How They Fit Into the Three Categories That Describe Them

Variables	Continuous vs. Discrete	Quantitative vs. Qualitative	Scale of Measurement
Sex (male, female)	Discrete	Qualitative	Nominal
Seasons (spring, summer, fall, winter)	Discrete	Qualitative	Nominal
Number of dreams recalled	Discrete	Quantitative	Ratio
Number of errors	Discrete	Quantitative	Ratio

(Continued)

TABLE 1.3 (Continued)

Variables	Continuous vs. Discrete	Quantitative vs. Qualitative	Scale of Measurement
Duration of drug abuse (in years)	Continuous	Quantitative	Ratio
Ranking of favorite foods	Discrete	Quantitative	Ordinal
Ratings of satisfaction (1 to 7)	Discrete	Quantitative	Interval
Body type (slim, average, heavy)	Discrete	Qualitative	Nominal
Score (from 0% to 100%) on an exam	Continuous	Quantitative	Ratio
Number of students in your class	Discrete	Quantitative	Ratio
Temperature (degrees Fahrenheit)	Continuous	Quantitative	Interval
Time (in seconds) to memorize a list	Continuous	Quantitative	Ratio
The size of a reward (in grams)	Continuous	Quantitative	Ratio
Position standing in line	Discrete	Quantitative	Ordinal
Political affiliation (Republican, Democrat)	Discrete	Qualitative	Nominal
Type of distraction (auditory, visual)	Discrete	Qualitative	Nominal
A letter grade (A, B, C, D, F)	Discrete	Qualitative	Ordinal
Weight (in pounds) of an infant	Continuous	Quantitative	Ratio
A college student's SAT score	Discrete	Quantitative	Interval
Number of lever presses per minute	Discrete	Quantitative	Ratio

Example 1.3

For each of the following examples, (1) name the variable being measured, (2) state whether the variable is continuous or discrete, and (3) state whether the variable is quantitative or qualitative.

a. A researcher records the month of birth among patients with schizophrenia. The month of birth (the variable) is discrete and qualitative.

b. A professor records the number of students absent during a final exam. The number of absent students (the variable) is discrete and quantitative.

c. A researcher asks children to choose which type of cereal they prefer (one with a toy inside or one without). He records the choice of cereal for each child. The choice of cereal (the variable) is discrete and qualitative.

d. A therapist measures the time (in hours) that clients continue a recommended program of counseling. The time in hours (the variable) is continuous and quantitative.

LEARNING CHECK 4

1. True or false: A ratio scale variable can be continuous or discrete.

2. State whether each of the following is continuous or discrete:

   (a) Delay (in seconds) it takes drivers to make a left-hand turn when a light turns green

   (b) Number of questions that participants ask during a research study

   (c) Type of drug use (none, infrequent, moderate, or frequent)

   (d) Season of birth (spring, summer, fall, or winter)

3. State whether the variables listed in Question 2 are quantitative or qualitative.

4. True or false: Qualitative variables can be continuous or discrete.

5. A researcher is interested in the effects of stuttering on social behavior with children. He records the number of peers a child speaks to during a typical school day. In this example, would the data be quantitative or qualitative?

Answers: 1. True; 2. (a) Continuous. (b) Discrete. (c) Discrete. (d) Discrete; 3. (a) Quantitative. (b) Quantitative. (c) Qualitative. (d) Qualitative; 4. False. Qualitative variables can only be discrete. 5. Quantitative.

1.6 RESEARCH IN FOCUS: EVALUATING DATA AND SCALES OF MEASUREMENT

While qualitative variables are often measured in behavioral research, this book will focus largely on quantitative variables. The reason is twofold: (1) Quantitative measures are more common in behavioral research, and (2) most statistical tests taught in this book are adapted for quantitative measures. Indeed, many researchers who measure qualitative variables will also measure those that are quantitative in the same study.

For example, Jones, Blackey, Fitzgibbon, and Chew (2010) explored the costs and benefits of social networking among college students. The researchers used a qualitative method to interview each student in their sample. In the interview, students could respond openly to questions asked during the interview. These researchers then summarized responses into categories related to learning, studying, and social life. For example, the following student response was categorized as an example of independent learning experience for employability: "I think it [social software] can be beneficial ... in the real working environment" (Jones et al., 2010, p. 780).

The limitation for this analysis is that categories are on a nominal scale (the least informative scale). So many researchers who record qualitative data also use some quantitative measures. For example, researchers in this study also asked students to rate

(Continued)

(Continued)

their usage of a variety of social software technologies, such as PowerPoint and personal websites, on a scale from 1 (*never*) to 4 (*always*). A fifth choice (*not applicable*) was also included on this rating scale. These ratings are on an interval scale, which allowed the researchers to also discuss *differences* related to how much students used social software technologies.

Inevitably, the conclusions we can draw with qualitative data are rather limited because these data are typically on a nominal scale. On the other hand, most statistics introduced in this book require that variables be measured on the more informative scales. For this reason, this book mainly describes statistical procedures for quantitative variables measured on an ordinal, interval, or ratio scale.

1.7 SPSS in Focus:
Entering and Defining Variables

Throughout this book, we present instructions for using the statistical software program SPSS by showing you how this software can make all the work you do by hand as simple as point and click. Before you read this SPSS section, please take the time to read the section titled "To the Student—How to Use SPSS With This Book" at the beginning of this book. That section provides an overview of the different views and features in SPSS. This software is an innovative statistical computer program that can compute any statistic taught in this book.

In this chapter, we discussed how variables are defined, coded, and measured. Let us see how SPSS makes this simple. Keep in mind that the Variable View display is used to define the variables you measure, and the Data View display is used to enter the scores you measured. When entering data, make sure that all values or scores are entered in each cell of the Data View spreadsheet. The biggest challenge is making sure you enter the data correctly. Entering even a single value incorrectly can alter the data analyses that SPSS computes. For this reason, always double-check the data to make sure the correct values have been entered.

We can use a simple example. Suppose you record the average GPA of students in one of three statistics classes. You record the following GPA scores for each class, given in Table 1.4.

TABLE 1.4   GPA Scores in Three Statistics Classes

Class 1	Class 2	Class 3
3.3	3.9	2.7
2.9	4.0	2.3
3.5	2.4	2.2
3.6	3.1	3.0
3.1	3.0	2.8

There are two ways you can enter these data: by column or by row. To *enter data by column*:

1. Open the Variable View tab, shown in Figure 1.7. In the Name column, enter your variable names as *class1*, *class2*, and *class3* (note that spaces are not allowed) in each row. Three rows should be active.

2. Because the data are to the tenths place, go to the Decimals column and reduce that value to 1 in each row.

FIGURE 1.7 SPSS Variable View for Entering Data by Column

Name	Type	Width	Decimals	Label	Values
class1	Numeric	8	1		None
class2	Numeric	8	1		None
class3	Numeric	8	1		None

3. Open the Data View tab. Notice that the first three columns are now labeled with the group names, as shown in Figure 1.8. Enter the data, given in Table 1.4, for each class in the appropriate column. The data for each group are now listed down each column.

FIGURE 1.8 Data Entry in SPSS Data View for Entering Data by Column

class1	class2	class3
3.3	3.9	2.7
2.9	4.0	2.3
3.5	2.4	2.2
3.6	3.1	3.0
3.1	3.0	2.8

There is another way to enter these data in SPSS: You can *enter data by row*. This requires *coding* the data. To begin, open a new SPSS data file and follow the instructions given here:

1. Open the Variable View tab, shown in Figure 1.9. Enter *classes* in the first row in the Name column. Enter *GPA* in the second row in the Name column.

2. Go to the Decimals column and reduce the value to 0 for the first row. You will see why we did this in the next step. Reduce the Decimals column value to 1 in the second row because we will enter GPA scores for this variable.

FIGURE 1.9   SPSS Variable View for Entering Data by Row

Name	Type	Width	Decimals	Label	Values
classes	Numeric	8	0		{1, class 1}...
GPA	Numeric	8	1		None

3. Go to the Values column and click on the small gray box with three dots. In the dialog box shown in Figure 1.10, enter *1* in the Value cell and *class 1* in the Label cell, and then select *Add*. Repeat these steps by entering *2* for *class 2* and *3* for *class 3*; then select OK. When you go back to the Data View tab, SPSS will now recognize *1* as *class 1*, *2* as *class 2*, and so on in the row you labeled *classes*.

FIGURE 1.10   SPSS Dialog Box for Coding the Variable

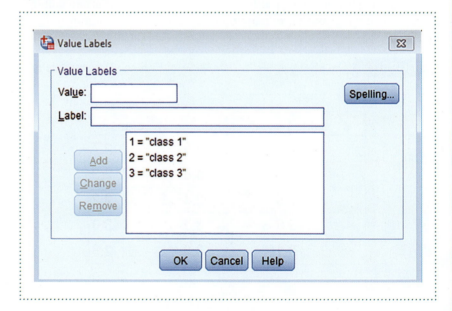

4. Open the Data View tab. In the first column, enter *1* five times, *2* five times, and *3* five times, as shown in Figure 1.11. This tells SPSS that there are five students in each class. In the second column, enter the GPA scores for each class by row, as shown in Figure 1.11. The data are now entered by row.

The data for all the variables are labeled, coded, and entered. If you do this correctly, SPSS will make summarizing, computing, and analyzing any statistic taught in this book fast and simple.

FIGURE 1.11 Data Entry in SPSS Data View for Entering Data by Row

classes	GPA
1	3.3
1	2.9
1	3.5
1	3.6
1	3.1
2	3.9
2	4.0
2	2.4
2	3.1
2	3.0
3	2.7
3	2.3
3	2.2
3	3.0
3	2.8

• • • CHAPTER SUMMARY ORGANIZED BY LEARNING OBJECTIVE

LO 1–2: **Distinguish between descriptive and inferential statistics; explain how samples and populations, as well as a sample statistic and population parameter, differ.**

- Statistics is a branch of mathematics used to summarize, analyze, and interpret a group of numbers or observations. Descriptive statistics are procedures used to summarize, organize, and make sense of a set of scores called *data*—typically presented graphically, in tabular form (in tables), or as summary statistics (single values). Inferential statistics are procedures that allow researchers to infer whether observations made with samples are also likely to be observed in the population.

- A population is a set of all individuals, items, or data of interest. A characteristic that describes a population is called a population parameter. A sample is a set of individuals, items, or data selected from a population of interest. A characteristic that describes a sample is called a sample statistic.

LO 3: **Describe three research methods commonly used in behavioral science.**

- The experimental design uses manipulation, randomization, and comparison/control to ensure enough control to allow researchers to draw cause-and-effect conclusions.

- The quasi-experimental design is structured similar to an experiment but lacks randomization and/or a comparison/control group.

- The correlational method is used to measure pairs of scores for each individual and examine the relationship between the variables.

LO 4: **State the four scales of measurement and provide an example for each.**

- Scales of measurement identify how the properties of numbers can change with different uses. Scales are characterized by three properties: order, difference, and ratio. There are four scales of measurement: nominal, ordinal, interval, and ratio. Nominal scales are typically coded (e.g., seasons, months, sex), ordinal scales indicate order alone (e.g., rankings, grade level), interval scales have equidistant scales and no true zero (e.g., rating scale values, temperature), and ratio scales

are also distributed in equal units but have a true zero (e.g., weight, height, calories).

LO 5–6: **Distinguish between quantitative and qualitative variables; distinguish between continuous and discrete variables.**

- A quantitative variable varies by amount, whereas a qualitative variable varies by class. A continuous variable is measured along a continuum, whereas a discrete variable is measured in whole units or categories. Hence, continuous but not discrete variables are measured at any place beyond the decimal point.

LO 7: **Enter data into SPSS by placing each group in a separate column and each group in a single column (coding is required).**

- SPSS can be used to enter and define variables. All variables are defined in the Variable View tab. The values recorded for each variable are listed in the Data View tab. Data can be entered by column or by row in the Data View tab. Listing data by row requires coding the variable. Variables are coded in the Variable View tab in the Values column (for more details, see Section 1.7).

••• KEY TERMS

coding
continuous variable
data
datum
dependent variable (DV)
descriptive statistics
discrete variable
equidistant scale
experiment
independent variable (IV)
inferential statistics
interval scale

levels of the
   independent variable
nominal scale
operational definition
ordinal scale
population
population parameter
qualitative variable
quantitative variable
quasi-independent variable
random assignment
ratio scale

raw score
research method
sample
sample statistic
scales of measurement
science
scientific method
score
statistics
true zero

••• END-OF-CHAPTER PROBLEMS

Factual Problems

1. Distinguish between descriptive and inferential statistics.

2. What is the difference between data and a raw score?

3. By definition, how is a sample related to a population?

4. State three commonly used research methods in behavioral science.

5. In an experiment, researchers measure two types of variables: independent and dependent variables.

    (a) Which variable is measured in each group?

    (b) Which variable is manipulated to create the groups?

6. State the four scales of measurement. Which scale of measurement is the most informative?

7. Can a nominal variable be numeric? Explain.

8. What is the main distinction between variables on an interval scale and those on a ratio scale of measurement?

9. A qualitative variable varies by _____; a quantitative variable varies by _____.

10. What are the two types of variables that can be quantitative?

Concept and Application Problems

11. State whether each of the following words best describes descriptive statistics or inferential statistics.

    (a) Summarize

    (b) Infer

    (c) Describe

12. State whether each of the following is true or false.

    (a) Graphs, tables, and summary statistics all illustrate the application of inferential statistics.

    (b) Inferential statistics are procedures used to make inferences about a population, given only a limited amount of data.

    (c) Descriptive statistics can be used to describe populations and samples of data.

13. A researcher measured behavior among all individuals in a small population. Are inferential statistics necessary to draw conclusions concerning this population? Explain.

14. Appropriately use the terms *sample* and *population* to describe the following statement: A statistics class has 25 students enrolled, but only 23 students attended class.

15. A researcher measures the height and income of participants and finds that taller men tend to earn greater incomes than do shorter men. What type of research method did the researcher use in this example? Explain.

16. A researcher demonstrates that eating breakfast in the morning causes increased alertness throughout the day. What research design must the researcher have used in this example? Explain.

17. On occasion, a sample can be larger than the population from which it was selected. Explain why this cannot be true.

18. State whether each of the following variables is an example of an independent variable or a quasi-independent variable. Only answer *quasi-independent* for variables that cannot be randomized.

    (a) Marital status

    (b) Political affiliation

    (c) Time of delay prior to recall

    (d) Environment of research setting

    (e) Years of education

    (f) Type of feedback (negative, positive)

19. To determine whether a new sleeping pill was effective, adult insomniacs received a pill (either real or fake), and their sleeping times were subsequently measured (in minutes) during an overnight observation period.

    (a) Identify the dependent variable in this study.

    (b) Identify the independent variable in this study.

20. A researcher tests whether mindfulness training reduces impulsive behavior in a sample of participants with a history of impulsivity.

    (a) Identify the independent variable in this study.

    (b) Identify the dependent variable in this study.

21. A study is conducted to test whether rewarding children in a cheer camp intermittently (4 times during the camp) or once at the end of the camp differentially bolsters how much they enjoy cheering.

    (a) Identify the independent and dependent variable in this study.

    (b) What is the scale of measurement of the independent variable?

22. Rank the scales of measurement in order from least informative to most informative.

23. What is the main disadvantage of measuring qualitative data? In your answer, also explain why quantitative research is most often applied in the behavioral sciences.

24. State whether each of the following describes a study measuring a qualitative or quantitative variable.

    (a) A researcher distributes open-ended questions to participants asking how they feel when they are in love.

    (b) A researcher records the blood pressure of participants during a task meant to induce stress.

    (c) A psychologist interested in drug addiction injects rats with an attention-inducing drug and then measures the rate of lever pressing.

    (d) A witness to a crime gives a description of the suspect to the police.

25. State whether each of the following is an example of a continuous or discrete variable.

    (a) Time in seconds to memorize a list of words

    (b) Number of students in a statistics class

    (c) Weight in pounds of newborn infants

    (d) SAT scores among college students

26. Fill in the table below to identify the characteristics of each variable.

Variable	Continuous vs. Discrete	Quantitative vs. Qualitative	Scale of Measurement
Sex (male, female)			
Seasons (spring, summer, fall, winter)			
Time of day			
Rating scale score			
Movie ratings (1 to 4 stars)			
Number of students in your class			
Temperature (degrees Fahrenheit)			
Time (in minutes) to prepare dinner			
Position standing in line			

Problems in Research

27. **Gun ownership in the United States.** Data from Gallup polls over a 40-year period show how gun ownership in the United States has changed. The results are described in the table below, with the percent of Americans who own guns given in each of five decades:

Year	%
1972	43
1982	42
1992	48
2002	40
2012	43

Source: Reported at http://www.gallup.com/poll/1645/Guns.aspx

(a) Are the percentages reported here an example of descriptive statistics or inferential statistics?

(b) Based on the percentages given in the table, how has gun ownership in the United States changed over the past 40 years?

28. **The curiosity of a child.** Jirout and Klahr (2012) were interested in understanding how to characterize and study curiosity in children. In their article, they note, "Although curiosity is an undeniably important aspect of children's cognitive development, a universally accepted [way to measure] curiosity does not exist" (Jirout & Klahr, 2012, p. 125). What type of definition, according to these authors, is needed for the term *curiosity*?

29. **Selecting samples from populations.** Grafström and Schelin (2014) conducted a study evaluating the selection of samples from populations.

They identified that "the main goal [of selecting samples] is to select a sample so that various parameters can be estimated with good precision" (Grafström & Schelin, 2014, p. 277).

(a) What does a parameter describe?

(b) What are the characteristics in a sample called that are used to estimate the various parameters that the authors refer to?

30. **Noise levels in hospital rooms.** Pope (2010) conducted a study to test if noise levels measured in decibels differed in medical/surgical nursing units compared to patient rooms. She found that noise levels were substantially higher in the patient rooms compared to the nursing units. In this study, state whether noise levels in decibels were each of the following:

(a) Continuous or discrete

(b) Qualitative or quantitative

(c) Nominal, ordinal, interval, or ratio scale

31. **Educational attainment and delirium.** Martins, Paiva, Simões, and Fernandes (2017) conducted a study aimed to "analyze the relationship between educational attainment and delirium [i.e., a serious disturbance in mental abilities]" (p. 95). Based on the aims described for the study, what type of research design was likely the one utilized in this study: experimental, nonexperimental, or correlational? Explain your answer.

32. **Describing the scales of measurement.** Landry (2015) stated, "[Scaled] data can be validly treated as interval" (p. 1348). Explain why data on a rating scale are often treated as interval scale data in the behavioral sciences.

Answers for even numbers are in Appendix D.

Sharpen your skills with **SAGE edge** at edge.sagepub.com/priviteraess2e

SAGE edge for Students provides a personalized approach to help you accomplish your coursework goals in an easy-to-use learning environment.

iStock/Sergey Nivans

2

Summarizing Data
Frequency Distributions in Tables and Graphs

• • • Learning Objectives

After reading this chapter, you should be able to:

1. Construct a simple frequency distribution for grouped and ungrouped data.

2. Determine whether data should be grouped or ungrouped.

3. Identify when it is appropriate to distribute the cumulative frequency, relative frequency, relative percent, cumulative relative frequency, and cumulative percent.

4. Identify percentile points and percentile ranks in a cumulative percent distribution.

5. Construct and interpret graphs for distributions of continuous data.

6. Construct and interpret graphs for distributions of discrete data.

7. Construct frequency distributions for quantitative and categorical data using SPSS.

8. Construct histograms, bar charts, and pie charts using SPSS.

Often, the types of data that interest you are simple counts. In other words, you often ask questions that relate to how often or how frequently something of interest occurs. An employer may ask, "When do most employees call off from work?" to decide about staffing; a college student may ask, "How often does an instructor receive positive ratings from his or her students?" to decide whether or not to enroll in a class; a frequent flyer may ask, "How frequently do popular airlines have flight delays?" to decide which airline to travel with. In each example, the decision being made is based upon how frequently or how often something occurs.

Likewise, frequencies have a big place in science. For example, many aspects of behavior are naturally categorical, such as obesity and mental health, where scientists are concerned with how many people fall into categories that can range from "normal" to higher levels of severity or risk. Behaviors in educational or school settings often relate to rankings where students are counted in various levels of ability from high to low achieving. In workplace settings, employees are often rated on their job performance, and the number of employees meeting versus below standards may be counted to track the quality of employee performance across an organization. Likewise, general demographic data, such as sex and race, are often recorded in research studies, and reported to disclose the types of participants observed in a research study. In this way, frequency data are often utilized in science, and it is therefore useful to have a set of procedures to simplify the presentation of how often or how frequently events and behaviors occur.

Statistics provides a useful way to accomplish the summary of frequencies, typically by summarizing them in tables or graphs. In this chapter, we will introduce many ways in which researchers summarize, organize, and make sense of frequency data to appropriately construct and accurately interpret many of the tables and graphs used to summarize data in behavioral research.

Master the content.

edge.sagepub.com/priviteraess2e

2.1 WHY SUMMARIZE DATA?

Suppose you scored 90% on your first statistics exam. How could you determine how well you did in comparison to the rest of the class? First you would need to consider the scores of the other students. If there were 20 students in the class, the listing of scores could look like Figure 2.1a. This listing is not particularly helpful because you cannot see at a glance how a score of 90% compares to the other grades. A more meaningful arrangement is to place the data in a summary table that shows the **frequency** of exam scores, which in this case is the number of scores for each grade range. When you arrange the scores in this way, as shown in Figure 2.1b, you can see that an exam score of 90% is extremely good. Only three students earned a score of 90% or higher, and most of the class earned lower scores.

This simple example illustrates the need to summarize data (recall from Chapter 1 that summarization is part of descriptive statistics), in that it can make the presentation and interpretation of a distribution of data clearer. Today, computers can construct just about any table or graph we need. But to understand what computers do, it helps to work through smaller data sets by hand. We do that in this chapter, starting with a discussion of frequency distribution tables and concluding with graphs of distributions for frequency data. In all, this chapter will help you appropriately construct and accurately interpret many of the tables and graphs used to summarize data in behavioral research.

FIGURE 2.1   Summarizing the Frequency of Scores

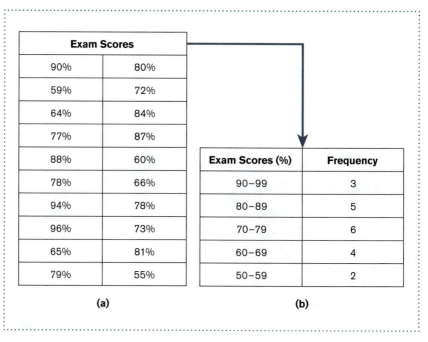

(a)   (b)

This figure shows (a) a list of 20 exam scores and (b) a summary table of the frequency of scores from that list.

A **frequency** is the number of times or how often a category, score, or range of scores occurs.

2.2 FREQUENCY DISTRIBUTIONS FOR GROUPED DATA

Frequency distributions summarize how often (or frequently) scores occur in a data set. Frequency distributions are most often published when researchers count the number of times that scores occur. Consider, for example, hypothetical data based on research often conducted for evaluating the time children spend watching television (Ansari & Crosnoe, 2016; Timperio, Crawford, Ball, & Salmon, 2017). The hypothetical values listed in Table 2.1 are the average number of minutes (rounded to the nearest whole number) that 50 healthy American children watched television per day in the previous year.

Table 2.1 is not really informative as presented. It is only a listing of 50 numbers. To make sense of this list, researchers will consider what makes these data interesting—that is, by determining how the results of this study can be more meaningful to someone wanting to learn something about children's television habits.

Simple Frequency Distribution

One way to make these data more meaningful is to summarize how often scores occur in this list using a **simple frequency distribution**. In a simple frequency distribution, we can summarize how often each individual score occurs (i.e., ungrouped data, defined in Section 2.5) or how often scores occur in defined groups or intervals (i.e., **grouped data**). Often we collect hundreds or even thousands of scores. With such large data sets with many different values recorded, it is generally clearer to summarize the frequency of scores in groups or **intervals**. When summarizing data this way, the data are called grouped data.

A **frequency distribution** is a summary display for a distribution of data organized or summarized in terms of how often a category, score, or range of scores occurs.

A **simple frequency distribution** is a summary display for (1) the frequency of each individual score or category (ungrouped data) in a distribution or (2) the frequency of scores falling within defined groups or intervals (grouped data) in a distribution.

Grouped data are a set of scores distributed into intervals, where the frequency of each score can fall into any given interval.

An **interval** is a discrete range of values within which the frequency of a subset of scores is contained.

TABLE 2.1 The Average Time (in minutes) That 50 Healthy American Children Watched Television per Day in the Previous Year

30	70	7	47	13
60	0	91	33	44
40	9	67	55	65
12	140	77	49	77
110	98	21	22	44
33	44	18	10	33
30	20	110	109	54
17	40	102	33	17
55	16	90	12	175
44	33	33	7	82

Table 2.1 lists 50 scores, which is large enough that we will need to summarize this list of scores into groups or intervals. To construct a simple frequency distribution for grouped data, follow three steps:

Step 1: Find the real range.

Step 2: Find the interval width.

Step 3: Construct the frequency distribution.

We will follow these three steps to construct a frequency distribution for the data given in Table 2.1.

Step 1: Find the real range. The **real range** is one more than the difference between the largest and smallest number in a list of data. In Table 2.1, the smallest value is 0, and the largest value is 175; therefore, 175 − 0 = 175. The *real range* is 175 + 1 = 176.

Step 2: Find the interval width. The **interval width** is the range of values contained in each interval of a grouped frequency distribution. To find this, we divide the real range by the number of intervals chosen. The recommended number of intervals is between 5 and 20. Anything less provides too little summary; anything more is often too confusing. Regardless, *you* choose the number of intervals. The computation for the interval width can be stated as follows:

FYI

Simple frequency distributions summarize how often scores occur. With larger data sets, the frequency of scores contained in discrete intervals is summarized (grouped data).

$$\text{Interval Width} = \frac{\text{Real Range}}{\text{Number of intervals}}$$

If we decide to split the data in Table 2.1 into 10 intervals, then the computation is $\frac{176}{10}$; hence, the interval width is 17.6. Rounding is necessary when the value for the interval width is not the same degree of accuracy as the original list. For example, the data listed in Table 2.1 are rounded to the ones place (i.e., the nearest whole number). Thus, the interval width should also be a whole number. If it is not, then the interval width should be *rounded up* to the nearest whole number. For this example, we round 17.6 up to an interval width of 18 (the nearest whole number).

The **real range** is one more than the difference between the largest and smallest values in a data set.

The **interval width** or **class width** is the range of values contained in each interval of a grouped frequency distribution.

Interval boundaries are the upper and lower limits for each interval in a grouped frequency distribution.

Step 3: Construct the frequency distribution. To construct the frequency distribution, we distribute the same number of intervals that we chose in Step 2. In this case, we chose 10 intervals. Table 2.2 shows that each interval has a width of 18. Notice that the first interval contains 18 times in seconds (0, 1, 2, 3, 4, 5, 6, 7, 8, 9, 10, 11, 12, 13, 14, 15, 16, 17), so it does have a width of 18. In a frequency distribution, the **interval boundaries** mark the cutoffs for a given interval. The **lower boundary** is the smallest value in each interval, and the **upper boundary** is the largest value in each interval.

Table 2.2 shows that each lower boundary begins one degree of accuracy greater than the previous upper boundary. This means that we add one whole number because this is the degree of accuracy of the data. (If the data were to the tenths place, then we would add .1; if the data were to the hundredths place, then we would add .01; and so on.) We again make the interval width 18 for the second interval and repeat this process until all 10 intervals are constructed. In all, there are four rules for creating a simple frequency distribution:

1. Each interval is defined (it has a lower and upper boundary). Intervals such as "or more" or "less than" should not be expressed.

2. Each interval is equidistant (the interval width is the same for each interval).

3. No interval overlaps (the same score cannot occur in more than one interval).

4. All values are rounded to the same degree of accuracy measured in the original data (or to the ones place for the data listed in Table 2.1).

The total counts in a frequency distribution should sum to the total number of counts made. Because we recorded data for 50 children, the frequency distribution must sum to 50; otherwise, we made a counting error. In all, the simple frequency distribution in Table 2.2 paints a picture of the data, so to speak—it conveys a more descriptive and meaningful way to look at the data.

Also, Table 2.2 shows that only two values fall at or above 126. It may be tempting here to combine the top three intervals into one **open interval**. In other words, we could list the interval as "126 and above" because only two values were counted. Often you will see open intervals published when **outliers** exist in a set of data, but be aware that this is not very informative. An outlier is an extreme score that falls substantially above or below most other scores in a distribution. In this example, 175 is an outlier in the data because this value falls substantially above most of the other values recorded. An open interval would make it less obvious that this outlier exists because the upper boundary of the interval would not be given; instead, the upper boundary would be left open.

Example 2.1 applies the steps for distributing the frequency of scores in a data set.

FYI

For grouped data, the frequencies are listed into equal-sized intervals that do not overlap. Hence, each score falls into one and only one interval.

FYI

Open intervals violate the first rule for simple frequency distributions and can make it difficult to identify if outliers exist in a data set.

The **lower boundary** is the smallest value in each interval of a frequency distribution; the **upper boundary** is the largest value in each interval of a frequency distribution.

An **open interval**, or **open class**, is an interval with no defined upper or lower boundary.

Outliers are extreme scores that fall substantially above or below most of the scores in a particular data set.

TABLE 2.2 Simple Frequency Distribution

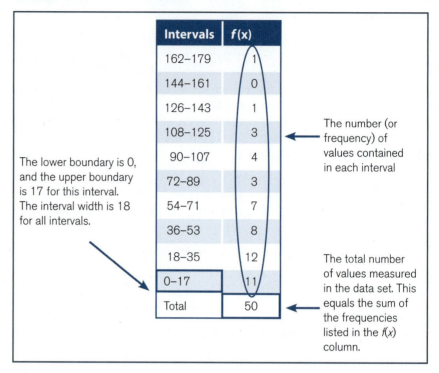

Intervals	f(x)
162–179	1
144–161	0
126–143	1
108–125	3
90–107	4
72–89	3
54–71	7
36–53	8
18–35	12
0–17	11
Total	50

The lower boundary is 0, and the upper boundary is 17 for this interval. The interval width is 18 for all intervals.

The number (or frequency) of values contained in each interval

The total number of values measured in the data set. This equals the sum of the frequencies listed in the f(x) column.

A simple frequency distribution for the average time in minutes that 50 healthy American children watched television per day in the previous year. In this table, f(x) denotes the column heading for the frequency (f) of scores (x) in each interval.

LEARNING CHECK 1

1. A _____ is a summary display for a distribution of data organized or summarized in terms of how often (or frequently) scores occur.

2. True or false: A researcher observes that a single parent works 42.25 hours per week. The degree of accuracy of 42.25 is to the hundredths place (.01).

3. Each of the following is a rule for the simple frequency distribution except:

   (a) Each interval is equidistant.

   (b) The same score cannot occur in more than one interval.

   (c) Each interval is defined (it has a lower and an upper boundary).

   (d) The interval width is equal to the number of intervals in a frequency distribution.

4. What is the recommended number of intervals that should be included in a simple frequency distribution?

5. Why is it generally inappropriate to include an open interval in a simple frequency distribution?

Answers: 1. Frequency distribution; 2. True; 3. d; 4. 5 to 20 intervals; 5. Including an open interval can make it difficult to identify if outliers exist in a data set.

Example 2.1

A topic of interest in industrial organizational psychology is studying issues of worker safety (Burt, 2015; Mullen, Kelloway, & Teed, 2017). To study this topic, a researcher records the number of complaints about safety filed by employees of 45 local small businesses over the previous 3 years. The results are listed in Table 2.3. In this example, we can construct a frequency distribution of these data.

TABLE 2.3	The Number of Safety Complaints That Employees at 45 Local Small Businesses Filed Over the Previous 3 Years

45	98	83	50	86
66	66	88	95	73
88	55	76	115	66
92	110	79	105	101
101	85	90	92	81
55	95	91	92	
78	66	73	58	
86	92	51	63	
91	77	88	86	
94	80	102	107	

Step 1: Find the real range. The smallest value in Table 2.3 is 45, and the largest value is 115; therefore, $115 - 45 = 70$. The real range is $70 + 1 = 71$.

Step 2: Find the interval width. We can split the data into eight intervals (again, you choose the number of intervals). The interval width is the real range divided by the number of intervals: $\frac{71}{8} = 8.88$. The original data are listed as whole numbers, so we round up to the nearest whole number. The nearest whole number is the degree of accuracy of the data. The interval width is 9.

Step 3: Construct the frequency distribution. The frequency distribution table is shown in Table 2.4. The first interval starts with the smallest value (45) and contains nine values. To construct the next interval, add one degree of accuracy, or one whole number in this example, and repeat the steps to construct the remaining intervals.

One important rule of thumb is to always summarize data in terms of how you want to describe them. For example, if you want to describe the frequency of safety complaints in discrete intervals, then a simple frequency distribution is a great way to summarize the data. But often, researchers want to describe frequencies "at or above" a certain value, or the percentage of people scoring "at least" a certain score. In these cases, it can be more effective to summarize frequency data cumulatively or as percents. Many of these additional summaries for frequency data are described here.

TABLE 2.4   Simple Frequency Distribution

Intervals	f(x)
108–116	2
99–107	5
90–98	11
81–89	9
72–80	7
63–71	5
54–62	3
45–53	3

A simple frequency distribution with eight intervals and an interval width of 9. The data are the number of complaints about safety that employees of 45 local small businesses filed over the previous 3 years.

Cumulative Frequency Distribution

When researchers want to describe frequencies above or below a certain value, they often report a **cumulative frequency distribution**. A cumulative frequency distributes the sum of frequencies across a series of intervals. You can add from the top or from the bottom; it really depends on how you want to discuss the data. To illustrate, we will use the data summarized in Table 2.4 (Example 2.1), which shows the frequencies of the number of complaints about safety for 45 small local businesses.

Suppose the researcher wants to describe these businesses as safe, at risk, or dangerous. She uses the following criteria to categorize these businesses: safe (fewer than 72 complaints filed), at risk (between 72 and 89 complaints filed), and dangerous (at least 90 complaints filed). Let us see how a cumulative frequency distribution can be a clearer way to describe these safety categories.

We can sum the frequencies beginning with the bottom frequency and adding up the table, as shown in the last column of Table 2.5. In the table, we began with the frequency in the bottom interval (3) and added the frequency above it to get 6 (3 + 3), added again to get the next frequency 11 (3 + 3 + 5), and repeated these steps until all frequencies were summed. The top frequency is equal to the total number of measures recorded (the total was 45 businesses in this example). This type of summary from the "bottom up" is most meaningful to discuss data in terms of "less than" or "at or below" a certain value or "at most." For example, "safe" businesses are those that report *fewer than* 72 complaints. In the cumulative frequency column, we find that 11 businesses are categorized as safe.

We can also sum the frequencies beginning with the top frequency and adding down the table, although this is less common. To do this, we follow the same steps shown in Table 2.5 but instead begin at the top of the table

A **cumulative frequency distribution** is a summary display that distributes the sum of frequencies across a series of intervals.

in the first column. Hence, in the table we begin with the frequency in the top interval (2) and add the frequency below it (5) to get 7 (2 + 5), add again (11) to get the next frequency 18 (2 + 5 + 11), and repeat these steps until all frequencies are summed. The bottom frequency will equal the total number of measures recorded (the total is 45 businesses in this example). This type of "top down" summary is more meaningful to discuss data in terms of "greater than" or "at or above" a certain value or "at least."

FYI

The cumulative frequency distribution describes the sum of scores across each range and always sums to the total number of scores in a distribution.

TABLE 2.5 A Cumulative Frequency Distribution Table With Calculations Shown in the Center Column

Intervals	Frequency, $f(x)$	Calculation →	Cumulative Frequency (Bottom Up)
108–116	2	3 + 3 + 5 + 7 + 9 + 11 + 5 + 2	45
99–107	5	3 + 3 + 5 + 7 + 9 + 11 + 5	43
90–98	11	3 + 3 + 5 + 7 + 9 + 11	38
81–89	9	3 + 3 + 5 + 7 + 9	27
72–80	7	3 + 3 + 5 + 7	18
63–71	5	3 + 3 + 5	11
54–62	3	3 + 3	6
45–53	3	3	3
	$N = 45$		

LEARNING CHECK 2

1. A _____ is a summary display that distributes the sum of frequencies across a series of intervals.

2. Cumulative frequencies can be added from the top _____ and the bottom _____.

3. When cumulating frequencies from the bottom up, you typically want to discuss the data in terms of:
   (a) "At most"
   (b) "Less than"
   (c) "At or below"
   (d) All of the above

4. True or false: Whether you cumulate a frequency distribution from the bottom up or the top down depends on how you want to discuss the data.

5. When cumulating frequencies from the top down, you typically want to discuss the data in terms of:
   (a) "Less than"
   (b) "At or above"
   (c) "At most"
   (d) All of the above

Answers: 1. Cumulative frequency distribution; 2. Down, up; 3. d; 4. True; 5. b.

Relative Frequency Distribution

When researchers summarize larger data sets (with thousands or even millions of counts), they often distribute the **relative frequency** of scores rather than counts. A relative frequency is a **proportion** from 0 to 1.0 that describes the portion of data in each interval. It is often easier to list the relative frequency of scores because a list with very large frequencies in each interval can be more confusing to read. The calculation for a relative frequency is as follows:

$$\text{Relative Frequency} = \frac{\text{Observed Frequency}}{\text{Total Frequency Count}}$$

Using the same data listed in Table 2.5, we can calculate relative frequency by dividing the frequency in each interval by the total frequency count. The relative frequency in each interval in Table 2.6 (from the top down) is

$$\frac{2}{45} = .04, \frac{5}{45} = .11, \frac{11}{45} = .24, \frac{9}{45} = .20, \frac{7}{45} = .16, \frac{5}{45} = .11, \frac{3}{45} = .07, \text{ and } \frac{3}{45} = .07.$$

The sum of relative frequencies across all intervals is 1.00, or, in this example, $\frac{45}{45} = 1.00$.

FYI

Relative percents and relative frequencies summarize the percentage and proportion of scores falling into each interval, respectively.

The **relative frequency distribution** is a summary display that distributes the proportion of scores in each interval. It is computed as the frequency in each interval divided by the total number of frequencies recorded.

A **proportion** is a part or portion of all measured data. The sum of all proportions for a distribution of scores is 1.0.

The **relative percent distribution** is a summary display that distributes the percentage of scores occurring in each interval relative to all scores distributed.

Relative Percent Distribution

A common way to summarize a relative frequency is to convert it to a relative percent because most readers find it easier to understand percents than decimals, perhaps because percents are the basis for awarding grades from grade school through college. To compute a **relative percent**, multiply the relative frequency by 100, which moves the decimal point two places to the right:

$$\text{Relative Percent} = \frac{\text{Observed Frequency}}{\text{Total Frequency Count}} \times 100$$

Percents range from 0% to 100% and can never be negative. The relative percent in each interval is given in the last column in Table 2.6. A relative percent provides the same information as a relative frequency; it is just that many people find it easier to read percents than decimals. The choice of which to use is up to the person compiling the data; there is no right or wrong approach because both provide the same information.

TABLE 2.6 The Relative Frequency of Scores in Each Interval (third column)

Intervals	Frequency, $f(x)$	Relative Frequency	Relative Percent
108–116	2	.04	4%
99–107	5	.11	11%
90–98	11	.24	24%
81–89	9	.20	20%
72–80	7	.16	16%
63–71	5	.11	11%
54–62	3	.07	7%
45–53	3	.07	7%
	$N = 45$	Total Rel. Freq. = 1.00	Total Rel. Percent = 100%

The calculation for each relative frequency is given in the text. The relative percent of scores in each interval is given in the last column.

LEARNING CHECK 3

1. When would a researcher construct a relative frequency table?

2. The sum of relative frequencies across all intervals is equal to _____.

3. Relative frequencies are commonly reported in academic journals as percents. Why?

4. True or false: A relative percent sums to the total frequency count.

Answers: 1. To summarize large data sets; 2. 1.00; 3. Readers often find percents easier to read than decimals; 4. False; A relative percent sums to 100%.

Cumulative Relative Frequency and Cumulative Percent Distribution

It is also useful to summarize relative frequencies and percents cumulatively for the same reasons described for cumulative frequencies. To distribute the **cumulative relative frequency**, add each relative frequency beginning at the top or bottom of the table. Table 2.7 lists the bottom-up cumulative relative frequency distribution for the business safety data, with calculations given in the table. To add from the bottom up in the table, we

The **cumulative relative frequency distribution** is a summary display that distributes the sum of relative frequencies across a series of intervals.

summed the relative frequency in each interval as we moved up the table. For the top-down summary, we would follow these same steps, except we would begin at the top of the table and sum down. The total cumulative relative frequency is equal to 1.00 (give or take rounding errors).

To distribute **cumulative percents**, we can sum the relative percent in each interval, following the same procedures for adding as we did for the cumulative relative frequencies. In a cumulative percent distribution, shown in the last column of Table 2.8, intervals are typically summed from the smallest to the largest score in a distribution (bottom up). The total cumulative percent is equal to 100% (give or take rounding errors). In the next section, we discuss the usefulness of a cumulative percent distribution for identifying percentile points and ranks.

A **cumulative percent distribution** is a summary display that distributes the sum of relative percents across a series of intervals.

TABLE 2.7 A Cumulative Relative Frequency Distribution Table With Calculations Shown in the Fourth Column

Intervals	Frequency, $f(x)$	Relative Frequency	Calculation →	Cumulative Relative Frequency (Bottom Up)
108–116	2	.04	.07 + .07 + .11 + .16 + .20 + .24 + .11 + .04	1.00
99–107	5	.11	.07 + .07 + .11 + .16 + .20 + .24 + .11	.96
90–98	11	.24	.07 + .07 + .11 + .16 + .20 + .24	.85
81–89	9	.20	.07 + .07 + .11 + .16 + .20	.61
72–80	7	.16	.07 + .07 + .11 + .16	.41
63–71	5	.11	.07 + .07 + .11	.25
54–62	3	.07	.07 + .07	.14
45–53	3	.07	.07	.07
	$N = 45$			

TABLE 2.8 A Cumulative Percentage of Scores Adding From the Bottom Up

Intervals	Frequency, $f(x)$	Relative Percent	Cumulative Percent (Bottom Up)
108–116	2	4%	100%
99–107	5	11%	96%
90–98	11	24%	85%
81–89	9	20%	61%
72–80	7	16%	41%
63–71	5	11%	25%
54–62	3	7%	14%
45–53	3	7%	7%
	$N = 45$	Total Rel. Percent = 100%	

2.3 IDENTIFYING PERCENTILE POINTS AND PERCENTILE RANKS

In some cases, it may be useful to identify the position or rank of an individual within a frequency distribution. You find cases like this in standardized testing, for example, in which you are given scores that indicate your rank as a percentage relative to others who took the same exam. Class standing is also based upon ranks, with students in the "top percent of the class" being among the best or highest-performing students. To identify the position or rank of an individual, we convert a frequency distribution to a cumulative percent distribution, then apply the steps identified in this section.

A cumulative percent distribution identifies percentiles, which are measures of the relative position of individuals or scores within a larger distribution. A percentile, specifically a **percentile point**, is the value of an individual or a score within a larger distribution. The corresponding percentile of a percentile point is the **percentile rank** of that score. Thus, the 75th percentile point, for example, is the value (the percentile point) below which 75% of scores in a distribution fall (the percentile rank). To find the percentile point in a cumulative percent distribution, we can follow four basic steps. In this section, we will apply these steps to identify the percentile point in a frequency distribution at the 75th percentile for the business safety data, which are reproduced in Table 2.9.

FYI

Cumulative relative frequencies and cumulative percents are a sum of the proportion and percent of scores, respectively, across intervals. These sum to 1.00 or 100%, respectively.

TABLE 2.9 The Cumulative Percentage of Scores for the Business Safety Data

Intervals	Frequency, f(x)	Cumulative Percent (Bottom Up)
108–116	2	100%
99–107	5	96%
90–98	**11**	**85%**
81–89	9	61%
72–80	7	41%
63–71	5	25%
54–62	3	14%
45–53	3	7%
	N = 45	

The 75th percentile falls at this interval

A **percentile point** is the value of a score on a measurement scale below which a specified percentage of scores in a distribution fall.

The **percentile rank** of a score is the percentage of scores with values that fall below a specified score in a distribution.

Step 1: Identify the interval within which a specified percentile point falls. In our example, we want to identify the 75th percentile point, which falls in the interval of 90–98. Note that each percentile given in Table 2.9 is the top percentage in each interval.

Step 2: Identify the real range for the interval identified. In our example, the interval that contains the 75th percentile point is the interval of 90–98 (this is the observed range). The real limits for this interval are 0.5 less than the lower limit and 0.5 greater than the upper limit. Hence, the real limits are 89.5 to 98.5. The width of the real range is therefore 9 points, or 1 point greater than the observed range. For the percentages, the range width is 24 percentage points (from 61% to 85%).

Interval	Percentages
98.5	85%
?	**75%**
89.5	61%

← We are looking for the percentile point at the 75th percentile.

Step 3: Find the position of the percentile point within the interval. To identify the position of the percentile point, first find the distance of the 75th percentile from the top of the interval. The 75th percentile is 10 points from the top of the interval. Next, divide 10 by the total range width of the percentages. Hence, 75% is 10 out of 24, or $\frac{10}{24}$ of the total interval.

As a final part for this step, multiply the fraction by the width of the real range, which is 9 points:

$$\frac{10}{24} \times 9 = 3.75 \text{ points}$$

Hence, the position of the percentile point is 3.75 points from the top of the interval.

Step 4: Identify the percentile point. In this example, the top of the interval is 98.5. We subtract 3.75 from that value to identify the percentile point at the 75th percentile: $98.5 - 3.75 = 94.75$. Thus, the percentile point at the 75th percentile is 94.75.

In all, you can follow these basic steps to find the percentile point at any percentile rank in a frequency distribution.

LEARNING CHECK 4

1. True or false: Cumulative relative frequencies are added from the top down or the bottom up.

2. Cumulative relative frequencies sum to _____ (give or take rounding error).

3. A student scores in the 80th percentile on an exam. What does this mean in comparison to all other students?

Answers: 1. True; 2. 1.00; 3. The student scored higher than 80% of all others who took the same exam.

2.4 SPSS in Focus:
Frequency Distributions for Quantitative Data

SPSS can be used to construct frequency distributions. In this section, we will construct a frequency distribution table for the business safety data first listed in Table 2.3, which are reproduced here for reference.

Data reproduced from Table 2.3.

45	98	83	50	86
66	66	88	95	73
88	55	76	115	66
92	110	79	105	101
101	85	90	92	81
55	95	91	92	
78	66	73	58	
86	92	51	63	
91	77	88	86	
94	80	102	107	

1. Click on the Variable View tab and enter *complaints* in the Name column. We will enter whole numbers, so go to the Decimals column and reduce the value to 0.

2. Click on the Data View tab and enter the 45 values from Table 2.3 in the column labeled *complaints.* You can enter the data in any order you wish, but make sure all the data are entered correctly.

3. Go to the menu bar and click Analyze, then Descriptive Statistics and Frequencies, to bring up the dialog box shown in Figure 2.2.

FIGURE 2.2 SPSS Dialog Box

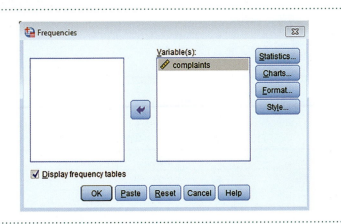

(Continued)

(Continued)

4. In the dialog box, select the *complaints* variable. When you click the arrow in the center, it will move *complaints* into the Variable(s): box to the right. Make sure the option to display frequency tables is selected.

5. Select OK, or select Paste and click the Run command. By clicking Paste, you open a syntax file shown in Figure 2.3 with the code SPSS will use to run your commands. You can save the syntax file instead of the output file we are about to create. The reason is simple: The syntax file does not take up a lot of computer memory space, but the output file does. To create the output file, click the Run command on the toolbar (the colored triangle pointing to the right).

FIGURE 2.3 SPSS Syntax File

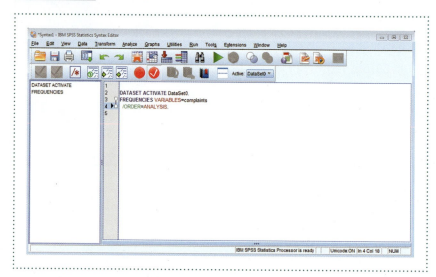

Table 2.10 shows the SPSS output file display. SPSS did not distribute these data into intervals as we did. Instead, every value in the original data set is listed (in numerical order from least to most) with frequencies, relative percents (middle two columns), and cumulative percents given for each value. Note that SPSS automatically groups data into intervals only with very large data sets.

TABLE 2.10 SPSS Output Display

complaints

		Frequency	Percent	Valid Percent	Cumulative Percent
Valid	45	1	2.2	2.2	2.2
	50	1	2.2	2.2	4.4
	51	1	2.2	2.2	6.7
	55	2	4.4	4.4	11.1

58	1	2.2	2.2	13.3
63	1	2.2	2.2	15.6
66	4	8.9	8.9	24.4
73	2	4.4	4.4	28.9
76	1	2.2	2.2	31.1
77	1	2.2	2.2	33.3
78	1	2.2	2.2	35.6
79	1	2.2	2.2	37.8
80	1	2.2	2.2	40.0
81	1	2.2	2.2	42.2
83	1	2.2	2.2	44.4
85	1	2.2	2.2	46.7
86	3	6.7	6.7	53.3
88	3	6.7	6.7	60.0
90	1	2.2	2.2	62.2
91	2	4.4	4.4	66.7
92	4	8.9	8.9	75.6
94	1	2.2	2.2	77.8
95	2	4.4	4.4	82.2
98	1	2.2	2.2	84.4
101	2	4.4	4.4	88.9
102	1	2.2	2.2	91.1
105	1	2.2	2.2	93.3
107	1	2.2	2.2	95.6
110	1	2.2	2.2	97.8
115	1	2.2	2.2	100.0
Total	45	100.0	100.0	

2.5 FREQUENCY DISTRIBUTIONS FOR UNGROUPED DATA

Although we have focused on grouped data (i.e., data grouped into intervals), it is not always necessary to group data when you summarize study results. When the dependent variable is qualitative or categorical, or the number of different scores is small, then the frequency of each individual score or category can be summarized. For data of this type, called **ungrouped data**, each measured score is listed in a frequency table; intervals are not constructed. Let us look at an example.

Suppose you come across an article suggesting that children younger than age 3 years should take at least two naps a day. The benefit of napping in children is certainly a topic of interest in the behavioral sciences (El-Sheikh, Arsiwalla, Staton, Dyer, & Vaughn, 2013; Lo, Dijk, & Groger, 2014). To see how many naps children actually get, you randomly ask a

Ungrouped data are a set of scores or categories distributed individually, where the frequency for each individual score or category is counted.

TABLE 2.11 A List of the Number of Naps That Children, Younger Than Age 3, Take per Day

0	2	1	0
0	2	1	0
2	3	2	2
3	3	2	3
1	4	3	2
2	1	2	0
3	2	2	1
0	3	3	2
2	2	1	0
2	1	0	1

sample of 40 primary caretakers of a child younger than age 3 how many naps their child takes per day, on average. Table 2.11 lists the hypothetical results. For these data, the caretakers gave one of five responses: 0, 1, 2, 3, or 4 naps per day. Grouping data with only five different responses makes little sense, especially because the recommended minimum number of intervals is five. Instead, the data should remain ungrouped. The frequency of ungrouped data is simply listed in a frequency table. We skip all the steps for creating the intervals and go straight to counting the frequency of each value. Each score represents its own count in a frequency distribution table, as shown in Table 2.12. Notice the important distinction: Grouped data have intervals, and ungrouped data do not.

TABLE 2.12 A Simple Frequency Distribution for Ungrouped Data

Number of Naps	$f(x)$
0	8
1	8
2	15
3	8
4	1
	$N = 40$

The data are the number of naps that children, younger than age 3, take per day.

Ungrouped data can be summarized using relative frequency, cumulative relative frequency, relative percent, and cumulative relative percent, just as grouped data can be. It again depends on how you want to describe the data. Summarizing ungrouped data is especially practical for data sets with only a few different scores and for qualitative or categorical variables. Data obtained for opinion and marketing polls, health categories (lean, healthy, overweight, and obese), or college year (freshman, sophomore, junior, and senior) are often summarized as ungrouped data. A research example for summarizing demographic data is given in Section 2.6.

FYI

Data are typically ungrouped for data sets with only a few different scores and for qualitative or categorical variables. For ungrouped data, the frequency of each individual score or category is counted.

2.6 RESEARCH IN FOCUS: SUMMARIZING DEMOGRAPHIC INFORMATION

Lau (2017) conducted a study to examine how social media use and social media multitasking impact academic performance among an undergraduate college sample of 342 students. To describe general characteristics of the students he sampled, the researcher included data, a portion of which is shown in Table 2.13. The table summarizes the subjects being studied and the class year for students (ungrouped, categorical data) in the study. The frequency and relative percent are given for each categorical variable.

TABLE 2.13 Demographic Information of Subject Studied and Class Year of Undergraduate Student Participants

Variable		Frequency	Relative Percent
Subject	Arts	51	14.9%
	Business	73	21.3%
	Education	19	5.6%
	Engineering	29	8.5%
	Law	8	2.3%
	Medicine	53	15.5%
	Science	47	13.7%
	Social Science	62	18.1%
Class Year	First year	123	36.0%
	Second year	85	24.9%
	Third year	75	21.9%
	Fourth year	57	16.7%
	Fifth year	2	0.6%

These data are adapted from Lau (2017).

(Continued)

(Continued)

Most academic journals require that researchers report relevant demographic information of human participants. In this study, the researcher reported demographic data that were relevant to his study. This study showed that using social media for academic purposes did not predict academic performance (i.e., cumulative grade point average), whereas using social media for nonacademic purposes (e.g., video gaming) and multitasking between many types of social media predicted worse academic performance.

2.7 SPSS in Focus: Frequency Distributions for Categorical Data

SPSS can be used to summarize categorical data that are ungrouped. We can use SPSS to create a frequency distribution for the following hypothetical example: A group of health practitioners wants to classify children in public schools as being lean, healthy, overweight, or obese; this type of classification is common (Centers for Disease Control and Prevention, 2016; Privitera, 2016). To do this, the researchers calculated the body mass index (BMI) score of 100 children. Based on the BMI scores, they classified 15 children as lean, 30 as healthy, 35 as overweight, and 20 as obese.

1. Click on the Variable View tab and enter *categories* in the Name column. In the second row, enter *frequencies* in the Name column. We will enter whole numbers, so go to the Decimals column and reduce the value to 0 for both rows.

2. We must code the data for the categorical variable. Click on the Values column and click on the small gray box with three dots. In the dialog box, enter *1* in the Values cell and *lean* in the Label cell, and then click Add. Repeat these steps by entering *2* for *healthy*, *3* for *overweight*, and *4* for *obese*, and then select OK. Now each level for the categorical variable is coded.

3. Click on the Data View tab and enter *1*, *2*, *3*, and *4* in the *categories* column. In the *frequencies* column, enter *15*, *30*, *35*, and *20* next to the corresponding numeric code.

4. Go to Data, then Weight cases . . ., to open up a dialog box. Select Weight cases by and move *frequencies* into the Frequency Variable: box. Now each frequency is matched to each level of the variable.

5. Go to the menu bar and click Analyze, then Descriptive Statistics and Frequencies, to bring up a dialog box.

6. In the dialog box, select the *categories* variable and click the arrow in the center to move *categories* into the box labeled Variable(s): to the right. Make sure the option to display frequency tables is selected.

7. Select OK, or select Paste and click the Run command (the triangle pointing to the right in the toolbar).

Notice that SPSS does not list the values as 1, 2, 3, and 4 in the output table shown in Table 2.14, although you entered these values in the *categories* column in Data View. Instead, SPSS lists the data as you labeled them in Step 2 in Variable View. This format makes it much easier to read the output file. Also, every category in the original data set is listed with frequencies, relative percents, and cumulative percents given.

TABLE 2.14   SPSS Output Display

Statistics

categories

N	Valid	100
	Missing	0

categories

		Frequency	Percent	Valid Percent	Cumulative Percent
Valid	lean	15	15.0	15.0	15.0
	healthy	30	30.0	30.0	45.0
	overweight	35	35.0	35.0	80.0
	obese	20	20.0	20.0	100.0
	Total	100	100.0	100.0	

LEARNING CHECK 5

1. What are the data called when the frequency of each individual score or category is listed?

2. When is it appropriate to summarize frequencies for ungrouped data?

Answers: 1. Ungrouped data; 2. When data sets have only a few different scores and for qualitative or categorical variables.

2.8 GRAPHING DISTRIBUTIONS: CONTINUOUS DATA

Researchers can also display frequency data graphically instead of in a table. Although using a table or graph to summarize frequency data is equally effective for the most part, graphs have the main advantage of being more visual and less intimidating than tables in many cases. In this section, we look at several ways to graph distributions of continuous data: histograms, frequency polygons, and ogives.

Histograms

Grouped data are often summarized graphically using **histograms**. Histograms are graphs that distribute the intervals along the horizontal scale (*x*-axis) and list the frequency of scores in each interval on the vertical scale (*y*-axis). To illustrate, we can construct a histogram for the data given in Figure 2.4, which shows the frequency table and the respective histogram for the time (in months) it took a sample of 200 college graduates to find employment. To construct a histogram, we follow three rules:

Rule 1: A vertical rectangle represents each interval, and the height of the rectangle equals the frequency recorded for each interval. This rule implies that the *y*-axis should be labeled as a number or count. The *y*-axis reflects the frequency of scores for each interval.

Rule 2: The base of each rectangle begins and ends at the upper and lower boundaries of each interval. This rule means that histograms cannot be constructed for open intervals because open intervals do not have an upper or a lower boundary. Also, each rectangle should have the same interval width.

Rule 3: Each rectangle touches adjacent rectangles at the boundaries of each interval. Histograms are used to summarize continuous data, such as the time (in months) it takes to find employment. The adjacent rectangles touch because it is assumed that the data are continuous. In other words, it is assumed that the data were measured along a continuum.

FYI

Histograms summarize the frequency of continuous data that are quantitative.

A **histogram** is a graphical display used to summarize the frequency of continuous data that are distributed in numeric intervals (grouped).

FIGURE 2.4 A Histogram

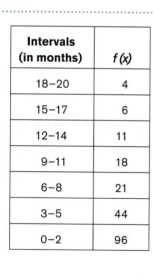

Intervals (in months)	f (x)
18–20	4
15–17	6
12–14	11
9–11	18
6–8	21
3–5	44
0–2	96

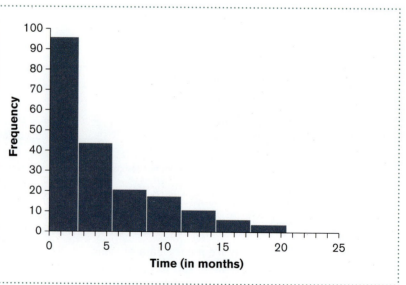

A frequency table (left) and histogram (right) summarizing the frequency distribution for the time (in months) that it took a sample of 200 college graduates to find employment.

Frequency Polygons

Another graph that can be used to summarize grouped data is the **frequency polygon**. A frequency polygon is a dot-and-line graph where the dot is the midpoint of each interval, and the line connects each dot. The midpoint of an interval is distributed along the *x*-axis and is calculated by adding the upper and lower boundaries of an interval and then dividing by 2. Figure 2.5 illustrates a frequency polygon for the same data used to construct the histogram in Figure 2.4. A histogram and a frequency polygon are equally effective at summarizing these data— the choice between the two depends on how you prefer to summarize the data.

Frequency polygons are dot-and-line graphs used to summarize the same types of data as histograms.

FYI

FIGURE 2.5 A Frequency Polygon

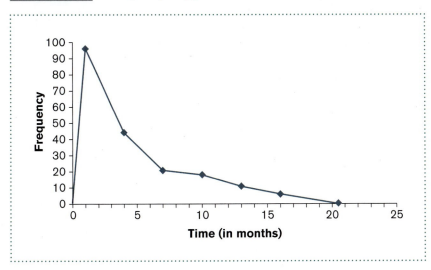

A frequency polygon summarizing the frequency distribution for the time (in months) that it took a sample of 200 college graduates to find employment.

Ogives

A dot-and-line graph can also be used to summarize cumulative percents. This type of graph, called an **ogive** (pronounced *oh-jive*), is used to summarize the cumulative percents of continuous data at the upper boundary of each interval. Figure 2.6 shows an ogive for the cumulative percent distribution, from the bottom up, for the same data used to construct the histogram in Figure 2.4. The *y*-axis of an ogive always ranges from 0% to 100% of the data.

Notice that each dot in an ogive is plotted at the upper boundary of each interval. Each dot represents the cumulative percent of scores at each interval. Plotting at the upper boundary of each interval is necessary because this point represents or contains all the scores in that interval.

A **frequency polygon** is a dot-and-line graph used to summarize the frequency of continuous data at the midpoint of each interval.

An **ogive** is a dot-and-line graph used to summarize the cumulative percent of continuous data at the upper boundary of each interval.

FIGURE 2.6   An Ogive

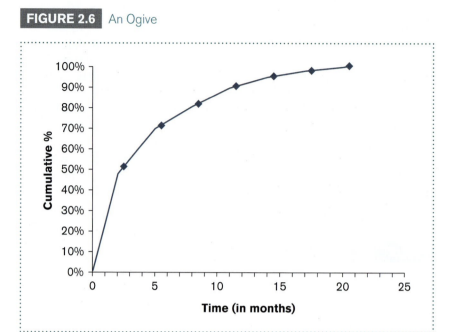

An ogive summarizing the cumulative percent distribution for the time (in months) that it took a sample of 200 college graduates to find employment.

LEARNING CHECK 6

1. All of the following are rules for constructing histograms except:

   (a) A vertical rectangle represents each interval, and the height of the rectangle equals the frequency recorded for each interval.

   (b) The base of each rectangle begins and ends at the upper and lower boundaries of each interval.

   (c) Each rectangle represents the frequency of all scores in a distribution.

   (d) Each rectangle touches adjacent rectangles at the boundaries of each interval.

2. True or false: Histograms are used to summarize ungrouped data, which is why each vertical rectangle touches the other.

3. A(n) _____ is a dot-and-line graph plotted at the midpoint of each interval, whereas a(n) _____ is a dot-and-line graph plotted at the upper boundary of each interval.

4. An ogive graphically summarizes what type of frequency distribution?

Answers: 1. c; 2. False. Histograms are used to summarize grouped data; 3. Frequency polygon, ogive; 4. A cumulative percent distribution.

2.9 GRAPHING DISTRIBUTIONS: DISCRETE AND CATEGORICAL DATA

Researchers often measure discrete variables—variables measured in whole units. For example, the number of traffic accidents and the number of college graduates are discrete variables because these variables are measured by counting one traffic accident or college graduate at a time. Researchers often measure categorical variables, which vary by class. Examples include race, gender, and marital status. Discrete and categorical data are graphed differently than continuous data because the data are measured in whole units or classes and not along a continuum. Two types of graphs for discrete and categorical data described here are bar charts and pie charts.

Bar Charts

Bar charts are much like histograms, except that the bars are separated from one another, whereas the vertical rectangles or bars on histograms touch each other. The separation between bars reflects the separation or "break" between the whole numbers or categories being summarized. For this reason, bar charts are appropriate for summarizing distributions of discrete and categorical data.

To construct a bar chart, list the whole units or categories along the x-axis, and distribute the frequencies along the y-axis. To illustrate, Figure 2.7 gives the frequency distribution and the respective bar chart for the number of naps that mothers give their children daily. (The original data for Figure 2.7 are given in Table 2.11.) The bar chart has two characteristics: (1) Each class or category is represented by a rectangle, and (2) each rectangle is separated along the x-axis. Again, the bar chart is nothing more

FYI

Bar charts are used to summarize discrete and categorical data. Bar charts are similar to histograms, except that the bars are separated to indicate discrete units or classes.

A **bar chart**, or **bar graph**, is a graphical display used to summarize the frequency of discrete and categorical data that are distributed in whole units or classes.

| FIGURE 2.7 | A Bar Chart |

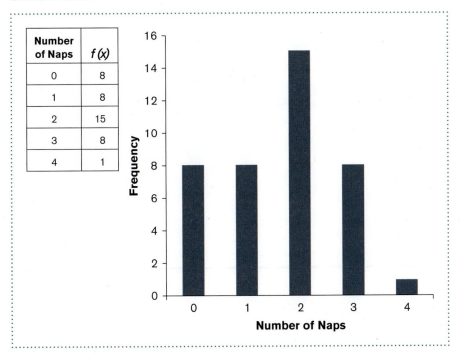

Number of Naps	f (x)
0	8
1	8
2	15
3	8
4	1

A frequency table (left) and a bar chart (right) summarizing the average number of naps per day that mothers give their children, who are younger than age 3.

than a histogram with the bars separated, which makes it more appropriate for summarizing discrete and categorical data.

Pie Charts

The **pie chart** is another graphical summary used almost exclusively for discrete and categorical data. Educators often teach children subtraction and other mathematical operations by "slicing up pieces of pie." Similarly, you can think of pie charts as slices or pieces of data. To construct a pie chart, we typically distribute data as relative percents. Consider Table 2.15, which displays the educational attainment in the United States of a sample of Americans in 2015.

Converting this distribution to a pie chart is simply a matter of finding the correct angles for each slice of pie. There are 360 degrees in a complete circle; therefore, we multiply each percentage by 3.6 (because 100 percent × 3.6 = 360°) to find the central angles of each **sector** (or category). The central angles for the data in Table 2.15 (from the top down and rounded to the nearest tenths place) are 41.1 × 3.6 = 147.9, 16.6 × 3.6 = 59.8, 9.8 × 3.6 = 35.3, 20.5 × 3.6 = 73.8, and 12.0 × 3.6 = 43.2. The total of all central angles will equal 360 degrees. Now dust off your protractor or use a computer program (such as Excel or SPSS) to construct the pie chart by slicing the pie into each angle you just calculated. The result is shown in Figure 2.8.

FYI

Pie charts look like a pie, with each slice typically representing the relative percent of scores in some category.

A **pie chart** is a graphical display in the shape of a circle that is used to summarize the relative percent of discrete and categorical data into sectors.

A **sector** is the particular portion of a pie chart that represents the relative percent of a particular class or category.

	The Frequency and Relative Percent of Educational
TABLE 2.15	Attainment of the Population 25 Years or Older in the United States, 2015

Level of Education	f(x)	Relative Percent
High school graduate (or less)	87,183	41.1%
Some college	35,212	16.6%
Associate's degree	20,788	9.8%
Bachelor's degree	43,485	20.5%
Advanced degree (beyond a bachelor's degree)	25,455	12.0%
Total	212,123	100.0%

Source: Table created based on data from the U.S. Census Bureau, Current Population Survey, 2015 Annual Social and Economic Supplement.

FIGURE 2.8 A Pie Chart for the Distribution of Educational Attainment of the Population 25 Years or Older in the United States, 2015

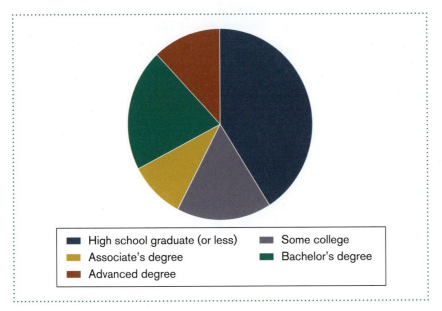

- High school graduate (or less)
- Associate's degree
- Advanced degree
- Some college
- Bachelor's degree

Source: Figure created based on data from the U.S. Census Bureau, Current Population Survey, 2015 Annual Social and Economic Supplement.

LEARNING CHECK 7

1. _____ are graphical displays similar to histograms, except that the vertical bars or rectangles do not touch.

2. In the following bar chart summarizing the frequency of exercise among a sample of college students, which category of exercise has the largest frequency?

3. True or false: The 360 degrees in a pie chart correspond to 100% of a data distribution.

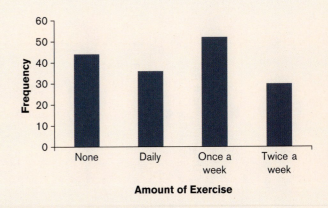

Answers: 1. Bar charts; 2. Most college students exercised once a week; 3. True.

MAKING SENSE DECEPTION DUE TO THE DISTORTION OF DATA

It was Mark Twain who once said *there are lies, damned lies, and statistics.* His statement identified that statistics can be deceiving—and so can interpreting them. Descriptive statistics are used to inform us. Therefore, being able to identify statistics and correctly interpret what they mean is an important part of the research process. Presenting data can be an ethical concern when the data are distorted in any way, whether on accident or intentionally. The

Figure 2.9   Two Graphical Displays for the Same Data

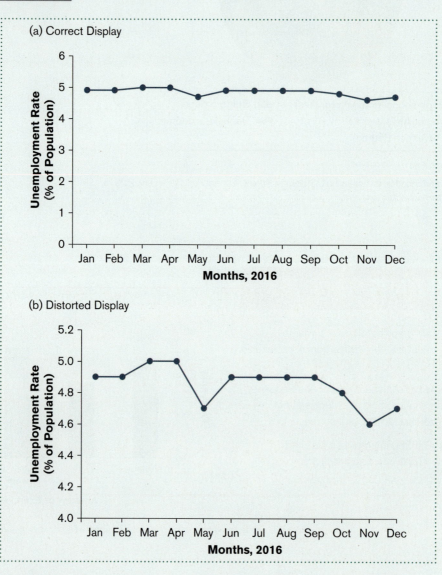

(a) This graph is a correct display, and (b) this is a display that is distorted because the *y*-axis does not begin at 0%. Data are of actual unemployment rates in the United States in 2016 (U.S. Bureau of Labor Statistics, 2017).

distortion of data can occur for data presented graphically or as summary statistics. Here, we will describe how the presentation of data can be distorted.

When a graph is distorted, it can deceive the reader into thinking differences exist, when in truth, differences are negligible (Privitera, 2017, 2018). Three common distortions to look for in graphs are (1) displays with an unlabeled axis, (2) displays with one axis altered in relation to the other axis, and (3) displays in which the vertical axis (y-axis) does not begin with 0. As an example of how a graphical display can be distorted, Figure 2.9 displays a frequency polygon for U.S. unemployment rates in 2016. Figure 2.9a displays the data correctly with the y-axis starting at 0%; Figure 2.9b displays the same data with the y-axis distorted and beginning at 4.0%. When the graph is distorted in this way, it can make the slope of the line appear steeper as if unemployment rates are substantially changing, although it is clear from Figure 2.9a that this is not the case—in fact, U.S. unemployment rates were rather stable in 2016. To avoid misleading or deceiving readers, pay attention to how data are displayed in graphs to make sure that the data are accurately and appropriately presented.

Distortion can also occur when presenting summary statistics. Two common distortions to look for with summary statistics are when data are omitted or differences are described in a way that gives the impression of larger differences than really are meaningful in the data. It can sometimes be difficult to determine if data are misleading or have been omitted, although some data can naturally be reported together—such as reporting the sample size with percentile distributions. For example, if we report that 75% of those surveyed preferred Product A to Product B, you may be inclined to conclude that Product A is a better product. However, if you were also informed that only four people were sampled, then 75% may not seem as convincing. Anytime you read a claim about results in a study, it is important to refer back to the data to confirm the extent to which the data support the claim being made by the author or authors of a research study.

FYI

Data presentation must not be distorted in order to prevent misleading interpretations of data.

2.10 **RESEARCH** IN FOCUS:
FREQUENCIES AND PERCENTS

Although graphs are often used to help the reader understand frequency data, bar charts and histograms are not always equally effective at summarizing percent data. For example, Hollands and Spence (1992, 1998) asked adult participants to identify relative percents displayed in bar charts and pie charts (similar to those presented in this chapter). Their studies showed that participants required more time and made larger errors looking at bar charts than when they looked at pie charts. They went on to show that participants also required more time as the number of bars in the graph increased, whereas increasing the number of slices in a pie chart did not have this effect. They explained that most bar graphs, especially for frequency data, are not distributed in percentage units; hence, the reader cannot clearly estimate a proportion by simply viewing the scale. This research suggests that when you want to convey data as percents, pie charts (and even ogives) would be a better choice for displaying the data.

©iStockphoto.com/ClaudioVentrella

2.11 SPSS in Focus:
Histograms, Bar Charts, and Pie Charts

To review, histograms are used for continuous or quantitative data, and bar charts and pie charts are used for discrete, categorical, or qualitative data. As an exercise to compare histograms, bar charts, and pie charts, we can construct these graphs for the same data, by treating the data as a simple set of general values. Suppose we measure the data shown in Table 2.16.

TABLE 2.16   A Sample of 20 Values

1	4	5	7
2	3	6	8
3	6	7	9
2	6	5	4
4	5	8	5

Because we are not defining these values, we can just call the variable "numbers." Here are the steps:

1. Click on the Variable View tab and enter *numbers* in the Name column. We will enter whole numbers, so go to the Decimals column and reduce the value to 0.

2. Click on the Data View tab and enter the 20 values in the column you labeled *numbers*. You can enter the data in any order you wish, but make sure all the data are entered correctly.

3. Go to the menu bar and click Analyze, then Descriptive Statistics and Frequencies, to bring up a dialog box.

4. In the dialog box, select the *numbers* variable and click the arrow in the center to move *numbers* into the box labeled Variable(s): to the right. Because we only want the graphs and charts in this example, make sure the option to display frequency tables is not selected (so unselect the check mark, which is shown in Figure 2.10).

5. Click the Charts option in the dialog box, which is shown in Figure 2.10. In the dialog box, you have the option to select bar charts, pie charts, or histograms. Select each option to see how each is displayed; however, you can only select one option at a time. After you make your selection, click Continue.

6. Select OK, or select Paste and click the Run command to construct each graph.

FIGURE 2.10   A Screenshot of the Dialog Boxes for Step 5

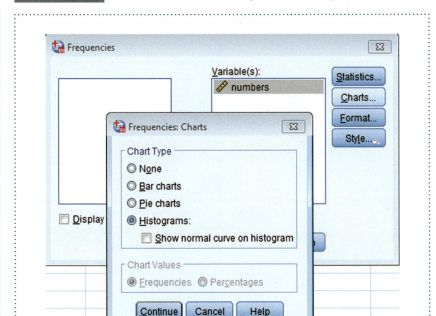

In this example, you can also display the frequency table with the graph by keeping the option to display frequency tables selected. In this way, SPSS gives you many options for summarizing data using tables and graphs.

••• CHAPTER SUMMARY ORGANIZED BY LEARNING OBJECTIVE

LO 1–2: **Construct a simple frequency distribution for grouped and ungrouped data; determine whether data should be grouped or ungrouped.**

- A frequency distribution is a summary display for a distribution of data organized or summarized in terms of how often or frequently scores occur.

- A simple frequency distribution for grouped data displays the frequency of data in intervals. Each interval is equidistant, no interval overlaps,

and the degree of accuracy for each interval is the same as in the original data. This distribution can be constructed using three steps:

Step 1: Find the real range.

Step 2: Find the interval width.

Step 3: Construct the frequency distribution.

- A simple frequency distribution for ungrouped data displays the frequency of categories or whole units when the number of different values collected is small. Because constructing intervals is not necessary for ungrouped data, skip straight to Step 3 to construct this frequency distribution.

LO 3: **Identify when it is appropriate to distribute the cumulative frequency, relative frequency, relative percent, cumulative relative frequency, and cumulative percent.**

- A cumulative frequency is a summary display that distributes the sum of frequencies across a series of intervals. You can sum from the top or the bottom depending on how you want to discuss the data. You add from the bottom up when discussing the data in terms of "less than" or "at or below" a certain value or "at most." You add from the top down when discussing the data in terms of "greater than" or "at or above" a certain value or "at least."

- A relative frequency is a summary display that distributes the proportion of scores in each interval. To compute a relative frequency, divide the frequency in each interval by the total number of scores counted. The relative frequency is reported when summarizing large data sets. To convert relative frequencies to relative percents, multiply each relative frequency by 100. Both summary displays convey the same information.

- Cumulative relative frequencies are summary displays for the sum of relative frequencies from the top down or the bottom up. These can be converted to cumulative relative percents by multiplying the cumulative relative frequency in each interval by 100. Cumulative relative percents can be distributed as percentile ranks, which indicate the percentage of scores at or below a given score.

LO 4: **Identify percentile points and percentile ranks in a cumulative percent distribution.**

- A cumulative percent distribution identifies percentiles, which are measures of the relative position of individuals or scores within a larger distribution. A percentile, specifically a percentile point, is the value of an individual or score within a larger distribution. The corresponding percentile of a percentile point is the percentile rank of that score.

- To find the percentile point in a cumulative percent distribution, follow four basic steps:

  Step 1: Identify the interval within which a specified percentile point falls.

  Step 2: Identify the real range for the interval identified.

  Step 3: Find the position of the percentile point within the interval.

  Step 4: Identify the percentile point.

LO 5: **Construct and interpret graphs for distributions of continuous data.**

- A histogram is a graphical display used to summarize the frequency of continuous data distributed in numeric intervals (grouped). Histograms are constructed by distributing the intervals along the x-axis and listing the frequencies of scores on the y-axis, with each interval connected by vertical bars or rectangles. The height of each rectangle reflects the frequency of scores in a given interval. Three rules for constructing histograms are as follows:

  Rule 1: A vertical rectangle represents each interval, and the height of the rectangle equals the frequency recorded for each interval.

  Rule 2: The base of each rectangle begins and ends at the upper and lower boundaries of each interval.

Rule 3: Each rectangle touches adjacent rectangles at the boundaries of each interval.

- A frequency polygon is a dot-and-line graph where the dot is the midpoint of each interval, and the line connects each dot. The midpoint of an interval is distributed along the *x*-axis and is calculated by adding the upper and lower boundaries of an interval and then dividing by 2.

- An ogive is a dot-and-line graph used to summarize the cumulative percent of continuous data at the upper boundary of each interval.

LO 6:   Construct and interpret graphs for distributions of discrete data.

- Bar charts are used to summarize discrete and categorical data. Bar charts are similar to histograms, except that the bars or rectangles are separated to indicate discrete units or classes. To construct a bar chart, list the whole units or categories along the *x*-axis, and distribute the frequencies along the *y*-axis.

- A pie chart is a graphical display in the shape of a circle that is used to summarize the relative percent of discrete and categorical data into sectors. Converting proportions to a pie chart requires finding the correct angles for each slice of the pie. To find the central angles of each sector (or category), multiply each relative percent by 3.6 (100 percent × 3.6 = 360°).

LO 7–8:   Construct frequency distributions for quantitative and categorical data using SPSS; construct histograms, bar charts, and pie charts using SPSS.

- SPSS can be used to create frequency distributions for quantitative and categorical data. Quantitative data are typically entered by column, whereas categorical data (which typically require coding) are entered by row. Frequency distributions for quantitative and categorical data are created using the Analyze, Descriptive Statistics, and Frequencies options in the menu bar. Whenever the levels of a variable are coded, a Weight cases . . . option must also be selected from the menu bar (for more details, see Sections 2.4 and 2.7).

- SPSS can be used to create histograms, bar charts, and pie charts. Each graph is created using the Analyze, Descriptive Statistics, and Frequencies options in the menu bar. This option will bring up a dialog box that will allow you to identify your variable and select the Charts option that gives you the option to select bar charts, pie charts, or histograms. Select each option to see how each summary is displayed (for more details, see Section 2.11).

• • • KEY TERMS

bar chart	frequency polygon	percentile point
bar graph	grouped data	percentile rank
class width	histogram	pie chart
cumulative frequency distribution	interval	proportion
cumulative percent distribution	interval boundaries	real range
	interval width	relative frequency distribution
cumulative relative frequency distribution	lower boundary	relative percent distribution
	ogive	sector
frequency	open class	simple frequency distribution
frequency distribution	open interval	ungrouped data
	outliers	upper boundary

• • • END-OF-CHAPTER PROBLEMS

Factual Problems

1. State the three steps used to construct a simple frequency distribution.

2. What is the key distinction between grouped and ungrouped data?

3. Researchers often prefer to report cumulative percents from the bottom up to explain how certain scores rank at or below other scores in a distribution. What is this type of summary called?

4. The upper boundary of one interval and the lower boundary of the next interval do not overlap in a simple frequency distribution. Why?

5. Is it necessary to compute the real range to construct a frequency distribution for (a) ungrouped data and (b) grouped data?

6. Frequency data are not always distributed in intervals. What types of data are not distributed in intervals?

7. State three rules for constructing a histogram.

8. Frequency polygons are plotted at the _____ of each interval, whereas ogives are plotted at the _____ of each interval.

9. Why would a researcher summarize data with a bar chart instead of a histogram?

10. Is a pie chart typically used to summarize continuous or discrete/categorical data?

Concept and Application Problems

11. Below is the number of times a commercial was shown displaying unhealthy foods during children's programming over each of 20 days.

    21, 8, 11, 9, 12, 10, 10, 5, 9, 18, 17, 3, 6, 14, 18, 16, 19, 3, 22, 7

    (a) Create a simple frequency distribution for these grouped data with four intervals.

    (b) Which interval had the largest frequency?

12. A researcher observed a rat respond for a food reward by pressing one of three levers in a cage. Pressing the lever to the right (R) produced no food reward, pressing the lever to the left (L) produced a single food pellet, and pressing the lever at the center (C) produced two food pellets. Because the center level produced the largest reward, the researcher hypothesized that the rat would press this lever most often. Each trial ended when the rat pressed a lever. The researcher recorded lever pressing for 30 trials:

    L, L, R, L, R, C, R, L, C, L, L, C, C, C, C, R, C, R, C, L, C, C, L, C, C, C, L, C, C, C, C

    (a) Create an ungrouped frequency distribution for these data.

    (b) Do these data support the hypothesis? Explain.

13. The following table shows a frequency distribution for grouped data. Notice that the frequency of scores, $f(x)$, does not add up to 15. If a total of 15 scores were actually counted, give a possible explanation for why the frequencies do not add up to 15.

Intervals	Frequency
0–5	4
5–10	6
10–15	3
15–20	5

14. A researcher reports the following frequency distribution for the time (in minutes) that college students spent on social networking

websites during class time. Identify three errors in this simple frequency distribution.

Class Time	Frequency
0–9	14
9–20	18
21–40	26
40+	12

15. In a study on romantic relationships, 240 romantically involved men were asked to choose their preference for an ideal night out with their partner. The frequency of men choosing (1) dinner and a movie, (2) a sporting event, (3) gambling/gaming, or (4) going out for drinks was recorded. Should these frequency data be grouped? Explain.

16. The lower boundaries for the number of tattoos among prison inmates are 1, 4, 7, 10, 13, and 16. List the value for each upper boundary in this distribution.

17. The upper boundaries for a distribution of waiting times (in seconds) in a grocery store aisle are 45, 56, 67, and 78. List the value for each lower boundary in this distribution.

18. The frequency of alcohol-related arrests during a single season at a sporting arena ranged from 0 to 17 arrests per game. What is the interval width if you choose to create a frequency distribution with six intervals?

19. A researcher records the number of dreams that 50 children recalled during the week prior to their first day at a new school.

Number of Dreams	Cumulative Frequency
4	50
3	44
2	30
1	12
0	5

(a) Convert this table to a percentile rank distribution.

(b) What is the number of dreams at the 60th percentile?

20. The following table shows the relative percent distribution for the time in seconds that it took 200 children with attention deficit disorder (ADD) to show symptoms of the disorder after a manipulation.

Time (in seconds)	Relative Percent
1–6	5%
7–12	5%
13–18	20%
19–24	20%
25–30	30%
31–36	20%

Assume that researchers determined that children who showed symptoms of ADD in 18 seconds or less qualified to participate in a new cognitive behavioral therapy trial thought to help reduce ADD symptoms. How many children qualify for this new treatment? *Hint:* First convert the data to a cumulative frequency distribution.

21. What type of graph for frequency data should you construct when distributing each of the following? Note that there may be more than one right answer.

(a) The number of students falling into an A, B, C, D, or F grade range

(b) The number of autistic children showing improvement following one of three behavioral therapies

(c) The number of men and women suffering from depression

(d) The time it takes a sample of college students to complete some memory task

22. Would it be most appropriate to use a bar chart or a histogram to summarize the frequency distribution of each of the following?

(a)   The delay to start a game in minutes

(b)   The number of students in each of three classrooms

(c)   The age (in years) that a sample of women first conceived

(d)   The direction of a person's eye movement (right, left, or center) when he or she is telling a lie

23.   The following is an incomplete simple frequency distribution table for the number of mistakes made during a series of military combat readiness training exercises. Find the missing values for A, B, and C.

Number of Mistakes	Frequency
6–**A**	1
B–5	3
0–2	**C**
	N = 16

24.   The following is an incomplete simple frequency distribution table for student grades on a college professor's statistics exam.

Grades (%)	Frequency
87–95	4
A–B	11
69–77	5
60–**C**	7
51–59	**D**
	N = 40

(a)   Find the missing values for A, B, C, and D.

(b)   If students scoring less than 69% on this exam receive a failing grade, was this a difficult test? Explain.

25.   The following bar graph summarizes the number of nights per week a sample of college students spent studying.

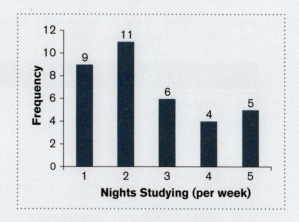

(a)   How many students were observed in this study?

(b)   How many students studied 3 nights per week?

(c)   How many students studied *at least* 3 nights per week?

26.   In a study on marital satisfaction, a researcher asks a sample of men to estimate how many times per week they say "I love you" to their spouse. The relative frequency distribution is given below for these data. Construct an ogive for these data. *Hint:* Convert these relative frequencies to cumulative percents before constructing an ogive.

Intervals	Relative Frequency
1–2	.20
3–4	.13
5–6	.17
7–8	.22
9–10	.18
11–12	.10

27.   A researcher records the season of birth in a sample of patients at a behavioral health clinic. The seasons recorded are winter, spring, spring, fall, summer, winter, fall, winter, winter, spring, winter, spring, winter, winter, summer, spring, winter, winter, fall, spring.

(a)   Construct a bar chart to summarize these data.

(b) Construct a pie chart to summarize these data.

28. Convert the following histogram to a frequency polygon. *Hint:* You must plot the midpoints of each interval to distribute a frequency polygon.

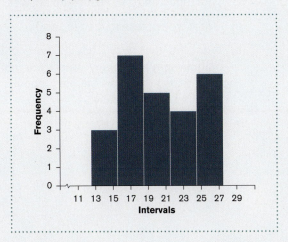

29. The following is a cumulative percent distribution for scores on a college readiness assessment in a population-based study with college students. Based on the data in this table, in which interval does the largest portion of college students fall?

Intervals	Cumulative Percent
120–139	100%
100–119	85%
80–99	70%
60–79	55%
40–59	35%
20–39	25%
0–19	15%

30. Using the data given in Question 29, what is the percentile point for the 50th percentile for the college readiness assessment data in a population-based study with college students?

Problems in Research

31. **Facebook's ad hoc groups.** Sormanen, Lauk, and Uskali (2017) conducted a study evaluating Facebook's ad hoc groups as a potential source of communicative networking power among users. As part of their study, they reported the following frequency distribution for members of categories of groups on Facebook.

Group Category Type	Frequency
Societal well-being movement	223
Community/discussion	233
Protest/support movement	94
Ideological movement	71
Law initiative	35

(a) Based on the table, what category is associated with the highest frequency of group members?

(b) What is the relative frequency for the category that is associated with the highest frequency of group members?

32. **Women in psychology then and now.** The following table lists the distribution of degrees in psychology conferred by degree-granting institutions, by sex and year. These and similar data are reported by the National Center for Education Statistics (NCES) at http://nces.ed.gov/programs/digest/.

Bachelor's Degrees	Males	Females
1970–1971	21,227	14,602
1980–1981	14,332	26,736
1990–1991	16,067	42,588
2000–2001	16,585	57,060
2005–2006	19,865	68,269

(a) Based on the data in this table, how has the number of degrees conferred in psychology changed by sex since 1970–1971?

(b) Is this a frequency distribution for grouped or ungrouped data? Explain.

33. **Women serving in the armed forces.** In February 2016, a CNN poll asked a sample of 1,001 adults nationwide if they think women in the armed services should get combat assignments on the same terms as men (reported at www.pollingreport.com). The opinions of adults nationwide were as follows: 36%, on the same terms as men; 51%, only if they want to; 12%, never; and 1%, unsure.

(a) What type of distribution is this?

(b) Is this a summary for grouped or ungrouped data? Explain.

34. **Perceptions of same-sex marriage.** In June 2016, a CBS News poll asked a sample of adults worldwide whether it should be legal or not legal for same-sex couples to marry (reported at www.pollingreport.com). The opinions of adults worldwide were as follows: 58%, legal; 33%, not legal; and 9%, unsure/no answer.

(a) What type of distribution is this?

(b) Knowing that 1,280 adults were polled nationwide, how many Americans polled felt that same-sex couples should be allowed to legally marry?

Answers for even numbers are in Appendix D.

Sharpen your skills with **SAGE edge at edge.sagepub.com/priviteraess2e**

SAGE edge for Students provides a personalized approach to help you accomplish your coursework goals in an easy-to-use learning environment.

$SAGE edge™

iStock/Sergey Nivens

©Can Stock Photo Inc./OG_vision

3 Summarizing Data
Central Tendency

• • • Learning Objectives

After reading this chapter, you should be able to:

1. Distinguish between a population mean and a sample mean.

2. Calculate and interpret the mean, the median, and the mode.

3. Calculate and interpret the weighted mean for two or more samples with unequal sample sizes.

4. Identify the characteristics of the mean.

5. Identify an appropriate measure of central tendency for different distributions and scales of measurement.

6. Compute the mean, the median, and the mode using SPSS.

Anytime we use a word like *usually*, *typically*, or *often*, we are in many ways describing what we think should happen. An employee may fail to meet a deadline that he *usually* meets; a basketball player may miss a shot that she *typically* makes; your roommate may pay her share of the rent late one month, although she *often* pays it on time. In each case, we are describing an occasion when the behavior we observe does not occur as it usually does. Of course, what is *usual* is not what always occurs, but it does give us a snapshot of the behaviors and events in our life. Put into statistical terms, it gives us a snapshot of what the center of a distribution looks like.

We often see sensational claims related to central tendency, such as a weight loss supplement claiming to help "people lose an average of 10 pounds in 7 days" or an insurance company claiming that "people who switch typically save about $300 per year." For everyday decisions, people typically like to know what will happen or, at least, to get a good sense of what should happen. In the behavioral sciences, central tendency is likewise vitally important for the decisions that researchers make. Researchers studying diagnosis of depression, for example, may ask questions pertaining to the types of symptoms expressed most often by patients to decide how to improve diagnosis; those studying obesity may ask questions pertaining to the average number of calories consumed per day to decide on dietary strategies for weight loss; those studying group dynamics may ask questions pertaining to the typical characteristics of strong leaders to decide how to best train leaders in a variety of settings. In each example, researchers use central tendency as a way to gauge decision making about a behavior.

Statistics provides a useful way to measure central tendency. In this chapter, we introduce many ways in which researchers measure this to understand the center of distributions and to summarize the data observed.

Master the content.

edge.sagepub.com/priviteraess2e

● ● ● **Chapter Outline**

3.1 INTRODUCTION TO CENTRAL TENDENCY

Suppose, before registering for a statistics class, a friend told you that students in Professor Smith's class earned higher grades on average than those in Professor Jones's class. On the basis of this information, you decided to register for Professor Smith's class. You did not need to know all the individual grades for each student in both classes to make your decision. Instead, your decision was based on knowledge of a single score or, in this case, a class average.

The class average in this example is a measure of **central tendency**. Measures of central tendency are single values that have a "tendency" to be near the "center" of a distribution. Although we lose some meaning anytime we reduce a set of data to a single score, statistical measures of central tendency ensure that the single score meaningfully represents a set of data. In this chapter, we will use three measures of central tendency to describe samples and populations of data: the mean, the median, and the mode.

Measures of central tendency are stated differently for populations and samples. Calculations of central tendency are largely the same for populations and samples of data, except for the notation used to represent **population size** and **sample size**. A population, as you may recall from Chapter 1, is a set of all scores from a given group; a sample is a subset of scores from this group or population. The size of a population is represented by a capital *N*; the size of a sample or subset of scores from a population is represented by a lowercase *n*. This notation, summarized here, distinguishes the size of a population from the size of a sample:

$$N = \text{Population size}$$

$$n = \text{Sample size}$$

In the sections that follow, we describe how measures of central tendency convey different information regarding scores in both populations and samples. We begin with the mean.

FYI

The size of a population is represented by a capital N*; the size of a sample is represented by a lowercase* n.

FYI

Measures of central tendency are values at or near the center of a distribution. Three common measures of central tendency are the mean, the median, and the mode.

Measures of **central tendency** are statistical measures for locating a single score that is most representative or descriptive of all scores in a distribution.

The **population size** is the number of individuals who constitute an entire group or population. The population size is represented by a capital *N*.

The **sample size** is the number of individuals who constitute a subset of those selected from a larger population. The sample size is represented by a lowercase *n*.

LEARNING CHECK 1

1. All measures of central tendency have a tendency to be at or near the _____ of a distribution.

2. ___ symbolizes the size of a population, whereas ___ symbolizes the size of a sample.

Answers: 1. Center; 2. *N*, *n*.

3.2 MEASURES OF CENTRAL TENDENCY

Although we use different symbols to represent the number of scores (*x*) in a sample (*n*) versus a population (*N*), the computation of central tendency is the same for samples and populations. Three measures of central tendency are introduced in this section: the mean, the median, and the mode.

The Mean

The most commonly reported measure of central tendency is the mean. The **mean**, also called an **arithmetic mean** or **average**, is the sum of (Σ) a set of scores (x) divided by the number of scores summed, in either a sample (n) or a population (N). The formulas for the population mean and the sample mean are as follows.

© Can Stock Photo Inc./victorburnside

The **population mean** is the sum of N scores (x) divided by N:

$$\mu = \frac{\Sigma x}{N}.$$

The **sample mean** is the sum of n scores (x) divided by n:

$$M = \frac{\Sigma x}{n}.$$

The symbol Σ (sigma) means "sum of," and the numbers or expression to the right of sigma are the items summed. In this formula, x represents each score (x) in a data set. The population mean is identified by the Greek letter *mu*, μ (pronounced "mew"); the sample mean is identified by an italicized M. You may sometimes see the sample mean identified with $\overline{X}$ (read "x-bar"). Although both notations are acceptable, M is the more common notation used to represent a sample mean in published research and thus is the notation used in this book.

The mean is often referred to as the "balance point" in a distribution. The balance point is not always at the exact center of a distribution, as this analogy will demonstrate. Pick up a pen with a cap and remove the cap. Then place the pen sideways on your index finger until it is balanced and parallel with the floor. Once you have steadied the pen, your finger represents the "balance point" of the distribution of the weight of that pen. In the same way, the mean is the balance point of a distribution of data. Now, put the cap back on the pen and balance it again on your index finger. To balance the pen, you had to move your finger toward the side with the cap, right? Now your finger is not at the center of the pen but closer to the cap. In the same way, the mean is not necessarily the middle value; it is the value that balances an entire distribution of numbers.

Remember that the computation of the mean does not change for samples and populations; just the notation used in the formula changes. To calculate the mean of a sample or a population, we do the same thing: We sum a set of scores and divide by the number of scores summed. Example 3.1 illustrates the computation of a population mean, and Example 3.2 illustrates the computation of a sample mean. Notice that the method of solution is the same in both examples.

FYI

The mean is the "balance point" in a distribution.

FYI

The mean is the sum of (Σ) a set of scores (x) divided by the number of scores summed, in either a sample (n) or a population (N).

The **mean**, also called an **arithmetic mean** or **average**, is the sum of a set of scores in a distribution, divided by the total number of scores summed.

The mean for a set of scores in an entire population is referred to as a **population mean**; the mean for a sample (or subset of scores from a population) is referred to as a **sample mean**.

Example 3.1

A clinical psychologist records the number of symptoms expressed for attention deficit disorder (ADD) by a group of five children (N = 5) in a teacher's classroom. Suppose this group is the only group of interest to the researcher. So this group constitutes the population of children that the researcher is interested in. The psychologist records the following number of symptoms in this population: 3, 6, 4, 7, and 5. To compute the population mean, first sum the recorded values:

$$\sum x = 3 + 6 + 4 + 7 + 5 = 25.$$

Then divide the total by the number of scores summed ($N = 5$):

$$\frac{\sum x}{N} = \frac{25}{5} = 5.0.$$

Children in this population expressed a mean of five symptoms ($\mu = 5.0$) for ADD.

Example 3.2

Suppose we create an experimental situation where a sample of participants must walk past a presumably scary portion of campus after dark. To measure fear, we record how quickly (in seconds) participants walk through the scary portion of campus after dark. The following times are recorded: 8, 9, 5, 5, 5, 10, 6, and 8. To compute the sample mean, first sum the recorded values:

$$\sum x = 8 + 9 + 5 + 5 + 5 + 10 + 6 + 8 = 56.$$

Then divide this total by the number of values summed ($n = 8$):

$$\frac{\sum x}{n} = \frac{56}{8} = 7.0.$$

Participants in this sample had a mean time of seven seconds ($M = 7.0$) to walk past the presumably scary portion of campus after dark.

LEARNING CHECK 2

1. The notation used in the formulas for sample mean and population mean differs. What notation differs in these formulas?

2. The calculation of a population mean and sample mean is the same. State in words how to compute the mean.

3. A scientist records the following sample of scores ($n = 6$): 3, 6, 4, 1, 10, and 12. What is the sample mean of these scores?

Answers: 1. The term N is used in the denominator for the population mean, and the term n is used in the denominator for the sample mean; 2. The mean is the sum of a set of scores, divided by the total number of scores summed; 3. $M = 6.0$.

The Weighted Mean

A **weighted mean** (denoted M_w) is the combined mean of two or more groups of scores in which the number of scores in each group is disproportionate or unequal.

Another popular measure of central tendency is the **weighted mean**. This statistic measures the mean of a group of disproportionate scores or samples of scores. A common application of this in behavioral science is when scores are measured in two or more samples with unequal sample sizes.

The term *disproportionate* refers to the fact that some samples have more scores than others (the samples are of disproportionate sizes). In this section, we will use the weighted mean in such a circumstance.

The formula for the weighted mean for samples of unequal size can be expressed as follows:

$$M_w = \frac{\Sigma(M \times n)}{\Sigma n} \text{ or } \frac{\text{weighted sum}}{\text{combined } n}.$$

M represents the mean of each sample, and n represents the size of each sample. In this formula, the sample size (n) is the weight for each mean. Using this formula, we will compute the combined mean for two or more samples of scores in which the number of scores in each sample is disproportionate or unequal. We will use the data in Table 3.1, which shows the mean fitness score for three samples consisting of participants who are lean, overweight, or obese.

TABLE 3.1	The Mean Fitness Score and Sample Size for Lean, Overweight, and Obese Participants

Sample	M	n
Lean	46	12
Overweight	58	14
Obese	73	30

Notice that the sample size for each group is not the same; more scores were used to compute the mean for some samples than others. If we computed the arithmetic mean, we would get the following result:

$$\text{Arithmetic mean}: \frac{46 + 58 + 73}{3} = 59.0.$$

The combined mean is 59.0. But this calculation is incorrect. It does not account for the number of scores that contributed to the calculation of each mean. As a general rule, larger sample sizes carry more weight in determining the overall weighted mean. Because more scores contributed to the mean in the sample of obese participants, for example, the sample mean in this group contributed more to the combined mean of all samples and is therefore given more weight.

To compute the weighted mean, we find the product, $M \times n$, for each sample. This gives us a weight for the mean of each sample. By adding these products, we arrive at the weighted sum:

$$\text{Weighted sum} = (46 \times 12) + (58 \times 14) + (73 \times 30) = 3,554.$$

FYI

A weighted mean can be used to compute the mean for multiple groups of scores when the size of each group is unequal.

Then, we divide the weighted sum by the combined sample size (n), which is computed by adding the sample sizes in the denominator:

$$M_w = \frac{3,554}{12+14+30} = 63.5.$$

The weighted mean for these samples is 63.5.

The weighted mean is larger than the arithmetic mean (63.5 vs. 59.0) because the larger sample (the sample of obese participants) scored higher on the fitness measure. Hence, the value of the weighted mean shifted toward the mean from the larger sample (or the sample with more weight). This makes the weighted mean an accurate statistic for computing the mean for samples with unequal sample sizes.

MAKING SENSE MAKING THE GRADE

Instructors often weight grades for college courses. Suppose your statistics course includes an exam, a quiz, and a final class project. The instructor considers the exam to be the most important measure of learning and so gives it the greatest weight. Table 3.2 shows this weighted distribution.

| TABLE 3.2 | Grading Distribution for Students in a Hypothetical Statistics Course |

Type of Measure	Points	Weight
Exam	100	60%
Quiz	100	20%
Final project	100	20%

In this example, we have three class assignments with unequal weights. The score for each assignment is represented as x in the formula, and the weight is represented as w (instead of n for sample size). Notice that the sum of the weights is 100% or 1.00, which means that the denominator will always sum to 1.00. In these cases, when the sum of the weights equals 1.00, the weighted mean is calculated by computing the weighted sum:

Weighted mean $= \sum (x \times w)$.

The exam, quiz, and final project are each worth the same number of points (100), but they are weighted differently. Suppose you score 70 points on the exam, 98 points on the quiz, and 100 points on the final project. If you compute an arithmetic mean to determine your grade, you would be wrong:

$$\frac{70+98+100}{300} = .89 \text{ or } 89\%.$$

Instead, you apply the formula for weighted means to calculate your final average because each grade was weighted. Without doing the calculation, you might guess (correctly) that it is going to be lower than 89%. After you multiply each grade by its weight, then sum each product, you can verify your hunch:

$$\sum (x \times w) = (70 \times .60) + (98 \times .20) + (100 \times .20) = .816 \text{ or } 81.6\%.$$

Your grade dropped from a B+ to a B− because your lowest score was on the most important (or most heavily weighted) measure of learning—the exam. You should be aware of this for any class you take. If an instructor puts particular weight on a certain graded assignment, then you should too. A weighted mean can substantially change a grade.

The Median

Suppose you measure the following set of scores: 2, 3, 4, 5, 6, 6, and 100. The mean of these scores is 18 (add up the seven scores and divide by 7). Yet, the score of 100 is an outlier in this data set, which causes the mean value to increase so much that the mean fails to reflect most of the data. The mean can be misleading when a data set has an outlier because the mean will shift toward the value of that outlier. For this reason, there is a need for alternative measures of central tendency. One measure is the **median**, which is the middle value in a distribution. The median value represents the midpoint of a distribution of scores where half the scores in a distribution fall above and half below its value. To find the median position, list a set of scores in numeric order and compute this formula:

$$\text{Median position} = \frac{n+1}{2}.$$

Locating the median is a little different for odd- and even-numbered sample sizes (n). Example 3.3 illustrates how to find the median for an odd-numbered sample size, and in Example 3.4 we will calculate the median for an even-numbered sample size.

FYI

The median is the midpoint in a distribution. If you list a set of scores in numeric order, the median is the middle score.

Example 3.3

When the number of scores in a distribution is odd, order the set of scores from least to most (or vice versa) and find the middle number. Let us find the median for the following list: 3, 6, 5, 3, 8, 6, 7 (n = 7).

First, place each score in numeric order: 3, 3, 5, 6, 6, 7, and 8. Then locate the position of the middle score: $\frac{7+1}{2} = 4$. Count four scores in (from the left or right; it does not matter); the median is 6.

Example 3.4

When the number of scores in a distribution is even, list the scores in numeric order and then average the middle two scores. Let us find the median for the following list: 3, 6, 5, 3, 8, 6 (n = 6).

First, place each score in numeric order: 3, 3, 5, 6, 6, and 8. The position of the median score is $\frac{6+1}{2} = 3.5$. Anytime you obtain a value to the tenths place (i.e., .5), you must average the two positions surrounding this answer. In this case, you average the third and fourth positioned values: $\frac{5+6}{2} = 5.5$. The median is 5.5.

Notice that to find the median, we find the middle score. The value of an outlier has little influence over the median. At the beginning of this section, we measured the following set of scores: 2, 3, 4, 5, 6, 6, and 100. The mean of these scores is M = 18. If you find the middle score, the median is 5. The value of the outlier did not distort the value of the median. To illustrate further, suppose that the seventh score in this set was not an outlier. So let us change 100 to something more in line with the other scores—we will change it to 9. With this change, the mean

FYI

Outliers in a data set influence the value of the mean but not the median.

The **median** is the middle value in a distribution of data listed in numeric order.

FYI

The 50th percentile of a cumulative percent distribution can be used to estimate the value of the median.

changes drastically from $M = 18$ to $M = 5$. The median, however, does not change: the median is still 5. Therefore, the median is more informative to describe data in a distribution with one or more outliers.

Graphically, the median can be estimated by a cumulative percent distribution. Because the median is located in the middle of a distribution, it is approximately at the 50th percentile of a cumulative percent distribution. To illustrate, suppose we measure the 20 scores listed in Table 3.3. The median of this distribution is 16. Figure 3.1 shows an *ogive* (introduced in Chapter 2) of the cumulative percent distribution for these data. Notice in the figure that the 50th percentile closely approximates the median of this distribution.

TABLE 3.3   A Hypothetical List of 20 Scores

2	7	18	29
3	8	21	34
4	11	21	34
4	12	26	37
5	14	29	44

FIGURE 3.1   An Ogive for the Cumulative Percent Distribution of Scores With a Median of 16

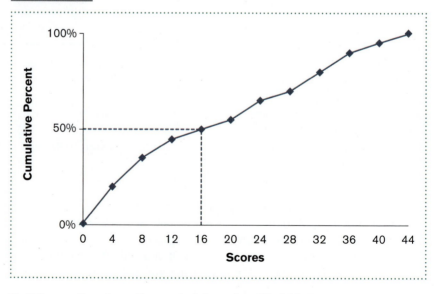

The 50th percentile can be used to approximate the median of this distribution.

LEARNING CHECK 3

1. The _____ is the combined mean of two or more groups of scores in which the number of scores in each group is disproportionate or unequal.

2. A researcher collects two samples of data. He finds the first sample ($n = 8$) has a mean of 5; the second sample ($n = 2$) has a mean of 10. What is the weighted mean of these samples?

3. What type of distribution is used to approximate the median?

4. The _____ is the preferred measure of central tendency when a data set has outliers.

Answers: 1. Weighted mean; 2. $M_w = \frac{(5.8) + (10.2)}{8 + 2} = 6.0$; 3. Cumulative percent distribution; 4. Median.

The Mode

In addition to the mean and median, a third common measure of central tendency is the **mode**. The mode is the score that occurs most often in a data set. One advantage of the mode is that it is simply a count; no calculations or formulas are necessary to compute a mode. To find the mode, list a set of scores in numeric order and count the score that occurs most often.

The mode is generally reported in research journals with other measures of central tendency, such as the mean and median. It is rarely used as the sole way of describing data. Let us work through Examples 3.5 and 3.6 to find the mode.

FYI

The mode reflects the score or scores that occur most often in a distribution. The mode is often reported in research journals with the mean or median.

Example 3.5

The following is a list of 20 golfers' scores on a difficult par-4 golf hole: 2, 3, 3, 3, 3, 3, 4, 4, 4, 4, 4, 4, 4, 4, 5, 5, 5, 5, 6, and 7. What score did these golfers card the most (mode) on this hole?

Table 3.4 lists these scores in a frequency distribution table. From this table, it is clear that most golfers scored a par 4 on this difficult hole. Therefore, the mode, or most common score on this hole, was par.

TABLE 3.4 The Frequency of Scores on a Hypothetical Par-4 Golf Hole

Score	f(x)
Eagle (2)	1
Birdie (3)	5
Par (4)	8
Bogey (5)	4
Double-bogey (6)	1
Triple-bogey (7)	1

The **mode** is the value in a data set that occurs most often or most frequently.

Example 3.6

A researcher recorded the number of symptoms for major depressive disorder (MDD) expressed in a small sample of 20 "at-risk" participants: 0, 4, 3, 6, 5, 2, 3, 3, 5, 4, 6, 3, 5, 6, 4, 0, 0, 3, 0, and 1. How many symptoms of MDD did participants in this sample most commonly express?

First list these scores in numeric order: 0, 0, 0, 0, 1, 2, 3, 3, 3, 3, 3, 4, 4, 4, 5, 5, 5, 6, 6, and 6. In doing so, we find that 3, which occurred five times, is the mode in this data set. Participants in this "at-risk" sample most often reported three symptoms of MDD.

LEARNING CHECK 4

1. The _____ is the value in a data set that occurs most often or most frequently.

2. Identify the mode: A study reports that women are more likely to ask for directions than men.

3. A researcher observes the following data set: 3, 5, 4, 4, 6, 7, 8, 2, 3, 2, 4, 2, 2, and 4. How many modes are in this distribution? State the value of each mode.

Answers: 1. Mode; 2. Women; 3. There are two modes: 2 and 4 each occur four times.

3.3 CHARACTERISTICS OF THE MEAN

Although each measure of central tendency is important for different reasons, the mean is the most reported statistic in behavioral science. Indeed, each subsequent chapter in this book will at least make mention of it. For this reason, it is important to introduce five key characteristics of the mean. Note in this discussion that the five characteristics emphasize that the mean reflects every score in a distribution.

Changing an Existing Score

Changing an existing score will change the mean. In essence, every score in a distribution affects the mean. Therefore, changing any existing score in a distribution will change the value of the mean. We can work with a sample of 10 quiz scores: 1, 6, 4, 2, 5, 9, 7, 4, 8, and 4. In this sample, $n = 10$ and $\Sigma x = 50$. The mean is 5.0:

$$M = \frac{\Sigma x}{n} = \frac{50}{10} = 5.0.$$

If we change one of the scores, the mean will change. For example, suppose that the instructor made a mistake grading one quiz and realized that the first score of 1 should be a 6. Although the number of scores is unchanged at $n = 10$, the sum of scores (Σx) increases from 50 to 55. The mean increases from 5.0 to 5.5:

$$M = \frac{\Sigma x}{n} = \frac{55}{10} = 5.5.$$

If you change the value of the numerator without changing the sample size n, then the value of the mean will change. In this example, the mean increased. As a rule, when you increase the value of an existing score, the mean will increase; when you decrease the value of an existing score, the mean will decrease.

Adding a New Score or Removing an Existing Score

Adding a new score or removing an existing score will change the mean, unless that value equals the mean. We can use the same sample of $n = 10$ quiz scores: 1, 6, 4, 2, 5, 9, 7, 4, 8, and 4, with $M = 5.0$. Suppose another student takes the quiz and scores a 2. The new list, with the added score, is $n = 11$ with the following values: 1, 6, 4, 2, 5, 9, 7, 4, 8, 4, and 2. Because this new score ($x = 2$) is less than the mean ($M = 5$), the mean will *decrease* or shift toward that smaller score. The mean decreases from 5.0 to 4.7:

$$M = \frac{\Sigma x}{n} = \frac{52}{11} = 4.7.$$

Now suppose the additional student scored an 8 instead. The new list, with the added score, is $n = 11$ with the following values: 1, 6, 4, 2, 5, 9, 7, 4, 8, 4, and 8. Because this new score ($x = 8$) is greater than the mean ($M = 5$), the mean will *increase* or shift toward that larger score. The mean increases from 5.0 to 5.3:

$$M = \frac{\Sigma x}{n} = \frac{58}{11} = 5.3.$$

Deleting a score from the original list of 10 quiz scores will also change the mean in a predictable way. Deleting a score below the mean will *increase* the value of the mean. Suppose one student drops out of the class, so we delete his score of 1 from the data set. The new list, after removing the deleted score, is $n = 9$ with the following values: 6, 4, 2, 5, 9, 7, 4, 8, and 4. The mean increases from 5.0 to 5.4:

$$M = \frac{\Sigma x}{n} = \frac{49}{9} = 5.4.$$

Deleting a score above the mean will *decrease* the value of the mean. Suppose the student who scored a 9 on the quiz drops out of the class. The new list, after removing the deleted score, is $n = 9$ with the following values: 1, 6, 4, 2, 5, 7, 4, 8, and 4. The mean decreases from 5.0 to 4.6:

$$M = \frac{\Sigma x}{n} = \frac{41}{11} = 4.6.$$

The only time that a change in a distribution of scores *does not change* the value of the mean is when the value that is added or removed is exactly equal to the mean. For example, here is the original list of quiz scores: 1, 6, 4, 2, 5, 9, 7, 4, 8, and 4, with $M = 5.0$.

Adding a 5 to this data set makes $n = 11$, and the $\sum x = 55$. The mean remains 5.0.

$$M = \frac{\sum x}{n} = \frac{55}{11} = 5.0.$$

Subtracting a 5 from this same data set makes $n = 9$, and the $\sum x = 45$. The mean again remains unchanged.

$$M = \frac{\sum x}{n} = \frac{45}{9} = 5.0.$$

In sum, the *mean* reflects the distance that each individual score deviates from the balance point of a distribution. The farther scores are from the mean, the more they pull the mean toward them to balance the distribution. Values exactly equal to the mean are zero distance from the mean, so the value of the mean does not need to change to keep the distribution balanced. This rule has many parts:

Part 1. Add a score above the mean and the mean will *increase*.

Part 2. Add a score below the mean and the mean will *decrease*.

Part 3. Delete a score below the mean and the mean will *increase*.

Part 4. Delete a score above the mean and the mean will *decrease*.

Part 5. Add or delete a score equal to the mean and the mean will *not change*.

FYI

The mean is a balance point of a distribution of scores. Its value shifts in a direction that balances a set of scores.

Adding, Subtracting, Multiplying, or Dividing Each Score by a Constant

Adding, subtracting, multiplying, or dividing each score in a distribution by a constant will cause the mean to change by that constant. To illustrate this, we will work through one example where we subtract a constant from each score and a second example where we multiply each score by a constant. We can begin with an example in which we subtract a constant from each score. Suppose you have five favorite meals consisting of 450, 500, 525, 550, and 600 calories (cal), respectively. For these data, $M = 525$ cal, as shown in the middle column in Table 3.5.

Suppose that each of these meals includes a 100-calorie portion of French fries. In a stunning series of research reports, though, you learn that fried foods are not good for your heart, so you subtract the French fries portion from each meal. In the rightmost column in Table 3.5, the 100-calorie portion of French fries is subtracted from the total calories in each meal. The reduction in calories is a constant: *Constant* $= -100$. Notice that when each value (measured in calories) is changed by the same constant (-100 cal), the mean is also changed by that constant. The mean is exactly 100 calories less without the French fries ($M = 425$). This rule applies when *every* score in the distribution is changed by the *same* constant.

To further illustrate this rule, we can use an example in which we multiply a constant by each score. Suppose you are a health practitioner conducting a study to determine whether people who eat more fat in their diets also tend to consume more calories. You find that five astonishingly health-conscious adults eat only 2, 3, 4, 5, and 6 grams of fat in their diets per week, respectively. For this study, the mean amount consumed is $M = 4$ grams of fat per week.

TABLE 3.5 The Calories in Each Meal With and Without the 100-Calorie Portion of French Fries

Meal	Meal With French Fries	Meal Without French Fries (−100 calories)
1	450	350
2	500	400
3	525	425
4	550	450
5	600	500
$n = 5$	$M = 525$	$M = 425$

Because the same constant (100 calories) was subtracted from each meal, the mean also decreased by 100.

Suppose you want to know how many calories of fat each adult consumed per week (instead of grams of fat). Fat contains 9 calories per gram, so we can multiply the weight (in grams) by 9 to find the number of calories consumed. Table 3.6 shows that multiplying each value in the original distribution by 9 also changes the mean by a multiple of 9. The mean is $M = 36$ calories (4 mean grams of fat × 9 cal per gram = 36 mean calories). Again, this rule applies when *every* score in the distribution is changed by the *same* constant.

FYI

Changing each score in a distribution by the same constant will likewise change the mean by that constant.

TABLE 3.6 The Grams of Fat and Calories of Fat Consumed per Week

Participants	Grams of Fat	Calories
A	2	18
B	3	27
C	4	36
D	5	45
E	6	54
$n = 5$	$M = 4$	$M = 36$

Because fat (in grams) was multiplied by the same constant (9 calories per gram of fat) for each participant, the mean also increased by a multiple of 9.

Summing the Differences of Scores From Their Mean

The sum of the differences of scores from their mean is zero. We can think of the mean as the balance point of a distribution of scores. What logically follows from this is to think of the mean as a zero point for a distribution as well. It is the only constant you can subtract from every score in a distribution, where the sum of the differences is equal to zero. Think of this as balancing weights on a scale. Only when the difference between the weights on each side of the scale is the same (difference = 0) will the weights on each side of the scale be balanced. Similarly, the balance point of a distribution of scores is the point where the difference of scores above the mean is the same as the difference of scores below the mean (difference = 0). The notation for describing the sum of (Σ) the differences of scores (x) from their mean (M) is $\Sigma(x - M)$.

FYI

The difference of each score from the mean always sums to zero, similar to placing weights on both sides of a scale. The mean would be located at the point that balances both ends—the difference in weight on each side would be zero.

To illustrate, we can use the following scores ($n = 5$): 1, 2, 5, 7, and 10. The mean of this distribution is $M = 5.0$. Now subtract 5 (the mean) from each score. Notice that the sum of the differences above the mean (the positive differences) is the same as the sum of the differences below the mean (the negative differences) in Table 3.7. The differences cancel out; the sum of the differences of scores from their mean is 0 $(\Sigma(x - M) = 0)$, as shown in Table 3.7. No other constant produces this result. Only when the mean is subtracted from each score in a distribution is the sum of the differences equal to zero. We will examine this characteristic again in Chapter 4.

TABLE 3.7   The Sum of the Differences of Scores From Their Mean

x	$(x - M)$
1	$(1 - 5) = -4$
2	$(2 - 5) = -3$
5	$(5 - 5) = 0$
7	$(7 - 5) = 2$
10	$(10 - 5) = 5$
$\Sigma x = 25$	$\Sigma(x - M) = 0$

When the mean ($M = 5$) is subtracted from each score (x), then summed, the solution is always zero (right column).

Summing the Squared Differences of Scores From Their Mean

The sum of the squared differences of scores from their mean is minimal. Suppose that we want to measure how far scores deviate from the mean. We could subtract each score from the mean and sum the deviations, but that will always produce a result equal to 0, as shown in Table 3.7. If we did this, then we would erroneously conclude that scores do not deviate from their mean. The solution to obtain a value greater than 0 is to square each deviation before summing. This produces the smallest possible positive number greater than 0, where larger outcomes indicate that scores deviate further from their mean. The notation for describing the sum of (Σ) the squared differences of scores (x) from their mean (M) is $\Sigma(x - M)^2$.

To illustrate, suppose we measure the same five scores ($n = 5$) from the previous example: 1, 2, 5, 7, and 10, with $M = 5.0$. If we substitute the values of x and M, we will obtain the following solution:

$$\Sigma(x - M)^2 = (1-5)^2 + (2-5)^2 + (5-5)^2 + (7-5)^2 + (10-5)^2$$
$$= (-4)^2 + (-3)^2 + (0)^2 + (2)^2 + (5)^2 = 16 + 9 + 0 + 4 + 25 = 54.$$

Table 3.8 shows the details of this calculation. The solution is 54, which is the smallest (or minimal) value for the sum of the squared differences of scores from their mean. Subtracting scores from any constant other than the mean will produce a greater value. If you substitute any positive or negative value other than the mean ($M = 5$), you will always obtain a solution greater than 54. We will examine this characteristic again in Chapter 4.

FYI

Summing the squared differences of each score from its mean produces a minimal solution. If you replace the mean with any other value, the solution will be larger.

TABLE 3.8 The Sum of the Squared Differences of Scores From Their Mean

x	(x – M)²
1	$(1 - 5)^2 = 16$
2	$(2 - 5)^2 = 9$
5	$(5 - 5)^2 = 0$
7	$(7 - 5)^2 = 4$
10	$(10 - 5)^2 = 25$
$\Sigma x = 25$	$\Sigma(x - M)^2 = 54$

In this example, 54 is the smallest possible solution. Subtracting any other value than the mean will produce a larger solution.

LEARNING CHECK 5

1. Which of the following will *decrease* the value of the mean?

   (a) Delete a score below the mean

   (b) Add a score below the mean

   (c) Add a score exactly equal to the mean

   (d) None of the above

2. From the choices in Question 1, which will *increase* the value of the mean?

3. From the choices in Question 1, which will have *no effect* on the mean?

4. State the characteristic of the mean that indicates that the mean is the "zero point" for a distribution of scores.

5. Suppose that you sum the squared differences of scores from their mean. What is always true about the result you obtain?

Answers: 1. b; 2. a; 3. c; 4. The sum of the differences of scores from their mean is zero; 5. The result is the smallest possible positive solution. Substituting any constant (other than the mean) will produce a larger result.

3.4 CHOOSING AN APPROPRIATE MEASURE OF CENTRAL TENDENCY

The measures of central tendency we have discussed—the mean, median, and mode—are used to summarize different types of data. The choice of which measure to select depends largely on the type of distribution and the scale of measurement of the data. In this section, we consider both factors to decide which measures of central tendency are most appropriate to describe a given set of data.

Using the Mean to Describe Data

The mean is typically used to describe data that are normally distributed and measures on an interval or ratio scale.

Describing Normal Distributions

The mean is used to describe data that are approximately normally distributed. The **normal distribution** is a symmetrical distribution in which scores are similarly distributed above and below the mean, the median, and the mode at the center of the distribution. The characteristics of the normal distribution are introduced in Chapter 5, which is an entire chapter devoted to describing this distribution—because a great deal of behavioral data approximate this type of distribution. The general structure and approximate shape of this distribution is shown in Figure 3.2. While the mean is used to summarize data that are approximately normally distributed, we could choose to describe these data with the median or mode, but the mean is most often used because all scores are included in its calculation (i.e., its value is most reflective of all the data).

FIGURE 3.2   The Normal Distribution

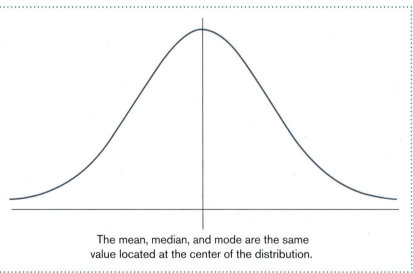

The mean, median, and mode are the same value located at the center of the distribution.

The **normal distribution** (also called the **symmetrical**, **Gaussian**, or **bell-shaped distribution**) is a theoretical distribution in which scores are symmetrically distributed above and below the mean, the median, and the mode at the center of the distribution.

The approximate shape of a normal distribution in which the mean, median, and mode are the same value located at the center of the distribution.

Describing Interval and Ratio Scale Data

The mean is used for data that can be described in terms of the *distance* that scores deviate from the mean. After all, one of the characteristics of the mean (described in Section 3.3) is that the mean balances a set of scores—in other words, the sum of the differences of scores from their mean is 0. For this reason, data that are described by the mean should meaningfully convey differences (or deviations) from the mean. Differences between two scores are meaningfully conveyed for data on an interval or ratio scale only. Hence, the mean is an appropriate measure of central tendency used to describe interval and ratio scale data.

Using the Median to Describe Data

The median is typically used to describe data distributions that are skewed and measures on an ordinal scale.

Describing Skewed Distributions

Some data can have scores that are unusually high or low that skew (or distort) a data set. A **skewed distribution** occurs whenever a data set includes a score or group of scores that fall substantially above (**positively skewed**) or substantially below (**negatively skewed**) most other scores in a distribution. Figure 3.3 illustrates how a skewed distribution shifts the value of the mean. In a normal distribution, the mean and mode are equal (they are both at the center of the distribution). Notice in Figure 3.3 that the value of the mean in a skewed distribution is pulled toward the skewed data points. In a positively skewed distribution, the mean is greater than the mode; in a negatively skewed distribution, the mean is less than the mode. The location of the median is actually unpredictable, and can fall on any side of the mode, depending on how the scores are distributed (Ottenbacher, 1993; Sinacore, Chang, & Falconer, 1992).

Scores that fall substantially above or below most other scores in a distribution will distort the value of the mean, making it a less meaningful measure for describing all data in a distribution. The value of the median, on the other hand, is not influenced by the value of these unusually high or low scores. For this reason, the median is more representative of all data in a skewed distribution and is therefore the most appropriate measure of central tendency to describe these types of distributions.

Describing Ordinal Scale Data

The median is used to describe ranked or ordinal data that convey *direction* only. For example, the fifth person to finish a task took longer than the first person to finish a task; a child in first grade is in a lower grade than a child in fourth grade. In both examples, the ordinal data convey direction (greater than or less than) only. Because the *distance* (or deviation) of ordinal scale scores from their mean is not meaningful, the median is an appropriate measure used to describe ordinal scale data.

FYI

The mean is typically used to describe interval and ratio scale data that are normally distributed.

FYI

The median is typically used to describe skewed distributions and ordinal scale data.

A **skewed distribution** is a distribution of scores that includes outliers or scores that fall substantially above or below most other scores in a data set.

A **positively skewed distribution** is a distribution of scores that includes one or a few scores that are substantially larger (toward the right tail in a graph) than most other scores.

A **negatively skewed distribution** is a distribution of scores that includes one or a few scores that are substantially smaller (toward the left tail in a graph) than most other scores.

The Position of the Mean and Median for Positively Skewed and Negatively Skewed Distributions, Relative to the Normal Distribution

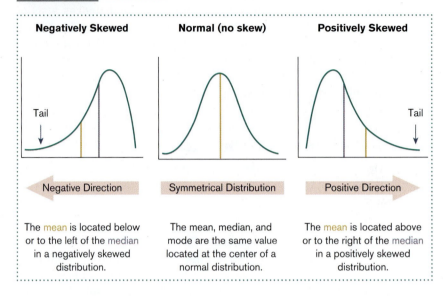

Notice that in each distribution shown here, the mode does not change, but the mean is pulled in the direction of the tail of a skewed distribution.

Using the Mode to Describe Data

The mode is typically used to describe data with modal distributions and measures on a nominal scale.

Describing Modal Distributions

The mode can be used to describe most data that are measured. Sometimes it can complement other measures of central tendency. In Section 3.1, for example, we identified that to choose between two professors teaching the same class, it would be informative to know the average or mean grade students earn in each class. In addition to knowing the mean grade that students earn in each class, it would be informative to know the grade that most students earn in each class (the mode). Both measures—the mean and mode—would be informative. Any distribution in which one or more scores occur most often is called a **modal distribution**. Modal distributions can come in a variety of shapes and sizes.

Unimodal distributions have a single mode. The normal distribution and the skewed distribution have one mode—both distributions are examples of a unimodal shape. The mode can be used with the mean to describe normal distributions. Likewise, the mode can be used with the median to describe skewed distributions.

Bimodal distributions, such as the one in Figure 3.4, have two modes. The mean and median are typically located between the two modes in a bimodal distribution, which often occurs when the data for two groups with unique characteristics are combined. For example, if you measured

A **modal distribution** is a distribution of scores in which one or more scores occur most often or most frequently.

A **unimodal distribution** is a distribution of scores in which one score occurs most often or most frequently. A unimodal distribution has one mode.

A **bimodal distribution** is a distribution of scores in which two scores occur most often or most frequently. A bimodal distribution has two modes.

the height of adult American men and women, you would find a roughly bimodal distribution, with most men reporting a height around 71 inches and most women reporting a height around 66 inches. The modes would be located at 71 inches and 66 inches, with the mean and median heights generally falling somewhere between the two modes.

Multimodal distributions have more than two modes; **nonmodal distributions**, such as the one in Figure 3.5, have no mode at all. For distributions such as these, the mode would be used to describe multimodal distributions only. Nonmodal distributions are essentially a straight line, with the frequency of each score being the same, so there is no mode. In this rare case, the mean or median, which are both located toward the center of a nonmodal distribution, can be used to describe these data.

FYI

The mode is typically used to describe modal distributions and nominal scale data.

FIGURE 3.4	The Location of the Mean, the Median, and the Mode for Bimodal Distributions

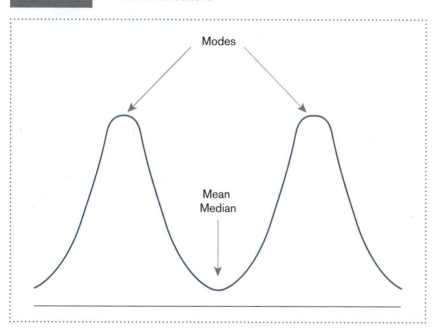

Note that the mean and median can be different values, but they are typically located between the two modes in a bimodal distribution.

Describing Nominal Scale Data

The mode is used to describe nominal data that identify something or someone, nothing more. Because a nominal scale value is not a *quantity*, it does not make sense to use the mean or median to describe these data. The mode is used instead. For example, the mean or median season of birth for patients with schizophrenia is not very meaningful or sensible. But describing these nominal data with the mode is meaningful by saying, for example, that most patients with schizophrenia are born in winter months. Anytime you see phrases such as *most often*, *typical*, or *common*, the mode is being used to describe these data. Table 3.9 summarizes when it is appropriate to use each measure of central tendency.

A **multimodal distribution** is a distribution of scores where more than two scores occur most often or most frequently. A multimodal distribution has more than two modes.

A **nonmodal distribution**, also called a **rectangular distribution**, is a distribution of scores where all scores occur at the same frequency. A nonmodal distribution has no mode.

FIGURE 3.5   A Nonmodal or Rectangular Distribution

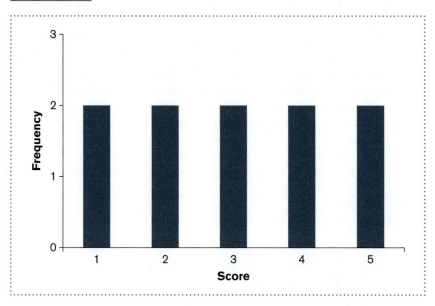

Notice that nonmodal distributions have no identifiable peak, or mode, in the distribution.

TABLE 3.9   A Summary for When It Is Appropriate to Use Each Measure of Central Tendency to Describe Data

Measure of Central Tendency	Shape of Distribution	Measurement Scale
Mean	Normal	Interval, ratio
Median	Skewed	Ordinal
Mode	Modal	Nominal

LEARNING CHECK 6

1. The mean is a preferred descriptive statistic:

   (a) For describing normal distributions

   (b) For summarizing interval scale measures

   (c) For summarizing ratio scale measures

   (d) All of the above

2. True or false: When the mean is greater than the mode, the distribution is negatively skewed.

3. True or false: The mean is a preferred measure for describing skewed distributions.

4. Which type of modal distribution would *not* be described using the mode?

   (a) Unimodal

   (b) Bimodal

   (c) Multimodal

   (d) Nonmodal

Answers: 1. d; 2. False. When the mean is less than the mode, the distribution is negatively skewed; 3. False. The median is the preferred measure; 4. d.

3.5

RESEARCH IN FOCUS:
DESCRIBING CENTRAL TENDENCY

Gulledge, Stahmann, and Wilson (2004) used the mean, the median, and the mode to describe several types of nonsexual romantic physical affection among dating and married students at a university in the northwest region of the United States. They defined nonsexual romantic physical affection as "any touch intended to arouse feelings of love in the giver or the recipient" (Gulledge et al., 2004, p. 609). They recorded the amount of time, or the number of times, students engaged in seven forms of affection (per week) based on self-reports. Table 3.10 shows a portion of their results.

TABLE 3.10   Data From Gulledge et al., 2004

Type of Affection	n	Mean	Median	Mode
Back rubs/massages[a]	177	30	20	0, 30
Caressing/stroking[a]	167	88	30	30
Cuddling/holding[a]	171	189	120	120
Holding hands[a]	168	138	60	60
Hugging[b]	174	34	21	20
Kissing on the face[b]	170	30	15	10
Kissing on the lips[b]	169	66	40	50

a. Measured as minutes per week.

b. Measured as times per week.

Table 3.10 shows the sample size (n) for each type of affection, in addition to the mean, the median, and the mode. By knowing these measures of central tendency, we can identify how students generally responded in this study. Looking at the data in Table 3.10, we can see that the distribution of back rubs/massages is bimodal (it has two modes: 0 and 30). Also, the mean is greater than the median and mode for each type of affection, indicating that the distribution for each type of affection is approximately positively skewed. The mean is larger because of unusually large scores—or a few respondents who apparently are very affectionate. The median indicates that most students responded below the mean (in most cases, well below the mean).

We are able to identify all this information based solely on three measures. Now suppose the researchers claim that the average student holds hands with a romantic partner for 138 minutes per week. While this is certainly true, you, being an informed reader, will quickly recognize that this conclusion is misleading. The median and mode indicate that most people actually spend less than half that time per week holding hands with romantic partners because the median and mode for this type of affection are only 60 minutes. Hence, understanding central tendency allows you to clearly describe and accurately interpret behavioral data in ways not otherwise possible.

© Hemera Technologies/Photos.com/Thinkstock

3.6 SPSS in Focus:
Mean, Median, and Mode

SPSS can be used to measure the mean, the median, and the mode for all sorts of data. In this section, we will work through a new example to compute each measure of central tendency. Suppose you want to study creativity using a paper clip, as has been used in prior studies on the topic (Feist, Reiter-Palmon, & Kaufman, 2017; Piffer, 2012). You give students a paper clip, and the time (in seconds) it takes the students to list 10 uses for the paper clip is recorded. Faster times are presumed to reflect greater creativity. Using the data shown in Table 3.11, we can use SPSS to compute the mean, the median, and the mode.

TABLE 3.11	The Time (in seconds) That It Took 20 Participants to Write Down 10 Uses for a Paper Clip on a Creativity Test	
41		80
65		80
123		64
46		59
48		51
87		36
38		80
90		143
132		122
115		100

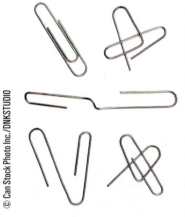

© Can Stock Photo Inc./DNKSTUDIO

1. Click on the Variable View tab and enter *creativity* in the Name column. We will enter whole numbers, so go to the Decimals column and reduce the value to 0.

2. Click on the Data View tab and enter the 20 values in the column labeled *creativity*.

3. Go to the menu bar and click Analyze, then Descriptive Statistics and Frequencies, to bring up a dialog box.

4. In the dialog box, select the *creativity* variable and click the arrow in the center to move creativity into the box labeled Variable(s): to the right. Make sure the option to display frequency tables is not selected, and then select Statistics to bring up another dialog box.

5. In the dialog box, select Mean, Median and Mode to the right; then select Continue.

6. Select OK, or select Paste and click the Run command.

Notice in Table 3.12 that the mean, the median, and the mode are the same—the value of each measure of central tendency is 80. Also, note that when multiple modes exist in the data, which is not the case for this data set, SPSS does not list the value for every mode. Instead, SPSS gives the value for the smallest mode and places the superscript *a* next to that modal value to indicate that other modes exist in the data.

TABLE 3.12 SPSS Output Table Showing the Mean, the Median, and the Mode

Statistics

creativity

N	Valid	20
	Missing	0
Mean		80.00
Median		80.00
Mode		80

● ● ● CHAPTER SUMMARY ORGANIZED BY LEARNING OBJECTIVE

LO 1: **Distinguish between a population mean and a sample mean.**

- The mean for a set of scores in an entire population is called a population mean; the mean for a sample (or subset of scores from a population) is called a sample mean. Each mean is computed the same but with different notation used to identify the sample size (*n*) and population size (*N*).

LO 2: **Calculate and interpret the mean, the median, and the mode.**

- Measures of central tendency are statistical measures for locating a single score that is most representative or descriptive of all scores in a distribution. Three measures of central tendency are the mean, the median, and the mode.

- The mean is the sum of a set of scores divided by the total number of scores summed:

  The population mean is the sum of *N* scores (*x*) divided by *N*:
  $$\mu = \frac{\Sigma x}{N}.$$

  The sample mean is the sum of *n* scores (*x*) divided by *n*: $M = \frac{\Sigma x}{n}$.

- The median is the middle score in a data set that is listed in numerical order in which half of all scores fall above and half fall below its value. Unlike the mean, the value of the median is not shifted in the direction of outliers—the median is always at the center or midpoint of a data set. To find the median position, list scores in numerical order and apply this formula:

$$\text{Median position} = \frac{n+1}{2}.$$

- The mode is the value in a data set that occurs most often or most frequently. The mode is often reported with the mean or the median.

LO 3:   Calculate and interpret the weighted mean for two or more samples with unequal sample sizes.

- The weighted mean is the combined mean of two or more groups of scores in which the number of scores in each group is disproportionate or unequal. The formula for the weighted mean of two or more samples with unequal sample sizes is $M_w = \dfrac{\sum(M \times n)}{\sum n}$.

LO 4:   Identify the characteristics of the mean.

- The mean has the following characteristics:

  (a) Changing an existing score will change the mean.

  (b) Adding a new score or removing an existing score will change the mean, unless that value equals the mean.

  (c) Adding, subtracting, multiplying, or dividing each score in a distribution by a constant will cause the mean to change by that constant.

  (d) The sum of the differences of scores from their mean is zero.

  (e) The sum of the squared differences of scores from their mean is minimal.

LO 5:   Identify an appropriate measure of central tendency for different distributions and scales of measurement.

- The *mean* is used to describe (1) data that are normally distributed and (2) interval and ratio scale data.

- The *median* is used to describe (1) data in a skewed distribution and (2) ordinal scale data.

- The *mode* is used to describe (1) any type of data with a value that occurs the most, although it is typically used together with the mean or the median, and (2) nominal scale data.

LO 6:   Compute the mean, the median, and the mode using SPSS.

- SPSS can be used to compute the mean, the median, and the mode. Each measure of central tendency is computed using the Analyze, then Descriptive Statistics and Frequencies, options in the menu bar. These actions will bring up a dialog box that will allow you to identify the variable and select the Statistics option to select and compute the mean, the median, and the mode (for more details, see Section 3.6).

• • • KEY TERMS

arithmetic mean	modal distribution	positively skewed
average	mode	rectangular distribution
bell-shaped distribution	multimodal distribution	sample mean
bimodal distribution	negatively skewed	sample size (n)
central tendency	nonmodal distribution	skewed distribution
Gaussian distribution	normal distribution	symmetrical distribution
mean	population mean	unimodal distribution
median	population size (N)	weighted mean

••• END-OF-CHAPTER PROBLEMS

Factual Problems

1. State the statistical notation for each of the following terms:

    (a) Population size

    (b) Sample size

    (c) Population mean

    (d) Sample mean

2. What is central tendency?

3. Which type of central tendency is always located at the center or in the middle of a distribution?

4. How do the sample mean and population mean differ?

5. List five characteristics of the mean.

6. When is the weighted mean equal to the arithmetic mean for combining the mean for two or more samples?

7. The mode is an appropriate measure for describing what types of data?

8. The median is an appropriate measure for describing what types of data?

9. The mean is an appropriate measure for describing what types of data?

10. What value represents:

    (a) The midpoint of a distribution? Explain.

    (b) The balance point of a distribution? Explain.

    (c) The zero point of a distribution? Explain.

Concept and Application Problems

11. The following frequency distribution table lists the time (in minutes) that participants were late for an experimental session. Compute the sample mean, median, and mode for these data.

Time (min)	Frequency
0	5
2	2
6	1
8	3
9	2

12. The following table lists the number of text messages sent per day in a sample of college students and a sample of their parents.

    (a) Compute the mean, the median, and the mode for the college students' and parents' data.

    (b) Based on the shape of the distribution for each sample, which measure of central tendency is most appropriate for describing each sample? Explain how describing each sample with only the most appropriate measure might be misleading.

College Students		Parents	
43	7	24	21
12	50	0	17
14	15	20	19
13	21	21	5
54	21	3	10

13. A researcher records the number of hours (per week) that adults spend on social media and finds that the data are distributed normally. Which measure of central tendency is most appropriate for describing these data?

14. A psychologist records the duration of natural labor (in hours) in a sample of 36 first-pregnancy mothers. Based on the duration data given in the following table, which measure of central tendency is most appropriate for describing

these data? *Hint:* Draw the shape of this distribution first.

1	5	6	2
7	3	4	7
10	7	5	6
4	3	2	11
5	9	8	5
6	6	9	7
4	5	6	4
8	8	10	9
8	7	6	3

15. A researcher records the levels of attraction for various fashion models among college students. He finds that mean levels of attraction are much higher than the median and mode for these data.

    (a) What is the shape of the distribution for the data described in this study?

    (b) Which measure of central tendency is most appropriate for describing these data? Explain.

16. A colleague measures the following heights (in inches) of 10 CEOs selected at random: 72, 75, 75, 66, 64, 79, 79, 75, 70, and 72. Which measure of central tendency is most appropriate for describing these data? *Hint:* Draw the shape of this distribution first.

17. A neuroscientist measures the reaction times (in seconds) during an experimental session in a sample of cocaine-addicted ($n = 8$), morphine-addicted ($n = 12$), and heroin-addicted rats ($n = 6$). Mean reaction times in each sample are 11, 18, and 13 seconds, respectively. What is the weighted mean for all three samples? *Hint:* The overall mean is not 14.0 seconds.

18. A family counselor records the number of sessions required for children to complete counseling following the loss of a family member. The counselor finds that most boys complete counseling in 12 sessions, whereas most girls require 15 sessions to complete counseling. If the data for boys and girls are combined, what type of distribution best describes the combined data?

19. A sports psychologist uses the body mass index (BMI) score to measure health in a sample of 60 athletes and determines that 20 are healthy, 26 are overweight, and 14 are obese. Which measure of central tendency is most appropriate for describing these data?

20. A cognitive psychologist was interested in the ability of men and women to multitask—a cognitive skill thought to engage short-term or working memory. The psychologist observed a sample of 5 men ($n = 5$) and 8 women ($n = 8$) and measured the number of tasks they could accurately complete within a short time frame. He found that men completed 2.3 tasks on average ($M = 2.3$), whereas women completed 4.5 tasks on average ($M = 4.5$). What is the weighted mean for both samples? *Hint:* The overall mean is not 3.4 tasks.

21. Based on the scale of measurement for each variable listed below, which measure of central tendency is most appropriate for describing the data?

    (a) The distance in miles that a group of athletes run to train for a marathon

    (b) The rankings of college undergraduate academic programs

    (c) The blood type (e.g., Type A, B, AB, O) of a group of participants

22. An instructor gives students a surprise quiz and records a mean grade of 12 points. What is the new mean value if the instructor does each of the following?

    (a) Adds 10 points to each quiz

    (b) Subtracts 2 points from each quiz

    (c) Doubles each quiz score

    (d) Divides each quiz score in half

23. Children participating at a one-week summer camp made five new friends on average during the first six days of camp. If each child made two more friends on the last day of camp, then

how many friends on average did the children make during the one-week summer camp?

24. A sample of 26 patients with major depressive disorder (MDD) showed an average of five symptoms of the disorder prior to diagnosis. What is the sum of the differences of scores from the mean in this example?

Based on the example below, answer Questions 25 to 28:

A group of researchers measures the weight of five participants prior to a clinical weight loss intervention. They record the following weights (in pounds): 200, 250, 150, 100, and 300 pounds. The mean is 200 pounds.

25. The researchers realize that the scale was not accurate for the individual weighing 300 pounds, so they reweigh that individual and record 250 pounds. Will the mean increase or decrease in this situation?

26. Instead, the researchers reweigh the 300-pound individual and record a new weight of 350 pounds. Will the mean increase or decrease in this situation?

27. Using the original example of five weights, the researchers add a sixth participant to the sample.

   (a) If the sixth participant weighs 240 pounds, will the mean increase, decrease, or not change?

   (b) If the sixth participant weighs 200 pounds, will the mean increase, decrease, or not change?

   (c) If the sixth participant weighs 180 pounds, will the mean increase, decrease, or not change?

28. The researchers implement their weight loss intervention with the original five participants and find that each participant loses exactly 10 pounds in the first three weeks. Without recalculating the mean, what is the new mean weight?

Problems in Research

29. **Family income in the middle class.** Bauer et al. (2011) identified the median income of a middle-class family in their sample to be $84,200 annually; the mean family income was $85,300 annually. In their data, the lowest family income reported in this group was $65,100 annually, and the highest family income reported was $103,400 annually. Based on the data given, was the mean an appropriate value to summarize these data? Explain.

30. **Gender differences with money.** Furnham, von Stumm, and Fenton-O'Creevy (2015), in a study about why males and females spend money, stated that "money was associated with generosity (money representing love) where males scored much lower than females, and autonomy (money representing freedom) where males scored higher than females. For males, more than females, money represented Power and Security" (Furnham et al., 2015, p. 701). Based on this citation, which sex (males, females) would be likely to have a higher mean score for each of the following?

   (a) Money representing love/generosity
   (b) Money representing freedom
   (c) Money representing power and security

31. **Helping smokers quit by race.** Patten and colleagues (2008) stated that "among non-smokers who indicated they were close to a smoker whom they thought should quit, Black [participants] were most often concerned about a family member whereas White [participants] endorsed concern most often for a friend" (p. 496). What are the most common concerns (or mode) for each race?

32. **The convenience of eating.** Privitera and Zuraikat (2014) conducted a study to test whether the proximity of food influences consumption. They placed a bowl of popcorn or apple slices in a container on a table (near) or 2 meters from a participant (far). Do the data

in the figure given here support their hypothesis that the more proximate the food, the more participants will eat of it? Explain.

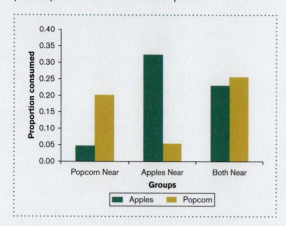

33. **Social support and stroke-induced aphasia.** Hilari and Northcott (2006) used a Social Support Survey (SSS) to gauge how well supported individuals suffering from stroke-induced aphasia (a language disorder) felt more than one year following the stroke. They reported that "in terms of social support, the SSS scores were *negatively skewed* with a mean of 3.69, suggesting that participants felt overall well supported" (Hilari & Northcott, 2006, p. 17). Based on their findings, what additional measure of central tendency would be appropriate to report with these data? Explain.

Answers for even numbers are in Appendix D.

Sharpen your skills with **SAGE edge at edge.sagepub.com/priviteraess2e**

SAGE edge for Students provides a personalized approach to help you accomplish your coursework goals in an easy-to-use learning environment.

⑤SAGE edge™

©Can Stock Photo Inc./OG_vision

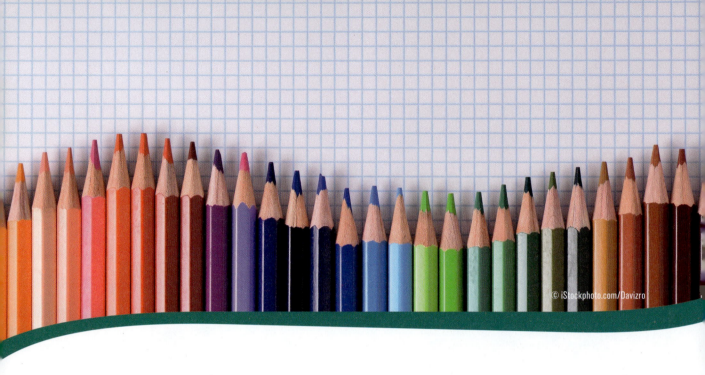

© iStockphoto.com/Davizro

4 Summarizing Data
Variability

• • • Learning Objectives

After reading this chapter, you should be able to:

1. Compute and interpret a range, interquartile range, and semi-interquartile range.

2. Compute and interpret the variance and standard deviation for a population and sample of data using the definitional formula.

3. Compute and interpret the variance and standard deviation for a population and sample of data using the computational formula.

4. Explain why the sample variance and population variance are computed differently.

5. State the characteristics of the standard deviation and explain the empirical rule.

6. Compute the range, variance, and standard deviation using SPSS.

You may notice that a friend does not always show up on time when you go out or that a movie showing is delayed some nights due to long lines, or your parents may have been frustrated with you on the rare nights you did not show up by your curfew. A simple night out with a friend to the movies can thus have a lot of variability—in terms of when your friend shows up, when the movie starts, and when you get home that night.

Most events and behaviors likewise do not occur exactly but instead have variability associated with their occurrence. For example, patients with a certain mental health disorder may express 5 symptoms of their disorder on average, but not all patients express exactly 5 symptoms; employee wellness programs may reduce employer health care costs by 15% on average, but not all wellness programs show this outcome; students in a statistics class may have scored an 80% on average on their test, but not all students scored an 80%. The key takeaway message is that variability, or the tendency for events and behaviors to vary—whether by patient, by program, or by student—is not at all surprising; it is expected. This makes variability important to understand in science inasmuch as it is part of the nature of the observations behavioral scientists make. Behavior varies, and understanding that variability is a vital part of utilizing data in science. In many ways, variability is a wider scope than central tendency. Whereas measures of central tendency take a snapshot of the center of a distribution (we did this in Chapter 3), variability widens the lens to capture an image of the entire distribution.

Statistics provides a useful way to measure variability. In this chapter, we introduce many ways in which researchers measure this to understand how data vary across all observations and to summarize the distribution of the data observed.

Master the content.

edge.sagepub.com/priviteraess2e

••• Chapter Outline

4.1 MEASURING VARIABILITY

FYI

Researchers measure variability to determine how dispersed scores are in a set of data. Measures of variability include the range, variance, and standard deviation.

Suppose you learn that the average college graduate earns about $50,000 per year within six months of graduating. This may seem like a fair starting income, but what about the income for all other graduates? Each graduate earns a college degree that qualifies him or her for a different type of job that can provide earnings well above or well below the average income. What is the highest income a college graduate can expect to earn? What is the lowest income? What percentage of college graduates earn above or below a certain income level? The idea here is that the mean, like the median and mode, informs you only of scores (or incomes in this example) at or near the center of a distribution but little to nothing of the remaining scores in a set of data.

Once we know the mean, we need to determine where all the other scores are in relation to the mean. As illustrated in Figure 4.1, we need a measure of **variability**—that is, a way to measure the dispersion or spread of scores around the mean. By definition, the variability of scores can never be negative; variability ranges from 0 to +∞ (positive infinity). If four students receive the same scores of 8, 8, 8, and 8 on some assessment, then their scores do not vary because they are all the same value—the variability is 0. However, if the scores are 8, 8, 8, and 9, then they do vary because at least one of the scores differs from the others. Thus, scores can either not vary (variability is 0) or vary (variability is greater than 0). A negative variability is meaningless.

The focus of this chapter is measures of variability: range, quartiles, interquartiles, variance, and standard deviation. As with central tendency, we explain how measures of variability are informative, descriptive, and useful for making sense of data.

FIGURE 4.1 What We Do Not Know About a Distribution Even When We Know the Mean

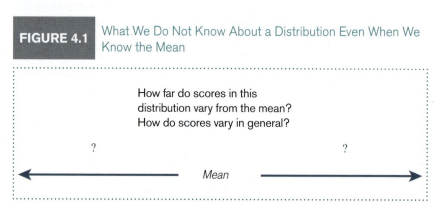

Notice that although we know the mean score in this distribution, we know nothing of the remaining scores. By computing measures of variability, we can determine how scores vary around the mean and how they vary in general.

4.2 THE RANGE AND INTERQUARTILE RANGE

Variability is a measure of the dispersion or spread of scores in a distribution and ranges from 0 to +∞.

The **range** is the difference between the largest value (L) and smallest value (S) in a data set.

The simplest way to describe how dispersed scores are is to identify the range of scores in a distribution. The **range** is the difference between the largest value (L) and smallest value (S) in a data set. The formula for the range can be stated as follows:

$$\text{Range} = L - S.$$

The range is most informative for data sets without outliers. For example, suppose you measure five scores: 1, 2, 3, 4, and 5. The range of these data is $5 - 1 = 4$. In this example, the range gives a fair description of the variability of these data. Now suppose your friend also measures five scores: 2, 4, 6, 8, and 100. The range of these data is $100 - 2 = 98$ because the outlier is the largest value in the data set. In this example, a range of 98 is misleading because only one value is greater than 8.

One way to resolve the problem of outliers when computing range is to compute an **interquartile range (IQR)**. An IQR is the range of scores in a distribution between the first quartile (Q_1) and the third quartile (Q_3). **Quartiles** split data into four equal parts (each containing 25% of the data). Hence, the IQR is the range of scores, minus the top and bottom 25% of scores, in a distribution. The top 25% of scores are above Q_3 (the 75th percentile); the bottom 25% of scores are below Q_1 (the 25th percentile). To compute an IQR, we therefore subtract the lower quartile (Q_1) from the upper quartile (Q_3):

$$IQR = Q_3 - Q_1.$$

Some statisticians also use the **semi-interquartile range (SIQR)**:

$$SIQR = \frac{Q_3 - Q_1}{2}, \text{ also represented as } SIQR = \frac{IQR}{2}.$$

The semi-interquartile range is used as a measure of half the distance between the upper (Q_3) and lower (Q_1) quartiles of a distribution. You can think of the SIQR as the mean IQR, with smaller SIQR values indicating less spread or variability of scores in a data set. Because the IQR excludes the top and bottom 25% of scores in a distribution, outliers have little influence over this value. However, while the SIQR is a good estimate of variability, it is also limited in that its estimate excludes half the scores in a distribution.

Although the range provides a simple measure of variability, the range accounts for only two values (the largest value and smallest value) in a distribution. Whether the data set has five scores or 5 million scores, calculations of the range consider only the largest value and smallest value in that distribution. The range in a data set of $n = 3$ may be very informative, but a typical data set for human participant research can be in the hundreds or

FYI

The range is the difference between the largest value and smallest value in a distribution. It is different from a real range (equal to the range plus one), which we calculated in Chapter 2 for continuous data.

FYI

The interquartile range (IQR) is the range of scores between the upper and lower quartiles of a distribution.

FYI

Calculations of the range consider only the largest value and smallest value in a data set.

The **interquartile range (IQR)** is the range of values between the upper (Q_3) and lower (Q_1) quartiles of a data set.

Quartiles are four equal parts or sections, each containing 25% of the data.

The **semi-interquartile range (SIQR)** is a measure of half the distance between the upper quartile (Q_3) and lower quartile (Q_1) of a data set and is computed by dividing the IQR in half.

4.3	**RESEARCH** IN FOCUS:
	REPORTING THE RANGE

Because we use only two values to find the range, it is seldom used as a primary measure of variability in behavioral science. The range is included in many research studies to summarize demographic information (e.g., age, weight, race) and to support other reported descriptive measures (e.g., life satisfaction, personality traits, social skills). For instance, researchers often use the range in addition to the mean (and standard deviation, introduced later in this chapter) to describe participants in a study. These values are often reported in summary tables such as Table 4.1.

(Continued)

(Continued)

TABLE 4.1	A Portion of the Descriptive Data Reported by Pérez Escoda and Alegre (2016)

Participant Variables	Mean (Range)
Emotional Awareness	7.17 (2.43–10.00)
Emotional Regulation	5.73 (0.46–9.62)
Social Skills	6.26 (2.42–9.75)
Life and Well-Being Skills	7.29 (2.11–10.00)
Life Satisfaction	25.15 (5.00–35.00)

The sample characteristics for 2,233 participants in a study evaluating how emotional intelligence moderates the relationship between various levels of life satisfaction (Pérez Escoda & Alegre, 2016).

Table 4.1 shows a summary of five characteristics of interest in a study conducted by Pérez Escoda and Alegre (2016). In this table, the researchers reported the mean and range of each characteristic. Notice that the range when given with the mean adds greater detail (i.e., more information) to our understanding of participant characteristics. The ranges for measures of emotional awareness and social skills, for example, are about the same, but the means differ. From these values, we can surmise that mean scores for social skills are closer to the center of the distribution (i.e., closer to the middle of the range) compared to scores for emotional awareness. We can also see that scores for life satisfaction, for example, are approximately negatively skewed, with the mean being closer to the high end of the range. When both the mean and the range are given, readers have more information for each measure than they would if the mean or the range were reported alone.

LEARNING CHECK 1

1. _____ is a measure of the dispersion or spread of scores in a distribution and ranges from 0 to +∞.

2. What is the formula for computing the range?

3. A researcher collects the following scores: 1, 2, 3, 4, 5, 6, 7, and 8. What is the range of these scores?

4. When data are divided into four equal parts, the data are split into _____.

5. A researcher records the number of times that 10 students cough during a final exam. He records the following data: 0, 0, 0, 3, 3, 5, 5, 7, 8, and 11. True or false: In this example, the range will be smaller than the interquartile range.

Answers: 1. Variability; 2. The range is the largest value (L) minus the smallest value (S) in a data set; 3. Range = 8 − 1 = 7; 4. Quartiles; 5. False. The range will be larger than the IQR.

even thousands. For this reason, many researchers favor other measures of variability to describe data sets.

4.4 THE VARIANCE

A preferred estimate of variability is the variance because it includes all scores, not just two extreme scores, to estimate variability. The **variance** measures the average squared distance that scores deviate from their mean. The value of the variance can be 0 (there is no variability) or greater than 0 (there is variability). A negative variance is meaningless. Unlike calculations of the mean, the formula for variance does change for samples and populations, in terms of both notation and calculation.

Population Variance

The **population variance** is represented by the square of the Greek symbol σ (or σ², stated as "sigma squared"). Calculations of population variance are used to measure the dispersion of scores from their mean. A population variance, which is computed only for an entire population of scores, is defined by the following formula:

$$\sigma^2 = \frac{\sum(x-\mu)^2}{N} \text{ or } \frac{SS}{N}.$$

In this formula, the expression $x - \mu$ is a **deviation**; it is the difference of each score from its mean. This value is squared, then summed, in the numerator: $\sum(x - \mu)^2$. The numerator for the variance formula is also called the **sum of squares (SS)** or the sum of the squared deviations of scores from their mean. The term N is the population size. To compute the population variance, we split the steps into two parts:

Part 1: Calculate the SS (the numerator).

Part 2: Divide the SS by the population size (N).

In Example 4.1, we apply each part to compute the population variance formula.

FYI

The variance is a preferred measure of variability because all scores are included in its computation. Variance can be computed for data in populations and samples.

FYI

To compute the population variance, the SS is divided by the population size (N).

Variance is a measure of variability for the average squared distance that scores deviate from their mean.

Population variance is a measure of variability for the average squared distance that scores in a population deviate from the mean. It is computed only when all scores in a given population are recorded.

A **deviation** is the difference of each score from its mean.

The **sum of squares (SS)** is the sum of the squared deviations of scores from their mean. The SS is the numerator in the variance formula.

Example 4.1

Suppose you want to determine how much your six closest friends actually know about you. This is the group of interest to you; your six closest friends constitute the population of interest. You quiz all six close friends about 10 facts you think they should know about you. Their scores on the quiz are 5, 10, 3, 7, 2, and 3. We will follow the steps to calculate the population variance (σ^2) of these scores.

Part 1: Calculate the SS. In Part 1, we follow four steps. To compute the SS,

(1) Identify each score: 5, 10, 3, 7, 2, and 3.

(2) Compute the population mean:

$$\mu = \frac{5+10+3+7+2+3}{6} = 5.$$

(3) Compute the squared deviation of each score from the mean. In other words, find how far each score is from the mean, and square it. To do this for each score,

subtract the mean, and then square the result. The computation for each score (x) is as follows:

$$x = 5: (5 - 5)^2 = 0$$

$$x = 10: (10 - 5)^2 = 25$$

$$x = 3: (3 - 5)^2 = 4$$

$$x = 7: (7 - 5)^2 = 4$$

$$x = 2: (2 - 5)^2 = 9$$

$$x = 3: (3 - 5)^2 = 4$$

(4) Sum the squared deviations. In other words, to find the SS, add up the answers from (3):

$$SS = 0 + 25 + 4 + 4 + 9 + 4 = 46.$$

Part 2: Divide the SS by the population size. The solution is the population variance. Thus, the population variance is SS divided by N:

$$\sigma^2 = \frac{SS}{N} = \frac{46}{6} = 7.67.$$

The population variance for the data in this example is $\sigma^2 = 7.67$.

LEARNING CHECK 2

1. Why is the variance a preferred measure of variability?

2. A researcher selects a population of eight scores where $SS = 72$. What is the population variance in this example?

3. Describe the sum of squares (SS) in words.

4. A researcher measures the following scores: 12, 14, 16, 18, and 20. Compute the SS for these data.

5. True or false: When all scores in a population are the same, the variance will always be equal to 0.

Answers: 1. Because it includes all scores in its computation; 2. $\sigma^2 = 9$; 3. SS is the sum of the squared deviations of scores from their mean; 4. $SS = 40$; 5. True.

FYI

To compute the sample variance, we divide the SS by one less than the sample size ($n - 1$).

Sample variance is a measure of variability for the average squared distance that scores in a sample deviate from the mean. It is computed when only a portion or sample of data is measured in a population.

Sample Variance

The **sample variance** is likewise used to measure how dispersed scores are from their mean when the data consist of less than an entire population of scores. The sample variance (denoted s^2) is defined by the following formula:

$$s^2 = \frac{\sum(x - M)^2}{n - 1} \text{ or } \frac{SS}{n - 1}.$$

Figure 4.2 shows that the numerator for the sample variance is computed in the same way as that for the population variance: The numerator is the SS. It is calculations in the denominator that differ for populations and samples. To compute the sample variance, we divide the *SS* by the sample size (*n*) minus 1. The notations for the mean (*M*) and the sample size (*n*) have also changed to account for the fact that the data are from a sample and not a population. To compute sample variance, we again split the steps into two parts:

Part 1: Calculate the *SS* (the numerator).

Part 2: Divide *SS* by (*n* − 1).

In Example 4.2, we compute the sample variance using the same data from Example 4.1. This allows us to directly compare calculations for both measures of variability.

FIGURE 4.2   The Steps to Compute the Sample Variance and Population Variance

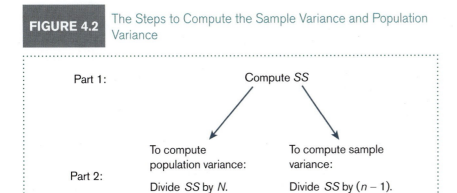

Notice that Part 1 is the same for computing the sample variance and population variance. Only computations in the denominator of the variance formula (Part 2) differ for sample variance and population variance.

Example 4.2

Suppose you have more than just six close friends, so the six close friends you quizzed in Example 4.1 now constitute a sample or portion of all your close friends. The sample of six scores from Example 4.1 was 5, 10, 3, 7, 2, and 3. We will follow the steps to calculate the sample variance (s^2) of these scores.

Part 1: Calculate the *SS*. Follow the same steps shown for Part 1 in Example 4.1. The steps to compute *SS* are the same for population variance and sample variance: *SS* = 46.

Part 2: Divide *SS* by (*n* − 1). The sample variance is $s^2 = \frac{SS}{n-1} = \frac{46}{(6-1)} = 9.20$.

The sample variance for the data in this example is $s^2 = 9.20$.

For populations and samples of data, the larger the value of the variance, the more dispersed or spread out scores are from their mean. For variance, keep in mind that values of sample variance and population variance can be very large—much larger than scores in the original data set.

FYI

Computations of SS are the same for population variance and sample variance. The change in computation is whether we divide SS by N (population variance) or by n − 1 (sample variance).

LEARNING CHECK 3

1. How does calculating the sample variance differ from calculating the population variance?

2. A researcher measures the following data: 3, 3, 3, 4, 4, and 4. What is the sample variance for these data?

3. True or false: A scientist measures the following data: 23, 23, 23, 23, 23, and 23. The value for the sample variance and population variance will be the same.

Answers: 1. The denominator for sample variance is $(n-1)$, not N; 2. $s^2 = 0.3$; 3. True because the variance is 0.

4.5 EXPLAINING VARIANCE FOR POPULATIONS AND SAMPLES

In this section, we look at the variance calculation in depth. In particular, we explain why we compute squared deviations in the numerator and why the denominator differs in the calculations for sample variance and population variance. Believe it or not, there is actually a good reason for this change beyond the cynical statistician's goal of just trying to confuse you.

The Numerator: Why Square Deviations From the Mean?

We can calculate how far each score is from its mean to determine how much variability there is in a data set. For example, suppose a set of data has a mean of 5. As shown in Figure 4.3, a score of 10 will deviate farther from the mean than a score of 3 in this data set. The idea here is that scores in a given data set will be at various distances from the mean. Some scores will deviate farther than others. Regardless of whether we have a sample or population of scores, in both cases we want to measure variability by determining how far a group of scores deviates from the mean. To compute variance, we square each deviation in the numerator. There are three reasons we square each deviation to compute SS:

1. The sum of the differences of scores from their mean is zero.

2. The sum of the squared differences of scores from their mean is minimal.

3. Squaring scores can be corrected by taking the square root.

The most straightforward way to measure variability is to subtract each score from its mean and to sum each deviation. The problem is that the sum will always be equal to zero (this was the fourth characteristic of the mean listed in Chapter 3). Table 4.2 shows an example of a small population of scores: 3, 5, and 7. Notice that the sum of the differences of scores from their mean is zero in the table. Here we would conclude that these scores do not vary from one another, but they do. To avoid this result, each deviation is squared to produce the smallest positive solution that is not zero.

The reason we square each deviation before summing is largely because of Reasons 2 and 3 listed on the previous page: We want to compute how far scores are from their mean without ending up with a solution equal to zero every time. Basically, we need to compute a positive value for variance that is not zero. Think of any solution to avoid this zero result as intentionally making an error. To minimize error, we need to ensure that the result we obtain is the smallest possible positive value—or the value with minimal error. The last characteristic of the mean listed in Chapter 3 showed that squaring each deviation before summing each deviation will produce the smallest possible positive solution. This is one reason for squaring deviations: It provides a solution with minimal error.

Another reason for squaring is that we can correct for this by taking the square root of the solution for variance (we will do this when we calculate *standard deviation* in Section 4.7). This is not a perfect correction, but it is a simple and appropriate way to correct for squaring each deviation. Whether we have a sample or population of scores, these rules are the same: In both cases, squaring each deviation provides a solution with minimal error that can be corrected by taking the square root of the variance.

FIGURE 4.3   A Hypothetical Data Set With a Score of 2, 3, and 10

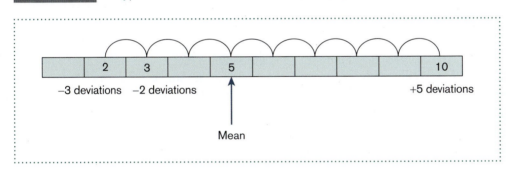

The mean is 5. Notice that a score of 10 is farther from the mean than a score of 2 or a score of 3 in this distribution. The distance that scores deviate from the mean can be used to measure the variability of scores in a data set.

TABLE 4.2   A List of Scores (left column) With a Mean of 5

x	x – Mean
3	3 – 5 = –2
5	5 – 5 = 0
7	7 – 5 = 2
	Sum of deviations = 0

The sum of the differences of each score from their mean is 0 (right column). The sum of the differences of scores from their mean will always equal 0.

FYI

The SS produces the smallest possible positive value for deviations of scores from their mean. The SS is computed in the same way for sample variance and population variance.

The Denominator: Sample Variance as an Unbiased Estimator

The population variance is computed by dividing the *SS* by the population size (*N*), whereas the sample variance is computed by dividing the *SS* by the sample size (*n*) minus 1. Why did statisticians choose to subtract 1 in the denominator of the sample variance? The following example will illustrate the reason and demonstrate why (*n* − 1) improves the sample variance calculation. Suppose we have a hypothetical population of three people (*N* = 3) who scored an 8 (Person A), 5 (Person B), and 2 (Person C) on a quiz. This hypothetical population has a variance of 6:

$$\sigma^2 = \frac{(8-5)^2 + (5-5)^2 + (2-5)^2}{3} = \frac{9+0+9}{3} = \frac{18}{3} = 6.$$

We know that this population has a variance of 6. On average, any sample we select from this population should also have a variance of 6. To determine this, we will take all samples of size two (*n* = 2) from this population of three. On average, we should find that the sample variance is equal to 6—it should be the same as the variance in the population. If it is not, then the sample variance is biased. Table 4.3 lists the nine possible samples of size two that could be selected from this population.

The last two columns in Table 4.3 show two ways to calculate sample variance. In Column C, *SS* is divided by *n* (not *n* − 1). Notice that when we do not subtract 1 in the denominator, the sample variance will underestimate the population variance on average. Hence, the sample variance is a **biased estimator** in that it will be less than the population variance on average (3 < 6). The following statement describes this rule:

The sample variance is biased: If $s^2 = \frac{SS}{n}$, then $s^2 < \sigma^2$ on average.

In Column D of Table 4.3, notice that, on average, the sample variance equals the population variance when we subtract 1 from *n* in the denominator (6 = 6). Making this simple change in the denominator makes the sample variance an **unbiased estimator**—its value will equal the population variance on average. The following statement describes this rule:

The sample variance is unbiased: If $s^2 = \frac{SS}{n-1}$, then $s^2 = \sigma^2$ on average.

On the basis of this example, you can see that only when we divide *SS* by (*n* − 1) to compute the sample variance will we produce a value that equals the population variance on average. This makes the sample variance unbiased in that, on average, the variance of the sample will equal the variance of the population from which the sample was selected. Therefore, to ensure that the sample variance is an unbiased estimator, we divide by (*n* − 1) to calculate sample variance.

A **biased estimator** is any sample statistic, such as the sample variance when we divide *SS* by *n*, obtained from a randomly selected sample that does not equal the value of its respective population parameter, such as a population mean, on average.

An **unbiased estimator** is any sample statistic, such as the sample variance when we divide *SS* by (*n* − 1), obtained from a randomly selected sample that equals the value of its respective population parameter, such as a population variance, on average.

TABLE 4.3	The Computation of Sample Variance (last two columns) Using n and $(n-1)$ in the Denominator		
A **Participants** **Sampled ($n=2$)**	**B** **Scores for Each** **Participant**	**C** s^2 **Using (n)**	**D** s^2 **Using** **($n-1$)**
A, A	8, 8	0	0
A, B	8, 5	2.25	4.50
A, C	8, 2	9.00	18.00
B, A	5, 8	2.25	4.50
B, B	5, 5	0	0
B, C	5, 2	2.25	4.50
C, A	2, 8	9.00	18.00
C, B	2, 5	2.25	4.50
C, C	2, 2	0	0
Mean sample variance:		$\frac{27}{9}=3.0$	$\frac{54}{9}=6.0$

FYI

When we divide SS by $(n-1)$, the sample variance is an unbiased estimator of the population variance. This is one reason why researchers place $(n-1)$ in the denominator of sample variance.

To compute the average sample variance in Columns C and D, we add up all possible values for sample variance listed in that column and divide by 9 (or the total number of samples that can be selected). In this example, each sample was selected from a population with a variance of 6. Notice that only when we divide SS by $(n-1)$ do we find that, on average, the sample variance is equal to the population variance—it is an unbiased estimator.

The Denominator: Degrees of Freedom

The denominator $(n-1)$ also tells us the **degrees of freedom (df) for sample variance**, which are the number of scores that are free to vary in a sample. Basically, if you know the mean of a data set and the value of all scores in that data set except one, you can perfectly predict the last score (i.e., the last score is not free to vary). Suppose, for example, we have a sample of three participants with a mean score of 4 ($M=4$). Table 4.4 shows a distribution with these three scores: 3, 4, and x. We know two scores (3 and 4) but not the last score (x). But the last score is not free, so we can find its value.

TABLE 4.4	The Degrees of Freedom for Variance

x	M	$x-M$
3	4	−1
4	4	0
x	4	?
		$\sum(x-M)=0$

Each score is free to vary in a distribution, except one $(n-1)$.

The **degrees of freedom (df) for sample variance** are the number of scores in a sample that are free to vary. All scores except one are free to vary in a sample: $n-1$.

FYI

The degrees of freedom for sample variance tell us that all scores are free to vary in a sample except one (n − 1). This term is placed in the denominator of the formula for sample variance.

Remember that the sum of the deviations of scores from their mean is zero. The deviation of the first score from its mean is −1 (3 − 4 = −1), and the deviation of the second score from its mean is 0 (4 − 4 = 0). Therefore, it must be the case that −1 + 0 + (x − 4) = 0. Thus, x = 5 because it is the only value for x that can make the solution to this equation equal to 0. Therefore, we can say that one score is not free to vary when the sample mean is known. In other words, scores used to compute sample variance are free to vary, except one. Because all scores in a sample (n) are free to vary except one (−1), we calculate the sample variance by dividing SS by only those scores that are free to vary in a sample (n − 1).

LEARNING CHECK 4

1. Why do we square each deviation in the numerator of variance?

2. How many scores are free to vary in a sample?

3. True or false: The sample variance is unbiased when dividing SS by (n − 1).

4. A researcher records five scores: 3, 4, 5, 6, and x. If the mean in this distribution is 5, then what is the value for x?

Answers: 1. We want to compute how far every score are from their mean without ending up with a solution equal to zero every time, and taking the square root of variance can correct for squaring each deviation in the numerator; 2. All scores, except one, are free to vary; 3. True; 4. x = 7.

4.6 THE COMPUTATIONAL FORMULA FOR VARIANCE

The formula we have used thus far to compute variance is called the **definitional formula for variance**. This formula literally defines the SS in the numerator, which is the sum of the squared differences of scores from their mean. The definitional formula for variance is as follows:

Definitional formula (population):

$$SS = \Sigma(x - \mu)^2, \text{ where } \sigma^2 = \frac{SS}{N}.$$

Definitional formula (sample):

$$SS = \Sigma(x - M)^2, \text{ where } s^2 = \frac{SS}{n-1}.$$

The **definitional formula for variance** is a way to calculate the population variance and sample variance that requires summing the squared differences of scores from their mean to compute the SS in the numerator.

The **computational formula for variance**, or the **raw scores method for variance**, is a way to calculate the population variance and sample variance without needing to sum the squared differences of scores from their mean to compute the SS in the numerator.

Computationally, there is a disadvantage to using the definitional formula—it is prone to rounding errors, especially when the mean has a decimal remainder. Squaring decimals often requires rounding, and the mean is often a decimal, resulting in rounding errors. As an alternative to this problem, statisticians derived the **computational formula for variance**, also called the **raw scores method for variance**. Notice in the formula that the computational method does not require us to calculate the mean to compute the SS. The computational formula for variance is as follows:

Computational formula (population):

$$SS = \sum x^2 - \frac{(\sum x)^2}{N}, \text{ where } \sigma^2 = \frac{SS}{N}.$$

Computational formula (sample):

$$SS = \sum x^2 - \frac{(\sum x)^2}{n}, \text{ where } s^2 = \frac{SS}{n-1}.$$

The notation in each formula distinguishes between a population (N) and a sample size (n). Before proceeding, keep in mind that with identical data sets, the computational formula will always produce the same solution as the definitional formula, give or take rounding error. The computational formula is actually a quicker way to calculate variance with large data sets. Example 4.3 demonstrates the equivalence of the two forms of the variance formula.

FYI

The computational formula for variance is a quicker way to compute variance by hand. To see a proof of how the computational formula is mathematically equivalent to the definitional formula, see the Student Study Site (edge.sagepub.com/priviteraess2e).

Example 4.3

A social psychologist studying emotion presented 20 participants ($n = 20$) with five pictures showing personal loss or tragedy and recorded the amount of time (in seconds) each participant spent looking at these pictures. Using the hypothetical data for this study given in Table 4.5, we will calculate the SS (or the numerator for variance) using both formulas.

TABLE 4.5 A List of the Amount of Time (in seconds) Each Participant ($n = 20$) Spent Looking at Pictures Showing Personal Loss or Tragedy

46	35	28	44
33	40	14	43
45	39	88	51
110	55	74	92
30	52	54	23

Calculate the SS using the definitional formula. To compute the SS, (1) identify each score, (2) compute the population mean, (3) compute the squared deviation of each score from the mean, and (4) sum the squared deviations. These calculations are shown in Table 4.6. For this example, $SS = 11,199.20$.

TABLE 4.6	Calculations Required for Computing the Sum of Squares (SS) Using the Definitional Formula in Example 4.3

x	M	x − M	(x − M)²
14	49.80	−35.80	1,281.64
23	49.80	−26.80	718.24
28	49.80	−21.80	475.24
30	49.80	−19.80	392.04
33	49.80	−16.80	282.24
35	49.80	−14.80	219.04
39	49.80	−10.80	116.64
40	49.80	−9.80	96.04
43	49.80	−6.80	46.24
44	49.80	−5.80	33.64
45	49.80	−4.80	23.04
46	49.80	−3.80	14.44
51	49.80	1.20	1.44
52	49.80	2.20	4.84
54	49.80	4.20	17.64
55	49.80	5.20	27.04
74	49.80	24.20	585.64
88	49.80	38.20	1,459.24
92	49.80	42.20	1,780.84
110	49.80	60.20	3,624.04
		$\sum(x - M) = 0$	$\sum(x - M)^2 = 11,199.20$

Although we found the answer, it took a lot of work. We had to calculate the mean, calculate 20 deviations from the mean, square 20 deviations from the mean, and then sum 20 squared deviations from the mean just to find the SS. To compute population variance, we divide SS by N; to compute sample variance, we divide SS by (n − 1). You can imagine how complex the calculation would be if the study had 100 or 1,000 scores. Let us solve the same problem using the computational formula to see whether it is any easier to compute.

Calculate SS using the computational formula. To compute SS, (1) identify each score and the size of the sample or population, (2) square each score, and (3) substitute the value in the formula. These calculations are shown in Table 4.7. Notice that we did not calculate the mean. We found all the information we need to compute the computational formula in only three steps. When we substitute the values given in Table 4.7, we get the following solution:

$$SS = \sum x^2 - \frac{\left(\sum x^2\right)}{n}$$

$$= 60{,}800 - \frac{(996)^2}{20}$$

$$= 11{,}199.20$$

As with the definitional formula, $SS = 11{,}199.20$, verifying that both formulas (definitional and computational) produce the same solution for SS.

| TABLE 4.7 | Calculations Required for Computing the Sum of Squares (SS) Using the Computational Formula in Example 4.3 |

x	x^2
14	196
23	529
28	784
30	900
33	1,089
35	1,225
39	1,521
40	1,600
43	1,849
44	1,936
45	2,025
46	2,116
51	2,601
52	2,704
54	2,916
55	3,025
74	5,476
88	7,744
92	8,464
110	12,100
$\sum x = 996$	$\sum x^2 = 60{,}800$

LEARNING CHECK 5

1. How is the computational formula different from the definitional formula for variance?

2. True or false: With identical data sets, the definitional and computational formula for sample variance will always produce the same solution, give or take rounding error.

3. A researcher measures the following sample of scores ($n = 3$): 1, 4, and 7. (a) Use the definitional formula to calculate variance. (b) Use the computational formula to calculate variance. (c) Are your answers the same?

Answers: 1. The computational formula does not require that we compute the mean to compute SS in the numerator; 2. True; 3. (a) 9. (b) 9. (c) Yes.

4.7 THE STANDARD DEVIATION

The **standard deviation**, also called the **root mean square deviation**, is the square root of the variance. Taking the square root of the variance basically "unsquares" the variance, and it is used as a measure for the average distance that scores deviate from their mean. The distance that scores deviate from their mean is measured as the number of standard deviations that scores deviate from their mean. The **population standard deviation** is represented by the Greek letter for a lowercase s, called sigma: σ. The **sample standard deviation** is represented by a lowercase s. In research reports, you may also see the sample standard deviation stated as SD. The notation for population standard deviation is as follows:

$$\sigma = \sqrt{\sigma^2} = \sqrt{\frac{SS}{N}} \ .$$

The notation for sample standard deviation is as follows:

$$s = \sqrt{s^2} = \sqrt{\frac{SS}{n-1}} \ .$$

To find the standard deviation, we first compute the variance and then take the square root of that answer. Remember that our objective is to find the average distance that scores deviate from their mean (the standard deviation) and not the average *squared* distance that scores deviate from their mean (the variance). Taking the square root of the variance will allow us to reach this objective. We compute the standard deviation in Example 4.4. To compute the standard deviation, we follow two steps:

Step 1: Compute the variance.

Step 2: Take the square root of the variance.

FYI

The standard deviation is the square root of the variance. It is used to determine the average distance that scores deviate from their mean.

The **standard deviation**, also called the **root mean square deviation**, is a measure of variability for the average distance that scores deviate from their mean. It is calculated by taking the square root of the variance.

The **population standard deviation** is a measure of variability for the average distance that scores in a population deviate from their mean. It is calculated by taking the square root of the population variance.

The **sample standard deviation** is a measure of variability for the average distance that scores in a sample deviate from their mean. It is calculated by taking the square root of the sample variance.

Example 4.4

A psychologist assumes that students will really miss their parents when they first leave for college. To test this assumption, she records the time (in minutes) that 10 freshman students ($n = 10$) talked to their parents during their first month of college. Using the data for this study given in Table 4.8, we can compute the variance and standard deviation.

TABLE 4.8	The Number of Minutes That 10 Students ($n = 10$) Spent Talking to Their Parents in Their First Month of College

450	560	250	630	280
300	340	435	355	700

Step 1: Compute the variance. Using the computational formula to calculate variance, we find n, Σx, and Σx^2. We know that $n = 10$, and Table 4.9 shows that $\Sigma x = 4,300$ and $\Sigma x^2 = 2,064,750$. When we substitute these values into the formula for sample variance, we find that $SS = 215,750$ (the numerator), and the sample variance is $s^2 = 23,972.22$.

$$s^2 = \frac{SS}{n-1} = \frac{2,064,750 - \frac{(4,300)^2}{10}}{10-1} = \frac{215,750}{9} = 23,972.22.$$

Step 2: Take the square root of the variance. We take the square root of the sample variance to find the standard deviation.

$$SD = \sqrt{s^2} = \sqrt{23,972.22} = 154.83.$$

The standard deviation is 154.83 minutes in this example. If you compute the mean for this sample, you will find that the mean time is 430 minutes. The standard deviation tells us that the distribution of times for all students (other than those responding at the mean) deviates an average distance of 154.83 minutes from the mean. In the next section, we explain how to interpret this result.

TABLE 4.9	Calculations for the Sum of Squares (SS) Using the Computational Formula for Example 4.4

x	x^2
250	62,500
280	78,400
300	90,000
340	115,600
355	126,025
435	189,225
450	202,500
560	313,600
630	396,900
700	490,000
$\Sigma x = 4,300$	$\Sigma x^2 = 2,064,750$

LEARNING CHECK 6

1. How do you compute standard deviation?

2. The standard deviation is a measure used to determine the average distance that each score deviates from _____.

3. The sample variance is 121. What is the standard deviation for this sample?

4. The population variance is 121. What is the standard deviation for this population?

Answers: 1. Take the square root of the variance; 2. The mean; 3. 11; 4. 11.

4.8 WHAT DOES THE STANDARD DEVIATION TELL US?

The standard deviation is an estimate for the average distance that scores deviate from the mean. When scores are concentrated near the mean, the standard deviation is small; when scores are scattered far from the mean, the standard deviation is larger. Yet, the standard deviation is more informative than this, particularly for data that are normally distributed. For normal distributions with any mean and any variance, we can make the following three statements:

1. At least 68% of all scores lie within one standard deviation of the mean.

2. At least 95% of all scores lie within two standard deviations of the mean.

3. At least 99.7% of all scores lie within three standard deviations of the mean.

FYI

For normal distributions, most scores (68%) fall within one standard deviation of the mean, and almost all scores (99.7%) fall within three standard deviations of the mean.

The **empirical rule** states that for data that are normally distributed, at least 99.7% of data lie within three standard deviations of the mean, at least 95% of data lie within two standard deviations of the mean, and at least 68% of data lie within one standard deviation of the mean.

These statements are often called the **empirical rule**. Empiricism is *to observe.* The name of this rule arises because many of the behaviors that researchers *observe* are approximately normally distributed. The empirical rule, then, is an approximation—the percentages are correct, give or take a few fractions of a standard deviation. Nevertheless, this rule is critical because of how specific it is for describing behavior.

To illustrate how useful the empirical rule is, consider how we can apply it to a sample data set and can come to some immediate conclusions about the distribution of scores. Suppose that a researcher selects a sample of 5,000 full-time employees and records the time (in hours per week) that they spend thinking about work when they are not working. These data are normally distributed with a mean equal to 12 ($M = 12$) and a standard deviation equal to 4 ($SD = 4$). Without knowing the time for each employee, we still know a lot about this sample. In fact, because the data are normally distributed, we can distribute at least 99.7% of the data simply by plotting three standard deviations above and below the mean, as shown in Figure 4.4. Notice that we add the SD value to M to plot standard deviations above the mean; to plot standard deviations below the mean, we subtract the SD value from M.

Although the researcher did not report the time (in hours) recorded for each individual employee in this sample, we know a lot about these data because we know the mean and the standard deviation. For example, we know that at least 68% of employees spent between 8 and 16 hours thinking about work when they were not working (per week), and we know that any time (in hours) beyond three standard deviations from the mean is unlikely. This makes the standard deviation a very descriptive measure for determining the average distance that each score is from the mean for data that are normally distributed.

FIGURE 4.4 The Empirical Rule

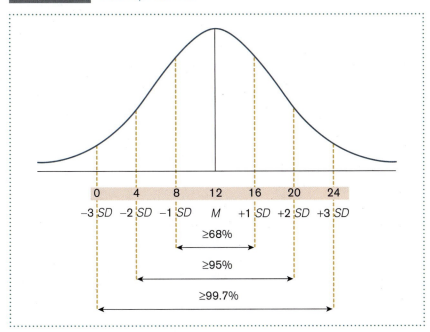

The proportion of scores under a normal curve at each standard deviation above and below the mean. The data are distributed as 12 ± 4 ($M \pm SD$).

Chebyshev's theorem defines the percentage of data from any distribution that will be contained within any number of standard deviations (where $SD > 1$).

MAKING SENSE STANDARD DEVIATION AND NONNORMAL DISTRIBUTIONS

The standard deviation (*SD*) also tells us about distributions that are not normally distributed. The Russian mathematician Pafnuty Chebyshev devised the theorem that explains the standard deviation for any distribution.

Chebyshev explained that the proportion of all data for any distribution (sample or population; normal or not)

must lie within *k* standard deviations above and below the mean, where *k* is greater than 1. **Chebyshev's theorem** is defined as follows:

$$1 - \frac{1}{k^2}, \text{ where } k \text{ is greater than 1.}$$

(Continued)

(Continued)

Notice that if k were one standard deviation (1 SD), the solution would be 0%. So this theorem can describe only the proportion of data falling within *greater* than 1 SD of the mean. Let us see how this theorem compares to the empirical rule. Recall that 95% of all data fall within 2 SD of the mean for normal distributions. Chebyshev's theorem explains that for any distribution *at least* 75% of the data fall within 2 SD of the mean:

$$1-\frac{1}{k^2}=1-\frac{1}{2^2}=.75 \text{ or } 75\%.$$

Recall that 99.7% of all data fall within 3 SD of the mean for normal distributions. Chebyshev's theorem explains that for any distribution *at least* 89% of the data fall within 3 SD of the mean:

$$1-\frac{1}{k^2}=1-\frac{1}{3^2}=.89 \text{ or } 89\%.$$

In fact, it would take 10 standard deviations (10 SD) from the mean to account for *at least* 99% of the data for nonnormal distributions according to Chebyshev's theorem:

$$1-\frac{1}{k^2}=1-\frac{1}{10^2}=.99 \text{ or } 99\%.$$

While the standard deviation is most precise for normal distributions, because most data fall within 3 SD of the mean, it is also informative for any other distribution. We can still define the percentage of scores that will fall within each standard deviation from the mean for any distribution. The informativeness of the standard deviation for any type of distribution makes it one of the most complete and meaningful measures for determining the variability of scores from their mean.

4.9 CHARACTERISTICS OF THE STANDARD DEVIATION

Although the standard deviation has many characteristics, we focus on four of the most fundamental ones for samples and populations.

1. **The standard deviation is always positive**: $SD \geq 0$. The standard deviation is a measure of variability. Data sets can either vary (be greater than 0) or not vary (be equal to 0) from the mean. A negative variability is meaningless.

2. **The standard deviation is used to describe quantitative data**. The standard deviation is a numeric value—it is the square root of the variance. For this reason, the standard deviation is used to describe quantitative data, which can be continuous or discrete.

3. **The standard deviation is most informative when reported with the mean**. The standard deviation is the average distance that scores deviate from their mean. It is therefore most informative to report the mean and the standard deviation together. For normally distributed data, knowing just the mean and standard deviation can inform the reader of the distribution for close to all the recorded data (at least 99.7% of data fall within 3 SD of the mean). A common way to see the mean and standard deviation reported in a scientific article is "mean plus or minus standard deviation" or $M \pm SD$. For example, if a data set consists of scores with $M = 16$ and $SD = 4$, then these values can be reported as 16 ± 4.

4. **The value for the standard deviation is affected by the value of each score in a distribution**. To change the standard deviation, you

must change the distance of scores from the mean and from each other. To illustrate this, consider two cases: one where changing scores in a distribution has no effect on standard deviation and another where the standard deviation is changed.

Adding or subtracting the same constant to each score will not change the value of the standard deviation. Suppose, for example, an instructor gives a quiz to eight students ($n = 8$) and obtains the following scores: 3, 5, 6, 6, 7, 7, 9, and 10. If we calculate the sample standard deviation of quiz scores, we get $SD = 2.20$.

After grading all the quizzes, the instructor decides that one of the questions was misleading, so he adds one point to every score. The distribution of scores is now shifted by +1; the new scores are 4, 6, 7, 7, 8, 8, 10, and 11. If we now recalculate the sample standard deviation of this new distribution of quiz scores, we again get $SD = 2.20$.

Figure 4.5 illustrates the reason the standard deviation is unchanged. Adding (or subtracting) the same constant to each score will not change the distance that scores deviate from the mean because the mean also changes by that constant. (In Chapter 3, we discussed how the mean changes.) Despite the change in each score, the average distance of each score from its mean remains the same, so the standard deviation also remains the same.

Multiplying or dividing each score using the same constant will cause the standard deviation to change by that constant. Suppose we throw a party for a friend with five balloons ($n = 5$); the balloons have radii of 1, 2, 3, 4, and 5 units. If we calculate the sample standard deviation for this distribution, we obtain $s = 1.58$.

Yet after much deep and profound consideration, we realize that the friend will never be happy with such inadequately blown-up balloons. We decide to blow up the balloons to double their size. The new radii are 2, 4, 6, 8, and 10 units (all we did was multiply each radius by 2). Notice in Figure 4.6 that the distance between each radius has doubled; each score is now separated by two units, not one. If we now recalculate the standard deviation for this new distribution of radii, we get $s = 3.16$ or $(1.58)^2$. Dividing all scores by the same constant will produce a similar result—the value for the standard deviation will be divided by that constant.

FYI

Adding or subtracting the same constant to each score will not change the distance that scores deviate from the mean. Hence, the standard deviation remains unchanged.

FYI

Multiplying or dividing each score using the same constant will cause the standard deviation to change by that constant.

FIGURE 4.5 A List of the Original Distribution of Scores (top row) and the New Distribution Created by Increasing Each Score by One Point (bottom row)

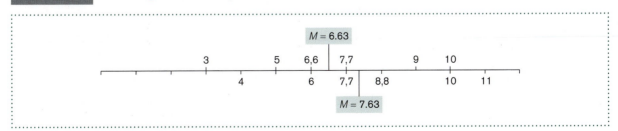

Adding one point to each score in the original data set did not change the distance each score was from its mean. Hence, the value of the standard deviation does not change.

A List of the Original Distribution of Scores (top row) and the New Distribution Created by Multiplying Each Score by 2 (bottom row)

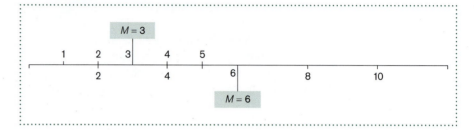

Multiplying each score by 2 doubled the distance each score was from its mean. Hence, the value for the standard deviation also doubled.

1. The empirical rule is stated for data with what type of distribution?

2. How many standard deviations from the mean will contain at least 99% of data *for any type of distribution*? Hint: Refer to the Making Sense section.

3. Each of the following is a characteristic of standard deviation, except:

   (a) The standard deviation is always positive.

   (b) The standard deviation is affected by the value of every score in a distribution.

   (c) The standard deviation is used to describe qualitative variables.

   (d) Standard deviations are almost always reported with the mean.

4. An instructor measures the following quiz scores: 6, 8, 7, and 9 ($SD = 1.29$). If the instructor subtracts two points from each quiz score, how will the value for the standard deviation change?

Answers: 1. Normal distribution; 2. ±10 SD; 3. c; 4. The standard deviation will not change ($SD = 1.29$).

4.10 SPSS in Focus:
Range, Variance, and Standard Deviation

In the SPSS in Focus section of Chapter 3, we utilized an example adapted from studies on creativity (Feist, Reiter-Palmon, & Kaufman, 2017; Piffer, 2012) to compute the mean, the median, and the mode for creativity, measured as the time (in seconds) it took participants to list 10 uses for a paper clip. The data for this example, originally given in Table 3.11, are reproduced here in Table 4.10. In this section, we will use these same data to compute the range, variance, and standard deviation.

1. Click on the Variable View tab and enter *creativity* in the Name column. We will enter whole numbers, so reduce the value in the Decimals column to 0.

2. Click on the Data View tab and enter the 20 values in the *creativity* column.

3. Go to the menu bar and click Analyze, then Descriptive Statistics and Frequencies, to display a dialog box.

4. When you select the *creativity* variable and click the arrow in the center of the dialog box, *creativity* will move into the box labeled Variable(s): to the right. Make sure the option to display frequency tables is not selected, and then click on Statistics to bring up another dialog box.

5. In this dialog box, select Std. deviation, Variance, and Range; then select Continue.

6. Select OK, or select Paste and click the Run command. Table 4.11 shows the SPSS output table.

TABLE 4.10 The Time (in seconds) That It Took a Group of 20 Participants to Write Down 10 Uses for a Paper Clip on a Creativity Test

41	80
65	80
123	64
46	59
48	51
87	36
38	80
90	143
132	122
115	100

This table originally appeared as Table 3.11 in Chapter 3.

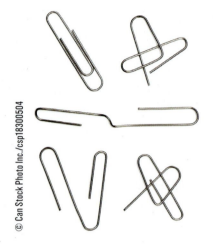

© Can Stock Photo Inc./csp18300504

| TABLE 4.11 | SPSS Output Table Displaying the Range, Variance, and Standard Deviation for the Creativity Data |

Statistics

creativity

N	Valid	20
	Missing	0
Std. Deviation		33.422
Variance		1117.053
Range		107

Recall from Chapter 3 that the mean for these data is 80. Knowing also the standard deviation of 33.42, we can immediate identify that the majority of the data (about 68%) fall between 46.58 and 113.42. All we did was subtract/add the standard deviation from/to the mean one time. We can do this again to identify where about 95% of the data fall, and so on based on the empirical rule. The idea here is that with only two values (i.e., the mean and standard deviation), we can get a very good sense of the distribution of these data without actually seeing the original list of raw scores. Thus, knowing the mean and the standard deviation is quite informative.

••• CHAPTER SUMMARY ORGANIZED BY LEARNING OBJECTIVE

LO 1:   **Compute and interpret a range, interquartile range, and semi-interquartile range.**

- The range is the difference between the largest value (L) and smallest value (S) in a data set. Although the range provides a simple measure for variability, it accounts for only two values (the largest value and smallest value) in a distribution.

- The interquartile range (IQR) is the range of a distribution of scores after the top and bottom 25% of scores in that distribution are removed.

$$IQR = Q_3 - Q_1.$$

- The semi-interquartile range (SIQR) is used as a measure of half the distance between Q_3 and Q_1.

$$SIQR = \frac{Q_3 - Q_1}{2}, \text{ also represented as } SIQR = \frac{IQR}{2}.$$

LO 2–3:   **Compute and interpret the variance and standard deviation for a population and sample of data using the definitional formula and the computational formula.**

- The variance is a measure of variability for the average squared distance that scores deviate from their mean. Its value is always greater than or equal to zero. The numerator in the variance formula is the sum of squares (SS). The denominator for population variance is N; the denominator for sample variance is $(n-1)$.

- The population variance is a measure of variability for the average squared distance that scores in a population deviate from the mean:

Population variance: $\sigma^2 = \dfrac{\Sigma(x-\mu)^2}{N}$ or $\dfrac{SS}{N}$.

- The sample variance is a measure of variability for the average squared distance that scores in a sample deviate from the mean:

Sample variance: $s^2 = \dfrac{\Sigma(x-M)^2}{n-1}$ or $\dfrac{SS}{n-1}$.

- The computational formula for variance is a way to calculate the population variance and sample variance without needing to compute the mean to compute SS in the numerator.

Computational formula (population):

$$SS = \Sigma x^2 - \dfrac{(\Sigma x)^2}{N}, \text{ where } \sigma^2 = \dfrac{SS}{N}.$$

Computational formula (sample):

$$SS = \Sigma x^2 - \dfrac{(\Sigma x)^2}{n}, \text{ where } s^2 = \dfrac{SS}{n-1}.$$

- The standard deviation is a measure of variability for the average distance that scores deviate from their mean and is calculated by taking the square root of the variance.

Population standard deviation: $\sigma = \sqrt{\sigma^2} = \sqrt{\dfrac{SS}{N}}$.

Sample standard deviation: $s = \sqrt{s^2} = \sqrt{\dfrac{SS}{n-1}}$.

LO 4: **Explain why the sample variance and population variance are computed differently.**

- The numerators for the sample variance and population variance do not differ. SS is the numerator in both formulas; only the denominators differ for two reasons. First, the sample variance is unbiased when we divide SS by $(n-1)$—on average, the variance of the sample will equal

the variance of the population from which the sample was selected. Second, all scores in a sample are free to vary except one when the mean is known. So we divide the SS by one less than the sample size, called the degrees of freedom (df) for sample variance.

LO 5: **State the characteristics of the standard deviation and explain the empirical rule.**

- The standard deviation is always positive. It is used to describe quantitative data, typically reported with the mean, and is affected by the value of each score in a distribution. Adding or subtracting the same constant to or from each score will not change the standard deviation. Multiplying or dividing each score using the same constant will cause the standard deviation to change by the constant.

- For normal distributions with any mean and any variance, we can make the following three statements using the empirical rule: (1) At least 68% of all scores lie within one standard deviation of the mean, (2) at least 95% of all scores lie within two standard deviations of the mean, and (3) at least 99.7% of all scores lie within three standard deviations of the mean.

LO 6: **Compute the range, variance, and standard deviation using SPSS.**

- SPSS can be used to compute the range, variance, and standard deviation. Each measure of variability is computed using the Analyze, Descriptive Statistics, and Frequencies options in the menu bar. These actions will bring up a dialog box that will allow you to identify the variable and select the Statistics option to select and compute the range, variance, and standard deviation (for more details, see Section 4.10).

••• KEY TERMS

biased estimator	empirical rule	sample standard deviation
Chebyshev's theorem	interquartile range (IQR)	sample variance
computational formula for	population standard deviation	semi-interquartile range (SIQR)
variance	population variance	standard deviation
definitional formula for variance	quartiles	sum of squares (SS)
degrees of freedom (df) for	range	unbiased estimator
sample variance	raw scores method for variance	variability
deviation	root mean square deviation	variance

••• END-OF-CHAPTER PROBLEMS

Factual Problems

1. You read a claim that variability is negative. Is this possible? Explain.

2. How many scores are included to compute the range?

3. What is the interquartile range?

4. Why is variance, as a measure of variability, preferred to the range, the IQR, and the SIQR?

5. What are the degrees of freedom for sample variance?

6. What does it mean to say that the sample variance is unbiased?

7. Explain why deviations from the mean are squared in the formula for variance.

8. What does the standard deviation measure?

9. Based on the empirical rule, what percentage of data fall within 1 SD, 2 SD, and 3 SD of the mean for data that are distributed normally?

10. State four characteristics of the standard deviation.

Concept and Application Problems

11. A social scientist measures the number of minutes (per day) that a small hypothetical population of college students spends online.

Student	Minutes	Student	Minutes
A	98	F	92
B	77	G	94
C	88	H	98
D	65	I	88
E	24	J	82

(a) What is the range of data in this population?

(b) What is the IQR of data in this population?

(c) What is the SIQR of data in this population?

(d) What is the population variance?

(e) What is the population standard deviation?

12. Suppose the researcher selects a sample of eight students from the population in Question 11. The sample consists of persons A, B, C, F, G, H, I, and J.

(a) What is the range of data in this sample?

(b) What is the IQR of data in this sample?

(c) What is the SIQR of data in this sample?

(d) What is the sample variance?

(e) What is the sample standard deviation?

13. If Sample 1 has a variance of 4 and Sample 2 has variance of 32, can we tell which sample had a larger range? If so, which sample had a greater range?

14. A behavioral scientist measures attention in a sample of 31 participants. To measure the variance of attention, she computes $SS = 120$ for this sample. (a) What are the degrees of

freedom for variance? (b) Compute the variance and standard deviation.

15. A psychopathologist records the number of criminal offenses among teenage drug users in a nationwide sample of 1,201 participants. To measure the variance of criminal offenses, he computes $SS = 10,800$ for this sample. (a) What are the degrees of freedom for variance? (b) Compute the variance and standard deviation.

16. A student computes a standard deviation of 12. Will the variance differ if 12 is the value for a population versus a sample standard deviation? Explain.

17. A student computes a variance of 9. Will the standard deviation differ if 9 is the value for a population versus a sample variance? Explain.

18. If the value of the SS remains constant, state whether each of the following will increase, decrease, or have no effect on the sample variance.

    (a) The sample size increases.

    (b) The degrees of freedom decrease.

    (c) The size of the population increases.

19. Suppose the population variance for a given population is 36. If we select all possible samples of a certain size from this population, then, on average, what will be the value of the sample variance?

20. State whether each of the following will increase, decrease, or have no effect on the population variance.

    (a) The sum of squares (SS) increases.

    (b) The sample size decreases.

    (c) The size of the population increases.

21. A researcher measures the time (in seconds) it takes a sample of five participants to complete a memory task. It takes four of the participants 5, 6, 6, and 7 seconds. If $M = 6$, then what must be the fifth time recorded?

22. A sample of 60 scores is distributed with $SS = 240$. What is the sample variance and sample standard deviation for this distribution?

23. If the example in Question 22 were a population of scores, would the values for the variance and standard deviation change? If so, how?

24. A psychologist measures a sample of scores on a love quiz, where $SD = 4$ points. State the new value for SD if the psychologist (a) adds 2 points to each quiz score and (b) doubles each quiz score.

25. An expert reviews a sample of 10 scientific articles ($n = 10$) and records the following number of errors in each article: 0, 4, 2, 8, 2, 3, 1, 0, 5, and 7. Compute the SS, the variance, and the standard deviation for this sample using the definitional and computational formulas.

26. A social psychologist records the age (in years) that a sample of eight participants first experienced peer pressure. The recorded ages for the participants are 14, 20, 17, 16, 12, 16, 15, and 16. Compute the SS, the variance, and the standard deviation for this sample using the definitional and computational formulas.

27. A professor records the time (in minutes) that it takes 16 students to complete an exam. Compute the SS, the variance, and the standard deviation (a) assuming the 16 students constitute a population and (b) assuming the 16 students constitute a sample.

23	32	44	20
25	14	29	41
43	21	39	33
48	38	50	40

28. A school administrator has students rate the quality of their education on a scale from 1 (*poor*) to 7 (*exceptional*). She claims that 99.7% of students rated the quality of their education between 3.5 and 6.5. If the mean rating is 5.0, then what is the standard deviation assuming the data are normally distributed? *Hint:* Use the empirical rule.

Problems in Research

29. **Conscientious Responders.** Marjanovic, Holden, Struthers, Cribbie, and Greenglass (2014) tested an index to discriminate between conscientious and random responders to surveys. As part of their study, they had participants complete the Conscientious Responders Scale (CRS; Marjanovic, Struthers, Cribbie, & Greenglass, 2014). The mean score for conscientious responders was 4.58, and the standard deviation was 1.16. Assuming the data are normally distributed in this example, would a score above 5.0 be unlikely? Explain.

30. **Showing love in marriage.** Schoenfeld, Bredow, and Huston (2012) had couples who were married complete a rating scale indicating their feelings of *love* for their partners—that is, "the extent to which [they] felt a sense of closeness, belonging, and attachment to their partners" (p. 1400). Higher ratings indicated greater love. In one phase of their study, they found that husbands rated their love as $M = 8.15$, $SD = 0.71$ (range = 4.56–9.00), while wives rated their love as $M = 8.38$, $SD = 0.71$ (range = 4.00–9.00). Based on the data reported, answer the following questions:

    (a) Do husbands and wives show a similar distribution in their ratings of love?

    (b) What is the approximate shape of the distribution in ratings of love among husbands and wives? Interpret what this means for how husbands and wives report their feelings of love.

31. **Total wellness among Citadel cadets.** Gibson and Myers (2006) investigated perceived wellness among freshman military cadets at the Citadel academy. Cadets completed the Five Factor Wellness Inventory to measure their perceived wellness pertaining to creative, coping, social, essential, and physical wellness. Total wellness scores ranged from 14.84 to 71.60, with $M \pm SD$ being 50.00 ± 9.99. Are these data approximately normally distributed? Explain.

32. **Acceptable height preferences.** Pérez Escoda and Alegre (2016) studied how emotional intelligence moderates the relationship between various levels of life satisfaction. As part of their study, they measured participant life satisfaction or their personal satisfaction with themselves. The following table lists a portion of the results. Based on the data reported, answer the following questions.

    (a) Which participant variable showed the greatest variability?

    (b) Approximately what type of distribution (positively skewed, negatively skewed, or normal) does each participant variable show? Explain your answer.

Participant Variable	Range		Descriptive Statistics	
	Min	Max	Mean	SD
Life Satisfaction	5.00	35.00	25.15	5.14
Satisfaction With Self	4.00	28.00	20.88	3.75

Answers for even numbers are in Appendix D.

Sharpen your skills with **SAGE edge** at edge.sagepub.com/priviteraess2e

SAGE edge for Students provides a personalized approach to help you accomplish your coursework goals in an easy-to-use learning environment.

$SAGE edge™

Part II

Probability and the Foundations of Inferential Statistics

© iStockphoto.com/Bennewitz

5 Probability, Normal Distributions, and *z* Scores

• • • Learning Objectives

After reading this chapter, you should be able to:

1. Identify and compute a simple probability.

2. Identify eight characteristics of the normal distribution.

3. Define the standard normal distribution and compute the standard normal transformation.

4. Locate proportions of area under any normal curve above the mean, below the mean, and between two scores.

5. Locate scores in a normal distribution with a given probability.

6. Convert raw scores to standard *z* scores using SPSS.

In your experiences with college, it is most certain that you have considered your *chances* along the way. Surely you were interested in your chances of being selected by a college, your chances of graduating college, and even your chances of obtaining a job after graduation. From college applications to job applications, you were and are interested in your chances or the *likelihood* that you will find success. In each example, you are applying probability to meaningfully navigate your path from college to employment and beyond.

You are applying probability anytime you ask, "How likely is something to occur?" It is not uncommon at all for questions like this to be asked. For instance, probability is often used in sports (e.g., the likelihood that a team will win or lose a game), in the news (e.g., the likelihood that a crime will occur in a neighborhood), at an airport (e.g., the likelihood that a flight will be delayed), in a weather report (e.g., the likelihood of rain in a forecast), in business (e.g., the likelihood of increased sales in a new market), and even for emphasis in everyday conversation (e.g., you may exclaim, "I'm 99% confident!"). These examples highlight how common probabilities are in our everyday experiences.

Understanding the likelihood of the observations we make is fundamental to the application of statistics. Many or even most behaviors that we observe are normally distributed where most people are behaving "normal" at or near the mean in a given general population. It is therefore especially useful to understand probability as it relates to this type of distribution. Ultimately statistics provides a useful way to measure probability, which is instrumentally important to the decisions that researchers make. In this chapter, we introduce many ways in which researchers use probability to understand the likelihood of the observations they make.

Master the content.

edge.sagepub.com/priviteraess2e

Chapter Outline

5.1 INTRODUCTION TO PROBABILITY

Although you may not notice variances and standard deviations too often in everyday life, you likely come across probabilities quite often. **Probability** is used to describe the likelihood that an outcome will occur. An outcome can be just about any observation of interest from behaviors to weather patterns. A casino, for example, may advertise a raffle where 10% of tickets will win a prize, an odds maker may tell you that the favored horse in the Kentucky Derby has 2-to-1 odds of winning, or a sportscaster may tell you that an all-star baseball player has a 3-in-10 chance of getting a hit. Probabilities are important in research as well. Researchers may report that the likelihood of detecting a disorder is 72%, that 1 in 4 women marry by their 20th birthday, or that about 24% of Americans age 25 or older have earned a bachelor's degree. In each example given here, probability was used to describe the likelihood of an outcome.

Probability can be used to predict any outcome that is not fixed. Thus, probability is used to identify the likelihood of a **random event**—any event in which the outcomes observed can vary. For example, if you flip a coin one time (the event), then it can land heads up or tails up (the outcomes). We can predict the likelihood of one outcome or the other, but the outcome itself can vary from one observation to the next. Probability is unnecessary for predicting a **fixed event**—any event in which the outcome observed does not change. For example, what is the probability that a life (the event) will end (the outcome)? The event is fixed: All living things die eventually. Estimating the probability of this event is not valuable. Yet, suppose we ask what the probability is that a car accident (the event) will result in loss of life (the outcome)? Now the event is random: Not all car accidents result in death.

5.2 CALCULATING PROBABILITY

In this section, we demonstrate how probabilities are calculated. By definition, probability is the frequency of times an outcome occurs divided by the total number of possible outcomes.

To calculate probability, we need to know two things. First, we need to know the number of total possible outcomes. For example, if we flip a fair coin one time, then one of two total outcomes is possible: heads or tails. The total number of possible outcomes is called the **sample space**. Second, we need to know how often an outcome of interest occurs. If we want to know how often heads occurs in one flip of a fair coin, we can count the number of times heads occurs in the total sample space. In this case, heads can occur one time per flip of a fair coin.

For any given random event, the probability, p, of an outcome, x, is represented as $p(x)$. The frequency, f, of times an outcome, x, occurs is represented as $f(x)$. The formula for probability then is the frequency of times an outcome occurs, $f(x)$, divided by the sample space or the total number of possible outcomes:

$$p(x) = \frac{f(x)}{sample\ space}.$$

To compute probability, we follow two steps: (1) find the sample space and (2) find $f(x)$. We will use these steps to compute probability in two hypothetical experiments.

FYI

Probability is a measure for the likelihood of observing an outcome in a random event.

FYI

Probability allows us to make predictions regarding random events.

Probability (symbolized as p) is the frequency of times an outcome occurs divided by the total number of possible outcomes.

A **random event** is any event in which the outcome observed can vary.

A **fixed event** is any event in which the outcome observed is always the same.

The **sample space** is the total number of possible outcomes that can occur in a given random event.

Suppose, in Experiment 1, we flip a fair coin one time and want to know what the probability is that we will flip heads. In Step 1, we find the sample space. The sample space for all possible outcomes is two: heads and tails:

Sample space: 2 (Heads, Tails).

In Step 2, we find *f*(*x*). In this example, we want to know the probability of flipping heads. Hence, we want to know how often heads will be the outcome. When we count the number of times heads occurs in our sample space, we find that heads occurs one time. We can now state the probability of flipping heads (the outcome) with one flip of a fair coin (the event) as follows:

$$p\left(\text{flipping heads}\right) = \frac{1}{2}.$$

Now let us work through an example related to conducting research. Suppose, in Experiment 2, we select a sample of one participant ($n = 1$) from a population of 10 participants ($N = 10$). We want to know the probability of selecting a man from this population, when the population consists of 4 men and 6 women. In Step 1, we find the sample space. The sample space for all possible outcomes is 10:4 men and 6 women in the population:

Sample space: 10 (4 men, 6 women).

In Step 2, we find *f*(*x*). In this example, we want to know the probability of selecting a man from this population. Hence, we want to know how often selecting a man will be the outcome. When we count the number of men in our sample space, we find that there are 4 men. We can now state the probability of selecting a man (the outcome) with one selection from this population (the event) as follows:

$$p\left(\text{selecting a man}\right) = \frac{4}{10}.$$

Again, probability is the frequency of a given outcome, *x*, divided by all possible outcomes or sample space. Flip a fair coin once, and you have a 1-in-2 probability of flipping heads; select one person from a population of size 10, where there are 4 men and 6 women in the population, and you have a 4-in-10 probability of selecting a male participant.

When you solve the probability formula, you can use two rules about probability to verify your answer:

1. **Probability varies between 0 and 1**. There are various ways to express a probability: It can be written as a fraction, decimal, percent, or proportion. No matter how you express the probability, its value must vary between 0 and 1. The probability of flipping heads in Experiment 1 was written as a fraction, but it would have been just as accurate if you wrote it as a decimal ($p = .50$), a percent ($p = 50\%$), or a proportion ($p = 1:1$, where the proportion is stated as heads to tails). Similarly, the probability of selecting a man in Experiment 2 was stated as a fraction, but it would have been just as accurate if you wrote it as a decimal ($p = .40$), a percent ($p = 40\%$), or a proportion ($p = 4:6$, where the proportion is stated as men to

FYI

Probability is the frequency of times an outcome occurs divided by the total number of possible outcomes.

FYI

Probability varies between 0 and 1 and is never negative. Hence, a specified outcome is either probable $(0 < p \leq 1)$ or improbable $(p = 0)$.

women). The closer to 1, the more probable an event is; the closer to 0, the less probable an event is.

2. **Probability can never be negative**. Similar to the logic given in Chapter 4 for variance, a negative probability is meaningless. An event is either probable (its probability is greater than 0 but never greater than 1) or improbable (its probability is equal to 0).

To this point, each step used to compute probability has been elaborated to help you see the sample space and count the frequency of times an outcome occurs. In Example 5.1, we work through an example in which we determine the value of the sample space and $f(x)$ without writing out the sample space.

Example 5.1

©iStockphoto.com/Thomas_EyeDesign

Black, Shaw, and Allen (2016) conducted a study on compulsive shopping. As part of their study, they asked participants who had been diagnosed with a compulsive shopping disorder to indicate whether their interest in shopping and spending increased/greatly increased, stayed the same, or decreased/greatly decreased since an initial interview. Of the 17 participants who responded, 4 said increased/greatly increased, 5 said same, and 8 said decreased/greatly decreased. Since the initial interview, what is the probability that the interest in shopping and spending among participants sampled had (a) increased/greatly increased, (b) stayed the same, and (c) decreased/greatly decreased?

Step 1: Find the sample space. In this study, 17 participants were observed; the sample space is 17.

Step 2: Find $f(x)$. We know that 4 said increased/greatly increased, $f(x) = 4$; 5 said same, $f(x) = 5$; and 8 said decreased/greatly decreased, $f(x) = 8$. Therefore, the probabilities for each response can be stated as follows:

(a) $p(\text{increased/greatly increased}) = \dfrac{4}{17} = .24$

(b) $p(\text{same}) = \dfrac{5}{17} = .29$

(c) $p(\text{decreased/greatly decreased}) = \dfrac{8}{17} = .47$

LEARNING CHECK 1

1. _____ is the proportion or fraction of times an outcome is likely to occur.

2. Distinguish between a random event and a fixed event.

3. A researcher has participants complete a computer task where they can choose to play one of 200 games. Of the 200 games, only 80 are set up so that participants can win the game.

   (a) What is the event in this example?

   (b) What is the outcome, x, in this example?

   (c) What is the probability that a participant will choose a game that he or she can win?

4. State whether each of the following is an appropriate probability.

   (a) $p = .88$ (b) $p = -.26$ (c) $p = 1.45$ (d) $p = 1.00$

Answers: 1. Probability; 2. Outcomes in a random event can vary, whereas outcomes in a fixed event are always the same; 3. (a) Selecting one game, (b) Selecting a game that a participant can win, (c) $p(x) = .40$; 4. (a) Yes, (b) No. A probability can never be negative, (c) No. A probability can never be greater than 1.0, (d) Yes.

5.3 PROBABILITY AND THE NORMAL DISTRIBUTION

Probability is important in the behavioral sciences, particularly when it is applied to understand the likelihood of behavior. When researchers study behavior, they find that in many physical, behavioral, and social measurement studies, the data are normally distributed. Many behaviors and individual characteristics are distributed normally, with very few people at the extremes relative to all others in a given general population. For example, most people express some level of aggression, a few are entirely passive, and a few express an abnormally high level of aggression. Most people have some moderate level of intelligence, a few score very low on intelligence, and a few score very high using the intelligence quotient (IQ) to measure intelligence.

Because most behavior is approximately normally distributed, we can use the empirical rule (introduced in Chapter 4) to determine the probability of obtaining a particular outcome (or behavior) in a research study. We know, for example, that scores closer to the mean are more probable or likely than scores farther from the mean when those scores are normally distributed. In this chapter, we therefore extend the concepts of probability to include situations in which we locate probabilities for scores in a **normal distribution**. In Chapter 6, we will extend the concepts of normal distributions to introduce how probability is applied to techniques in sampling using *sampling distributions*.

FYI

The behavioral data that researchers measure often tend to approximate a normal distribution.

5.4 CHARACTERISTICS OF THE NORMAL DISTRIBUTION

Because the normal distribution is central to our understanding of the likelihood of observing many behaviors of interest to researchers, it is important to consider how this distribution is characterized. In 1733, Abraham de Moivre introduced the normal distribution, first discussed in Chapter 3, as a mathematical approximation to the binomial distribution, although de Moivre's 1733 work was not widely recognized until the accomplished statistician Karl Pearson rediscovered it in 1924. The shape of the curve in a normal distribution can drop suddenly at the tails, or the tails can be stretched out. Figure 5.1 shows three examples of normal distributions—notice in the figure that a normal distribution can vary in appearance. So what makes a set of data normally distributed? In this section, we introduce eight characteristics that make a set of data normally distributed:

1. **The normal distribution is mathematically defined.** The shape of a normal distribution is specified by an equation relating each score (distributed along the *x*-axis) with each frequency (distributed along the *y*-axis):

$$Y = \left(\frac{1}{\sigma\sqrt{2\pi}} e^{-\frac{1}{2}\left(\frac{x-\mu}{\sigma}\right)^2} \right).$$

The **normal distribution**, also called the **symmetrical**, **Gaussian**, or **bell-shaped distribution**, is a theoretical distribution in which scores are symmetrically distributed above and below the mean, the median, and the mode at the center of the distribution.

It is not necessary to memorize this formula. It is important to understand that rarely do behavioral data fall exactly within the limits of this
formula. When we say that data are normally distributed, we mean that
the data approximate a normal distribution. The normal distribution is
so exact that it is simply impractical to think that behavior can fit exactly
within the limits defined by this formula.

FIGURE 5.1   Three Examples of a Normal Distribution With Different
Means and Standard Deviations

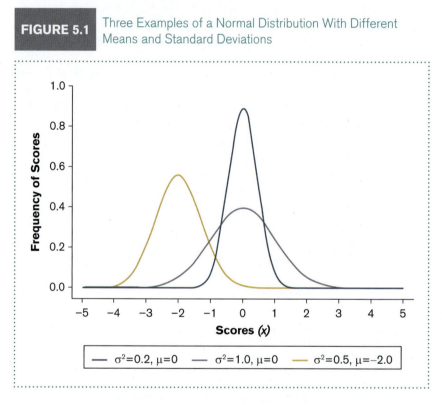

2. **The normal distribution is theoretical.** This characteristic follows
   from the first in that it emphasizes that data can be normally distributed in theory—although rarely do we observe behaviors that
   are exactly normally distributed. Instead, behavioral data typically
   approximate a normal distribution. As you will see in this chapter,
   we can still use the normal distribution to describe behavior so
   long as the behaviors being described are approximately normally
   distributed.

3. **The mean, median, and mode are all located at the 50th percentile.** In a normal distribution, the mean, the median, and the mode
   are the same value at the center of the distribution. So half the data
   (50%) in a normal distribution fall above the mean, the median, and
   the mode, and half the data (50%) fall below these measures.

4. **The normal distribution is symmetrical.** The normal distribution
   is symmetrical in that the distribution of data above the mean is
   the same as the distribution of data below the mean. If you were to
   fold a normal curve in half, both sides of the curve would exactly
   overlap.

5. **The mean can equal any value.** The normal distribution can be defined by its mean and standard deviation. The mean of a normal distribution can equal any number from positive infinity ($-\infty$) to negative infinity ($-\infty$):

$$-\infty \leq M \leq +\infty.$$

6. **The standard deviation can equal any positive value.** The standard deviation (*SD*) is a measure of variability. Data can vary (*SD* > 0) or not vary (*SD* = 0). A negative standard deviation is meaningless. In the normal distribution, then, the standard deviation can be any positive value greater than 0.

7. **The total area under the curve of a normal distribution is equal to 1.0.** The area under the normal curve has the same characteristics as probability: Portions of it vary between 0 and 1 and can never be negative. In this way, the area under the normal curve can be used to determine the probabilities at different points along the distribution. In Characteristic 3, we stated that 50% of all data fall above and 50% fall below the mean. This is the same as saying that half (.50) of the area under the normal curve falls above and half of the area (.50) falls below the mean. The total area, then, is equal to 1.0. Figure 5.2 shows the proportions of area under the normal curve 3 *SD* above and below the mean (±3 *SD*).

8. **The tails of a normal distribution are asymptotic.** In a normal distribution, the tails are asymptotic, meaning that as you travel away from the mean the tails of the distribution are always approaching the x-axis but never touch it. Because the tails of the normal distribution go out to infinity, this characteristic allows for the possibility of outliers (or scores far from the mean) in a data set.

FYI

Most behavioral data approximate a normal distribution. Rarely are behavioral data exactly normally distributed.

FYI

In a normal distribution, 50% of all data fall above the mean, the median, and the mode, and 50% fall below these measures.

FYI

In a normal distribution, the mean can equal any value between +∞ and −∞; the standard deviation can equal any positive value greater than 0.

FYI

Proportions of area under a normal curve are used to determine the probabilities for normally distributed data.

FYI

The tails of a normal distribution never touch the x-axis, so it is possible to observe outliers in a data set that is normally distributed.

FIGURE 5.2   The Proportion of Area Within Each Standard Deviation of the Mean

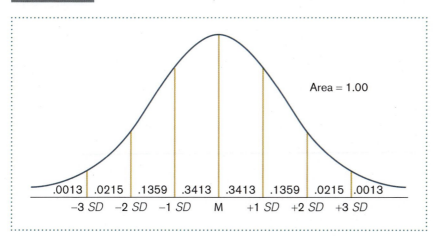

The total area is equal to 1.00. Note that these proportions follow the empirical rule as illustrated in Chapter 4, Figure 4.4.

RESEARCH IN FOCUS:
THE STATISTICAL NORM

Researchers often use the word *normal* to describe behavior in a study but with little qualification for what exactly constitutes normal behavior. Researchers studying the links between obesity and sleep have stated that short sleepers are at a higher risk of obesity compared to "normal" sleepers (see Theorell-Haglöw, Berglund, Berne, & Lindberg, 2014), and researchers studying mental health and cognition describe changes in clinically "normal" adults (see Machulda et al., 2017). What do researchers mean when they say that sleeping or change is normal?

Statistically speaking, normal behavior is defined by the *statistical norm*, which is data that fall within about 2 *SD* of the mean in a normal distribution. Figure 5.3 shows that about 95% of all data fall within 2 *SD* of the mean in a normal distribution—these data

FIGURE 5.3   The Statistical Norm

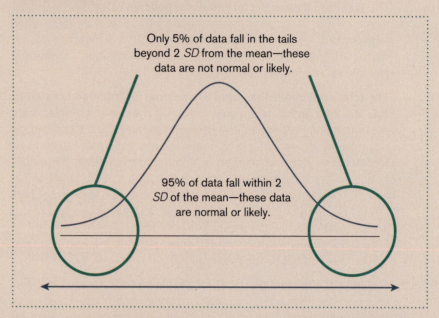

Behavioral data that fall within 2 *SD* of the mean are regarded as normal (or likely) because these data fall near the mean. Behavioral data that fall outside of 2 *SD* from the mean are regarded as not normal (or not likely) because these data fall far from the mean in a normal distribution.

are normal only inasmuch as they fall close to the mean. Data that are more than 2 *SD* from the mean are characteristic of less than 5% of data in that distribution—these data are not normal only inasmuch as they fall far from the mean.

LEARNING CHECK 2

1. All of the following characteristics are true about a normal distribution, except:

   (a) The mean can be any positive or negative number.

   (b) The variance can be any positive number.

   (c) The shape of the normal distribution is symmetrical.

   (d) The tails of a normal distribution touch the x-axis at 3 *SD* from the mean.

2. A normal distribution has a mean equal to 5. What is the value of the median and mode in this distribution?

3. The area under a normal curve ranges between 0 and 1 and can never be negative. What type of statistic also has these same characteristics?

4. What term is often used to describe behavior that falls within 2 *SD* of the mean in a normal distribution?

Answers: 1. d; 2. Median = 5, mode = 5; 3. Probability; 4. Normal or statistical norm.

5.6 THE STANDARD NORMAL DISTRIBUTION AND z SCORES

In a normal distribution, the mean can be any positive or negative number, and the standard deviation can be any positive number (see Characteristics 5 and 6). For this reason, we could combine values of the mean and standard deviation to construct an infinite number of normal distributions. To find the probability of a score in each and every one of these normal distributions would be quite overwhelming.

As an alternative, statisticians found the area under one normal curve, called the "standard," and stated a formula to convert all other normal distributions to this standard. As stated in Characteristic 7, the area under the normal curve is a probability at different points along the distribution. The "standard" curve is called the **standard normal distribution** or **z distribution**, which has a mean of 0 and a standard deviation of 1. Scores on the x-axis in a standard normal distribution are called **z scores**.

The standard normal distribution is one example of a normal distribution. Figure 5.4 shows the area, or probabilities, under the standard normal curve at each z score. The numerical value of a z score specifies the distance or standard deviation of a value from the mean. (Thus, z = +1 is one standard deviation above the mean, z = −1 is one standard deviation below the mean, and so on.) Notice that the probabilities given for the standard normal distribution are the same as those shown in Figure 5.2. The probabilities are the same because the proportion of area under the normal curve is the same at each standard deviation for all normal distributions.

Because we know the probabilities under a standard normal curve, we can convert all other normal distributions to this standard. By doing so, we can find the probabilities of scores in any normal distribution using probabilities listed for the standard normal distribution. To convert any normal distribution to a standard normal distribution, we compute

FYI

The standard normal distribution is one of the infinite normal distributions—it has a mean of 0 and standard deviation of 1.

FYI

The z transformation formula converts any normal distribution to the standard normal distribution with a mean equal to 0 and standard deviation equal to 1.

The **standard normal distribution**, or **z distribution**, is a normal distribution with a mean equal to 0 and a standard deviation equal to 1. The standard normal distribution is distributed in z score units along the x-axis.

A **z score** is a value on the x-axis of a standard normal distribution. The numerical value of a z score specifies the distance or the number of standard deviations that a value is above or below the mean.

FIGURE 5.4	The Proportion of Total Area (total area = 1.0) Under the Standard Normal Curve

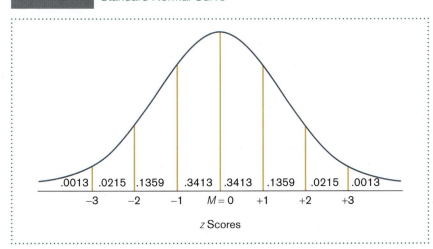

The "standard" normal distribution is one example of a normal distribution. Hence, the areas in this figure are identical to those given in Figure 5.2.

The **standard normal transformation** or **z transformation** is a formula used to convert any normal distribution with any mean and any variance to a standard normal distribution with a mean equal to 0 and a standard deviation equal to 1.

the **standard normal transformation**, or **z transformation**. The formula for the z transformation is

$$z = \frac{x - \mu}{\sigma} \text{ for a population of scores, or}$$

$$z = \frac{x - M}{SD} \text{ for a sample of scores.}$$

We use the z transformation to locate where a score in any normal distribution would be in the standard normal distribution. To illustrate, we will compute a z transformation in Example 5.2 and ask a more conceptual question in Example 5.3.

Example 5.2

A researcher measures the farthest distance (in feet) that students moved from a podium during a class presentation. The data were normally distributed with $M = 12$ and $SD = 2$. What is the z score for $x = 14$ feet?

Because $M = 12$ and $SD = 2$, we can find the z score for $x = 14$ by substituting these values into the z transformation formula:

$$z = \frac{14 - 12}{2} = 1.00.$$

Figure 5.5a shows the original normal distribution of scores (x) with $M = 12$ and $SD = 2$. Notice that in Figure 5.5b, a score of $x = 14$ in the

FIGURE 5.5   Computing the z Transformation for a Sample With $M = 12$ and $SD = 2$

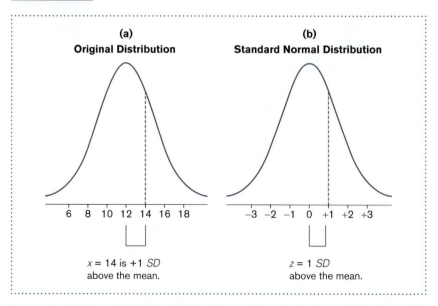

A score of $x = 14$ in the original distribution is located at $z = 1.0$ in a standard normal distribution, or 1 SD above the mean.

©iStockphoto.com/DIMUSE

original distribution is exactly one z score, or one standard deviation, above the mean in a standard normal distribution.

Example 5.3

Suppose we want to determine the z score for the mean of a normal distribution. The z transformation for the mean of any normal distribution will always equal what z score value?

The mean is always at the center of a normal distribution. If you substitute the mean for z in the z transformation, the solution will always be 0. In other words, when $M = x$, the solution for the z transformation is 0.

FYI

The mean in any normal distribution corresponds to a z score equal to 0.

5.7 A BRIEF INTRODUCTION TO THE UNIT NORMAL TABLE

The proportion of area under the standard normal distribution is given in the **unit normal table**, or **z table**, in Table C.1 in Appendix C. A portion of the table is shown in Table 5.1. The unit normal table has three columns: A, B, and C. This section will familiarize you with each column in the table.

Column A lists the z scores. The table lists only positive z scores, meaning that only z scores at or above the mean are listed in the table. For negative z scores below the mean, you must realize that the normal distribution is symmetrical. The areas listed in Columns B and C for each z score below the mean are the same as those for z scores listed above the mean in the unit normal table. In Column A, z scores are listed from $z = 0.00$ at the mean to $z = 4.00$ above the mean.

Column B lists the area between a z score and the mean. The first value for the area listed in Column B is .0000, which is the area between the mean ($z = 0$) and $z = 0$ (the mean). Notice that the area between the mean and a z score of 1.00 is .3413—the same value given in Figure 5.4. As a z score moves away from the mean, the proportion of area between that score and the mean increases closer to .5000, or the total area above the mean.

Column C lists the area from a z score toward the tail. The first value for the area listed in Column C is .5000, which is the total area above the mean. As a z score increases and therefore moves closer to the tail, the area between that score and the tail decreases closer to .0000.

Keep in mind that the normal distribution is used to determine the probability of a certain outcome in relation to all other outcomes. For example, to describe data that are normally distributed, we ask questions about observing scores greater than ___, scores less than ___, or scores among the top or bottom ___%, or the likelihood of scoring within a range of values. In each case, we are interested in the probability of an outcome in relation to all other normally distributed outcomes. Finding the area, and therefore probability, of any value in a normal distribution is introduced in Section 5.8.

The **unit normal table** or **z table** is a type of probability distribution table displaying a list of z scores and the corresponding probabilities (or proportions of area) associated with each z score listed.

TABLE 5.1 A Portion of the Unit Normal Table in Table C.1 in Appendix C

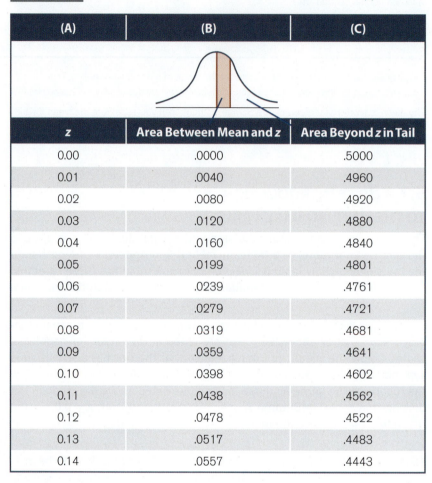

z	Area Between Mean and z	Area Beyond z in Tail
0.00	.0000	.5000
0.01	.0040	.4960
0.02	.0080	.4920
0.03	.0120	.4880
0.04	.0160	.4840
0.05	.0199	.4801
0.06	.0239	.4761
0.07	.0279	.4721
0.08	.0319	.4681
0.09	.0359	.4641
0.10	.0398	.4602
0.11	.0438	.4562
0.12	.0478	.4522
0.13	.0517	.4483
0.14	.0557	.4443

Source: Based on J. E. Freund (2004). *Modern elementary statistics* (11th ed.). Upper Saddle River, NJ: Pearson Prentice Hall.

FYI

To estimate probabilities under the normal curve, we determine the probability of a certain outcome in relation to all other outcomes.

LEARNING CHECK 3

1. A set of data is normally distributed with a mean equal to 10 and a standard deviation equal to 3. Compute a z transformation for each of the following scores in this normal distribution:

   (a) –2   (b) 10   (c) 3   (d) 16   e) 0

2. Identify the column in the unit normal table for each of the following:

   (a) The z scores

   (b) The area from each z score toward the tail

   (c) The area between each z score and the mean

3. Complete the following sentence: The normal distribution is used to determine the probability of a certain outcome _____ to all other outcomes.

Answers: 1. (a) $z = \frac{-2-10}{3} = -4.00$, (b) $z = \frac{10-10}{3} = 0$, (c) $z = \frac{3-10}{3} = -2.33$, (d) $z = \frac{16-10}{3} = 2.00$, (e) $z = \frac{0-10}{3} = -3.33$; 2. (a) Column A, (b) Column C, (c) Column B; 3. In relation or relative.

5.8 LOCATING PROPORTIONS

The area at each z score is given as a proportion in the unit normal table. Hence, we can use the unit normal table to locate the proportion or probability of a score in a normal distribution. To locate the proportion, and therefore the probability, of scores in any normal distribution, we follow two steps:

Step 1: Transform a raw score (x) into a z score.

Step 2: Locate the corresponding proportion for the z score in the unit normal table.

In Examples 5.4 and 5.5, we follow these steps to locate the proportion associated with scores above the mean. In Examples 5.6 and 5.7, we follow these steps to locate the proportion associated with scores below the mean. In Example 5.8, we follow these steps to locate the proportion between two scores. In each example, we show the normal curve and shade the region under the curve that we are locating.

FYI

For normally distributed data, we use the unit normal table to find the probability of obtaining an outcome in relation to all other outcomes.

Locating Proportions Above the Mean

Example 5.4

A sample of scores is normally distributed with $M = 8$ and $SD = 2$. What is the probability of obtaining a score greater than 12?

Figure 5.6 shows the normal curve for this distribution. The shaded region in Figure 5.6 represents the proportion, or probability, of obtaining a score greater than 12. We apply the two steps to find the proportion associated with this shaded region.

Step 1: To transform a raw score (x) to a z score, we compute a z transformation. In this example, $x = 12$. The z transformation is

$$z = \frac{12-8}{2} = \frac{4}{2} = 2.00.$$

A score equal to 12 in the distribution illustrated in Figure 5.6 is located 2.00 z scores (or 2 SD) above the mean in a standard normal distribution.

Step 2: In this example, we are looking for the proportion from $z = +2.00$ toward the tail. To locate the proportion, look in Column A in Table C.1 in Appendix C for a z score equal to 2.00. The proportion toward the tail is listed in Column C. The proportion greater than 12 in the original distribution is

$$p = .0228.$$

The probability is $p = .0228$ of obtaining a score greater than 12.

FIGURE 5.6   A Normal Distribution With $M = 8$ and $SD = 2$

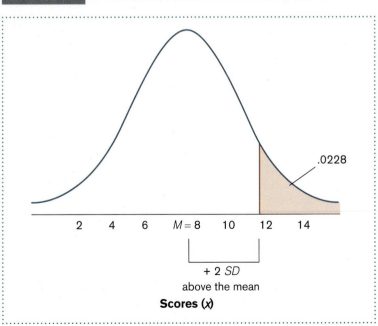

The shaded region shows the proportion of scores that are at or above 12 in this distribution.

Example 5.5

© iStockphoto.com / monkeybusinessimages

To investigate how mindful employees are of job-related tasks, a researcher develops a survey to determine the amount of time employees at a local business spend off-task during the day; such a topic is of interest to those who study workplace behavior and performance (Katz-Navon, Unger-Aviram, & Block, 2016; Wilson, Bennett, Gibson, & Alliger, 2012). After observing all employees, she reports that employees spent 5.2 ± 1.6 ($M \pm SD$) minutes off-task during the day. Assuming the data are normally distributed, what is the probability that employees in this study spent less than 6 minutes off-task during the day?

Figure 5.7 shows the distribution of times. The shaded regions in Figure 5.7 represent the proportion, or probability, of obtaining a time less than 6 minutes. We apply the two steps to find the proportion associated with the shaded region.

Step 1: To transform a raw score (x) to a z score, we compute a z transformation. In this example, $x = 6$. The z transformation is

$$z = \frac{6-5.2}{1.6} = \frac{0.8}{1.6} = 0.50.$$

In the distribution shown in Figure 5.7, a time equal to 6 minutes is located 0.50 z scores, or half a standard deviation, above the mean in a standard normal distribution.

Step 2: In this example, we are looking for the proportion from $z = 0.50$ back to the mean, and then we will add .5000, which is the total proportion of area below the mean. To locate the proportion, we look in Column A in Table C.1 in Appendix C for a z score equal to 0.50.

FIGURE 5.7   A Normal Distribution With $M = 5.2$ and $SD = 1.6$

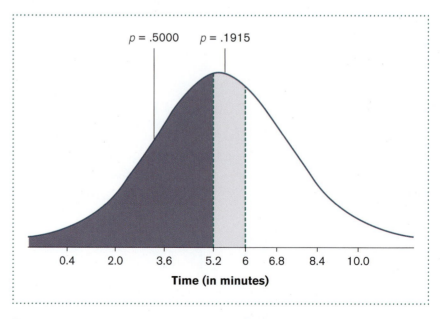

The shaded region is the proportion at or below a score of 6 in this distribution.

The proportion from $z = 0.50$ to the mean given in Column B is $p = .1915$. Add .1915 to the proportion below the mean ($p = .5000$) to find the total proportion:

$$p = .1915 + .5000 = .6915.$$

The probability is $p = .6915$ that employees spent less than 6 minutes off-task during the day.

FYI

The total area is .5000 above the mean and .5000 below the mean in a normal distribution.

Locating Proportions Below the Mean

Example 5.6

Researchers are often interested in depression across many different groups, which can be measured using the Beck Depression Inventory (BDI-II; Beck, Steer, & Brown, 1996). Individuals who experience chronic pain are one such group for which depression is of interest to researchers (Knaster, Estlander, Karlsson, Kaprio, & Kalso, 2016; Lopez, Pierce, Gardner, & Hanson, 2013). Using data based on reports in published research, suppose a group of veterans who experience chronic pain scored 24.0 ± 12.0 ($M \pm SD$) on the BDI-II, where higher scores indicate more severe depression. According to conventions, a score of 13 or less is regarded as a score in the minimal depression range. Assuming these data are normally distributed, what is the probability that veterans who experience chronic pain scored in the minimal depression range (13 or less)?

Figure 5.8 is a normal curve showing this distribution of scores. The shaded region in Figure 5.8 is the proportion, or probability, of scores at or less than 13 on this inventory. We can follow the two steps to find the proportion associated with the shaded region.

FIGURE 5.8 A Normal Distribution With $M = 24.0$ and $SD = 12.0$

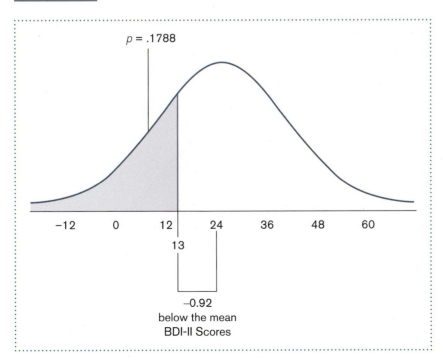

The shaded region is the proportion at or below a score of 13 in this distribution.

Step 1: To transform a raw score (x) to a z score, we compute a z transformation. In this example, $x = 13$. The z transformation is

$$z = \frac{13-24}{12} = -\frac{11}{12} = -0.92.$$

In the distribution shown in Figure 5.8, a score equal to 13 is located 0.92 z scores, or standard deviations, below the mean in a standard normal distribution. The negative sign indicates that the z score is located below the mean.

FYI

In the standard normal distribution, z scores above the mean are positive; z scores below the mean are negative.

Step 2: In this example, we are looking for the proportion toward the lower tail. To locate the proportion, we look in Column A in Table C.1 in Appendix C. We find $z = 0.92$ in the table. Again, the normal distribution is symmetrical. A proportion given for a positive z score will be the same for a corresponding negative z score. The proportion for a z score of 0.92 toward the lower tail is listed in Column C. The proportion is

$$p = .1788.$$

Hence, the probability is $p = .1788$ that a veteran given this depression measure scored in the minimal depression range (a score of 13 or less) on the BDI-II.

Example 5.7

Memory is a factor often studied in patients who experience trauma where it is possible that memory is impaired (Brown, Mapleston, & Nairn, 2012; Segovia, Strange, & Takarangi, 2017; Yu, Washington, & Kernie, 2016). One type of metric used to measure memory among stroke patients is the Cognistat (Kiernan, Mueller, & Langston, 1987), which includes a series of tests with a higher raw score indicating more severe impairment. Using data based on reports in published research, suppose a large sample of stroke patients scored 7.5 ± 2.5 ($M \pm SD$) on the Cognistat metric. Assuming these data are normally distributed, what is the probability that a stroke patient in this sample scored 4.1 or higher on this metric?

The shaded region in Figure 5.9 reflects the proportion, or probability, of a score 4.1 or higher on this metric. We will follow the two steps to find the proportion associated with the shaded region.

FIGURE 5.9   A Normal Distribution With $M = 7.5$ and $SD = 2.5$

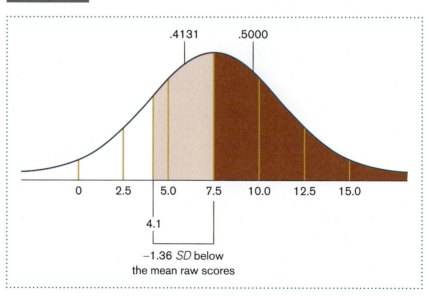

The shaded region is the proportion at or above a score of 4.1 in this distribution.

Step 1: To transform a raw score (*x*) to a *z* score, we compute a *z* transformation. In this example, *x* = 4.1. The *z* transformation is

$$z = \frac{4.1 - 7.5}{2.5} = -\frac{3.4}{2.5} = -1.36.$$

In the distribution shown in Figure 5.9, a score equal to 4.1 is located 1.36 *z* scores, or standard deviations, below the mean in a standard normal distribution.

Step 2: In this example, we are looking for the proportion from *z* = −1.36 to the mean, and then we will add .5000, which is the total proportion of area above the mean. To locate the proportion, search Column A in Table C.1 in Appendix C for a *z* score equal to 1.36. (Remember that a proportion given for a positive *z* score is the same for a corresponding negative *z* score.) The proportion given in Column B is *p* = .4131. Add .4131 to the proportion of area above the mean (*p* = .5000) to find the proportion:

$$p = .4131 + .5000 = .9131.$$

The probability is *p* = .9131 that a patient in this sample scored 4.1 or higher on the Cognistat metric.

FYI

Because the normal distribution is symmetrical, probabilities associated with positive z scores are the same for corresponding negative z scores.

Locating Proportions Between Two Values

Example 5.8

In recent studies, researchers have tested the possible benefits of gum chewing on academic performance in an educational environment (Johnston, Tyler, Stansberry, Moreno, & Foreyt, 2012; Tucha & Simpson, 2011). Using data based on reports in published research, adult students who chew gum while in class improve 20 ± 9 (*M* ± *SD*) points on a standardized math test the second time they take it. Assuming these data are normally distributed, what is the probability that a student who chews gum will score between 11 and 29 points higher the second time he or she takes the standardized math test?

Jupiterimages/Stockbyte/Thinkstock

Figure 5.10 is a normal curve showing this distribution. The shaded region in Figure 5.10 is the proportion, or probability, associated with scores between 11 and 29 on the math test. To find the proportion in the shaded regions, we apply the two steps for each score, *x*:

Step 1 for *x* = 11: To transform a raw score (*x*) to a *z* score, we compute a *z* transformation. In this example, *x* = 11. The *z* transformation is

$$z = \frac{11 - 20}{9} = -\frac{9}{9} = -1.00.$$

In the distribution shown in Figure 5.10, a score equal to 11 is located 1.00 *z* score, or one standard deviation, below the mean in a standard normal distribution.

Step 2 for *x* = 11: Find the *z* score 1.00 in Column A of Table C.1 in Appendix C, and then look in Column B for the proportion between −1.00 and the mean: *p* = .3413.

To find the total proportion between the two scores, we will add .3413 to the proportion associated with the second score (*x* = 29).

Step 1 for $x = 29$: Compute the z transformation for $x = 29$:

$$z = \frac{29-20}{9} = \frac{9}{9} = 1.00.$$

A score equal to 29 in the distribution illustrated in Figure 5.10 is located 1.00 z score above the mean in a standard normal distribution.

Step 2 for $x = 29$: The proportion between the mean and a z score of 1.00 is the same as that for -1.00: $p = .3413$. The total proportion between 11 and 29 is the sum of the proportion for each score:

$$p = .3413 + .3413 = .6826.$$

The probability is $p = .6826$ that a student will score between 11 and 29 points higher the second time he or she takes the standardized math test.

FIGURE 5.10   A Normal Distribution With $M = 20$ and $SD = 9$

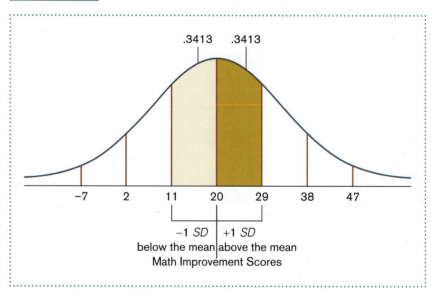

The shaded region is the proportion of scores between $x = 11$ and $x = 29$ in this distribution.

LEARNING CHECK 4

1. State the two steps for locating the proportion of scores in any normal distribution.

2. Find the probability of a score at or above the following z scores:

    (a) 1.23

    (b) −2.50

    (c) 0.50

3. Find the probability of a score at or below the following z scores:

    (a) 0.08

    (b) −1.00

    (c) 2.90

4. Find the probability of a score between the following *z* scores:

    (a) The mean and 1.40

(b) −1.00 and 1.00

(c) 60 and 1.20

Answers: 1. Step 1: Transform a raw score (*x*) into a *z* score. Step 2: Locate the corresponding probability for that *z* score in the unit normal table; 2. (a) *p* = .1093, (b) *p* = .9938, (c) *p* = .3085; 3. (a) *p* = .5319, (b) *p* = .1587, (c) *p* = .9981; 4. (a) *p* = .4192, (b) *p* = .6826, (c) *p* = .1592.

5.9 LOCATING SCORES

In a normal distribution, we can also find the scores that fall within a given proportion, or percentile, using the unit normal table. Finding scores in a given percentile can be useful in certain situations, such as when instructors grade "on a curve" with, say, the top 10% earning As. In this example, the unit normal table can be used to determine which scores will receive an A—that is, which scores fall in the top 10%. To find the cutoff score for a given proportion, we follow two steps:

Step 1: Locate a *z* score associated with a given proportion in the unit normal table.

Step 2: Transform the *z* score into a raw score (*x*).

In Examples 5.9 and 5.10, we will apply these steps to locate scores that fall within a given proportion in a normal distribution. In each example, we will show the normal distribution and shade the proportion under the curve that we are given.

FYI

The unit normal table can be used to locate scores that fall within a given proportion or percentile.

Example 5.9

Many researchers are interested in studying intelligence in many groups and populations, with a popular measure of intelligence being the IQ test (Hafer, 2017; Naglieri, 2015). In the general healthy population, scores on an IQ test are normally distributed with 100 ± 15 (μ ± σ). Based on this distribution of IQ scores, what is the minimum score required on this test to have an intelligence score in the top 10% of scores in this distribution?

© iStockphoto.com / PeopleImages

Figure 5.11 shows this distribution of scores. The shaded region in Figure 5.11 is the top 10% (*p* = .1000) of scores—we need to find the cutoff or lowest score, *x*, in this shaded region. We will apply the two steps to locate the cutoff score for the top 10% of data:

Step 1: The top 10% of scores is the same as *p* = .1000 toward the tail. To locate the *z* score associated with this proportion, we look for *p* = .1000 in Column C of the unit normal table in Table C.1 in Appendix C. The *z* score is *z* = 1.28. A *z* score equal to 1.28 is the cutoff for the top 10% of data.

Step 2: We need to determine which score, *x*, in the distribution shown in Figure 5.11 corresponds to a *z* score equal to 1.28. Because *z* = 1.28, we can substitute this value into the *z* transformation formula:

$$1.28 = \frac{x-100}{15}.$$

First, multiply both sides of the equation by 15 to eliminate the fraction:

$$(15)1.28 = \left(\frac{x-100}{15}\right)(15)$$
$$19.2 = x - 100.$$

To find the solution for *x*, add 100 to each side of the equation:

$$119.2 = x.$$

A score of 119.2 on the IQ test is the cutoff for the top 10% of scores in this distribution.

FIGURE 5.11 Locating Scores for Example 5.9

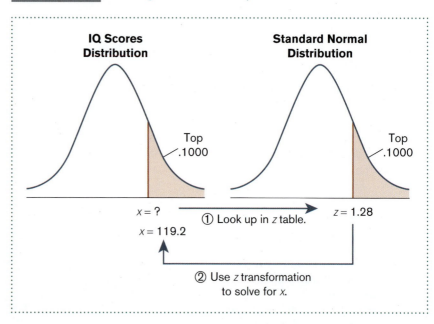

An IQ score greater than 119.2 represents the top 10% of intelligence scores in this distribution. Steps 1 and 2 show the method used to locate the cutoff score for the top 10% of scores in this normal distribution.

Example 5.10

Let us use the same IQ data for intelligence from Example 5.9, with a distribution of 100 ± 15 (*M* ± *SD*). Based on this distribution of IQ scores, what is the cutoff score for the bottom 25% of scores in this distribution?

Figure 5.12 shows this distribution. The shaded region in Figure 5.12 is the bottom 25% (*p* = .2500). We need to find the cutoff score, *x*, for this shaded region. We follow the two steps to locate the cutoff score that falls in the bottom 25%.

Step 1: The bottom 25% of scores is $p = .2500$ toward the tail. To locate the z score associated with this proportion, we look for $p = .2500$ in Column C of the unit normal table in Table C.1 in Appendix C. Because $p = .2500$ falls between z scores of 0.67 and 0.68 in the table, we compute the average of the two z scores: $z = 0.675$. Keep in mind that this z score is actually negative because it is located below the mean. A z score equal to –0.675 is the cutoff for the bottom 25% of data in this distribution.

Step 2: We need to determine which score, x, in the distribution shown in Figure 5.12 corresponds to a z score equal to –0.675. Because $z = -0.675$, we substitute this value into the z-transformation formula:

$$-0.675 = \frac{x-100}{15}.$$

First, multiply both sides of the equation by 15 to eliminate the fraction:

$$(15)(-0.675) = \left(\frac{x-100}{15}\right)(15) - 10.125 = x - 100.$$

To find the solution for x, add 100 to each side of the equation. The solution given here is rounded to the nearest hundredths place:

$$89.88 = x.$$

A score equal to 89.88 on the IQ test is the cutoff for the bottom 25% of scores in this distribution.

FYI

The unit normal table can be used to locate a cutoff score for a given proportion for data that are normally distributed.

FYI

The unit normal table allows us to locate raw scores, x, and determine probabilities, p, for data that are normally distributed.

FIGURE 5.12 Locating Scores for Example 5.10

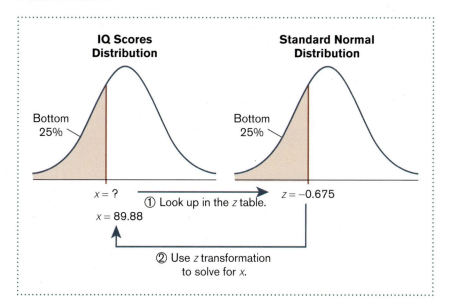

An IQ score less than 89.88 represents the bottom 25% of intelligence scores in this distribution. Steps 1 and 2 show the method used to locate the cutoff score for the bottom 25% of scores in this normal distribution.

MAKING SENSE STANDARD DEVIATION
AND THE NORMAL DISTRIBUTION

Keep in mind that the standard deviation is very informative, particularly for normally distributed data. To illustrate, consider that when students get an exam grade back, they often compare their grade to the grades of others in the class. Suppose, for example, that two professors give an exam, where the top 10% of scores receive an A grade. You take the exam given by Professor 1 and receive an 80

on the exam. Figure 5.13a shows that grades for that exam were 76 ± 2.0 ($M \pm SD$).

You then ask your friend how he did on Professor 2's exam and find that he scored an 84 on the same exam. Figure 5.13b shows that grades for that exam were 76 ± 8.0 ($M \pm SD$).

FIGURE 5.13   Exam Scores in the Top 10% of a Distribution

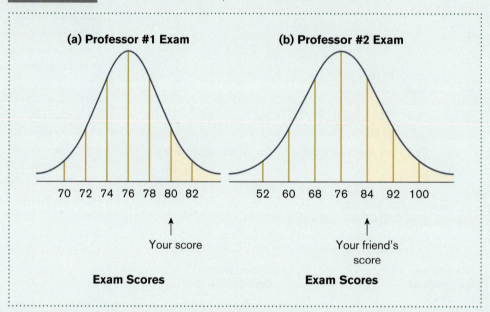

A distribution of exam scores with your grade on Professor 1's exam (a) and your friend's grade on Professor 2's exam (b). $M = 76$ in both distributions, but the standard deviations are different.

Because the mean grade is the same in both distributions, you might conclude that your friend performed better on the exam than you did, but you would be wrong. To see why, we can follow the steps to locate the cutoff score for earning an A on the exam, which is the top 10% of scores in each distribution.

The lowest score you can get and still receive an A on Professor 1's exam is the following:

Step 1: The top 10% of scores is $p = .1000$ toward the tail located in Column C in the unit normal table. The z score associated with $p = .1000$ is $z = 1.28$.

Step 2: Substitute 1.28 for z in the z transformation formula and solve for x:

$$1.28 = \frac{x-76}{2}.$$

$x - 76 = 2.56$ (multiply both sides by 2).

$x = 78.56$ (solve for x).

Your score on Professor 1's exam was an 80. Your score is in the top 10%; you earned an A on the exam.

The lowest score you can get and still receive an A on Professor 2's exam is the following:

Step 1: We already located this z score. The z score associated with the top 10% is $z = 1.28$.

Step 2: Substitute 1.28 for z in the z transformation equation and solve for x:

$$1.28 = \frac{x - 76}{8} \ .$$

$x - 76 = 10.24$ (multiply both sides by 8).

$x = 86.24$ (solve for x).

Your friend's score on Professor 2's exam was an 84. This score is outside the top 10%; your friend did not earn an A on the exam. Therefore, your 80 is an A,

and your friend's 84 is not, even though the mean was the same in both classes. The mean tells you only the average outcome—the standard deviation tells you the distribution of all other outcomes. Your score was lower than your friend's score, but you outperformed a larger percentage of your classmates than your friend did. The standard deviation is important because it gives you information about how your score compares relative to all other scores.

FYI

To find the probabilities of scores in a normal distribution, you must know the mean and standard deviation in that distribution.

LEARNING CHECK 5

1. State the two steps for locating the cutoff score for a given proportion of data.

2. What are the z scores associated with the following probabilities toward the tail in a normal distribution?

    (a) .4013

    (b) .3050

    (c) .0250

    (d) .0505

3. State the z score that most closely approximates the following probabilities:

    (a) Top 10% of scores

    (b) Bottom 10% of scores

    (c) Top 50% of scores

Answers: 1. Step 1: Locate the z score associated with a given proportion in the unit normal table. Step 2: Transform the z score into a raw score (x); 2. (a) $z = 0.25$, (b) $z = 0.51$, (c) $z = 1.96$, (d) $z = 1.64$; 3. (a) $z \approx 1.28$, (b) $z \approx -1.28$, (c) $z = 0$.

5.10 SPSS in Focus:
Converting Raw Scores to Standard z Scores

SPSS can be used to compute a z transformation for a given data set. To demonstrate how SPSS computes z scores, suppose you evaluate the effectiveness of an SAT remedial tutoring course with 16 students who plan to retake the standardized exam. Table 5.2 lists the number of points that each student gained on the exam after taking the remedial course. We will use SPSS to convert these data into z scores.

(Continued)

(Continued)

TABLE 5.2	The Number of Points Gained on the SAT Exam After Taking a Remedial Course, for 16 Students		
+500	+950	+780	+800
+750	+880	+800	+680
+600	+990	+800	+550
+900	+560	+450	+600

1. Click on the Variable View tab and enter *SAT* in the Name column. We will enter whole numbers, so reduce the value to 0 in the Decimals column.

2. In the Data View tab, enter the 16 values in the column labeled *SAT.* Go to the menu bar and click Analyze, then Descriptive Statistics and Descriptives, to display a dialog box.

3. In the dialog box, select *SAT* and click the arrow to move it into the Variable(s): box. Select the "Save standardized values as variables" box, shown in the left side of Figure 5.14.

4. Select OK, or select Paste and click the Run command.

SPSS will create two outputs. First, it will create the output table shown in Table 5.3. The output table contains the sample size, the minimum and maximum score, the mean, and the standard deviation. Second, SPSS creates an additional column of *z* scores in the Data View tab, shown in the right side of Figure 5.14. The added column is labeled with *Z* and then your variable name. In this example, we named the variable SAT, so the column is labeled ZSAT. Each *z* score in the ZSAT column is the number of standard deviations that the corresponding score in the original SAT column is from the mean.

TABLE 5.3   SPSS Output Table

Descriptive Statistics

	N	Minimum	Maximum	Mean	Std. Deviation
SAT	16	450	990	724.38	166.011
Valid N (listwise)	16				

FIGURE 5.14 The Dialog Box for Step 3 (left side) and the Data View With the ZSAT Column Listing z Scores for Each of the 16 Scores (right side)

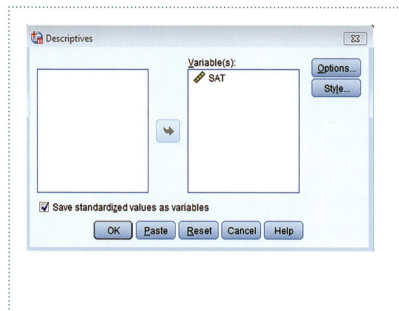

SAT	ZSAT
500	-1.35157
750	.15436
600	-.74920
900	1.05791
950	1.35910
880	.93744
990	1.60005
560	-.99015
780	.33507
800	.45554
800	.45554
450	-1.65275
800	.45554
680	-.26730
550	-1.05038
600	-.74920

••• CHAPTER SUMMARY ORGANIZED BY LEARNING OBJECTIVE

LO 1: Identify and compute a simple probability.

- Probability (symbolized as *p*) is the frequency of times an outcome occurs divided by the total number of possible outcomes. Probability varies between 0 and 1 and is never negative.

- To calculate the probability of an outcome for a random variable, *x*, use

the formula for $p(x)$, where $f(x)$ is the frequency of times an outcome occurs, and the sample space is the total number of outcomes possible:

$$p(x) = \frac{f(x)}{\text{sample space}}.$$

- The two steps to compute the probability formula are (1) find the sample space and (2) find $f(x)$.

LO 2:   Identify eight characteristics of the normal distribution.

- The normal distribution is a theoretical distribution in which scores are symmetrically distributed above and below the mean, the median, and the mode at the center of the distribution.

Eight characteristics of a normal distribution are as follows:

1. The normal distribution is mathematically defined.
2. The normal distribution is theoretical.
3. The mean, the median, and the mode are all located at the 50th percentile.
4. The normal distribution is symmetrical.
5. The mean can equal any value.
6. The standard deviation can equal any positive value.
7. The total area under the curve of a normal distribution is equal to 1.00.
8. The tails of a normal distribution are asymptotic.

LO 3:   Define the standard normal distribution and compute the standard normal transformation.

- The standard normal distribution, or z distribution, is a normal distribution with a mean equal to 0 and a standard deviation equal to 1. The standard normal distribution is distributed in z score units along the x-axis.

- The standard normal transformation, or z transformation, is an equation that converts any normal distribution with any mean and any positive standard deviation into a standard normal distribution with a mean equal to 0 and a standard deviation equal to 1:

For a population: $z = \frac{x - \mu}{\sigma}$.

For a sample: $z = \frac{x - M}{SD}$.

- The probabilities of z scores in a standard normal distribution are listed in the unit normal table in Table C.1 in Appendix C.

LO 4:   Locate proportions of area under any normal curve above the mean, below the mean, and between two scores.

- To locate the proportion, and therefore probabilities, for scores in any normal distribution, we follow two steps:

  Step 1: Transform a raw score (x) into a z score.

  Step 2: Locate the corresponding proportion for the z score in the unit normal table.

LO 5:   Locate scores in a normal distribution with a given probability.

- To locate scores that fall within a given proportion, or probability, we follow two steps:

  Step 1: Locate a z score associated with a given proportion in the unit normal table.

  Step 2: Transform the z score into a raw score (x).

LO 6:   Convert raw scores to standard z scores using SPSS.

- SPSS can be used to convert raw scores to standard z scores. After entering the data for each variable, raw scores are converted to standard z scores using the Analyze, Descriptive Statistics, and Descriptives options in the menu bar. These actions will allow you to select the "Save standardized values as variables" option to convert raw scores to standard z scores (for more details, see Section 5.10).

• • • KEY TERMS

bell-shaped distribution	random event	unit normal table
fixed event	sample space	z distribution
Gaussian distribution	standard normal distribution	z score
normal distribution	standard normal transformation	z table
probability	symmetrical distribution	z transformation

• • • END-OF-CHAPTER PROBLEMS

Factual Problems

1. Describe in words how to compute $p(x)$.

2. State two characteristics of a probability.

3. The normal distribution is symmetrical. What does this mean?

4. What type of distribution is most commonly applied to behavioral research?

5. A normal distribution has a mean of 0 and a standard deviation of −1.0. Is this possible? Explain.

6. What are the values of the mean and the standard deviation in the standard normal distribution?

7. What is a z score?

8. State the standard normal transformation formula in words.

9. What are two steps to locate proportions under the normal curve?

10. What are two steps to locate the cutoff score for a given proportion?

Concept and Application Problems

11. A hypothetical population consists of eight individuals ages 13, 14, 17, 20, 21, 22, 24, and 30 years.

    (a) What is the probability that a person in this population is a teenager?

    (b) What is the probability of selecting a participant who is at least 20 years old?

    (c) What is the probability of selecting a participant older than 30?

12. On the basis of statistics from the previous 3 years, a maternity ward states that 97% of patients say they are satisfied with their birthing experience. If 100,000 patients gave birth in that maternity ward over the previous 3 years, then how many patients do we expect were not satisfied with their visit?

13. Using the unit normal table, find the proportion under the standard normal curve that lies to the right of each of the following:

    (a) $z = 1.00$
    (b) $z = -1.05$
    (c) $z = -2.80$
    (d) $z = 0$
    (e) $z = 1.96$

14. Using the unit normal table, find the proportion under the standard normal curve that lies to the left of each of the following:

    (a) $z = 0.50$
    (b) $z = -1.32$
    (c) $z = 0$
    (d) $z = -1.96$
    (e) $z = -0.10$

15. Using the unit normal table, find the proportion under the standard normal curve that lies between each of the following:

    (a) The mean and $z = 0$
    (b) The mean and $z = 1.96$

(c) $z = -1.50$ and $z = 1.50$

(d) $z = -0.30$ and $z = -0.10$

(e) $z = 1.00$ and $z = 2.00$

16. State whether the first area is bigger, the second area is bigger, or the two areas are equal in each of the following situations:

   (a)   The area to the left of $z = 1.00$ and the area to the right of $z = -1.00$

   (b)   The area to the left of $z = 1.00$ and the area to the left of $z = -1.00$

   (c)   The area between the mean and $z = 1.20$ and the area to the right of $z = 0.80$

   (d)   The area to the left of the mean and the area between $z = \pm1.00$

   (e)   The area to the right of $z = 1.65$ and the area to the right of $z = -1.65$

17. An athletics coach states that player run times (in seconds) for a 100-meter dash are normally distributed with a mean equal to 0.12 and a standard deviation equal to 0.02 second. What percentage of players on the team run the 100-meter dash in 0.14 seconds or faster (i.e., in less time)?

18. State the z score that is the cutoff for each of the following:

   (a)   The top 5% of scores

   (b)   The bottom 2.5% of scores

   (c)   The top 69.5% of scores

   (d)   The top 50% of scores

   (e)   The bottom 50% of scores

19. A sample of final exam scores is normally distributed with a mean equal to 20 and a variance equal to 25.

   (a)   What percentage of scores is between 15 and 25?

   (b)   What raw score is the cutoff for the top 10% of scores?

   (c)   What is the probability of a score less than 27?

   (d)   What is the proportion below 13?

20. A college administrator states that the average high school GPA for incoming freshman students is normally distributed with a mean

equal to 3.30 and a standard deviation equal to 0.20. If students with a GPA in the top 10% will be offered a scholarship, then what is the minimum GPA required to receive the scholarship?

21. A set of scores measuring aggression is normally distributed with a mean equal to 23 and a standard deviation equal to 2.5. Find the proportion:

   (a)   To the left of $x = 19.0$

   (b)   To the right of $x = 25.5$

   (c)   Between the mean and $x = 19.0$

   (d)   To the left of $x = 25.5$

   (e)   To the right of $x = 19.0$

22. A set of data is normally distributed with a mean of 3.5 and a standard deviation of 0.6. State whether the first area is bigger, the second area is bigger, or the two areas are equal in each of the following situations for these data:

   (a)   The area above the mean and the area below the mean

   (b)   The area between 2.9 and 4.1 and the area between 3.5 and 4.7

   (c)   The area between the mean and 3.5 and the area above 5.3

   (d)   The area below 3.6 and the area above 3.4

   (e)   The area between 4.1 and 4.7 and the area between 2.9 and 3.5

23. A normal distribution has a mean equal to 45. What is the standard deviation of this normal distribution if 2.5% of the proportion under the curve lies to the right of $x = 50.88$?

24. A normal distribution has a mean equal to 10. What is the standard deviation of this normal distribution if the cutoff for the top 5% is $x = 12.47$?

25. A normal distribution has a standard deviation equal to 10. What is the mean of this normal distribution if the probability of scoring below $x = 10$ is .5000?

26. A normal distribution has a standard deviation equal to 32. What is the mean of this normal distribution if the probability of scoring above $x = 200$ is .0228?

Problems in Research

27. **The inaccuracy of lie detection.** Maureen O'Sullivan (2007) stated that research on expert lie detection is "based on three assumptions: 1) Lie detection is an ability that can be measured; 2) This ability is distributed like many other abilities (i.e., normally); 3) Therefore, only a very few people will be highly accurate" (p. 118). How does this researcher know that very few people will be highly accurate at lie detection?

28. **The empirical rule and normal distributions.** Ruxton, Wilkinson, and Neuhäuser (2015) stated that "researchers will frequently be required to consider whether a sample of data appears to have been drawn from a normal distribution" (p. 249). Based on the empirical rule, why is it informative to know whether a set of data is normally distributed?

29. **Visual sequential memory and poor spellers.** Holmes, Malone, and Redenbach (2008) found that good readers and good spellers correctly read 93.8 ± 2.9 (*M* ± *SD*) words from a spelling list. On the other hand, average readers and poor spellers correctly read 84.8 ± 3.0 (*M* ± *SD*) words from the same spelling list. Assuming these data are normally distributed,

    (a) What percentage of participants correctly read at least 90 words in the good readers and good spellers group?

    (b) What percentage of participants correctly read at least 90 words in the average readers and poor spellers group?

30. **Preferences for specific body parts: The eyes.** Montoya (2007) asked 56 men and 82 women to rate 21 different body parts on a scale of 1 (*no opinion*) to 5 (*very desirable*). They found that men and women rated the eyes similarly, with an average rating of about 3.77 ± 1.23 (*M* ± *SD*). Assuming these data are normally distributed,

    (a) What percentage of participants rated the eyes at least a 5 (*very desirable*)?

    (b) What percentage rated the eyes at most a 1 (*no opinion*)?

31. **Multicultural perceptions in education.** Yang and Montgomery (2013) studied how teachers and prospective teachers perceive diversity in an educational environment. In their study, participants responded with their level of agreement to many statements regarding diversity on a scale from –5 (*most unlike me*) to +5 (*most like me*); the median value, 0, indicated a neutral rating. One item stated, "Some cultural groups are not prepared enough to achieve in America" (Yang & Montgomery, 2013, p. 32). The researchers ranked the responses to each item and found that the response to this item was associated with a *z* score of –0.76. In this example, find the proportion of area to the right of –0.76.

32. **Can eating slower reduce how much we eat in a meal?** In one variation of a study conducted by Privitera, Cooper, and Cosco (2012), participants were asked to eat fast or slow, and the amount consumed in their meal was recorded. In this study, participants who ate slowly consumed 627 ± 183 kilocalories (*M* ± SD); participants who ate fast consumed 670 ± 184 kilocalories. Assuming these data are normally distributed,

    (a) In which group, the slow group or the fast group, was it more likely that participants consumed greater than 700 kilocalories in their meal?

    (b) In which group, the slow group or the fast group, was it more likely that participants consumed less than 600 kilocalories in their meal?

Answers for even numbers are in Appendix D.

Sharpen your skills with **SAGE edge at edge.sagepub.com/priviteraess2e**

SAGE edge for Students provides a personalized approach to help you accomplish your coursework goals in an easy-to-use learning environment.

Marek Uliasz/iStock/Thinkstock

6 Characteristics of the Sample Mean

••• Learning Objectives

After reading this chapter, you should be able to:

1. Define *sampling distribution*.

2. Compare theoretical and experimental sampling strategies.

3. Identify three characteristics of the sampling distribution of the sample mean.

4. Calculate the mean and standard error of a sampling distribution of the sample mean and draw the shape of this distribution.

5. Explain the relationship between standard error, standard deviation, and sample size.

6. Compute z transformations for the sampling distribution of the sample mean.

7. Summarize the standard error of the mean in APA format.

8. Compute the estimate for the standard error of the mean using SPSS.

Consider how often you hear about "new findings from research . . ." Just from social media, for example, you may see studies showing that "social media-related online traffic outperforms overall traffic from late afternoon to nighttime," that "the average Instagram user is more engaged per post than Twitter and Facebook users," or that, "on average, including a photo in a social media post increases engagement." Keep in mind that, of course, not all social media users are observed to make these claims. In each case, these studies used samples of social media users (i.e., a portion of all users) to get a better understanding of the behavior of the population (i.e., all social media users). This indubitably leads to a critical question: How well does the behavior of a portion of social media users (i.e., samples) inform us about the actual behavior of all social media users (i.e., the population)?

In a broader context, it is important to be critical about the informativeness of samples for drawing conclusions about populations. How well do observations with samples truly generalize or inform us about a population? Can we trust the findings reported when samples of data are used? The most commonly reported and highly utilized statistic to describe behavior is the sample mean. At a fundamental level, it is practical to ask, "Is the sample mean unbiased?" In other words, on average, does it correctly estimate a population mean; and if it does not correctly estimate the population mean, then how far "off" is it, or how much of an "error" will we make?

Given that most research is conducted using samples in the behavioral sciences, it should not surprise you that samples are actually quite informative about the populations from which they are selected. In this chapter, we evaluate the questions asked in this opening section to see just how useful the mean in a sample is for estimating the mean in a population.

Master the content.

edge.sagepub.com/priviteraess2e

• • • Chapter Outline

6.1 SELECTING SAMPLES FROM POPULATIONS

In Chapter 5, we computed the probability of obtaining any score in a normal distribution by converting the scores in a normal distribution to z scores and then using the unit normal table to locate the probability of each z score. We can apply these same steps to inferential statistics—specifically in situations in which we select samples from populations. The use of z scores and the normal distribution in this chapter lays the theoretical foundation for our use of inferential statistics in Chapters 7 to 14.

Inferential Statistics and Sampling Distributions

In inferential statistics, researchers select a sample or portion of data from a much larger population. They then measure a sample statistic they are interested in, such as the mean or variance in a sample. But they do not measure a sample mean, for example, to learn about the mean in that sample. Instead, they select a sample mean to learn more about the mean in a population. As illustrated in Figure 6.1, you may ask a few students (the sample) how they scored on an exam to compare your score to theirs. You do this, though, to learn more about how you did compared to the entire class (the population), not just those few students. In a similar way, researchers select samples to learn more about populations.

When researchers measure sample statistics such as the mean and variance, they do so to estimate the value of the mean and variance in a population. But how well do sample statistics, such as the sample mean and sample variance, estimate the value of population parameters, such as the population mean and population variance? What is the probability that a sample statistic will be smaller than, larger than, or exactly equal to the value of a population parameter? These questions can be answered, in part, by applying our knowledge of normal distributions from Chapter 5.

In this chapter, we compare the mean and variance in a sample to the mean and variance in a small hypothetical population. We make this comparison by constructing a **sampling distribution**, which is a distribution of the mean and variance for all possible samples of a given size from a population. We can then compare the statistics we obtain in the samples to the value of the mean and variance in the hypothetical population. By doing so, we will answer the two questions asked in the previous paragraph.

Sampling and Conditional Probabilities

To avoid bias, researchers use a random procedure to select a sample from a given population. For samples to be selected at random, all individuals in a population must have an equal chance of being selected—so the probability of selecting each participant must be the same.

To illustrate the requirements for random sampling, suppose you place eight squares facedown on a desk in front of you. Two squares are marked A, two are marked B, two are marked C, and two are marked D. To select two squares at random, we must ensure that each square has the same probability of being selected. The most common sampling method in behavioral research is **sampling without replacement**, meaning that after we select a square, we do not replace that square before selecting a second square.

FYI

Researchers measure a mean and variance in a sample to gauge the value of the mean and variance in a population.

A **sampling distribution** for the mean is a distribution of all sample means that could be obtained in samples of a given size from the same population.

Sampling without replacement is a method of sampling in which each participant or item selected is not replaced before the next selection. This method of sampling is the most common method used in behavioral research.

FIGURE 6.1 Selecting Samples From Populations

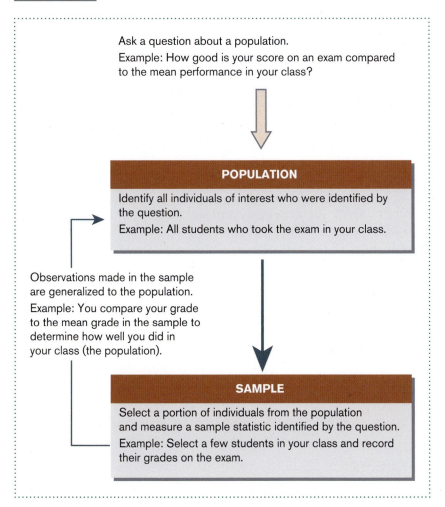

Ask a question about a population.
Example: How good is your score on an exam compared to the mean performance in your class?

POPULATION

Identify all individuals of interest who were identified by the question.
Example: All students who took the exam in your class.

Observations made in the sample are generalized to the population.
Example: You compare your grade to the mean grade in the sample to determine how well you did in your class (the population).

SAMPLE

Select a portion of individuals from the population and measure a sample statistic identified by the question.
Example: Select a few students in your class and record their grades on the exam.

In inferential statistics, researchers use the sample statistics they measure in a sample to make inferences about the characteristics, or population parameters, in a population of interest.

Let us find the probability of selecting a square marked A on the first draw and a square marked A on the second draw using this sampling method.

First draw: The probability of selecting a square marked A is the number of squares marked A divided by the total number of squares on the desk:

$$p(\text{square marked A on first draw}) = \frac{2}{8} = .25.$$

Second draw: We do not replace the square marked A. If we selected a square marked A on the first draw, then only seven squares remain, one of which is marked A. The probability of selecting a square marked A is the number of squares marked A divided by the total number of squares remaining on the desk:

$$p(\text{square marked A on second draw}) = \frac{1}{7} = .14.$$

Using the typical sampling method in behavioral science, we find that the probabilities of each selection are not the same because we did not replace each selection. To ensure that each individual or item has the same probability of being selected, we can use **sampling with replacement**, in which each individual or item is replaced after each selection.

Although sampling with replacement is a more random sampling method, it is typically not necessary in behavioral research because the populations of interest are large. In a population of 100 women, for example, the probability of selecting the first woman is $p = \frac{1}{100} = .01$. The probability of selecting the second woman if we sample without replacement is $p = \frac{1}{99} = .01$. When we round to the hundredths place, these probabilities are identical because the total number of individuals in the population is so large. As the population size increases, the changes in probabilities become minimal. Therefore, with large populations, random samples can be selected, even when we use a sampling without replacement method.

FYI

Sampling without replacement means that the probability of each selection is conditional. The probabilities of each selection are not the same.

LEARNING CHECK 1

1. A researcher uses a sample _____ to make inferences about the value of a population _____ of interest.

2. Which method for sampling is associated with equal probabilities for each selection, even with small sample sizes?

3. The number of left-handed people in a hypothetical population of 25 students is 8. What is the probability of selecting 2 left-handed people from this population when:

    (a) Sampling *with* replacement?

    (b) Sampling *without* replacement?

4. Which sampling method is the most commonly used in behavioral research?

Answers: 1. Statistic, parameter; 2. Sampling with replacement 3. (a) $\frac{8}{25} \times \frac{8}{25} = .10$, (b) $\frac{8}{25} \times \frac{7}{24} = .09$; 4. Sampling without replacement.

6.2 SELECTING A SAMPLE: WHO'S IN AND WHO'S OUT?

Sampling with replacement is a method of sampling in which each participant or item selected is replaced before the next selection. Replacing before the next selection ensures that the probability for each selection is the same. This method of sampling is used in the development of statistical theory.

A **sample design** is a specific plan or protocol for how individuals will be selected or sampled from a population of interest.

Once we identify a population of interest, we need to determine a **sample design** for selecting samples from the population. A sample design is a plan for how individuals will be selected from a population of interest. There are many appropriate sample designs, and all of them address the following two questions:

1. Does the order of selecting participants matter?

2. Do we replace each selection before the next draw?

The first question determines how often people in a population can be selected. Both questions determine the number of samples of a given size that can be selected from a given population. Answering both questions leads to two strategies for sampling, which we describe in this section. One strategy, called theoretical sampling, is used in the development of statistical theory. The second strategy, called experimental sampling, is the most common strategy used in behavioral research. Figure 6.2 shows how we can apply each strategy.

Sampling Strategy:
The Basis for Statistical Theory

We defined statistics in Chapter 1 as a branch of mathematics used to summarize, analyze, and interpret a group of numbers or observations. This branch of mathematics is based on theoretical proofs that show how statistical methods can be used to describe and interpret observations. Theoretical sampling, then, is used in the development of the theories that have led to statistics as a branch of mathematics.

To develop theories of sampling, statisticians answered yes to both questions stated above. To select samples from populations, the order of selecting people mattered, and each person selected was replaced before selecting again. To illustrate, suppose we select as many samples of two participants as possible from a population of three individuals (A, B, and C). In theoretical sampling:

1. Order matters. If two participants (A and B) are selected from a population, then selecting Participant A first, then B, differs from selecting Participant B first, then A. Each of these samples is regarded as a different possible sample that can be selected from this population.

2. We sample with replacement. This means that a sample of Participant A and then Participant A again is a possible sample because we replaced Participant A before making the second selection.

Table 6.1 shows that we can select nine possible samples of size 2 from a population of three people using theoretical sampling. To determine the total number of samples of any size that can be selected from a population of any size using theoretical sampling, use the following computation:

$$\text{Total number of samples possible} = N^n.$$

Let us verify the results shown in Table 6.1, in which we had samples of two participants ($n = 2$) from a population of three people ($N = 3$). If we substitute these values into the computation, we obtain the following:

$$N^n = 3^2 = 9 \text{ samples.}$$

We use this computation for a larger population and larger sample size in Example 6.1.

FYI

In theoretical sampling, the order of selecting individuals matters, and each individual selected is replaced before sampling again.

FIGURE 6.2	The Effect of Replacement and Order Changes on the Many Possible Samples That Can Be Drawn From a Given Population

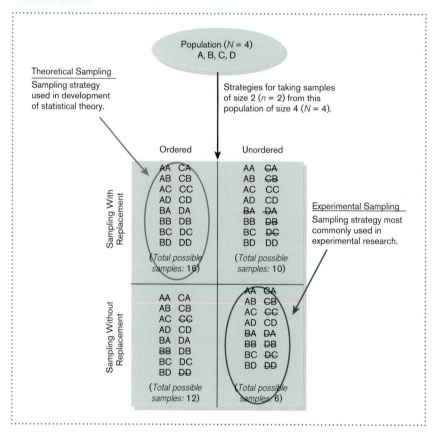

In this example, all possible samples of size 2 ($n = 2$) are taken from this population of size 4 ($N = 4$). Notice that theoretical sampling allows for the most possible samples (16), whereas experimental sampling allows for the fewest possible samples (6).

TABLE 6.1	Total Number of Samples of Size 2 ($n = 2$) From a Population of Size 3 ($N = 3$) Using Theoretical Sampling

Total Possible Samples ($n = 2$)
AA
AB
AC
BA
BB
BC
CA
CB
CC

Example 6.1

A researcher selects a sample of size 3 ($n = 3$) from a population of size 10 ($N = 10$). How many possible samples of size 3 can be selected using theoretical sampling?

To find the answer, we substitute the sample size (n) and population size (N) into the computation. The total number of samples possible using theoretical sampling is $N^n = 10^3 = 1,000$ samples.

Sampling Strategy: Most Used in Behavioral Research

In practice, however, we select diverse samples. For most studies in behavioral science, order does not matter because we do not care about the order in which participants are selected. Also, we usually do not want to select the same person twice for the same study, so we sample without replacement. Experimental sampling, then, is the strategy used by the experimenters who engage in behavioral research.

To illustrate the sampling strategy used in behavioral research, suppose we select as many samples of two participants as possible from a population of three people (A, B, and C). In experimental sampling:

1. Order does not matter. If two participants, A and B, are selected from a population, then selecting Participant A first, then B, is the same as selecting Participant B first, then A. These samples are counted as one sample and not as separate samples. In the example given in Figure 6.2, this was one criterion by which samples were crossed out for experimental sampling.

2. We sample without replacement. This means that the same participant can never be sampled twice. So samples of AA, BB, and CC from the population in this example are not possible. In the example given in Figure 6.2, this was the second criterion by which samples were crossed out for experimental sampling.

Table 6.2 shows that three different samples are possible if we select samples of size 2 from a population of size 3 using experimental sampling. To determine the total number of samples of any size that can be selected from a population of any size using experimental sampling, use the following computation:

$$\text{Total number of samples possible} = \frac{N!}{n!(N-n)!}.$$

Let us use this computation to verify the results in Table 6.2 in which we selected as many samples of two individuals ($n = 2$) from a population of three individuals ($N = 3$):

$$\frac{N!}{n!(N-n)!} = \frac{3!}{2!(3-2)!} = \frac{3 \times 2 \times 1}{2 \times 1 \times 1} = 3.$$

We use this computation for a larger population and larger sample size in Example 6.2.

FYI

In experimental sampling, the order of selecting individuals does not matter, and each individual selected is not replaced before selecting again.

| TABLE 6.2 | Total Number of Samples of Size 2 ($n = 2$) From a Population of Size 3 ($N = 3$) Using Experimental Sampling |

Total Possible Samples ($n = 2$)
AB
AC
CB

Example 6.2

In Example 6.1, a researcher selected a sample of size 3 ($n = 3$) from a population of size 10 ($N = 10$). Using this same example, how many possible samples of size 3 can be selected using experimental sampling?

To find the answer, we substitute the sample size (n) and population size (N) into the computation. The total number of samples possible is as follows:

$$\frac{N!}{n!(N-n)!} = \frac{10!}{3!(10-3)!} = \frac{10 \times 9 \times 8 \times 7 \times 6 \times 5 \times 4 \times 3 \times 2 \times 1}{3 \times 2 \times 1 \times 7 \times 6 \times 5 \times 4 \times 3 \times 2 \times 1} = 120.$$

LEARNING CHECK 2

1. State the two criteria for theoretical sampling.

2. A researcher draws a sample of size 4 ($n = 4$) from a population of size 50 ($N = 50$). How many possible samples of this size can the researcher draw using theoretical sampling?

3. State the two criteria for experimental sampling.

4. A researcher draws a sample of size 2 ($n = 2$) from a population of size 5 ($N = 5$). How many possible samples of this size can the researcher draw using experimental sampling?

Answers: 1. Order matters, and we sample with replacement; 2. $50^4 = 6{,}250{,}000$ possible samples; 3. Order does not matter, and we sample without replacement; 4. $\frac{5 \times 4 \times 3 \times 2 \times 1}{2 \times 1 \times 3 \times 2 \times 1} = 10$ samples.

6.3 SAMPLING DISTRIBUTIONS: THE MEAN

In behavioral research, we often measure a sample mean to estimate the value of a population mean. To determine how well a sample mean estimates a population mean, we need to identify a population of interest and then determine the distribution of the sample means for all possible samples of a given size that can be selected from that population—thus, we need to construct a sampling distribution.

Because statisticians used theoretical sampling to learn about the characteristics of the mean, we also will use this sampling strategy to select samples from a population. We can use the sampling distribution we construct in this section to see how well a sample mean estimates the value of a population mean.

To construct a sampling distribution, let us identify a hypothetical population of three people ($N = 3$) who took a psychological assessment. Person A scored an 8, Person B scored a 5, and Person C scored a 2 on this assessment. Because we know all three scores in this population, we can identify the mean in this population (we will identify the variance in Section 6.4). Then we can construct a sampling distribution of the mean to determine how the sample means we could select from this population compare to the population mean we calculated.

The population mean for $N = 3$: The population mean (μ) is computed by summing all scores in the population, then dividing by the population size:

$$\mu = \frac{8+5+2}{3} = 5.0.$$

To find the sampling distribution for $n = 2$, we use the possible samples from Table 6.1, which lists all the possible samples of size 2 that can be drawn from a population of three people using theoretical sampling. These nine samples are repeated in Table 6.3 along with the scores and sample means we would have measured in those samples using the assessment scores we listed for each person.

In the last column in Table 6.3, ΣM is the sum of the sample means. The average sample mean (μ_M) is computed by dividing the sum of the sample means (ΣM) by the total number of samples summed (nine samples). Using the data in this table, we will find that the sample mean is related to the population mean in three ways: The sample mean is an unbiased estimator, follows the central limit theorem, and has a minimum variance.

TABLE 6.3 The Participants, Individual Scores, and Sample Means for Each Possible Sample of Size 2 From a Population of Size 3

Participants Sampled ($n = 2$)	Scores for Each Participant	Sample Mean for Each Sample (M)
A, A	8, 8	8.0
A, B	8, 5	6.5
A, C	8, 2	5.0
B, A	5, 8	6.5
B, B	5, 5	5.0
B, C	5, 2	3.5
C, A	2, 8	5.0
C, B	2, 5	3.5
C, C	2, 2	2.0
$N^n = 9$ samples		$\Sigma M = 45$
		$\mu_M = \frac{45}{9} = 5.0$

Unbiased Estimator

A sample mean is an *unbiased estimator* (defined in Chapter 4) when the sample mean we obtain in a randomly selected sample equals the value of the population mean on average. We know that the population mean in our hypothetical example is equal to 5.0. The mean of the sampling distribution of sample means is the sum of the sample means we could select ($\sum M$) divided by the total number of samples summed:

$$\mu_M = \frac{45}{9} = 5.0$$

On average, we can expect the sample mean from a randomly selected sample to be equal to the population mean. The sample mean, then, is an unbiased estimator of the value of the population mean. In statistical terms, $M = \mu$, on average. We can state this as a rule for the sample mean:

$$\text{When } M = \frac{\sum x}{n}, \text{ then } M = \mu \text{ on average.}$$

Central Limit Theorem

We know that, on average, the sample mean is equal to the population mean. But what about all other possible values of the sample mean that we could obtain? We can distribute all other possible sample means by listing the value of each possible sample mean on the *x*-axis and the frequency of times it occurs on the *y*-axis of a graph. Figure 6.3b shows that the sample means selected from this population are normally distributed, and this will always be the case regardless of the distribution of scores in the population. Notice in Figure 6.3a that the frequency of scores in the original population is nonmodal. Although the population of scores is not normally distributed, the sample means selected from this population are normally distributed. This outcome is described by the **central limit theorem**.

The central limit theorem has an important implication: It means that the probability distribution for obtaining a sample mean from a population is normal. From the empirical rule, then, we know that at least 95% of all possible sample means we could select from a population are within two standard deviations (*SD*) of the population mean.

Minimum Variance

The variance of a normal distribution can be any positive number, and defining the variance can give us an idea of how far the value of a sample mean can deviate from the value of the population mean. To compute the variance, we use the same formula that was introduced in Chapter 4 except that we use the notation for a sampling distribution. The formula for the variance of the sampling distribution of the sample means (symbolized as σ^2_M) is as follows:

$$\sigma^2_M = \sum \frac{(M - \mu_M)^2}{N^n}.$$

FYI

The sample mean is an unbiased estimator of the value of the population mean.

FYI

The central limit theorem explains that the shape of a sampling distribution of sample means tends toward a normal distribution, regardless of the distribution in the population.

The **central limit theorem** explains that regardless of the distribution of scores in a population, the sampling distribution of sample means selected at random from that population will approach the shape of a normal distribution, as the number of samples in the sampling distribution increases.

FIGURE 6.3   The Central Limit Theorem

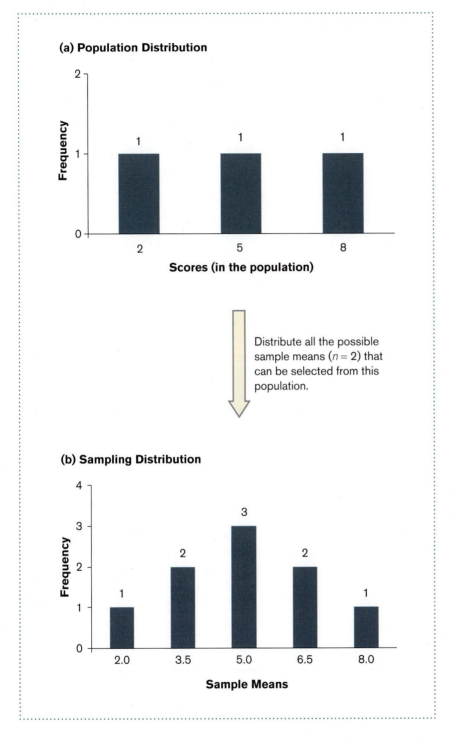

The hypothetical population has a nonmodal distribution (a), yet the possible sample means ($n = 2$) are approximately normally distributed (b).

In this formula, M is the sample mean in each possible sample, μ_M is the mean of the sampling distribution (this equals the population mean, $\mu_M = 5$), and N^n is the total number of possible samples that can be selected (nine possible samples). The variance when the population mean is $\mu_M = 5$ and $N^n = 9$ is as follows:

$$\sigma_M^2 = \frac{(2-5)^2}{9} + \frac{(3.5-5)^2}{9} + \frac{(3.5-5)^2}{9} + \frac{(5-5)^2}{9} + \frac{(5-5)^2}{9} + \frac{(5-5)^2}{9} + \frac{(6.5-5)^2}{9} + \frac{(6.5-5)^2}{9}$$

$$+ \frac{(8-5)^2}{9} = \frac{27}{9} = 3.0.$$

FYI

The standard error of the mean is the standard deviation of the sampling distribution of sample means.

The variance equals 3.0. The standard deviation of a sampling distribution is called the **standard error of the mean** (*SEM* or σ_M), or simply the **standard error** (*SE*). The standard error tells us how far possible sample means deviate from the value of the population mean. To compute the standard error, we take the square root of the variance:

$$\sigma_M = \sqrt{\sigma_M^2} = \sqrt{3.0} = 1.73.$$

The value 1.73 is the smallest possible value we could obtain for the standard error. If we used any value for the mean other than the population mean ($\mu = 5$) to compute the standard error, then the solution would be larger. In this way, all other possible values for the sample mean vary minimally from the population mean.

Overview of the Sample Mean

In all, three characteristics of the sample mean make it a good estimate of the value of the population mean:

1. The sample mean is an unbiased estimator. On average, the sample mean we obtain in a randomly selected sample will equal the value of the population mean.

2. A distribution of sample means follows the central limit theorem. That is, regardless of the shape of the distribution in a population, the distribution of sample means selected from the population will approach the shape of a normal distribution, as the number of samples in the sampling distribution increases.

3. A distribution of sample means has minimum variance. The sampling distribution of sample means will vary minimally from the value of the population mean.

The **standard error of the mean**, or **standard error**, is the standard deviation of a sampling distribution of sample means. It is the standard error or distance that sample mean values deviate from the value of the population mean.

6.4 THE STANDARD ERROR OF THE MEAN

In Section 6.3, we introduced that the standard error of the mean is the standard deviation of a sampling distribution of sample means. In the example of a hypothetical population with a mean of 5.0, we found that the variance of the sampling distribution of sample means was equal to

LEARNING CHECK 3

1. If a random sample is selected from a population with a mean equal to 15, then what can we expect the value of the sample mean to be on average?

2. A(n) _____ is any sample statistic obtained from a randomly selected sample that equals the value of its respective population parameter on average.

3. Suppose a population consists of a positively skewed distribution of scores. If we select all possible samples of size 10 from this population, then what will be the approximate shape of the sampling distribution of sample means?

4. What is the standard error of the mean (σ_M) when the variance of the sampling distribution of sample means (σ^2_M) is equal to (a) 4, (b) 144, and (c) 1,225?

5. The _____ states that regardless of the distribution of scores in a population, the sampling distribution of sample means selected from that population will approach the shape of a normal distribution, as the number of samples in the sampling distribution increases.

Answers: 1. $\mu_M = 15$; 2. Unbiased estimator; 3. Normal distribution; 4. (a) $\sqrt{4} = 2$, (b) $\sqrt{144} = 12$, (c) $\sqrt{1,225} = 35$; 5. Central limit theorem.

$\sigma^2_M = 3.0$. The standard error of the mean was equal to the square root of the variance, or $\sigma_M = 1.73$. In this section, we introduce a new formula to find the variance (σ^2_M) and standard error (σ_M) of a sampling distribution of sample means.

To compute the variance of the sampling distribution of sample means, divide the population variance (σ^2) by the sample size (n). If we substitute the population variance (6) and sample size (2) from the original example into the formula, we find that the variance of the sampling distribution of sample means is equal to 3.0:

$$\sigma^2_M = \frac{\sigma^2}{n} = \frac{6}{2} = 3.0.$$

This is the same value we computed in Section 6.3 for the variance of the sampling distribution of sample means. The standard error of the mean is the square root of the variance. We can write the shortcut formula as follows:

$$\sigma_M = \sqrt{\frac{\sigma^2}{n}} = \frac{\sigma}{\sqrt{n}}.$$

If we take the square root of the variance, we obtain the same value we computed in Section 6.3 for the standard error of the mean:

$$\sigma_M = \sqrt{3.0} = 1.73.$$

Researchers fully understand that when they select a sample, the mean they measure will not always be equal to the population mean. They

©iStockphoto.com/bo1982

FYI

To compute the standard error of the mean, divide the population standard deviation by the square root of the sample size.

understand that two random samples selected from the same population can produce different estimates of the same population mean, which is called **sampling error**. The standard error of the mean is a numeric measure of sampling error, with larger values indicating greater sampling error or greater differences that can exist from one sample to the next.

In Example 6.3, we apply the characteristics of the sample mean to distribute the mean and standard error of a sampling distribution.

Example 6.3

Participants in a random sample of 100 college students are asked to state the number of hours they spend studying during finals week. Among all college students at this school (the population), the mean study time is equal to 20 hours per week, with a standard deviation equal to 15 hours per week. Construct a sampling distribution of the mean.

To construct the sampling distribution, we must (1) identify the mean of the sampling distribution, (2) compute the standard error of the mean, and (3) distribute the possible sample means 3 *SEM* above and below the mean.

Because the sample mean is an unbiased estimator of the population mean, the mean of the sampling distribution is equal to the population mean. The mean of this sampling distribution is equal to 20. The standard error is the population standard deviation (15) divided by the square root of the sample size (100):

$$\sigma_M = \frac{\sigma}{\sqrt{n}} = \frac{15}{\sqrt{100}} = 1.50.$$

The sampling distribution of the sample mean for a sample of size 100 from this population is normal with a mean equal to 20 and a standard error equal to 1.50. We know the sampling distribution is normal because of the central limit theorem. Figure 6.4 shows this sampling distribution. From the empirical rule, we know that at least 95% of all sample means will be within 3 hours of the value of the population mean ($\mu = 20$). In other words, at least 95% of the sample means we could select from this population will be between $M = 17$ hours and $M = 23$ hours.

FYI

The larger the standard deviation in the population, the larger the standard error.

Sampling error is the extent to which sample means selected from the same population differ from one another. This difference, which occurs by chance, is measured by the standard error of the mean.

| **FIGURE 6.4** | The Sampling Distribution of Sample Means for Samples of Size 100 Selected From a Population With a Mean of 20 and Standard Deviation of 15 |

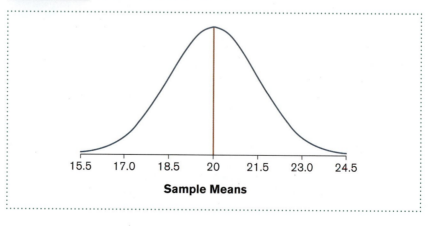

Sample Means

6.5 FACTORS THAT DECREASE STANDARD ERROR

The standard error can increase or decrease depending on the sample size and the value of the population standard deviation. First, as the population standard deviation (σ) decreases, the standard error decreases. That is, the less scores in a population deviate from the population mean, the less possible it is that sample means will deviate from the population mean. Suppose, for example, that we select samples of size 2 ($n = 2$) from one of five populations having a population standard deviation equal to $\sigma_1 = 4$, $\sigma_2 = 9$, $\sigma_3 = 16$, $\sigma_4 = 25$, and $\sigma_5 = 81$. Figure 6.5 shows that the standard error decreases as the population standard deviation decreases.

Second, as the sample size (n) increases, the standard error decreases. The larger the sample, the more data you collect, and the closer your estimate of the population mean will be. Suppose, for example, that we select samples of size 4 ($n = 4$), 9 ($n = 9$), 16 ($n = 16$), 25 ($n = 25$), and 81 ($n = 81$) from a single population with a standard deviation equal to 4. Figure 6.6 shows that the standard error decreases as the sample size increases. This result is called the **law of large numbers**.

FIGURE 6.5   Population Standard Deviation and *SEM*

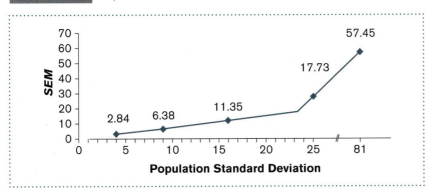

As the standard deviation in the population decreases, the standard error of the mean (*SEM*), or the distance that sample means deviate from the population mean, also decreases.

FIGURE 6.6   The Law of Large Numbers

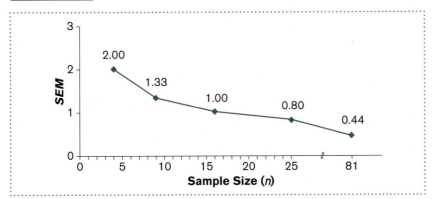

As the sample size increases, the standard error of the mean (*SEM*) decreases, so sample means deviate closer to the population mean as sample size increases.

FYI

The law of large numbers explains that the larger the sample size, the smaller the standard error.

The **law of large numbers** states that increasing the number of observations or samples in a study will decrease the standard error. Hence, larger samples are associated with closer estimates of the population mean on average.

6.6 SPSS in Focus:
Estimating the Standard Error of the Mean

Researchers rarely know the value of the population standard deviation, which is in the numerator of the formula for standard error. It is more common to estimate the standard error by substituting the sample standard deviation in place of the population standard deviation in the formula for standard error. SPSS makes this substitution to compute an estimate of standard error. The formula, which is discussed further in Chapter 8, is as follows:

$$s_M = \frac{s}{\sqrt{n}}.$$

SPSS is designed to estimate the standard error using this formula. To illustrate, suppose we measure the individual reaction times (in seconds) for a team of 10 firefighters to respond to an emergency call. The reaction times are 93, 66, 30, 44, 20, 100, 35, 58, 70, and 81. Let us use SPSS to estimate the standard error of these data:

FIGURE 6.7　The SPSS Dialog Box in Step 5

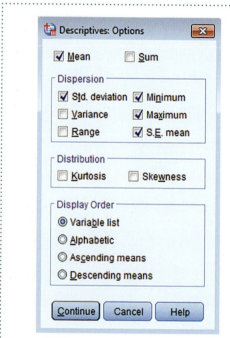

1. Click on the Variable View tab and enter *reaction* in the Name column. We will enter whole numbers, so reduce the value to 0 in the Decimals column.

2. Click on the Data View tab and enter the 10 values in the column labeled *reaction.*

3. Go to the menu bar and click Analyze, then Descriptive Statistics and Descriptives, to display a dialog box.

4. In the dialog box, select the *reaction* variable and click the arrow to move it into the box labeled Variable(s): to the right. Click the Options . . . tab to bring up a new dialog box.

5. In the new dialog box, shown in Figure 6.7, select S.E. mean in the Dispersion box and click Continue.

6. Select OK, or select Paste and click the Run command.

The SPSS output table, shown in Table 6.4, gives the value for the standard error as 8.596. We can double-check that the value of the standard error is correct because the SPSS output table also gives us the value of the sample standard deviation and sample size. When we enter these values into the formula for standard error, we obtain the same result given in the table:

$$\text{Standard error} = \frac{s}{\sqrt{n}} = \frac{27.183}{\sqrt{10}} \approx 8.596.$$

TABLE 6.4   The SPSS Output Table

	N Statistic	Minimum Statistic	Maximum Statistic	Mean Statistic	Std. Error	Std. Deviation Statistic
					The value of standard error	
reaction	10	20	100	59.70	8.596	27.183
Valid N (listwise)	10					

Descriptive Statistics

The standard error of the mean is circled in the table.

6.7   APA IN FOCUS:
REPORTING THE STANDARD ERROR

The standard error of the mean is often reported in research journals using the American Psychological Association (APA) guidelines. The *Publication Manual of the American Psychological Association* (APA, 2010) recommends any combination of three ways to report the standard error: in the text, in a table, or in a graph.

Reporting *SEM* in the text. The standard error can be reported directly in the text. For example, DeVoe and House (2012) reported the effects of thinking about money on happiness as follows:

> Those participants randomly assigned to calculate their expected hourly wage showed no increase in happiness after the leisure period ($M = 3.47$, $SEM = 1.12$) compared to before the leisure period ($M = 3.56$, $SEM = 0.99$). (p. 468)

Reporting *SEM* in a table. The standard error can be reported in a table. For example, the standard error can be displayed as $M \pm SEM$, as shown in Table 6.5. The table provides a concise way to summarize the mean and standard error of many measures.

Reporting *SEM* in a graph. The standard error can also be reported in a graph. The standard error is displayed as a vertical bar extending above and below each mean plot, as shown in Figure 6.8, or mean bar, as shown in Figure 6.9.

TABLE 6.5   Reporting *SEM* in a Table

Life Satisfaction Score	Responses (*M ± SEM*)
Home without therapy	5.05 ± 0.08
Home with mono-disciplinary therapy	4.67 ± 0.14
Home with outpatient rehabilitation program	5.09 ± 0.15
Clinical rehabilitation in a nursing home	4.08 ± 0.28
Clinical rehabilitation in a rehabilitation center	5.06 ± 0.06

Participant responses on a scale from –3 (*completely disagree*) to +3 (*completely agree*) to statements concerning product samples in a buffet. Means are given plus and minus *SEM*.

Source: Adapted from Oosterveer, Mishre, van Oort, Bodde, and Aerden (2017).

(Continued)

(Continued)

FIGURE 6.8 Using Error Bars in a Line Graph

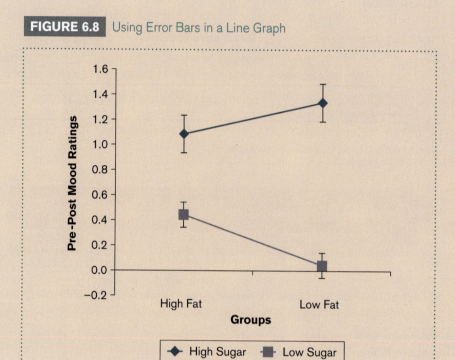

Mean change in ratings of mood after viewing images of foods that were high or low in fat and high or low in sugar. More positive ratings indicate more positive mood change. Vertical lines represent *SEM*.

Source: Adapted from Privitera, Antonelli, and Creary (2013).

FIGURE 6.9 Using Error Bars in a Bar Graph

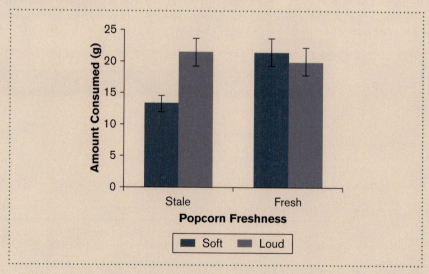

Total amount consumed in grams of popcorn (stale versus fresh) while watching a movie clip that was played at differing volumes (soft, loud). Vertical lines represent *SEM*.

Source: Adapted from Privitera, Diaz, and Haas (2014).

LEARNING CHECK 4

1. Assuming the population standard deviation is known, state the formula for the standard error of the mean in words.

2. A psychologist selects a sample of 36 children from a population with a standard deviation of 12. Compute the standard error for this example.

3. Increasing the _____ will decrease the standard error.

4. Decreasing the _____ will decrease the standard error.

5. What are three ways that the standard error is reported in research journals?

Answers: 1. It is the population standard deviation divided by the square root of the sample size; 2. $\sigma_M = \frac{12}{\sqrt{36}} = 2.0$; 3. Sample size; 4. Population standard deviation; 5. The standard error is reported in the text of an article, in a table, or in a graph.

6.8 STANDARD NORMAL TRANSFORMATIONS WITH SAMPLING DISTRIBUTIONS

We can find the probability of obtaining any sample mean using the standard normal distribution because we know from the central limit theorem that the sampling distribution of the mean is approximately normal. We can thus convert any sampling distribution with any mean and standard error to a standard normal distribution by applying the z transformation (introduced in Chapter 5). Using the notation for a sampling distribution, the z transformation can be stated as follows:

$$z = \frac{M - \mu_M}{\sigma_M}.$$

Because the mean of the sampling distribution of the mean, μ_M, equals the population mean, μ, we can also write the z transformation as follows:

$$z = \frac{M - \mu}{\sigma_M}.$$

To locate the proportion, and therefore the probability, of selecting a sample mean in any sampling distribution, we follow two steps:

Step 1: Transform a sample mean (M) into a z score.

Step 2: Locate the corresponding proportion for the z score in the unit normal table.

In Example 6.4, we follow these steps to locate the probability of obtaining a sample mean from a given population with a known mean and variance.

FYI

The z transformation is used to determine the likelihood of measuring a particular sample mean, from a population with a given mean and variance.

Example 6.4

©iStockphoto.com/KenanOlgun

The GRE General Test, a standardized exam required by many graduate schools for applying to their graduate programs, was recently revised. For two sections in the revised test, the verbal reasoning and quantitative reasoning sections, the new scoring system is based on scores that range from 130 to 170 on each section. Based on population-based data of all examinees who tested between July 2012 and June 2015, Table 6.6 lists an estimate for the mean and standard deviation of scores in the population. Using these data, what is the probability of selecting a random sample of 100 college students who scored a mean of 153 or better (a) on the verbal section and (b) on the quantitative section?

TABLE 6.6   An Estimate for the Mean and Standard Deviation of GRE Scores in the General Population

GRE Section	μ	σ
Verbal	151	9
Quantitative	152	10

Source: Adapted from data provided at http://www.ets.org/s/gre/pdf/concordance_information.pdf (Educational Testing Service, 2017).

We can apply the steps to find the proportion under the normal curve for each section of the GRE General Test.

Verbal section. To compute the z transformation, we need to know M, μ, and σ_M:

1. M is the sample mean: $M = 153$.

2. μ is the mean of the population, which is also the mean of the sampling distribution of sample means: $\mu = \mu_M = 151$.

3. σ_M is the standard error and is calculated as $\dfrac{\sigma}{\sqrt{n}} = \dfrac{9}{\sqrt{100}} = 0.9$.

Step 1: To transform a sample mean (M) to a z score, we compute a z transformation. In this example, $M = 153$. The z transformation is as follows:

$$z = \frac{153\text{-}151}{0.9} = 2.22.$$

Step 2: In the unit normal table, the probability of selecting a sample mean of 153 or better on the verbal section (toward the tail) is $p = .0132$.

Quantitative section. To compute the z transformation, we again need to know M, μ, and σ_M:

1. M is the sample mean: $M = 153$.

2. μ is the mean of the population, which is also the mean of the sampling distribution of sample means: $\mu = \mu_M = 152$.

3. σ_M is the standard error and is calculated as $\frac{\sigma}{\sqrt{n}} = \frac{10}{\sqrt{100}} = 1.0$.

Step 1: To transform a sample mean (M) to a z score, we compute a z transformation. In this example, $M = 153$. The z transformation is as follows:

$$z = \frac{153-152}{1} = 1.00.$$

Step 2: In the unit normal table, the probability of selecting a sample mean of 153 or better on the quantitative section (toward the tail) is $p = .1587$.

In this example, the probability of selecting a sample mean of 153 or better on the verbal section is very small ($p = .0132$), whereas the probability of selecting a sample mean of 153 or better on the quantitative section is much higher ($p = .1587$). We can use the z transformation to locate the probability of obtaining any sample mean because the sampling distribution of the mean always tends toward a normal distribution.

LEARNING CHECK 5

1. What formula is used to find the probability of obtaining a sample mean from a given population?

2. Compute a z transformation to find the z score, given the following measures: $\mu = 5$, $\sigma_M = 1.5$, $M = 8$.

3. Explain the following statement in words: $\mu_M = \mu$.

Answers: 1. The standard normal transformation or z transformation; 2. $z = \frac{8-5}{1.5} = 2.00$; 3. The mean of the sampling distribution of sample means is equal to the value of the population mean.

••• CHAPTER SUMMARY ORGANIZED BY LEARNING OBJECTIVE

LO 1:   **Define *sampling distribution*.**

- A sampling distribution is a distribution of all sample means or sample variances that could be obtained in samples of a given size from the same population.

LO 2:   **Compare theoretical and experimental sampling strategies.**

- The theoretical sampling strategy is a sampling method in which we sample with replacement and the order in which a participant is selected matters.

- Sampling with replacement is a method of sampling in which each participant or item selected is replaced before the next draw.

- The experimental sampling strategy is a sampling method in which we sample without replacement and the order in which a participant is selected does not matter.

- Sampling without replacement is a method of sampling in which each participant or item selected is not replaced before the next draw.

LO 3–4:   **Identify three characteristics of the sampling distribution of the sample mean; calculate the mean and standard error of a sampling distribution of the**

sample mean and draw the shape of this distribution.

- The sample mean has the following three characteristics:

  a. The sample mean is an unbiased estimator. On average, the sample mean we obtain in a randomly selected sample will equal the value of the population mean.

  b. A distribution of sample means follows the central limit theorem. Regardless of the shape of the distribution in a population, the distribution of sample means selected at random from the population will approach the shape of a normal distribution, as the number of samples in the sampling distribution increases.

  c. A distribution of sample means has minimum variance. The sampling distribution of the mean will vary minimally from the value of the population mean.

- The variance of the sampling distribution of sample means equals the population variance divided by the sample size:

$$\sigma_M^2 = \frac{\sigma^2}{n}.$$

- The standard error of the mean is the standard deviation of the sampling distribution of the sample means. It is the square root of the variance:

$$\sigma_M = \sqrt{\sigma_M^2} = \sqrt{\frac{\sigma^2}{n}} = \frac{\sigma}{\sqrt{n}}.$$

LO 5:   **Explain the relationship between standard error, standard deviation, and sample size.**

- As the population standard deviation (σ) increases, standard error increases. Hence, the farther scores in a population deviate from the mean in a population, the farther possible

sample means can deviate from the value of the population mean.

- As the sample size (n) increases, standard error decreases. Hence, the more data you collect, the closer your estimate of the value of the population mean. This relationship is explained by the law of large numbers.

LO 6:   **Compute z transformations for the sampling distribution of the sample mean.**

- Using the notation for sample means, the z transformation formula can be stated as follows:

$$z = \frac{M - \mu_M}{\sigma_M} \text{ or } z = \frac{M - \mu}{\sigma_M}.$$

- To locate the proportion of area, and therefore probabilities, of sample means in any sampling distribution, we follow two steps:

  Step 1: Transform a sample mean (M) into a z score.

  Step 2: Locate the corresponding proportion for the z score in the unit normal table.

LO 7:   **Summarize the standard error of the mean in APA format.**

- The standard error is most often reported in the text, in a table, or in a graph. When data are reported in the text or in a table, they are usually reported with the value of the mean. In a graph, the standard error is displayed as a vertical bar extending above and below each mean plot or mean bar.

LO 8:   **Compute the estimate for the standard error of the mean using SPSS.**

- SPSS can be used to compute an estimate of the standard error of the mean. An estimate for the standard error is computed using the Analyze, Descriptive Statistics, and Descriptives options in the menu bar. These actions will bring up a dialog box that will allow you to identify your variable, select Options, and choose the S.E. mean option to compute an estimate of the standard error (for more details, see Section 6.6).

• • • KEY TERMS

central limit theorem

law of large numbers

sample design

sampling distribution

sampling error

sampling with replacement

sampling without replacement

standard error

standard error of the mean

• • • END-OF-CHAPTER PROBLEMS

Factual Problems

1. What is a sampling distribution?

2. Explain how conditional probabilities are related to sampling without replacement.

3. Distinguish between sampling with replacement and sampling without replacement.

4. Distinguish between sampling where order matters and sampling where order does not matter.

5. The sample mean is an unbiased estimator of the population mean. Explain this statement.

6. Define the central limit theorem.

7. Explain why the following statement is true: $\mu = \mu_M$.

8. Can the mean of a sampling distribution be a negative value? Explain.

9. The sampling distribution of the sample mean approximates the shape of what type of distribution?

10. What values do you need to know to compute the formula for standard error?

11. The standard error measure is the standard deviation for what type of distribution?

12. How would the standard error change if (a) the population standard deviation increased and (b) the sample size increased?

Concept and Application Problems

13. A statistics instructor wants to measure the effectiveness of his teaching skills in a class of 102 students ($N = 102$). He selects students by waiting at the door to the classroom prior to his lecture and pulling aside every third student to give him or her a questionnaire.

    (a) Is this sample design an example of random sampling? Explain.

    (b) Assuming that all students attend his class that day, how many students will he select to complete the questionnaire?

14. A local high school is interested in studying how teacher perceptions of students, as being intelligent or not, affect the success of freshman students in the classroom. The school creates an Excel spreadsheet listing all freshman students in alphabetical order and places their names into one of two columns. All students listed in the second column are selected to participate in this study. Is this sample design an example of random sampling? Explain.

15. A support group has 12 patients who attend each week. Suppose 3 patients are selected at random to participate in a study. How many different samples of this size can be selected from this population of 12 patients using (a) experimental sampling and (b) theoretical sampling?

16. Using the theoretical sampling strategy, how many samples of size 4 ($n = 4$) can be drawn from a population of size:

    (a) $N = 5$? (b) $N = 8$? (c) $N = 16$? (d) $N = 50$?

17. Using the experimental sampling strategy, how many samples of size 3 ($n = 3$) can be drawn from a population of size:

    (a) $N = 5$?   (b) $N = 6$?   (c) $N = 7$?   (d) $N = 8$?

18. The sample mean is an unbiased estimator of the population mean. What do we expect the sample mean to be equal to when the population mean is equal to:

    (a) $\mu = 8$?   (b) $\mu = 0$?   (c) $\mu = 20$?

    (d) $\mu = \infty$?   (e) $\mu = -40$?   (f) $\mu = 0.03$?

19. Using the central limit theorem, what is the distribution of sample means when the population distribution is:

    (a) rectangular?

    (b) normal?

    (c) positively skewed?

    (d) nonmodal?

    (e) multimodal?

    (f) negatively skewed?

20. State whether each of the following statements is true or false. If false, then explain what would make the statement true.

    (a) The central limit theorem explains why the mean is always at the center of a distribution.

    (b) The standard error of the mean is the standard deviation of a sampling distribution of sample means.

    (c) The mean of a sampling distribution is equal to the population mean from which samples are selected.

21. State whether each of the following statements concerning the sample mean is true or false. If false, then explain what would make the statement true.

    (a) The value of the sample mean equals the population mean on average.

    (b) The value of the sample mean can vary from sample to sample.

(c) There is more than a 5% probability of selecting a sample mean that is farther than 2 SEM from the population mean.

(d) The sampling distribution of sample means is approximately normally distributed.

22. A population with a positively skewed distribution of scores has a mean of 5 and a standard deviation of 4.

    (a) What is the shape of the sampling distribution of the mean for this population?

    (b) What is the mean of the sampling distribution for this population?

    (c) Suppose a researcher selects two samples from this population and records a sample mean of 3.5 in each sample. If Sample A is $n = 12$ and Sample B is $n = 20$, in which sample will a sample mean of 3.5 be less likely? Explain.

23. A population is normally distributed with a mean of 56 and a standard deviation of 12.

    (a) What is the mean of the sampling distribution (μ_M) for this population?

    (b) If a sample of 36 participants is selected from this population, what is the standard error of the mean (σ_M)?

    (c) Sketch the shape of this distribution with $M \pm 3$ SEM.

24. A population is normally distributed with a mean of –30 and a standard deviation of 4.

    (a) What is the mean of the sampling distribution (μ_M) for this population?

    (b) If a sample of 16 participants is selected from this population, what is the standard error of the mean (σ_M)?

    (c) Sketch the shape of this distribution with $M \pm 3$ SEM.

25. A population of scores is normally distributed with a standard deviation equal to 7. State whether the standard error will increase, decrease, or remain unchanged if the value of the population standard deviation is changed to:

    (a) $\sigma = 10$ (b) $\sigma = 2$ (c) $\sigma = \dfrac{28}{4}$

    (d) $\sigma = 0$ (e) $\sigma = 7.5$ (f) $\sigma = \dfrac{4}{20}$

26. A sample of 26 scores is selected from a normally distributed population. State whether the standard error will increase or decrease if the sample size is changed to:

(a) $n = 36$ (b) $n = 5$ (c) $n = 28$ (d) $n = 25$

Problems in Research

27. **Sampling from the population.** Olesen, Butterworth, Leach, Kelaher, and Pirkis (2013) selected a sample of 8,315 respondents from a population of about 22 million people who live in Australia to study the effects of mental health on employment status.

    (a) Set up the calculation used to determine how many possible samples of 8,315 respondents are possible from this population of 22 million people using theoretical sampling.

    (b) Would more samples be possible if the researchers used experimental sampling?

28. **Classroom assessment: Sampling and the population.** Ryan (2006) reported about the effectiveness of an assignment given to students during a statistics class. The in-class assignment was aimed at helping students understand sampling distributions. In this study, participants selected 120 samples of size 3 from a population of 5 scores (0, 0, 0, 3, and 6) using the theoretical sampling strategy.

    (a) How many possible samples can be drawn from this population?

    (b) What is the population mean?

    (c) What is the population standard deviation?

29. **Classroom assessment: Central limit theorem.** In the Ryan (2006) study described in Question 28, participants selected 120 samples of size 3 from a population of 5 scores (0, 0, 0, 3, and 6) using theoretical sampling. Based on this example,

    (a) What is the shape of the population distribution? *Hint:* Graph the frequency distribution of the population of scores: 0, 0, 0, 3, and 6.

    (b) What is the shape of the sampling distribution of sample means? *Hint:* You do not need calculations to answer this question.

30. **Classroom assessment: Standard error.** In the Ryan (2006) study described in Question 28, participants selected 120 samples of size 3 from a population of 5 scores (0, 0, 0, 3, and 6) using theoretical sampling. Ryan reported the mean and standard error for the theoretical sampling distribution listed in the following table. Compute the formula for standard error to confirm the value of the standard error shown in the table.

	Theoretical Sampling Distribution
Mean	1.80
Standard error	1.39

31. **Physical activity and enhanced mood.** Williams, Dunsiger, Jennings, and Marcus (2012) conducted a study to test how enhanced mood during exercise can increase the likelihood of physical activity in the future. They reported that at 6 months of physical activity, mood scores (rated on a scale from −5 to +5) after a walking exercise were 3.3 ± 1.2, and at 12 months, mood scores after a walking exercise were 3.3 ± 1.3 (mean ± standard error). Assuming these data are normally distributed, use the steps to conduct a z transformation to determine the following probabilities:

    (a) What is the probability that a sample mean selected from this population would show no change (0) or a negative change (less than 0) at 6 months of physical activity?

    (b) What is the probability that a sample mean selected from this population would show no change (0) or a negative change (less than 0) at 12 months of physical activity?

32. **The importance of sampling distributions.** Turner and Dabney (2015) stated, "Sampling distributions play a key role in the process of statistical inference" (p. 23). Explain what the researchers meant by this statement.

Answers for even numbers are in Appendix D.

Sharpen your skills with **SAGE edge at edge.sagepub.com/priviteraess2e**

SAGE edge for Students provides a personalized approach to help you accomplish your coursework goals in an easy-to-use learning environment.

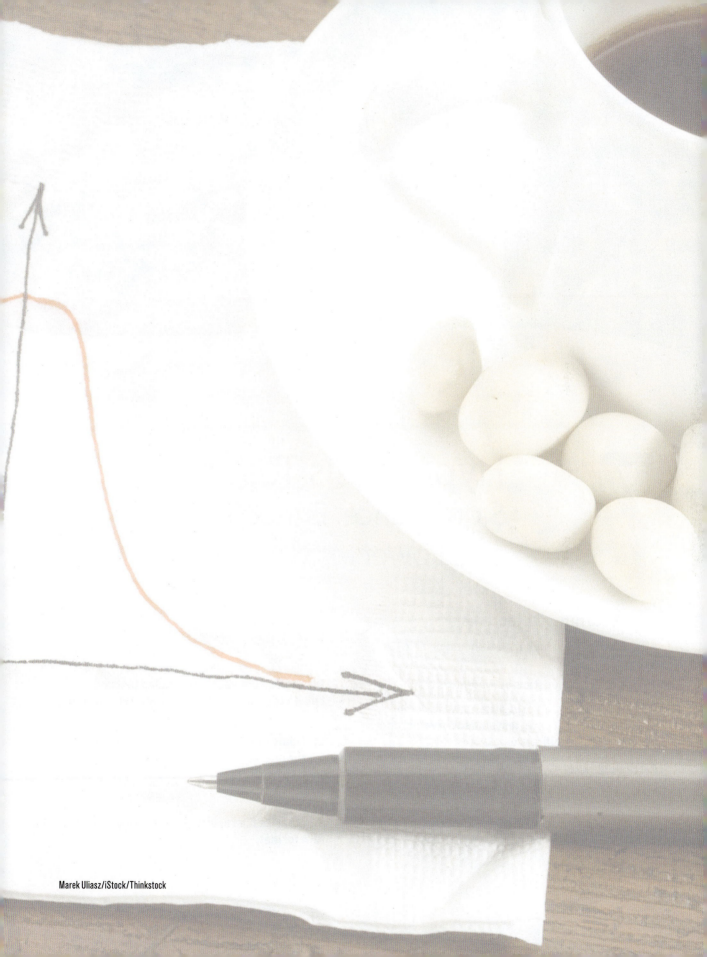

Marek Uliasz/iStock/Thinkstock

cosmin4000/iStock/Thinkstock

7

Hypothesis Testing
Significance, Effect Size, and Power

• • • **Learning Objectives**

After reading this chapter, you should be able to:

1. Identify the four steps of hypothesis testing.

2. Define null hypothesis, alternative hypothesis, level of significance, test statistic, *p* value, and statistical significance.

3. Define Type I error and Type II error, and identify the type of error that researchers control.

4. Calculate the one-sample *z* test and interpret the results.

5. Distinguish between a one-tailed test and a two-tailed test, and explain why a Type III error is possible only with one-tailed tests.

6. Elucidate effect size and compute a Cohen's *d* for the one-sample *z* test.

7. Define *power* and identify six factors that influence power.

8. Summarize the results of a one-sample *z* test in APA format.

The word *hypothesis* is loosely used in everyday language to describe an educated guess. We often informally state hypotheses about behaviors (e.g., who is the most outgoing among your friends) and events (e.g., which team will win the big game). Informally stating hypotheses in everyday language helps us describe or organize our understanding of the behaviors and events we experience from day to day.

In science, hypotheses are stated and tested more formally with the purpose of acquiring knowledge. The value of understanding the basic structure of the scientific process requires an understanding of how researchers test their hypotheses. Behavioral science is about understanding behaviors and events. You are in many ways a behavioral scientist in that you already hypothesize about many behaviors and events, albeit informally. Formally, hypothesis testing in science is similar to a board game, which has many rules to control, manage, and organize how you are allowed to move game pieces on a game board. Most board games, for example, have rules that tell you how many spaces you can move on the game board at most at a time, and what to do if you pick up a certain card or land on a certain spot on the game board. The rules, in essence, define the game. Each board game makes most sense if players follow the rules.

Likewise, in science, we ultimately want to gain an understanding of the behaviors and events we observe. The steps we follow in hypothesis testing allow us to gain this understanding and draw conclusions from our observations with certainty. In a board game, we follow rules to establish a winner; in hypothesis testing, we follow rules or steps to establish conclusions from the observations we make. In this chapter, we explore the nature of hypothesis testing as it is used in science and the types of information it provides about the observations we make.

Master the content.

edge.sagepub.com/priviteraess2e

• • • Chapter Outline

7.1 INFERENTIAL STATISTICS AND HYPOTHESIS TESTING

We use inferential statistics because it allows us to observe samples to learn more about the behavior in populations that are often too large or inaccessible to observe. We use samples because we know how they are related to populations. For example, suppose the average score on a standardized exam in a given population is 150. In Chapter 6, we showed that the sample mean is an unbiased estimator of the population mean—if we select a random sample from a population, then on average the value of the sample mean will equal the value of the population mean. In our example, if we select a random sample from this population with a mean of 150, then, on average, the value of a sample mean will equal 150. On the basis of the central limit theorem, we know that the probability of selecting any other sample mean value from this population is normally distributed.

In behavioral research, we select samples to learn more about populations of interest to us. In terms of the mean, we measure a sample mean to learn more about the mean in a population. Therefore, we will use the sample mean to describe the population mean. We begin by stating a **hypothesis** about the value of a population mean, and then we select a sample and measure the mean in that sample. On average, the value of the sample mean will equal that of the population mean. The larger the difference or discrepancy between the sample mean and population mean, the less likely it will be that the value of the population mean we hypothesized is correct. This type of experimental situation, using the example of standardized exam scores, is illustrated in Figure 7.1.

A **hypothesis** is a statement or proposed explanation for an observation, a phenomenon, or a scientific problem that can be tested using the research method. A hypothesis is often a statement about the value for a parameter in a population.

Hypothesis testing or **significance testing** is a method for testing a claim or hypothesis about a parameter in a population, using data measured in a sample. In this method, we test a hypothesis by determining the likelihood that a sample statistic would be selected if the hypothesis regarding the population parameter were true.

FIGURE 7.1   The Sampling Distribution for a Population With a Mean Equal to 150

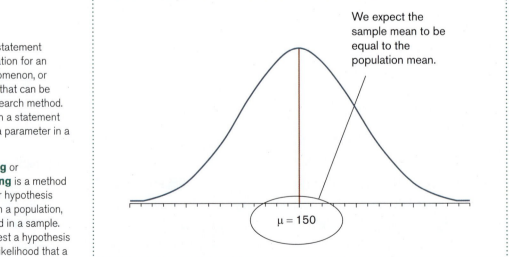

We expect the sample mean to be equal to the population mean.

μ = 150

If 150 is the correct population mean, then the sample mean will equal 150, on average, with outcomes farther from the population mean being less and less likely to occur.

The method of evaluating samples to learn more about characteristics in a given population is called **hypothesis testing**. Hypothesis testing is really a systematic way to test claims or ideas about a group or population. To illustrate, let us use a simple example concerning social media use. According to estimates reported by Mediakix (2016), the average consumer spends roughly 120 minutes (or 2 hours) a day on social media. Suppose we want to test if pre-millennial-generation consumers use social media comparably to the average consumer. To make a test, we record the time (in minutes) that a sample of pre-millennial consumers use social media per day, and compare this to the average of 120 minutes per day that all consumers (the population) use social media. The mean we measure for these pre-millennial consumers is a sample mean. We can then compare the mean in our sample to the population mean for all consumers ($\mu = 120$ minutes).

The method of hypothesis testing can be summarized in four steps. We describe each of these four steps in greater detail in Section 7.2.

1. To begin, we identify a hypothesis or claim that we feel should be tested. For example, we decide to test whether the mean number of minutes per day that pre-millennial consumers spend on social media is 120 minutes per day (i.e., the average for all consumers).

2. We select a criterion upon which we decide whether the hypothesis being tested should be accepted or not. For example, the hypothesis is whether or not pre-millennial consumers spend 120 minutes using social media per day. If pre-millennial consumers use social media similar to the average consumer, then we expect the sample mean will be about 120 minutes. If pre-millennial consumers spend more or less than 120 minutes using social media per day, then we expect the sample mean will be some value much lower or higher than 120 minutes. However, at what point do we decide that the discrepancy between the sample mean and 120 minutes (i.e., the population mean) is so big that we can reject the notion that pre-millennial consumers use social media similar to the average consumer? In Step 2 of hypothesis testing, we answer this question.

3. Select a sample from the population and measure the sample mean. For example, we can select a sample of 1,000 pre-millennial consumers and measure the mean time (in minutes) that they use social media per day.

4. Compare what we observe in the sample to what we expect to observe if the claim we are testing—that pre-millennial consumers spend 120 minutes using social media per day—is true. We expect the sample mean will be around 120 minutes. The smaller the discrepancy between the sample mean and population mean, the more likely we are to decide that pre-millennial consumers use social media similar to the average consumer (i.e., about 120 minutes per day). The larger the discrepancy between the sample mean and population mean, the more likely we are to decide to reject that claim.

Hypothesis testing or **significance testing** is a method for testing a claim or hypothesis about a parameter in a population, using data measured in a sample. In this method, we test a hypothesis by determining the likelihood that a sample statistic would be selected if the hypothesis regarding the population parameter were true.

LEARNING CHECK 1

1. On average, what do we expect the sample mean to be equal to?

2. True or false: Researchers select a sample from a population to learn more about characteristics in that sample.

Answers: 1. The population mean; 2. False. Researchers select a sample from a population to learn more about characteristics in the population from which the sample was selected.

7.2 FOUR STEPS TO HYPOTHESIS TESTING

The goal of hypothesis testing is to determine the likelihood that a sample statistic would be selected if the hypothesis regarding a population parameter were true. In this section, we describe the four steps of hypothesis testing that were briefly introduced in Section 7.1:

Step 1: State the hypotheses.

Step 2: Set the criteria for a decision.

Step 3: Compute the test statistic.

Step 4: Make a decision.

FYI

Hypothesis testing is a method of testing whether hypotheses about a population parameter are likely to be true.

Step 1: State the hypotheses. We begin by stating the value of a population mean in a **null hypothesis**, which we presume is true. For the example of social media use, we can state the null hypothesis that pre-millennial consumers use an average of 120 minutes of social media per day:

$$H_0: \mu = 120.$$

This is a starting point so that we can decide whether or not the null hypothesis is likely to be true, similar to the presumption of innocence in a courtroom. When a defendant is on trial, the jury starts by assuming that the defendant is innocent. The basis of the decision is to determine whether this assumption is true. Likewise, in hypothesis testing, we start by assuming that the hypothesis or claim we are testing is true. This is stated in the null hypothesis. The basis of the decision is to determine whether this assumption is likely to be true.

The **null hypothesis (H_0)**, stated as the *null*, is a statement about a population parameter, such as the population mean, that is assumed to be true, and a hypothesis test is structured to decide whether or not to reject this assumption.

An **alternative hypothesis (H_1)** is a statement that directly contradicts a null hypothesis by stating that the actual value of a population parameter is less than, greater than, or not equal to the value stated in the null hypothesis.

The key reason we are testing the null hypothesis is because we think it is wrong. We state what we think is wrong about the null hypothesis in an **alternative hypothesis**. In a courtroom, the defendant is assumed to be innocent (this is the null hypothesis so to speak), so the burden is on a prosecutor to conduct a trial to show evidence that the defendant is not innocent. In a similar way, we assume the null hypothesis is true, placing the burden on the researcher to conduct a study to show evidence that the null hypothesis is unlikely to be true. Regardless, we always make a decision about the null hypothesis (that it is likely or unlikely to be true). The alternative hypothesis is needed for Step 2.

The null and alternative hypotheses must encompass all possibilities for the population mean. For the example of social media use, we can state that the value in the null hypothesis is not equal to ($\neq$) 120 minutes. In this way, the null hypothesis value ($\mu = 120$ minutes) and the alternative hypothesis value ($\mu \neq 120$) encompass all possible values for the population mean. If we believe that pre-millennial consumers use more than (>) or less than (<) 120 minutes of social media per day, then we can make a "greater than" or "less than" statement in the alternative hypothesis—this type of alternative is described in Example 7.2 (page 206). Regardless of the decision alternative, the null and alternative hypotheses must encompass all possibilities for the value of the population mean.

FYI

In hypothesis testing, we conduct a study to test whether the null hypothesis is likely to be true.

MAKING SENSE TESTING THE NULL HYPOTHESIS

A decision made in hypothesis testing relates to the null hypothesis. This means two things in terms of making a decision:

1. Decisions are made about the null hypothesis. Using the courtroom analogy, a jury decides whether a defendant is guilty or not guilty. The jury does not make a decision of guilty or *innocent* because the defendant is assumed to be innocent. All evidence presented in a trial is to show that a defendant is guilty. The evidence either shows guilt (decision: guilty) or does not (decision: not guilty). In a similar way, the null hypothesis is assumed to be correct. A researcher conducts a study showing evidence that this assumption is unlikely (we reject the null hypothesis) or fails to do so (we retain the null hypothesis).

2. The bias is to do nothing. Using the courtroom analogy, for the same reason the courts would rather let the guilty go free than send the innocent to prison, researchers would rather do nothing (accept previous notions of truth stated by a null hypothesis) than make statements that are not correct. For this reason, we assume the null hypothesis is correct, thereby placing the burden on the researcher to demonstrate that the null hypothesis is not likely to be correct. Keep in mind, however, that when we retain the null hypothesis, this does not mean that the null hypothesis is correct. Instead, it means that there is insufficient evidence to reject it; it is not possible to *prove* the null hypothesis.

Step 2: Set the criteria for a decision. To set the criteria for a decision, we state the **level of significance** for a hypothesis test. This is similar to the criterion that jurors use in a criminal trial. Jurors decide whether the evidence presented shows guilt *beyond a reasonable doubt* (this is the criterion). Likewise, in hypothesis testing, we collect data to test whether or not the null hypothesis is retained, based on the likelihood of selecting a sample mean from a population (the likelihood is the criterion). The likelihood or level of significance is typically set at 5% in behavioral research studies. When the probability of obtaining a sample mean would be less than 5% if the null hypothesis were true, then we conclude that the sample we selected is too unlikely, and thus we reject the null hypothesis.

The alternative hypothesis is identified so that the criterion can be specifically stated. Remember that the sample mean will equal the population mean on average if the null hypothesis is true. All other possible values of the sample mean are normally distributed (central limit theorem). The empirical rule tells us that at least 95% of all sample means fall within

Level of significance, or **significance level**, is a criterion of judgment upon which a decision is made regarding the value stated in a null hypothesis. The criterion is based on the probability of obtaining a statistic measured in a sample if the value stated in the null hypothesis were true.

FYI

In behavioral science, the criterion or level of significance is typically set at 5%. When the probability of obtaining a sample mean would be less than 5% if the null hypothesis were true, then we reject the value stated in the null hypothesis.

The **test statistic** is a mathematical formula that identifies how far or how many standard deviations a sample outcome is from the value stated in a null hypothesis. It allows researchers to determine the likelihood of obtaining sample outcomes if the null hypothesis were true. The value of the test statistic is used to make a decision regarding a null hypothesis.

about 2 standard deviations (*SD*) of the population mean, meaning that there is less than a 5% probability of obtaining a sample mean that is beyond approximately 2 *SD* from the population mean. For the example of social media use, we can look for the probability of obtaining a sample mean beyond 2 *SD* in the upper tail (greater than 120), the lower tail (less than 120), or both tails (not equal to 120). Figure 7.2 shows the three decision alternatives for a hypothesis test; to conduct a hypothesis test, you choose only one alternative. How to choose an alternative is described in this chapter. No matter what test you compute, the null and alternative hypotheses must encompass all possibilities for the population mean.

Step 3: Compute the test statistic. Suppose we observe the sample and record a sample mean equal to 100 minutes (*M* = 100) that pre-millennial consumers use social media per day. Of course, we did not observe everyone in the population, so to make a decision, we need to evaluate how likely this sample outcome is if the population mean stated in the null hypothesis (120 minutes per day) is true. To determine this likelihood, we use a **test statistic**, which tells us how far, or how many standard deviations, a sample mean is from the population mean. The larger the value of the test statistic, the farther the distance, or number of standard deviations, a sample mean outcome is from the population mean stated in the null hypothesis. The value of the test statistic is used to make a decision in Step 4.

FIGURE 7.2   The Three Decision Alternatives for a Hypothesis Test

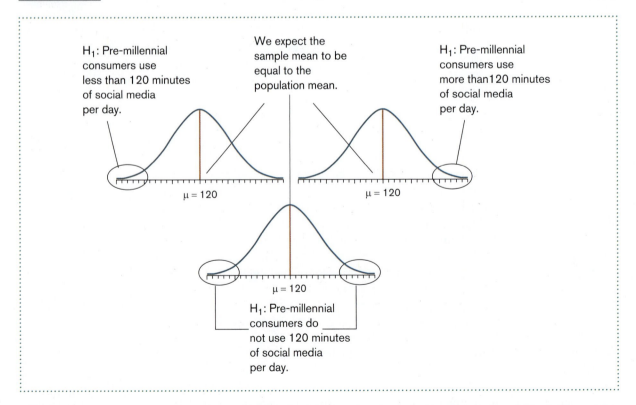

H_1: Pre-millennial consumers use less than 120 minutes of social media per day.

We expect the sample mean to be equal to the population mean.

H_1: Pre-millennial consumers use more than 120 minutes of social media per day.

$\mu = 120$

$\mu = 120$

$\mu = 120$

H_1: Pre-millennial consumers do not use 120 minutes of social media per day.

Although a decision alternative can be stated in only one tail, the null and alternative hypotheses should encompass all possibilities for the population mean.

Step 4: Make a decision. We use the value of the test statistic to make a decision about the null hypothesis. The decision is based on the probability of obtaining a sample mean, given that the value stated in the null hypothesis is true. If the probability of obtaining a sample mean is less than or equal to 5% when the null hypothesis is true, then the decision is to reject the null hypothesis. If the probability of obtaining a sample mean is greater than 5% when the null hypothesis is true, then the decision is to retain the null hypothesis. In sum, there are two decisions a researcher can make:

1. Reject the null hypothesis. The sample mean is associated with a low probability of occurrence when the null hypothesis is true. For this decision, we conclude that the value stated in the null hypothesis is wrong; it is rejected.

2. Retain the null hypothesis. The sample mean is associated with a high probability of occurrence when the null hypothesis is true. For this decision, we conclude that there is insufficient evidence to reject the null hypothesis; this does not mean that the null hypothesis is correct. It is not possible to *prove* the null hypothesis.

The probability of obtaining a sample mean, given that the value stated in the null hypothesis is true, is stated by the ***p* value**. The *p* value is a probability: It varies between 0 and 1 and can never be negative. In Step 2, we stated the criterion or probability of obtaining a sample mean at which point we will decide to reject the value stated in the null hypothesis, which is typically set at 5% in behavioral research. To make a decision, we compare the *p* value to the criterion we set in Step 2.

When the *p* value is less than 5% ($p < .05$), we reject the null hypothesis, and when $p = .05$, the decision is also to reject the null hypothesis. When the *p* value is greater than 5% ($p > .05$), we retain the null hypothesis. The decision to reject or retain the null hypothesis is called **significance**. When the *p* value is less than or equal to .05, we *reach significance*; the decision is to reject the null hypothesis. When the *p* value is greater than .05, we *fail to reach significance*; the decision is to retain the null hypothesis. Figure 7.3 summarizes the four steps of hypothesis testing.

FYI

We use the value of the test statistic to make a decision regarding the null hypothesis.

FYI

Researchers make decisions regarding the null hypothesis. The decision can be to retain the null ($p > .05$) or reject the null ($p \leq .05$).

A ***p* value** is the probability of obtaining a sample outcome, given that the value stated in the null hypothesis is true. The *p* value for obtaining a sample outcome is compared to the level of significance or criterion for making a decision.

Significance, or **statistical significance**, describes a decision made concerning a value stated in the null hypothesis. When the null hypothesis is rejected, we reach significance. When the null hypothesis is retained, we fail to reach significance.

LEARNING CHECK 2

1. State the four steps of hypothesis testing.

2. The decision in hypothesis testing is to retain or reject which hypothesis: null or alternative?

3. The criterion or level of significance in behavioral research is typically set at what probability value?

4. A test statistic is associated with a *p* value less than .05. What is the decision for this hypothesis test?

5. If the null hypothesis is rejected, did we reach significance?

Answers: 1. Step 1: State the hypotheses. Step 2: Set the criteria for a decision. Step 3: Compute the test statistic. Step 4: Make a decision; 2. Null hypothesis; 3. The level of significance is typically set at .05; 4. Reject the null hypothesis; 5. Yes.

FIGURE 7.3   A Summary of the Four Steps of Hypothesis Testing

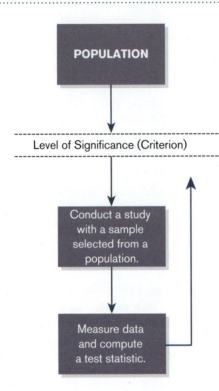

STEP 1: State the hypotheses. A researcher states a null hypothesis about a value in the population (H_0) and an alternative hypothesis that contradicts the null hypothesis.

STEP 2: Set the criteria for a decision. A criterion is set upon which a researcher will decide whether to retain or reject the value stated in the null hypothesis.

A sample is selected from the population, and a sample mean is measured.

STEP 3: Compute the test statistic. This will produce a value that can be compared to the criterion that was set before the sample was selected.

POPULATION

Level of Significance (Criterion)

Conduct a study with a sample selected from a population.

Measure data and compute a test statistic.

STEP 4: Make a decision. If the probability of obtaining a sample mean is less than or equal to 5% when the null is true, then reject the null hypothesis. If the probability of obtaining a sample mean is greater than 5% when the null is true, then retain the null hypothesis.

If 150 is the correct population mean, then the sample mean will equal 150, on average, with outcomes farther from the population mean being less and less likely to occur.

7.3 HYPOTHESIS TESTING AND SAMPLING DISTRIBUTIONS

The application of hypothesis testing is rooted in an understanding of the sampling distribution of the mean. In Chapter 6, we showed three characteristics of the mean, two of which are particularly relevant in this section:

1. The sample mean is an unbiased estimator of the population mean. On average, a randomly selected sample will have a mean equal to that in the population. In hypothesis testing, we begin by stating the null hypothesis. We expect that, if the null hypothesis is true, then a random sample selected from a given population will have a sample mean equal to the value stated in the null hypothesis.

2. Regardless of the distribution in a given population, the sampling distribution of the sample mean is approximately normal. Hence,

the probabilities of all other possible sample means we could select are normally distributed. Using this distribution, we can therefore state an alternative hypothesis to locate the probability of obtaining sample means with less than a 5% chance of being selected if the value stated in the null hypothesis is true. Figure 7.2 shows that we can identify sample mean outcomes in one or both tails using the normal distribution.

To locate the probability of obtaining a sample mean in a sampling distribution, we must know (1) the population mean and (2) the standard error of the mean (*SEM*; introduced in Chapter 6). Each value is entered in the test statistic formula computed in Step 3, thereby allowing us to make a decision in Step 4. To review, Table 7.1 displays the notations used to describe populations, samples, and sampling distributions. Table 7.2 summarizes the characteristics of each type of distribution.

TABLE 7.1 A Review of the Notations Used for the Mean, Variance, and Standard Deviation in Populations, Samples, and Sampling Distributions

Characteristic	Population	Sample	Sampling Distribution
Mean	μ	M or $\bar{X}$	$\mu_M = \mu$
Variance	σ^2	s^2 or SD^2	$\sigma_M^2 = \dfrac{\sigma^2}{n}$
Standard deviation	σ	s or SD	$\sigma_M = \dfrac{\sigma}{\sqrt{n}}$

TABLE 7.2 A Review of the Key Differences Between Population, Sample, and Sampling Distributions

	Population Distribution	Sample Distribution	Distribution of Sample Means
What is it?	Scores of all persons in a population	Scores of a select portion of persons from the population	All possible sample means that can be selected, given a certain sample size
Is it accessible?	Typically, no	Yes	Yes
What is the shape?	Could be any shape	Could be any shape	Normal distribution

LEARNING CHECK 3

1. For the following statements, write *increases* or *decreases* as an answer. The likelihood that we reject the null hypothesis (increases or decreases):

    (a) The closer the value of a sample mean is to the value stated by the null hypothesis.

    (b) The farther the value of a sample mean is from the value stated in the null hypothesis.

2. A researcher selects a sample of 49 students to test the null hypothesis that the average student exercises 90 minutes per week. What is the mean for the sampling distribution for this population of interest if the null hypothesis is true?

Answers: 1. (a) Decreases; (b) Increases; 2. 90 minutes per week.

7.4 MAKING A DECISION: TYPES OF ERROR

In Step 4, we decide whether to retain or reject the null hypothesis. Because we are observing a sample and not an entire population, it is possible that our decision about a null hypothesis is wrong. Table 7.3 shows that there are four decision alternatives regarding the truth and falsity of the decision we make about a null hypothesis:

1. The decision to retain the null hypothesis is correct.

2. The decision to retain the null hypothesis is incorrect.

3. The decision to reject the null hypothesis is correct.

4. The decision to reject the null hypothesis is incorrect.

We investigate each decision alternative in this section. Because we will observe a sample, and not a population, it is impossible to know for sure the truth in the population. So for the sake of illustration, we will assume we know this. This assumption is labeled as Truth in the Population in Table 7.3. In this section, we introduce each decision alternative.

TABLE 7.3   Four Outcomes for Making a Decision

		Decision	
		Retain the Null Hypothesis	**Reject the Null Hypothesis**
Truth in the Population	True	CORRECT $1 - \alpha$	TYPE I ERROR α
	False	TYPE II ERROR β	CORRECT $1 - \beta$ POWER

The decision can be either correct (correctly reject or retain the null hypothesis) or wrong (incorrectly reject or retain the null hypothesis).

FYI

A Type II error, or beta (β) error, is the probability of incorrectly retaining the null hypothesis.

Decision: Retain the Null Hypothesis

When we decide to retain the null hypothesis, we can be correct or incorrect. The correct decision is to retain a true null hypothesis. This decision is called a null result or null finding. This is usually an uninteresting decision because the decision is to retain what we already assumed. For this reason, a null result alone is rarely published in scientific journals for behavioral research.

The incorrect decision is to retain a false null hypothesis: a "false negative" finding. This decision is an example of a **Type II error**, or **beta (β) error**. With each test we make, there is always some probability that the decision is a Type II error. In this decision, we decide not to reject previous notions of truth that are in fact false. While this type of error is often regarded as less problematic than a Type I error (defined in the next paragraph), it can be problematic in many fields, such as in medicine where testing of treatments could mean life or death for patients.

Decision: Reject the Null Hypothesis

When we decide to reject the null hypothesis, we can be correct or incorrect. The incorrect decision is to reject a true null hypothesis: a "false positive" finding. This decision is an example of a **Type I error**. With each test we make, there is always some probability that our decision is a Type I error. A researcher who makes this error decides to reject previous notions of truth that are in fact true. Using the courtroom analogy, making this type of error is analogous to finding an innocent person guilty. To minimize this error, we therefore place the burden on the researcher to demonstrate evidence that the null hypothesis is indeed false.

Because we assume the null hypothesis is true, we control for Type I error by stating a level of significance. The level we set, called the **alpha level** (symbolized as α), is the largest probability of committing a Type I error that we will allow and still decide to reject the null hypothesis. This criterion is usually set at .05 ($\alpha = .05$) in behavioral research. To make a decision, we compare the alpha level (or criterion) to the *p* value (the actual likelihood of obtaining a sample mean, if the null were true). When the *p* value is less than the criterion of $\alpha = .05$, we decide to reject the null hypothesis; otherwise, we retain the null hypothesis.

The correct decision is to reject a false null hypothesis. In other words, we decide that the null hypothesis is false when it is indeed false. This decision is called the **power** of the decision-making process because it is the decision we aim for. Remember that we are only testing the null hypothesis because we think it is wrong. Deciding to reject a false null hypothesis, then, is the power, inasmuch as we learn the most about populations when we accurately reject false notions of truth about them. This decision is the most published result in behavioral research.

FYI

Researchers directly control for the probability of a Type I error by stating an alpha (α) level.

FYI

The power in hypothesis testing is the probability of correctly rejecting a value stated in the null hypothesis.

Type II error, or **beta (β) error**, is the probability of retaining a null hypothesis that is actually false.

Type I error is the probability of rejecting a null hypothesis that is actually true. Researchers directly control for the probability of committing this type of error by stating an alpha level.

An **alpha (α) level** is the level of significance or criterion for a hypothesis test. It is the largest probability of committing a Type I error that we will allow and still decide to reject the null hypothesis.

The **power** in hypothesis testing is the probability of rejecting a false null hypothesis. Specifically, it is the probability that a randomly selected sample will show that the null hypothesis is false when the null hypothesis is indeed false.

LEARNING CHECK 4

1. What type of error do we directly control?

2. What type of error is associated with decisions to retain the null hypothesis?

3. What type of error is associated with decisions to reject the null hypothesis?

4. State the two correct decisions that a researcher can make.

Answers: 1. Type I error; 2. Type II error; 3. Type I error; 4. Retain a true null hypothesis and reject a false null hypothesis.

FYI

The one-sample z test is used to test hypotheses about a population mean when the population variance is known.

FYI

Nondirectional tests are used to test hypotheses when we are interested in any alternative to the null hypothesis.

The **one-sample *z* test** is a statistical procedure used to test hypotheses concerning the mean in a single population with a known variance.

Nondirectional tests, or **two-tailed tests**, are hypothesis tests in which the alternative hypothesis is stated as *not equal to* (≠) a value stated in the null hypothesis. Hence, the researcher is interested in any alternative to the null hypothesis.

7.5 TESTING FOR SIGNIFICANCE: EXAMPLES USING THE *z* TEST

We use hypothesis testing to make decisions about parameters in a population. The type of test statistic we use in hypothesis testing depends largely on what is known in a population. When we know the mean and standard deviation in a single population, we can use the **one-sample *z* test**, which we use in this section to illustrate the four steps of hypothesis testing.

Recall that we can state one of three alternative hypotheses: A population mean is greater than (>), less than (<), or not equal to (≠) the value stated in a null hypothesis. The alternative hypothesis determines which tail of a sampling distribution to place the level of significance in, as illustrated in Figure 7.2. In this section, we will use an example for a directional and a nondirectional hypothesis test.

Nondirectional Tests ($H_1: \neq$)

In Example 7.1, we use the one-sample *z* test for a **nondirectional**, or **two-tailed, test**, where the alternative hypothesis is stated as *not equal to* (≠) the null hypothesis. For this test, we will place the level of significance in both tails of the sampling distribution. We are therefore interested in any alternative to the null hypothesis. This is the most common alternative hypothesis tested in behavioral science.

Example 7.1

© iStockphoto.com/kali9

A common measure of intelligence is the intelligence quotient (IQ) test (Hafer, 2017; Naglieri, 2015) in which scores in the general healthy population are approximately normally distributed with 100 ± 15 ($\mu \pm \sigma$). Suppose we select a sample of 100 graduate students to identify if the IQ of those students is significantly different from that of the general healthy adult population. In this sample, we record a sample mean equal to 103 (*M* = 103). Compute the one-sample *z* test to decide whether to retain or reject the null hypothesis at a .05 level of significance ($\alpha = .05$).

Step 1: State the hypotheses. The population mean IQ score is 100; therefore, $\mu = 100$ is the null hypothesis. We are testing whether the null hypothesis is (=) or is not ($\neq$) likely to be true among graduate students:

$H_0: \mu = 100$ Mean IQ scores are equal to 100 in the population of graduate students.

$H_1: \mu \neq 100$ Mean IQ scores are not equal to 100 in the population of graduate students.

Step 2: Set the criteria for a decision. The level of significance is .05, which makes the alpha level $\alpha = .05$. To locate the probability of obtaining a sample mean from a given population, we use the standard normal distribution. We will locate the z scores in a standard normal distribution that are the cutoffs, or **critical values**, for sample mean values with less than a 5% probability of occurrence if the value stated in the null hypothesis ($\mu = 100$) is true.

FYI

For two-tailed tests, the alpha is split in half and placed in each tail of a standard normal distribution.

FYI

A critical value marks the cutoff for the rejection region.

In a nondirectional (two-tailed) hypothesis test, we divide the alpha value in half so that an equal proportion of area is placed in the upper and lower tail. Table 7.4 gives the critical values for one- and two-tailed tests at .05, .01, and .001 levels of significance. Figure 7.4 displays a graph with the critical values for Example 7.1 shown. In this example, $\alpha = .05$, so we split this probability in half:

$$\text{Splitting } \alpha \text{ in half: } \frac{\alpha}{2} = \frac{.05}{2} = .0250 \text{ in each tail.}$$

To locate the critical values, we use the unit normal table given in Table C.1 in Appendix C and look up the proportion .0250 toward the tail in Column C. This value, .0250, is listed for a z score equal to $z = 1.96$. This is the critical value for the upper tail of the standard normal distribution. Because the normal distribution is symmetrical, the critical value in the bottom tail will be the same distance below the mean, or $z = -1.96$. The regions beyond the critical values, displayed in Figure 7.4, are called the **rejection regions**. If the value of the test statistic falls in these regions, then the decision is to reject the null hypothesis; otherwise, we retain the null hypothesis.

Step 3: Compute the test statistic. Step 2 sets the stage for making a decision because the criterion is set. The probability is less than 5% that we will obtain a sample mean that is at least 1.96 standard deviations above or below the value of the population mean stated in the null hypothesis. In this step, we will compute a test statistic to determine whether the sample mean we selected is beyond or within the critical values we stated in Step 2.

The test statistic for a one-sample z test is called the **z statistic**. The z statistic converts any sampling distribution into a standard normal distribution. The z statistic is therefore a z transformation. The solution of the formula gives the number of standard deviations, or

A **critical value** is a cutoff value that defines the boundaries beyond which less than 5% of sample means can be obtained if the null hypothesis is true. Sample means obtained beyond a critical value will result in a decision to reject the null hypothesis.

The **rejection region** is the region beyond a critical value in a hypothesis test. When the value of a test statistic is in the rejection region, we decide to reject the null hypothesis; otherwise, we retain the null hypothesis.

The **z statistic** is an inferential statistic used to determine the number of standard deviations in a standard normal distribution that a sample mean deviates from the population mean stated in the null hypothesis.

TABLE 7.4	Critical Values for One- and Two-Tailed Tests at Three Commonly Used Levels of Significance

| Level of Significance (α) | Type of Test | |
	One-Tailed	Two-Tailed
.05	+1.645 or −1.645	± 1.96
.01	+2.33 or −2.33	± 2.58
.001	+3.09 or −3.09	± 3.30

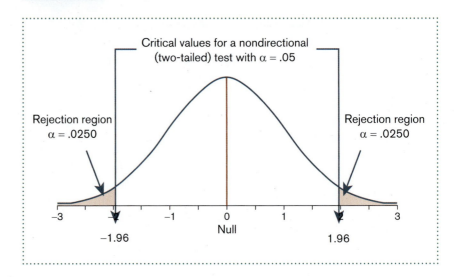

FIGURE 7.4   The Critical Values (± 1.96) for a Nondirectional (two-tailed) Test With a .05 Level of Significance

z scores, that a sample mean falls above or below the population mean stated in the null hypothesis. We can then compare the value of the z statistic, called the **obtained value**, to the critical values we determined in Step 2. The z statistic formula is the sample mean minus the population mean stated in the null hypothesis, divided by the standard error of the mean:

$$z \text{ statistic: } z_{\text{obt}} = \frac{M - \mu}{\sigma_M}, \text{where } \sigma_M = \frac{\sigma}{\sqrt{n}}.$$

To calculate the z statistic, first compute the standard error (σ_M), which is the denominator for the z statistic:

$$\sigma_M = \frac{\sigma}{\sqrt{n}} = \frac{15}{\sqrt{100}} = 1.50.$$

Then compute the z statistic by substituting the values of the sample mean, $M = 103$; the population mean stated by the null hypothesis, $\mu = 100$; and the standard error we just calculated, $\sigma_M = 1.50$:

$$z_{\text{obt}} = \frac{M - \mu}{\sigma_M} = \frac{103 - 100}{1.50} = 2.00.$$

FYI

The z statistic measures the number of standard deviations, or z scores, that a sample mean falls above or below the population mean stated in the null hypothesis.

The **obtained value** is the value of a test statistic. This value is compared to the critical value(s) of a hypothesis test to make a decision. When the obtained value exceeds a critical value, we decide to reject the null hypothesis; otherwise, we retain the null hypothesis.

Step 4: Make a decision. To make a decision, we compare the obtained value to the critical values. We reject the null hypothesis if the obtained value exceeds a critical value. Figure 7.5 shows that the obtained value ($z_{\text{obt}} = 2.00$) is greater than the critical value; it falls in the rejection region. The decision for this test is to reject the null hypothesis.

The probability of obtaining $z_{\text{obt}} = 2.00$ is stated by the p value. To locate the p value or probability of obtaining the z statistic, we refer to the unit normal table in Table C.1 in Appendix C. Look for a z score equal to 2.00 in Column A, then locate the probability toward the tail in Column C. The value is .0228. Finally, multiply the value given in

FIGURE 7.5 Making a Decision for Example 7.1

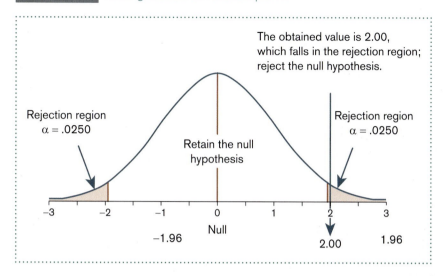

Because the obtained value falls in the rejection region (it is beyond the critical value in the upper tail), we decide to reject the null hypothesis.

Column C by the number of tails for alpha. Because this is a two-tailed test, we multiply .0228 by 2: $p = (.0228) \times 2$ tails $= .0456$. Table 7.5 summarizes how to determine the p value for one- and two-tailed tests.

We found in Example 7.1 that if the null hypothesis were true, then $p = .0456$ that we would have selected this sample mean from this population. The criterion we set in Step 2 was that the probability must be less than 5% or $p = .0500$ that we would obtain a sample mean if the null hypothesis were true. Because p is less than 5%, we decide to reject the null hypothesis. We conclude that the mean IQ score among graduate students in this population is not 100 (the value stated in the null hypothesis). Instead, we found that the mean was significantly larger than 100.

FYI

A nondirectional test is conducted when it is impossible or highly unlikely that a sample mean will fall in the direction opposite to that stated in the alternative hypothesis.

TABLE 7.5 Determining the p Value

	One-Tailed Test	**Two-Tailed Test**
Number of tails	1	2
Probability	p	p
p value calculation	$1p$	$2p$

To find the p value for the z statistic, find its probability (toward the tail) in the unit normal table and multiply this probability by the number of tails for alpha.

Directional Tests (H_1: > or H_1: <)

An alternative to the nondirectional test is a **directional**, or **one-tailed**, **test**, where the alternative hypothesis is stated as *greater than* (>) the null hypothesis or *less than* (<) the null hypothesis. For an upper-tail critical test, or a "greater than" statement, we place the level of significance in the

Directional tests, or **one-tailed tests**, are hypothesis tests in which the alternative hypothesis is stated as greater than (>) or less than (<) a value stated in the null hypothesis. Hence, the researcher is interested in a specific alternative to the null hypothesis.

upper tail of the sampling distribution. So we are interested in any alternative greater than the value stated in the null hypothesis. This test can be used when it is impossible or highly unlikely that a sample mean will fall below the population mean stated in the null hypothesis.

For a lower-tail critical test, or a "less than" statement, we place the level of significance or critical value in the lower tail of the sampling distribution. So we are interested in any alternative less than the value stated in the null hypothesis. This test can be used when it is impossible or highly unlikely that a sample mean will fall above the population mean stated in the null hypothesis.

To illustrate how to make a decision using the one-tailed test, we work in Example 7.2 with an example in which such a test could be used.

Example 7.2

Researchers in areas of child development and education are often interested in evaluating methods to promote reading proficiency and academic success (Crosnoe, Benner, & Davis-Kean, 2016; Phillips, Norris, Hayward, & Lovell, 2017). Suppose, for example, researchers were interested in looking at improvement in reading proficiency among elementary school students following a reading program. In this example, the reading program should, if anything, improve reading skills, so if any outcome were possible, it should be to see improvement. For this reason, we could use a one-tailed test to evaluate these data. Suppose elementary school children in the general population show reading proficiency increases of 12 ± 4 ($\mu \pm \sigma$) points on a given standardized measure. If we select a sample of 25 elementary school children in the reading program and record a sample mean improvement in reading proficiency equal to 14 ($M = 14$) points, then we compute the one-sample z test at a .05 level of significance to determine if the reading program was effective.

Step 1: State the hypotheses. The population mean is 12, and we are testing whether the alternative is greater than (>) this value:

H_0: $\mu \le 12$ With the reading program, mean improvement is at most 12 points in the population.

H_1: $\mu > 12$ With the reading program, mean improvement is greater than 12 points in the population.

Notice a key change for one-tailed tests: The null hypothesis encompasses outcomes in all directions that are opposite the alternative hypothesis. In other words, the directional statement is incorporated into the statement of both hypotheses. In this example, the reading program is intended to improve reading proficiency. Therefore, a one-tailed test is used because there is a specific, expected, logical direction for the effect if the reading program were effective. The null hypothesis therefore states that the expected effect will not occur (that mean improvement will be at most 12 points), and the alternative hypothesis states that the expected effect will occur (that mean improvement will be greater than 12 points).

Step 2: Set the criteria for a decision. The level of significance is .05, which makes the alpha level $\alpha = .05$. To determine the critical value for an upper-tail critical test, we locate the probability .0500 toward the tail in Column C in the unit normal table in Table C.1 in

©iStockphoto.com/ Mari

Appendix C. The z score associated with this probability is between $z = 1.64$ and $z = 1.65$. The average of these z scores is $z = 1.645$, which is the critical value or cutoff for the rejection region. Figure 7.6 shows that, for this test, we place the entire rejection region, or alpha level, in the upper tail of the standard normal distribution.

FIGURE 7.6   The Critical Value (1.645) for a Directional (upper-tail critical) Hypothesis Test at a .05 Level of Significance

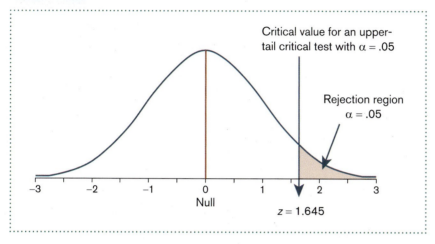

When the test statistic exceeds 1.645, we reject the null hypothesis; otherwise, we retain the null hypothesis.

Step 3: Compute the test statistic. Step 2 sets the stage for making a decision because the criterion is set. The probability is less than 5% that we will obtain a sample mean that is at least 1.645 standard deviations above the value of the population mean stated in the null hypothesis. In this step, we compute a test statistic to determine whether or not the sample mean we selected is beyond the critical value we stated in Step 2.

To calculate the z statistic, first compute the standard error (σ_M), which is the denominator for the z statistic:

$$\sigma_M = \frac{\sigma}{\sqrt{n}} = \frac{4}{\sqrt{25}} = 0.80.$$

Then compute the z statistic by substituting the values of the sample mean, $M = 14$; the population mean stated by the null hypothesis, $\mu = 12$; and the standard error we just calculated, $\sigma_M = 0.80$:

$$z_{obt} = \frac{M - \mu}{\sigma_M} = \frac{14 - 12}{0.80} = 2.50.$$

Step 4: Make a decision. To make a decision, we compare the obtained value to the critical value. We reject the null hypothesis if the obtained value exceeds the critical value. Figure 7.7 shows that the obtained value ($z_{obt} = 2.50$) is greater than the critical value; it falls in the rejection region. The decision is to reject the null hypothesis. To locate the p value or probability of obtaining the z statistic, we refer to the unit normal table in Table C.1 in Appendix C. Look for a z score equal to 2.50 in Column A, then locate the probability toward the tail in Column C. The p value is .0062 ($p = .0062$). We do not double the p value for one-tailed tests.

FYI

For one-tailed tests, the alpha level is placed in a single tail of a distribution.

FIGURE 7.7   Making a Decision for Example 7.2

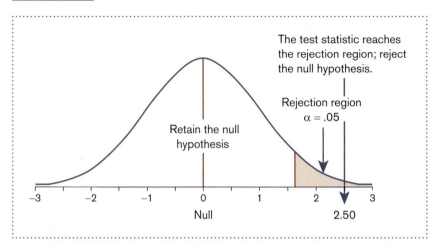

Because the obtained value falls in the rejection region (it is beyond the critical value of 1.645), we decide to reject the null hypothesis.

FYI

Two-tailed tests are more conservative and eliminate the possibility of committing a Type III error. One-tailed tests are associated with greater power, assuming the value stated in the null hypothesis is false.

FYI

For a Type III error, the "wrong tail" refers to the opposite tail from where a difference was observed and would have otherwise been significant.

A **Type III error** is a type of error possible with one-tailed tests in which a decision would have been to reject the null hypothesis, but the researcher decides to retain the null hypothesis because the rejection region was located in the wrong tail.

We found in Example 7.2 that if the null hypothesis were true, then $p = .0062$ that we would have selected a sample mean of 14 from this population. The criterion we set in Step 2 was that the probability must be less than 5% that we would obtain a sample mean if the null hypothesis were true. Because p is less than 5%, we decide to reject the null hypothesis that mean improvement in this population is equal to 12. Instead, we found that the reading program significantly improved reading proficiency scores more than 12 points.

The decision in Example 7.2 was to reject the null hypothesis using a one-tailed test. One problem that can arise, however, is if scores go in the opposite direction than what was predicted. In other words, for one-tailed tests, it is possible in some cases to place the rejection region in the wrong tail. Thus, we predict that scores will increase, and instead they decrease, and vice versa. When we fail to reject a null hypothesis because we placed the rejection region in the wrong tail, we commit a type of error called a **Type III error** (Kaiser, 1960). We make a closer comparison of one-tailed and two-tailed hypothesis tests in the next section.

7.6   **RESEARCH** IN FOCUS: DIRECTIONAL
VERSUS NONDIRECTIONAL TESTS

Kruger and Savitsky (2006) conducted a study in which they performed two tests on the same data. They completed an upper-tail critical test at $\alpha = .05$ and a two-tailed test at $\alpha = .10$. As shown in Figure 7.8, these are similar tests, except in the upper-tail test, all the alpha level is placed in the upper tail, and in the two-tailed test, the alpha level is split so that .05 is placed in each tail. When the researchers showed these results to a group of participants, they found that participants were more persuaded by a significant result when it was described as a one-tailed test, $p < .05$, than when it was described as a two-tailed test, $p < .10$. This was interesting because the two results were identical—both tests were associated with the same critical value in the upper tail.

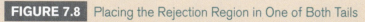

FIGURE 7.8 Placing the Rejection Region in One of Both Tails

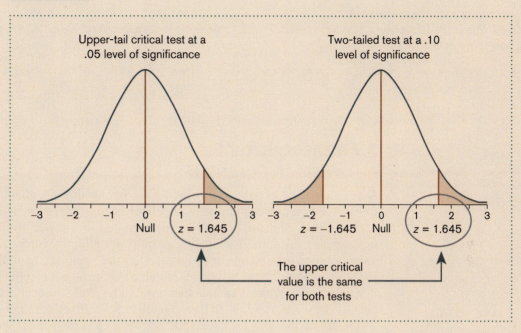

When $\alpha = .05$, all of that value is placed in the upper tail for an upper-tail critical test. The two-tailed equivalent would require a test with $\alpha = .10$, such that .05 is placed in each tail. Note that the normal distribution is symmetrical, so the cutoff in the lower tail is the same distance below the mean (-1.645; the upper tail is $+1.645$).

Most editors of peer-reviewed journals in behavioral research will not publish the results of a study where the level of significance is greater than .05. Although the two-tailed test, $p < .10$, was significant, it is unlikely that the results would be published in a peer-reviewed scientific journal. Reporting the same results as a one-tailed test, $p < .05$, makes it more likely that the data will be published.

The two-tailed test is more conservative; it makes it more difficult to reject the null hypothesis. It also eliminates the possibility of committing a Type III error. The one-tailed test, though, is associated with greater power. If the value stated in the null hypothesis is false, then a one-tailed test will make it easier to detect this (i.e., lead to a decision to reject the null hypothesis). Because the one-tailed test makes it easier to reject the null hypothesis, it is important that we justify that an outcome can occur in only one direction. Justifying that an outcome can occur in only one direction is difficult for much of the data that behavioral researchers measure. For this reason, most studies in behavioral research are two-tailed tests.

LEARNING CHECK 5

1. Is the following set of hypotheses appropriate for a directional or a nondirectional hypothesis test?

    $H_0: \mu = 35$

    $H_1: \mu \neq 35$

2. A researcher conducts a one-sample z test. The z statistic for the upper-tail critical test at a .05 level of significance is $z_{obt} = 1.84$. What is the decision for this test?

(Continued)

(Continued)

3. A researcher conducts a hypothesis test and finds that $p = .0689$. What is the decision for a hypothesis test at a .05 level of significance?

4. Which type of test, one-tailed or two-tailed, is susceptible to the possibility of committing a Type III error?

Answers: 1. A nondirectional (two-tailed) test; 2. Reject the null hypothesis; 3. Retain the null hypothesis; 4. One-tailed test.

7.7 MEASURING THE SIZE OF AN EFFECT: COHEN'S *d*

A decision to reject the null hypothesis means that an effect is significant. For a one-sample test, an **effect** is the difference between a sample mean and the population mean stated in the null hypothesis. In Examples 7.1 and 7.2 we found a significant effect, meaning that the sample mean was significantly larger than the value stated in the null hypothesis. Hypothesis testing identifies whether or not an effect exists in a population. When a sample mean would be likely to occur if the null hypothesis were true ($p > .05$), we decide that an effect does not exist in a population; the effect is not significant. When a sample mean would be unlikely to occur if the null hypothesis were true (typically less than a 5% likelihood, $p < .05$), we decide that an effect does exist in a population; the effect is significant. Hypothesis testing does not, however, inform us of how big the effect is.

To determine the size of an effect, we compute **effect size**. There are two ways to calculate the size of an effect. We can determine

1. how far scores shifted in the population, and

2. the percent of variance that can be explained by a given variable.

Effect size is most meaningfully reported with significant effects when the decision was to reject the null hypothesis. If an effect is not significant, as in instances when we retain the null hypothesis, then we are concluding that an effect does not exist in a population. It makes little sense to compute the size of an effect that we just concluded does not exist. In this section, we describe how far scores shifted in the population using a measure of effect size called Cohen's *d*.

Cohen's *d* measures the number of standard deviations an effect is shifted above or below the population mean stated by the null hypothesis. The formula for Cohen's *d* replaces the standard error in the denominator of the test statistic with the population standard deviation (J. Cohen, 1988):

$$\text{Cohen's } d = \frac{M - \mu}{\sigma}.$$

For a single sample, an **effect** is the difference between a sample mean and the population mean stated in the null hypothesis. In hypothesis testing, an effect is not significant when we retain the null hypothesis; an effect is significant when we reject the null hypothesis.

Effect size is a statistical measure of the size of an effect in a population, which allows researchers to describe how far scores shifted in the population, or the percent of variance that can be explained by a given variable.

Cohen's *d* is a measure of effect size in terms of the number of standard deviations that mean scores shifted above or below the population mean stated by the null hypothesis. The larger the value of *d*, the larger the effect in the population.

The value of Cohen's *d* is zero when there is no difference between two means, and it gets farther from zero as the difference gets larger. To interpret values of *d*, we refer to **Cohen's effect size conventions** outlined in Table 7.6. The sign of *d* indicates the direction of the shift. When values of *d* are positive, an effect shifted above the population mean; when values of *d* are negative, an effect shifted below the population mean.

FYI

Hypothesis testing determines whether or not an effect exists in a population. Effect size measures the size of an observed effect from small to large.

TABLE 7.6 Cohen's Effect Size Conventions

Description of Effect	Effect Size (d)
Small	$d < 0.2$
Medium	$0.2 < d < 0.8$
Large	$d > 0.8$

In Example 7.3, we will determine the effect size for the research study in Example 7.2 to illustrate how significance and effect size can be interpreted for the same set of data.

Cohen's effect size conventions are standard rules for identifying small, medium, and large effects based on typical findings in behavioral research.

Example 7.3

In Example 7.2, we tested if a reading program could effectively improve reading proficiency scores in a group of elementary school children. Scores in the general population show reading proficiency increases of 12 ± 4 ($\mu \pm \sigma$) points on a given standardized measure. In our sample of children who took the reading program, mean proficiency scores improved by 14 points. In Example 7.3, we will determine the effect size for this test using Cohen's *d*.

The numerator for Cohen's *d* is the difference between the sample mean ($M = 14$) and the population mean ($\mu = 12$). The denominator is the population standard deviation ($\sigma = 4$):

$$d = \frac{M - \mu}{\sigma} = \frac{14 - 12}{4} = 0.50.$$

We conclude that the observed effect shifted 0.50 standard deviations above the mean in the population. This way of interpreting effect size is illustrated in Figure 7.9. For our example, we are stating that students in the reading program scored 0.50 standard deviations higher, on average, than students in the general population. This interpretation is most meaningfully reported when the decision was to reject the null hypothesis, as we did in Example 7.2. Table 7.7 compares the basic characteristics of hypothesis testing and effect size.

FIGURE 7.9   Effect Size for Example 7.3

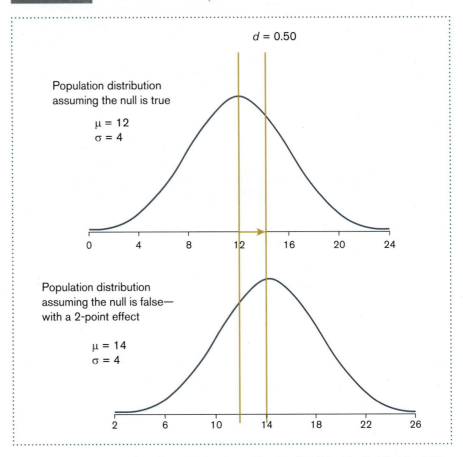

Cohen's *d* estimates the size of an effect in the population. A 2-point effect (14 − 12 = 2) shifted the distribution of scores in the population by 0.50 standard deviations.

TABLE 7.7   Distinguishing Characteristics for Hypothesis Testing and Effect Size

	Hypothesis (Significance) Testing	Effect Size (Cohen's *d*)
What value is being measured?	*p* value	*d*
What type of distribution is the test based upon?	Sampling distribution	Population distribution
What does the test measure?	The probability of obtaining a measured sample mean	The size of a measured effect in the population
What can be inferred from the test?	Whether an effect exists in a population	The size of an effect from small to large
Can this test stand alone in research reports?	Yes, but a test statistic is increasingly reported with effect size	No, effect size is most often reported with a test statistic

LEARNING CHECK 6

1. _____ measures the size of an effect in a population, whereas _____ measures whether an effect exists in a population.

2. The scores for a population are normally distributed with a mean equal to 25 and standard deviation equal to 6. A researcher selects a sample of 36 students and measures a sample mean equal to 23. For this example,

   (a) What is the value of Cohen's d?

   (b) Is this effect size small, medium, or large?

Answers: 1. Effect size, hypothesis testing; 2. (a) $d = \dfrac{23-25}{6} = -0.33$, (b) Medium effect size.

7.8 EFFECT SIZE, POWER, AND SAMPLE SIZE

One advantage of knowing effect size, d, is that its value can be used to determine the power of detecting an effect in hypothesis testing. The likelihood of detecting an effect, called *power*, is critical in behavioral research because it lets the researcher know the probability that a randomly selected sample will lead to a decision to reject the null hypothesis, if the null hypothesis is false. In this section, we describe how effect size and sample size are related to power.

The Relationship Between Effect Size and Power

As effect size increases, power increases. To illustrate, we will use a random sample of quiz scores in two statistics classes shown in Table 7.8. Notice that only the standard deviation differs between these populations. Using the values given in Table 7.8, we already have enough information to compute effect size:

$$\text{Effect size for Class 1: } d = \frac{M-\mu}{\sigma} = \frac{40-38}{10} = 0.20.$$

$$\text{Effect size for Class 2: } d = \frac{M-\mu}{\sigma} = \frac{40-38}{2} = 1.00.$$

TABLE 7.8 Characteristics for Two Hypothetical Populations of Quiz Scores

Class 1	Class 2
$M_1 = 40$	$M_2 = 40$
$\mu_1 = 38$	$\mu_2 = 38$
$\sigma_1 = 10$	$\sigma_2 = 2$

The numerator for each effect size estimate is the same. The mean difference between the sample mean and the population mean is 2 points. Although there is a 2-point effect in both Class 1 and Class 2, Class 2 is associated with a much larger effect size in the population because the standard deviation is smaller. Because a larger effect size is associated with greater power, we should find that it is easier to detect the 2-point effect in Class 2. To determine whether this is true, suppose we select a sample of 30 students ($n = 30$) from each class and measure the same sample mean value that is listed in Table 7.8. Let us determine the power of each test when we conduct an upper-tail critical test at a .05 level of significance.

To determine the power, we will first construct the sampling distribution for each class, with a mean equal to the population mean and standard error equal to $\frac{\sigma}{\sqrt{n}}$:

$$\text{Sampling distribution for Class 1: Mean: } \mu_M = 38$$

$$\text{Standard error}: \frac{\sigma}{\sqrt{n}} = \frac{10}{\sqrt{30}} = 1.82$$

$$\text{Sampling distribution for Class 2: Mean: } \mu_M = 38$$

$$\text{Standard error}: \frac{\sigma}{\sqrt{n}} = \frac{2}{\sqrt{30}} = 0.37$$

If the null hypothesis is true, then the sampling distribution of the mean for alpha (α), the type of error associated with a true null hypothesis, will have a mean equal to 38. We can now determine the smallest value of the sample mean that is the cutoff for the rejection region, where we decide to reject that the true population mean is 38. For an upper-tail critical test using a .05 level of significance, the critical value is 1.645. We can use this value to compute a z transformation to determine what sample mean value is 1.645 standard deviations above 38 in a sampling distribution for samples of size 30:

$$\text{Cutoff for } \alpha \text{ (Class 1): } 1.645 = \frac{M-38}{1.82}$$

$$M = 40.99$$

$$\text{Cutoff for } \alpha \text{ (Class 2): } 1.645 = \frac{M-38}{0.37}$$

$$M = 38.61$$

If we obtain a sample mean equal to 40.99 or higher in Class 1, then we will reject the null hypothesis. If we obtain a sample mean equal to 38.61 or higher in Class 2, then we will reject the null hypothesis. To determine the power for this test, we assume that the sample mean we selected ($M = 40$) is the true population mean—we are therefore assuming that the null hypothesis is false. We are asking the following question: If we are correct and there is a 2-point effect, then what is the probability that we will detect the effect? In other words, what is the probability that a sample randomly selected from this population will lead to a decision to reject the null hypothesis?

If the null hypothesis is false, then the sampling distribution of the mean for β, the type of error associated with a false null hypothesis, will have a mean equal to 40. This is what we believe is the true population mean, and this is the only change; we do not change the standard error. Figure 7.10 shows the sampling distribution for Class 1, and Figure 7.11 shows the sampling distribution for Class 2, assuming the null hypothesis is correct (top graph) and assuming the 2-point effect exists (bottom graph).

If we are correct, and the 2-point effect exists, then we are much more likely to detect the effect in Class 2 for $n = 30$. Class 1 has a small effect size ($d = 0.20$). Even if we are correct, and a 2-point effect does exist in this population, then of all the samples of size 30 we could select from this population, only about 29% (power = .2946) will show the effect (i.e., lead to a decision to reject the null). The probability of correctly rejecting the null hypothesis (power) is low.

Class 2 has a large effect size ($d = 1.00$). If we are correct, and a 2-point effect does exist in this population, then of all the samples of size 30 we could select from this population, nearly 100% (power = .9999) will show the effect (i.e., lead to a decision to reject the null). The probability of correctly rejecting the null hypothesis (power) is high.

FYI

As the size of an effect increases, the power to detect the effect also increases.

FIGURE 7.10 Small Effect Size and Low Power for Class 1

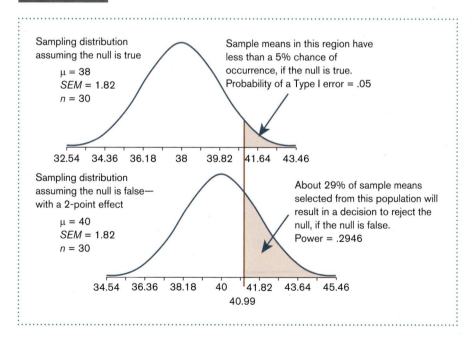

In this example, when alpha is .05, the critical value or cutoff for alpha is 40.99. When α = .05, notice that only about 29% of samples will detect this effect (the power). So even if the researcher is correct, and the null is false (with a 2-point effect), only about 29% of the samples he or she selects at random will result in a decision to reject the null hypothesis.

FIGURE 7.11 Large Effect Size and High Power for Class 2

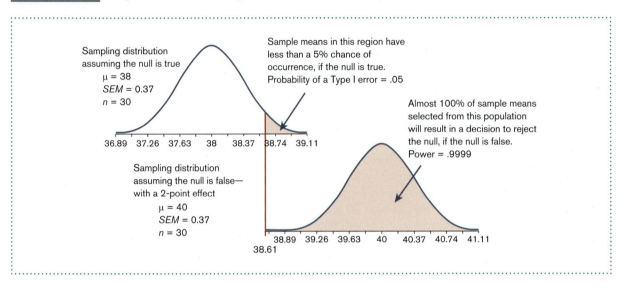

In this example, when alpha is .05, the critical value or cutoff for alpha is 38.61. When $\alpha = .05$, notice that practically any sample will detect this effect (the power). So if the researcher is correct, and the null is false (with a 2-point effect), nearly 100% of the samples he or she selects at random will result in a decision to reject the null hypothesis.

FYI

Increasing sample size increases power by reducing standard error, thereby increasing the value of the test statistic in hypothesis testing.

The Relationship Between Sample Size and Power

One common solution to overcome low effect size is to increase the sample size. Increasing sample size decreases standard error, thereby increasing power. To illustrate, we can compute the test statistic for the one-tailed significance test for Class 1, which had a small effect size. The data for Class 1 are given in Table 7.8 for a sample of 30 participants. The test statistic for Class 1 when $n = 30$ is

$$z_{obt} = \frac{M - \mu}{\frac{\sigma}{\sqrt{n}}} = \frac{40 - 38}{\frac{10}{\sqrt{30}}} = 1.10.$$

For a one-tailed test that is upper-tail critical, the critical value is 1.645. The value of the test statistic (+1.10) does not exceed the critical value (+1.645), so we retain the null hypothesis.

Suppose we increase the sample size to $n = 100$ and again measure a sample mean of $M = 40$. The test statistic for Class 1 when $n = 100$ is

$$z_{obt} = \frac{M - \mu}{\frac{\sigma}{\sqrt{n}}} = \frac{40 - 38}{\frac{10}{\sqrt{100}}} = 2.00.$$

The critical value is still 1.645. The value of the test statistic (+2.00), however, now exceeds the critical value (+1.645), so we reject the null hypothesis.

Notice that increasing the sample size alone led to a decision to reject the null hypothesis, despite testing for a small effect size in the population. Hence, increasing sample size increases power: It makes it more likely that we will detect an effect, assuming that an effect exists in a given population.

LEARNING CHECK 7

1. As effect size increases, what happens to the power?

2. As effect size decreases, what happens to the power?

3. When a population is associated with a small effect size, what can a researcher do to increase the power of the study?

4. True or false: The effect size, power, and sample size of a study can affect the decisions we make in hypothesis testing.

Answers: 1. Power increases; 2. Power decreases; 3. Increase the sample size (n); 4. True.

7.9 ADDITIONAL FACTORS THAT INCREASE POWER

The power is the likelihood of detecting an effect. Behavioral research often requires a great deal of time and money to select, observe, measure, and analyze data. For this reason, the institutions that offer substantial funding for research studies want to know that they are spending their money wisely and that researchers conduct studies that will show results. Consequently, to receive a research grant, researchers are often required to state the likelihood that they will detect an effect they are studying, assuming they are correct. In other words, researchers must disclose the power of their studies.

The typical standard for power is .80. Researchers try to make sure that at least 80% of the samples they select will show an effect when an effect exists in a population. In Section 7.8, we showed that increasing effect size and sample size increases power. In this section, we introduce four additional factors that influence power.

Increasing Power: Increase Effect Size, Sample Size, and Alpha

Increasing effect size, sample size, and the alpha level will increase power. Section 7.8 showed that increasing effect size and sample size increases power; here we discuss increasing alpha. The alpha level is the probability of a Type I error, and it is the rejection region for a hypothesis test. The larger the rejection region, the greater the likelihood of rejecting the null hypothesis, and the greater the power will be. Hence, increasing the size

FYI

To increase power, increase effect size, sample size, and alpha; and decrease beta, population standard deviation, and standard error.

of the rejection region in the upper tail in Example 7.2 (by placing all of the rejection region in one tail) increased the power of that hypothesis test. Similarly, increasing alpha will increase the size of the rejection region, thereby increasing power. That being said, it is widely accepted that alpha can never be stated at a value larger than .05. Simply increasing alpha is not a practical solution to increase power. Instead, the more practical solutions are to increase sample size, or structure your study to observe a large effect between groups.

Increasing Power: Decrease Beta, Standard Deviation (σ), and Standard Error

Decreasing beta error (β) increases power. In Table 7.3, β is given as the probability of a Type II error, and $1 - \beta$ is given as the power. The lower β is, the greater the solution will be for $1 - \beta$. For example, say $\beta = .20$. In this case, $1 - \beta = (1 - .20) = .80$. If we decrease β, say, to $\beta = .10$, the power will increase: $1 - \beta = (1 - .10) = .90$. Hence, decreasing beta error increases power.

Decreasing the population standard deviation (σ) and standard error (σ_M) will also increase power. The population standard deviation is the numerator for computing standard error. Decreasing the population standard deviation will decrease the standard error, thereby increasing the value of the test statistic. To illustrate, suppose that we select a sample from a population of students with quiz scores equal to 10 ± 8 ($\mu \pm \sigma$). We select a sample of 16 students from this population and measure a sample mean equal to 12. In this example, the standard error is

$$\sigma_M = \frac{\sigma}{\sqrt{n}} = \frac{8}{\sqrt{16}} = 2.00.$$

To compute the z statistic, we subtract the sample mean from the population mean and divide by the standard error:

$$z_{obt} = \frac{M - \mu}{\sigma_M} = \frac{12 - 10}{2} = 1.00.$$

An obtained value equal to 1.00 does not exceed the critical value for a one-tailed test (critical value = 1.645) or a two-tailed test (critical values = ±1.96). The decision is to retain the null hypothesis.

If the population standard deviation is smaller, the standard error will be smaller, thereby making the value of the test statistic larger. Suppose, for example, that we reduce the population standard deviation to 4. The standard error in this example is now

$$\sigma_M = \frac{\sigma}{\sqrt{n}} = \frac{4}{\sqrt{16}} = 1.0.$$

To compute the z statistic, we subtract the sample mean from the population mean and divide by this smaller standard error:

$$z_{obt} = \frac{M - \mu}{\sigma_M} = \frac{12 - 10}{1} = 2.00.$$

An obtained value equal to 2.00 does exceed the critical value for a one-tailed test (critical value = 1.645) and a two-tailed test (critical values = ±1.96). Now the decision is to reject the null hypothesis. Assuming that an effect exists in the population, decreasing the population standard deviation decreases standard error and increases the power to detect an effect. Table 7.9 lists each factor that increases power.

TABLE 7.9 A Summary of Factors That Increase Power—the Probability of Rejecting a False Null Hypothesis

To increase power:	
Increase	**Decrease**
d (Effect size)	β (Type II error)
n (Sample size)	σ (Standard deviation)
α (Type I error)	σ_M (Standard error)

7.10 SPSS in Focus:
A Preview for Chapters 8 to 14

In the behavioral sciences, it is rare that we know the value of the population variance, so the z test is not a common hypothesis test. It is so uncommon that there is no (direct) way to compute a z test in SPSS, although SPSS can be used to compute all other test statistics described in this book. For each analysis, SPSS provides output analyses that indicate the significance of a hypothesis test and the information needed to compute effect size and even power. SPSS is an easy-to-use, point-and-click statistical software that can be used to compute nearly any statistic or measure used in behavioral research. For this reason, many researchers use SPSS software to analyze their data.

7.11 APA IN FOCUS: REPORTING THE TEST STATISTIC AND EFFECT SIZE

To report the results of a z test, we report the test statistic, p value (stated to no more than the thousandths place), and effect size of a hypothesis test. Here is how we could report the significant result for the z statistic in Example 7.2:

Children in the reading program showed significantly greater improvement ($M = 14$) in reading proficiency scores compared to expected improvement in the general population ($\mu = 12$), $z = 2.50$, $p = .006$ ($d = 0.50$).

(Continued)

(Continued)

Notice that when we report a result, we do not state that we reject or retain the null hypothesis. Instead, we report whether a result is significant (the decision was to reject the null hypothesis) or not significant (the decision was to retain the null hypothesis). Also, you are not required to report the exact p value, although it is recommended. An alternative is to report it in terms of $p < .05$, $p < .01$, or $p < .001$. In our example, we could state $p < .01$ for a p value actually equal to .006.

Finally, notice that the means are also listed in the summary of the data. Often we can also report standard deviations, which is recommended by the APA. An alternative would be to report the means in a figure or table to illustrate a significant effect, with error bars given in a figure to indicate the standard error of the mean. In this way, we can report the value of the test statistic, p value, effect size, means, standard deviations, and standard error all in one sentence and a figure or table.

• • • CHAPTER SUMMARY ORGANIZED BY LEARNING OBJECTIVE

LO 1:   **Identify the four steps of hypothesis testing.**

- Hypothesis testing, or significance testing, is a method of testing a claim or hypothesis about a parameter in a population, using data measured in a sample. In this method, we test a hypothesis by determining the likelihood that a sample statistic would be selected if the hypothesis regarding the population parameter were true. The four steps of hypothesis testing are as follows:

   Step 1: State the hypotheses.

   Step 2: Set the criteria for a decision.

   Step 3: Compute the test statistic.

   Step 4: Make a decision.

LO 2:   **Define null hypothesis, alternative hypothesis, level of significance, test statistic, p value, and statistical significance.**

- The null hypothesis (H_0) is a statement about a population parameter, such as the population mean, that is assumed to be true.

- The alternative hypothesis (H_1) is a statement that directly contradicts a null hypothesis by stating that the

actual value of a population parameter, such as the mean, is less than, greater than, or not equal to the value stated in the null hypothesis.

- Level of significance is a criterion of judgment upon which a decision is made regarding the value stated in a null hypothesis. The criterion is based on the probability of obtaining a statistic measured in a sample if the value stated in the null hypothesis were true.

- The test statistic is a mathematical formula that allows researchers to determine the likelihood or probability of obtaining sample outcomes if the null hypothesis were true. The value of a test statistic can be used to make inferences concerning the value of a population parameter stated in the null hypothesis.

- A p value is the probability of obtaining a sample outcome, given that the value stated in the null hypothesis is true. The p value of a sample outcome is compared to the level of significance.

- Significance, or statistical significance, describes a decision made concerning a value stated in the null hypothesis. When a null hypothesis is rejected, a result is significant. When a null hypothesis is retained, a result is not significant.

LO 3:   **Define Type I error and Type II error, and identify the type of error that researchers control.**

- We can decide to retain or reject a null hypothesis, and this decision can be correct or incorrect. Two types of errors in hypothesis testing are called Type I and Type II errors.

- A Type I error is the probability of rejecting a null hypothesis that is actually true. The probability of this type of error is determined by the researcher and stated as the level of significance or alpha level for a hypothesis test.

- A Type II error is the probability of retaining a null hypothesis that is actually false.

LO 4:   **Calculate the one-sample z test and interpret the results.**

- The one-sample z test is a statistical procedure used to test hypotheses concerning the mean in a single population with a known variance. The test statistic for this hypothesis test is

$$z_{\text{obt}} = \frac{M - \mu}{\sigma_M}, \text{where } \sigma_M = \frac{\sigma}{\sqrt{n}}.$$

- Critical values, which mark the cutoffs for the rejection region, can be identified for any level of significance. The value of the test statistic is compared to the critical values. When the value of a test statistic exceeds a critical value, we reject the null hypothesis; otherwise, we retain the null hypothesis.

LO 5:   **Distinguish between a one-tailed test and two-tailed test, and explain why a Type III error is possible only with one-tailed tests.**

- Nondirectional (two-tailed) tests are hypothesis tests in which the alternative hypothesis is stated as *not equal to* (≠) a value stated in the null hypothesis. So we are interested in any alternative to the null hypothesis.

- Directional (one-tailed) tests are hypothesis tests in which the alternative hypothesis is stated as *greater than* (>) or *less than* (<) a value stated in the null hypothesis. So we are interested in a specific alternative to the null hypothesis.

- A Type III error is a type of error possible with one-tailed tests in which a result would have been significant in one tail, but the researcher retains the null hypothesis because the rejection region was placed in the wrong or opposite tail.

LO 6:   **Elucidate effect size and compute a Cohen's *d* for the one-sample *z* test.**

- Effect size is a statistical measure of the size of an observed effect in a population, which allows researchers to describe how far scores shifted in the population, or the percent of variance that can be explained by a given variable.

- Cohen's *d* is used to measure how far scores shifted in a population and is computed using the following formula:

$$\text{Cohen's } d = \frac{M - \mu}{\sigma}.$$

- To interpret the size of an effect, we refer to Cohen's effect size conventions, which are standard rules for identifying small, medium, and large effects based on typical findings in behavioral research. These conventions are given in Table 7.6.

LO 7:   **Define *power* and identify six factors that influence power.**

- In hypothesis testing, power is the probability that a sample selected at random will show that the null hypothesis is false when the null hypothesis is indeed false.

- To increase the power of detecting an effect in a given population:
  a. Increase effect size (d), sample size (n), and alpha (α).
  b. Decrease beta error (β), population standard deviation (σ), and standard error (σ_M).

LO 8:   Summarize the results of a one-sample z test in APA format.

- To report the results of a z test, we report the test statistic, p value, and effect size of a hypothesis test. In addition, a figure or table can be used to summarize the means and standard error or standard deviation measured in a study.

• • • KEY TERMS

alpha (α) level	hypothesis testing	significance
alternative hypothesis (H_1)	level of significance	significance level
beta (β) error	nondirectional tests	significance testing
Cohen's d	null hypothesis (H_0)	statistical significance
Cohen's effect size conventions	obtained value	test statistic
critical value	one-sample z test	two-tailed tests
directional tests	one-tailed test	Type I error
effect	p value	Type II error
effect size	power	Type III error
hypothesis	rejection region	z statistic

• • • END-OF-CHAPTER PROBLEMS

Factual Problems

1. State the four steps of hypothesis testing.

2. What are two decisions that a researcher makes in hypothesis testing?

3. What is the power in hypothesis testing?

4. What is a Type II error (β)?

5. What is a Type I error (α)?

6. What are the critical values for a one-sample nondirectional (two-tailed) z test at a .05 level of significance?

7. Is a one-tailed test associated with greater power than a two-tailed test? Explain.

8. How are the rejection regions, the probability of a Type I error, the level of significance, and the alpha level related?

9. Alpha (α) is used to measure the error for decisions concerning true null hypotheses. What is beta (β) error used to measure?

10. What three factors can be decreased to increase power?

11. What three factors can be increased to increase power?

12. Distinguish between the significance and the effect size of a result.

Concept and Application Problems

13. A researcher conducts a hypothesis test and concludes that his hypothesis is correct. Explain why this conclusion is never an appropriate decision in hypothesis testing.

14. Explain why the following statement is true: The population standard deviation is always larger than the standard error when the sample size is greater than one ($n > 1$).

15. The weight (in pounds) for a population of school-aged children is normally distributed with a mean equal to 135 ± 20 pounds ($\mu \pm \sigma$). Suppose we select a sample of 100 children ($n = 100$) to test whether children in this population are gaining weight at a .05 level of significance.

    (a) What is the null hypothesis? What is the alternative hypothesis?

    (b) What is the critical value for this test?

    (c) What is the mean of the sampling distribution?

    (d) What is the standard error of the mean for the sampling distribution?

16. A researcher selects a sample of 30 participants and makes the decision to retain the null hypothesis. She conducts the same study testing the same hypothesis with a sample of 300 participants and makes the decision to reject the null hypothesis. Give a likely explanation for why the two samples led to different decisions.

17. A researcher conducts a one-sample z test and makes the decision to reject the null hypothesis. Another researcher selects a larger sample from the same population, obtains the same sample mean, and makes the decision to retain the null hypothesis using the same hypothesis test. Is this possible? Explain.

18. Determine the level of significance for a hypothesis test in each of the following populations given the specified standard error and critical values. *Hint:* Refer to the values given in Table 7.4:

    (a) $\mu = 100$, $\sigma_M = 8$, critical values: 84.32 and 115.68

    (b) $\mu = 100$, $\sigma_M = 6$, critical value: 113.98

    (c) $\mu = 100$, $\sigma_M = 4$, critical value: 86.8

19. For each p value stated below, (1) what is the decision for each if $\alpha = .05$, and (2) what is the decision for each if $\alpha = .01$?

    (a) $p = .1000$

    (b) $p = .0050$

    (c) $p = .0250$

    (d) $p = .0001$

20. For each obtained value stated below, (1) what is the decision for each if $\alpha = .05$ (one-tailed test, upper-tail critical), and (2) what is the decision for each if $\alpha = .01$ (two-tailed test)?

    (a) $z_{obt} = 2.10$

    (b) $z_{obt} = 1.70$

    (c) $z_{obt} = 2.75$

    (d) $z_{obt} = -3.30$

21. Will each of the following increase, decrease, or have no effect on the value of a test statistic for the one-sample z test?

    (a) The sample size is increased.

    (b) The sample variance is doubled.

    (c) The population variance is decreased.

    (d) The difference between the sample mean and population mean is decreased.

22. The physical fitness score for a population of police officers at a local police station is 72, with a standard deviation of 7 on a 100-point physical endurance scale. Suppose the police chief selects a sample of 49 local police officers from this population and records a mean physical fitness rating on this scale equal to 74. He conducts a one-sample z test to determine whether physical endurance increased at a .05 level of significance.

    (a) State the value of the test statistic and whether to retain or reject the null hypothesis.

    (b) Compute effect size using Cohen's d.

23. A national firm reports mean earnings of $75 \pm 12 ($\mu \pm \sigma$) per unit sold over the lifetime of the company. A competing company over the past 36 reporting periods had reported mean earnings equal to $78 per unit sold. Conduct a one-sample z test to determine whether mean earnings (in dollars per unit) are larger (compared to that reported by the national firm) at a .05 level of significance.

    (a) State the value of the test statistic and whether to retain or reject the null hypothesis.

    (b) Compute effect size using Cohen's d.

24. A local school reports that the average grade point average (GPA) in the entire school is

a mean score of 2.66, with a standard deviation of 0.40. The school announces that it will be introducing a new program designed to improve GPA scores at the school. What is the effect size (d) for this program if it is expected to improve GPA by:

(a) 0.05 points?

(b) 0.10 points?

(c) 0.40 points?

25. Will each of the following increase, decrease, or have no effect on the value of Cohen's d?

(a) The population variance is increased.

(b) The sample size is decreased.

(c) The sample variance is reduced.

(d) The difference between the sample and population mean is increased.

26. State whether the effect size for a 1-point effect $(M - \mu = 1)$ is small, medium, or large given the following population variances:

(a) $\sigma = 1$

(b) $\sigma = 2$

(c) $\sigma = 4$

(d) $\sigma = 6$

27. As α increases, so does the power to detect an effect. Why, then, do we restrict α from being larger than .05?

28. Will increasing sample size (n) increase or decrease the value of standard error? Will this increase or decrease power?

Problems in Research

29. **Directional versus nondirectional hypothesis testing.** Cho and Abe (2013) provided a commentary on the appropriate use of one-tailed and two-tailed tests in behavioral research. In their discussion, they outlined the following hypothetical null and alternative hypotheses to test a research hypothesis that males self-disclose more than females:

$H_0: \mu_{males} - \mu_{females} \leq 0$

$H_1: \mu_{males} - \mu_{females} > 0$

(a) What type of test is set up with these hypotheses, a directional test or a nondirectional test?

(b) Do these hypotheses encompass all possibilities for the population mean? Explain.

30. **The one-tailed tests.** In their book, *Common Errors in Statistics (and How to Avoid Them)*, Good and Hardin (2003) wrote, "No one will know whether your [one-tailed] hypothesis was conceived before you started or only after you had examined the data" (p. 347). Why do the authors state this as a concern for one-tailed tests?

31. **The value of a *p* value.** In a critical commentary on the use of significance testing, Charles Lambdin (2012) explained, "If a $p < .05$ result is

'significant,' then a $p = .067$ result is not 'marginally significant'" (p. 76). Explain what the author is referring to in terms of the two decisions that a researcher can make.

32. **Describing the *z* test.** In an article describing hypothesis testing with small sample sizes, Collins and Morris (2008) provided the following description for a z test: "Z is considered significant if the difference is more than roughly two standard deviations above or below zero (or more precisely, $|Z| > 1.96$)" (p. 464). Based on this description,

(a) Are the authors referring to critical values for a one-tailed z test or a two-tailed z test?

(b) What alpha level are the authors referring to?

33. **Sample size and power.** Davis and Loprinzi (2016) evaluated a hypothesis related to engaging children, adolescents, and adults in physical activity. As part of their study, they reported a sample size of 106 children, 128 adolescents, and 440 adults. Assuming equal effect sizes across these age groups, which age group is likely to be associated with greater power to detect effects of physical activity? Explain.

34. **Making decisions in hypothesis testing.** Toll, Kroesbergen, and Van Luit (2016) tested their hypothesis regarding real math difficulties among children. In their study, the authors concluded: "Our hypothesis [regarding math difficulties] was confirmed" (p. 429). In this example, what decision did the authors make: Retain or reject the null hypothesis?

Answers for even numbers are in Appendix D.

Sharpen your skills with **SAGE edge at edge.sagepub.com/priviteraess2e**

SAGE edge for Students provides a personalized approach to help you accomplish your coursework goals in an easy-to-use learning environment.

$SAGE edge™

cosmin4000/iStock/Thinkstock

Part III

Making Inferences About One or Two Means

iStockphoto.com/JohnnyGreig

8

Testing Means
One-Sample *t* Test With Confidence Intervals

There are cases where making comparisons using only a single sample can be quite informative, especially where there are known standards or criteria for comparison. Many of us are familiar with standards or criteria that we often use to gauge how we are doing. Educational standards, for example, are often what we strive to meet (e.g., cutoff score requirements to pass state or national assessments), or health criteria are guidelines for us to assess how healthy we are (e.g., minimal cutoffs for cholesterol levels or body mass index scores for obesity). In each example, a specific standard or criteria is identified, which in turn is used to inform us about something of interest to us (e.g., whether or not we are passing educational standards or meeting health criteria).

In hypothesis testing, standards or criteria can be of interest to us as well. In these types of situations, we typically want to test how a sample of scores compares to some known standard or criterion. For example, researchers may want to compare health scores in a sample of adults who care for family members with mental health disorders to an average health score in the general population (the criterion) to learn about possible detrimental effects on health in this sample; in education, researchers may compare math scores on a standardized assessment at local elementary schools to the national average (the criterion) to learn about the effectiveness of a new curriculum. Anytime we compare one sample of scores to a standard or criterion (typically a known average), we are making "one-sample" comparisons.

In this chapter, we explore the nature of hypothesis testing with one sample, how to compute and interpret observed effects, and the informativeness of hypothesis testing for making comparisons with one sample. We further explore other ways of adding information about the nature of observed effects and how to appropriately interpret them.

Master the content.

edge.sagepub.com/priviteraess2e

● ● ● **Chapter Outline**

8.1 Going From *z* to *t*

In the discussion of hypothesis testing in Chapter 7, we introduced the one-sample *z* test. To compute the test statistic for a one-sample *z* test, we must know the value of the population variance. However, it is rare in behavioral science that we know the variance of a population, in which case we cannot compute the *z* statistic:

$$z_{obt} = \frac{M - \mu}{\sigma_M}, \text{where } \sigma_M = \frac{\sigma}{\sqrt{n}}.$$

To compute this *z* statistic formula, we need to know the population standard deviation, which requires that we know the variance. If we do not know the population variance, then we cannot compute the value for *z*. We need an alternative test statistic that can be computed when the population variance is unknown.

An alternative to the *z* statistic was proposed by William Sealy Gosset (Student, 1908), a scientist working with the Guinness brewing company to improve brewing processes in the early 1900s. Because Guinness prohibited its employees from publishing "trade secrets," Gosset obtained approval to publish his work only under the condition that he used a pseudonym ("Student"). He proposed substituting the sample variance for the population variance in the formula for standard error. When this substitution is made, the formula for error is called the **estimated standard error (s_M)**:

$$\text{Estimated standard error: } s_M = \sqrt{\frac{s^2}{n}} = \frac{SD}{\sqrt{n}}.$$

The substitution is possible because, as explained in Chapter 7, the sample variance is an unbiased estimator of the population variance: On average, the sample variance equals the population variance. Using this substitution, an alternative test statistic can be introduced for one sample when the population variance is unknown. The formula, known as a *t* **statistic**, is as follows for one sample:

$$t_{obt} = \frac{M - \mu}{s_M}, \text{where } s_M = \frac{SD}{\sqrt{n}}.$$

Gosset showed that substituting the sample variance for the population variance led to a new sampling distribution known as the *t* **distribution,** which is also known as **Student's** *t* referring to the pseudonym Gosset used when publishing his work. In Figure 8.1, you can see how similar the *t* distribution is to the normal distribution. The difference is that the *t* distribution has greater variability in the tails because the sample variance is not always equal to the population variance. Sometimes the estimate for variance is too large; sometimes the estimate is too small. This leads to a larger probability of obtaining sample means farther from the population mean. Otherwise, the *t* distribution shares all the same characteristics as the normal distribution: It is symmetrical and asymptotic, and its mean, median, and mode are all located at the center of the distribution.

The **estimated standard error** is an estimate of the standard deviation of a sampling distribution of sample means selected from a population with an unknown variance. It is an estimate of the standard error or standard distance that sample means deviate from the value of the population mean stated in the null hypothesis.

The *t* **statistic**, known as *t* **observed** *or* *t* **obtained**, is an inferential statistic used to determine the number of standard deviations in a *t* distribution that a sample mean deviates from the mean value or mean difference stated in the null hypothesis.

The *t* **distribution**, or **Student's** *t*, is a normal-like distribution with greater variability in the tails than a normal distribution because the sample variance is substituted for the population variance to estimate the standard error in this distribution.

FIGURE 8.1   A Normal Distribution and Two *t* Distributions

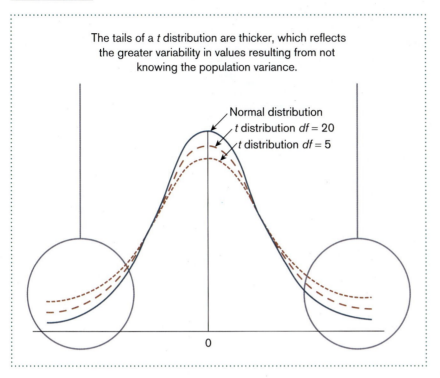

The tails of a *t* distribution are thicker, which reflects the greater variability in values resulting from not knowing the population variance.

Normal distribution
t distribution *df* = 20
t distribution *df* = 5

0

Notice that the normal distribution has less variability in the tails; otherwise, these distributions share the same characteristics.

Source: www.unl.edu

8.2 THE DEGREES OF FREEDOM

The *t* distribution is associated with **degrees of freedom (*df*)**. In Chapter 4, we identified that the degrees of freedom for sample variance equal $n - 1$. Because the estimate of standard error for the *t* distribution is computed using the sample variance, the degrees of freedom for the *t* distribution are also $n - 1$. The *t* distribution is a sampling distribution in which the estimated standard error is computed using the sample variance in the formula. As sample size increases, the sample variance more closely approximates the population variance. The result is that there is less variability in the tails as sample size increases. So the shape of the *t* distribution changes (the tails approach the *x*-axis faster) as the sample size is increased. Each changing *t* distribution is thus associated with the same degrees of freedom as for sample variance: $df = n - 1$.

8.3 READING THE *t* TABLE

To locate probabilities and critical values in a *t* distribution, we use a *t* table, such as Table 8.1, which reproduces part of Table C.2 in Appendix C. In the *t* table, there are six columns of values listing alpha levels for one-tailed tests (top heading) and two-tailed tests (lower heading). The rows show the degrees of freedom (*df*) for a *t* distribution.

FYI

The degrees of freedom for a t distribution are equal to the degrees of freedom for sample variance: n − 1.

The **degrees of freedom (*df*)** for a *t* distribution are equal to the degrees of freedom for sample variance for a given sample: $n - 1$. Each *t* distribution is associated with specified degrees of freedom; as sample size increases, the degrees of freedom also increase.

TABLE 8.1 A Portion of the *t* Table Adapted From Table C.2 in Appendix C

	Proportion in One Tail					
	.25	.10	.05	.025	.01	.005
	Proportion in Two Tails Combined					
df	.50	.20	.10	.05	.02	.01
1	1.000	3.078	6.314	12.706	31.821	63.657
2	0.816	1.886	2.920	4.303	6.965	9.925
3	0.765	1.638	2.353	3.182	4.541	5.841
4	0.741	1.533	2.132	2.776	3.747	4.604
5	0.727	1.476	2.015	2.571	3.365	4.032
6	0.718	1.440	1.943	2.447	3.143	3.707
7	0.711	1.415	1.895	2.365	2.998	3.499
8	0.706	1.397	1.860	2.306	2.896	3.355
9	0.703	1.383	1.833	2.282	2.821	3.250
10	0.700	1.372	1.812	2.228	2.764	3.169

Source: Table III in Fisher, R. A., & Yates, F. (1974). *Statistical tables for biological, agricultural and medical research* (6th ed.). London, England: Longman Group Ltd. (previously published by Oliver and Boyd Ltd., Edinburgh). Adapted and reprinted with permission of Addison Wesley Longman.

To use this table, you need to know the sample size (*n*), the alpha level (α), and the location of the rejection region (in one or both tails). For example, if we select a sample of 11 students, then $n = 11$, and $df = 10$ ($n - 1 = 10$). To find the *t* distribution with 10 degrees of freedom, we look for 10 listed in the rows. The critical values for this distribution at a .05 level of significance appear in the column with that probability listed: For a one-tailed test, the critical value is 1.812 for an upper-tail critical test and −1.812 for a lower-tail critical test. For a two-tailed test, the critical values are ±2.228. Each critical value identifies the cutoff for the rejection region, beyond which the decision will be to reject the null hypothesis for a hypothesis test.

Keep in mind that a *t* distribution is an estimate of a normal distribution. The larger the sample size, the more closely a *t* distribution estimates a normal distribution. When the sample size is so large that it equals the population size, we describe the sample size as infinite. In this case, the *t* distribution is a normal distribution. You can see this in the *t* table in Appendix C. The critical values at a .05 level of significance are ±1.960 for a two-tailed *t* test with infinite (∞) degrees of freedom and 1.645 (upper-tail critical) or −1.645 (lower-tail critical) for a one-tailed test. These are the same critical values listed in the unit normal table at a .05 level of significance.

In terms of the null hypothesis, in a small sample, there is a greater probability of obtaining sample means that are farther from the value stated in the null hypothesis. As sample size increases, obtaining sample means that are farther from the value stated in the null hypothesis becomes less likely. The result is that critical values get smaller as sample size increases.

FYI

The t table lists critical values for six levels of significance for one- and two-tailed tests.

LEARNING CHECK 1

1. What is the main limitation of the z test in behavioral research?

2. The _____ is a normal-like distribution with greater variability in the tails than a normal distribution because the sample variance is substituted for the population variance to estimate the standard error in this distribution.

3. How does increasing sample size affect the estimate of the population variance?

4. What is the calculation for the degrees of freedom of a t distribution?

5. What are the degrees of freedom for each of the following samples?

   (a) $n = 12$ (b) $n = 22$ (c) $n = 5$ (d) $n = 30$

6. Assuming $\alpha = .05$, what is the critical value in each of the following t distributions?

   (a) $df = 10$, two-tailed test

   (b) $df = 30$, one-tailed test (lower-tail critical)

   (c) $df = \infty$, two-tailed test

   (d) $df = 15$, one-tailed test (upper-tail critical)

Answers: 1. It requires that the population variance is known, and behavioral researchers rarely know the value of the population variance; 2. t distribution; 3. As sample size increases, the sample variance more closely approximates the population variance; 4. $n - 1$; 5. (a) $df = 11$, (b) $df = 21$, (c) $df = 4$, (d) $df = 29$; 6. (a) ± 2.228, (b) -1.697, (c) ± 1.96, (d) 1.753.

8.4 COMPUTING THE ONE-SAMPLE *t* TEST

In this section, we compute the alternative for a one-sample z test, called the **one-sample *t* test**, which is used to compare a mean value measured in a sample to a known value in the population. Specifically, this test is used to test hypotheses concerning a single group mean selected from a population with an unknown variance. Table 8.2 summarizes the differences and similarities between the z test and t test. To compute the one-sample t test, we make three assumptions:

1. *Normality.* We assume that data in the population being sampled are normally distributed. This assumption is particularly important for small samples. In larger samples ($n > 30$), the standard error is smaller, and this assumption becomes less critical as a result.

2. *Random sampling.* We assume that the data we measure were obtained from a sample that was selected using a random sampling procedure. It is considered inappropriate to conduct hypothesis tests with nonrandom samples.

The **one-sample t test** is a statistical procedure used to compare a mean value measured in a sample to a known value in the population. It is specifically used to test hypotheses concerning the mean in a single population with an unknown variance.

FYI

Three assumptions for a one-sample t *test are normality, random sampling, and independence.*

3. *Independence.* We assume that each outcome or observation is independent, meaning that one outcome does not influence another. Specifically, outcomes are independent when the probability of one outcome has no effect on the probability of another outcome. Using random sampling usually satisfies this assumption.

In Example 8.1, we compute the one-sample *t* test using the four steps to hypothesis testing introduced in Chapter 7.

TABLE 8.2   The Differences and Similarities Between the *z* Test and *t* Test

	z Test	*t* Test
What is the obtained value?	*z* statistic, *p* value	*t* statistic, *p* value
What distribution is used to locate the probability of obtaining a sample mean?	Normal distribution	*t* distribution
What is the denominator of the test statistic?	Standard error	Estimated standard error
Do we know the population variance?	Yes	No. The sample variance is used to estimate the population variance
Are degrees of freedom required for this test?	No, because the population variance is known	Yes. The degrees of freedom for a *t* test are equal to the degrees of freedom for sample variance for a given sample: $n - 1$
What does the test measure?	The probability of obtaining a measured sample outcome	
What can be inferred from the test?	Whether or not the null hypothesis should be rejected	

Example 8.1

iStock.com/monkeybusinessimages

Social functioning is the ability for an individual to interact or adapt in a normal or usual way in social environments. This area of research is of interest to behavioral researchers, particularly in medical or clinical settings, and those who study human development (Albert, Salvi, Saracco, Bogetto, & Maina, 2007; Cozolino, 2014; Taber-Thomas & Tranel, 2012). As an example for a one-sample *t* test, Albert et al. (2007) asked if relatives who care for patients with obsessive-compulsive disorder (OCD) are as healthy as those in the general healthy population. In their study, they recorded the social functioning of relatives of patients with OCD using a 36-item short-form health survey (SF-36), with scores ranging from 0 (*worst possible health*) to 100 (*best possible health*). They cited that the mean social functioning score in the general healthy population of interest was 77.43. Using a sample data set that approximates their findings, we will test whether the mean score in the sample data given in Table 8.3 significantly differs from that in the general population at a .05 level of significance.

Step 1: State the hypotheses. The population mean is 77.43, and we are testing whether (=) or not (≠) the population mean differs from the sample mean:

$H_0: \mu = 77.43$ For relatives who care for patients with OCD, the mean social functioning score is 77.43, same as that in the general healthy population.

$H_1: \mu \neq 77.43$ For relatives who care for patients with OCD, the mean social functioning score is not equal to 77.43.

Step 2: Set the criteria for a decision. The level of significance for this test is .05. We are computing a two-tailed test with $n - 1$ degrees of freedom. With $n = 18$, the degrees of freedom for this test are $18 - 1 = 17$. To locate the critical values, we find 17 listed in the rows of Table C.2 in Appendix C and go across to the column for a .05 proportion in two tails combined. The critical values are ±2.110. Figure 8.2 shows the t distribution, with rejection regions beyond the critical values.

We will compare the value of the test statistic with these critical values. If the value of the test statistic is beyond a critical value (either greater than +2.110 or less than −2.110), then there is less than a 5% chance we would obtain that outcome if the null hypothesis were correct, so we reject the null hypothesis; otherwise, we retain the null hypothesis.

Step 3: Compute the test statistic. In this example, we can compute the sample mean and standard deviation for the data given in Table 8.3. As introduced in Chapter 3, the sample mean is the sum of all scores divided by the number of scores summed: $M = 62.00$. As introduced in Chapter 4, to compute the sample standard deviation, first subtract and square the

| TABLE 8.3 | SF-36 Scores for a Sample of 18 Relatives Who Care for Patients With OCD |

Social Functioning Scores (SF-36)
20
60
48
92
50
82
48
90
30
68
43
54
60
62
94
67
63
85

FIGURE 8.2 Setting the Criteria for a Decision

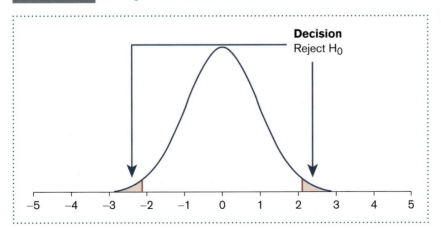

The shaded regions represent the rejection regions with critical values equal to ±2.110 for a t distribution with $df = 17$. If the value of the test statistic falls in the shaded region, we reject the null hypothesis; otherwise, we retain the null hypothesis.

difference of each score from the sample mean and divide by $n - 1$, then take the square root: $SD = 20.94$.

We will compare the sample mean to the population mean stated in the null hypothesis: $\mu = 77.43$. To find the t statistic, we first compute the estimated standard error. To compute the estimated standard error, which is the denominator of the t statistic, we divide the sample standard deviation (SD) by the square root of the sample size (n). In this example, $SD = 20.94$, and $n = 18$:

$$s_M = \frac{SD}{\sqrt{n}} = \frac{20.94}{\sqrt{18}} = 4.94.$$

Find the t statistic by substituting the values for the sample mean, $M = 62.00$; the population mean stated in the null hypothesis, $\mu = 77.43$; and the estimated standard error we just calculated, $s_M = 4.94$:

$$t_{obt} = \frac{M - \mu}{s_M} = \frac{62.00 - 77.43}{4.94} = -3.126.$$

FYI

The t table lists critical values for t distributions with various degrees of freedom.

FYI

The test statistic for a one-sample t test is the difference between the sample mean and population mean stated by the null hypothesis, divided by the estimated standard error.

Step 4: Make a decision. To decide to reject or retain the null hypothesis, we compare the obtained value ($t_{obt} = -3.126$) to the critical values. Figure 8.3 shows that the obtained value falls beyond the critical value in the lower tail; it falls in the rejection region. The decision is to reject the null hypothesis. If this result were reported in a research journal, it would look something like this:

Social functioning scores among relatives who care for patients with OCD ($M = 62.00$) were significantly lower than scores in the general healthy population, $t(17) = -3.126$, $p < .05$.

FIGURE 8.3   Making a Decision for Example 8.1

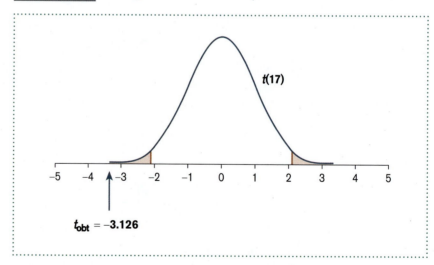

The value of the test statistic falls in the rejection region. Therefore, we reject the null hypothesis.

LEARNING CHECK 2

1. What are three assumptions of the one-sample *t* test?

2. Researchers record the number of errors on some behavioral task for 15 participants. They report a sample mean equal to 6 ± 1 ($M \pm SD$). What is the critical value for a two-tailed test with $\alpha = .01$?

3. Using the same study described in Question 2 with $\alpha = .01$, what is the decision if the following values for the test statistic are obtained?

   (a) 2.558   (b) 1.602   (c) 2.999   (d) −3.404

Answers: 1. Normality, random sampling, and independence; 2. ± 2.977; 3. (a) Retain the null hypothesis, (b) Retain the null hypothesis, (c) Reject the null hypothesis, (d) Reject the null hypothesis.

8.5 EFFECT SIZE FOR THE ONE-SAMPLE *t* TEST

As described in Chapter 7, hypothesis testing identifies whether or not an effect exists in a population. When we decide to retain the null hypothesis, we conclude that an effect does not exist in the population. When we decide to reject the null hypothesis, we conclude that an effect does exist in the population. However, hypothesis testing does not tell us how large the effect is.

In Example 8.1, we concluded that mean social functioning scores among relatives who care for patients with OCD are significantly lower than those in the general healthy population. To determine the size of an effect, we compute effect size, which gives an estimate of the size of an effect in the population. Three measures of effect size for the one-sample *t* test are described in this section: estimated Cohen's *d* and two measures of proportion of variance (eta-squared and omega-squared).

Estimated Cohen's *d*

The estimate of effect size that is most often used with a *t* test is the **estimated Cohen's *d***. In the Cohen's *d* measure introduced with the *z* test in Chapter 7, the population standard deviation was placed in the denominator of the formula. When the population standard deviation is unknown, we substitute it with the sample standard deviation because it gives an unbiased estimate of the population standard deviation. The estimated Cohen's *d* formula is as follows:

$$d = \frac{M - \mu}{SD}.$$

In Example 8.1, $M = 62.00$, $\mu = 77.43$, and $SD = 20.94$. The estimated Cohen's *d* for Example 8.1 is

$$d = \frac{62.00 - 77.43}{20.94} = -0.74.$$

An **estimated Cohen's *d*** is a measure of effect size in terms of the number of standard deviations that mean scores shift above or below the population mean stated by the null hypothesis. The larger the value of estimated Cohen's *d*, the larger the effect in the population.

FYI

The sample standard deviation is used to estimate the population standard deviation in the estimated Cohen's d formula.

We conclude that being a relative who cares for a patient with OCD reduces mean social functioning scores by 0.74 standard deviations below the mean in the general healthy population. The effect size conventions (J. Cohen, 1988) given in Chapter 7, Table 7.6 (p. 211), and in the second column of Table 8.4 show that this is a medium effect size. We could report this measure with the significant *t* test in Example 8.1 by stating,

> Social functioning scores among relatives who care for patients with OCD (*M* = 62.00) were significantly lower than scores in the general healthy population, $t(17) = -3.126$, $p < .05$ ($d = -0.74$).

Proportion of Variance

Another measure of effect size is to estimate the **proportion of variance** that can be accounted for by some **treatment**. A treatment, which is any unique characteristic of a sample or any unique way that a researcher treats a sample, can change the value of a dependent variable. A treatment is associated with variability in a study. Proportion of variance estimates how much of the variability in a dependent variable can be accounted for by the treatment. In the proportion of variance formula, the variability explained by a treatment is divided by the total variability observed:

$$\text{Proportion of variance} = \frac{\text{variability explained}}{\text{total variability}}.$$

In Example 8.1, we found that relatives who care for patients with OCD had significantly lower social functioning scores compared to the general healthy population. The unique characteristic of the sample in this study was that the participants were relatives of patients with OCD. The variable we measured (i.e., the dependent variable) was social functioning scores. Measuring proportion of variance determines how much of the variability in the dependent variable (social functioning scores) can be explained by the treatment (the fact that the participants were relatives of patients with OCD). Here, we introduce here two measures of proportion of variance: eta-squared (η^2) and omega-squared (ω^2).

Eta-Squared (η^2)

Eta-squared is a measure of proportion of variance that can be expressed in a single formula based on the result of a *t* test:

$$\eta^2 = \frac{t^2}{t^2 + df}.$$

The **proportion of variance** is a measure of effect size in terms of the proportion or percent of variability in a dependent variable that can be explained or accounted for by a treatment.

In hypothesis testing, a **treatment** is any unique characteristic of a sample or any unique way that a researcher treats a sample.

In this formula, *t* is the value of the *t* statistic, and *df* is the degrees of freedom. In this example, $t_{obt} = -3.126$, and $df = 17$. To find variance, we square the standard deviation. Thus, in the eta-squared formula, we square the value of *t* to find the proportion of variance. The proportion of variance for the data in Example 8.1 is

$$\eta^2 = \frac{(-3.126)^2}{(-3.126)^2 + 17} = .36.$$

We conclude that 36% of the variability in social functioning (the dependent variable) can be explained by the fact that participants were relatives who care for patients with OCD (the treatment). We could report this measure with the significant t test in Example 8.1 by stating,

> Social functioning scores among relatives who care for patients with OCD ($M = 62.00$) were significantly lower than scores in the general healthy population, $t(17) = -3.126$, $p < .05$ ($\eta^2 = .36$).

The third column in Table 8.4 displays guidelines for interpreting a small, medium, and large effect for η^2. Using this table, we find that $\eta^2 = .36$ is a large effect. When we used estimated Cohen's d, we concluded that it was a medium effect size. This discrepancy is partly due to eta-squared being biased. Although eta-squared is a popular measure of proportion of variance, it tends to overestimate the proportion of variance explained by a treatment. To correct for this bias, many researchers use a modified eta-squared formula, called omega-squared.

FYI

Eta-squared tends to overestimate the size of an effect in a population. Omega-squared corrects for this bias.

TABLE 8.4	The Size of an Effect Using Estimated Cohen's d and Two Measures of Proportion of Variance		
Description of Effect	**d**	**η^2**	**ω^2**
Trivial	—	$\eta^2 < .01$	$\omega^2 < .01$
Small	$d < 0.2$	$.01 < \eta^2 < .09$	$.01 < \omega^2 < .09$
Medium	$0.2 < d < 0.8$	$.10 < \eta^2 < .25$	$.10 < \omega^2 < .25$
Large	$d > 0.8$	$\eta^2 > .25$	$\omega^2 > .25$

Omega-Squared (ω^2)

Omega-squared is also the variability explained by a treatment, divided by the total variability observed. The change in the formula of proportion of variance is that 1 is subtracted from t^2 in the numerator:

$$\omega^2 = \frac{t^2 - 1}{t^2 + df}.$$

Subtracting 1 in the numerator reduces the estimate of effect size. Hence, omega-squared will always give a smaller or more conservative estimate of effect size, making it less biased than eta-squared. Using the omega-squared formula, the proportion of variance for the data in Example 8.1 is

$$\omega^2 = \frac{(-3.126)^2 - 1}{(-3.126)^2 + 17} = .33.$$

We conclude that 33% of the variability in social functioning (the dependent variable) can be explained by the fact that participants were relatives who care for patients with OCD (the treatment). In the last column in Table 8.4, we find that the value of omega-squared, while smaller than that of eta-squared, is also a large effect size. We could report this measure with the significant t test in Example 8.1 by stating,

> Social functioning scores among relatives who care for patients with OCD ($M = 62.00$) were significantly lower than scores in the general healthy population, $t(17) = -3.126$, $p < .05$ ($\omega^2 = .33$).

LEARNING CHECK 3

1. An estimated Cohen's d substitutes which value in the formula to estimate the population standard deviation?

2. A researcher compares the mean grade point average (GPA) of college students with a full-time job to the mean GPA of the general population of college students. In this example, identify (a) the dependent variable and (b) the treatment.

3. State whether each of the following values for estimated Cohen's d has a small, medium, or large effect size.

   (a) 0.40   (b) 1.20   (c) 0.05   (d) 0.10

4. A researcher reports that a sample of workers with high-stress careers slept significantly less than workers in the general population, $t(48) = 2.36$, $p < .05$. Compute eta-squared for this one-sample t test.

5. What measure, eta-squared or omega-squared, gives a more conservative or smaller estimate of proportion of variance?

Answers: 1. Sample standard deviation; 2. (a) GPA, (b) Having a full-time job; 3. (a) Medium, (b) Large, (c) Small, (d) Small; 4. $\eta^2 = .10$; 5. Omega-squared.

8.6 CONFIDENCE INTERVALS FOR THE ONE-SAMPLE t TEST

In Example 8.1, we stated a null hypothesis regarding the value of the mean in a population. We then computed a test statistic to determine the probability of obtaining a sample outcome if the null hypothesis were true. In our example, the probability of obtaining the sample outcome was less than 5% if the null hypothesis were true, so we rejected the null hypothesis; otherwise, we would have decided to retain the null hypothesis. Using hypothesis testing, the goal was to learn more about the value of a mean in a population of interest by deciding whether to retain or reject the null hypothesis.

We can also learn more about the mean in a population using a different procedure without ever deciding to retain or reject a null hypothesis. An alternative approach requires only that we set limits for the population parameter within which it is likely to be contained. The goal of this alternative approach, called **estimation**, is the same as that in hypothesis testing for Example 8.1—to learn more about the value of a mean in a population of interest.

There are two types of estimates: a point estimate and an interval estimate. When using one sample, a **point estimate** is the sample mean we measure. The advantage of using point estimation is that the *point estimate*, or sample mean, is an unbiased estimator—that is, the sample mean will equal the population mean on average. The disadvantage of using point estimation is that we have no way of knowing for sure whether a sample mean equals the population mean. One way to resolve this disadvantage is, instead of giving just one value, we identify a range of values within which we can be confident that any one of those values is equal to the population mean. The interval or range of possible values within which a population parameter is likely to be contained is called the **interval estimate**. Most often, the point estimate and interval estimate are given together. Thus, researchers report the sample mean (a point estimate) and give an interval within which a population mean is likely to be contained (an *interval estimate*). The interval estimate, often reported as a **confidence interval**, is stated within a given **level of confidence**, which is the likelihood that an interval contains an unknown population mean.

Using estimation, we use the sample mean as a point estimate, and we use the standard error to determine the interval estimate. The standard error is used to find the range of sample means within which the population mean is likely to be contained. To illustrate, we will revisit Example 8.1 and compute the confidence intervals at a 95% level of confidence for the data analyzed using the one-sample *t* test.

To find the confidence intervals for a one-sample *t* test, we need to evaluate an estimation formula. We will use the estimation formula to identify the upper and lower confidence limits within which the unknown population mean is likely to be contained. The estimation formula for the one-sample *t* test is as follows:

$$M \pm t(s_M).$$

In all, we follow three steps to estimate the value of a population mean using a point estimate and an interval estimate:

Step 1: Compute the sample mean and standard error.

Step 2: Choose the level of confidence and find the critical values at that level of confidence.

Step 3: Compute the estimation formula to find the confidence limits.

FYI

A point estimate is a sample mean or a sample mean difference. An interval estimate is the interval or range of values within which an unknown population mean is likely to be contained.

FYI

The estimation formula for a t test is used when we estimate the mean or the mean difference in populations with an unknown variance.

Estimation is a statistical procedure in which a sample statistic is used to estimate the value of an unknown population parameter. Two types of estimation are point estimation and interval estimation.

A **point estimate** is the use of a sample statistic (e.g., a sample mean) to estimate the value of a population parameter (e.g., a population mean).

An **interval estimate**, often reported as a **confidence interval**, is an interval or range of possible values within which a population parameter is likely to be contained.

Level of confidence is the probability or likelihood that an interval estimate will contain an unknown population parameter (e.g., a population mean).

In Example 8.1, we use the three steps to compute the estimation formula for the one-sample *t* test.

Step 1: Compute the sample mean and the estimated standard error. The sample mean, which is the point estimate of the population mean, is equal to $M = 62.00$ (we already computed this value for Example 8.1 in Step 3 of hypothesis testing).

The estimated standard error, s_M, is the sample standard deviation divided by the square root of the sample size (we already computed this value as well for Example 8.1 in Step 3 of hypothesis testing):

$$s_M = \frac{SD}{\sqrt{n}} = \frac{20.94}{\sqrt{18}} = 4.94.$$

Step 2: Choose the level of confidence and find the critical values at that level of confidence. In this example, we chose the 95% confidence interval (CI). The critical value at this level of confidence will be the same as we found in Step 2 for Example 8.1 using hypothesis testing. The 95% level of confidence corresponds to a two-tailed test at a .05 level of significance using hypothesis testing. Thus, the critical value for the interval estimate is 2.110.

To explain further how this critical value was determined, remember that in a sampling distribution, 50% of sample means fall above the sample mean we selected, and 50% fall below it. We are looking for the 95% of sample means that surround the sample mean we selected, meaning the 47.5% of sample means above and the 47.5% of sample means below the sample mean we selected. This leaves only 2.5% of sample means remaining in the upper tail and 2.5% in the lower tail. Table 8.5 shows how different levels of confidence using estimation correspond to different two-tailed levels of significance (α) using hypothesis testing. Referring to Table 8.5, we find that a 95% CI corresponds to a two-tailed test at a .05 level of significance. To find the critical value at this level of confidence, we look in the t table in Table C.2 in Appendix C. The degrees of freedom are 17 ($df = n - 1$ for a one-sample t test). The critical value for the interval estimate is 2.110.

TABLE 8.5	Levels of Significance Using Hypothesis Testing and the Corresponding Levels of Confidence Using Estimation

Level of Confidence	Level of Significance (α level, two-tailed)
99%	.01
95%	.05
90%	.10
80%	.20

Step 3: Compute the estimation formula to find the confidence limits for a 95% confidence interval. To compute the formula, multiply t by the estimated standard error:

$$t(s_M) = 2.110(4.94) = 10.42.$$

Add 10.42 to the sample mean to find the upper confidence limit:

$$M + (s_M) = 62 + 10.42 = 72.42.$$

Subtract 10.42 from the sample mean to find the lower confidence limit:

$$M - t(s_M) = 62 - 10.42 = 51.58.$$

As shown in Figure 8.4, the 95% confidence interval in this population is between a score of 51.58 and a score of 72.42 on the social functioning measure. We can estimate within a 95% level of confidence that the mean social functioning of relatives of patients with OCD using a 36-item short-form health survey (SF-36) is between 51.58 and 72.42 in the population. We are 95% confident that the population mean falls within this range because 95% of all sample means we could have selected from this population fall within the range of sample means we specified.

FYI

When the value stated by a null hypothesis is outside a confidence interval, this indicates a significant effect in the population.

FIGURE 8.4 In Example 8.1, the 95% Confidence Interval Is 51.58 to 72.42

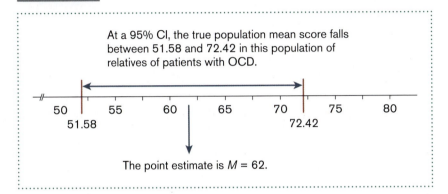

At a 95% CI, the true population mean score falls between 51.58 and 72.42 in this population of relatives of patients with OCD.

The point estimate is $M = 62$.

8.7 INFERRING SIGNIFICANCE AND EFFECT SIZE FROM A CONFIDENCE INTERVAL

Notice that we did not make a decision using estimation, other than to state confidence limits for a 95% confidence interval. When we evaluated these same data with hypothesis testing in Example 8.1, we selected a sample to decide whether or not to reject the null hypothesis. While we do not "make a decision" per se using estimation, we can use the confidence limits to determine what the decision would have been using hypothesis testing. In terms of the decisions we make in hypothesis testing,

1. If the value stated by a null hypothesis is inside a confidence interval, the decision is to retain the null hypothesis (not significant).

2. If the value stated by a null hypothesis is outside the confidence interval, the decision is to reject the null hypothesis (significant).

In terms of significance, Figure 8.5 shows that a score of 77.43 (the value of the null hypothesis) does not fall within the confidence interval identified. Because 77.43 does not fall within the 95% CI of 51.58 to 72.42, we would have decided to reject the null hypothesis using hypothesis testing, which was the decision we made in Example 8.1.

In terms of effect size, when the value stated by a null hypothesis is outside the confidence interval, we can interpret effect size using the confidence limits. Thus we estimate effect size as a range of values, and not using an exact value, as we did using Cohen's *d* and proportion of variance. Specifically, the effect size for a confidence interval is a range or interval, where the lower effect size estimate is the difference between the value stated in the null hypothesis and the lower confidence limit; the upper effect size estimate is the difference between the value stated in the null hypothesis and the upper confidence limit. Effect size can then be interpreted in terms of a shift in the population. To identify the effect size of the confidence interval for Example 8.1, we estimate that social functioning health is between 5.01 and 25.85 points worse in the population of relatives who care for patients with OCD than in the general healthy population, as also shown in Figure 8.5.

FIGURE 8.5   Effect Size for Example 8.1

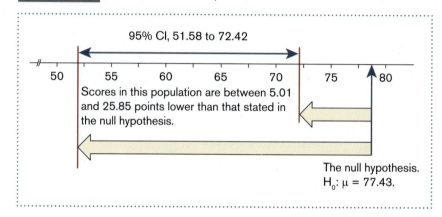

In Example 8.1, the effect size for the confidence interval is between 5.01 and 25.85 points lower in the population of relatives who care for patients with OCD than in the general healthy population.

LEARNING CHECK 4

1. State the estimation formula for a one-sample t test.

2. A researcher measures $M = 3.406$ and $SD = 4.0$ in one sample of 16 participants. What is the 95% CI (confidence interval) for these data using the estimation formula for a one-sample t test?

3. A researcher notes that the null hypothesis of $\mu = 6$ is not contained within the 95% confidence interval. Based on this result, would the decision have been to retain or reject the null hypothesis using hypothesis testing?

Answers: 1. $M \pm t(s_M)$; 2. The 95% CI is between 1.275 and 5.537; 3. Reject the null hypothesis.

8.8 SPSS in Focus:
One-Sample t Test and Confidence Intervals

SPSS can be used to compute the one-sample t test. To illustrate how to compute this test in SPSS and how the output tables in SPSS match with the data we computed by hand, let us compute this test using the same data given for Example 8.1 in Table 8.3. For reference, the social functioning scores in the sample of 18 relatives who care for patients with OCD were 20, 60, 48, 92, 50, 82, 48, 90, 30, 68, 43, 54, 60, 62, 94, 67, 63, and 85. We will compare these scores to the mean in the general healthy population ($\mu = 77.43$) using a .05 level of significance ($\alpha = .05$).

1. Click on the Variable View tab and enter *health* in the Name column. We will enter whole numbers for this variable, so reduce the value in the Decimals column to 0.

2. Click on the Data View tab and enter the 18 values in the column labeled *health*.

3. Go to the menu bar and click Analyze, then Compare Means and One-Sample T Test, to display the dialog box shown in Figure 8.6.

4. In the dialog box, select the variable *health* and click the arrow in the middle to move this variable to the Test Variable(s): box. To adjust the confidence intervals for this test, select Options . . . in the dialog box. Because the default confidence interval is set at a 95% CI, we do not have to adjust this.

5. The Test Value: box is set with a default value equal to 0. The value in this box is the value of the general population score stated in the null hypothesis. Type the value *77.43* in the Test Value: box.

6. Select OK, or select Paste and click the Run command.

In Table 8.6, the top table displays the sample size, the sample mean, the sample standard deviation, and the estimated standard error. The bottom table displays the obtained value for *t*, the degrees of freedom, the *p* value, the mean difference between the sample mean and the test value, and the confidence intervals.

FIGURE 8.6 SPSS Dialog Box for Steps 3 to 6

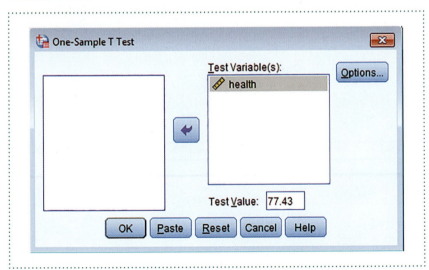

(Continued)

Notice that the confidence limits in the SPSS output table do not match those we computed for Example 8.1. This is because we computed confidence intervals for the actual raw scores on the social functioning measure. SPSS, however, gives the effect size for the confidence interval. The mean scores for relatives who care for patients with OCD in Example 8.1 shifted between 5.01 and 25.85 points *below* the mean score in the general healthy population. These values, −5.01 and −25.85 points, are the confidence limits displayed in the SPSS output table, give or take rounding.

Also, note that although SPSS does not compute effect size for the *t* test, the SPSS output table does include all the information needed to compute effect size. The formulas are restated here with the names of the headings in the SPSS output table where you will find the values needed to compute each estimate:

$$\text{Estimated Cohen's } d = \frac{\text{Mean Difference}}{\text{Std. Deviation}}.$$

$$\text{Proportion of variance} : \eta^2 = \frac{(t)^2}{(t)^2 + df}.$$

| **TABLE 8.6** | SPSS Output Table for the One-Sample *t* Test With the 95% Confidence Interval Given in the Table |

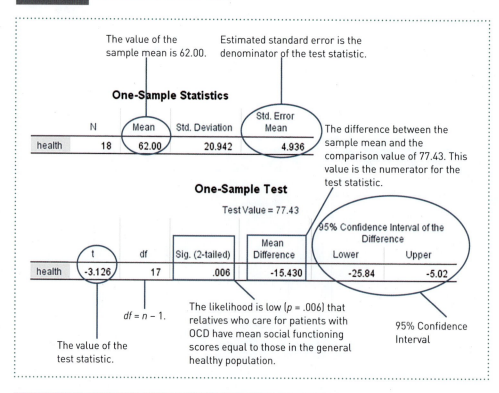

8.9 | APA IN FOCUS: REPORTING THE *t* STATISTIC AND CONFIDENCE INTERVALS

When reporting the results of a *t* test, we include the value of the test statistic, degrees of freedom, *p* value, and effect size. To illustrate, here is how we reported the results for the one-sample *t* test in Example 8.1:

> Social functioning scores among relatives who care for patients with OCD ($M = 62.00$) were significantly lower than scores in the general healthy population, $t(17) = -3.126$, $p < .05$ ($\omega^2 = .33$).

Many scientific journals will not publish the results of a study without the standard deviations or estimated standard errors reported with a *t* test. It is your choice whether to summarize these values in a figure, a table, or the written report, but they must be reported. Cohen's *d*, eta-squared (η^2), and omega-squared (ω^2) are all acceptable measures of effect size, although Cohen's *d* is most often reported as an effect size estimate with the *t* test. To report the results of estimation in scientific journals, we state the level of confidence, point estimate, and interval estimate of each confidence interval. For example, we could report the confidence interval for the one-sample *t* test in Example 8.1 as follows:

> Social functioning was worse among relatives of patients with OCD ($M = 62.00$) than in the general healthy population (95% confidence interval [CI] 51.58–72.42).

• • • CHAPTER SUMMARY ORGANIZED BY LEARNING OBJECTIVE

LO 1: **Explain why a *t* distribution is associated with $n - 1$ degrees of freedom and describe the information that is conveyed by the *t* statistic.**

- The *t* distribution is a normal-like distribution with greater variability in the tails than a normal distribution because the sample variance is substituted for the population variance to estimate the standard error in this distribution.

- The *t* distribution is a sampling distribution for *t* statistic values that are computed using the sample variance to estimate the population variance in the formula. As sample size increases, the sample variance more closely estimates the population variance. The result is that there is less variability in the tails of a *t* distribution as the sample size increases. Each *t* distribution is associated with

the same degrees of freedom as sample variance for a given sample: $df = n - 1$.

- The *t* statistic is an inferential statistic used to determine the number of standard deviations in a *t* distribution that a sample mean deviates from the mean value or mean difference stated in the null hypothesis.

LO 2: **Calculate the degrees of freedom for a one-sample *t* test and locate critical values in the *t* table.**

- The degrees of freedom for a *t* distribution are equal to the degrees of freedom for sample variance: $n - 1$. As the degrees of freedom increase, the tails of the corresponding *t* distribution change, and sample outcomes in the tails become less likely.

- The degrees of freedom for a one-sample *t* test are $(n - 1)$.

LO 3–4: **Identify the assumptions for the one-sample *t* test; compute a one-sample *t* test and interpret the results.**

- We compute a one-sample *t* test to compare a mean value measured in a sample to a known value in the population. It is specifically used to test hypotheses concerning a single population mean from a population with an unknown variance. We make three assumptions for this test: normality, random sampling, and independence.

- The larger the value of the test statistic, the less likely a sample mean would be to occur if the null hypothesis were true, and the more likely we are to reject the null hypothesis. The test statistic for a one-sample *t* test is the difference between the sample mean and population mean, divided by the estimated standard error:

$$t_{obt} = \frac{M - \mu}{s_M}, \text{where } s_M = \frac{SD}{\sqrt{n}}.$$

- The estimated standard error is an estimate of the standard deviation of a sampling distribution of sample means. It is an estimate of the standard error or standard distance that sample means can be expected to deviate from the value of the population mean stated in the null hypothesis.

LO 5: **Compute and interpret effect size and proportion of variance for a one-sample *t* test.**

- Effect size measures the size of an observed difference in a population. For the one-sample *t* test, this measure estimates how far, or how many standard deviations, an effect shifts in a population. The formula for estimated Cohen's *d* for the one-sample *t* test is

$$d = \frac{M - \mu}{SD}.$$

- Proportion of variance is a measure of effect size in terms of the proportion or percent of variability in a dependent variable that can be explained by a treatment. In hypothesis testing, a treatment is considered any unique characteristic of a sample or any unique way that a researcher treats a sample. Two measures of proportion of variance are computed in the same way for all *t* tests:

$$\text{Using eta-squared}: \eta^2 = \frac{t^2}{t^2 + df}.$$

$$\text{Using omega-squared}: \omega^2 = \frac{t^2 - 1}{t^2 + df}.$$

LO 6: **Describe the process of estimation and identify two types of estimation.**

- Estimation is a statistical procedure in which a sample statistic is used to estimate the value of an unknown population parameter. Two types of estimation are point estimation and interval estimation.

- Point estimation is the use of a sample statistic (e.g., a sample mean) to estimate the value of a population parameter (e.g., a population mean).

- Interval estimation is a statistical procedure in which a sample of data is used to find the interval or range of possible values within which a population parameter is likely to be contained.

- In research studies that use estimation, we report the sample mean (a point estimate) and the interval within which a population mean is likely to be contained (an interval estimate).

LO 7: **Compute and interpret confidence intervals for the one-sample *t* test.**

- The three steps to estimation are as follows:

  Step 1: Compute the sample mean and standard error.

Step 2: Choose the level of confidence and find the critical values at that level of confidence.

Step 3: Compute the estimation formula to find the confidence limits.

- The estimation formula for the one-sample t test is $M \pm t(s_M)$.

LO 8: **Summarize the results of a one-sample t test in APA format.**

- To report the results of a one-sample t test, state the test statistic, degrees of freedom, p value, and effect size. In addition, a figure or table is often used to summarize the means and standard error or standard deviations measured in a study. While this information can be included in the written report, it is often more concise to include it in a table or figure.

- To report the results of estimation for the one-sample t test, state the level of confidence, point estimate, and interval estimate of each confidence interval.

LO 9: **Compute a one-sample t test and identify confidence intervals using SPSS.**

- SPSS can be used to compute a one-sample t test using the Analyze, Compare Means, and One-Sample T Test options in the menu bar. These actions will display a dialog box that allows you to identify the variable, enter the comparison or null hypothesis value for the test, adjust the confidence level, and run the test (for more details, see Section 8.8).

••• KEY TERMS

confidence interval (CI)
degrees of freedom (*df*)
estimated Cohen's *d*
estimated standard error
estimation
interval estimate

level of confidence
one-sample *t* test
point estimate
proportion of variance
Student's *t*
t distribution

t observed
t obtained
treatment
t statistic

••• END-OF-CHAPTER PROBLEMS

Factual Problems

1. What test is used as an alternative to the z test when the population variance is unknown?

2. The sample variance is used in the formula for standard error when the population variance is not known. Why is it appropriate to substitute the sample variance for the population variance?

3. How does our estimate of the population variance change as the sample size increases? Explain.

4. Why are the degrees of freedom for the t distribution and the degrees of freedom for sample variance the same?

5. Name the t test used in hypothesis testing to evaluate the mean observed in one sample.

6. Name three measures used to estimate effect size for the one-sample t test.

7. Name two measures of proportion of variance for the one-sample t test. Which measure is the most conservative?

8. Define point estimation and interval estimation.

9. Who determines the level of confidence for an interval estimate?

10. What are the three steps to compute an estimation formula?

Concept and Application Problems

11. In the following studies, state whether the one-sample *t* test is an appropriate test statistic to analyze data. If not, then explain why it is not appropriate.

    (a) A study testing whether night-shift workers sleep the recommended 8 hours per day

    (b) A study measuring differences in attitudes about morality among people who self-identify as liberal or conservative

    (c) A study evaluating the body mass index (BMI) score of athletes compared to the general population

12. The values listed below are the obtained values for a *t* statistic. (1) What is your decision for each if *df* = 30 and α = .05 for a two-tailed test? (2) What is your decision for each if *df* = 30, and we change to α = .01 for an upper-tail critical test?

    (a) $t_{obt} = 2.050$

    (b) $t_{obt} = 1.680$

    (c) $t_{obt} = 2.834$

    (d) $t_{obt} = 3.030$

13. Will each of the following increase, decrease, or have no effect on the value of the test statistic in a one-sample *t* test?

    (a) The sample variance is doubled.

    (b) The level of significance is reduced from .05 to .01.

    (c) The sample size is increased.

    (d) The difference between the sample and population mean is increased.

14. State the critical values for a one-sample *t* test given the following conditions:

    (a) Two-tailed test, α = .05, *n* = 12

    (b) One-tailed test, lower-tail critical, α = .01, *df* = 15

    (c) Two-tailed test, α = .01, *df* = 26

    (d) One-tailed test, upper-tail critical, α = .05, *n* = 30

15. State the total degrees of freedom for the following *t* tests:

    (a) *n* = 12 for a one-sample *t* test

    (b) Critical value = 1.645 for a one-tailed test, α = .05

16. A researcher tests the null hypothesis that the mean intelligence score in the population of adult learners using the standard IQ test is μ = 100. In his sample, he identifies a 95% CI = 99.1 to 102.3. What would the decision have been for this test using the one-sample *t* test? Explain your answer.

17. Researchers report a 95% CI = 1.56 to 5.77. What would the decision be for a hypothesis test if the null hypothesis were:

    (a) μ = 0?

    (b) μ = 3?

    (c) μ = 6?

18. A social psychologist notes that the average time a person spends on social media is 2 hours a day. The researcher wants to test whether new parents spend more or less time than 2 hours on social media. She records the following number of hours spent on social media in a sample of 15 new parents: 0, 4, 1, 2, 2, 3, 0, 4, 3, 5, 2, 1, 1, 0, 2.

    (a) Test the hypothesis of whether new parents spend more or less than 2 hours a day on social media using a .05 level of significance. State the value of the test statistic and the decision to retain or reject the null hypothesis.

    (b) Compute effect size using estimated Cohen's *d*.

19. A school psychologist notes that the average number of times that students are disruptive during class is 1.4 (μ = 1.4) times per day. Following recent classroom policy changes, the psychologist tests if the number of disruptions during class has changed. He records the following number of disruptions observed during a class day: 2, 4, 3, 5, 4, 1, 1, and 4.

(a) Test the hypothesis that the number of complaints has increased or decreased using a .05 level of significance. State the value for the test statistic and the decision to retain or reject the null hypothesis.

(b) Compute effect size using estimated Cohen's d.

20. While researching lifestyle changes to improve heart health, you come across a research article reporting that the average American in the population consumes about 2,700 calories per day. You come across another article that refutes this, stating that a sample of Americans consumed significantly less than this mean standard on average, $t(50) = 2.993$, $p < .05$ $(\eta^2 = .15)$. Based on the information provided, answer the following questions:

(a) Does the test statistic show a significant effect?

(b) What is the proportion of variance for this effect?

21. Listening to music has long been thought to enhance intelligence, especially during infancy and childhood. To test whether this is true, a researcher records the number of hours that eight high-performing students listened to music per day for 1 week. The data are listed in the table.

Music Listening per Day (in hours)
4.2
4.8
5.0
3.8
4.2
5.5
4.1
4.4

(a) Find the confidence limits at a 95% CI for this sample.

(b) Suppose the null hypothesis states that students listen to 3.5 hours of music per day. What would the decision be for a two-tailed hypothesis test at a .05 level of significance?

22. An instructor implements a new teaching strategy in the classroom by using a teaching strategy to teach a sample of six students. After the instruction, he gives each student a test out of 100 possible points to test their recall. The scores are listed in the table.

Score on the Exam
65
73
77
70
68
67

(a) Find the confidence limits at a 90% CI for this one sample.

(b) If the mean grade in the entire class is $\mu = 75$ points, then did the new teaching strategy improve grades compared to the mean grade in the entire class (the population)?

23. A social psychologist records the number of outbursts in a sample of different classrooms at a local school. Based on the statement below, what are the sample size, decision (retain or reject the null hypothesis), and effect size in this study?

The number of outbursts among students at this local school $(M = 3)$ was significantly less than that in the general population, $t(39) = 4.19$, $p < .05$ $(d = 0.25)$.

24. Using Cohen's d, state whether a 3-point treatment effect $(M - \mu = 3)$ is small, medium, or large for a one-sample t test, given the following values for the sample standard deviation:

(a) $SD = 3$ (b) $SD = 6$ (c) $SD = 12$
(d) $SD = 24$

25. A researcher computes the following 95% CI = 12 to 24. What is the point estimate for this 95% CI?

26. Suppose a researcher has participants rate how much their mood improves following an exercise on a bipolar scale from −3 (*much worse*) to +3 (*much improved*), with the midpoint, 0, indicating no change in mood. If following the exercise the researcher reports a 95% CI = 0.5 to 1.3, did she observe a significant increase in mood? Explain.

Problems in Research

27. **Controlling the alpha level.** In an article evaluating the utility of *t* tests for biomedical research, Kreinovich and Servin (2015) explained that "for the *t* test, we estimate a statistic *t*. The hypothesis is confirmed, with given confidence α" (Kreinovich & Servin, 2015, p. 95). From this statement, what value for α is likely the given confidence the authors are referring to?

28. **Estimating effect size.** Yuan and Maxwell (2005) investigated how the power of a study influences the decisions researchers make in an experiment. In their introduction concerning effect size, they stated that "the exact true effect size is generally unknown even after the experiment. But one can estimate the effect size . . . [and] when the sample size is large, the estimated effect size is near the true effect size" (Yuan & Maxwell, 2005, p. 141).

    (a) Why is the "exact true effect size" generally unknown even after the experiment? Explain.

    (b) How does increasing the sample size improve our estimate of effect size when we use estimated Cohen's *d*?

29. **Calculating a *t* test.** In a review that, in part, reviewed *t* tests, Wall Emerson (2017) made the following two statements (p. 194):

    Statement 1: "The *t* statistic [is] calculated by taking the [mean] difference . . . and dividing that difference by the square root of a measure of variance which is divided by the number of scores in the dataset."

    Statement 2: "The *t* statistic and the measure of degrees of freedom allows the researcher to evaluate whether the result is significant by comparing [the result] to a table of values describing the way *t* values are distributed."

    Based on the statements above, (a) what value for the denominator of the *t* statistic is explained in Statement 1, and (b) what is the name of the distribution for *t* values referred to in Statement 2?

30. **Assumptions for the one-sample *t* test.** In a critical evaluation of the one-sample *t* test, Rochon and Kieser (2011) explained that "a one-sample *t* test is used when inference about the population mean μ is made for a sample of *n* independent observations" (p. 411). Identify the assumption for the one-sample *t* test that the authors refer to. Explain your answer.

31. **Using CIs for statistical inference.** In an article contrasting hypothesis testing with the use of confidence intervals, Hoekstra, Johnson, and Kiers (2012) explained, "When a CI is used only to determine whether the null value lies within the interval, the statistical inference is no different than determining whether the outcome of a *t* test is significant or not" (p. 1041). Explain what statistical inference can be made when the value of the null hypothesis "lies within the interval."

32. **The usefulness of confidence intervals.** To clarify the kind of information conveyed by a level of confidence, Thompson (2007) stated, "CIs are extremely useful because they convey not only our point estimate, but also, via the width of the intervals, something about the precision of our estimates" (p. 427). What is the name of the estimate that conveys the width of the intervals?

Answers for even numbers are in Appendix D.

Sharpen your skills with **SAGE edge at edge.sagepub.com/priviteraess2e**

SAGE edge for Students provides a personalized approach to help you accomplish your coursework goals in an easy-to-use learning environment.

⑤SAGE edge™

©iStockphoto.com/nastinka

9

Testing Means
Two-Independent-Sample
t Test With Confidence Intervals

● ● ● **Learning Objectives**

After reading this chapter, you should be able to:

1. Describe the between-subjects design, and identify two appropriate sampling methods used to select independent samples.

2. Calculate the degrees of freedom for a two-independent-sample *t* test and locate critical values in the *t* table.

3. Identify the assumptions for a two-independent-sample *t* test.

4. Compute a two-independent-sample *t* test and interpret the results.

5. Compute and interpret effect size and proportion of variance for a two-independent-sample *t* test.

6. Compute and interpret confidence intervals for a two-independent-sample *t* test.

7. Summarize the results of a two-independent-sample *t* test in APA format.

8. Compute a two-independent-sample *t* test and identify confidence intervals using SPSS.

Making comparisons between two groups is actually something we do quite often. At camp, we may compare which of two "cabins" showed the best survival skills; at a sporting event, we may compare whether east coast or west coast teams perform better; or in a classroom, we may compare whether students in an advanced or a basic-level class scored better on a standardized assessment. In each example, we can make comparisons between two groups. We can compare the number of survival skills mastered by campers in each of two cabins, compare the winning percentage of east coast and west coast sports teams, or compare the grades of students in an advanced and a basic-level class on an assessment in a classroom.

In hypothesis testing, there are often cases where making comparisons between two samples or two groups can be quite informative, especially when the researcher hypothesizes that the two samples or two groups are different. In the basic structure of such a study, the two groups or samples represent the independent variable. For the examples above, the two cabins, the two types of teams (east coast, west coast), and the two classes (basic, advanced) would be the independent/quasi-independent variables. The basic structure of such a test is to measure the same dependent variable in each of two groups. Again, for the examples above, the number of survival skills mastered, the winning percentage of the teams, and the scores on the assessment would be the dependent variables. The null hypothesis for such a test would be that the dependent variable is not different between the two groups; the alternative hypothesis would state that the two groups are different.

In this chapter, we explore the nature of hypothesis testing with two samples, how to compute and interpret observed effects, and the informativeness of hypothesis testing for making comparisons between the two groups. We further explore other ways of adding information about the nature of observed effects and how to appropriately interpret them.

Master the content.

edge.sagepub.com/priviteraess2e

••• Chapter Outline

9.1 INTRODUCTION TO THE BETWEEN-SUBJECTS DESIGN

In the last two chapters, we applied the steps to hypothesis testing using data recorded in a single sample. However, common research situations in the behavioral sciences include the comparison of differences between many samples or groups. In the next two chapters, we look at situations in which data are recorded in two groups or samples. There are two basic designs in which two groups or samples are observed. We can observe the same participants two times and compare differences between Time 1 and Time 2. This type of design is described in Chapter 10. A second way, introduced in this chapter, is to observe two groups or samples and select *different* participants for each group and compare differences between them. This type of design is called the **between-subjects design** and is the design introduced in this chapter.

With two groups, we can then compare differences between the groups. Each group or sample is represented by a level of a factor. For example, we could observe learning outcomes during a study session held in a low- or well-lit room. In this example, lighting is the factor, and it has two levels: low lit and well lit. Each level of the factor constitutes a group in the design for which we will compare differences in learning outcomes. To conduct the between-subjects design, participants are selected in a certain way, and a particular test statistic is used to compare differences between two groups. How participants are selected to two groups and how the test statistic is used to analyze measured data are introduced in this chapter.

9.2 SELECTING SAMPLES FOR COMPARING TWO GROUPS

Using the between-subjects design, different participants are observed in each group, and differences are compared between groups. When different participants are observed in each group, the sample is called an **independent sample**. Figure 9.1 shows two ways to select two independent samples.

The first way, shown in Figure 9.1a, is to select a sample from two populations. This type of sampling is commonly used to conduct quasi-experiments for situations in which the levels of a factor are preexisting. For example, suppose we hypothesize that students who pay for their own college education, without financial assistance, will study more. We record the time spent studying in a sample of students who, prior to the study, were paying their tuition with or without financial assistance. Referring to Figure 9.1a, Population 1 consists of students who pay for their education with financial assistance; Population 2 consists of students who pay for their college education without financial assistance. Each sample is selected from a different population, so each sample constitutes a different group.

The second way to select independent samples, shown in Figure 9.1b, is to select one sample from the same population and randomly assign participants in the sample to groups. This type of sampling is commonly used in experiments that include randomization, manipulation, and a comparison/control group. The only way to achieve an experiment is to randomly assign participants selected from a single population to different groups.

A **between-subjects design** is a research design in which different participants are observed one time in each group or at each level of one factor.

An **independent sample** is a type of sample in which different participants are independently observed one time in each group.

FIGURE 9.1 Two Ways in Which to Select Independent Samples

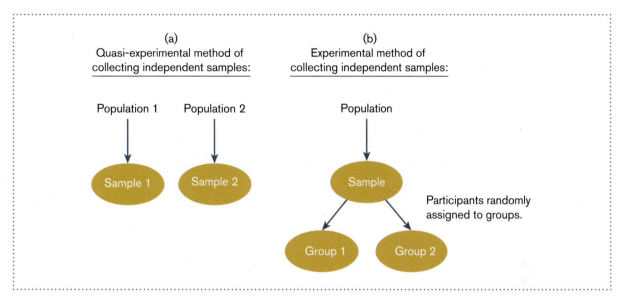

Part (b) shows the sampling method most commonly used to conduct an experiment.

For example, suppose we hypothesize that paying students for earning higher grades will improve their performance on an exam. To test this, we could select a group of students and have them study a word list and test their recall. In one group, participants are paid for better scores, and in a second group, participants are not paid. Referring to Figure 9.1b, the population would be college students, from which each sample was selected and randomly assigned to be paid (Group 1) or not paid (Group 2) for earning grades.

9.3 VARIABILITY AND COMPARING DIFFERENCES BETWEEN TWO GROUPS

With two groups, we use the test statistic to evaluate if two groups are different (we reach significance; a decision to reject the null hypothesis) or are the same (we fail to reach significance; a decision to retain the null hypothesis). In terms of evaluating the difference between two groups, we are really determining the extent to which scores between the groups are overlapping. The less that scores in two groups overlap, the more likely we are to decide that two groups are different. To illustrate how we will identify if two groups are different, Figure 9.2 shows data for two hypothetical experiments in which there is a 3-point treatment effect between two groups in both experiments; that is, the mean difference between the two groups is 3.0. When scores do not overlap, shown in Figure 9.2a, all scores for the group receiving Treatment A are smaller than scores for the group receiving Treatment B. This result indicates that the groups are likely different—Treatment A likely produced the 3-point effect because individuals at each level, or in each group, are behaving differently.

FIGURE 9.2 A Hypothetical Example of Two Experiments in Which There Is No Overlap (a) in One Experiment and There Is Overlap (b) in Scores Between Groups in the Second Experiment

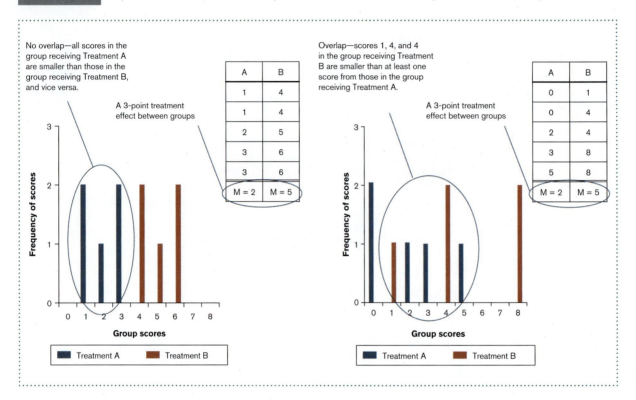

When scores do overlap, shown in Figure 9.2b, then any observed difference between two or more groups in an experiment is likely due to random variability, or error. Although the same 3-point treatment effect was observed in Figure 9.2b, some participants receiving Treatment B behaved as if they received Treatment A; that is, their scores overlap with the scores of those receiving Treatment A. When scores overlap with those for other groups, it indicates that the 3-point treatment effect between groups is likely not significant—greater overlap increases the amount of error measured. Hence, the two groups are less likely to be different when participant responding substantially overlaps from one group to the next.

In this chapter, we evaluate whether or not there is a difference between two groups using a *t* test adapted for situations in which different participants are independently observed in two groups. We again use the *t* distribution to make a decision, same as we did for the one-sample *t* test in Chapter 8.

9.4 COMPUTING THE TWO-INDEPENDENT-SAMPLE *t* TEST

Many studies aim to compare scores between two groups, as this is a common type of study conducted in the behavioral sciences. Making a comparison is useful because it allows the researcher to gain an insight into how two unique conditions or groups differ. For example, a research study may examine differences in multitasking between men and women, differences in happiness between pet owners and non–pet owners, or differences in recall between participants randomly assigned to use one of two learning strategies. In each study, researchers measure two means (one mean in each group) and then compare differences between the groups. The **two-independent-sample t test** is used to compare the mean difference between two groups—specifically, to test hypotheses regarding the difference between two population means.

In terms of the null hypothesis, we state the mean difference that we expect in the population and compare it to the difference we observe between the two sample means in our sample. Table 9.1 shows two ways to state the difference between two means in a population. For a two-independent-sample t test concerning two population means, we make four assumptions:

1. *Normality.* We assume that data in each population being sampled are normally distributed. This assumption is particularly important for small samples because the standard error is typically much larger. In larger sample sizes ($n > 30$), the standard error is smaller, and this assumption becomes less critical as a result.

2. *Random sampling.* We assume that the data we measure were obtained from samples that were selected using a random sampling procedure. It is generally considered inappropriate to conduct hypothesis tests with nonrandom samples.

3. *Independence.* We assume that each measured outcome or observation is independent, meaning that one outcome does not influence another. Specifically, outcomes are independent when the probability of one outcome has no effect on the probability of another outcome. Using random sampling usually satisfies this assumption.

4. *Equal variances.* We assume that the variances in each population are equal to each other. This assumption is usually satisfied when the larger sample variance is not greater than two times the smaller:

$$\frac{\text{larger } s^2}{\text{smaller } s^2} < 2.$$

Example 9.1 demonstrates how to compute the two-independent-sample t test using the four steps of hypothesis testing.

TABLE 9.1   Two Ways to State That There Is No Difference Between Two Population Means

Statement	Meaning
$\mu_1 - \mu_2 = 0$ $\mu_1 = \mu_2$	There is no difference between two population means.

FYI

Four assumptions for a two-independent-sample t test are normality, random sampling, independence, and equal variances.

The **two-independent-sample t test** is a statistical procedure used to compare the mean difference between two independent groups. This test is specifically used to test hypotheses concerning the difference between two population means, where the variance in one or both populations is unknown.

Example 9.1

© iStockphoto.com/Rawpixel Ltd

One behavioral strategy believed to reduce food intake is to eat slower, which presumably provides more time for physiological fullness signals to initiate (Azrin, Brooks, Kellen, Ehle, & Vinas, 2008; Privitera, 2016; Privitera, Cooper, & Cosco, 2012). To test this possibility, suppose we compare two groups given the same buffet of foods to consume: One group is instructed to eat fast, and another group is instructed to eat slowly. We record the number of calories consumed in the meal, as given in Table 9.2 (adapted from data reported by Privitera, Cooper, et al., 2012). Test whether rate of eating (slowly or fast) influenced amount consumed in a meal using a .05 level of significance.

| TABLE 9.2 | The Number of Calories Consumed in a Meal Between Groups Asked to Eat Slowly or Fast |

Group Eating Slowly	Group Eating Fast
700	450
450	800
850	750
600	700
450	550
550	650
Mean = 600	Mean = 650
SD = 154.92	*SD* = 130.38

The participant data, group means, and standard deviations for each group in the rate of eating study in Example 9.1. The data represent the number of calories consumed in a meal.

Step 1: State the hypotheses. The null hypothesis states that there is no difference between the two groups, and we are testing whether (=) or not (≠) there is a difference:

H_0: $\mu_1 - \mu_2 = 0$ No difference; rate of eating has no effect on the number of calories consumed in a meal.

H_1: $\mu_1 - \mu_2 \neq 0$ Rate of eating does have an effect on the number of calories consumed in a meal.

Step 2: Set the criteria for a decision. The level of significance for this test is .05. We are computing a two-tailed test, so we place the rejection region in both tails. For the *t* test, the degrees of freedom for each group or sample are $n - 1$. To find the degrees of freedom for two samples, then, we add the degrees of freedom in each sample. This can be found using one of three methods:

Method 1: df for two-independent-sample t test $= df_1 + df_2$.

Method 2: df for two-independent-sample t test $= (n_1 - 1) + (n_2 - 1)$.

Method 3: df for two-independent-sample t test $= N - 2$.

FYI

We can add the degrees of freedom for each sample to find the degrees of freedom for a two-independent-sample t *test.*

As summarized in Table 9.3, we can add the degrees of freedom for each sample using the first two methods. In the third method, N is the total sample size for both groups combined, and we subtract 2 from this value. Each method will produce the same result for degrees of freedom. The degrees of freedom for each sample in Example 9.1 are $6 - 1 = 5$. Thus, the degrees of freedom for the two-independent-sample t test are the sum of these degrees of freedom:

$$df = 5 + 5 = 10.$$

Locate 10 degrees of freedom in the leftmost column in the t table in Table C.2 in Appendix C. Move across the columns to find the critical value for a .05 proportion in two tails combined. The critical values for this test are ±2.228. The rejection region beyond these critical values is shown in the t distribution in Figure 9.3.

We will compare the value of the test statistic with these critical values. If the value of the test statistic is beyond a critical value (either greater than +2.228 or less than −2.228), then there is less than a 5% chance we would obtain that outcome if the null hypothesis were correct, so we reject the null hypothesis; otherwise, we retain the null hypothesis.

TABLE 9.3 Computing the Degrees of Freedom for a t Test

Type of t Test	Sample 1		Sample 2	Total df
One-sample t test	$(n - 1)$	$+$	$-$	$(n - 1)$
Two-independent-sample t test	$(n_1 - 1)$	$+$	$(n_2 - 1)$	$(n_1 - 1) + (n_2 - 1)$

Step 3: Compute the test statistic. In this example, we will compare the difference in the sample means between groups: 600 calories in Group Eating Slowly compared to 650 calories in Group Eating Fast. The difference between these sample means is 50 calories. We will compute the test statistic to determine how many standard deviations a sample mean difference of 50 calories is from a mean difference equal to 0 stated in the null hypothesis.

In the formula for a two-independent-sample t test, we subtract the mean difference between the sample means ($M_1 - M_2 = -50$) from the mean difference stated in the null ($\mu_1 - \mu_2 = 0$). We then divide this difference by the combined standard error in both samples, called the **estimated standard error for the difference** ($s_{M_1 - M_2}$), which is computed using the following formula:

$$s_{M_1 - M_2} = \sqrt{\frac{s_p^2}{n_1} + \frac{s_p^2}{n_2}} \, .$$

The **estimated standard error for the difference** is an estimate of the standard deviation of a sampling distribution of mean differences between two sample means. It is an estimate of the standard error or standard distance that mean differences can be expected to deviate from the mean difference stated in the null hypothesis.

FIGURE 9.3   Setting the Criteria for a Decision

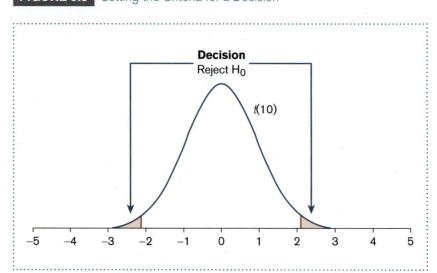

The shaded region shows the rejection region with critical values equal to ±2.228 for a *t* distribution with *df* = 10. If the value of the test statistic falls in the shaded region, we reject the null hypothesis; otherwise, we retain the null hypothesis.

Hence, the *t* statistic for a two-independent-sample *t* test is

$$t_{obt} = \frac{(M_1 - M_2) - (\mu_1 - \mu_2)}{s_{M_1 - M_2}}.$$

To find the estimated standard error for the difference in the denominator, we need to compute s_p^2, which is the **pooled sample variance**. A pooled sample variance is the mean sample variance for two samples. When the sample size is unequal, the variance is a weighted mean so that the pooled sample variance is weighted toward the sample mean computed from the larger sample size—the larger *n* is, the better the estimate of sample variance will be. The formula for computing pooled sample variance when the sample size is different in each group is

$$s_p^2 = \frac{s_1^2(df_1) + s_2^2(df_2)}{df_1 + df_2}.$$

The **pooled sample variance** is the mean sample variance of two samples. When the sample size is unequal, the variance in each group or sample is weighted by its respective degrees of freedom.

The degrees of freedom are the weights in the formula. When we have equal sample sizes, we do not have to weight each sample variance by its respective degrees of freedom. Thus, we can compute the pooled sample variance by adding the two sample variances and dividing by 2 when the sample size is equal or the same in each group:

$$s_p^2 = \frac{s_1^2 + s_2^2}{2}.$$

MAKING SENSE THE POOLED SAMPLE VARIANCE

When we have equal sample sizes, we do not have to weigh the sample variances by their degrees of freedom. We compute a straightforward arithmetic mean of the two sample variances. To illustrate, suppose we have two samples with the size and variance listed in Table 9.4. Notice both samples are the same size and therefore have the same degrees of freedom: Both samples have 19 degrees of freedom. If we substitute the values of s^2 and df into the

TABLE 9.4 The Sample Size and Variance for Two Hypothetical Samples

Sample	
1	2
$n_1 = 20$	$n_2 = 20$
$S_1^2 = 12$	$S_2^2 = 18$

formula for the pooled sample variance with unequal sample sizes, we obtain

$$s_p^2 = \frac{s_1^2(df_1) + s_2^2(df_2)}{df_1 + df_2} = \frac{12(19) + 18(19)}{19 + 19} = 15.$$

Notice that the value for the pooled sample variance is the middle value between the two sample variances (12 and 18) when the sample sizes are equal. If we substitute the values of s^2 and df into the formula for the pooled sample variance with equal sample sizes, we obtain the same value for the pooled sample variance:

$$s_p^2 = \frac{s_1^2 + s_2^2}{2} = \frac{12 + 18}{2} = 15.$$

Both formulas for pooled sample variance produce the same result when $n_1 = n_2$. Only when the sample sizes are unequal is it necessary to weight each sample variance by its respective degrees of freedom.

To compute the test statistic, we (1) compute the pooled sample variance, (2) compute the estimated standard error for the difference, and (3) compute the test statistic for the two-independent-sample t test. For reference, Table 9.5 lists the values needed in each step.

TABLE 9.5 Data From Example 9.1 Needed to Compute the t Statistic

Group Eating Slowly	Group Eating Fast
$n_1 = 6$	$n_2 = 6$
$df_1 = 5$	$df_2 = 5$
$M_1 = 600$	$M_2 = 650$
$S_1^2 = 24,000$	$S_2^2 = 17,000$

1. Compute the pooled sample variance. Because the sample sizes are equal in each group, we can compute the pooled sample variance using the simpler formula. Table 9.2 gives the standard deviation in each group. The standard deviation is the square root of the variance. So to find the variance for each group, simply square the standard deviation in each group. In our example, the

sample variance for Group Eating Slowly is $(154.92)^2 = 24,000$, and the sample variance for Group Eating Fast is $(130.38)^2 = 17,000$. The pooled sample variance is as follows:

$$S_p^2 = \frac{24,000 + 17,000}{2} = 20,500.$$

2. Compute the estimated standard error for the difference. We substitute the pooled sample variance and sample size into the following formula:

$$s_{M_1-M_2} = \sqrt{\frac{s_p^2}{n_1} + \frac{s_p^2}{n_2}} = \sqrt{\frac{20,500}{6} + \frac{20,500}{6}} = 82.66.$$

3. Compute the test statistic for the two-independent-sample t test. We substitute the mean difference we observed ($600 - 650 = -50$), the mean difference stated in the null hypothesis (0), and the estimated standard error for the difference (82.66) into the test statistic formula:

$$t_{obt} = \frac{(M_1-M_2) - (\mu_1-\mu_2)}{s_{M_1-M_2}} = \frac{-50 - 0}{82.66} = -0.605.$$

FYI

The two-independent-sample t test measures the number of standard deviations in a t distribution that a mean difference between two groups deviates from the mean difference stated in the null hypothesis.

Step 4: Make a decision. To decide whether or not to reject the null hypothesis, we compare the obtained value to the critical values. Figure 9.4 shows that the obtained value ($t_{obt} = -0.605$) does not exceed the critical values; it does not fall in the rejection region. The decision is to retain the null hypothesis, same as the decision made in the Privitera, Cooper, et al. (2012) study. If this null result were reported in a research journal, it would look something like this:

Rate of eating, either slowly ($M = 600$ calories) or fast ($M = 650$ calories), failed to produce significant differences in food intake between groups, $t(10) = -0.605$, $p > .05$.

FIGURE 9.4   Making a Decision for Example 9.1

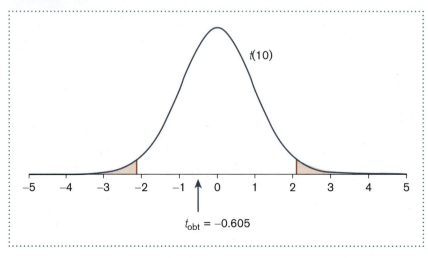

$t_{obt} = -0.605$

The value of the test statistic does not fall in the rejection region. Therefore, we retain the null hypothesis.

LEARNING CHECK 1

1. What are the four assumptions for the two-independent-sample t test?

2. What value is placed in the denominator for the two-independent-sample t test?

3. A researcher measures the time it takes 13 men and 15 women to complete multiple tasks in a study. She compares the mean difference between men and women using the two-independent-sample t test. What is the critical value for this test if she conducts a two-tailed test at a .05 level of significance?

4. Using the same example as in Question 3, what is the researcher's decision if she reports the following values for the test statistic?

    (a) 2.558   (b) 1.602   (c) 2.042   (d) –2.500

Answers: 1. Normality, random sampling, independence, and equal variances; 2. The estimated standard error for the difference; 3. ±2.056; 4. (a) Reject the null hypothesis, (b) Retain the null hypothesis, (c) Retain the null hypothesis, (d) Reject the null hypothesis.

9.5 EFFECT SIZE FOR THE TWO-INDEPENDENT-SAMPLE t TEST

Hypothesis testing is used to identify whether an effect exists in one or more populations of interest. When we reject the null hypothesis, we conclude that an effect does exist in the population. When we retain the null hypothesis, we conclude that an effect does not exist in the population, which was the decision in Example 9.1. However, for the purposes of identifying effect size, we will compute effect size for the test in Example 9.1 to determine the effect size of this result or mean difference. We will identify three measures of effect size for the two-independent-sample t test: estimated Cohen's d and the same two measures of proportion of variance (eta-squared and omega-squared).

Estimated Cohen's d

As stated in Section 8.5 in Chapter 8, estimated Cohen's d is most often used with the t test. When the estimated Cohen's d is used with the two-independent-sample t test, we place the difference between two sample means in the numerator and the **pooled sample standard deviation** (or square root of the pooled sample variance) in the denominator. The pooled sample standard deviation is an estimate for the pooled or mean standard deviation for the difference between two population means. The formula for an estimated Cohen's d for the two-independent-sample t test is

$$\text{Estimated Cohen's } d : \frac{M_1 - M_2}{\sqrt{s_p^2}}.$$

In Example 9.1, $M_1 = 600$, $M_2 = 650$, and $\sqrt{s_p^2} = \sqrt{20{,}500} = 143$ (rounded to the nearest whole number). The estimated Cohen's d for Example 9.1 is

$$d = \frac{600 - 650}{143} = -0.35.$$

The **pooled sample standard deviation** $\left(\sqrt{s_p^2}\right)$ is the combined sample standard deviation of two groups or samples. It is computed by taking the square root of the pooled sample variance. This measure estimates the standard deviation for the difference between two population means.

Although we concluded that an effect does not exist in the population, the effect size of the difference between groups observed was medium based on effect size conventions given in Chapter 8, Table 8.4 (p. 239). We can report this estimate with the *t* test in Example 9.1 by stating,

Rate of eating, either slowly (*M* = 600 calories) or fast (*M* = 650 calories), failed to produce significant differences in food intake between groups, *t*(10) = −0.605, *p* > .05 (*d* = −0.35).

Proportion of Variance

Another measure of effect size is proportion of variance, which estimates the proportion of variance in a dependent variable that can be explained by some treatment. In Example 9.1, this measure can describe the proportion of variance in calories consumed (the dependent variable) that can be explained by whether participants ate slowly or fast (the treatment). Two measures of proportion of variance for the two-independent-sample *t* test are eta-squared and omega-squared. These measures are computed in the same way for all *t* tests.

Eta-Squared (η²)

Eta-squared is one measure of proportion of variance that can be expressed in a single formula based on the result of a *t* test:

$$\eta^2 = \frac{t^2}{t^2 + df}.$$

In Example 9.1, the test statistic $t = -0.605$, and $df = 10$. The proportion of variance for Example 9.1 is

$$\eta^2 = \frac{(-0.605)^2}{(-0.605)^2 + 10} = .04.$$

We conclude that 4% of the variability in calories consumed can be explained by whether participants ate slowly or fast. Based on the effect size conventions listed in Chapter 8, Table 8.4 (p. 239), this result is a small effect size. We can report this estimate with the significant *t* test in Example 9.1 by stating,

Rate of eating, either slowly (*M* = 600 calories) or fast (*M* = 650 calories), failed to produce significant differences in food intake between groups, *t*(10) = −0.605, *p* > .05 (η² = .04).

Omega-Squared (ω²)

As described in Section 8.5 in Chapter 8, we compute omega-squared by subtracting 1 from t^2 in the numerator of the eta-squared formula. This makes the estimate of effect size smaller than eta-squared, thereby making omega-squared a less biased measure. However, one limitation for this estimate when used with the *t* test is that it will be negative when *t* is less than 1. Because a negative proportion is meaningless, omega-squared cannot be computed for this *t* test because *t* is less than 1 in Example 9.1. That being said, note in the *t* table in Table C.2 that the smallest critical values associated with tests at a .05 level of significance are 1.645 (one-tailed tests) and ±1.96 (two-tailed tests). Any effect for *t* that is significant must therefore have a value of *t* greater than or equal to 1.645. Hence, while omega-squared cannot be computed for Example 9.1, it can be computed for any significant effect using the *t* test.

In Example 9.1, eta-squared estimated a small effect size whereas estimated Cohen's *d* estimated a medium effect size for the rate of eating data. While different measures of effect size do not always make the same estimates, there is little consensus as to which is the superior measure. Thus, each measure is regarded as an acceptable estimate of effect size in the published scientific literature.

FYI

The pooled sample standard deviation is used as an unbiased estimate for the standard deviation of the difference between two population means in the formula for estimated Cohen's d.

FYI

Proportion of variance is calculated using the same formula for one-sample and two-independent-sample t tests.

FYI

Omega-squared can only be computed for a t test when t ≥ 1.

LEARNING CHECK 2

1. What is the denominator for computing an estimated Cohen's *d* for a two-independent-sample *t* test?

2. If the difference between two means is 4, then what will the estimated Cohen's *d* value be with a pooled sample standard deviation of each of the following?

   (a) 4   (b) 8   (c) 16   (d) 40

3. The value of the test statistic for a two-independent-sample *t* test is 2.400. Using eta-squared, what is the proportion of variance when the degrees of freedom are 30?

4. Using the same example as in Question 3, what is the proportion of variance using omega-squared?

Answers: 1. The pooled sample standard deviation; 2. (a) $\frac{4}{4} = 1.00$ (large effect size), (b) $\frac{4}{8} = 0.50$ (medium effect size), (c) $\frac{4}{16} = 0.25$ (medium effect size), (d) $\frac{4}{40} = 0.10$ (small effect size); 3. $\eta^2 = \frac{(2.400)^2}{(2.400)^2 + 30} = .16$ (medium effect); 4. $\omega^2 = \frac{(2.400)^2 - 1}{(2.400)^2 + 30} = .13$ (medium effect).

9.6 CONFIDENCE INTERVALS FOR THE TWO-INDEPENDENT-SAMPLE *t* TEST

In Example 9.1, we stated a null hypothesis regarding the mean difference in a population. We then computed a test statistic to determine the probability of obtaining a sample outcome if the null hypothesis were true. In our example, the probability of obtaining the sample outcome was greater than 5% if the null hypothesis were true, so we retained the null hypothesis. Using hypothesis testing, the goal was to learn more about the mean difference in a population of interest by deciding whether to retain or reject the null hypothesis.

We can also learn more about the mean difference in a population using a different procedure without ever deciding to retain or reject a null hypothesis. The alternative approach requires only that we set limits for the population parameter within which it is likely to be contained. The goal of this alternative approach, called *estimation*, is the same as that in hypothesis testing for Example 9.1—to learn more about the value of a mean in a population of interest.

To use estimation, we identify the sample mean (a point estimate) and give an interval within which a population mean is likely to be contained (an interval estimate). Same as we did for the one-sample *t* test in Chapter 8, we find the interval estimate, often reported as a confidence interval, and state it within a given level of confidence, which is the likelihood that an interval contains an unknown population mean. To illustrate, we will revisit Example 9.1, and using the same data, we will compute the confidence intervals at a 95% level of confidence using the three steps to estimation first introduced in Chapter 8. For a two-independent-sample *t* test, the estimation formula is

$$M_1 - M_2 \pm t(s_{M_1 - M_2}).$$

Step 1: Compute the sample mean and standard error. The difference between the two sample means is $M_1 - M_2 = -50$ calories. Therefore, the mean difference or point estimate of the population mean difference is -50 (we already computed this value for Example 9.1 in Step 3 of hypothesis testing).

The estimated standard error for the difference, $s_{M_1 - M_2}$, is equal to 82.66 (we already computed this value as well for Example 9.1 in Step 3 of hypothesis testing).

Step 2: Choose the level of confidence and find the critical values at that level of confidence. In this example, we want to find the 95% confidence interval (CI), so we choose a 95% level of confidence. Remember, in a sampling distribution, 50% of the differences between two sample means fall above the mean difference we selected in our sample, and 50% fall below it. We are looking for the 95% of differences between two sample means that surround the mean difference we measured in our sample. A 95% CI corresponds to a two-tailed test at a .05 level of significance. To find the critical value at this level of confidence, we look in the *t* table in Table C.2 in Appendix C. The degrees of freedom are 10 ($df = N - 2$ for two independent samples). The critical value for the interval estimate is $t = 2.228$.

Step 3: Compute the estimation formula to find the confidence limits for a 95% confidence interval. Because we are estimating the difference between two sample means in the population with an unknown variance, we use the $M_1 - M_2 \pm t(s_{M_1 - M_2})$ estimation formula.

To compute the formula, multiply *t* by the estimated standard error for the difference:

$$t(s_{M_1 - M_2}) = 2.228\,(82.66) = 184.17.$$

Add 184.17 to the sample mean difference to find the upper confidence limit:

$$M_1 - M_2 + t(s_{M_1 - M_2}) = -50 + 184.17 = 134.17.$$

Subtract 184.17 from the sample mean difference to find the lower confidence limit:

$$M_1 - M_2 - t(s_{M_1 - M_2}) = -50 - 184.17 = -234.17.$$

As shown in Figure 9.5, the 95% confidence interval in this population is between +134.17 and −234.17 calories. We can estimate within a 95% level of confidence that the difference between groups is between +134.17 and −234.17 calories. We are 95% confident that the mean difference in the population falls within this range because 95% of all sample mean differences we could have selected from this population fall within the range of sample mean differences we specified.

 FIGURE 9.5 In Example 9.1, the 95% Confidence Interval Is −234.17 to +134.17 Calories

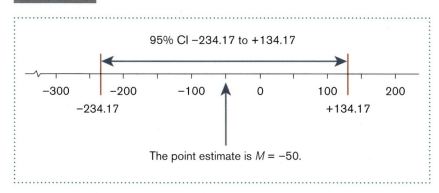

9.7 INFERRING SIGNIFICANCE AND EFFECT SIZE FROM A CONFIDENCE INTERVAL

Notice that we did not make a decision using estimation, other than to state confidence limits for a 95% confidence interval. When we evaluated these same data with hypothesis testing in Example 9.1, we selected a sample to decide whether or not to reject the null hypothesis. While we do not "make a decision" per se using estimation, we can use the confidence limits to determine what the decision would have been using hypothesis testing. As stated in Chapter 8, in terms of the decisions we make in hypothesis testing,

1. If the value stated by a null hypothesis is inside the confidence interval, the decision is to retain the null hypothesis (not significant).

2. If the value stated by a null hypothesis is outside the confidence interval, the decision is to reject the null hypothesis (significant).

Using these rules, we can thus determine the decision we would have made using hypothesis testing. In Example 9.1, we identified a null hypothesis that the mean difference was 0 between Groups Eating Slowly and Eating Fast. Because a mean difference of 0 falls within the 95% CI of +134.17 and −234.17 (i.e., it is a possible value for the mean difference in the population), we would have decided to retain the null hypothesis using hypothesis testing, which was the decision we made using hypothesis testing.

FYI

When the value stated by a null hypothesis is outside the confidence interval, this indicates a significant effect in the population.

In terms of effect size, when the value stated by a null hypothesis is outside the confidence interval, we can interpret effect size using the confidence limits. Specifically, the effect size for a confidence interval is a range or interval, where the lower effect size estimate is the difference between the value stated in the null hypothesis and the lower confidence limit; the upper effect size estimate is the difference between the value stated in the null hypothesis and the upper confidence limit. Effect size can then be interpreted in terms of a shift in the population. However, because the value stated in the null hypothesis (0) was contained inside the confidence interval for Example 9.1, we cannot estimate an effect size for this example.

9.8 SPSS in Focus: Two-Independent-Sample *t* Test and Confidence Intervals

SPSS can be used to compute the two-independent-sample *t* test. To illustrate how to compute this test in SPSS and how the output tables in SPSS match with the data we computed by hand, let us compute this test using the same data originally given for Example 9.1 in Table 9.2. For reference, Table 9.6 restates the original data for this example, which we will enter into SPSS. We will compare these data between groups using a .05 level of significance ($\alpha = .05$).

| TABLE 9.6 | The Number of Calories Consumed in a Meal Between Groups Asked to Eat Slowly or Fast |

Group Eating Slowly	Group Eating Fast
700	450
450	800
850	750
600	700
450	550
550	650

These data for Example 9.1 are restated here from data originally given in Table 9.2.

1. Click on the Variable View tab and enter *groups* in the Name column. In the second row, enter *intake* in the Name column. We will enter whole numbers, so reduce the value in the Decimals column to 0.

2. In the row labeled *groups*, click on the small gray box with three dots in the Values column. In the dialog box, enter *1* in the value cell and *Slowly* in the label cell, and then click Add. Then enter *2* in the value cell and *Fast* in the label cell, and then click *Add.* Select OK.

3. Click on the Data View tab. In the *groups* column, enter *1* in the first six cells, then *2* in the next six cells. In the *intake* column, enter the calorie intakes for each group in the cells that correspond with the codes for each group listed in the first column.

4. Go to the menu bar and click Analyze, then Compare Means and Independent-Samples *T* Test, to display the dialog box shown in Figure 9.6.

5. Using the arrows, select *intake* and move it into the Test Variable(s): box; select *groups* and move it into the Grouping Variable: box. Two question marks will appear in the Grouping Variable: box. To adjust the confidence intervals for this test, select Options . . . in the dialog box. Because the default confidence interval is set at a 95% CI, we do not have to adjust this.

6. To define the groups, click Define Groups . . . to bring up a new dialog box. Enter *1* in the Group 1: box, enter *2* in the Group 2: box, and then click Continue. Now a *1* and *2* will appear in the Grouping Variable: box instead of question marks.

7. Select OK, or select Paste and click the Run command.

FIGURE 9.6   SPSS Dialog Box for Steps 4 to 7

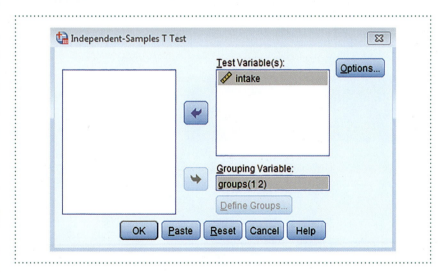

Table 9.7 shows the output. The top table displays the sample size, mean, standard deviation, and standard error for both groups. The bottom table displays a summary for the *t* test. The effect size is not given, although you can use the data given in the output tables to compute effect size.

(Continued)

(Continued)

Also, notice that the bottom table gives the numerator (Mean Difference column) and denominator (Std. Error Difference column) for the *t* test. If we substitute the values in the SPSS output table into the formula, we will obtain the same values for the test statistic computed in Example 9.1.

The confidence limits are also given in the SPSS output table. The lower and upper confidence limits, which are circled in the SPSS output table, match those we already computed, give or take rounding. Using these 95% confidence limits, we conclude that it is likely that there is no difference in calories consumed between groups instructed to eat slowly or fast because 0 falls within the interval specified.

| **TABLE 9.7** | SPSS Output Table for the Two-Independent-Sample *t* Test With the 95% Confidence Interval Given in the Table |

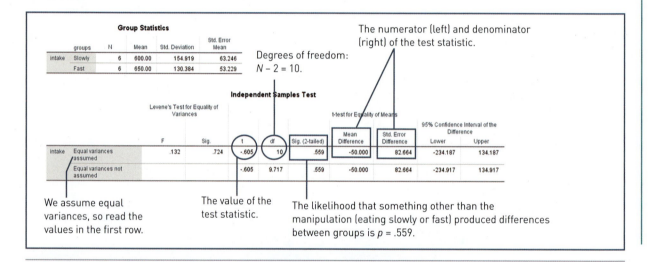

9.9 APA IN FOCUS: REPORTING THE *t* STATISTIC AND CONFIDENCE INTERVALS

When reporting the results of a *t* test, we include the value of the test statistic, degrees of freedom, *p* value, and effect size. In addition, a figure or table is often used to summarize the means and standard error or standard deviations measured in the study. While this information can be included in the written results of the study, it is often more concise to do so in a table or figure.

Many scientific journals will not publish the results of a study without the standard deviations or estimated standard errors reported with a *t* test. It is your choice whether to summarize these values in a figure, a table, or the written report, but they must be reported. Cohen's *d*, eta-squared (η^2), and omega-squared (ω^2) are all acceptable measures of effect size, although Cohen's *d* is most often reported as an effect size estimate with the *t* test. To report the results of estimation in scientific journals, we state the level of confidence, point estimate, and interval estimate of each confidence interval. For example, we could report the confidence interval for the two-independent-sample *t* test in Example 9.1 as follows:

Rate of eating, either slowly (*M* = 600 calories) or fast (*M* = 650 calories), failed to produce significant differences in food intake between groups, (mean [95% CI] = –50 [–234.17 to +134.17]).

••• CHAPTER SUMMARY ORGANIZED BY LEARNING OBJECTIVE

LO 1: **Describe the between-subjects design, and identify two appropriate sampling methods used to select independent samples.**

- A between-subjects design is a research design in which different participants are observed one time in each group or at each level of one factor. With two groups, we can then compare differences between the groups.

  o Differences between the groups selected can then be evaluated by determining the extent to which scores in each group overlap. The less overlap in scores between groups, the more likely we are to decide to reject the null hypothesis.

- When different participants are observed in each group, the sample is called an independent sample. To select independent samples, we can (a) select a sample from two populations or (b) select one sample from the same population and randomly assign participants in the sample to groups.

LO 2–3: **Calculate the degrees of freedom for a two-independent-sample t test and locate critical values in the t table; identify the assumptions for a two-independent-sample t test.**

- The degrees of freedom for a two-independent-sample t test are $(n_1 - 1) + (n_2 - 1)$, or $N - 2$.

- We compute a two-independent-sample t test to compare the mean difference between two groups. This test is specifically used to test hypotheses concerning the difference between two population means from one or two populations with unknown variances. We make four assumptions for this test: normality, random sampling, independence, and equal variances.

LO 4: **Compute a two-independent-sample t test and interpret the results.**

- The larger the value of the test statistic, the less likely a sample mean would be to occur if the null hypothesis were true, and the more likely we are to reject the null hypothesis. The test statistic for a two-independent-sample t test is the mean difference between two samples minus the mean difference stated in the null hypothesis, divided by the estimated standard error for the difference:

$$t_{obt} = \frac{(M_1 - M_2) - (\mu_1 - \mu_2)}{s_{M_1 - M_2}}, \text{where}$$

$$s_{M_1 - M_2} = \sqrt{\frac{s_p^2}{n_1} + \frac{s_p^2}{n_2}} \text{ and } s_p^2 = \frac{s_1^2(df_1) + s_2^2(df_2)}{df_1 + df_2}.$$

- The estimated standard error for the difference is an estimate of the standard deviation of a sampling distribution of mean differences between two sample means. It is an estimate of the standard error or distance that mean differences can deviate from the mean difference stated in the null hypothesis.

LO 5: **Compute and interpret effect size and proportion of variance for a two-independent-sample t test.**

- Estimated Cohen's d can be used to estimate effect size for the two-independent-sample t test. This measure estimates how far, or how many standard deviations, an observed mean difference is shifted in one or two populations. The formula for estimated Cohen's d for the two-independent-sample t test is

$$d = \frac{M_1 - M_2}{\sqrt{s_p^2}}.$$

- The computation and interpretation of proportion of variance are the same for all *t* tests.

LO 6: **Compute and interpret confidence intervals for the two-independent-sample *t* test.**

- The three steps to estimation are as follows:

  Step 1: Compute the sample mean and standard error.

  Step 2: Choose the level of confidence and find the critical values at that level of confidence.

  Step 3: Compute the estimation formula to find the confidence limits.

- The estimation formula for the two-independent-sample *t* test is $M_1 - M_2 \pm t(s_{M_1 - M_2})$.

LO 7: **Summarize the results of a two-independent-sample *t* test in APA format.**

- To report the results of a two-independent-sample *t* test, state the test statistic, degrees of freedom,

p value, and effect size. In addition, a figure or table is often used to summarize the means and standard error or standard deviations measured in a study. While this information can be included in the written report, it is often more concise to include it in a table or figure.

- To report the results of estimation for the two-independent-sample *t* test, state the level of confidence, point estimate, and interval estimate of each confidence interval.

LO 8: **Compute a two-independent-sample *t* test and identify confidence intervals using SPSS.**

- SPSS can be used to compute a two-independent-sample *t* test using the Analyze, Compare Means, and Independent-Samples T Test options in the menu bar. These actions will display a dialog box that allows you to identify the groups, adjust the confidence level, and run the test (for more details, see Section 9.8).

• • • KEY TERMS

between-subjects design
estimated standard error for the
  difference

independent sample
pooled sample
  standard deviation

pooled sample variance
two-independent-sample *t* test

• • • END-OF-CHAPTER PROBLEMS

Factual Problems

1. What is the between-subjects design?

2. When an independent sample is selected, are the same or different participants observed in each group?

3. Of the two ways to select two samples described in this chapter, which type of sampling is commonly used in experiments?

4. Explain how overlap in scores between two groups can help to identify whether a difference observed is likely to be significant.

5. What is the calculation of the degrees of freedom for the two-independent-sample *t* test?

6. Name three measures used to estimate effect size for the two-independent-sample *t* test.

7. Name two measures of proportion of variance. Which measure is the least conservative?

8. What value is used to estimate the population standard deviation of the difference between two means in the formula for estimated Cohen's *d*?

9. What measure of effect size is most often reported with the *t* test?

Concept and Application Problems

11. In the following studies, state whether you would use a one-sample *t* test or a two-independent-sample *t* test.

    (a) A study testing whether night-shift workers sleep the recommended 8 hours per day

    (b) A study measuring differences in attitudes about morality among men and women

    (c) An experiment measuring differences in brain activity among rats placed on either a continuous or an intermittent reward schedule

12. State the degrees of freedom for the *t* test for each of the following situations in which two groups are observed.

    (a) A study in which 12 participants are assigned to one group and 15 participants are assigned to a second group

    (b) A study in which 30 participants are selected, then half are observed in Group 1, and half in Group 2

    (c) A study in which researchers compare the standardized test scores between a class of 20 psychology students and a class of 26 biology students

13. State the total degrees of freedom for the following *t* tests:

    (a) $n = 12$ for a one-sample *t* test

    (b) Critical value = 1.645 for a one-tailed test, $\alpha = .05$

    (c) $df_1 = 12$, $n_2 = 19$ for a two-independent-sample *t* test

    (d) Critical value = 63.657 for a two-tailed test, $\alpha = .01$

14. Will each of the following increase, decrease, or have no effect on the critical value of a two-independent-sample *t* test?

    (a) The sample size is increased.

    (b) The level of significance is reduced from .05 to .01.

    (c) The pooled sample variance is doubled.

15. State the critical values for a two-independent-sample *t* test given the following conditions:

    (a) Two-tailed test, $\alpha = .01$, total $df = 26$

    (b) One-tailed test, lower-tail critical, $\alpha = .01$, $df = 15$ for each group

    (c) Two-tailed test, $\alpha = .05$, $n = 12$ in each group

    (d) One-tailed test, upper-tail critical, $\alpha = .05$, n for both groups combined is 30

16. Will each of the following increase, decrease, or have no effect on the value of the test statistic for a two-independent-sample *t* test?

    (a) The total sample size is increased.

    (b) The level of significance is reduced from .05 to .01.

    (c) The pooled sample variance is doubled.

17. A researcher reports the following confidence interval for a comparison of the difference between two groups: 95% CI −12.0 [−30.0 to 6.0]. If there was no difference between groups, then a difference of 0 was expected.

    (a) What would the decision have likely been if the researcher tested this hypothesis with hypothesis testing at a .05 level of significance? Explain.

    (b) What is the value of the point estimate?

18. A researcher reports the following confidence interval to determine whether or not there is a difference between two groups (i.e., whether or not the difference is larger than 0): 95% CI 2.0 [0.2 to 3.8].

    (a) What would the decision have likely been if the researcher tested this hypothesis with hypothesis testing at a .05 level of significance? Explain.

    (b) What is the value of the point estimate?

10. What are the three steps to compute an estimation formula?

19. While researching lifestyle changes to improve happiness, you come across a research article reporting that pet owners self-reported greater overall happiness compared to those who do not own a pet, $t(50) = 2.993$, $p < .05$. Based on the information provided, answer the following questions:

    (a) Does the test statistic show a significant effect? Explain.

    (b) Would the confidence interval for this effect envelop 0? Explain.

20. A study evaluating the effects of parenting style (authoritative, permissive) on child well-being observed 20 children (10 from parents who use an authoritative parenting style and 10 from parents who use a permissive parenting style). Children between the ages of 12 and 14 completed a standard child health questionnaire where scores can range between 0 and 100, with higher scores indicating greater well-being. The scores are given in the table.

Authoritative Parenting Style	Permissive Parenting Style
60	80
65	75
70	55
65	85
80	90
50	65
75	70
55	65
60	70
70	80

    (a) Test whether or not child health scores differ between groups using a .05 level of significance. State the value of the test statistic and the decision to retain or reject the null hypothesis.

    (b) Compute effect size using estimated Cohen's d.

21. Individual actions can play a large role in the overall health of our planet. A researcher interested in evaluating environmentally friendly behaviors evaluated how often people recycle (per month) based on whether they have an overall optimistic or an overall pessimistic attitude toward eco-friendly behaviors. The results from this hypothetical study are given in the table.

Pessimistic	Optimistic
3	4
0	9
4	6
2	8
1	9
6	5
3	6
5	8
0	6
5	7

    (a) Test whether or not recycling behaviors differed between groups using a .05 level of significance. State the value of the test statistic and the decision to retain or reject the null hypothesis.

    (b) Compute effect size using eta-squared (η^2).

22. A social psychologist records the number of outbursts among students at two schools. Assuming the same number of students were observed at each school, what is the sample size at each school, the decision (to retain or reject the null hypothesis), and the effect size for this study, based on the following statement?

    The number of outbursts among students at the small school ($M = 3$) was significantly less than the number recorded at the large school ($M = 5$), $t(38) = 4.19$, $p < .05$ ($d = 0.25$).

23. A researcher records the number of words recalled by students presented with a list of words for one minute. In one group, students were presented with the list of words in color; in a second group, the same words were presented in black and white. An equal number of students were in each group. Based on the statement below, state the sample size in each group, the decision (to retain or reject the null hypothesis), and the effect size in this study.

   Participants recalled significantly more words when the words were presented in color ($M = 12.4$ words) versus black and white ($M = 10.9$ words), $t(48) = 2.009$, $p < .05$ ($\eta^2 = .18$).

24. A researcher reports a value of .28 for the effect size estimate. State the size of this effect as small, medium, or large, assuming the value is for (a) Cohen's d, (b) eta-squared, and (c) omega-squared.

25. Using Cohen's d, state whether a 3-point treatment effect ($M_1 - M_2 = 3$) is small, medium, or large for a two-independent-sample t test, given the following values for the pooled sample variance:

   (a) $s_p^2 = 9$ (b) $s_p^2 = 36$

   (c) $s_p^2 = 576$ (d) $s_p^2 = 144$

Problems in Research

26. **Power and degrees of freedom.** In an explanation regarding the use of t tests, Zimmerman (2012) implied that power is greater for a test associated with $n - 1$ degrees of freedom compared to a test associated with $N - 2$ degrees of freedom—assuming that the total sample sizes are equal (i.e., $n = N$). Based on the information provided,

   (a) Which t test is associated with $n - 1$ degrees of freedom? Which t test is associated with $N - 2$ degrees of freedom?

   (b) Referring to the t table, explain why the statement about power is true.

27. **Identifying tests for two samples.** Özdemir (2013) stated, "when trying to detect and describe differences between two independent groups, by far the most common strategy is to use the arithmetic mean as a measure of location and Student's t test as a method" (p. 322). What is the name of the t test the author is referring to?

28. **Athletics and academic achievement among elementary school children.** Dyke (2014) showed that students who participated in school sports had higher standardized test scores in both reading and math than those who did not, in a sample of 1,605 fourth- and fifth-grade boys and girls. What statistical test was likely performed to determine this outcome? Explain.

29. **Distress and coping among high school students.** In a comparison of coping strategies used among distressed and nondistressed high school students, Lin and Yusoff (2013) identified the following 95% CI for the difference in the use of self-blame as a coping strategy: −0.76 (−1.08 to −0.45). If the null hypothesis was that the difference in self-blame as a coping strategy was 0 between distressed and nondistressed high school students, then what was the decision for this test at a .05 level of significance? Explain.

30. **Assumptions for the two-independent-sample t test.** Bakker and Wicherts (2014) identified that researchers will often exclude outliers in data sets that are nonnormal prior to conducting a two-independent-sample t test. While their findings showed that the practice of removing outliers was not appropriate, why would researchers want to remove outliers in the first place?

31. **Sociodemographic differences in lung cancer worry.** Hahn (2017) evaluated sociodemographic differences in how people worry about lung cancer. Some of the differences observed across demographics of interest were between males and females [$t(45) = 0.69$; higher mean worry among men], smokers and nonsmokers [$t(45) = 2.69$; higher mean worry among smokers], and whether or not a person

graduated high school [$t(45) = 2.56$; higher mean worry among those who did not graduate high school]. However, at least one of these results were not statistically significant. Use the information provided to state which *t* test or *t* tests did not reach the .05 level of significance in this study.

(a) Compute the proportion of variance using omega-squared.

(b) Suppose the pooled sample standard deviation for this test is 0.74. Using this value, compute estimated Cohen's *d*.

32. **Skewness and the assumptions for *t* tests.** Rietveld and van Hout (2015) explained that skewness is an important feature of the data as it relates to "assumptions of *t* tests" (p. 158). Which assumption does skewness relate to? Explain.

Answers for even numbers are in Appendix D.

Sharpen your skills with **SAGE edge at edge.sagepub.com/priviteraess2e**

SAGE edge for Students provides a personalized approach to help you accomplish your coursework goals in an easy-to-use learning environment.

$SAGE edge™

©iStockphoto.com/nastinka

©iStockphoto.com/Shalith

10 Testing Means
Related-Samples *t* Test
With Confidence Intervals

••• Learning Objectives

After reading this chapter, you should be able to:

1. Describe two types of research designs used when selecting related samples.

2. Explain why difference scores are computed for the related-samples *t* test.

3. State three advantages for selecting related samples.

4. Calculate the degrees of freedom for a related-samples *t* test and locate critical values in the *t* table.

5. Identify the assumptions for the related-samples *t* test.

6. Compute a related-samples *t* test and interpret the results.

7. Compute and interpret effect size and proportion of variance for a related-samples *t* test.

8. Compute and interpret confidence intervals for a related-samples *t* test.

9. Summarize the results of a related-samples *t* test in APA format.

10. Compute a related-samples *t* test and identify confidence intervals using SPSS.

Making comparisons over time is often an important part of observing "improvement" or "change." In a classroom, we may want to see how a new curriculum improves student performance on a standardized assessment; or in business, we may want to see how customer service scores change after a new marketing strategy is implemented. We often make observations over time in our daily lives as well, whether it is observing how our grade point average changes from one semester to another or how much money we have in our savings account from before to after college.

In hypothesis testing, there are often cases where making comparisons between two groups over time can be quite informative, especially when the researcher hypothesizes that the two groups are different (i.e., that some change or improvement is expected). In the basic structure of such a study, two groups represent the independent variable. For example, suppose we want to study how music makes us feel when we work out. As part of such a study, we may have participants exercise while listening to music one day and not listening to music on another day, and each time ask them how their mood changed after their workout. For this study, listening (music, no music) would be the independent variable. Here we are observing the same participants two times: one time with and one time without music. The basic structure of such a test is to measure the same dependent variable in each of the two groups. For this example, mood change would be the dependent variable. The null hypothesis for such a test would be that there is no difference between the two groups; the alternative hypothesis would then state that there is a difference.

In this chapter, we explore the nature of hypothesis testing when participants are observed over time, how to compute and interpret observed effects, and the informativeness of hypothesis testing for making comparisons over time. We further explore other ways of adding information about the nature of observed effects and how to appropriately interpret them.

Master the content.
edge.sagepub.com/priviteraess2e

● ● ● Chapter Outline

10.1 RELATED-SAMPLES DESIGNS

In Chapter 9, we introduced a hypothesis test for situations in which we observe independent samples. An independent sample is one in which different participants are observed one time in each group. However, it can often be preferred, even necessary, to observe the same participants in each group or condition, such as when we observe the effects of learning before and after an educational intervention, or when we observe the effectiveness of a behavioral intervention on reducing symptoms of depression. In each case, it makes most sense, and is even necessary, to observe the same participants over time.

In this chapter, we describe such a hypothesis test for observing **related samples**—that is, samples in which the participants are observed in more than one treatment or matched on common characteristics. There are two types of research designs commonly used to select related samples: the repeated-measures design and the matched-pairs design. While these research designs are analyzed in the same way, the data are collected differently for each. Both research designs are briefly described in this section.

The Repeated-Measures Design

The most common related-samples design is the **repeated-measures design**, in which each participant is observed repeatedly. Table 10.1 shows a situation with two treatments. In a repeated-measures design, each participant (n_1, n_2, etc.) is observed twice (once in each treatment). We can create repeated measures by using a pre-post design or a within-subjects design.

Using the **pre-post design**, we measure a dependent variable for participants observed before (pre) and after (post) a treatment. For example, we can measure athletic performance (the dependent variable) in a sample of athletes before and after a training camp. We can compare the difference in athletic performance before and after the camp. This type of repeated-measures design is limited to observing participants two times (i.e., before and after a treatment).

In a **related sample**, also called a **dependent sample**, participants are related. Participants can be related in one of two ways: They are observed in more than one group (a repeated-measures design), or they are matched, experimentally or naturally, based on common characteristics or traits (a matched-pairs design).

The **repeated-measures design** is a research design in which the same participants are observed in each treatment. Two types of repeated-measures designs are the pre-post design and the within-subjects design.

The **pre-post design** is a type of repeated-measures design in which researchers measure a dependent variable for participants before (pre) and after (post) a treatment.

TABLE 10.1	In a Repeated-Measures Design With Two Treatments, n Participants Are Observed Two Times

Treatment 1		Treatment 2
n_1	–	n_1
n_2	–	n_2
n_3	–	n_3
n_4	–	n_4
n_5	–	n_5

Using the **within-subjects design**, we observe participants across many treatments but not necessarily before and after a treatment. For two samples, suppose we want to study the effects of exercise on memory. We can select a sample of participants and have them take a memory test after completing an anaerobic exercise, and again after completing an aerobic exercise. In this example, we observe participants twice, but not necessarily before and after a treatment. Anytime the same participants are observed in each group, either pre-post or within-subjects, we are using the repeated-measures design to observe related samples.

The Matched-Pairs Design

The matched-pairs design is also used to study related samples. In the **matched-pairs design**, participants are selected and then matched, experimentally or naturally, based on common characteristics or traits. The matched-pairs design is limited to observing two groups, where pairs of participants are matched. Using this design, Table 10.2 shows a situation with two treatments. In a matched-pairs design, different, yet matched, participants (n_1, n_2, etc.) are observed in each treatment, and scores from each matched pair of participants are compared.

We can obtain matched pairs in one of two ways: experimental manipulation or natural occurrence. Matching through experimental manipulation is typical for research studies in which the researcher manipulates the traits or characteristics upon which participants are matched. We can match pairs of participants on any number of variables, including their level of intelligence, their personality type, their eating habits, their level of education, and their sleep patterns. We could measure these characteristics and then match participants. For example, we could measure intelligence and then match the two participants scoring the highest, the two participants scoring the next highest, and so on. Matching through experimental manipulation requires that we measure some trait or characteristic before we match participants into pairs.

FYI

Two types of designs for selecting related samples are the repeated-measures and matched-pairs designs.

FYI

In a repeated-measures design, the same participants are observed in each treatment. Two types of repeated-measures designs are the pre-post and within-subjects designs.

FYI

In a matched-pairs design, participants are matched based on the characteristics that they share. Matched pairs can be obtained either experimentally or through natural occurrence.

TABLE 10.2 In a Matched-Pairs Design, *n* Pairs Are Matched and Observed One Time

Treatment 1		Treatment 2
n_1	–	n_2
n_3	–	n_4
n_5	–	n_6
n_7	–	n_8
n_9	–	n_{10}

The **within-subjects design** is a type of repeated-measures design in which researchers observe the same participants across many treatments but not necessarily before and after a treatment.

The **matched-pairs design**, also called the **matched-subjects design** or **matched-samples design**, is a research design in which participants are selected and then matched, experimentally or naturally, based on common characteristics or traits.

Matching through natural occurrence is typical for quasi-experiments in which participants are matched based on preexisting traits. The preexisting traits are typically biological or physiological in nature. For example, we could match participants based on genetics (e.g., biological twins) or family affiliation (e.g., brothers, sisters, or cousins). Each trait or characteristic is inherent to the participant. There is no need to measure this in order to pair participants. Instead, the participants are already matched naturally. Pairs of identical twins or brothers, for example, are paired together naturally. One member of each pair is assigned to a group or a treatment, and differences between pairs of scores are observed. Anytime participants are matched on common traits, either experimentally or through natural occurrence, we are using the matched-pairs design to select related samples. Figure 10.1 summarizes the designs used with related samples.

FIGURE 10.1 Two Designs Associated With Selecting Related Samples: The Repeated-Measures Design and the Matched-Pairs Design

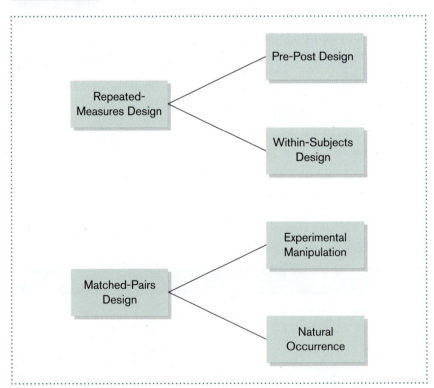

Repeated measures can be selected by observing participants before and after a treatment (pre-post design) or across treatments (within-subjects design). Matched pairs can be selected through experimental manipulation or natural occurrence.

LEARNING CHECK 1

1. How do related samples differ from independent samples?

2. Name two types of repeated-measures designs.

3. Distinguish between the repeated-measures design and the matched-pairs design.

4. A researcher records the amount of computer use (in hours per day) in a sample of students and then matches the students based on their amount of computer use. Is this an example of matching through experimental manipulation or matching through natural occurrence?

Answers: 1. In related samples, participants are related because they are either observed more than once or matched on common traits. In independent samples, participants are not related because different participants are observed in each group; 2. Pre-post design and within-subjects design; 3. Each participant is observed at least two times in the repeated-measures design. In the matched-pairs design, each pair of participants is matched and observed one time; 4. Matching through experimental manipulation.

10.2 INTRODUCTION TO THE RELATED-SAMPLES *t* TEST

When we select two related samples, we can compare differences using the **related-samples *t* test**. To use this test, we start by stating the null hypothesis for the mean difference between pairs of scores in a population, and we then compare this to the difference we observe between paired scores in a sample. The related-samples *t* test is different from the two-independent-sample *t* test in that first we subtract one score in each pair from the other to obtain the **difference score** for each participant; then we compute the test statistic.

There is a good reason for finding the difference between scores in each pair before computing the test statistic using a related-samples *t* test: It eliminates the source of error associated with observing different participants in each group or treatment. When we select related samples, we observe the same, or matched, participants in each group, not different participants. So we can eliminate this source of error.

Consider the hypothetical data shown in Table 10.3 for four participants (A, B, C, and D) observed in two groups (Q and Z). Table 10.3 identifies three places where differences can occur with two groups. The null hypothesis makes a statement about the mean difference between groups, which is the difference we are testing. Any other difference is called **error** because the differences cannot be attributed to having different groups.

As shown in Table 10.4, when we reduce pairs of scores to a single column of difference scores, we eliminate the between-persons error that was illustrated in Table 10.3. Between-persons error is associated with differences associated with observing different participants in each group or treatment. However, using the related-samples design, we observe the same (or matched) participants in each group, not different participants,

The **related-samples *t* test** is a statistical procedure used to test hypotheses concerning two related samples selected from populations in which the variance in one or both populations is unknown.

A **difference score** is a score or value obtained by subtracting one score from another. In a related-samples *t* test, difference scores are obtained prior to computing the test statistic.

For a *t* test, the term **error** refers to any unexplained difference that cannot be attributed to, or caused by, having different treatments. The standard error of the mean is used to measure the error or unexplained differences in a statistical design.

TABLE 10.3   A Hypothetical Set of Data of Four Participants

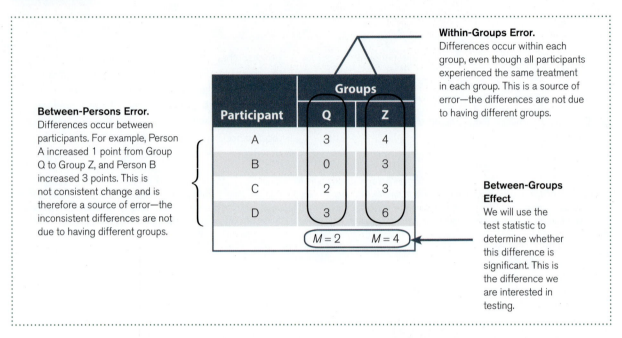

Between-Persons Error.
Differences occur between participants. For example, Person A increased 1 point from Group Q to Group Z, and Person B increased 3 points. This is not consistent change and is therefore a source of error—the inconsistent differences are not due to having different groups.

Within-Groups Error.
Differences occur within each group, even though all participants experienced the same treatment in each group. This is a source of error—the differences are not due to having different groups.

Between-Groups Effect.
We will use the test statistic to determine whether this difference is significant. This is the difference we are interested in testing.

Participant	Groups	
	Q	**Z**
A	3	4
B	0	3
C	2	3
D	3	6
	$M = 2$	$M = 4$

There are three places where differences can occur. Mean differences (the between-groups effect) are the differences we are testing. The other two places where differences occur are regarded as errors in that they have nothing to do with having different groups.

TABLE 10.4   A Hypothetical Set of Data of the Same Four Participants in Table 10.3

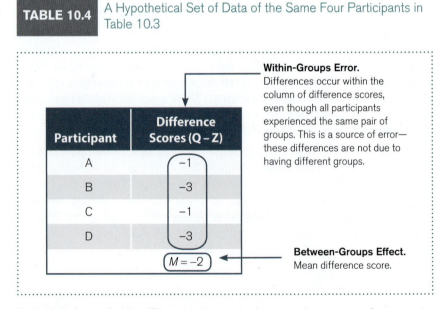

Within-Groups Error.
Differences occur within the column of difference scores, even though all participants experienced the same pair of groups. This is a source of error—these differences are not due to having different groups.

Between-Groups Effect.
Mean difference score.

Participant	Difference Scores (Q – Z)
A	−1
B	−3
C	−1
D	−3
	$M = -2$

Notice that when we find the difference between paired scores, only one source of error remains (within-groups error). The between-persons error is eliminated when the same or matched participants are observed in each group.

so we can eliminate this source of error before computing the test statistic. Error in a study is measured by the estimate of standard error. Eliminating between-persons error makes the total value of error smaller, thereby reducing standard error. In Chapter 8, we showed that reducing standard error increases the power of detecting an effect. This is a key advantage of computing difference scores prior to computing the test statistic: It reduces standard error, thereby increasing the power to detect an effect.

FYI

Computing difference scores prior to computing the test statistic reduces error by eliminating one possible source of error, thereby increasing the power of a hypothesis test.

Advantages for Selecting Related Samples

Selecting related samples has many advantages and disadvantages. Because most of the disadvantages pertain specifically to a repeated-measures design and not a matched-pairs design, we introduce only the advantages that pertain to both designs. There are three key advantages for selecting related samples compared to selecting independent samples in behavioral research:

1. Selecting related samples can be more practical. It is more practical in that selecting related samples may provide a better way to test your hypotheses. This is especially true for research areas in learning and development in which researchers must observe changes in behavior or development over time or between matched pairs of participants. For example, it can be more practical to observe the behavior of the same participants before and after a treatment (repeated measures) or to compare how well participants of similar ability master a task (matched samples).

2. Selecting related samples reduces standard error. Computing difference scores prior to computing the test statistic eliminates the between-persons source of error, which reduces the estimate of standard error. Using the same data, this means that the value for the estimate of standard error for a related-samples t test will be smaller than that for a two-independent-sample t test.

3. Selecting related samples increases power. It follows from the second advantage that reducing the estimate for standard error will increase the value of the test statistic. Using the same data, a related-samples t test is more likely than a two-independent-sample t test to result in a decision to reject the null hypothesis. Hence, the related-samples t test is associated with greater power to detect an effect.

Thus, selecting related samples has distinct advantages that are practical and can increase power. The remainder of this section elucidates the test statistic and degrees of freedom for a related-samples t test, which is used to analyze data for related samples with two groups.

The Test Statistic

The test statistic for a related-samples t test is similar to the test statistics introduced in Chapters 8 and 9 for one group. The mean differences are placed in the numerator, and the estimate of standard error is placed in the denominator. For a related-samples t test, in the numerator, we subtract the mean difference between two related samples (M_D) from the mean difference stated in the null hypothesis (μ_D):

$$M_D - \mu_D.$$

The estimate of standard error is placed in the denominator of the test statistic for a related-samples t test. The standard error for a distribution of mean difference scores, called the **estimated standard error for difference scores (s_{MD})**, is computed using the following formula:

$$s_{MD} = \sqrt{\frac{s_D^2}{n_D}} = \frac{s_D}{\sqrt{n_D}}.$$

By placing the mean differences in the numerator and the estimated standard error for difference scores in the denominator, we obtain the formula for the test statistic for a related-samples t test:

$$t_{obt} = \frac{M_D - \mu_D}{s_{MD}}.$$

The test statistic for a related-samples t test estimates the number of standard deviations in a t distribution that a sample mean difference falls from the population mean difference stated in the null hypothesis. The larger the value of the test statistic, the less likely a sample mean difference would occur if the null hypothesis were true, thereby making it more likely that we will decide to reject the null hypothesis.

FYI

The degrees of freedom for the related-samples t *test equal the number of difference scores minus 1:* df = (n_D – 1).

Degrees of Freedom

To compute the test statistic, we first reduce each pair of scores to one column of difference scores. Hence, the degrees of freedom for the related-samples t test equal the number of difference scores minus 1: $df = (n_D - 1)$.

FYI

Two assumptions for a related-samples t *test are normality and independence within groups.*

Assumptions

There are two assumptions we make to compute the related-samples t test:

The **estimated standard error for difference scores (s_{MD})** is an estimate of the standard deviation of a sampling distribution of mean difference scores. It is an estimate of the standard error or standard distance that the mean difference scores deviate from the mean difference score stated in a null hypothesis.

1. *Normality.* We assume that data in the population of difference scores are normally distributed. Again, this assumption is most important for small sample sizes. With larger samples ($n > 30$), the standard error is smaller, and this assumption becomes less critical as a result.

2. *Independence within groups.* The samples are related or matched between groups. However, we must assume that difference scores were obtained from different individuals within each group or treatment.

LEARNING CHECK 2

1. Why do we find the difference between pairs of scores (compute difference scores) before computing the test statistic for a related-samples *t* test?

2. What is the value for the degrees of freedom for each example listed below?

   (a) A study comparing 10 matched pairs of scores

   (b) A study involving 18 participants observed two times

3. What value is placed in the denominator of the test statistic for the related-samples *t* test?

4. What are the assumptions for a related-samples *t* test?

Answers: 1. Computing difference scores eliminates the between-persons error, thereby increasing the power of the test; 2. (a) *df* = 9, (b) *df* = 17; 3. Estimated standard error for difference scores; 4. Normality and independence within groups.

10.3 COMPUTING THE RELATED-SAMPLES *t* TEST

Two designs associated with selecting related samples are the repeated-measures design and the matched-pairs design. In Example 10.1, we compute the related-samples *t* test for a study using the repeated-measures design. However, the same procedures described here can also be applied to compute the related-samples *t* test for a study using the matched-pairs design.

FYI

The null and alternative hypotheses make statements about a population of mean difference scores.

Example 10.1

One area of focus in many areas of psychology and in education is on understanding and promoting reading among children and adults (Kent, Wanzek, & Al Otaiba, 2012; Reese, 2015; White, Chen, & Forsyth, 2010). Suppose we conduct a study with this area of focus by testing if teacher supervision influences the time that elementary school children read. To test this, we stage two 6-minute reading sessions and record the time in seconds that children spend reading in each session. In one session, the children read with a teacher present in the room; in another session, the same group of children read without a teacher present. The difference in time spent reading in the presence versus absence of a teacher is recorded. Table 10.5 lists the results of this hypothetical study with difference scores given. Test whether or not reading times differ using a .05 level of significance.

© iStockphoto.com/CEFutcher

| **TABLE 10.5** | The Time (in seconds) Spent Reading in a Sample of Eight Students in the Presence and Absence of a Teacher |

	Teacher		
Participants	**Present**	**Absent**	**Difference Scores**
1	220	210	(220 – 210) = 10
2	245	220	(245 – 220) = 25
3	215	195	(215 – 195) = 20
4	260	265	(260 – 265) = –5
5	300	275	(300 – 275) = 25
6	280	290	(280 – 290) = –10
7	250	220	(250 – 220) = 30
8	310	285	(310 – 285) = 25

Difference scores are given in the last column.

Step 1: State the hypotheses. Because we are testing whether (=) or not (≠) a difference exists, the null hypothesis states that there is no mean difference, and the alternative hypothesis states that there is a mean difference:

H_0: $\mu_D = 0$ There is no mean difference in time spent reading in the presence versus absence of a teacher.

H_1: $\mu_D \neq 0$ There is a mean difference in time spent reading in the presence versus absence of a teacher.

Step 2: Set the criteria for a decision. The level of significance for this test is .05. This is a two-tailed test for the mean difference between two related samples. The degrees of freedom for this test are $df = 8 - 1 = 7$. We locate 7 degrees of freedom in the far-left column of the t table in Table C.2 in Appendix C. Move across to the column to find the critical values for a .05 proportion in two tails. The critical values for this test are ±2.365. Figure 10.2 shows the t distribution and the rejection regions beyond these critical values.

We will compare the value of the test statistic to these critical values. If the value of the test statistic falls beyond either critical value (±2.365), then there is less than a 5% chance we would obtain that outcome if the null hypothesis were true, so we reject the null hypothesis; otherwise, we retain the null hypothesis.

Step 3: Compute the test statistic. To compute the test statistic, we (1) compute the mean, variance, and standard deviation of difference scores; (2) compute the estimated standard error for difference scores; then (3) compute the test statistic.

(1) Compute the mean, variance, and standard deviation of difference scores. Keep in mind that the sign (negative or positive) of difference scores matters when we compute the mean and standard deviation. To compute the mean, we sum the difference scores (ΣD) and divide by the number of difference scores summed (n_D):

$$M_D = \frac{\Sigma D}{n_D} = \frac{120}{8} = 15.$$

FIGURE 10.2 Setting the Criteria for a Decision

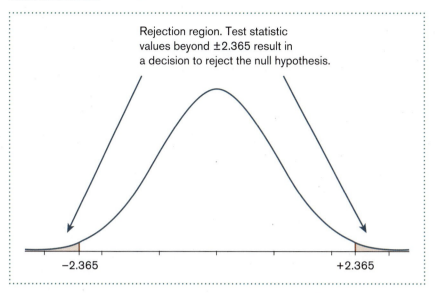

Rejection region. Test statistic
values beyond ±2.365 result in
a decision to reject the null hypothesis.

−2.365   +2.365

The shaded areas show the rejection regions for a t distribution with $df = 7$. The critical value cutoffs are ±2.365. If the value of the test statistic falls in the shaded area, then we choose to reject the null hypothesis; otherwise, we retain the null hypothesis.

To compute the variance, we use the computational formula for sample variance (p. 114). Table 10.6 shows the calculations for computing D and D^2 using this formula:

$$s_D^2 = \frac{SS}{n_D - 1}, \text{ where } SS = \sum D^2 - \frac{(\sum D)^2}{n_D}$$

$$SS = 3{,}400 - \frac{(120)^2}{8} = 1{,}600.$$

$$s_D^2 = \frac{1{,}600}{8-1} = 228.57.$$

TABLE 10.6 Calculations for the Variance of Difference Scores

D	D²
10	100
25	625
20	400
−5	25
25	625
−10	100
30	900
25	625
$\sum D = 120$	$\sum D^2 = 3{,}400$

The first column lists the same difference scores as those in the last column of Table 10.5.

FYI

The mean difference and the estimated standard error for difference scores are entered in the formula for a related-samples t test.

To compute the standard deviation, we take the square root of the variance:

$$s_D = \sqrt{s_D^2} = \sqrt{228.57} = 15.12.$$

(2) Compute the estimated standard error for difference scores (s_{MD}). We substitute 15.12 for s_D and 8 for n_D:

$$s_{MD} = \frac{s_D}{\sqrt{n_D}} = \frac{15.12}{\sqrt{8}} = 5.35.$$

(3) Compute the test statistic. We substitute 15 for M_D, 0 for μ_D (this is the value stated in the null hypothesis), and 5.35 for s_{MD}:

$$t_{obt} = \frac{M_D - \mu_D}{s_{MD}} = \frac{15-0}{5.35} = 2.804.$$

Step 4: Make a decision. To make a decision, we compare the obtained value to the critical value. We reject the null hypothesis if the obtained value exceeds the critical value. Figure 10.3 shows that the obtained value ($t_{obt} = 2.804$) exceeds the upper critical value; it falls in the rejection region. The decision is to reject the null hypothesis. If we were to report this result in a research journal, it would look something like this:

> Elementary school children spent significantly more time reading in the presence of a teacher than when the teacher was absent, $t(7) = 2.804$, $p < .05$.

FIGURE 10.3 Making a Decision for Example 10.1

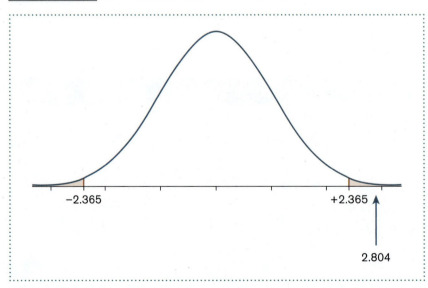

The test statistic falls in the rejection region (it is beyond the critical value). Hence, we reject the null hypothesis.

MAKING SENSE INCREASING POWER BY REDUCING ERROR

As illustrated in Table 10.3, there are three places where scores can differ: Two are attributed to error (within groups and between persons), and one is tested by the null hypothesis (between groups). When we compute difference scores, we eliminate one of the sources of error (i.e., between-persons error), as illustrated in Table 10.4, thereby increasing the power of a related-samples t test compared to the two-independent-sample t test. To see how this increases power, we can take another look at Example 10.1.

In Example 10.1, the null hypothesis was that the mean difference equals 0, and we computed the following test statistic:

$$t_{obt} = \frac{mean\ difference}{estimate\ for\ error} = \frac{15}{5.35} = 2.804,\ p < .05.$$

The test statistic reached significance; we decided to reject the null hypothesis. Now, let us suppose that different participants were assigned to each group and we obtained the same data shown in Table 10.5. In that case, we would compute the two-independent-sample t test, and we would not reduce the scores in each group to one column of difference scores.

When the two columns (teacher present, teacher absent) are not reduced to one column of difference scores, error is computed with both between persons and within groups as sources of error. When we compute the two-independent-sample t test, the mean difference is still 15, but our estimate for standard error will therefore be larger because both sources of error are included in its calculation. When we analyze these data using the test statistic for the two-independent-sample t test, we obtain

$$t_{obt} = \frac{mean\ difference}{estimate\ for\ error} = \frac{15}{18.10} = 0.829,\ p > .05.$$

Notice that the estimate for standard error in the denominator is indeed larger. In this case, our decision will change as a result. Using the two-independent-sample t test, we have not detected the effect or mean difference between groups. Instead, for the two-independent-sample t test, we decide to retain the null hypothesis. All other things being equal, the related-samples t test reduces our estimate of standard error. Thus, as a general rule, the related-samples t test will have greater power to detect an effect or mean difference than the two-independent-sample t test.

LEARNING CHECK 3

1. What is the test statistic for a related-samples t test with a mean difference equal to 5 and an estimated standard error for difference scores equal to each of the following?

    (a) 2.5   (b) 5.0   (c) 10.0

2. The test statistic for a related-samples t test is +2.100. Using a .05 level of significance, would you retain or reject the null hypothesis under each of the following conditions?

    (a) $df = 10$, two-tailed test

    (b) $df = 30$, one-tailed test (upper-tail critical)

    (c) $df = 20$, two-tailed test

    (d) $df = 40$, one-tailed test (lower-tail critical)

3. How does computing difference scores increase the power of a related-samples t test compared to a two-independent-sample t test?

Answers: 1. (a) $t_{obt} = \frac{5}{2.5} = 2.000$, (b) $t_{obt} = \frac{5}{5} = 1.000$, (c) $t_{obt} = \frac{5}{10} = 0.500$; 2. (a) Retain the null hypothesis, (b) Reject the null hypothesis, (c) Reject the null hypothesis, (d) Retain the null hypothesis; 3. Computing difference scores eliminates between-persons error, thereby reducing the estimate for standard error in the denominator.

10.4 MEASURING EFFECT SIZE FOR THE RELATED-SAMPLES *t* TEST

FYI

The standard deviation of difference scores is used to estimate the population standard deviation in the formula for Cohen's d.

Hypothesis testing identifies whether or not an effect exists. In Example 10.1, we concluded that an effect does exist—elementary school children spent significantly more time reading in the presence of a teacher than when the teacher was absent; we rejected the null hypothesis. The size of this effect is determined by measures of effect size. We will compute effect size for Example 10.1 because the decision was to reject the null hypothesis for that hypothesis test. There are three measures of effect size for the related-samples *t* test: estimated Cohen's *d* and two measures of proportion of variance (eta-squared and omega-squared).

Estimated Cohen's *d*

An estimated Cohen's *d* is the most common measure of effect size used with the *t* test. For two related samples, *d* measures the number of standard deviations that mean difference scores shifted above or below the population mean difference stated in the null hypothesis. The larger the value of *d*, the larger the effect in the population. To compute estimated Cohen's *d* with two related samples, we place the mean difference between two samples in the numerator and the standard deviation of the difference scores to estimate the population standard deviation in the denominator:

$$d = \frac{M_D}{s_D}.$$

In Example 10.1, the mean difference was $M_D = 15$, and the standard deviation of difference scores was $s_D = 15.12$. The estimated Cohen's *d* is

$$d = \frac{15}{15.12} = 0.99.$$

We conclude that time spent reading in the presence of a teacher is 0.99 standard deviations longer than when the teacher is absent for the population. The effect size conventions listed in Chapter 7, Table 7.6 (p. 211), and Chapter 8, Table 8.4 (p. 239), show that this is a large effect size ($d > 0.8$). We could report this measure with the significant *t* test in Example 10.1 by stating,

> Elementary school children spent significantly more time reading in the presence of a teacher than when the teacher was absent, $t(7) = 2.804$, $p < .05$ ($d = 0.99$).

Proportion of Variance

Another measure of effect size is proportion of variance. Specifically, this is an estimate of the proportion of variance in a dependent variable that can be explained by a treatment. In Example 10.1, we can measure the proportion of variance in time spent reading (the dependent variable) that can be explained by whether children read more in the presence or absence of a teacher (the treatment). Two measures of proportion of variance for the related-samples *t* test are eta-squared and omega-squared.

The calculations are the same as those for the one-sample and two-independent-sample t tests.

In Example 10.1, we found that elementary school children spent significantly more time reading in the presence of a teacher than when the teacher was absent, $t(7) = 2.804$, $p < .05$. To compute eta-squared, we substitute $t = 2.804$ and $df = 7$:

$$\eta^2 = \frac{t^2}{t^2 + df} = \frac{(2.804)^2}{(2.804)^2 + 7} = .53.$$

Using eta-squared, we conclude that 53% of the variability in time spent reading can be explained by whether or not the teacher was present.

Again, eta-squared tends to overestimate the size of an effect. To correct for this, we can compute omega-squared. To compute omega-squared, we subtract 1 from t^2 in the numerator of the eta-squared formula, thereby reducing the value of the proportion of variance. To compute omega-squared, we again substitute $t = 2.804$ and $df = 7$:

$$\omega^2 = \frac{t^2 - 1}{t^2 + df} = \frac{(2.804)^2 - 1}{(2.804)^2 + 7} = .46.$$

Using omega-squared, we conclude that 46% of the variability in time spent reading can be explained by whether or not the teacher was present. The effect size conventions listed in Chapter 8, Table 8.4 (p. 239), show that both measures of proportion of variance estimate a large effect size in the population. We would report only one measure in a research journal. Using omega-squared, we could report this measure with the significant t test in Example 10.1 by stating,

FYI

Proportion of variance is computed in the same way for all t tests.

Elementary school children spent significantly more time reading in the presence of a teacher than when the teacher was absent, $t(7) = 2.804$, $p < .05$ ($\omega^2 = .46$).

LEARNING CHECK 4

1. What is the denominator for the estimated Cohen's d when used with the related-samples t test?

2. The mean difference between two related samples is 4.00. What is the value for an estimated Cohen's d if a sample standard deviation for the difference scores in this example is equal to (a) 4 and (b) 40?

3. A psychologist reports that the value of the test statistic for two related samples is 2.400. If the degrees of freedom are 20, then what is the value for eta-squared? Is this a small, medium, or large effect size?

4. Using the same data as in Question 3, what is the proportion of variance explained using omega-squared? Is this a small, medium, or large effect size?

Answers: 1. The standard deviation for the difference scores; 2. (a) $d = \frac{4}{4} = 1.00$, (b) $d = \frac{4}{40} = 0.10$; 3. $\eta^2 = \frac{(2.400)^2}{(2.400)^2 + 20} = .22$ (medium effect size); 4. $\omega^2 = \frac{(2.400)^2 - 1}{(2.400)^2 + 20} = .18$ (medium effect size).

10.5 CONFIDENCE INTERVALS
FOR THE RELATED-SAMPLES t TEST

In Example 10.1, we stated a null hypothesis regarding the mean difference in a population. We can also learn more about the mean difference in a population using a different procedure without ever deciding to retain or reject a null hypothesis. The alternative approach requires only that we set limits for the population parameter within which it is likely to be contained. The goal of this alternative approach, called *estimation*, is the same as that in hypothesis testing for Example 10.1—to learn more about the value of a mean in a population of interest.

To use estimation, we identify the sample mean (a point estimate) and give an interval within which a population mean is likely to be contained (an interval estimate). Same as we did for the t tests in Chapter 8 and Chapter 9, we find the interval estimate, often reported as a confidence interval, and state it within a given level of confidence, which is the likelihood that an interval contains an unknown population mean. To illustrate, we will revisit Example 10.1, and using the same data, we will compute the confidence intervals at a 95% level of confidence using the three steps to estimation first introduced in Chapter 8. For a related-samples t test, the estimation formula is

$$M_D \pm t(s_{MD}).$$

Step 1: Compute the sample mean and standard error. The mean difference, which is the point estimate of the population mean difference, is equal to $M_D = 15$.

The estimated standard error for difference scores, s_{MD}, is equal to 5.35.

Step 2: Choose the level of confidence and find the critical values at that level of confidence. In this example, we want to find the 95% confidence interval, so we choose a 95% level of confidence. Remember, in a sampling distribution, 50% of the mean differences fall above the mean difference we selected in our sample, and 50% fall below it. We are looking for the 95% of mean differences that surround the mean difference we selected in our sample. A 95% CI corresponds to a two-tailed test at a .05 level of significance. To find the critical value at this level of confidence, we look in the t table in Table C.2 in Appendix C. The degrees of freedom are 7 ($df = n_D - 1$ for two related samples). The critical value for the interval estimate is $t = 2.365$.

Step 3: Compute the estimation formula to find the confidence limits for a 95% confidence interval. Because we are estimating the mean difference between two related samples from a population with an unknown variance, we use the $M_D \pm t(s_{MD})$. estimation formula.

To compute the formula, multiply t by the estimated standard error for difference scores:

$$t(s_{MD}) = 2.365(5.35) = 12.65.$$

Add 12.65 to the sample mean difference to find the upper confidence limit:

$$M_D + t(s_{MD}) = 15 + 12.65 + 27.65.$$

Subtract 12.65 from the sample mean difference to find the lower confidence limit:

$$M_D - t(s_{MD}) = 15 - 12.65 = 2.35.$$

As shown in Figure 10.4, the 95% confidence interval in this population is between 2.35 and 27.65 seconds. We can estimate within a 95% level of confidence that the children spent more time reading with the teacher present than with no teacher present during a 6-minute session.

FIGURE 10.4	In Example 10.1, the 95% Confidence Interval Is 2.35 to 27.65 Seconds

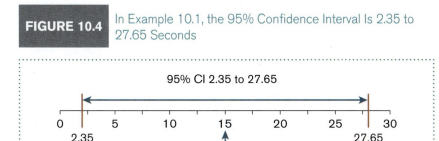

10.6 INFERRING SIGNIFICANCE AND EFFECT SIZE FROM A CONFIDENCE INTERVAL

Notice that we did not make a decision using estimation, other than to state confidence limits for a 95% confidence interval. When we evaluated these same data with hypothesis testing in Example 10.1, we selected a sample to decide whether or not to reject the null hypothesis. While we do not "make a decision" per se using estimation, we can use the confidence limits to determine what the decision would have been using hypothesis testing. As first stated in Chapter 8, in terms of the decisions we make in hypothesis testing,

1. If the value stated by a null hypothesis is inside the confidence interval, the decision is to retain the null hypothesis (not significant).

2. If the value stated by a null hypothesis is outside the confidence interval, the decision is to reject the null hypothesis (significant).

Using these rules, we can thus determine the decision we would have made using hypothesis testing. In Example 10.1, we identified a null hypothesis that the mean difference was 0 between groups. Because a mean difference of 0 falls outside the 95% CI of 2.35 and 27.65 seconds (i.e., it is not a possible value for the mean difference in the population), we would have decided to reject the null hypothesis using hypothesis testing, which was the decision we made using hypothesis testing.

In terms of effect size, when the value stated by a null hypothesis is outside the confidence interval, we can interpret effect size using the confidence limits. Specifically, the effect size for a confidence interval is a range or interval, where the lower effect size estimate is the difference between the value stated in the null hypothesis and the lower

FYI

When the value stated by a null hypothesis is outside the confidence interval, this indicates a significant effect in the population.

confidence limit; the upper effect size estimate is the difference between the value stated in the null hypothesis and the upper confidence limit. Effect size can then be interpreted in terms of a shift in the population. For Example 10.1, we can estimate within a 95% level of confidence that the mean difference in time spent reading in the presence of a teacher is between 2.35 and 27.65 seconds longer than with no teacher present during a 6-minute session.

10.7 SPSS in Focus:
Related-Samples *t* Test and Confidence Intervals

In Example 10.1, we tested whether teacher supervision influences the time that elementary school children read. We used a two-tailed test at a .05 level of significance and decided to reject the null hypothesis. Thus, we concluded that elementary school children spent significantly more time reading in the presence of a teacher than when the teacher was absent, $t(7) = 2.804$, $p < .05$. We can confirm this result using SPSS.

1. Click on the Variable View tab and enter *present* in the Name column. In the second row, enter *absent* in the Name column. We will enter whole numbers, so reduce the value in the Decimals column to 0.

2. Click on the Data View tab. Enter the data in each column as shown in Table 10.7.

TABLE 10.7 Data View in SPSS for Step 2

present	absent
220	210
245	220
215	195
260	265
300	275
280	290
250	220
310	285

3. Go to the menu bar and click Analyze, then Compare Means and Paired-Samples T Test, to display the dialog box shown in Figure 10.5.

FIGURE 10.5 SPSS Dialog Box for Steps 3 to 5

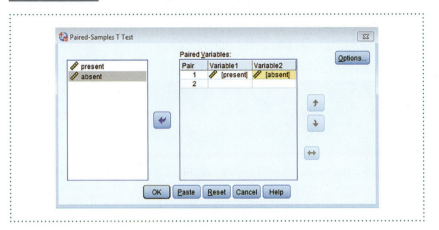

4. In the dialog box, select *present* and *absent* in the left box and move them to the right box using the arrow in the middle. The variables should be side by side in the box to the right. To adjust the confidence intervals for this test, select Options . . . in the dialog box. Because the default confidence interval is set at a 95% CI, we do not have to adjust this.

5. Select OK, or select Paste and click the Run command.

TABLE 10.8 The SPSS Output Table for the Related-Samples *t* Test

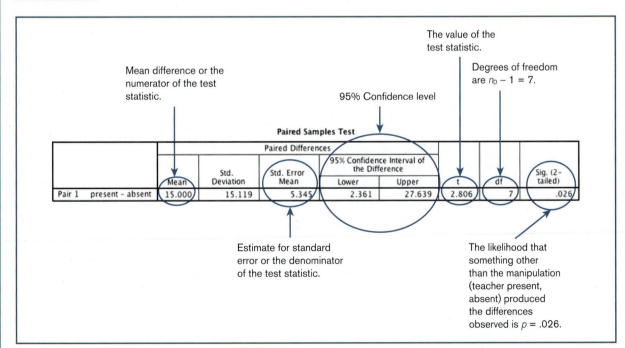

The value of the test statistic.

Degrees of freedom are $n_D - 1 = 7$.

Mean difference or the numerator of the test statistic.

95% Confidence level

Paired Samples Test

		Paired Differences					t	df	Sig. (2-tailed)
		Mean	Std. Deviation	Std. Error Mean	95% Confidence Interval of the Difference				
					Lower	Upper			
Pair 1	present – absent	15.000	15.119	5.345	2.361	27.639	2.806	7	.026

Estimate for standard error or the denominator of the test statistic.

The likelihood that something other than the manipulation (teacher present, absent) produced the differences observed is $p = .026$.

(Continued)

(Continued)

Notice that the calculations we made match the results displayed in the output table shown in Table 10.8, give or take a small discrepancy due to rounding. These same step-by-step directions for using SPSS can be used to compute the repeated-measures design (shown in this section) and the matched-pairs design. Finally, note that SPSS gives the confidence intervals for this test in the output table.

10.8 APA IN FOCUS: REPORTING THE *t* STATISTIC AND CONFIDENCE INTERVALS

To summarize a related-samples *t* test, we report the test statistic, degrees of freedom, and *p* value. In addition, we summarize the means and standard error or standard deviations measured in the study in a figure or table or in the main text. When reporting results, though, it is not necessary to identify the type of *t* test computed in a results section. The type of *t* test that was used is typically reported in a data analysis section that precedes the results section, where the statistics are reported.

• • • CHAPTER SUMMARY ORGANIZED BY LEARNING OBJECTIVE

LO 1: Describe two types of research designs used when selecting related samples.

- In a related sample, participants are related. Participants can be related in one of two ways: They are observed in more than one group (a repeated-measures design), or they are matched, experimentally or naturally, based on common characteristics or traits (a matched-pairs design).

- The repeated-measures design is a research design in which the same participants are observed in each treatment. Two types of repeated-measures designs are the pre-post design and the within-subjects design.

- The matched-pairs design is a research design in which participants are selected, then matched, experimentally or naturally, based on common characteristics or traits.

LO 2: Explain why difference scores are computed for the related-samples *t* test.

- To test the null hypothesis, we state the mean difference between paired scores in the population and compare this to the difference between paired scores in a sample. A related-samples *t* test is different from a two-independent-sample *t* test in that we first find the difference between the paired scores and then compute the test statistic. The difference between two scores in a pair is called a difference score.

- Computing difference scores eliminates between-persons error. This error is associated with differences associated with observing different participants in each group or treatment. Because we observe the same (or matched) participants in each treatment, not different participants, we can eliminate this source of error before computing the test statistic. Removing this error reduces the value of the estimate of standard error, which increases the power to detect an effect.

LO 3: **State three advantages for selecting related samples.**

- Three advantages for selecting related samples are that selecting related samples (1) can be more practical, (2) reduces standard error, and (3) increases power.

LO 4–6: **Calculate the degrees of freedom for a related-samples *t* test and locate critical values in the *t* table; identify the assumptions for the related-samples *t* test; compute a related-samples *t* test and interpret the results.**

- The related-samples *t* test is a statistical procedure used to test hypotheses concerning two related samples selected from related populations in which the variance in one or both populations is unknown.

- The degrees of freedom for a related-samples *t* test are the number of difference scores minus 1: $df = (n_D - 1)$.

- To compute a related-samples *t* test, we assume normality and independence within groups. The test statistic for a related-samples *t* test concerning the difference between two related samples is as follows:

$$t_{obt} = \frac{M_D - \mu_D}{s_{MD}}, \text{where } s_{MD} = \frac{s_D}{\sqrt{n_D}}.$$

LO 7: **Compute and interpret effect size and proportion of variance for a related-samples *t* test.**

- Estimated Cohen's *d* is the most popular estimate of effect size used with the *t* test. It is a measure of effect size in terms of the number of standard deviations that mean difference

scores shifted above or below the population mean difference stated in the null hypothesis. To compute estimated Cohen's *d* with two related samples, divide the mean difference (M_D) between two samples by the standard deviation of the difference scores (s_D):

$$d = \frac{M_D}{s_D}.$$

- Another measure of effect size is proportion of variance. Specifically, this is an estimate of the proportion of variance in the dependent variable that can be explained by a treatment. Two measures of proportion of variance for the related-samples *t* test are eta-squared and omega-squared. These measures are computed in the same way for all *t* tests:

$$\text{Using eta-squared: } \eta^2 = \frac{t^2}{t^2 + df}.$$

$$\text{Using omega-squared: } \omega^2 = \frac{t^2 - 1}{t^2 + df}.$$

LO 8: **Compute and interpret confidence intervals for a related-samples *t* test.**

- The three steps to estimation are as follows:

  Step 1: Compute the sample mean and standard error.

  Step 2: Choose the level of confidence and find the critical values at that level of confidence.

  Step 3: Compute the estimation formula to find the confidence limits.

- The estimation formula for the related-samples *t* test is $M_D \pm t(s_{MD})$.

LO 9: **Summarize the results of a related-samples *t* test in APA format.**

- To report the results of a related-samples *t* test, state the test statistic, the degrees of freedom, the p value, and the effect size. In addition, summarize the means and the standard error or the standard deviations measured in the study in a figure or a table or in the text. Finally, note that the type of t test computed is reported in a data analysis section that precedes the results section, where the statistics are reported.

LO 10:   Compute a related-samples t test and identify confidence intervals using SPSS.

- SPSS can be used to compute a related-samples t test using the Analyze, Compare Means, and Paired-Samples T Test options in the menu bar. These actions will display a dialog box that allows you to identify the groups and run the test (for more details, see Section 10.7).

• • • KEY TERMS

dependent sample
difference scores
error
estimated standard error for
    difference scores

matched-pairs design
matched-samples design
matched-subjects design
pre-post design
related sample

related-samples t test
repeated-measures design
within-subjects design

• • • END-OF-CHAPTER PROBLEMS

Factual Problems

1. How are related samples different from independent samples?

2. Name two research designs in which related samples are selected.

3. Which type of repeated-measures design can only be used with two groups?

4. State two ways for matching pairs of participants using the matched-pairs research design.

5. Define difference scores. How does using difference scores increase the power of a related-samples t test?

6. Describe in words what the degrees of freedom are for a related-samples t test.

7. State three advantages for using related samples in behavioral research.

8. How does computing difference scores change the value of the estimate of standard error in the denominator of the test statistic for a related-samples t test?

9. What are the assumptions for a related-samples t test?

10. Is the related-samples t test computed differently for a repeated-measures design and a matched-pairs design? Explain.

11. Describe in words the formula for an estimated Cohen's d for two related samples.

12. What are the three steps to compute an estimation formula?

Concept and Application Problems

13. For each example, state whether the one-sample, two-independent-sample, or related-samples t test is most appropriate. If it is a related-samples t test, indicate whether the test is a repeated-measures design or a matched-pairs design.

(a) A researcher matches right-handed and left-handed siblings to test whether right-handed siblings express greater emotional intelligence than left-handed siblings.

(b) A professor tests whether students sitting in the front row score higher on an exam than students sitting in the back row.

(c) A graduate student selects a sample of 25 participants to test whether the average time students attend to a task is greater than 30 minutes.

(d) A principal at a local school wants to know how much students gain from being in an honors class. He gives students in an honors English class a test prior to the school year and again at the end of the school year to measure how much students learned during the year.

14. State the degrees of freedom and the type of test (repeated measures or matched pairs) for the following examples of measures for a related-samples t test:

(a) The difference in coping ability in a sample of 20 brothers and sisters paired based on their relatedness

(b) The difference in comprehension before and after an experimental training seminar in a sample of 30 students

(c) The difference in relationship satisfaction in a sample of 25 pairs of married couples

(d) The difference in athletic performance at the beginning and end of an athletic season for 12 athletes

15. What are the difference scores for the following list of scores for participants observed at two times?

Time 1	Time 2
4	8
3	2
5	7
4	6
6	3

16. Using the data listed in Question 15,

(a) Compute the mean difference (M_D), standard deviation (s_D), and standard error for the difference scores (s_{MD}).

(b) Sketch a graph of the distribution of mean difference scores $(M_D \pm s_D)$.

(c) Sketch a graph of the sampling distribution of mean difference scores $(M_D \pm s_{MD})$.

17. Would each of the following increase, decrease, or have no effect on the value of the test statistic for a related-samples t test?

(a) The sample size is increased.

(b) The estimated standard error for difference scores is doubled.

(c) The level of significance is reduced from .05 to .01.

(d) The mean difference is decreased.

18. What is the value of the test statistic for a related-samples t test given the following measurements?

(a) $n_D = 16$, $M_D = 4$, and $s_D = 8$

(b) $M_D = 4$ and $s_{MD} = 8$

(c) $n_D = 64$, $M_D = 8$, and $s_D = 16$

(d) $M_D = 8$ and $s_{MD} = 16$

19. A statistics tutor wants to assess whether her remedial tutoring has been effective for her five students. Using a pre-post design, she records the grades for a group of students prior to and after receiving her tutoring. The grades recorded are given in the table.

Tutoring	
Before	**After**
2.4	3.0
2.5	2.8
3.0	3.5
2.9	3.1
2.7	3.5

(a) Test whether or not her tutoring is effective at a .05 level of significance. State the value of the test statistic and the decision to retain or reject the null hypothesis.

(b) Compute effect size using estimated Cohen's *d*.

20. Published reports indicate that a brain region called the nucleus accumbens (NAc) is involved in interval timing, which is the perception of time in the seconds-to-minutes range. To test this, researchers investigated whether removing the NAc interferes with rats' ability to time the presentation of a liquid reward. Using a conditioning procedure, the researchers had rats press a lever for a reward that was delivered after 16 seconds. The time that eight rats responded the most (peak responding) was recorded before and after a surgery to remove the NAc. The peak responding times are given in the table.

Peak Interval Timing	
Before NAc Surgery	After NAc Surgery
15	20
14	26
16	20
16	18
17	25
18	21
15	18
16	23

(a) Test whether or not the difference in peak responding changed at a .05 level of significance (two-tailed test). State the value of the test statistic and the decision to retain or reject the null hypothesis.

(b) Compute effect size using estimated Cohen's *d*.

21. A health psychologist tests a new intervention to determine if it can change healthy behaviors among children. To conduct the test, the researcher gives one group of children an intervention, and a second group is given a control task without the intervention. The number of healthy behaviors observed in the children during a 5-minute observation are given in the table.

Intervention	
Yes	No
7	5
4	6
7	5
7	6
7	5
6	5

(a) Test whether or not the number of healthy behaviors differ at a .05 level of significance. State the value of the test statistic and the decision to retain or reject the null hypothesis.

(b) Compute effect size using eta-squared.

22. A clinical psychologist noticed that the siblings of his obese patients are often not overweight. He hypothesized that the normal-weight siblings consume fewer daily calories than the obese patients. To test this using a matched-pairs design, he compared the daily caloric intake of obese patients to that of a "matched" normal-weight sibling. The calories consumed for each sibling pair are given in the table.

Normal-Weight Sibling	Overweight Sibling
1,600	2,000
1,800	2,400
2,100	2,000
1,800	3,000
2,400	2,400
2,800	1,900
1,900	2,600
2,300	2,450
2,000	2,000
2,050	1,950

(a) Test whether or not obese patients consumed significantly more calories than their normal-weight siblings at a .05 level of significance. State the value of the test statistic and the decision to retain or reject the null hypothesis.

(b) Compute effect size using omega-squared.

(c) Did the results support the researcher's hypothesis? Explain.

23. State whether each of the following related-samples t tests is significant for a two-tailed test at a .05 level of significance.

(a) $t(30) = 3.220$

(b) $t(12) = 2.346$

(c) $t(18) = 2.034$

(d) $t(60) = 1.985$

24. A researcher develops an advertisement aimed at increasing how much the public trusts a federal organization. She asks participants to rate their level of trust for the organization before and after viewing an advertisement. Higher ratings indicate greater trust. From the following findings reported in APA format, interpret these results by stating the research design used (repeated measures or matched pairs), the sample size, the decision, and the effect size.

Participants rated the federal organization as significantly more trustworthy ($M_D = +4$ points) after viewing the advertisement, $t(119) = 4.021$, $p < .05$, $d = 0.88$.

25. A researcher records the amount of time (in minutes) that parent–child pairs spend on social networking sites to test whether they show any generational differences. From the following findings reported in APA format, interpret these results by stating the research design used (repeated measures or matched pairs), the sample size, the decision, and the effect size.

Parents spent significantly less time on social networking sites compared to their children ($M_D = -42$ minutes), $t(29) = 4.021$, $p < .05$, $d = 0.49$.

26. Would each of the following increase, decrease, or have no effect on the value of estimated Cohen's d for the related-samples t test?

(a) The sample standard deviation for difference scores is increased.

(b) The estimated standard error for difference scores is increased.

(c) The mean difference is increased.

27. An instructor believes that students do not retain as much information from a lecture on a Friday compared to a lecture on a Monday. To test this belief, the instructor teaches a small sample of college students preselected material from a single topic on statistics on a Friday and on a Monday. All students receive a test on the material. The differences in exam scores for material taught on Friday minus Monday are listed in the following table.

Difference Scores (Friday – Monday)
+3.4
−1.6
+4.4
+6.3
+1.0

(a) Find the confidence limits at a 95% CI for these related samples.

(b) Can we conclude that students retained more of the material taught in the Monday class?

28. A researcher hypothesizes that children will eat more of foods wrapped in familiar packaging than the same foods wrapped in plain packaging. To test this hypothesis, she records the number of bites that 24 children take of a food given to them wrapped in fast-food packaging versus plain packaging. If the mean difference (fast-food packaging minus plain packaging) is $M_D = 12$, and $s_{MD} = 2.4$, then:

(a) Find the confidence limits at a 95% CI for these related samples.

(b) Can we conclude that wrapping foods in familiar packaging increased the number of bites that children took compared to plain packaging?

Problems in Research

29. **The mental health of rescue workers deployed in the 2010 Haiti earthquake.** In a questionnaire-based study, van der Velden, van Loon, Benight, and Eckhardt (2012) looked at factors of mental health among rescue workers before (Time 1) and 3 months after (Time 2) deployment to Haiti following the January 2010 earthquake. The following table summarizes some of the results reported in this study. Based on the results given, which mental health problems were significantly worse among the rescue workers following deployment to Haiti?

	Deployment		
Mental Health Problem	Pre-deployment M (SD)	Post-deployment M (SD)	Significance (p)
Anxiety symptoms	10.08 (0.27)	10.40 (0.20)	.414
Depression symptoms	16.29 (0.73)	16.10 (0.30)	.048
Somatic problems	12.37 (0.82)	12.33 (0.68)	.771
Sleeping problems	3.37 (0.71)	3.27 (0.75)	.468
Hostility	6.13 (0.55)	6.10 (0.41)	.931
Interpersonal sensitivity	18.72 (1.54)	18.14 (0.35)	.002

30. **The within-subjects design.** Son and Lee (2015) used a "within-subjects repeated measures design" (p. 2277) to evaluate the effect of the amount of rice carbohydrates consumed during mealtime on blood pressure in older people with hypotension. Explain what the researchers mean by a within-subjects repeated-measures design.

31. **Post-traumatic stress disorder (PTSD) following 9/11.** Levitt, Malta, Martin, Davis, and Cloitre (2007) evaluated the effectiveness of cognitive behavioral therapy (CBT) for treating PTSD and related symptoms for survivors of the 9/11 attacks on the World Trade Center (WTC). They used a pretest–posttest design to see if CBT was successful at reducing the symptoms of PTSD and related symptoms of depression. They used the Modified PTSD Symptom Scale Self-Report (MPSS-SR) questionnaire to measure symptoms of PTSD and the Beck Depression Inventory (BDI) self-report questionnaire to measure symptoms of depression. For both questionnaires, lower scores indicated fewer symptoms. The authors reported the following results:

> Pre- to post-treatment t tests for the WTC sample revealed significant decreases in scores on the MPSS-SR, ($t(37) = 12.74$, $p < .01$); as well as on the BDI ($t(34) = 7.36$, $p < .01$). (Levitt et al., 2007, p. 1427)

(a) Was this a repeated-measures design or a matched-pairs design?

(b) Which questionnaire (MPSS-SR or BDI) was completed by more participants?

(c) Did the authors find support for their hypothesis? Explain.

32. **The impact of a mentoring program for highly aggressive children.** Faith, Fiala, Cavell, and Hughes (2011) examined the impact of a mentoring program for elementary school–aged children on attitudes that mentors and children have about mentoring. Faith et al. reported that children's and mentors' ratings of the openness of the mentor significantly decreased from before to after the mentoring program, $t(101) = 12.51$.

(a) What was the sample size for this test?

(b) Was a repeated-measures or a matched-pairs design used in this study?

(c) Compute eta-squared for the effect reported.

33. **Simulating workload in an emergency department nursing triage.** Dubovsky and colleagues (2017) evaluated the utility of a new emergency

department nursing triage for incorporating research applications using a simulation for how it impacted the workload of staff. They measured a variety of factors related to workload, including mental demand, physical demand, and performance. The following table summarizes a portion of their results analyzed using the related-samples t test.

Measures	Mean (SD) for Overall Workload Rating		t	Degrees of Freedom
	Typical Day at Work	During Simulation		
Mental demand	67.0 (20.8)	77.5 (16.9)	−1.64	9
Physical demand	46.5 (24.8)	14.5 (20.2)	2.82	9
Performance	32.0 (22.6)	51.5 (17.6)	−1.84	9

(a) Using the information provided, find and state the critical value for a two-tailed test at a .05 level of significance, and identify which measures reached a decision to reject the null hypothesis at this significance level.

(b) Using the information provided, find and state the critical value for a one-tailed test at a .05 level of significance, and identify which measures reached a decision to reject the null hypothesis at this significance level.

(c) Which measure, if any, led to a decision to reject the null hypothesis for a one-tailed test, but not for a two-tailed test?

34. **Confidence intervals, significance, and effect size.** Zou (2007) noted in an article that confidence intervals "encompass significance tests and provide an estimate of the magnitude of the effect" (p. 399). What does "the magnitude of the effect" refer to in this citation?

Answers for even numbers are in Appendix D.

Sharpen your skills with **SAGE edge at edge.sagepub.com/priviteraess2e**

SAGE edge for Students provides a personalized approach to help you accomplish your coursework goals in an easy-to-use learning environment.

$SAGE edge™

©iStockphoto.com/Shaiith

Part IV

Making Inferences About the Variability of Two or More Means

©iStockphoto.com/PeopleImages

11 One-Way Analysis of Variance
Between-Subjects and Within-Subjects (Repeated-Measures) Designs

• • • Learning Objectives

After reading this chapter, you should be able to:

1. Identify the analysis of variance test and when it is used for tests of a single factor.

2. Identify each source of variation in a one-way between-subjects ANOVA and a one-way within-subjects ANOVA.

3. Calculate the degrees of freedom and locate critical values for a one-way between-subjects ANOVA and a one-way within-subjects ANOVA.

4. Identify the assumptions for a one-way between-subjects ANOVA and a one-way within-subjects ANOVA.

5. Follow the steps to compute a one-way between-subjects ANOVA and a one-way within-subjects ANOVA, and interpret the results.

6. Compute and interpret Tukey's HSD post hoc test and identify the most powerful post hoc test alternatives.

7. Compute and interpret proportion of variance for the one-way between-subjects ANOVA and the one-way within-subjects ANOVA.

8. Delineate the power of between-subjects and within-subjects designs for the one-way ANOVAs.

9. Summarize the results of the one-way between-subjects ANOVA and the one-way within-subjects ANOVA in APA format.

10. Compute and select an appropriate post hoc test for a one-way between-subjects ANOVA and a one-way within-subjects ANOVA using SPSS.

We would not be able to capture the full scope of observing behavior if our observations were limited to observing just two groups or observing participants at only two times. Many types of comparisons would reveal more about the nature of behavior when we make multiple observations, whether between more than two different groups or when we observe the same groups more than two times. Examples include variables that naturally have more than two levels (e.g., seasons, months, or trimesters), variables that can be manipulated to have more than two levels (e.g., learning tasks: recall, recognition, and relearning; types of persuasion: ethos, pathos, logos, statistics, deliberation, and refutation), and comparisons where a third control group is needed (e.g., adding a "no treatment" group to compare the effectiveness of two treatments, A and B, for a mental health disorder).

In hypothesis testing, there are often cases where making comparisons between more than two groups can be quite informative. In the basic structure of such a study, the groups represent the independent variable. For the examples above, the seasons, months, trimesters, learning tasks, types of persuasion, and treatments/control would be the independent variable for each test; the levels of each variable would be the groups. We can observe the same or different participants across all the levels of each variable. The basic structure of such a test is to measure the same dependent variable in each group, as we did when observing only two groups. The null hypothesis would be that group means do not vary; the alternative hypothesis would state that the group means do vary.

In this chapter, we explore the nature of hypothesis testing when observations are made across more than two levels of a factor, how to compute and interpret observed effects, and the informativeness of hypothesis testing for making such comparisons. We further explore other ways of adding information about the nature of observed effects and how to appropriately interpret them.

Master the content.

edge.sagepub.com/priviteraess2e

● ● ● Chapter Outline

11.1 AN INTRODUCTION TO ANALYSIS OF VARIANCE

In hypothesis testing, the t tests are limited in that they can only be used to test for differences in one group or between two groups. However, researchers often ask questions that require the observation of more than two groups. In such research situations, we need a new test statistic because as the number of groups increases, so does the number of comparisons that need to be made between groups.

To illustrate the need for a new test statistic, consider a research situation in which participants are given negative or positive feedback regarding an exam to see how that subsequently influences their self-esteem. In this example, there are only two groups; however, in a typical behavioral research study, it is essential to also include a control group in which feedback is not given—thus, a group in which the manipulation (type of feedback) is omitted. Now we have three groups, or three levels of the factor (feedback: positive, negative, and none), and as illustrated in Figure 11.1, we also have three ways in which we can compare differences between these groups. The number of groups or **levels of the factor** are symbolized as k. When many pairs of group means can differ, we analyze the variance of group means using a new hypothesis test called an **analysis of variance (ANOVA)**. This test, which is introduced in this chapter, is one of the most popular hypothesis tests used in the behavioral sciences.

FIGURE 11.1   Differences Between Groups When $k = 3$

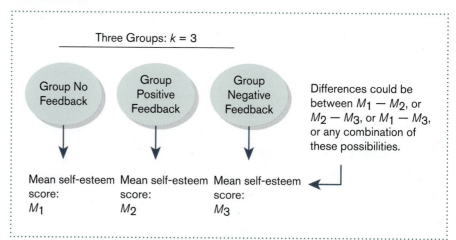

Note that as the number of groups increases, so does the number of pairs of group means that can differ.

The **levels of the factor**, symbolized as k, are the number of groups or different ways in which an independent or quasi-independent variable is observed.

An **analysis of variance (ANOVA)** is a statistical procedure used to test hypotheses for one or more factors concerning the variance among two or more group means ($k \geq 2$) where the variance in one or more populations is unknown.

In terms of the use of notation, it is a bit different. The notation used to identify the sample size for the t tests is different from that used with the ANOVA. For the ANOVA, n represents the number of participants per group (not sample size), and *N* represents the number of total participants in a study (not population size).

$$n = \text{number of participants per group}$$

$$N = \text{total number of participants in a study}$$

When *n* is the same or equal in each group, we state that $N = k \times n$. To illustrate, suppose we measure the time spent talking during three types of classes (a psychology class, a biology class, and a sociology class). In this example, we have one factor (type of class) with three levels ($k = 3$). If five students are in each class, then the sample size (*n*) equals 5, and the total number of students observed is $N = 3 \times 5 = 15$.

In this chapter, we introduce the ANOVA for one factor in which the same (within-subjects) or different (between-subjects) participants are observed at each level, or in each group. The word *subjects* refers to the design that describes how participants are observed—whether the same or different participants are observed. When the same participants are observed across the levels of a factor, we use the within-subjects design (defined in Chapter 10). For example, to see whether students preferred celery or carrots as a healthy snack, we could use the same group and subject the participants to two treatments (e.g., first the celery and then the carrots). When different participants are observed at each level of a factor, we use the between-subjects design (defined in Chapter 9). For example, to see whether students preferred celery or carrots as a healthy snack, we could use two groups and give one group the celery and the other group the carrots. We begin this chapter by introducing the ANOVA for the between-subjects design.

An ANOVA measures the variance among two or more group means.

For an ANOVA, k is the number of groups, n is the number of participants per group, and N is the total number of participants in a study.

In a one-way between-subjects ANOVA, different participants are observed at each level of one factor.

LEARNING CHECK 1

1. The _____ is a statistical procedure used to test hypotheses for one or more factors concerning the variance among two or more group means ($k \geq 2$) where the variance in one or more populations is unknown.

2. What is the total sample size for each example, assuming that *n* is equal in each group?

   (a) $k = 4, n = 12$ (b) $k = 3, n = 8$ (c) $N = 28$

Answers: 1. Analysis of variance (ANOVA); 2. (a) $4 \times 12 = 48$, (b) $3 \times 8 = 24$, (c) 28.

11.2 THE BETWEEN-SUBJECTS DESIGN FOR ANALYSIS OF VARIANCE

When different participants are observed in each group or at each level of one factor with two or more levels, we compute interval and ratio scale data using the **one-way between-subjects ANOVA**. The *one-way* in the name of this hypothesis test indicates the number of factors being tested in the study. In a one-way ANOVA, we test one factor. If we tested two factors, we would call the test a two-way ANOVA. If we tested three factors, then it would be a three-way ANOVA, and so on.

Sources of Variation and the Test Statistic

The one-way between-subjects ANOVA evaluates if the means in each group significantly vary. If group means are equal, then the variance of group means is equal to 0 (the means do not vary). The larger the differences are between group means, the larger the variance of group means will be. In all, there are two key ways in which means can vary—each way is called a **source of variation**: between groups and within groups.

The variance of the group means is called **between-groups variation**. This source of variation is shown in Table 11.1 for an example in which we observe students in one of three classes. This variance is placed in the numerator of the test statistic. Another source of variation is error, or any unexplained variation that cannot be attributed to, or caused by, having different groups. The variation attributed to error or chance, called **within-groups variation**, is also shown in Table 11.1. This variance is placed in the denominator of the test statistic, just as our estimate of standard error

FYI

There are two sources of variation in a one-way between-subjects ANOVA: one attributed to differences between groups and one associated with observing different participants in each group (within groups).

FYI

The test statistic for an ANOVA measures the variance attributed to the mean differences between groups (MS_{BG}) divided by the variance attributed to error (MS_E).

A **one-way between-subjects ANOVA** is a statistical procedure used to test hypotheses for one factor with two or more levels concerning the variance among group means. This test is used when different participants are observed at each level of a factor and the variance in any one population is unknown.

A **source of variation** is any variation that can be measured in a study. In the one-way between-subjects ANOVA, there are two sources of variation: variation attributed to differences between group means and variation attributed to error.

Between-groups variation is the variation attributed to mean differences between groups.

Within-groups variation is the variation attributed to mean differences within each group. This source of variation cannot be attributed to or caused by having different groups and is therefore called error variation.

TABLE 11.1	Between-Groups and Within-Groups Variation for the One-Way Between-Subjects ANOVA

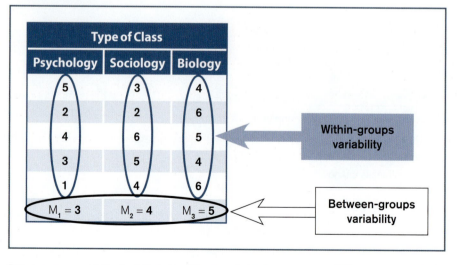

Between-groups variation is attributed to differences between group means. Within-groups variation is attributed to variation that has nothing to do with having different groups.

was placed in the denominator for the *t* tests. This makes the general form of the test statistic, F_{obt}, for a one-way between-subjects ANOVA:

$$F_{obt} = \frac{\text{variance attributed to group differences}}{\text{variance attributed to chance}}.$$

The variances measured in an ANOVA test are computed as mean squares. A mean square is a variance. The two terms, *variance* and *mean square*, are synonyms—they mean the same thing. The formula for the test statistic, called the **F statistic**, is the variance between groups, or **mean square between groups (MS_{BG})**, divided by the variance within groups, or **mean square within groups**. Mean square within groups is more commonly called **mean square error (MS_E)**. The formula for the test statistic is

$$F_{obt} = \frac{MS_{BG}}{MS_E} \quad \text{or} \quad \frac{\text{variance between groups}}{\text{variance within groups}}.$$

Degrees of Freedom and the *F* Distribution

The distribution of possible outcomes for the test statistic of an ANOVA is positively skewed. The distribution, called the **F distribution**, is derived from a sampling distribution of *F* ratios and is illustrated in Figure 11.2. An *F* ratio reflects the between-groups variance. When

FIGURE 11.2   The *F* Distribution

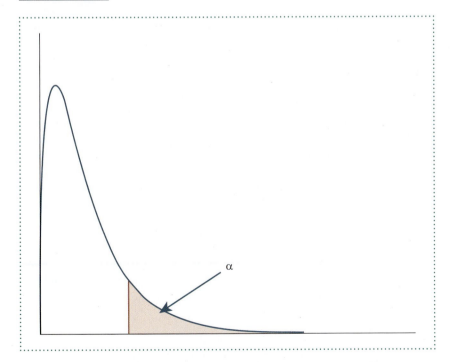

The rejection region or alpha level (α) is placed in the upper tail of an *F* distribution because values farther from 0 indicate outcomes that are less likely to occur if the null hypothesis is true.

The **F statistic**, or **F obtained (F_{obt})**, is the test statistic for an ANOVA. It is computed as the mean square (or variance) between groups divided by the mean square (or variance) within groups.

Mean square between groups (MS_{BG}) is the variance attributed to differences between group means. It is the numerator of the test statistic.

Mean square error (MS_E), or **mean square within groups**, is the variance attributed to differences within each group. It is the denominator of the test statistic.

An **F distribution** is a positively skewed distribution derived from a sampling distribution of *F* ratios.

group means are exactly the same, the F ratio is equal to 0 because the variance of group means (i.e., the value placed in the numerator) will equal 0. The larger the differences are between group means, the larger the F ratio becomes. The test statistic is used to determine how large or disproportionate the differences are between group means compared to the variance expected to occur by chance.

To understand the relationship between the F statistic and the null hypothesis, keep in mind that the F statistic evaluates how much variance is due to the groups (placed in the numerator) and how much variance is due to error (placed in the denominator). When the variance attributed to the groups is equal to the variance attributed to error, then $F = 1.0$ (the numerator and denominator are the same value; anything divided by itself is equal to 1.0). Thus, the traditional expectation is that F will equal 1.0 when the null hypothesis is true that the group means do not differ. However, this assumes that the group means vary in some way (i.e., that the group means are not all exactly equal—so that a variance larger than 0 is computed in the numerator). When the group means are exactly the same value, however, $F = 0$ (because the variance of the group means is 0); this is also an expectation when the null hypothesis is true.

The degrees of freedom for a one-way between-subjects ANOVA are equal to those for sample variance: $N - 1$. However, there are two sources of variation for the one-way between-subjects ANOVA. For this reason, we must split the total degrees of freedom ($N - 1$) into two parts: one for each source of variation.

The variance in the numerator is attributed to differences between group means. The degrees of freedom for this variance are called the **degrees of freedom numerator** or **degrees of freedom between groups** (df_{BG}). The degrees of freedom for this variance are the number of groups (k) minus 1:

$$df_{BG} = k - 1.$$

The variance in the denominator is attributed to error. The degrees of freedom for this variance are called the **degrees of freedom error (df_E)**, **degrees of freedom within groups**, or **degrees of freedom denominator**. The degrees of freedom for this variance are the total sample size (N) minus the number of groups (k):

$$df_E = N - k.$$

The reason for the reference to numerator and denominator for degrees of freedom is that there are two sets of degrees of freedom: one for the variance placed in the numerator of the test statistic (between groups) and one for the variance placed in the denominator of the test statistic (error variance). This is shown here:

The **degrees of freedom between groups (df_{BG})** or **degrees of freedom numerator** are the degrees of freedom associated with the variance of the group means in the numerator of the test statistic. They are equal to the number of groups (k) minus 1.

The **degrees of freedom error (df_E)**, **degrees of freedom within groups**, or **degrees of freedom denominator** are the degrees of freedom associated with the error variance in the denominator. They are equal to the total sample size (N) minus the number of groups (k).

$$F_{obt} = \frac{\text{variance between groups}}{\text{variance within groups}} \longleftarrow \text{degrees of freedom} \longrightarrow \frac{k-1}{N-k}.$$

Note that changing any one of the degrees of freedom will change the shape of the *F* distribution. As the value for *k*, *N*, or *n* increases, so too will the total degrees of freedom. As the total degrees of freedom increase, the *F* distribution becomes less skewed, meaning that the tails of the *F* distribution pull closer to the *y*-axis. In terms of the critical values for an ANOVA, as degrees of freedom increase, the critical values get smaller. Smaller critical values are associated with greater power. Hence, as the degrees of freedom increase, the power to detect an effect also increases.

To locate the critical values for an ANOVA, we use an *F* table, which is given in Table C.3 in Appendix C. The *F* table in Appendix C lists the critical values at a .05 and .01 level of significance; the values in boldface are for a .01 level of significance. Table 11.2 shows a portion of the *F* table. To use the table, locate the degrees of freedom numerator listed in the columns

TABLE 11.2 A Portion of the *F* Table Given in Table C.3 in Appendix C

Degrees of Freedom Denominator	Degrees of Freedom Numerator			
	1	2	3	4
1	161 **4,052**	200 **5,000**	216 **5,403**	225 **5,625**
2	18.51 **98.49**	19.00 **99.00**	19.16 **99.17**	19.25 **99.25**
3	10.13 **34.12**	9.55 **30.92**	9.28 **29.46**	9.12 **28.71**
4	7.71 **21.20**	6.94 **18.00**	6.59 **16.69**	6.39 **15.98**
5	6.61 **16.26**	5.79 **13.27**	5.41 **12.06**	5.19 **11.39**
6	5.99 **13.74**	5.14 **10.92**	4.76 **9.78**	4.53 **9.15**
7	5.59 **13.74**	4.74 **9.55**	4.35 **8.45**	4.12 **7.85**
8	5.32 **11.26**	4.46 **8.65**	4.07 **7.59**	3.84 **7.01**
9	5.12 **10.56**	4.26 **8.02**	3.86 **6.99**	3.63 **6.42**
10	4.96 **10.04**	4.10 **7.56**	3.71 **6.55**	3.48 **5.99**
11	4.84 **9.65**	3.98 **7.20**	3.59 **6.22**	3.36 **5.67**
12	4.75 **9.33**	3.89 **6.93**	3.49 **5.95**	3.26 **5.41**

The degrees of freedom numerator is listed in the columns; the degrees of freedom denominator is listed in the rows.

and then the degrees of freedom denominator listed down the rows. The critical value is the entry found at the intersection of the two degrees of freedom. As an example, for a one-way ANOVA with 2 and 12 degrees of freedom at a .05 level of significance, the critical value is 3.89.

Keep in mind that the *F* distribution is positively skewed. It begins at 0 and is skewed toward positive values. So the critical value for all tests is placed in the upper tail. Negative outcomes are not possible in an *F* distribution.

LEARNING CHECK 2

1. Name the source of variation in the numerator and the source of variation in the denominator of the test statistic for the one-way between-subjects ANOVA.

2. A researcher computes an ANOVA with 4 and 12 degrees of freedom. What is the critical value for this test at a .05 level of significance?

Answers: 1. Between-groups variation is in the numerator, and within-groups variation is in the denominator; 2. 3.26.

11.3 COMPUTING THE ONE-WAY BETWEEN-SUBJECTS ANOVA

In this section, we compute the one-way between-subjects ANOVA. We compute this test when we compare two or more group means, in which different participants are observed in each group. In terms of differences, the null hypothesis states that each mean is the same or equal: H_0: $\mu_1 = \mu_2 = \mu_k$, where *k* is the number of groups. However, we compute and compare variances in an ANOVA: the variance attributed to the groups and the variance attributed to error/chance. It is therefore most appropriate to state the null hypothesis and the alternative hypothesis in a way that mathematically matches the test we will compute, just as we did for the *t* tests when we compared mean differences. Strictly speaking, we compute variances, not differences, in an ANOVA. In terms of variance, which is directly measured to conduct this test, the null hypothesis states that group means (μ) do not vary (σ^2) in the population:

$$H_0: \sigma_\mu^2 = 0.$$

The alternative hypothesis states that group means (μ) in the population do vary (σ^2):

$$H_1: \sigma_\mu^2 > 0.$$

In terms of variance, group means either vary ($\sigma_\mu^2 > 0$) or do not vary ($\sigma_\mu^2 = 0$). A negative variance is meaningless. For this reason, the alternative hypothesis is always a "greater than" statement. Also, note that variance corresponds to differences. When group means vary, they also differ; when group means do not vary, they also do not differ.

There are four assumptions associated with the one-way between-subjects ANOVA:

1. *Normality.* We assume that data in the population or populations being sampled from are normally distributed. This assumption is particularly important for small sample sizes. In larger samples, the overall variance is reduced, and this assumption becomes less critical as a result.

2. *Random sampling.* We assume that the data we measure were obtained from a sample that was selected using a random sampling procedure. It is generally considered inappropriate to conduct hypothesis tests with nonrandom samples.

3. *Independence.* We assume that the probabilities of each measured outcome in a study are independent or equal. Using random sampling usually satisfies this assumption.

4. *Homogeneity of variance.* We assume that the variance in each population is equal to that of the others. Violating this assumption can inflate the value of the variance in the numerator of the test statistic, thereby increasing the likelihood of committing a Type I error (incorrectly rejecting the null hypothesis; defined in Chapter 7, p. 201).

FYI

Four assumptions for a one-way between-subjects ANOVA are normality, random sampling, independence, and homogeneity of variance.

Computing the Test Statistic: Evaluating Significance

ANOVA is also used to measure variability across groups. Because we compute variance across groups, the sample size (*n*) must be equal in each group—it is necessary that the same number of scores are averaged in each group. Most researchers plan for equal samples by making sure that the same number of participants are observed in each group. Sometimes this is too difficult or impractical to accomplish. In these circumstances, the best alternative is to increase the sample size to minimize problems associated with averaging a different number of scores in each group.

In Example 11.1, we follow the four steps in hypothesis testing to compute a one-way between-subjects ANOVA.

Example 11.1

Employee turnover is a common concern among businesses and organizational psychologists. Stress levels at a workplace are often cited as a key reason for increased employee turnover, which is the rate at which employees leave a company, thereby impacting costs needed to hire new employees (DeTienne, Agle, Phillips, & Ingerson, 2012; Morrell, 2016; Saridakis & Cooper, 2016). As an example of one such study in this area of research, suppose we ask new employees at a company how long they feel they will remain with the company. Employees are assigned to groups based on how stressful they rated the workplace: 10 employees rated the company as a high-stress workplace, 10 as moderately stressful, and 10 as low

© iStockphoto.com/Steve Debenport

stress. The times in years that employees said they would stay with the company are given in Table 11.3. We will conduct an ANOVA to analyze the significance of these data at a .05 level of significance.

| | | | TABLE 11.3 | The Times in Years That Employees Said They Would Stay With the Company Among Employees Who Rated the Workplace as Being a High-, Moderate-, or Low-Stress Environment |

Perceived Stress Level of Workplace			
Low	Moderate	High	$[k=3]$
3.4	3.5	2.9	
3.2	3.6	3.0	
3.0	2.7	2.6	
3.0	3.5	3.3	
3.5	3.8	3.7	
3.8	2.9	2.7	
3.6	3.4	2.4	
4.0	3.2	2.5	
3.9	3.3	3.3	
2.9	3.1	3.4	$[N = k \times n = 30]$
$n_1 = 10$	$n_2 = 10$	$n_3 = 10$	

FYI

The null hypothesis for an ANOVA states that group means in the population do not vary; the alternative hypothesis states that group means in the population do vary.

FYI

The rejection region is always located in the upper tail of the F distribution, so the critical value is always positive.

Step 1: State the hypotheses. In terms of differences, the null hypothesis states that each mean is the same as or equal to the others: $H_0: \mu_1 = \mu_2 = \mu_k$, where k is the number of groups. In terms of variance, which is directly measured to conduct this test, the null hypothesis states that group means (μ) do not vary (σ^2) in the population. Thus, the null hypothesis states that group means in the population do not vary (variance = 0); the alternative hypothesis states that group means in the population do vary (variance > 0):

$H_0: \sigma_\mu^2 = 0$. Group means do not vary between groups in the employee population.

$H_1: \sigma_\mu^2 > 0$. Group means do vary between groups in the employee population.

Step 2: Set the criteria for a decision. The level of significance for this test is .05. The degrees of freedom between groups are $k - 1$:

$$df_{BG} = 3 - 1 = 2.$$

The degrees of freedom error are $N - k$:

$$df_E = 30 - 3 = 27.$$

To locate the critical value for an ANOVA with 2 and 27 degrees of freedom, find where 2 and 27 intersect in Table C.3 in Appendix C. The critical value for this test is 3.35. Figure 11.3 shows where this critical value falls in an F distribution. The region in the upper tail is the rejection region for this test.

We will compare the value of the test statistic with this critical value. If the value of the test statistic falls beyond the critical value (at or greater than 3.35), then we reject the null hypothesis; otherwise, we retain the null hypothesis.

Step 3: Compute the test statistic. We compute the F statistic to determine the total variance attributed to differences between group means relative to the variance attributed to error. There are many different ways to compute a mean square. We will describe this analysis in four stages: preliminary calculations, intermediate calculations, computing the sum of squares, and completing the F table.

FIGURE 11.3   The F Distribution With 2 and 27 Degrees of Freedom

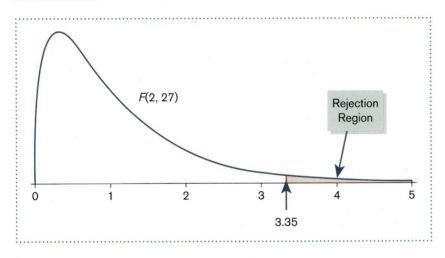

The alpha level (α) is placed in the upper tail at or above 3.35.

Stage 1: Preliminary calculations: Find Σx, Σx_T, Σx^2, Σx_T^2, n, and k. These preliminary calculations are shown in Table 11.4. Each calculation made in the table is described here.

1. Find k and n. We have three groups, $k = 3$, and 10 participants are in each group, $n = 10$.

2. Find Σx and Σx_T. Sum the scores in each group: Σx. The grand total Σx_T is the sum of scores in all groups combined.

3. Find Σx^2 and Σx_T^2. Square each score, and then sum the squared scores in each group: Σx^2. The sum of the squared scores in all groups combined is Σx_T^2.

Stage 2: Intermediate calculations: Find [1], [2], and [3]. In Stage 1, we computed the values needed to make calculations in Stage 2. There are three calculations in Stage 2:

First, we compute a correction factor by squaring the grand total Σx_T and dividing by the total sample size (N):

$$[1]\frac{\left(\Sigma x_T\right)^2}{N} = \frac{(97.10)^2}{30} = 314.28.$$

TABLE 11.4   Preliminary Calculations for the One-Way Between-Subjects ANOVA in Example 11.1

Perceived Stress Level of Workplace			
Low	Moderate	High	← $k = 3$
3.4	3.5	2.9	
3.2	3.6	3.0	
3.0	2.7	2.6	
3.0	3.5	3.3	
3.5	3.8	3.7	
3.8	2.9	2.7	
3.6	3.4	2.4	
4.0	3.2	2.5	
3.9	3.3	3.3	
2.9	3.1	3.4	
$n_1 = 10$	$n_2 = 10$	$n_3 = 10$	$N = 30$
$\sum x_1 = 34.30$	$\sum x_2 = 33.00$	$\sum x_3 = 29.30$	$\sum x_T = 97.10$
$\sum x_1^2 = 119.07$	$\sum x_2^2 = 119.07$	$\sum x_3^2 = 90.50$	$\sum x_T^2 = 319.47$

Second, we divide the sum of squared scores in each group by the sample size in each group:

$$[2] \ \sum \frac{x^2}{n} = \frac{(34.30)^2}{10} + \frac{(33.00)^2}{10} + \frac{(29.80)^2}{10} = 315.35.$$

Third, we restate the sum of the squared scores in all groups combined:

$$[3] \ \sum x_T^2 = 319.47.$$

We can use these values to compute sum of squares (SS) for each source of variation in the ANOVA. SS is the numerator for variance (see Chapter 4). Hence, the calculations we make in Stage 3 will give us the numerator in the formula for variance for each source of variation.

Stage 3: Computing the sum of squares (SS) for each source of variation.

The **sum of squares between groups (SS_{BG})** is the difference between Calculation [2] and Calculation [1] in Stage 2:

$$SS_{BG} = [2] - [1] = 315.35 - 314.28 = 1.07.$$

The **sum of squares total (SS_T)** is the difference between Calculation [3] and Calculation [1] in Stage 2:

$$SS_T = [3] - [1] = 319.47 - 314.28 = 5.19.$$

Sum of squares between groups (SS_{BG}) is the sum of squares attributed to variability between groups.

Sum of squares total (SS_T) is the overall sum of squares across all groups.

The **sum of squares error (SS_E)** is the sum of squares total minus the sum of squares between groups:

$$SS_E = SS_T - SS_{BG} = 5.19 - 1.07 = 4.12.$$

Stage 4: Completing the F table. The F table lists the sum of squares (SS), degrees of freedom (df), mean squares (MS), and value of the test statistic. The calculations in the table are described below and are listed in Table 11.5. Table 11.6 is the completed F table.

FYI

In Stage 3, we compute the numerator (SS) for the variance between and within groups.

TABLE 11.5 An F Table With the Formulas for Completing the Table

Source of Variation	SS	df	MS	F_{obt}
Between groups	1.07	$k - 1 = 2$	$\frac{SS_{BG}}{df_{BG}}$	$\frac{MS_{BG}}{MS_E}$
Within groups (error)	4.12	$N - k = 27$	$\frac{SS_E}{df_E}$	
Total	5.19	$N - 1 = 29$		

The first column of values in the F table lists the sum of squares (we computed SS in Stage 3). The second column lists the degrees of freedom (we computed df in Step 2). We will use these values to compute the mean squares for the test statistic. The formula for variance is SS divided by df, so we divide across each row to compute each mean square.

To compute the variance or mean square between groups, we divide SS_{BG} by df_{BG}:

$$MS_{BG} = \frac{SS_{BG}}{df_{BG}} = \frac{1.07}{2} = 0.535.$$

Likewise, to compute the variance or mean square error, we divide SS_E by df_E:

$$MS_E = \frac{SS_E}{df_E} = \frac{4.12}{27} = 0.152.$$

The formula for the test statistic is the mean square between groups (0.535) divided by the mean square error (0.152):

$$F_{obt} = \frac{MS_{BG}}{MS_E} = \frac{0.535}{0.152} = 3.52.$$

Step 4: Make a decision. To make a decision, we compare the obtained value to the critical value. As shown in Figure 11.4, the obtained value (3.52) is greater than the critical value (3.35); it falls in the rejection region. The decision is to reject the null hypothesis.

Table 11.7 summarizes the procedures used to compute a one-way between-subjects ANOVA.

Sum of squares within groups, or **sum of squares error (SS_E)**, is the sum of squares attributed to variability within each group.

FYI

The mean squares for each source of variation are computed by dividing SS by df for each source of variation.

TABLE 11.6 The Completed F Table for Example 11.1

Source of Variation	SS	df	MS	F_{obt}
Between groups	1.07	2	0.535	3.52*
Within groups (error)	4.12	27	0.152	
Total	5.19	29		

An asterisk (*) next to the F statistic indicates significance or a decision to reject the null hypothesis.

FIGURE 11.4 Making a Decision

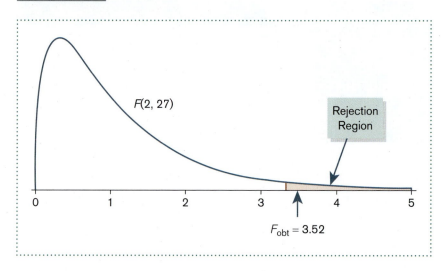

$F(2, 27)$

Rejection Region

$F_{obt} = 3.52$

The test statistic, F_{obt}, reaches the rejection region, so we choose to reject the null hypothesis. At least one pair of group means significantly differs.

TABLE 11.7 The Steps Used to Compute a One-Way Between-Subjects ANOVA

Steps for Computing a One-Way Between-Subjects ANOVA		
Terminology	**Statement**	**Meaning**
Step 1: State the hypotheses.		
Null hypothesis	$\sigma_\mu^2 = 0$	Population means do not vary.
Alternative hypothesis	$\sigma_\mu^2 > 0$	Population means do vary.
Step 2: Set the criteria for a decision.		
Degrees of freedom between groups	$df_{BG} = k - 1$	The number of groups minus 1

Steps for Computing a One-Way Between-Subjects ANOVA		
Terminology	**Statement**	**Meaning**
Degrees of freedom error	$df_E = N - k$	The number of total participants minus the number of groups
Degrees of freedom total	$df_T = N - 1$	The number of total participants minus 1
Step 3: Compute test statistic.		
STAGE 1		
Groups	k	The number of groups or levels of a factor
Participants	n, N	The number of participants per group (n) and overall (N)
Grand total	Σx_T	The sum of all scores in a study
Total sum of squared scores	Σx_T^2	The sum of all scores individually squared in a study
STAGE 2		
[1]	$\frac{(\Sigma x_T)^2}{N}$	The correction factor
[2]	$\Sigma \frac{x^2}{n}$	The "uncorrected" variation between groups
[3]	Σx_T^2	The "uncorrected" total variation in a study
STAGE 3		
Sum of squares between groups	$SS_{BG} = [2] - [1]$	The sum of squared deviations between groups
Sum of squares total	$SS_T = [3] - [1]$	The sum of squared deviations in all groups
Sum of squares error	$SS_E = SS_T - SS_{BG}$	The sum of squared deviations within groups (error)
STAGE 4		
Mean square between groups	$MS_{BG} = \frac{SS_{BG}}{df_{BG}}$	The variance between groups. This is the numerator of the test statistic.
Mean square error	$MS_E = \frac{SS_E}{df_E}$	The variance within groups (error). This is the denominator of the F statistic.
F statistic formula	$F_{obt} = \frac{MS_{BG}}{MS_E}$	The obtained value of the test statistic for an ANOVA
Step 4: Make a decision.		
Decision criterion	—	When $F_{obt} < F_{crit}$, retain the null hypothesis. When $F_{obt} \geq F_{crit}$, reject the null hypothesis.

MAKING SENSE MEAN SQUARES AND VARIANCE

To compute a variance, or mean square, we compute sum of squares (SS), which is the numerator for sample variance, and degrees of freedom (df), which is the denominator for sample variance:

$$\text{Sample variance} = \frac{SS}{df}.$$

For an ANOVA, the formula is the same. To find the variance or mean square attributed to differences between groups, we divide SS_{BG} by df_{BG}. To find the variance or mean square attributed to error, we divide SS_E by df_E. The procedures for computing SS and df for an ANOVA may be a bit different, but the formula for variance is still the same. Computing a mean square is the same as computing a variance:

$$MS = \frac{SS}{df} \text{ for between groups and error variance.}$$

The test statistic for an ANOVA, then, is a ratio used to determine whether the variance attributed to differences between groups (MS_{BG}) is significantly larger than the variance attributed to error (MS_E).

Measuring Effect Size: Eta-Squared and Omega-Squared

In Example 11.1, we concluded that the group means significantly varied by group. We can also determine the size of this effect using the proportion of variance. A proportion of variance is used to measure how much variability in the dependent variable (time in years) can be accounted for by the levels of the factor (the perceived stress of the workplace). Two measures of proportion of variance are eta-squared (η^2 or R^2) and omega-squared (ω^2).

Using eta-squared, the symbol R^2 may be used instead of η^2. Eta-squared is computed as the sum of squares between groups divided by the sum of squares total:

$$R^2 = \eta^2 = \frac{SS_{BG}}{SS_T}.$$

In Example 11.1, Table 11.6 shows that $SS_{BG} = 1.07$ and $SS_T = 5.19$. The value for eta-squared is

$$\eta^2 = \frac{1.07}{5.19} = .21.$$

We conclude that 21% of the variability in how long employees said they would stay with their company can be accounted for by the perceived stress of the workplace. Based on the effect size conventions listed in the second column of Table 8.4 in Chapter 8 (p. 239), this is a medium effect size.

Using eta-squared can be biased in that it tends to overestimate the proportion of variance explained by the levels of a factor. To correct for the overestimate, we can use omega-squared to estimate proportion of variance. This estimate has two advantages over eta-squared:

FYI

Eta-squared is often reported as R² for an ANOVA test.

1. It corrects for the size of error by including MS_E in the formula.

2. It corrects for the number of groups by including the degrees of freedom between groups (df_{BG}) in the formula.

The formula for omega-squared is

$$\omega^2 = \frac{SS_{BG} - df_{BG}(MS_E)}{SS_T + MS_E}.$$

In Example 11.1, Table 11.6 shows that $SS_{BG} = 1.07$, $df_{BG} = 2$, $MS_E = 0.152$, and $SS_T = 5.19$. The value for omega-squared is

$$\omega^2 = \frac{1.07 - 2(0.152)}{5.19 + 0.152} = .14.$$

We conclude that 14% of the variability in how long employees said they would stay with their company can be accounted for by the perceived stress of the workplace. This is a smaller estimate than eta-squared but still a medium effect size based on the effect size conventions listed in the third column of Table 8.4 in Chapter 8 (p. 239). Here is how we might report omega-squared with the significant result (simply replace omega-squared with eta-squared to report that effect size measure):

> The one-way analysis of variance showed that how long employees stated they would stay with the company depended on their perceived stress level of the workplace, $F(2, 27) = 3.52$, $p < .05$ $(\omega^2 = .14)$.

Different measures of effect size do not give the same estimates, and there is little consensus as to which is the superior measure. This lack of consensus is something to be aware of when reading reports of effect size in scientific journals.

FYI

Omega-squared corrects for the number of groups and the size of error in an ANOVA test.

LEARNING CHECK 3

1. State the four assumptions for the one-way between-subjects ANOVA.

2. If $SS_{BG} = 40$ in a one-way between-subjects ANOVA with five groups, what is the numerator of the F statistic?

3. Make a decision given the following values for the F statistic in a test with 3 and 20 degrees of freedom.

    (a) $F_{obt} = 3.05$ (b) $F_{obt} = 4.00$ (c) $F_{obt} = 5.35$

4. A mean square is the same as what descriptive statistic?

5. Which measure, eta-squared or omega-squared, gives a larger estimate of proportion of variance for the same data?

Answers: 1. Normality, random sampling, independence, and homogeneity of variance. 2. $MS_{BG} = \frac{40}{4} = 10$; 3. (a) Retain the null hypothesis, (b) Reject the null hypothesis, (c) Reject the null hypothesis; 4. Variance; 5. Eta-squared.

11.4 POST HOC TESTS: AN EXAMPLE USING TUKEY'S HSD

When the decision is to retain the null hypothesis for an ANOVA, we stop the analysis. No pairs of group means are significantly different. As shown in Figure 11.5, following a decision to retain the null hypothesis, we stop, start over, consider an alternative study, and begin again.

FIGURE 11.5 Following an ANOVA: A Decision Chart for When to Compute Post Hoc Tests

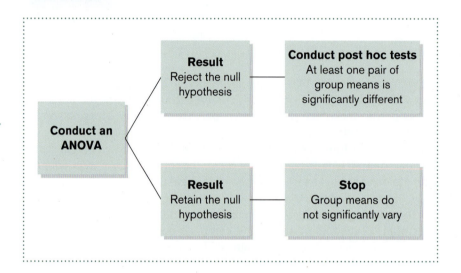

FYI

When the ANOVA is significant, conduct post hoc tests to determine which pair or pairs of group means significantly differ. When the ANOVA is not significant, stop; no group means significantly differ.

FYI

Experimentwise alpha is the alpha level stated for multiple tests conducted on the same data.

A **post hoc test** is a statistical procedure computed following a significant ANOVA to determine which pair or pairs of group means significantly differ. These tests are necessary when $k > 2$ because multiple comparisons are needed. When $k = 2$, only one comparison is made because only one pair of group means can be compared.

A **pairwise comparison** is a statistical comparison for the difference between two group means. A post hoc test evaluates all possible pairwise comparisons for an ANOVA with any number of groups.

Experimentwise alpha is the aggregated alpha level, or probability of committing a Type I error for all tests, when multiple tests are conducted on the same data.

Testwise alpha is the alpha level, or probability of committing a Type I error, for each test or pairwise comparison made on the same data.

The decision in Example 11.1, however, was to reject the null hypothesis: The test was significant. A significant ANOVA indicates that at least one pair of group means significantly differs. However, this test does not tell us which pairs of means differ. To determine which pairs differ, we compute **post hoc tests** or "after-the-fact" tests. These tests evaluate the difference for all possible pairs of group means, called **pairwise comparisons**. With only two groups ($k = 2$), post hoc tests are not needed because only one pair of group means can be compared. With more than two groups ($k > 2$), multiple comparisons must be made, so post hoc tests are necessary.

All post hoc tests are aimed at making sure that no matter how many tests we compute, the overall likelihood of committing a Type I error is .05. In other words, all post hoc tests control for **experimentwise alpha**, which is the overall alpha level for multiple tests conducted on the same data. The alpha level for each test is called **testwise alpha**.

In Example 11.1, we stated an experimentwise alpha equal to .05 for all tests. Post hoc tests are used to control for experimentwise alpha, thereby making the overall alpha or probability of a Type I error for all pairwise comparisons combined equal to .05. Figure 11.6 lists five tests used to control for experimentwise alpha. The tests in the figure are listed from most conservative (associated with the least power) to most liberal (associated with the greatest power).

For a between-subjects test, the two most conservative tests are the Scheffé test and the Bonferroni procedure. For a between-subjects design (defined in Chapter 9), both post hoc tests tend to be too conservative—in a way, these post hoc tests do too good of a job of controlling for experimentwise alpha. However, the Bonferroni procedure is only too conservative when the number of pairwise comparisons is greater than three. Because we made three pairwise comparisons in Example 11.1, this procedure would not have been too conservative in that case.

FYI

All post hoc tests control for experimentwise alpha.

FIGURE 11.6   A Ranking of Some of the Most Conservative and Liberal Post Hoc Tests

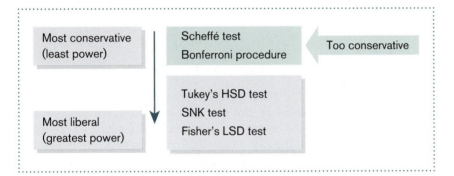

While the Scheffé test and Bonferroni procedure are good post hoc tests, they are generally considered too conservative for a between-subjects ANOVA design. HSD = honestly significant difference; LSD = least significant difference; SNK = Student-Newman-Keuls.

The remaining three post hoc tests are Fisher's least significant difference (LSD) test, the Student-Newman-Keuls (SNK) test, and Tukey's honestly significant difference (HSD) test. Each test has drawbacks as well, although all tend to have a better balance between making it too easy (too liberal) and making it too difficult (too conservative) to reject the null hypothesis. In this section, we describe the most conservative (Tukey's HSD) of these post hoc tests. The steps to compute Tukey's HSD are as follows, although note that only Step 2 would be different to compute any of the three post hoc tests identified here:

Step 1: Compute the test statistic for each pairwise comparison.

Step 2: Compute the critical value for each pairwise comparison.

Step 3: Make a decision to retain or reject the null hypothesis for each pairwise comparison.

Step 1: Compute the test statistic for each pairwise comparison. The test statistic for each pairwise comparison is the difference between the largest and the smallest group mean. We compute the test statistic in the same way for both post hoc tests. The test statistic for each comparison is as follows:

Comparison 1: Low Stress and High Stress: 3.43 − 2.98 = 0.45.

Comparison 2: Moderate Stress and High Stress: 3.30 − 2.98 = 0.32.

Comparison 3: Low Stress and Moderate Stress: 3.43 − 3.30 = 0.13.

Tukey's HSD is a conservative pairwise comparison in that it will lead to larger critical values than the SNK and LSD tests. However, it generally does a sufficient job at controlling for experimentwise alpha, while not making it overly difficult to lead to a decision to reject the null hypothesis. Here, we will compute the critical value (Step 2) and make a decision (Step 3).

Step 2: Compute the critical value for each pairwise comparison. The critical value is computed using the following statistic:

$$\text{Tukey's HSD}: q_{\alpha}\sqrt{\frac{MS_E}{n}}.$$

In this formula, q is the **studentized range statistic**. We must find this value in the studentized range statistic table in Table C.4 in Appendix C. Table 11.8 shows a portion of this table. To locate values for q in Table C.4, we need to know df_E and the real range (r). For Tukey's HSD test, the real range, r, is equal to the number of groups, k, in a study. In Example 11.1, we observed three groups; therefore, $r = 3$.

In Table C.4, we move across to 3 in the columns and down to 27 (the value for df_E) in the rows. Because 27 is not in the table, the most conservative rule is to use the next smallest value, which is 26 in the table. We use the q value at 3 and 26: $q = 3.52$. For this test, $MS_E = 0.152$ and $n = 10$, and the critical value for Tukey's HSD is

$$3.52\sqrt{\frac{0.152}{10}} = 0.43.$$

Step 3: Make a decision to retain or reject the null hypothesis for each pairwise comparison. The value 0.43 is the critical value for each pairwise comparison. For each comparison, we decide that the two groups are significantly different if the test statistic is larger than the critical value we computed. The decision for each comparison is given below (an asterisk is included to indicate significance where applicable):

Comparison 1: Low Stress and High Stress: 3.43 − 2.98 = 0.45* (reject the null hypothesis; the test statistic value, 0.45, is larger than 0.43).

Comparison 2: Moderate Stress and High Stress: 3.30 − 2.98 = 0.32 (retain the null hypothesis; the test statistic value, 0.32, is less than 0.43).

The **studentized range statistic** (**q**) is a statistic used to determine critical values for comparing pairs of means at a given range. This statistic is used in the formula to find the critical value for Tukey's HSD post hoc test.

TABLE 11.8	A Portion of the Studentized Range Statistic Table in Table C.4 in Appendix C

df_E	Range			
	2	3	4	5
6	3.46	4.34	4.90	5.30
	5.24	6.32	7.02	7.55
7	3.34	4.17	4.68	5.06
	4.95	5.91	6.54	7.00
8	3.26	4.05	4.53	4.89
	4.75	5.64	6.21	6.63
9	3.20	3.95	4.42	4.76
	4.60	5.43	5.95	6.34
10	3.15	3.88	4.33	4.66
	4.48	5.27	5.77	6.14
11	3.11	3.82	4.27	4.59
	4.38	5.16	5.63	5.98
12	3.08	3.78	4.20	4.51
	4.32	5.05	5.50	5.84

Comparison 3: Low Stress and Moderate Stress: 3.43 − 3.30 = 0.13 (retain the null hypothesis; the test statistic value, 0.13, is less than 0.43).

Only Comparison 1 is significant. Thus, we conclude that employees are willing to stay longer with a company if they perceive the workplace as a low-stress environment compared to employees who perceive the same workplace as a high-stress environment. If we were to report this result in a research journal, it would look something like this:

The one-way analysis of variance reached significance, $F(2, 27) = 3.52$, $p < .05$, with the time employees said they would stay with the company being significantly greater among employees who perceived the workplace environment as low stress compared to those who perceived the same workplace as a high-stress environment (Tukey's HSD, $p < .05$). Otherwise, no significant differences were evident ($p > .05$).

LEARNING CHECK 4

1. All post hoc tests compute critical values that control for what value?

2. The following is an ANOVA summary table for a significant result ($p < .05$):

	SS	df	MS	F_{obt}
Between groups	66.08	2	33.04	3.815
Error	181.88	21	8.66	
Total	247.96	23		

If the means in each group are 4.00 (Group A), 6.63 (Group B), and 8.00 (Group C), then which pairs of groups are significantly different using Tukey's HSD test?

Answers: 1. Experimentwise alpha; 2. Only Group A and Group C significantly differ.

11.5 SPSS in Focus:
The One-Way Between-Subjects ANOVA

There are two commands for computing a one-way between-subjects ANOVA using SPSS—the One-Way ANOVA and the GLM Univariate commands. Using the data given in Table 11.9, which is reproduced from data originally given in Table 11.3, we will confirm our conclusion using the One-Way ANOVA command:

TABLE 11.9 Data for Example 11.1, Reproduced From Data Originally Given in Table 11.3

Perceived Stress Level of Workplace		
Low	Moderate	High
3.4	3.5	2.9
3.2	3.6	3.0
3.0	2.7	2.6
3.0	3.5	3.3
3.5	3.8	3.7
3.8	2.9	2.7
3.6	3.4	2.4

Perceived Stress Level of Workplace		
Low	**Moderate**	**High**
4.0	3.2	2.5
3.9	3.3	3.3
2.9	3.1	3.4

1. Click on the Variable View tab and enter *groups* in the Name column. Go to the Decimals column for this row only and reduce the value to 0 (we use only whole numbers to code groups). To label the groups, click on the small gray box with three dots in the Values column to display a dialog box. In the dialog box, enter *1* in the value cell and *Low* in the label cell, and then click Add; enter *2* in the value cell and *Moderate* in the label cell, and then click Add; enter *3* in the value cell and *High* in the label cell, and then click Add. Click OK.

2. Still in the Variable View, enter *length* in the Name column in the second row. We will list the length of time employees said they would stay with the company (rounded to the tenths place), so go to the Decimals column for this row only and reduce the value to 1.

3. Click on the Data View tab. In the *groups* column, enter *1* in the first 10 cells, *2* in the next 10 cells, and *3* in the next 10 cells. These values (1, 2, and 3) are the codes for each group. In the *length* column, enter the length data in the cells that correspond with the codes for each group listed in the first column.

4. Go to the menu bar and click Analyze, then Compare Means and One-Way ANOVA, to display the dialog box shown in Figure 11.7.

FIGURE 11.7 Dialog Box for Steps 4 and 5

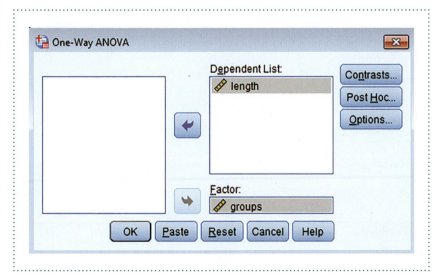

(Continued)

(Continued)

5. Using the appropriate arrows, move *groups* into the Factor: box to identify the groups. Move *length* into the Dependent List: box.

6. Click the Post Hoc option to display the new dialog box shown in Figure 11.8. Notice that each post hoc test listed in Figure 11.6 is an option in SPSS in Figure 11.8. Select Tukey (this differs from the Tukey's-b option) and click Continue.

FIGURE 11.8   Dialog Box for Step 6

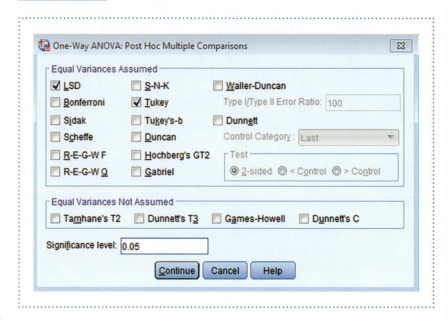

7. Select OK, or select Paste and click the Run command.

Notice that the ANOVA table, shown in Table 11.10, is similar to the one we computed for Example 11.1. In addition, SPSS gives us the exact p value for this test in the last column. Table 11.11 displays the SPSS output for the post hoc tests.

TABLE 11.10   The SPSS Output Table Using the One-Way ANOVA Command for Example 11.1

ANOVA

length

	Sum of Squares	df	Mean Square	F	Sig.
Between Groups	1.073	2	.536	3.517	.044
Within Groups	4.117	27	.152		
Total	5.190	29			

TABLE 11.11   The SPSS Output Table for the Post Hoc Comparisons Using Tukey's HSD Test

Multiple Comparisons

Dependent Variable: length

	(I) groups	(J) groups	Mean Difference (I-J)	Std. Error	Sig.	95% Confidence Interval Lower Bound	Upper Bound
Tukey HSD	Low	Moderate	.1300	.1746	.740	-.303	.563
		High	.4500*	.1746	.040	.017	.883
	Moderate	Low	-.1300	.1746	.740	-.563	.303
		High	.3200	.1746	.178	-.113	.753
	High	Low	-.4500*	.1746	.040	-.883	-.017
		Moderate	-.3200	.1746	.178	-.753	.113
LSD	Low	Moderate	.1300	.1746	.463	-.228	.488
		High	.4500*	.1746	.016	.092	.808
	Moderate	Low	-.1300	.1746	.463	-.488	.228
		High	.3200	.1746	.078	-.038	.678
	High	Low	-.4500*	.1746	.016	-.808	-.092
		Moderate	-.3200	.1746	.078	-.678	.038

*. The mean difference is significant at the 0.05 level.

The post hoc comparisons in Table 11.11 label each group. At the top, you see Low with Moderate; High is placed next to it. You read the table as comparisons across the rows. The first comparison is Low and Moderate. If there is no asterisk next to the value given in the Mean Difference column, then those two means do not differ (note that the p value, which indicates a significant difference when p is less than .05, is also given in the Sig. column). The next comparison is Low and High. This post hoc comparison is significant, as indicated by the asterisk, which confirms the conclusions we made in Example 11.1.

11.6 THE WITHIN-SUBJECTS DESIGN FOR ANALYSIS OF VARIANCE

When the same participants are observed across two or more levels of one factor, we are using the within-subjects design, also called the repeated-measures design (defined in Chapter 10). Using the within-subjects design, we compute interval and ratio scale data using the **one-way within-subjects ANOVA**. The term *one-way* indicates that we are testing one factor. The term *within-subjects*, also called *repeated-measures*, indicates that the same participants are observed in each group. Hence, using the within-subjects design, n participants are each observed k times. For example,

A **one-way within-subjects ANOVA**, also called a **one-way repeated-measures ANOVA**, is a statistical procedure used to test hypotheses for one factor with two or more levels concerning the variance among group means. This test is used when the same participants are observed at each level of a factor and the variance in any one population is unknown.

suppose that in a study of troop morale, 20 soldiers were observed six times. In that case, $n = 20$, and $k = 6$.

The test statistic is the same for the within-subjects and between-subjects designs using an ANOVA. It is the variance or mean square between groups divided by the variance or mean square error:

$$F_{obt} = \frac{MS_{BG}}{MS_E} = \frac{\text{variance between groups}}{\text{variance within groups}}.$$

There are three sources of variation in the one-way within-subjects ANOVA: between-groups, within-groups, and between-persons variation. The between-groups and within-groups variation is the same as that for the between-subjects design. Each source of variation is illustrated in Table 11.12 for a hypothetical study with three groups: A, B, and C.

The within-groups and between-persons sources of variation are regarded as "error," or variation that cannot be explained by having different groups. The **between-persons variation**, which is a new source of variation, is calculated and removed from the denominator of the test statistic. It is a source of variation associated with the differences between

FYI

The one-way within-subjects (repeated-measures) ANOVA is used to analyze data when the same participants are observed across two or more levels of one factor.

The **between-persons variation** is the variance attributed to differences between person means averaged across groups. Because the same participants are observed across groups using a within-subjects design, this source of variation is removed or omitted from the error term in the denominator of the test statistic for within-subjects designs.

	Three Sources of Variation in a Within-Subjects
TABLE 11.12	Design: Between Groups and Two Sources of Error Variation—Between Persons and Within Groups

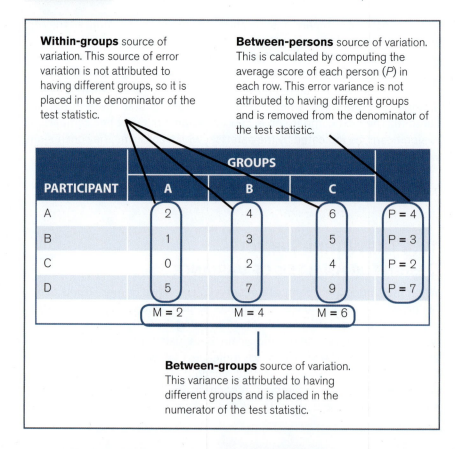

Within-groups source of variation. This source of error variation is not attributed to having different groups, so it is placed in the denominator of the test statistic.

Between-persons source of variation. This is calculated by computing the average score of each person (P) in each row. This error variance is not attributed to having different groups and is removed from the denominator of the test statistic.

PARTICIPANT	GROUPS			
	A	B	C	
A	2	4	6	P = 4
B	1	3	5	P = 3
C	0	2	4	P = 2
D	5	7	9	P = 7
	M = 2	M = 4	M = 6	

Between-groups source of variation. This variance is attributed to having different groups and is placed in the numerator of the test statistic.

person means averaged across groups. In a within-subjects design, we can assume that any differences in the characteristics of participants across groups are the same because the same people are observed in each group. For this reason, between-persons variation can be measured and then removed from the error term in the denominator of the test statistic.

Although there are two sources of error in a within-subjects design, this does not mean that we have more error variation in this design compared to the between-subjects design. Think of error variation as a pie with two slices. In the between-subjects design, we measure the whole pie and place it all in the denominator of the test statistic. In the within-subjects design, we cut this same pie into two slices and then remove the between-persons slice. The remaining portion of pie is placed in the denominator of the test statistic.

FYI

There are two sources of error variation in the one-way within-subjects ANOVA: one associated with observing different participants in each group (within groups) and one associated with observing the same participants across groups (between persons).

LEARNING CHECK 5

1. How are participants observed using the within-subjects design?

2. State the three sources of variation in the one-way within-subjects ANOVA.

3. Which source of error is removed from the denominator of the test statistic in the one-way within-subjects ANOVA?

Answers: 1. Using the within-subjects design, the same participants are observed across groups; 2. Between groups, between persons, and within groups variation; 3. Between-persons variation.

11.7 COMPUTING THE ONE-WAY WITHIN-SUBJECTS ANOVA

In this section, we will compute the one-way within-subjects ANOVA, which is the hypothesis test when the same participants are observed in each group (within-subjects design). We must make four assumptions to compute the one-way within-subjects ANOVA:

1. *Normality.* We assume that data in the population or populations being sampled from are normally distributed. This assumption is particularly important for small sample sizes. In larger samples, the overall variance of sample outcomes is reduced, and this assumption becomes less critical as a result.

2. *Independence within groups.* The same participants are observed between groups. Within each group, different participants are observed. For this reason, we make the assumption that participants are independently observed within groups but not between groups.

3. *Homogeneity of variance.* We assume that the variance in each population is equal to that in the others.

4. *Homogeneity of covariance.* We assume that participant scores in each group are related because the same participants are observed across or between groups. The reasons for this assumption are rather complex and beyond the scope of this book.

FYI

Four assumptions for the one-way within-subjects ANOVA are normality, independence within groups, homogeneity of variance, and homogeneity of covariance.

Together, the assumptions of homogeneity of variance and homogeneity of covariance are called *sphericity.* Note that if we violate the assumption of sphericity, then the value of the variance in the numerator of the test statistic can be inflated, which can increase the likelihood of committing a Type I error (or incorrectly rejecting the null hypothesis, defined in Chapter 7, p. 201).

Computing the Test Statistic: Evaluating Significance

In Example 11.2, we will use a new example and follow the four steps in hypothesis testing to compute the one-way within-subjects ANOVA.

Example 11.2

An important area of research targets efforts to reduce drug use to include the use of antismoking advertisement campaigns that facilitate the cessation and prevention of smoking among teens and adults (Farrelly et al., 2012; Institute of Medicine, 2015; Lee, Cappella, Lerman, & Strasser, 2013). As an example of a research study in this area, suppose a researcher wants to determine which of three advertisements is most likely to encourage teens not to smoke. To assess the impact of each advertisement, she asks a sample of teenagers to view each ad and to rate the ad's effectiveness on a scale from 1 (*not at all effective*) to 7 (*very effective*). One ad uses words only (no-cues condition). A second ad uses a generic abstract picture (generic-cues condition). A third ad shows a picture of a teenager smoking and coughing (smoking-related-cues condition). Using the data listed in Table 11.13, we will conduct the one-way within-subjects ANOVA to analyze the significance of these data at a .05 level of significance.

TABLE 11.13 The Results of a Within-Subjects Study Design in Which Participants Rated the Effectiveness of Three Different Types of Antismoking Advertisements in Example 11.2

Person	Cues		
	No Cues	**Generic Cues**	**Smoking-Related Cues**
A	2	5	5
B	3	5	6
C	1	4	5
D	4	5	7
E	4	3	6
F	5	4	7
G	2	2	6

Step 1: State the hypotheses. The null hypothesis states that group means in the population do not vary (variance = 0); the alternative hypothesis states that group means in the population do vary (variance > 0):

$H_0: \sigma_\mu^2 = 0$. Mean ratings for each advertisement do not vary in the population.

$H_1: \sigma_\mu^2 > 0$. Mean ratings for each advertisement do vary in the population.

Step 2: Set the criteria for a decision. The level of significance for this test is .05. The total degrees of freedom are $(kn) - 1$, which is $(3 \times 7) - 1 = 20$. We will split these total degrees of freedom into three parts for each source of variation. The degrees of freedom between groups are $k - 1$:

$$df_{BG} = 3 - 1 = 2.$$

The **degrees of freedom between persons** are $n - 1$:

$$df_{BP} = 7 - 1 = 6.$$

The degrees of freedom error are $(k - 1)(n - 1)$:

$$df_E = 2 \times 6 = 12.$$

The test statistic is the variance between groups (MS_{BG}) divided by the variance attributed to error (MS_E). The corresponding degrees of freedom for the test statistic are the degrees of freedom numerator or between groups ($df_{BG} = 2$) and the degrees of freedom denominator or error ($df_E = 12$):

$$F_{obt} = \frac{MS_{BG}}{MS_E} \xleftarrow{\text{Degrees of freedom}} \frac{df_{BG}}{df_E}.$$

Hence, we are locating the critical value for an ANOVA with 2 and 12 degrees of freedom. To locate the critical value, find where these degrees of freedom intersect in Table C.3 in Appendix C. The critical value for this test is 3.89. We will again use the F distribution to make a decision about the null hypothesis, as we do for all ANOVA tests. The critical value and rejection region for Example 11.2 are shown in Figure 11.9.

FYI

The null hypothesis for an ANOVA states that group means in the population do not vary; the alternative hypothesis states that group means in the population do vary.

FYI

The rejection region is always placed in the upper tail of the F distribution for an ANOVA.

FIGURE 11.9 An F Distribution With 2 and 12 Degrees of Freedom

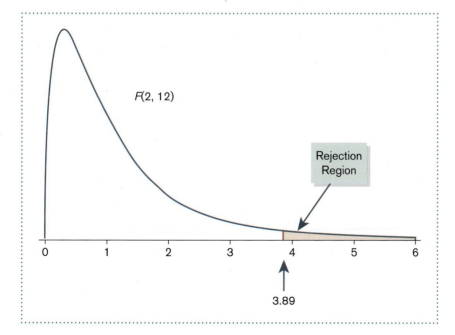

$F(2, 12)$

Rejection Region

3.89

The rejection region is placed in the upper tail at or above 3.89.

The **degrees of freedom between persons (df_{BP})** are the degrees of freedom associated with the variance of person means averaged across groups. They are equal to the number of participants (n) minus 1.

We will compare the test statistic with this critical value. If the value of the test statistic falls beyond the critical value (greater than 3.89), then we reject the null hypothesis; otherwise, we retain the null hypothesis.

Step 3: Compute the test statistic. We compute the F statistic to determine the total variance attributed to differences between group means relative to the variance attributed to error. There are many different ways to compute a mean square. We will again describe this analysis in four stages: preliminary calculations, intermediate calculations, computing the sum of squares, and completing the F table.

Stage 1: Preliminary calculations—find Σx, $\Sigma x_2^2 = 109$, $\Sigma x_3^2 = 90.50$, $\Sigma x_T^2 = 319.47$, ΣP, n, and k. These preliminary calculations are shown in Table 11.14. Each calculation made in the table is the same as described for the between-subjects design, except that we also sum the person scores. Each calculation is described here.

| TABLE 11.14 | Preliminary Calculations for the One-Way Within-Subjects ANOVA in Example 11.2 |

| Person | Cues | | | ΣP |
	No Cues	Generic Cues	Smoking-Related Cues	
A	2	5	5	12
B	3	5	6	14
C	1	4	5	10
D	4	5	7	16
E	4	3	6	13
F	5	4	7	16
G	2	2	6	10
	$\Sigma x_1 = 21$	$\Sigma x_2 = 28$	$\Sigma x_3 = 42$	$\Sigma x_T = 91$
	$\Sigma x_1^2 = 75$	$\Sigma x_2^2 = 120$	$\Sigma x_3^2 = 256$	$\Sigma x_T^2 = 451$

1. Find k and n. In this study, seven participants ($n = 7$) are observed across three groups ($k = 3$).

2. Find Σx and Σx_T. Sum the scores in each group: Σx. The grand total Σx_T is the sum of scores in all groups combined.

3. Find Σx^2 and Σx_T^2. Square each score, and then sum the squared scores in each group: Σx^2. The sum of the squared scores in all groups combined is Σx_T^2.

4. Find ΣP. Sum across the rows for each person. The sum of person scores is $2 + 5 + 5 = 12$ for Person A, $3 + 5 + 6 = 14$ for Person B, and so on. The total of these scores equals the grand total ($\Sigma P = \Sigma X_T = 91$).

Stage 2: Intermediate calculations—find [1], [2], [3], and [4]. In Stage 1, we computed the values needed to make calculations in Stage 2. There are four calculations in Stage 2 (the first three calculations are the same as those described for the between-subjects design).

First, we compute a correction factor by squaring the grand total Σx_T and dividing by the total number of observations ($k \times n$):

$$[1]\frac{\left(\Sigma x_T\right)^2}{k \times n} = \frac{(91)^2}{3 \times 7} = 394.33.$$

Second, we divide the sum of squared scores in each group by the sample size for each group:

$$[2]\ \Sigma \frac{x^2}{n} = \frac{(21)^2}{7} + \frac{(28)^2}{7} + \frac{(42)^2}{7} = 427.$$

Third, we restate the sum of the squared scores in all groups combined:

$$[3]\ \Sigma x_T^2 = 451.$$

Fourth, we divide the sum of squared person scores by the number of groups:

$$[4]\ \Sigma \frac{P^2}{k} = \frac{12^2}{3} + \frac{14^2}{3} + \frac{10^2}{3} + \frac{16^2}{3} + \frac{13^2}{3} + \frac{16^2}{3} + \frac{10^2}{3} = 407.$$

We can use these values to compute the sum of squares (SS) for each source of variation in the ANOVA. The calculations we make in Stage 3 will give us the numerator in the formula for variance, or SS, for each source of variation.

Stage 3: Computing the sum of squares (SS) for each source of variation.

The sum of squares between groups (SS_{BG}) is the difference between Calculation [2] and Calculation [1] in Stage 2:

$$SS_{BG} = [2] - [1] = 427 - 394.33 = 32.67.$$

The sum of squares total (SS_T) is the difference between Calculation [3] and Calculation [1] in Stage 2:

$$SS_T = [3] - [1] = 451 - 394.33 = 56.67.$$

The **sum of squares between persons (SS_{BP})** is the difference between Calculation [4] and Calculation [1] in Stage 2:

$$SS_{BP} = [4] - [1] = 407 - 394.33 = 12.67.$$

The sum of squares within groups, called the sum of squares error (SS_E), is the sum of squares total minus the sum of squares between groups and between persons:

$$SS_E = SS_T - SS_{BG} - SS_{BP} = 56.67 - 32.67 - 12.67 = 11.33.$$

Stage 4: Completing the F table. The F table lists the sum of squares (SS), the degrees of freedom (df), the mean squares (MS), and the value of the test statistic. The calculations in the F table are described here and listed in Table 11.15. Table 11.16 is the completed F table.

The **sum of squares between persons (SS_{BP})** is the sum of squares attributed to variability in participant scores across groups.

TABLE 11.15 The *F* Table With the Formulas for Completing the Table Given

Source of Variation	SS	df	MS	F_{obt}
Between groups	32.67	$k - 1 = 2$	$\frac{SS_{BG}}{df_{BG}}$	$\frac{MS_{BG}}{MS_E}$
Between persons	12.67	$n - 1 = 6$	$\frac{SS_{BP}}{df_{BP}}$	
Within groups (error)	11.33	$(k - 1)(n - 1) = 12$	$\frac{SS_E}{df_E}$	
Total	56.67	$(kn) - 1 = 20$		

FYI

In Stage 3, we compute SS for the variance between groups, between persons, and within groups.

FYI

Calculations of SS between persons are unique to the one-way within-subjects ANOVA. All remaining calculations of SS are the same as those computed using the one-way between-subjects ANOVA.

The first column of values in the *F* table lists the sum of squares (we computed these in Stage 3). The second column lists the degrees of freedom (we computed these in Step 2). We will use these values to compute the mean squares for the test statistic. The formula for variance is *SS* divided by *df*, so we divide across each row to compute each mean square.

To compute the variance or mean square between groups, we divide SS_{BG} by df_{BG}:

$$MS_{BG} = \frac{SS_{BG}}{df_{BG}} = \frac{32.67}{2} = 16.34.$$

To compute the variance or **mean square between persons**, which is the variance attributed to differences between persons across groups, we divide SS_{BP} by df_{BP}:

$$MS_{BP} = \frac{SS_{BP}}{df_{BP}} = \frac{12.67}{6} = 2.11.$$

To compute the variance or mean square error, we divide SS_E by df_E:

$$MS_E = \frac{SS_E}{df_E} = \frac{11.33}{12} = 0.94.$$

The formula for the test statistic is mean square between groups (16.34) divided by mean square error (0.94):

$$F_{obt} = \frac{MS_{BG}}{MS_E} = \frac{16.34}{0.94} = 17.30.$$

TABLE 11.16 The Completed *F* Table for Example 11.2

Source of Variation	SS	df	MS	F_{obt}
Between groups	32.67	2	16.34	17.30*
Between persons	12.67	6	2.11	
Within groups (error)	11.33	12	0.94	
Total	56.67	20		

Mean square between persons (MS_{BP}) is a measure of the variance attributed to differences in scores between persons.

The asterisk (*) indicates significance.

Step 4: Make a decision. To make a decision, we compare the obtained value to the critical value. As shown in Figure 11.10, the obtained value (17.30) is greater than the critical value (3.89); it falls well into the rejection region. The decision is to reject the null hypothesis.

FIGURE 11.10   Making a Decision

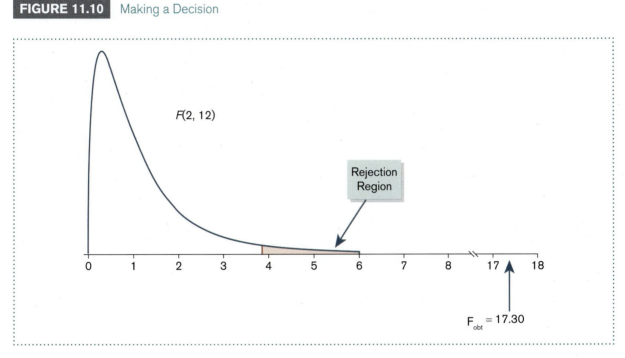

The test statistic, F_{obt}, reaches the rejection region, so we choose to reject the null hypothesis. At least one pair of group means significantly differs.

Table 11.17 summarizes the procedures used to compute a one-way within-subjects ANOVA.

TABLE 11.17   The Steps Used to Compute a One-Way Within-Subjects ANOVA

Steps for Computing a One-Way Within-Subjects ANOVA		
Terminology	**Formula**	**Meaning**
Step 1: State the hypotheses.		
Null hypothesis	$\sigma_{\mu}^2 = 0$	Population means do not vary.
Alternative hypothesis	$\sigma_{\mu}^2 > 0$	Population means do vary.
Step 2: Set the criteria for a decision.		
Degrees of freedom between groups	$df_{BG} = k - 1$	The number of groups minus 1
Degrees of freedom between persons	$df_{BP} = n - 1$	The number of participants per group minus 1

(Continued)

TABLE 11.17 (Continued)

Steps for Computing a One-Way Within-Subjects ANOVA		
Terminology	**Formula**	**Meaning**
Degrees of freedom error	$df_E = (k-1)(n-1)$	The degrees of freedom between groups multiplied by the degrees of freedom between persons
Degrees of freedom total	$df_T = (kn) - 1$	The number of groups multiplied by the number of participants, minus 1
Step 3: Compute the test statistic.		
STAGE 1		
Groups	k	The number of groups or levels of a factor
Participants	n	The number of participants per group (n)
Grand total	Σx_T	The sum of all scores in a study
Sum of person scores	ΣP	The sum of scores for each person
Sum of squared scores	Σx_T^2	The sum of all scores individually squared in a study
STAGE 2		
[1]	$\dfrac{\left(\Sigma x_T\right)^2}{k \times n}$	The correction factor
[2]	$\Sigma \dfrac{x^2}{n}$	The "uncorrected" between-groups variation
[3]	Σx_T^2	The "uncorrected" total variation in a study
[4]	$\Sigma \dfrac{P^2}{k}$	The "uncorrected" between-persons variation
STAGE 3		
Sum of squares between groups	$SS_{BG} = [2] - [1]$	The sum of squared deviations between groups
Sum of squares between persons	$SS_{BP} = [4] - [1]$	The sum of squared deviations between persons
Sum of squares total	$SS_T = [3] - [1]$	The sum of squared deviations in all groups
Sum of squares error	$SS_E = SS_T - SS_{BG} - SS_{BP}$	The sum of squared deviations within each group
STAGE 4		
Mean square between groups	$MS_{BG} = \dfrac{SS_{BG}}{df_{BG}}$	The variance between groups. This is the numerator of the test statistic.

Steps for Computing a One-Way Within-Subjects ANOVA		
Terminology	**Formula**	**Meaning**
Mean square between persons	$MS_{BP} = \dfrac{SS_{BP}}{df_{BP}}$	The variance between persons averaged across groups
Mean square error	$MS_E = \dfrac{SS_E}{df_E}$	The variance within groups. This is the denominator of the test statistic.
F statistic formula	$F_{obt} = \dfrac{MS_{BG}}{MS_E}$	The obtained value of the test statistic for an ANOVA
Step 4: Make a decision.		
Decision criterion	—	When $F_{obt} < F_{crit}$, retain the null hypothesis. When $F_{obt} \geq F_{crit}$, reject the null hypothesis.

Measuring Effect Size:
Partial Eta-Squared and Partial Omega-Squared

In Example 11.2, we concluded that the group means significantly varied by group. We can also determine the size of the effect using the proportion of variance. A proportion of variance is used to measure how much variability in the dependent variable (ratings of effectiveness) can be accounted for by the levels of the factor (the different types of ads). Two measures of proportion of variance for the within-subjects design are partial eta-squared (η_P^2) and partial omega-squared (ω_P^2).

Using a partial proportion of variance, we remove or partial out the between-persons variation before calculating the proportion of variance. We do this because the between-persons variation was removed from the denominator of the test statistic for the one-way within-subjects ANOVA; thus it is also removed when calculating effect size.

Using partial eta-squared, we remove the sum of squares between persons from the sum of squares total in the denominator. There are two ways we can remove the sum of squares between persons. We can subtract the sum of squares between persons from the sum of squares total:

$$\eta_P^2 = \frac{SS_{BG}}{SS_T - SS_{BP}},$$

or we can add the sum of squares between groups and sum of squares error. This will leave the sum of squares between persons out of the denominator:

$$\eta_P^2 = \frac{SS_{BG}}{SS_{BG} + SS_E}.$$

In Example 11.2, Table 11.16 shows that $SS_{BG} = 32.67$ and $SS_T - SS_{BP} = 44$. The value of partial eta-squared using either formula is

$$\eta_P^2 = \frac{32.67}{44} = .74.$$

We conclude that 74% of the variability in ratings can be explained by the type of ad being rated. Using the effect size conventions listed in the second column of Table 8.4 in Chapter 8 (p. 239), we determine that this is a large effect size.

One limitation for using partial eta-squared is that it can be biased in that it tends to overestimate effect size. A more conservative measure of effect size is partial omega-squared. This estimate has two advantages over partial eta-squared:

1. It corrects for the size of error by including MS_E in the formula.

2. It corrects for the number of groups by including the degrees of freedom between groups (df_{BG}) in the formula.

To compute partial omega-squared, we remove the sum of squares between persons from the sum of squares total in the denominator of the omega-squared formula, same as we did for partial eta-squared. There are two ways we can remove this sum of squares. We can subtract the sum of squares between persons from the sum of squares total in the denominator:

$$\omega_P^2 = \frac{SS_{BG} - df_{BG}(MS_E)}{(SS_T - SS_{BP}) + MS_E},$$

or we can add the sum of squares between groups and sum of squares error. This will leave the sum of squares between persons out of the denominator:

$$\omega_P^2 = \frac{SS_{BG} - df_{BG}(MS_E)}{(SS_{BG} + SS_E) + MS_E}.$$

In Example 11.2, Table 11.16 shows that $SS_{BG} = 32.67$, $df_{BG} = 2$, $MS_E = 0.94$, and $SS_T - SS_{BP} = 44$. The value for partial omega-squared using either formula is

$$\omega_P^2 = \frac{32.67 - 2(0.94)}{44 + 0.94} = .69.$$

We conclude that 69% of the variability in ratings can be explained by the type of ad being rated. Using the effect size conventions listed in the third column of Table 8.4 in Chapter 8 (p. 239), we determine that this is a large effect size. Here is how we might report the significant result using partial omega-squared in this example as our measure of effect size:

FYI

Partial measures of proportion of variance are used to estimate the effect size for the one-way within-subjects ANOVA.

FYI

The formulas for partial eta-squared and partial omega-squared have between-persons variation removed or partialled out of the denominator.

A one-way analysis of variance showed that ratings of effectiveness for the three advertisements significantly varied, $F(2, 12) = 17.30$, $p < .05$ ($\omega_P^2 = .69$).

LEARNING CHECK 6

1. State the four assumptions for the one-way within-subjects ANOVA.

2. Given the following values, compute the F statistic: $SS_{BG} = 10$, $SS_E = 25$, $df_{BG} = 2$, $df_E = 25$.

3. Make a decision given the following test statistic values for a one-way within-subjects ANOVA with 4 and 30 degrees of freedom.

(a) $F_{obt} = 2.50$ (b) $F_{obt} = 2.80$ (c) $F_{obt} = 4.00$

4. Which estimate (partial eta-squared or partial omega-squared) gives a larger estimate of proportion of variance?

Answers: 1. Normality, independence within groups, homogeneity of variance, and homogeneity of covariance; 2. $F_{obt} = 5.00$; 3. (a) Retain the null hypothesis, (b) Reject the null hypothesis, (c) Reject the null hypothesis; 4. Partial eta-squared.

11.8 POST HOC TESTS
FOR THE WITHIN-SUBJECTS DESIGN

In Example 11.2, we decided to reject the null hypothesis: At least one pair of group means significantly differs. Because we have more than two groups, we need to make multiple pairwise comparisons using a post hoc test to determine which pair or pairs of group means significantly differ. The post hoc test analyzes differences for all possible pairs of group means or pairwise comparisons. Mean ratings in Example 11.2 are 3.0 (Group No Cue), 4.0 (Group Generic Cue), and 6.0 (Group Smoking-Related Cue). In Example 11.2, then, there are three possible pairwise comparisons:

Comparison 1: Generic Cue and No Cue: $4.0 - 3.0 = 1.0$.

Comparison 2: Smoking-Related Cue and Generic Cue: $6.0 - 4.0 = 2.0$.

Comparison 3: Smoking-Related Cue and No Cue: $6.0 - 3.0 = 3.0$.

All post hoc tests ensure that no matter how many tests we compute, the overall likelihood of committing a Type I error is .05. In other words, all post hoc tests control for experimentwise alpha, which is the overall alpha level for multiple tests conducted on the same data. Here we can use the same post hoc tests identified in Figure 11.6 for the between-subjects design. Tukey's HSD is a common post hoc test, for example—the calculations for this test are shown in Section 11.4. That being said, of the post hoc tests listed in the figure, the Bonferroni procedure is probably best adapted for use following a significant one-way within-subjects ANOVA. However, keep in mind that this procedure gets too conservative as k increases. With a larger number of comparisons, more specialized tests beyond the scope of this book, such as trend analysis, are recommended.

FYI

Post hoc tests are computed following a significant one-way ANOVA to determine which pair or pairs of group means significantly differ.

11.9 SPSS in Focus:
The One-Way Within-Subjects ANOVA

In Example 11.2, we concluded that ratings of effectiveness for the three advertisements significantly varied, $F(2, 12) = 17.30$, $p < .05$. A Bonferroni procedure showed that participants rated the effectiveness of an ad with smoking-related cues higher compared to an ad with no cues and compared to an ad with generic cues. We will use SPSS to confirm the calculations we computed in Example 11.2.

1. Click on the Variable View tab and enter *nocue* in the Name column; enter *gencue* in the Name column below it; enter *smokecue* in the Name column below that. We will enter whole numbers, so reduce the value in the Decimals column to 0 in each row.

2. Click on the Data View tab. Enter the data for each group in the appropriate column, as shown in the background of Figure 11.11.

FIGURE 11.11   SPSS Views for Steps 2, 5, and 6

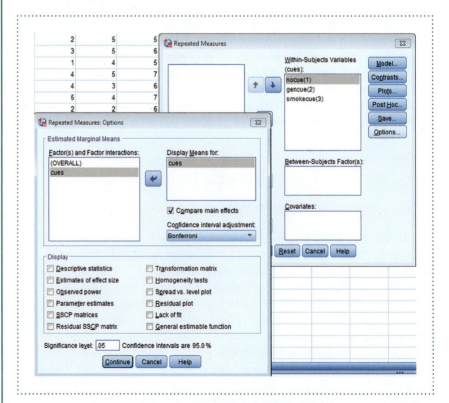

The SPSS Data View with data entry in each cell for Step 2 shown (left background). Also shown is the dialog box for Step 5 (right), and the dialog box for Step 6 (front).

3. Go to the menu bar and click Analyze, then General Linear Model and Repeated Measures, to display the dialog box shown in Figure 11.12.

4. In the Within-Subject Factor Name box, label the within-subjects factor. Enter *cues* in this box. Because this factor has three levels, enter *3* in the Number of Levels box. These actions will illuminate the Add option. Click Add, then Define to display a new dialog box for Step 5.

5. Using the appropriate arrows, move each column into the Within-Subjects Variables (cues) box, as shown in Figure 11.11 (upper right image).

6. To compute effect size and make post hoc comparisons, you can select Options to display a new dialog box. We will not do that here because we did not actually compute a post hoc test for this example in the chapter. However, for reference, the dialog box for doing this is shown in the bottom left image in Figure 11.11. Select Continue.

7. Select OK, or select Paste and click the Run command.

FIGURE 11.12 Dialog Box for Steps 3 to 4

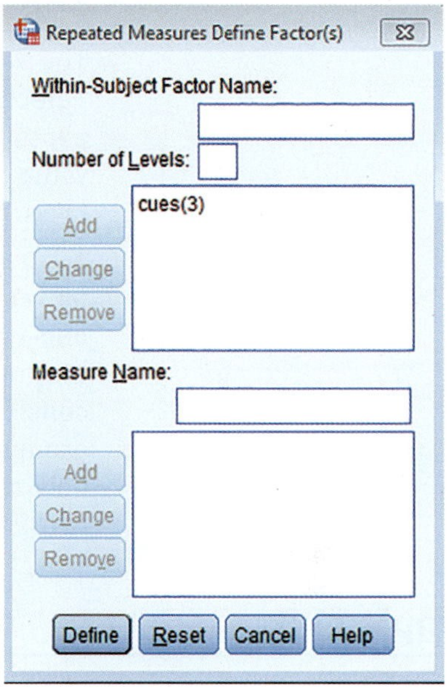

TABLE 11.18 SPSS Output *F* Table for Example 11.2

Tests of Within-Subjects Effects

Measure: MEASURE_1

Source		Type III Sum of Squares	df	Mean Square	F	Sig.
cues	Sphericity Assumed	32.667	2	16.333	17.294	.000
	Greenhouse-Geisser	32.667	1.323	24.698	17.294	.002
	Huynh-Feldt	32.667	1.552	21.050	17.294	.001
	Lower-bound	32.667	1.000	32.667	17.294	.006
Error(cues)	Sphericity Assumed	11.333	12	.944		
	Greenhouse-Geisser	11.333	7.936	1.428		
	Huynh-Feldt	11.333	9.311	1.217		
	Lower-bound	11.333	6.000	1.889		

Because we assume sphericity, read only the top row for cues and Error(cues) to find the values needed in this table.

Table 11.18 displays the SPSS output table for the ANOVA. Because we assume sphericity, read only the first row in each variable cell. Notice that the between-persons variation is not given in this table. SPSS removes this variation from the error term, leaving only the within-groups error. When we read only the first row in each cell and recognize that the between-persons variation is not given, we see that Table 11.18 is similar to Table 11.16, which we computed for Example 11.2.

11.10 A COMPARISON OF WITHIN-SUBJECTS AND BETWEEN-SUBJECTS DESIGNS FOR ANOVA: IMPLICATIONS FOR POWER

The within-subjects design is generally associated with more power to detect an effect than the between-subjects design. Eliminating the between-persons error makes the denominator of a test statistic smaller and the value of a test statistic larger, thereby increasing the power of the test.

However, for the ANOVA, we also adjust the degrees of freedom. So subtracting the between-persons variation will not always increase the power of a one-way within-subjects ANOVA. Instead, the power of the one-way within-subjects ANOVA is largely based on the assumption that observing the same participants across groups will result in more consistent responding, or changes in the dependent variable, between groups. We use two hypothetical data sets in Example 11.3 to see how consistency influences the power of the one-way within-subjects ANOVA.

Example 11.3

©iStockphoto.com/JacobStudio

Table 11.19 shows the results of two hypothetical studies measuring lever pressing in rats, which is a common behavioral task utilized in rodent studies (Kirkpatrick & Hall, 2005; Lattal, St. Peter, & Escobar, 2013). In each study, a group of four rats pressed a lever to receive a small, medium, or large reward. Rats were run on successive trials, and the number of lever presses on a given trial were recorded. In both hypothetical studies, the group means were identical. We will compare the data for each hypothetical study.

TABLE 11.19   The Data Measured in Study 1 (top) and Study 2 (bottom)

Study 1 (Consistent Responding)			
Reward Size			
Subject	**Small**	**Medium**	**Large**
A	2	3	4
B	1	2	3
C	3	4	5
D	0	2	4
Means:	1.50	2.75	4.00

| Study 2 (Inconsistent Responding) | | | |
| Reward Size | | | |
Subject	Small	Medium	Large
A	2	2	4
B	3	3	3
C	1	4	4
D	0	2	5
Means:	1.50	2.75	4.00

Note that the group means are the same in both studies.

Between-subjects design: If we observed different subjects in each group, then each study would be a between-subjects design, and we would use a one-way between-subjects ANOVA. In the between-subjects design, we place all of the error term in the denominator, so both studies would give the same value for error variance in the *F* table. Table 11.20 shows the results of the one-way between-subjects ANOVA, which would apply to both studies. For both studies, we decide to reject the null hypothesis; the variance between groups is significant.

TABLE 11.20   Between-Subjects Design

Source of Variation	SS	df	MS	F_{obt}
Between groups	12.50	2	6.25	5.79*
Within groups (error)	**9.75**	**9**	**1.08**	
Total	22.25	11		

The completed *F* table for Study 1 and Study 2 using a one-way between-subjects ANOVA. Both studies will result in the same *F* table because the individual scores and the group means are the same for each group. Values for within-groups error are given in bold.

If we assume that these results reflect a true effect in the population, then the **observed power** of each study is .72. We expect 72% of the samples we select to detect this effect and show a significant result using the between-subjects design. How does this power compare to the power of the within-subjects design? We will answer this question here.

Within-subjects design (high consistency): If we observed the same subjects in each group, then each study would be a within-subjects design, and we would compute a one-way within-subjects ANOVA. For both studies, the variance attributed to having different groups is the same because the group means are the same. The variance in the numerator, then, will be the same for both studies. However, the value of each measure of error variation (between persons and within groups) will depend on the consistency of subject responses in each group.

Be aware that there is some criticism for estimating power this way (for a detailed review, see Hoenig & Heisey, 2001).

Consistency refers to the extent to which the dependent variable (number of lever presses in this example) changes in an identifiable or predictable pattern across groups. Let us look at Study 1. Table 11.19 shows that responses in Study 1 always increased as the reward increased. Subject A increased from 2 to 3 to 4; Subject D from 0 to 2 to 4. There is high consistency in subject responses across groups. When changes in the dependent variable

FYI

The within-subjects design is more powerful than the between-subjects design when changes in the dependent variable are consistent across groups.

Observed power is a type of post hoc or retrospective power analysis that is used to estimate the likelihood of detecting a population effect, assuming that the observed results in a study reflect a true effect in the population.

are consistent across groups, most of the error variation is attributed to the between-persons source of variation, as shown in Figure 11.13. Table 11.21 shows that the one-way within-subjects ANOVA for Study 1 will result in a very large value of the test statistic. The decision in Study 1 is to reject the null hypothesis; the variance between groups is significant.

If we assume that the decision for Study 1 reflects a true effect in the population, then the observed power of this study is .99. The power increased compared to an analysis using the between-subjects design. We now expect 99% of the samples we select to detect this effect and show a significant result. The within-subjects design is more powerful than the between-subjects design when changes in the dependent variable are consistent across groups.

FIGURE 11.13   Error Variation for Study 1 Using a Within-Subjects Design

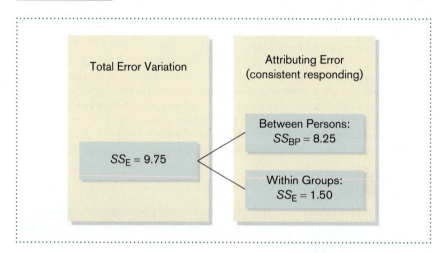

When there is consistent responding, most of the error variation is attributed to the between-persons source of variation.

TABLE 11.21   Within-Subjects Design (high consistency)

Source of Variation	SS	df	MS	F_{obt}
Between groups	12.50	2	6.25	25.00*
Between persons	8.25	3	2.75	
Within groups (error)	**1.50**	**6**	**0.25**	
Total	22.25	11		

The completed *F* table for Study 1 using a one-way within-subjects ANOVA. Notice that *SS* within groups is small because most of the variation attributed to error was attributed to between-persons variation. Values for within-groups error are given in bold.

Within-subjects design (low consistency): Suppose we also compute the one-way within-subjects ANOVA for Study 2. In Study 2, changes in the dependent variable are not consistent. For example, referring to Table 11.19, Subject D increased from 0 to 2 to 5, but Subject B showed no change. Because the group means are the same as those in Study 1, the numerator will be the same. However, when changes in the dependent variable are not consistent across groups, most of the error variation is attributed to the within-groups source of error (see Figure 11.14). Table 11.22 shows that the one-way within-subjects ANOVA for Study 2 will result in a much smaller value of the test statistic compared to the test statistic we computed in Study 1. The decision in Study 2 is to retain the null hypothesis; the variance between groups is not significant.

If we assume that the decision in Study 2 reflects a true effect in the population, then the observed power of this study is .51. We now expect only 51% of our samples to detect this effect and show a significant result. The test for Study 2 is now less powerful than the one-way between-subjects ANOVA we first computed. Hence, when changes in the dependent variable across groups are not consistent, the within-subjects design can actually be less powerful than the between-subjects design.

The power of a within-subjects design depends on the consistency of changes in the dependent variable because both the sum of squares and the degrees of freedom for error are reduced. Unless we remove a large amount of variation from the within-groups error term, we could actually end up with a larger mean square error in the denominator, making the within-subjects design less powerful than the between-subjects design. In all, we can state the following rules for the power of the one-way within-subjects ANOVA:

1. As SS_{BP} increases, power increases.
2. As SS_E decreases, power increases.
3. As MS_E decreases, power increases.

FIGURE 11.14   Error Variation for Study 2 Using a Within-Subjects Design

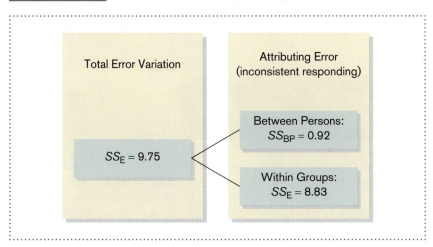

When there is inconsistent responding, most of the error variation is attributed to the within-groups or error source of variation.

TABLE 11.22   Within-Subjects Design (low consistency)

Source of Variation	SS	df	MS	F_{obt}
Between groups	12.50	2	6.25	4.25
Between persons	0.92	3	0.31	
Within groups (error)	**8.83**	**6**	**1.47**	
Total	22.25	11		

The completed *F* table for Study 2 using a one-way within-subjects ANOVA. Notice that the *SS* within groups is larger because most of the variation attributed to error was attributed to this source of variation. Values for within-groups error are given in bold.

LEARNING CHECK 7

1. The following table lists data from a hypothetical study measuring the time (in seconds) it takes participants to complete each of three tasks (easy, moderate, difficult).

Easy	Moderate	Difficult
9	14	15
7	9	17
10	12	16
6	8	9
7	8	13

(a) Are changes in the dependent variable consistent? Explain.

(b) Is this within-subjects design associated with high power? Explain.

2. What are three rules for increasing the power of a one-way within-subjects ANOVA?

Answers: 1. (a) Yes. The dependent variable increases for each participant across groups. (b) Yes, because changes in the dependent variable are consistent. This will increase the value of the test statistic, thereby increasing power; 2. To increase power, increase SS_{BP}, and decrease SS_E, and MS_E.

11.11 # APA IN FOCUS: REPORTING THE RESULTS OF THE ONE-WAY ANOVAS

To summarize the results of a one-way ANOVA test, we report the test statistic, the degrees of freedom, and the p value. We also report the effect size for significant analyses. We can summarize the means, standard error, or standard deviations measured in a study in a figure or a table or in the main text of the article. To report the results of a post hoc test, identify which post hoc test you computed and the p value for significant results. An example for reporting these values for between-subjects and within-subjects designs has been shown at the end of each analysis in this chapter. Typically, the group means and standard error for a study are also given in a table or graph.

• • • CHAPTER SUMMARY ORGANIZED BY LEARNING OBJECTIVE

LO 1: Identify the analysis of variance test and when it is used for tests of a single factor.

- An analysis of variance (ANOVA) is a statistical procedure used to test hypotheses for one or more factors concerning the variance among two or more group means, where the variance in one or more populations is unknown. The one-way ANOVA test can be computed for one factor in which the same (within-subjects) or different (between-subjects) participants are observed at each level, or in each group.

LO 2: **Identify each source of variation in a one-way between-subjects ANOVA and a one-way within-subjects ANOVA.**

- A source of variation is any variation that can be measured in a study. In the one-way between-subjects ANOVA, there are two sources of variation: variation attributed to differences between group means (between-groups variation) and variation attributed to error (within-groups variation).

- For the within-subjects design, there is one additional source of variation that is attributed to observing the same participants in each group (between-persons variation). This source of error variation is removed before computing the test statistic for a one-way within-subjects ANOVA.

LO 3: **Calculate the degrees of freedom and locate critical values for a one-way between-subjects ANOVA and a one-way within-subjects ANOVA.**

- The degrees of freedom for a one-way between-subjects ANOVA are the degrees of freedom between groups ($df_{BG} = k - 1$) and the degrees of freedom within groups or degrees of freedom error ($df_E = N - k$).

- The degrees of freedom for a one-way within-subjects ANOVA are the degrees of freedom between groups ($df_{BG} = k - 1$), the degrees of freedom between persons ($df_{BP} = n - 1$), and the degrees of freedom error [$df_E = (k - 1)(n - 1)$].

- To locate the critical values for an ANOVA, use the F table in Table C.3 in Appendix C. To use the table, locate the degrees of freedom numerator listed in the columns and then the degrees of freedom denominator listed down the rows. The critical value is the entry found at the intersection of the two degrees of freedom.

LO 4–5: **Identify the assumptions for a one-way between-subjects ANOVA and a one-way within-subjects ANOVA; follow the steps to compute a one-way between-subjects ANOVA and a one-way within-subjects ANOVA, and interpret the results.**

- Four assumptions for the one-way between-subjects ANOVA are normality, random sampling, independence, and homogeneity of variance. Four assumptions for the one-way within-subjects ANOVA are normality, independence within groups, homogeneity of variance, and homogeneity of covariance.

- The test statistic for any one-way ANOVA is $F_{obt} = \dfrac{MS_{BG}}{MS_E}$.

- The general steps for conducting any one-way ANOVA are as follows:

  Step 1: State the hypotheses.

  Step 2: Set the criteria for a decision.

  Step 3: Compute the test statistic.

  Stage 1: Preliminary calculations.

  Stage 2: Intermediate calculations.

  Stage 3: Computing the SS for each source of variation.

  Stage 4: Completing the F table.

  Step 4: Make a decision.

LO 6: **Compute and interpret Tukey's HSD post hoc test and identify the most powerful post hoc test alternatives.**

- A post hoc test is a statistical procedure computed following a significant ANOVA to determine which pair or pairs of group means significantly differ. These tests are necessary when $k > 2$ because multiple comparisons are needed. When $k = 2$, the two means must significantly differ; this is the only comparison.

- To compute Tukey's HSD post hoc test, follow three steps:

  Step 1: Compute the test statistic for each pairwise comparison.

Step 2: Compute the critical value for each pairwise comparison.

Step 3: Make a decision to retain or reject the null hypothesis for each pairwise comparison.

- Post hoc tests all control for experimentwise alpha. Post hoc tests are given from most to least powerful in Figure 11.6.

LO 7:   Compute and interpret proportion of variance for the one-way between-subjects ANOVA and the one-way within-subjects ANOVA.

- Proportion of variance estimates how much of the variability in the dependent variable can be accounted for by the levels of the factor. Two measures of proportion of variance for the between-subjects design are eta-squared (η^2 or R^2) and omega-squared (ω^2).

- Two measures of proportion of variance using the within-subjects design are partial eta-squared (η_P^2) and partial omega-squared (ω_P^2). To compute each measure, we partial out the between-persons variation before computing effect size.

LO 8:   Delineate the power of between-subjects and within-subjects designs for the one-way ANOVAs.

- Consistency refers to the extent to which the dependent measure changes in an identifiable or predictable pattern across groups. As consistency increases, the power to detect an effect also increases. Increased consistency increases the value of SS_{BP} and decreases the value of SS_E and MS_E.

LO 9:   Summarize the results of the one-way between-subjects ANOVA and the one-way within-subjects ANOVA in APA format.

- To summarize a one-way ANOVA test, we report the test statistic, degrees of freedom, and *p* value. You should also report the effect size for significant analyses. The means and standard error or standard deviations measured in a study can be summarized in a figure or table or in the main text. To report the results of a post hoc test, you must identify which post hoc test you computed and the *p* value for significant results.

LO 10:   Compute and select an appropriate post hoc test for a one-way between-subjects ANOVA and a one-way within-subjects ANOVA using SPSS.

- To compute the one-way between-subjects ANOVA using the One-Way ANOVA command in SPSS, select the Analyze, Compare Means, and One-Way ANOVA options in the menu bar. These actions will display a dialog box that allows you to identify the variables, choose an appropriate post hoc test, and run the analysis (for more details, see Section 11.5).

- SPSS can be used to compute the one-way within-subjects ANOVA using the Analyze, General Linear Model, and Repeated Measures options in the menu bar. These actions will display a dialog box that allows you to identify the variables, choose an appropriate post hoc test, and run the analysis (for more details, see Section 11.9).

• • • KEY TERMS

analysis of variance (ANOVA)
between groups variation
between-persons variation

degrees of freedom between groups
degrees of freedom between persons

degrees of freedom denominator
degrees of freedom error
degrees of freedom numerator
degrees of freedom within groups

experimentwise alpha	observed power	studentized range statistic (q)
F distribution	one-way between-subjects	sum of squares between groups
F obtained	ANOVA	sum of squares between persons
F statistic	one-way repeated-measures	sum of squares error
levels of the factor	ANOVA	sum of squares total
mean square between groups	one-way within-subjects ANOVA	sum of squares within groups
mean square between persons	pairwise comparison	testwise alpha
mean square error	post hoc test	within-groups variation
mean square within groups	source of variation	

• • • END-OF-CHAPTER PROBLEMS

Factual Problems

1. Explain the meaning of the following terms for an ANOVA: (a) *one-way*, (b) *between-subjects*, (c) *within-subjects.*

2. A researcher conducts two studies. Study 1 uses a one-way between-subjects ANOVA, and Study 2 uses a within-subjects ANOVA. If the number of groups and participants per group are the same in each study, then in which study was the total number of participants larger? Explain.

3. A researcher conducts a one-way ANOVA in which one independent variable has four levels.

    (a) How many different groups are in this study?

    (b) How many different factors are in this study?

4. Name two sources of variation in the one-way between-subjects ANOVA.

5. State in words the null hypothesis for a one-way ANOVA.

6. Define the following terms:

    (a) Sum of squares between groups

    (b) Sum of squares error

    (c) Mean square between groups

    (d) Mean square error

7. A mean square is the same as what type of descriptive statistic?

8. A researcher rejects the null hypothesis for a one-way between-subjects ANOVA, where $k = 4$. What is the next step in the analysis?

9. Define experimentwise alpha. What type of test controls for experimentwise alpha?

10. A within-subjects ANOVA is computed when the same or different participants are observed in each group?

11. What type of effect size measure is used for (a) a one-way between-subjects ANOVA and (b) a one-way within-subjects ANOVA?

12. Which effect size measure, eta-squared or omega-squared, is a more conservative estimate of effect size?

Concept and Application Problems

13. State the degrees of freedom error in each of the following between-subjects tests.

    (a) A researcher tests how nervous public speakers get in front of a small, medium, or large audience. Ten participants are randomly assigned to each group.

    (b) A high school counselor has 12 students in each of four classes rate how much they like their teacher.

    (c) A consultant measures job satisfaction in a sample of 15 supervisors, 15 managers, and 15 executives at a local firm.

14. State whether the following situations describe a between-subjects design or a within-subjects design.

    (a) A biopsychologist tests the time course for the release of a neurohormone before, during, and following a task thought to cause its release.

    (b) A sport psychologist compares mental functioning in a sample of athletes in four different sports.

    (c) A college professor compares the average class grade for students in each of three sections of a statistics course.

    (d) A behavioral psychologist allows a sample of children to play with four toys of various colors and has them rate how much they like playing with each toy. The psychologist compares mean ratings for each toy.

15. What is the decision at a .05 level of significance for each of the following tests? *Hint:* Find the critical value for each test; then make a decision.

    (a) $F(3, 26) = 3.00$
    (b) $F(5, 20) = 2.54$
    (c) $F(4, 30) = 2.72$
    (d) $F(2, 12) = 3.81$

16. State whether a post hoc test is necessary for each of the following results. Explain your answer for each result.

    (a) $F(1, 18) = 6.29, p < .05$
    (b) $F(4, 55) = 3.98, p < .05$
    (c) $F(2, 33) = 2.03, p > .05$

17. A researcher records the following data for each of four groups. Can an F statistic be computed for these data? Explain your answer.

Group A	Group B	Group C	Group D
3	8	2	5
3	8	2	5
3	8	2	5
3	8	2	5

18. A researcher records the following data for each of three groups. What is the value of the F statistic? Explain your answer.

Group A	Group B	Group C
8	9	12
4	6	0
7	1	12
5	8	0

19. The following is an incomplete F table summarizing the results of a study of the variance of life satisfaction scores among unemployed, retired, part-time, and full-time employees.

Source of Variation	SS	df	MS	F
Between groups			16	
Within groups (error)		36		
Total	128			

    (a) Complete the F table and make a decision to retain or reject the null hypothesis.

    (b) Compute omega-squared (ω^2).

    (c) Is the decision to retain or reject the null hypothesis?

20. The following is an incomplete F table summarizing the results of a study of the variance of reaction times during a training exercise in a sample of 14 ($n = 14$) highly experienced, moderately experienced, and inexperienced athletes.

Source of Variation	SS	df	MS	F
Between groups				
Within groups (error)	50			
Total	80			

    (a) Complete the F table for this between-subjects design.

    (b) Compute eta-squared (η^2).

    (c) Is the decision to retain or reject the null hypothesis?

21. To test whether animal subjects consume the same amounts of sweet-tasting solutions, a researcher has 10 subjects consume one of three sweet-tasting solutions: sucrose, saccharin, or Polycose. The amount consumed (in milliliters) of each solution is given in the table for this between-subjects design.

Type of Sweet-Tasting Solution		
Sucrose	Saccharin	Polycose
12	6	12
10	7	9
9	9	10
8	8	13
10	4	11
6	6	9
8	11	6
7	8	8
11	10	10
10	7	11

(a) Complete the F table and make a decision to retain or reject the null hypothesis.

(b) Compute Tukey's HSD post hoc test and interpret the results.

22. Iconic memory is a type of memory that holds visual information for about half a second (0.5 second). To demonstrate this type of memory, participants were shown three rows of four letters for 50 milliseconds. They were then asked to recall as many letters as possible, with a 0-, 0.5-, or 1.0-second delay before responding. Researchers hypothesized that longer delays would result in poorer recall. The number of letters correctly recalled is given in the table for this between-subjects design.

(a) Complete the F table and make a decision to retain or reject the null hypothesis.

(b) Compute Tukey's HSD post hoc test and interpret the results.

Delay Before Recall		
0	0.5	1.0
12	8	4
11	4	4
6	10	2
10	6	5
8	3	7
7	5	2

23. To test whether arousal or stress levels increase as the difficulty of a task increases, eight participants were asked to complete an easy, typical, or difficult task. Their galvanic skin response (GSR) was recorded. A GSR measures the electrical signals of the skin in units called microSiemens (μS), with higher signals indicating greater arousal or stress. The data for each task are given in the table for this between-subjects design.

Difficulty of Task		
Easy	Typical	Difficult
2.6	5.6	9.0
3.9	4.5	5.6
3.4	3.7	3.5
1.2	2.0	7.8
2.1	3.3	6.4
1.2	4.6	7.5
1.8	3.1	4.4
2.2	2.0	3.8

(a) Complete the F table and make a decision to retain or reject the null hypothesis.

(b) Compute Tukey's HSD post hoc test and interpret the results.

24. A researcher is interested in how perceptions of climate change influence consumer spending. He selects a sample of 10 environmentalists with strong perceptions of climate change

and has them report how much they spend on a variety of "typical" items. These items were categorized as detrimental, safe, or helpful to the environment. The following is an incomplete F table for this hypothetical study using the one-way within-subjects ANOVA.

Source of Variation	SS	df	MS	F_{obt}
Between groups			198	
Between persons	234			
Within groups (error)				
Total	1,278	29		

(a) Complete the F table and make a decision to retain or reject the null hypothesis.

(b) Compute effect size using partial eta-squared: η_P^2.

25. A child psychologist treated four children who were afraid of snakes with a behavioral modification procedure called systematic desensitization. In this procedure, children were slowly introduced to a snake over four treatment sessions. Children rated how fearful they were of the snake before the first session (baseline) and following each treatment session. Higher ratings indicated greater fear. The hypothetical data are listed in the table. Complete the F table for this within-subjects design and make a decision to retain or reject the null hypothesis.

Baseline	Sessions			
	1	2	3	4
7	7	5	4	3
7	6	6	4	4
6	6	7	7	3
7	7	5	4	3

26. In a study on attention and performance of memory tasks, six participants attended a 1-hour lecture on a topic chosen at random. Following this lecture, they received a survey testing their knowledge of the topics covered. After each 15-minute interval of the lecture, participants were asked 10 questions concerning facts covered. The table lists the number of incorrect answers recorded in each interval in this hypothetical study. Complete the F table for this within-subjects design and make a decision to retain or reject the null hypothesis.

15-Minute Intervals			
First	Second	Third	Last
1	5	4	0
0	4	3	2
2	7	7	1
2	5	4	2
3	3	7	1
0	4	5	1

Problems in Research

27. **The "ways" that participants are observed.** Rouder, Morey, Verhagen, Swagman, and Wagenmakers (2016) evaluated the nature of various ANOVA designs. In their analysis, they stated,

> If a factor is manipulated in a [A] manner, then each participant observes one level of the factor. Conversely, if a factor is manipulated in a [B] manner, then

each participant observes all levels of the factor. (Rouder et al., 2016, p. 9)

Fill in the blank for [A] and [B] using the following two choices: between-subjects; within-subjects.

28. **The assumptions of an ANOVA test.** In an article that explored alternatives for the one-way between-subjects ANOVA, Cribbie, Fiksenbaum, Keselman, and Wilcox (2012)

explained that "the ANOVA can be a valid and powerful test for identifying treatment effects; but, when the assumptions underlying the test are violated, the results from the test are typically unreliable and invalid" (p. 57). What four assumptions for the one-way between-subjects ANOVA are the authors referring to?

29. **Power and the within-subjects design.** In an article applying models that use repeated measures, Thomas and Zumbo (2012) identified that the within-subjects ANOVA "can have . . . high power" (p. 42). As also identified in this chapter for the one-way within-subjects ANOVA, state the three rules for identifying when the within-subjects design is likely to be a more powerful test than a between-subjects design.

30. **Estimating effect size.** Peng and Chen (2014) evaluated effect size estimates for various tests. In their paper, they stated that "The [two] popular effect size indices were found to be . . . Cohen's d, and η^2" (p. 43). Which effect size measure is reported with an ANOVA?

31. **Computer anxiety and usage frequency.** Using a rating scale, Tekinarslan (2008) measured computer anxiety among university students who use the computer very often, often, sometimes, and seldom. Below are the results of the one-way between-subjects ANOVA.

(a) What is the total sample size (N) and number of groups observed (k)?

(b) Was the sample size per group equal in all groups? Explain.

Source of Variation	SS	df	MS	F
Between groups	1,959.79	3	653.26	21.16*
Within groups (error)	3,148.61	102	30.86	
Total	5,108.41	105		

32. **Social comparisons and prosocial behavior.** To check that a manipulation of social comparison made in the study was effective, Yip and Kelly (2013) computed a one-way between-subjects ANOVA and reported the following result for one such check: $F(2, 120) = 6.42$. Based on the information given, answer the following questions.

(a) How many groups were compared in this test?

(b) How many participants were observed in this study?

(c) Was the outcome of this test significant at a .05 level of significance?

Answers for even numbers are in Appendix D.

Sharpen your skills with **SAGE edge** at edge.sagepub.com/priviteraess2e

SAGE edge for Students provides a personalized approach to help you accomplish your coursework goals in an easy-to-use learning environment.

$SAGE edge™

12 Two-Way Analysis of Variance
Between-Subjects Factorial Design

©iStockphoto.com/vvmich

• • • **Learning Objectives**

After reading this chapter, you should be able to:

1. Describe how the complexity of the two-way ANOVA differs from that of the *t* tests and one-way ANOVAs.

2. Define and explain the following terms: *cell*, *main effect*, and *interaction*.

3. Identify the assumptions and list the order of interpretation for outcomes in the two-way between-subjects ANOVA.

4. Calculate the degrees of freedom for the two-way between-subjects ANOVA and locate critical values in the *F* table.

5. Compute the two-way between-subjects ANOVA and interpret the results.

6. Identify when it is appropriate to compute simple main effect tests and analyze a significant interaction.

7. Compute and interpret proportion of variance for the two-way between-subjects ANOVA.

8. Summarize the results of the two-way between-subjects ANOVA in APA format.

9. Compute the two-way between-subjects ANOVA using SPSS.

In nature, rarely is one isolated factor causing changes in a dependent variable, and this is especially true in the behavioral sciences. Many types of comparisons would therefore reveal more about the nature of behavior if we made observations across the levels of two or more factors. Consider, for example, the emotions we feel (e.g., happiness, love), the nature of our development (e.g., taste preferences, personality), and how we perform on the job (e.g., motivation, leadership styles). Is it reasonable to assume that one factor in nature causes us to feel, develop, and work in a certain way? No, of course not. Naturally, we can imagine many possible "causes" that can impact how we feel, develop, and work—from genetic and biological to environmental.

In hypothesis testing, there are often cases where making observations across the levels of two or more factors can be quite informative. In the basic structure of such a study, two factors are combined, and the combination of the levels of those two factors creates the groups. For example, we may look at how viewing images of "comfort" foods impacts mood. We can show images of foods that are high or low in fat and high or low in sugar. Here, we have two factors (fat, sugar), each with two levels (high, low). The combination of those levels creates the groups. We can observe the same or different participants across the combination of levels of each factor. As usual, we measure the same dependent variable in each group; in our example, the dependent variable would be mood. The null hypothesis for such a test would be that group means do not vary; the alternative hypothesis would state that the group means do vary.

In this chapter, we explore the nature of hypothesis testing when observations are made across the levels of two or more factors, how to compute and interpret observed effects, and the informativeness of hypothesis testing for making such comparisons. We further explore other ways of adding information about the nature of observed effects and how to appropriately interpret them.

Master the content.

edge.sagepub.com/priviteraess2e

● ● ● Chapter Outline

12.1 INTRODUCTION TO FACTORIAL DESIGNS

To this point, the complexity of statistical design has varied in two ways:

1. We changed the levels of one factor. In Chapters 8, 9, and 10, we described tests for differences within one group and between two groups or levels of one factor. In Chapter 11, we described tests for the variance of more than two groups or levels of one factor.

2. We changed how participants were observed. In Chapters 9 and 11, we described tests in which different participants were observed in each group or at each level of one factor (between-subjects design; defined in Chapter 9). In Chapters 10 and 11, we described tests in which the same participants were observed in each group or across the levels of one factor (within-subjects design; defined in Chapter 10).

In each statistical design, we included the levels of a single factor. In this chapter, we describe a new way to change the complexity of a design—we add a second factor that will be observed in the same study. Adding a second factor is particularly useful because many factors likely contribute to the behaviors we observe, similar to how multiple ingredients contribute to the foods we eat, as abstractly illustrated in the chapter title image. In behavioral science, there are two common reasons we observe two factors in a single study.

First, a hypothesis may require that we observe two factors. As an example of one such hypothesis from an area of research studying the value and usefulness of books in the classroom (Bell & Limber, 2010; Silvers & Kreiner, 1997; Weiten, Halpern, & Bernstein, 2012), suppose we state that the higher the difficulty level of a book, the less students will comprehend when there is highlighting in the book. This hypothesis identifies two factors: the presence of highlighting (yes, no) and book difficulty (easy, difficult). To test this hypothesis, then, we must observe the levels of both factors at the same time. The structure of this design is illustrated in Table 12.1. If we measure comprehension as a test score, then on the basis of our hypothesis, we expect scores to be lowest in the group with a difficult book that has highlighting in it.

Second, adding a second factor allows us to control or account for threats to validity. Broadly defined, *validity* is the extent to which we demonstrate the effect we claim to be demonstrating. For example, suppose we state the hypothesis that the more positive a teacher is with his or her students, the more students will like their teacher. To test this hypothesis, we could randomly assign a sample of teachers to interact positively or negatively with students in a classroom setting, then have students rate how much they like the teacher.

One possible threat to the validity of our hypothesis or claim is the subject being taught. Maybe ratings reflect the subject taught and not the teacher interaction. We could account for this possibility by adding the subject taught as a factor in the study. Suppose we tested this hypothesis using a sample that consisted of biology and psychology teachers. As illustrated

TABLE 12.1   The Structure of a Study That Combines the Levels of Two Factors

		Highlighting	
		No	**Yes**
Book Difficulty	**Easy**	Group Easy, No	Group Easy, Yes
	Difficult	Group Difficult, No	Group Difficult, Yes

If the hypothesis is correct, then we expect this group to have the lowest test scores.

On the basis of the hypothesis, we expect that participants reading the difficult book with highlighting in it (Group Difficult, Yes) will have the lowest scores.

in Table 12.2, we can include the subject taught as a second factor. On the basis of our hypothesis, we expect the type of teacher interaction (positive, negative) and not the subject taught (biology, psychology) to be associated with differences in ratings. We included the subject taught as a factor only to account for it as a possible threat to the validity of our claim.

TABLE 12.2   The Structure of a Study That Combines the Levels of Two Factors

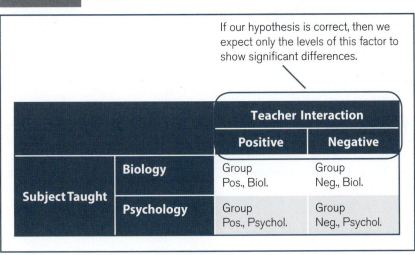

If our hypothesis is correct, then we expect only the levels of this factor to show significant differences.

		Teacher Interaction	
		Positive	**Negative**
Subject Taught	**Biology**	Group Pos., Biol.	Group Neg., Biol.
	Psychology	Group Pos., Psychol.	Group Neg., Psychol.

On the basis of the hypothesis, we expect the type of interaction (positive, negative) and not the subject taught (biology, psychology) to be associated with differences in ratings.

12.2 STRUCTURE AND NOTATION FOR THE TWO-WAY ANOVA

The research design for a study in which the levels of two or more factors are combined is called a **factorial design**. In a factorial design with

FYI

When the levels of two factors are combined, we use the two-way ANOVA to analyze the data.

The **factorial design** is a research design in which participants are observed across the combination of levels of two or more factors.

two factors, we use the **two-way ANOVA** to analyze the data, and this also leads to new terminology. The new terminology and notation for the two-way ANOVA are described in this section.

In a two-way ANOVA, each factor is identified with a letter in alphabetical order: Factor A, then Factor B. Separating the factors with a multiplication sign and listing only the letters can simplify this notation. For example, we can state a two-way ANOVA as an A × B ANOVA. The multiplication sign represents a "by" statement; we read this test as an "A by B" ANOVA.

More common is to identify the levels of each factor numerically. For example, if we measure how quickly (in seconds) subjects respond to a stimulus that varies in size (small, medium, large) and color (bright, dark), we might designate Factor A as size and Factor B as color. Factor A has three levels (small, medium, large), and Factor B has two levels (bright, dark). Using the levels of each factor, we can state this test as a 3 × 2 (read "3 by 2") ANOVA. Each number represents the levels of each factor. Table 12.3 shows the structure of this hypothetical study with two factors.

TABLE 12.3   The Structure of a Hypothetical Study With Two Factors

		Factor A (Size)		
		1 (Small)	2 (Medium)	3 (Large)
Factor B (Color)	1 (Light)	A_1B_1	A_2B_1	A_3B_1
	2 (Dark)	A_1B_2	A_2B_2	A_3B_2

Each cell is a combination of levels of each factor. For example, the combination of Factor A Level 2 (medium) with Factor B Level 1 (light) is A_2B_1.

The **two-way ANOVA** is a statistical procedure used to test hypotheses concerning the variance of groups created by combining the levels of two factors. This test is used when the variance in any one population is unknown.

A **cell** is the combination of one level from each factor, as represented in a cross tabulation. Each cell is a group in a research study.

A **complete factorial design** is a research design in which each level of one factor is combined or crossed with each level of the other factor, with participants observed in each cell or combination of levels.

We often arrange the data for a two-way ANOVA in a table, and when we do, there is special notation to indicate each entry. The levels of Factor A are symbolized as p, and the levels of Factor B are symbolized as q. The combination of one level from each factor is represented in the table as a **cell**. To calculate the number of cells in a two-way ANOVA, we multiply the levels of each factor:

$$\text{Total number of cells} = pq.$$

The number of cells is the number of groups in a study. In other words, each combination of one level from each factor creates a new group. In the example for a 3 × 2 ANOVA shown in Table 12.3, the number of cells is $pq = 3 \times 2 = 6$; there are six groups in this study. In this chapter, we introduce only **complete factorial designs**, where each level of each factor is combined. For example, if subjects were not observed in each cell shown in Table 12.3, then the ANOVA would not be a complete factorial design. In this book, we do not cover situations in which some cells are empty. These situations require statistical procedures beyond the scope of this book.

For a factorial design with two factors in which we use a two-way ANOVA to analyze the data, we can observe the same or different participants in each group or cell. When different participants are observed at each level of one factor, we call the factor a **between-subjects factor**. When the same participants are observed across the levels of one factor, we call the factor a **within-subjects factor**. In this chapter, we evaluate a two-way ANOVA when both factors are between-subjects factors.

FYI

Each cell is a group created by the unique combination of one level from each factor. Hence, the total number of cells (pq) is equal to the total number of groups in a study.

LEARNING CHECK 1

1. State two reasons that we observe two factors in a single study.

2. A researcher measures stress in a group of participants who travel different distances to work (none, short commute, long commute) from different demographic areas (urban, rural). In this example:

    (a) State the number of factors.

    (b) State the number of levels of each factor.

Answers: 1. The hypothesis requires the observation of two factors, and to control or account for threats to validity; 2. (a) Two (distance of commute and demographic area), (b) Three (distance of commute) and two (demographic area).

12.3 DESCRIBING VARIABILITY: MAIN EFFECTS AND INTERACTIONS

In this chapter, we introduce an analysis of variance using the 2-between or between-subjects factorial design called the **two-way between-subjects ANOVA**. When we combine the levels of two factors in which different participants are observed in each cell, four sources of variation can be measured: One source is error variation, and three sources are between-groups variation, which is variation associated with having different groups. We will conduct a hypothesis test for each between-groups variation. With a one-way ANOVA, we only have one source of between-groups variation, so we conduct only one hypothesis test. For the two-way between-subjects ANOVA, we have three sources of between-groups variation, so we will conduct three hypothesis tests. Each source of variation, the *F* statistic for each, and each hypothesis test are introduced in this section.

Sources of Variability

Figure 12.1 identifies four sources of variation that arise when we combine the levels of two factors and observe different participants in each cell or combination of levels. One source of variation is associated with differences attributed to error, which is variation that has nothing to do with differences associated with having different groups. The other three sources of variation are associated with differences between group means for each factor and for the combination of levels of each factor. Each source

A **between-subjects factor** is a type of factor in which different participants are observed at each level of the factor.

A **within-subjects factor** is a type of factor in which the same participants are observed across the levels of the factor.

The **two-way between-subjects ANOVA** is a statistical procedure used to test hypotheses concerning the combination of levels of two factors using the 2-between or between-subjects design.

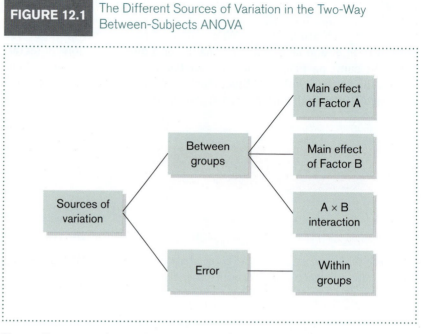

FIGURE 12.1   The Different Sources of Variation in the Two-Way Between-Subjects ANOVA

There are three sources of variation between groups and one source of error (within groups).

of variation for the two-way between-subjects ANOVA is described in this section.

One source of variation is associated with differences in participant scores within each group (located in the cells of a table summary). This variation, called *within-groups variation*, is also called *error* because it cannot be attributed to differences between group means. This is the same error variation measured for the *t* tests and one-way ANOVAs. Table 12.4 shows that this source of variation is located in the cells of a table summary for a 2 × 2 between-subjects ANOVA with $n = 5$ participants in each group. Because participants in each cell experience the same treatment, differences in participant scores in each cell or group cannot be attributed to differences between group means. As it is for the *t* tests and one-way ANOVAs, this source of error is placed in the denominator of the test statistic. The test statistic for the two-way between-subjects ANOVA follows the same general form used for the one-way ANOVAs:

$$F_{obt} = \frac{\text{variance between groups}}{\text{error variance}}.$$

Three between-groups sources of variation, or three ways that group means can be compared, are also shown in Table 12.4. Each set of group means is a source of variation that can be measured. We can measure the variation of group means across the levels of Factor A (the column means in Table 12.4) and across the levels of Factor B (the row means in

Table 12.4). These sources of variation are called **main effects**, and each is a source of between-groups variation:

1. Main effect of Factor A

2. Main effect of Factor B

Notice also that we can compute the mean at each combination of levels for each factor or in each cell. The third between-groups variation is associated with the variance of group means in each cell (the cell means in Table 12.4). This source of variation is called an **interaction**, and this is the third source of between-groups variation:

3. The interaction of Factors A and B, called the A × B interaction

In an analysis of variance, we want to decide whether group means significantly vary. In the two-way between-subjects ANOVA, there are three ways that the group means can vary (in the rows, columns, and cells). Therefore, we must compute three hypothesis tests: one for each source of between-groups variation. We make two main effect tests (one for Factor A and one for Factor B) and one interaction test (one for the combination of levels for Factors A and B). The within-groups (or error) variation is the denominator for each test. The test statistic for each test is described here.

Testing Main Effects

The hypothesis test for each main effect (one for Factor A and one for Factor B) determines whether group means significantly vary across the levels of a single factor. In a table summary, such as that given in Table 12.4, we compare the variance of row and column means. To compute the test statistic for a main effect, we place the between-groups variance of one factor in the numerator and the error variance in the denominator. We again measure the variance as a mean square (MS), same as we did for the one-way ANOVAs. The test statistic for the main effect of Factor A is

$$F_A = \frac{\text{variance of group means for Factor A}}{\text{variance attributed to error}} = \frac{MS_A}{MS_E}$$

The test statistic for the main effect of Factor B is

$$F_B = \frac{\text{variance of group means for Factor B}}{\text{variance attributed to error}} = \frac{MS_B}{MS_E}$$

A significant main effect indicates that group means significantly vary across the levels of one factor, independent of the second factor. To illustrate, suppose the data in Table 12.4 are quiz scores, where Factor A is whether students studied for a quiz (no, yes) and Factor B is their class attendance (high, low). Table 12.5 identifies each main effect and shows how each would be interpreted, if significant. Notice that we interpret a

FYI

There are four sources of variation in a two-way between-subjects ANOVA: two main effects, one interaction, and error (within groups).

A **main effect** is a source of variation associated with mean differences across the levels of a single factor. In the two-way ANOVA, there are two factors and therefore two main effects: one for Factor A and one for Factor B.

An **interaction** is a source of variation associated with the variance of group means across the combination of levels of two factors. It is a measure of how cell means at each level of one factor change across the levels of a second factor.

TABLE 12.4   A Cross Tabulation Illustrating the Sources of Variability in the Two-Way Between-Subjects ANOVA

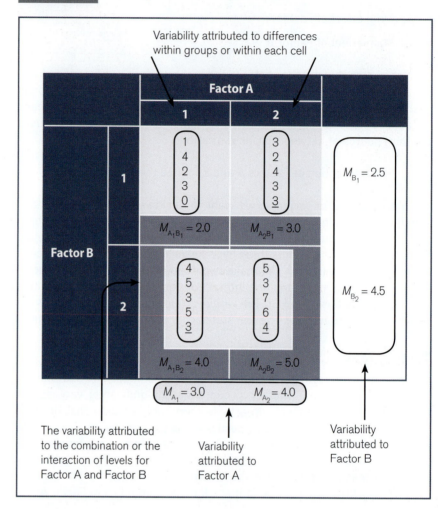

The within-groups (or error) variation is associated with differences in participant scores within each cell, which has nothing to do with differences attributed to having different groups. The other three sources of variation are associated with differences between group means: one for Factor A (main effect), one for Factor B (main effect), and one for the combination of levels for Factors A and B (interaction).

FYI

A main effect reflects differences between row and column means in a table summary.

significant main effect similar to the interpretation of significant results using the one-way ANOVA.

Testing the Interaction

The hypothesis test for the combination of levels of two factors is called an A × B interaction test, where each letter refers to one factor (A or B). The interaction test determines whether group means at each level of one factor significantly change across the levels of a second factor. To put it another way, a significant interaction indicates that differences in group means across the levels of one factor depend on which level of the second

TABLE 12.5 Main Effects

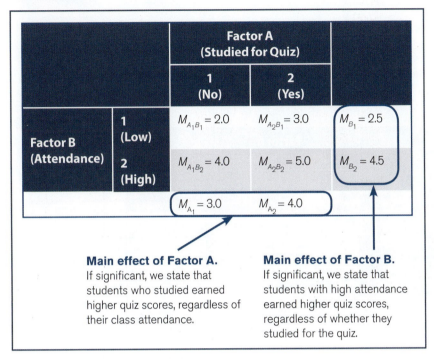

Main effect of Factor A.
If significant, we state that students who studied earned higher quiz scores, regardless of their class attendance.

Main effect of Factor B.
If significant, we state that students with high attendance earned higher quiz scores, regardless of whether they studied for the quiz.

The main effect for each factor reflects the difference between the row and column means in the table. There are two main effects (one for Factor A and one for Factor B) in a two-way ANOVA.

factor you look at. In a table summary, such as that given in Table 12.4, we compare the variance of cell means.

To compute the test statistic for an interaction, we place the between-groups variance for the combination of levels for two factors (the cell means) in the numerator and the error variance in the denominator. We again measure the variance as a mean square (*MS*). The test statistic for the A × B interaction test is

$$F_{A \times B} = \frac{\text{variance of cell means}}{\text{variance attributed to error}} = \frac{MS_{A \times B}}{MS_E}$$

A significant interaction indicates that group means across the levels for one factor significantly vary depending on which level of the second factor you look at. To illustrate this interpretation, let us go back again to the quiz scores study, where Factor A is whether students studied for a quiz (no, yes) and Factor B is class attendance (high, low). Table 12.6 identifies four ways to interpret the A × B interaction. For each interpretation, we look across the levels of one factor at each level of the second factor. Which interpretation we use to describe the interaction depends largely on how we want to describe the data.

The pattern of an interaction can be obvious when it is graphed. To graph an interaction, we plot the cell means for each combination of

TABLE 12.6   Interaction

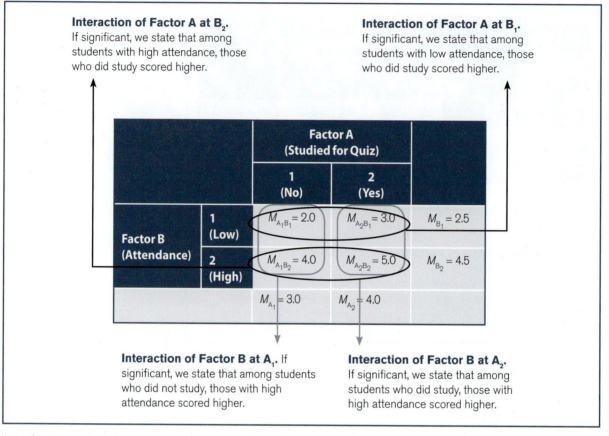

Interaction of Factor A at B₂.
If significant, we state that among students with high attendance, those who did study scored higher.

Interaction of Factor A at B₁.
If significant, we state that among students with low attendance, those who did study scored higher.

Interaction of Factor B at A₁. If significant, we state that among students who did not study, those with high attendance scored higher.

Interaction of Factor B at A₂.
If significant, we state that among students who did study, those with high attendance scored higher.

A significant interaction indicates that group means at each level of one factor significantly change across the levels of a second factor. For the interaction in a two-way ANOVA, we analyze cell or group means inside the table.

factors. Figure 12.2 shows a graph of the cell means for the studying and class attendance example. There are two ways to interpret this graph:

1. When the two lines are parallel, this indicates that a significant interaction is not likely.

2. When the two lines touch or cross, this indicates that there is a possible significant interaction.

The pattern in Figure 12.2 shows that an interaction between class attendance and studying is unlikely. Parallel lines indicate that changes across the levels of both factors are constant. In other words, it does not matter which level of a second factor you look at; the differences between group means will be the same. When the lines are not parallel, this indicates that changes are not constant; thus, changes in group means across

FIGURE 12.2   The Cell Means From the Study in Tables 12.5 and 12.6

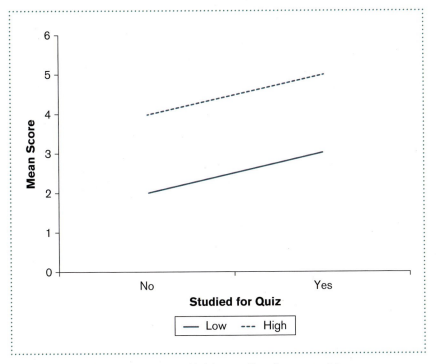

The graph indicates that an interaction is not likely because these lines are parallel.

the levels of one factor vary across the levels of the second factor. We compute the two-way between-subjects ANOVA to determine whether these changes are significant.

MAKING SENSE GRAPHING INTERACTIONS

The pattern of an interaction can appear many ways graphically. Figure 12.3 displays six graphs for two factors, A and B, using hypothetical data. Parallel lines indicate that two factors change in a similar pattern. Graphs (a), (b), and (c) illustrate this parallel pattern. These graphs indicate that an interaction is unlikely to be observed.

On the other hand, Graphs (d), (e), and (f) illustrate patterns where the lines touch or cross. When looking at a graph, imagine that the lines extend beyond the limits of the graph. For example, notice that Graph (f)

has two lines that do not touch or cross. But if the lines continued, they would eventually cross. Hence, Graph (f) is an example of a pattern where the lines touch or cross. When the distance between two lines changes, or is not parallel, this indicates that an interaction is possible. However, keep in mind that data do not always follow simple patterns. The graphical displays of interactions described here can be used as a general rule. It is not possible, however, to know for sure if an interaction is significant until we analyze the data statistically.

FIGURE 12.3 Six Hypothetical Results for Two Factors (A and B)

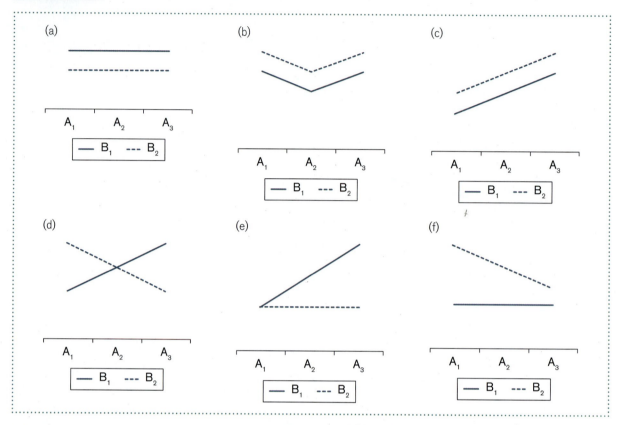

In this example, Factor A has three levels (A_1, A_2, and A_3), and Factor B has two levels (B_1 and B_2) in each graph. Possible interactions are evident in Graphs (d), (e), and (f).

FYI

When two lines are not parallel, meaning that they touch or cross, this indicates that an interaction is possible.

FYI

The interaction reflects differences between cell means in a table summary.

Outcomes and Order of Interpretation

We compute three hypothesis tests using the two-way between-subjects ANOVA, and each hypothesis test is an independent test. Any combination of these three tests could be significant when we compute the two-way between-subjects ANOVA. In all, there are eight possible outcomes we could obtain:

1. All three hypothesis tests are not significant.
2. Significant main effect of Factor A only
3. Significant main effect of Factor B only
4. Significant main effect of Factor A and Factor B
5. Significant A × B interaction only
6. Significant main effect of Factor A and an A × B interaction
7. Significant main effect of Factor B and an A × B interaction
8. All three hypothesis tests are significant.

A significant main effect shows that group means vary across the levels of a single factor. A significant interaction is informative because it indicates that mean differences cannot be readily explained by the levels of a single factor; it indicates that mean differences across the levels of one factor depend on which level of the second factor you look at. Therefore, we analyze a significant interaction before analyzing a significant main effect. Hence, if we obtain Outcomes 6 to 8 from the list above, then we typically examine the interaction first.

LEARNING CHECK 2

1. What are three sources of between-groups variation in the two-way between-subjects ANOVA?

2. What is the denominator for each hypothesis test in the two-way between-subjects ANOVA?

3. What is the pattern in a graph that indicates that a significant interaction is possible?

4. A researcher computes the two-way between-subjects ANOVA, and the results show a significant main effect and a significant interaction. Which significant result should the researcher analyze first?

Answers: 1. Factor A (main effect), Factor B (main effect), and the combination of levels for Factors A and B (A × B interaction); 2. Variance attributed to error or, specifically, mean square error; 3. A pattern where two lines are not parallel; instead, the lines touch or cross; 4. The significant interaction.

12.4 COMPUTING THE TWO-WAY BETWEEN-SUBJECTS ANOVA

In this section, we will compute the two-way between-subjects ANOVA. We use the two-way between-subjects ANOVA when we combine the levels of two factors using the 2-between or between-subjects design. We must make four assumptions to compute the two-way between-subjects ANOVA:

1. *Normality.* We assume that data in the population or populations being sampled from are normally distributed. This assumption is particularly important for small sample sizes. In larger samples, the overall variance is reduced, and this assumption becomes less critical as a result.

2. *Random sampling.* We assume that the data we measure were obtained from a sample that was selected using a random sampling procedure. It is generally considered inappropriate to conduct hypothesis tests with nonrandom samples.

3. *Independence.* We assume that the probabilities of each measured outcome in a study are independent or equal. Using random sampling usually satisfies this assumption.

FYI

A significant interaction is typically analyzed before analyzing significant main effects, if any.

4. *Homogeneity of variance.* We assume that the variance in each population is equal to that in the others. Violating this assumption can increase the likelihood of committing a Type I error (defined in Chapter 7, p. 201).

In Example 12.1, we follow the four steps in hypothesis testing to compute a two-way between-subjects ANOVA.

Example 12.1

The more sugar people consume (increased exposure), the more they tend to like sugary foods (Di Lorenzo & Youngentob, 2013; Mennella & Bobowski, 2015; Privitera, 2016). As an example from this area of research, suppose a researcher hypothesizes that a person's level of sugar exposure can interfere or distract him or her during a computer task when food is present. To test this, the researcher uses the estimated daily intake scale for sugar (EDIS-S; Privitera & Wallace, 2011) to group participants by their level of exposure to sugars (low, moderate, high exposure). All participants then complete a computer task at a table with a buffet of sugary foods (buffet present) or a stack of papers (buffet absent) on the table. Slower times to complete the computer task indicate greater interference or distraction. The times it took participants to complete the computer task in each group are given in Table 12.7. We will compute the two-way between-subjects ANOVA to analyze the significance of these data using a .05 level of significance.

TABLE 12.7   Data for Example 12.1

Buffet of Sugary Foods (Factor B)		Exposure to Sugars (Factor A)		
		Low	**Moderate**	**High**
	Absent	8	10	13
		7	12	9
		9	15	11
		10	8	8
		12	6	13
		8	9	12
		$M = 9$	$M = 10$	$M = 11$
	Present	5	15	15
		8	10	12
		5	8	15
		6	9	16
		5	7	12
		7	11	14
		$M = 6$	$M = 10$	$M = 14$

The data for a 3 × 2 ANOVA that gives the times (in seconds) it took 36 participants ($n = 6$ per cell or group) to complete a computer task. Cell means are given at the bottom in each cell.

©iStockphoto.com/grinvalds

FIGURE 12.4 The Cell Means in Example 12.1

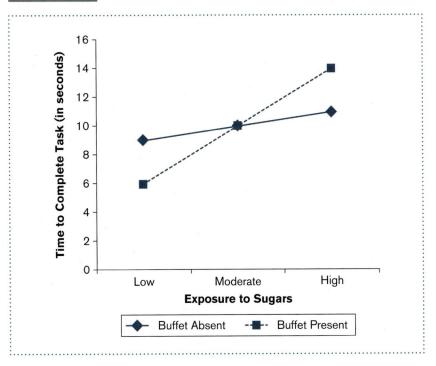

The lines in the graph cross, indicating that a significant interaction is possible between exposure to sugars and the buffet.

Let us start by graphing the interaction. The graph in Figure 12.4 plots the six cell means given in Table 12.7. When we distribute Factor A (exposure to sugars) on the x-axis and then plot the cell means, we find that the two lines touch or cross. This pattern indicates that the interaction could be significant. The only way to know for sure is to compute a two-way between-subjects ANOVA for these data. We begin by stating our hypotheses.

Step 1: State the hypotheses. The null hypothesis states that the group means for exposure to sugars (main effect), buffet (main effect), and both factors combined (interaction) do not vary (variance = 0) in the population; the alternative hypothesis states that the group means do vary (variance > 0) in the population:

$H_0: \sigma^2_{\mu's} = 0$. Mean times to complete the computer task do not vary by exposure to sugars, buffet, and/or the combination of these two factors.

$H_1: \sigma^2_{\mu's} > 0$. Mean times to complete the computer task do vary by exposure to sugars, buffet, and/or the combination of these two factors.

Step 2: Set the criteria for a decision. The level of significance for this test is .05. We must compute the degrees of freedom to find the critical values for each hypothesis test. There are four sources of variation in the two-way between-subjects ANOVA, and we compute degrees of freedom for each source of variation.

The degrees of freedom for Factor A (exposure) are $p - 1$:

$$df_A = 3 - 1 = 2.$$

The degrees of freedom for Factor B (buffet) are $q - 1$:

$$df_B = 2 - 1 = 1.$$

To compute the degrees of freedom for the A × B interaction, we multiply the degrees of freedom for Factor A by the degrees of freedom for Factor B, or $(p-1)(q-1)$:

$$df_{A \times B} = 2(1) = 2.$$

The degrees of freedom error are the total number of cells (pq) multiplied by the degrees of freedom for each cell $(n-1)$, or $pq(n-1)$.

$$df_E = (3)(2)(6-1) = 30.$$

The total degrees of freedom are equal to the total number of participants, minus 1, which are the degrees of freedom for variance: $N-1$, or $(npq)-1$. We can add up the degrees of freedom we just computed or calculate $(npq)-1$ to find the total degrees of freedom:

$$df_T = 2 + 1 + 2 + 30 = 35.$$

$$df_T = (6 \times 3 \times 2) - 1 = 35.$$

We will compute three hypothesis tests: one for each main effect and one for the interaction. Each hypothesis test requires a different critical value. We will find critical values for each hypothesis test in Step 4 because it will be easier to see why the critical values are computed differently for each test if we wait until Step 4 to find the critical values.

Step 3: Compute the test statistic. For each hypothesis test, we compute the F statistic. The F statistic can be used to determine the total variance attributed to Factor A (exposure), Factor B (buffet), or the combination of Factors A and B relative to the variance attributed to error. We compute the test statistic for each hypothesis test using a four-stage process, similar to that used for the one-way ANOVAs.

TABLE 12.8   Preliminary Calculations for the Two-Way Between-Subjects ANOVA in Example 12.1

		Exposure to Sugars (Factor A)			
		Low	**Moderate**	**High**	
Buffet of Sugary Foods (Factor B)	**Absent**	$\Sigma x = 54$ $\Sigma x^2 = 502$	$\Sigma x = 60$ $\Sigma x^2 = 650$	$\Sigma x = 66$ $\Sigma x^2 = 748$	$\Sigma x = 180$
	Present	$\Sigma x = 36$ $\Sigma x^2 = 224$	$\Sigma x = 60$ $\Sigma x^2 = 640$	$\Sigma x = 84$ $\Sigma x^2 = 1,190$	$\Sigma x = 180$
		$\Sigma x = 90$	$\Sigma x = 120$	$\Sigma x = 150$	$\Sigma x_T = 360$ $\Sigma x^2_T = 3,954$

Stage 1: Preliminary calculations: Find Σx in each cell and across each row and column, Σx_T, Σx^2 in each cell, Σx^2_T, n, p, and q. These preliminary calculations are shown in Table 12.8. Each calculation made in the table is described here.

1. Find n, p, and q. The number of participants per cell is $n = 6$. Exposure to sugars is Factor A, and the buffet is Factor B. Hence, $p = 3$ (the levels of Factor A) and $q = 2$ (the levels of Factor B). The total number of participants in this study is therefore $npq = 36$ participants.

2. Find Σx and Σx_T. Sum the scores (Σx) in each cell. Sum the row and the column totals by adding across the rows and columns, respectively. The grand total (Σx_T) is the sum of the cell totals.

3. Find Σx^2 and Σx_T^2. Square each score, then sum the squared scores in each cell. For example, in the top left cell (low exposure, buffet absent), we sum = 502. The sum of the squared scores across cells is equal to the total sum of squared scores: Σx_T^2.

Stage 2: Intermediate calculations: Find [1], [2], [3], [4], and [5].

In Stage 1, we computed the values needed to make calculations in Stage 2. We will use the values we compute in Stage 2 to find the sum of squares for each source of variation in Stage 3. There are five calculations in Stage 2:

First we compute a correction factor by squaring the grand total (Σx_T) and dividing by the total sample size (npq):

$$[1]\ \frac{(\Sigma x_T)^2}{npq} = \frac{(360)^2}{36} = 3{,}600.$$

Second, we restate the sum of the squared scores in all cells:

$$[2]\ \Sigma x_T^2 = 3{,}954.$$

Third, we calculate variation attributed to Factor A (exposure) by dividing the sum of squared scores in each column total (A) by the number of scores summed in each column (nq):

$$[3]\ \frac{\Sigma A^2}{nq} = \frac{90^2 + 120^2 + 150^2}{6 \times 2} = 3{,}750.$$

Fourth, we calculate variation attributed to Factor B (buffet) by dividing the sum of squared scores in each row total (B) by the number of scores summed in each row (np):

$$[4]\ \frac{\Sigma B^2}{np} = \frac{180^2 + 180^2}{6 \times 3} = 3{,}600.$$

Last, we calculate variation attributed to the interaction (exposure × buffet) by dividing the sum of squared scores in each cell total (AB) by the number of scores in each cell (n).

$$[5]\ \frac{\Sigma AB^2}{n} = \frac{54^2 + 60^2 + 66^2 + 36^2 + 60^2 + 84^2}{6} = 3{,}804.$$

Stage 3: Computing the sum of squares (SS) for each source of variation. SS is the numerator for the variance. We will compute the variance (a mean square) for each main effect, the interaction, error, and the total. So we compute SS for each source of variation and SS total.

The sum of squares for Factor A (SS_A) is the difference between Calculation [3] and Calculation [1] in Stage 2:

$$ss_A = [3] - [1] = 3{,}750 - 3{,}600 = 150.$$

The sum of squares for Factor B (SS_B) is the difference between Calculation [4] and Calculation [1] in Stage 2:

$$ss_B = [4] - [1] = 3{,}600 - 3{,}600 = 0.$$

The sum of squares for the A × B interaction ($SS_{A \times B}$) is Calculation [5] minus Calculation [1] in Stage 2, minus the sum of squares for Factors A and B:

$$ss_{A \times B} = [5] - [1] - ss_A - ss_B = 3{,}804 - 3{,}600 - 150 - 0 = 54.$$

The sum of squares error (SS_E) is the difference between Calculation [2] and Calculation [5] in Stage 2:

$$ss_E = [2] - [5] = 3{,}954 - 3{,}804 = 150.$$

The sum of squares total (SS_T) is the difference between Calculation [2] and Calculation [1] in Stage 2:

$$ss_T = [2] - [1] = 3{,}954 - 3{,}600 = 354.$$

Stage 4: Completing the F table. The F table lists SS, df, MS, and the test statistic value for each hypothesis test. The calculations in the F table are described here and listed in Table 12.9.

The first column of values in the F table lists the sum of squares (we computed these in Stage 3). The second column lists the degrees of freedom (we computed these in Step 2). We will use these values to compute the mean square (or variance) for each source of variation. The formula for variance is SS divided by df, so we divide across each row to compute each mean square.

TABLE 12.9 The F Table for a Two-Way Between-Subjects ANOVA, With Formulas for Completing the Table Given

Source of Variation	SS	df	MS	F
Factor A (exposure)	150	$p - 1$	$\dfrac{SS_A}{df_A}$	$F_A = \dfrac{MS_A}{MS_E}$
Factor B (buffet)	0	$q - 1$	$\dfrac{SS_B}{df_B}$	$F_B = \dfrac{MS_B}{MS_E}$
A × B (exposure × buffet)	54	$(p-1)(q-1)$	$\dfrac{SS_{A \times B}}{df_{A \times B}}$	$F_{A \times B} = \dfrac{MS_{A \times B}}{MS_E}$
Error (within groups)	150	$pq(n-1)$	$\dfrac{SS_E}{df_E}$	
Total	354	$npq - 1$		

Notice that mean square error (MS_E) is the denominator for each hypothesis test.

The variance or mean square for Factor A is

$$MS_A = \frac{ss_A}{df_A} = \frac{150}{2} = 75.$$

The variance or mean square for Factor B is

$$MS_B = \frac{ss_B}{df_B} = \frac{0}{1} = 0.$$

The variance or mean square for the A × B interaction is

$$MS_{A \times B} = \frac{ss_{A \times B}}{df_{A \times B}} = \frac{54}{2} = 27.$$

The variance or mean square for error is

$$MS_E = \frac{SS_E}{df_E} = \frac{150}{30} = 5.$$

The test statistic is basically the same as that for the one-way ANOVAs: It is the mean square between groups divided by the mean square error. For a two-way between-subjects ANOVA, we compute a different hypothesis test for each source of between-groups variation: one for each main effect and one for the interaction.

The test statistic for Factor A (exposure) is

$$F_A = \frac{MS_A}{MS_E} = \frac{75}{5} = 15.00.$$

To find the critical value, we need to know the degrees of freedom for Factor A and for error. The degrees of freedom numerator (for Factor A) is 2. The degrees of freedom denominator (for error) is 30. We locate the critical value in Table C.3 in Appendix C. At a .05 level of significance, the critical value associated with 2 and 30 degrees of freedom is 3.32.

The test statistic for Factor B (buffet) is

$$F_B = \frac{MS_B}{MS_E} = \frac{0}{5} = 0.$$

To find the critical value, we need to know the degrees of freedom for Factor B and for error. The degrees of freedom numerator (for Factor B) is 1. The degrees of freedom denominator (for error) does not change (30). At a .05 level of significance, the critical value associated with 1 and 30 degrees of freedom given in Table C.3 in Appendix C is 4.17.

The test statistic for the A × B (exposure × buffet) interaction is

$$F_{A\times B} = \frac{MS_{A\times B}}{MS_E} = \frac{27}{5} = 5.40.$$

To find the critical value, we need to know the degrees of freedom for the A × B interaction and for error. The degrees of freedom numerator (for the interaction) is 2. The degrees of freedom denominator (for error) does not change (30). At a .05 level of significance, the critical value associated with 2 and 30 degrees of freedom given in Table C.3 in Appendix C is 3.32.

Table 12.10 shows the completed F table for Example 12.1. We can now make a decision for each hypothesis test in Step 4.

TABLE 12.10   The Completed F Table for Example 12.1

Source of Variation	SS	df	MS	F
Factor A (exposure)	150	2	75	15.00*
Factor B (buffet)	0	1	0	0
A × B (exposure × buffet)	54	2	27	5.40*
Error (within groups)	150	30	5	
Total	354	35		

An asterisk indicates significance at $p < .05$.

Step 4: Make a decision. We will make a decision for each hypothesis test by comparing the value of the test statistic to the critical value.

Main effect of Factor A (exposure) is significant: $F_A = 15.00$ exceeds the critical value of 3.32; we reject the null hypothesis.

Main effect of Factor B (buffet) is not significant: $F_B = 0$ does not exceed the critical value of 4.17; we retain the null hypothesis.

The A × B interaction (exposure × buffet) is significant: $F_{A \times B} = 5.40$ exceeds the critical value of 3.32; we reject the null hypothesis.

Table 12.11 summarizes the procedures used to compute the two-way between-subjects ANOVA. If we were to report the result for Example 12.1 in a research journal, it would look something like this:

> Using a two-way between-subjects ANOVA, a significant main effect of exposure, $F(2, 30) = 15.00$, $p < .05$, and a significant exposure × buffet interaction, $F(2, 30) = 5.40$, $p < .05$, were evident. A main effect of buffet (present, absent) was not evident ($F = 0$).

This study is an example of Outcome 6 in the list of eight possible outcomes given under the last subheading of Section 12.3. The significant interaction confirms the pattern we observed in Figure 12.4. We know from the interaction that at least one pair of the six cell means significantly differs. Now we have to determine which pairs of cell means differ. The interaction was significant, so analyzing this result is the next step.

TABLE 12.11 Summary of the Process for the Two-Way Between-Subjects ANOVA

Terminology	Formula	Meaning
Step 1: State the hypotheses.		
Null hypotheses	$\sigma_A^2 = 0$	The levels of Factor A do not vary.
	$\sigma_B^2 = 0$	The levels of Factor B do not vary.
	$\sigma_{A \times B}^2 = 0$	Cell means do not vary.
Alternative hypotheses	$\sigma_A^2 > 0$	The levels of Factor A vary.
	$\sigma_B^2 > 0$	The levels of Factor B vary.
	$\sigma_{A \times B}^2 = 0$	Cell means vary.
Step 2: Set the criteria for a decision.		
Degrees of freedom for Factor A	$df_A = p - 1$	The levels of Factor A minus 1
Degrees of freedom for Factor B	$df_B = q - 1$	The levels of Factor B minus 1
Degrees of freedom for the A × B interaction	$df_{A \times B} = (p - 1)(q - 1)$	The df for Factor A multiplied by the df for Factor B
Degrees of freedom error (within groups)	$df_E = pq(n - 1)$	The total number of cells multiplied by the df within each cell

Terminology	Formula	Meaning
Degrees of freedom total	$df_T = npq - 1$	The total number of participants minus 1
Step 3: Compute the test statistic.		
STAGE 1		
Levels of Factor A	p	Number of levels for Factor A
Levels of Factor B	q	Number of levels for Factor B
Total cells	pq	Total number of cells (or groups) in a study
Sample size	npq	Total sample size
Grand total	Σx_T	The sum of all cell totals
Sum of squared scores	Σx_T^2	The sum of all individually squared scores in each cell
STAGE 2		
[1]	$\dfrac{\left(\Sigma x_T\right)^2}{npq}$	The correction factor
[2]	Σx_T^2	The "uncorrected" total variation in a study
[3]	$\dfrac{\Sigma A^2}{nq}$	The "uncorrected" variation attributed to Factor A
[4]	$\dfrac{\Sigma B^2}{np}$	The "uncorrected" variation attributed to Factor B
[5]	$\dfrac{\Sigma AB^2}{n}$	The "uncorrected" variation attributed to the A × B interaction
STAGE 3		
Sum of squares for Factor A	$SS_A = [3] - [1]$	The sum of the squared deviations for Factor A
Sum of squares for Factor B	$SS_B = [4] - [1]$	The sum of the squared deviations for Factor B
Sum of squares for the A × B interaction	$SS_{A \times B} = [5] - [1] - SS_A - SS_B$	The sum of the squared deviations for the A × B interaction
Sum of squares error (within groups)	$SS_E = [2] - [5]$	The sum of the squared deviations within each cell
Sum of squares total	$SS_T = [2] - [1]$	The sum of the squared deviations in all cells
STAGE 4		
Mean square for Factor A	$MS_A = \dfrac{SS_A}{df_A}$	The variance for Factor A

(Continued)

TABLE 12.11 (Continued)

Terminology	Formula	Meaning
Mean square for Factor B	$MS_B = \dfrac{SS_B}{df_B}$	The variance for Factor B
Mean square for the A × B interaction	$MS_{A\times B} = \dfrac{SS_{A\times B}}{df_{A\times B}}$	The variance for the combined levels of Factor A and Factor B
Mean square error (within groups)	$MS_E = \dfrac{SS_E}{df_E}$	The variance within each cell. This is the denominator for all three hypothesis tests.
Hypothesis test for Factor A	$F_A = \dfrac{MS_A}{MS_E}$	The test statistic for Factor A
Hypothesis test for Factor B	$F_B = \dfrac{MS_B}{MS_E}$	The test statistic for Factor B
Hypothesis test for the A × B interaction	$F_{A\times B} = \dfrac{MS_{A\times B}}{MS_E}$	The test statistic for the A × B interaction
Step 4: Make a decision.		
General decision criterion	—	When $F_{obt} < F_{crit}$, retain the null hypothesis. When $F_{obt} \geq F_{crit}$, reject the null hypothesis.

LEARNING CHECK 3

1. State four assumptions of the two-way between-subjects ANOVA.

Source of Variation	SS	df	MS	F
Factor A (self-esteem)	18			
Factor B (family size)	30			
A × B (self-esteem × family size)	42			
Error (within treatments)	75			
Total	165			

2. A researcher conducts a study to determine whether parents with different levels of self-esteem (low, high) and family size (1, 2, 3, 4, or 5 children) display different parenting styles. Six parents ($n = 6$ per cell) were observed using a between-subjects design. Based on the information given here and in the table, answer the following questions. Hint: First complete the F table.

   (a) What are the degrees of freedom for the A × B interaction?

   (b) What is the value of mean square error?

   (c) What is the value for the test statistic for each main effect and for the interaction?

3. Make a decision for each hypothesis test in Question 2.

Answers: 1. Normality, random sampling, independence, and homogeneity of variance. 2. (a) 4, (b) 1.50, (c) $F_A = 12.0$, $F_B = 5.0$, $F_{A\times B} = 7.0$; 3. Reject the null hypothesis for all hypothesis tests.

12.5 ANALYZING MAIN EFFECTS AND INTERACTIONS

If the decision is to retain the null hypothesis for all three hypothesis tests, then we stop: No pairs of group means significantly vary. However, when the decision is to reject the null hypothesis for even one of the three hypothesis tests, then we analyze the data further. If main effects are significant, then we conduct post hoc tests (as described in Chapter 11). If the interaction is significant, we analyze it using **simple main effect tests**.

Simple main effect tests are hypothesis tests used to analyze a significant interaction by comparing mean differences or simple main effects of one factor at each level of a second factor. After we compute simple main effect tests, we then compute post hoc tests for the significant simple main effects that we find. Figure 12.5 shows the steps for analyzing a significant two-way ANOVA. In this section, we describe how to compute and interpret simple main effect tests for a significant interaction.

FYI

The null hypothesis for a two-way ANOVA states that group means do not vary in the population for each factor or for both factors combined.

FYI

A mean square is the same as a variance. It is SS divided by df for each source of variation.

FIGURE 12.5   The Steps Following a Two-Way ANOVA

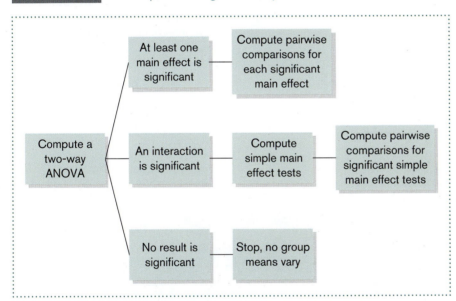

The Interaction: Simple Main Effect Tests

A significant interaction indicates that at least one pair of group means for the A × B interaction (in the cells of a table summary) significantly differs. To analyze the interaction, we first need to know what question we want to answer. We follow three steps to analyze the interaction:

Step 1: Choose how to describe the data.

Step 2: Compute simple main effect tests.

Step 3: Compute pairwise comparisons.

Step 1: Choose how to describe the data. Table 12.12 shows two ways to interpret the interaction and five potential questions that can be asked.

Simple main effect tests are hypothesis tests used to analyze a significant interaction by comparing the mean differences or simple main effects of one factor at each level of a second factor.

One way to interpret the interaction is to analyze the rows, leading to Q1 and Q2 in the table; the second way is to analyze the columns, leading to Q3, Q4, and Q5 in the table. We first choose which way we want to describe or interpret the data—typically determined by how to best answer the hypothesis being tested.

One way to interpret the interaction is to look in the table at how cell means for Factor A (exposure) change at each level of Factor B (buffet). This leads to two questions:

Q1: Does greater exposure to sugars interfere with completing a computer task when the buffet is absent?

Q2: Does greater exposure to sugars interfere with completing a computer task when the buffet is present?

By limiting our comparisons to one level of Factor B (buffet) at a time, we can compare the cell means for Factor A (exposure). In other words, we can compare the cell means at each level of exposure when the buffet was absent (top row of cells in Table 12.12) and make a separate comparison when the buffet was present (bottom row of cells in Table 12.12).

TABLE 12.12   Analyzing the Interaction

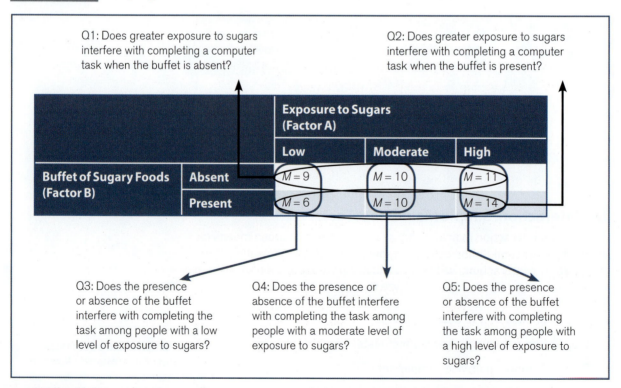

A significant interaction indicates that at least one pair of cell means is significantly different. There are two ways to analyze the A × B interaction. Analyzing across the rows addresses two questions (Q1 and Q2). Analyzing down the columns addresses three questions (Q3, Q4, and Q5) in this example.

A second way to interpret the interaction is to look in the table at how the cell means for Factor B (buffet) change at each level of Factor A (exposure). This leads to three questions:

Q3: Does the presence or absence of the buffet interfere with completing the task among people with a low level of exposure to sugars?

Q4: Does the presence or absence of the buffet interfere with completing the task among people with a moderate level of exposure to sugars?

Q5: Does the presence or absence of the buffet interfere with completing the task among people with a high level of exposure to sugars?

By limiting our comparisons to one level of Factor A (exposure) at a time, we can compare the cell means for Factor B (buffet). In other words, we can compare the cell means at each level of buffet for persons with low exposure (left column of cells in Table 12.12), make a separate comparison for persons with moderate exposure (middle column of cells in Table 12.12), and make another separate comparison for persons with high exposure (right column of cells in Table 12.12).

To decide whether we want to answer Q1 and Q2 or Q3, Q4, and Q5, we need to determine which questions best address the hypothesis. In the exposure and buffet study, we want to determine whether a buffet of foods interferes with completing a computer task when the buffet is present (sugary foods are placed on the desk) versus absent (stacks of papers are placed on the desk). We can determine this by answering Q1 and Q2, so let us choose to answer these two questions.

Step 2: Compute simple main effect tests. To answer Q1, we will compare the top row of cell means in Table 12.12 for the buffet-absent group. To answer Q2, we will compare the bottom row of cell means in Table 12.12 for the buffet-present group. We will answer Q1 first.

To answer Q1, we compare the top three cells in Table 12.12. Because different participants were assigned to each group or cell in this study, we can compute these data using a one-way between-subjects ANOVA (taught in Chapter 11)—this is the simple main effect test we will use. Table 12.13 shows the data for the top row of cells (originally given in Table 12.7) and the F table for the simple main effect test. On the basis of the results shown in the F table, we decide to retain the null hypothesis. As expected, we conclude that a person's level of exposure to sugars does not interfere with the time it takes to complete a computer task when the buffet is absent.

To answer Q2, we compare the bottom three cells in Table 12.12. Because different participants were assigned to each group or cell in this study, we again compute these data using a one-way between-subjects ANOVA—this is the simple main effect test we will use. Table 12.14 shows the data for the bottom row of cells (originally given in Table 12.7) and the F table for the simple main effect test. On the basis of the results shown in the F table, we decide to reject the null hypothesis. As expected, we conclude that a person's level of exposure to sugars interferes with the time it takes to complete a computer task when the buffet is present.

TABLE 12.13 Simple Main Effect Test for When the Buffet Was Absent

Exposure to Sugars		
Low	Moderate	High
5	15	15
8	10	12
5	8	15
6	9	16
5	7	12
7	11	14

Source of Variation	SS	df	MS	F
Between groups (exposure)	12	2	6.000	1.023
Error (within groups)	88	15	5.867	
Total	100	17		

The decision is to retain the null hypothesis. We decide that increased exposure to sugars does not interfere with completing the computer task when the buffet is absent (i.e., when stacks of paper are on the desk).

TABLE 12.14 Simple Main Effect Test for When the Buffet Was Present

Exposure to Sugars		
Low	Moderate	High
8	10	13
7	12	9
9	15	11
10	8	8
12	6	13
8	9	12

Source of Variation	SS	df	MS	F
Between groups (exposure)	192	2	96.00	23.23*
Error (within groups)	62	15	4.133	
Total	254	17		

The decision is to reject the null hypothesis. We decide that increased exposure to sugars interferes with the completion of a computer task when the buffet of sugary foods is present. An asterisk indicates significance at $p < .05$.

In Example 12.1, the researcher hypothesized that a person's level of sugar exposure can interfere or distract him or her during a computer task when food is present. We had participants with different levels of exposure to sugars complete a computer task with and without the buffet present. We measured the time it took participants to complete the computer task and used a two-way between-subjects ANOVA to analyze the data. The simple effect tests we just computed confirmed this original hypothesis: The time it took to complete the computer task significantly varied when the buffet was present but not when it was absent.

Step 3: Compute pairwise comparisons. In this step, we compute post hoc tests to analyze only the significant simple main effect tests we computed in Step 2. In this case, we will compare all possible pairs of cell means in the bottom row—to analyze the cell means for the significant simple main effect test for the buffet-present condition.

Step 3 is necessary only when we compare more than two cells. With two cells, only one pair of means can be compared; multiple pairwise comparisons are therefore unnecessary. For Example 12.1, multiple pairwise comparisons are necessary because we compared three cells or groups. The mean in each group in the bottom row of cells was $M = 6$ in the low-exposure group, $M = 10$ in the moderate-exposure group, and $M = 14$ in the high-exposure group.

In Chapter 11, we introduced Tukey's honestly significant difference (HSD) post hoc test, so let us use this test to compare each pair of cell means. For this post hoc test, the test statistic is the difference between each pair of group means. The critical value for each pairwise comparison is 3.05 (refer to Chapter 11 for a description of how to find the critical value using this post hoc test). Each pairwise comparison and the decision for each comparison are as follows:

Comparison 1: high exposure and low exposure: $14 - 6 = 8.00$ (reject the null hypothesis; the test statistic value, 8.00, is greater than 3.05).

Comparison 2: moderate exposure and low exposure: $10 - 6 = 4.00$ (reject the null hypothesis; the test statistic value, 4.00, is greater than 3.05).

Comparison 3: high exposure and moderate exposure: $14 - 10 = 4.00$ (reject the null hypothesis; the test statistic value, 4.00, is greater than 3.05).

The results show that every pairwise comparison is significant. Hence, the more exposure participants had with sugars, the slower they were to complete a computer task when the buffet was present but not absent. If we were to report the outcome of this analysis in a research journal, it would look something like this:

A two-way between-subjects ANOVA showed a significant main effect of exposure, $F(2, 30) = 15.00$, $p < .05$, and a significant exposure × buffet interaction, $F(2, 30) = 5.40$, $p < .05$. Simple main effect tests showed that times to complete the task were significantly different when the buffet was present, $F(2, 15) = 23.23$, $p < .001$, but not when it was absent ($p > .05$). The more exposure participants had to sugars, the slower their times were to complete the computer task when the buffet was present (Tukey's HSD, $p < .05$).

Main Effects: Pairwise Comparisons

If an interaction is significant, you should analyze the interaction. It may also be necessary to analyze significant main effects, particularly if such an outcome is predicted by the hypothesis being tested. To analyze a significant main effect, you skip straight to Step 3 and compute pairwise comparisons. Keep in mind that in a table summary, the main effects are located outside the table—we compare the row or column means for a single factor, independent of the second factor. The sample size at each level of a single factor will be larger than the sample size per cell. In Example 12.1, a significant main effect of exposure was evident. Table 12.15 reorganizes the data for this test. Notice that $n = 12$ participants per group because participants in the buffet-absent and buffet-present cells were combined at each level of the exposure factor.

TABLE 12.15   Data for Analyzing the Main Effect

	Exposure to Sugars		
	Low	**Moderate**	**High**
Scores for when the buffet was absent	8	10	13
	7	12	9
	9	15	11
	10	8	8
	12	6	13
	8	9	12
Scores for when the buffet was present	5	15	15
	8	10	12
	5	8	15
	6	9	16
	5	7	12
	7	11	14
Means	$M = 7.5$	$M = 10$	$M = 12.5$

The data in this table are from Table 12.7. To analyze the significant main effect, the buffet-absent and buffet-present groups are combined at each level of exposure. Hence, $n = 12$ per group.

LEARNING CHECK 4

1. State the steps for analyzing an interaction.

2. Simple main effect tests compare mean differences or simple main effects of one factor at _____ of a second factor.

3. Which of the following is the next step to analyze a significant A × B interaction in a two-way between-subjects ANOVA?

   (a) Compute simple main effect tests

   (b) Compute pairwise comparisons

   (c) Compute a two-way ANOVA

4. What is the next step for analyzing a significant main effect?

Answers: 1. Step 1: Choose how to describe the data. Step 2: Compute simple main effect tests. Step 3: Compute pairwise comparisons; 2. Each level; 3. (a); 4. Compute pairwise comparisons on the row means, the column means, or both.

12.6 MEASURING EFFECT SIZE FOR MAIN EFFECTS AND THE INTERACTION

We can compute effect size using proportion of variance for each effect tested using the two-way between-subjects ANOVA. Proportion of variance estimates how much of the variability in the dependent variable (time it took to complete the computer task) can be explained by each group (the two main effects and the interaction). Two measures of proportion of variance are eta-squared and omega-squared. In this section, we measure effect size for the significant results obtained in Example 12.1.

Eta-Squared (η² or R²)

Eta-squared can be computed for each main effect and the interaction. It is the sum of squares of the main effect or interaction divided by the sum of squares total. Based on the results given in Table 12.10, $SS_A = 150$ and $SS_T = 354$. The proportion of variance for Factor A is

$$\eta_A^2 \frac{SS_A}{SS_T} = \frac{150}{354} = .43.$$

We conclude that 43% of the variability in the time it took to complete the computer task can be explained by the participants' level of exposure to sugars. To find the proportion of variance for the significant A × B interaction, we substitute the sum of squares for the interaction, $SS_{A \times B} = 54$, into the numerator of the formula:

$$\eta_{A \times B}^2 = \frac{SS_{A \times B}^2}{SS_T} = \frac{54}{354} = .15.$$

We conclude that 15% of the variability in the time it took to complete the computer task can be explained by the combination of the two factors.

FYI
A significant interaction indicates that at least one pair of cell means significantly differs.

FYI
There are many ways to analyze an interaction depending on the questions researchers want to answer.

FYI
Making multiple pairwise comparisons in Step 3 is necessary only when we compare more than two cell means.

FYI
We analyze each significant main effect by making pairwise comparisons for the row means, the column means, or both in a summary table.

FYI
Two measures of proportion of variance are eta-squared and omega-squared. These measures can be computed for each main effect and the interaction.

The proportion of variance for the interaction is less informative than for the main effects because a significant interaction must be analyzed further. For this reason, many researchers will analyze the interaction first and report an effect size only for the significant simple main effects.

Omega-Squared (ω^2)

Omega-squared can be computed for each main effect and the interaction. This measure is less biased than eta-squared in that it

1. corrects for the size of error by including MS_E in the formula, and

2. corrects for the number of groups by including the degrees of freedom for the main effect or interaction in the formula.

The formula for omega-squared is the same as that given in Chapter 11, except we substitute SS and df for each main effect or the interaction. The proportion of variance for Factor A is

$$\omega_A^2 = \frac{SS_A - df_A (MS_E)}{SS_T + MS_E} = \frac{150 - 2(5)}{354 + 5} = .39.$$

We conclude that 39% of the variability in the time it took to complete the computer task can be explained by the participants' level of exposure to sugars. The proportion of variance for the A × B interaction is

$$\omega_{A \times B}^2 = \frac{SS_{A \times B} - df_{A \times B} (MS_E)}{SS_T + MS_E} = \frac{54 - 2(5)}{354 + 5} = .12.$$

FYI

Omega-squared is a more conservative estimate of proportion of variance than eta-squared.

We conclude that 12% of the variability in the time it took to complete the computer task can be explained by the combination of the two factors.

LEARNING CHECK 5

1. Using the data given in the following F table:

   (a) Compute eta-squared for each hypothesis test.

   (b) Compute omega-squared for each hypothesis test.

2. Which measure for proportion of variance is more conservative (eta-squared or omega-squared)?

Source of Variation	SS	df	MS	F
Factor A	12	1	12	4.0
Factor B	48	2	24	8.0
A × B	60	2	30	10.0
Error	90	30	3	
Total	210	35		

Answers: 1. (a) $\eta_A^2 = \frac{12}{210} = .06$, $\eta_B^2 = \frac{48}{210} = .23$, $\eta_{A \times B}^2 = \frac{60}{210} = .29$; (b) $\omega_A^2 = \frac{12 - 1(3)}{210 + 3} = .04$, $\omega_B^2 = \frac{48 - 2(3)}{210 + 3} = .20$, $\omega_{A \times B}^2 = \frac{60 - 2(3)}{210 + 3} = .25$; 2. Omega-squared.

12.7 SPSS in Focus:
The Two-Way Between-Subjects ANOVA

In Example 12.1, we tested whether levels of exposure to sugars interfered with the time it took participants to complete a computer task in the presence or absence of a buffet of sugary foods. We concluded that participants with more exposure to sugars took longer to complete the computer task when the buffet of sugary foods was present. Using the same data as in Example 12.1, we will use SPSS to confirm the calculations that we computed for these data.

1. Click on the Variable View tab and enter *buffet* in the Name column; enter *exposure* in the Name column below it; enter *duration* in the Name column below that. We will enter whole numbers, so reduce the value in the Decimals column to 0 in each row.

2. In the row named *buffet*, click on the small gray box with three dots in the Values column. In the dialog box, enter *1* in the value cell and *absent* in the label cell, and then click Add. Then enter *2* in the value cell and *present* in the label cell, and then click Add. Select OK.

3. In the row named *exposure*, follow the same directions stated in Step 2, except enter *1* for *low*, *2* for *moderate*, and *3* for *high*.

4. Click on the Data View tab. In the *buffet* column, enter *1* in the first 18 cells, then enter *2* in the next 18 cells.

5. In the *exposure* column, enter *1* in the first six cells, then enter 2 in the next six cells, then enter *3* in the next six cells. Repeat this: Enter *1* in the next six cells, enter *2* in the next six cells, and enter *3* in the next six cells. We have now set up the groups. For example, the first six cells read 1, 1; these codes identify the group with the buffet absent and low exposure to sugars.

6. In the *duration* column, enter the data for the duration of time to complete the task in the cells that correspond with the codes for each group listed in the first and second columns. A portion of the Data View is shown in Table 12.16.

7. Go to the menu bar and click Analyze, then General Linear Model and Univariate, to display a dialog box.

8. Using the appropriate arrows, move *buffet* and *exposure* into the Fixed Factor(s): box. Move the dependent variable, *duration*, into the Dependent Variable: box.

9. Click Options to display a new dialog box. In the Factor(s) and Factor Interactions box, move the two main effects and interaction into the Display Means for: box by using the arrow. Click Continue.

10. Select Post Hoc . . . to display a new dialog box. Use the arrow to move both main effects in the Factor(s) box into the Post Hoc Tests

(Continued)

(Continued)

TABLE 12.16   A Partial Display of the SPSS Data View for Example 12.1

buffet	exposure	duration
1	1	8
1	1	7
1	1	9
1	1	10
1	1	12
1	1	8
1	2	10
1	2	12
1	2	15
1	2	8
1	2	6
1	2	9
1	3	13
1	3	9
1	3	11
1	3	8
1	3	13
1	3	12
2	1	5
2	1	8
2	1	5
2	1	6
2	1	5
2	1	7
2	2	15
2	2	10
2	2	8
2	2	9
2	2	7

for: box. Select the Tukey box for the pairwise comparison for the main effects. (Note: SPSS does not perform simple effect tests by default. If you obtain a significant interaction, you will have to conduct these tests separately.) To obtain an estimate of the power for each hypothesis test, select Observed power and click Continue.

11.   Select OK, or select Paste and click the Run command.

The SPSS output table, shown in Table 12.17, has many more rows than we included in the ANOVA table in Table 12.10. Referring to Table 12.17, read only the rows labeled *buffet*, *exposure*, *buffet * exposure*, *Error*, and *Corrected Total*—ignore the rest. When we look only at those five rows, it now looks much like Table 12.10. These results confirm our conclusion that we have a buffet × exposure interaction and a main effect of exposure.

TABLE 12.17   The Output Table for SPSS

The first four rows and the last row circled here provide a summary for the two-way between-subjects ANOVA that is similar to the ANOVA table given in Table 12.10.

Tests of Between-Subjects Effects

Dependent Variable:times

Source	Type III Sum of Squares	df	Mean Square	F	Sig.	Noncent. Parameter	Observed Power[b]
Corrected Model	204.000[a]	5	40.800	8.160	.000	40.800	.998
Intercept	3600.000	1	3600.000	720.000	.000	720.000	1.000
buffet	.000	1	.000	.000	1.000	.000	.050
exposure	150.000	2	75.000	15.000	.000	30.000	.998
buffet * exposure	54.000	2	27.000	5.400	.010	10.800	.805
Error	150.000	30	5.000				
Total	3954.000	36					
Corrected Total	354.000	35					

a. R Squared = .576 (Adjusted R Squared = .506)
b. Computed using alpha = .05

12.8 APA IN FOCUS: REPORTING THE RESULTS OF THE TWO-WAY ANOVAS

To summarize any type of two-way ANOVA, we report the test statistic, the degrees of freedom, and the *p* value for each significant main effect and interaction. The effect size should also be reported for each significant hypothesis test and for the simple main effect tests. To report the results of a post hoc test, identify the name of the post hoc test used and the *p* value for the test. The means and standard error or standard deviations measured in a study can be summarized in a figure or table or in the main text. For example, here is an appropriate summary of the results obtained in Example 12.1, using eta-squared to estimate effect size and Tukey's HSD as the post hoc test:

A two-way between-subjects ANOVA showed a significant main effect of exposure, $F(2, 30) = 15.00$, $p < .05$, and a significant exposure × buffet interaction, $F(2, 30) = 5.40$, $p < .05$. Simple main effect tests showed that times to complete the task were significantly different when the buffet was present, $F(2, 15) = 23.23$, $p < .001$, but not when it was absent ($p > .05$). The more exposure participants had to sugars, the slower their times to complete the computer task when the buffet was present (Tukey's HSD, $p < .05$). Table 12.18 displays the means and standard deviations for each factor and the results for each hypothesis test.

In two sentences and a table, we summarized all of our work in this chapter: the test statistic, degrees of freedom, and *p* value for each test; effect size for both significant effects; post hoc tests; and the means and standard deviations for each group. In sum, this is a clear and concise summary of the two-way between-subjects ANOVA.

(Continued)

(Continued)

TABLE 12.18 The Mean (*M*) and Standard Deviation (*SD*) in Seconds for Each Factor and Interaction in Example 12.1

Factor		M	SD	F	p Value
Buffet				0.00	1.000
	Absent	10.00	2.43		
	Present	10.00	3.87		
Exposure to Sugars				15.00*	< .001
	Low	7.50	2.15		
	Moderate	10.00	2.86		
	High	12.50	2.39		
Buffet × Exposure				5.40*	.010
Buffet absent	**Low exposure**	9.00	1.79		
	Moderate exposure	10.00	3.16		
	High exposure	11.00	2.10		
Buffet present	**Low exposure**	6.00	1.26		
	Moderate exposure	10.00	2.83		
	High exposure	14.00	1.67		

Results for each hypothesis test are also given. An asterisk indicates significance at *p* < .05.

• • • CHAPTER SUMMARY ORGANIZED BY LEARNING OBJECTIVE

LO 1: **Describe how the complexity of the two-way ANOVA differs from that of the *t* tests and one-way ANOVAs.**

- A two-way ANOVA is more complex in that the levels of two factors (not one factor) are observed in a single study. Like the *t* tests and the one-way ANOVA, the two-way ANOVA can be used when different participants are observed in each group or at each level of one factor (between-subjects design) and when the same participants are observed in each group or across the levels of a factor (within-subjects design).

- Two common reasons for observing two factors in a single study are (1) the hypothesis requires the observation of two factors, and (2) to control or account for threats to validity.

LO 2: Define and explain the following terms: *cell, main effect,* and *interaction.*

- A cell is the combination of one level from each factor. Each cell is a group in a study.
- A main effect is a source of variation associated with mean differences across the levels of a single factor.
- An interaction is a source of variation associated with the variance of group means across the combination of levels for two factors. It is a measure of how cell means at each level of one factor change across the levels of a second factor.

LO 3: Identify the assumptions and list the order of interpretation for outcomes in the two-way between-subjects ANOVA.

- Four assumptions for the two-way between-subjects ANOVA are normality, random sampling, independence, and homogeneity of variance.
- In the two-way between-subjects ANOVA, there are three sources of between-groups variation and one source of error variation:
  1. Between-groups variation is a measure of the variance of the group means. Three sources of between-groups variation are the following:

     Main effect of Factor A

     Main effect of Factor B

     Interaction of Factors A and B, called the A × B interaction
  2. Within-groups (error) variation is a measure of the variance of scores in each group (or within the cells of a summary table). This source of error is the denominator for each hypothesis test.

- If significant, an interaction is typically analyzed first using the two-way between-subjects ANOVA.

LO 4: Calculate the degrees of freedom for the two-way between-subjects ANOVA and locate critical values in the *F* table.

- The degrees of freedom for a two-way between-subjects ANOVA are as follows:

  Degrees of freedom for Factor A: $df_A = p - 1$.

  Degrees of freedom for Factor B: $df_B = q - 1$.

  Degrees of freedom for the A × B interaction: $df_{A \times B} = (p - 1)(q - 1)$.

  Degrees of freedom error: $df_E = pq(n - 1)$.

  Degrees of freedom total: $df_T = npq - 1$.

- To find the critical value for each hypothesis test, use the degrees of freedom for the factor or interaction that is being tested and the degrees of freedom error.

LO 5: Compute the two-way between-subjects ANOVA and interpret the results.

- The test statistics for the main effects and interaction are as follows:

  Main effect for Factor A: $F_A = \frac{MS_A}{MS_E}$.

  Main effect for Factor B: $F_B = \frac{MS_B}{MS_E}$.

  A × B interaction: $F_{A \times B} = \frac{MS_{A \times B}}{MS_E}$.

- The steps for conducting a two-way between-subjects ANOVA are as follows:

  Step 1: State the hypotheses.

  Step 2: Set the criteria for a decision.

  Step 3: Compute the test statistic.

  Stage 1: Preliminary calculations.

  Stage 2: Intermediate calculations.

  Stage 3: Computing sums of squares (*SS*).

  Stage 4: Completing the *F* table.

  Step 4: Make a decision.

LO 6:   **Identify when it is appropriate to compute simple main effect tests and analyze a significant interaction.**

- Simple main effect tests are appropriate to analyze a significant interaction. If an interaction is significant, then the interaction is analyzed first. To analyze a significant interaction, follow three steps:

  Step 1: Choose how to describe the data.

  Step 2: Compute simple main effect tests.

  Step 3: Compute pairwise comparisons.

- Simple main effect tests are hypothesis tests used to analyze a significant interaction by comparing the mean differences or the simple main effects for one factor at each level of a second factor.

LO 7:   **Compute and interpret proportion of variance for the two-way between-subjects ANOVA.**

- One measure of proportion of variance for the two-way between-subjects ANOVA is eta-squared:

  Factor A: $\eta_A^2 = \frac{SS_A}{SS_T}$,

  Factor B: $\eta_B^2 = \frac{SS_B}{SS_T}$,

  A × B interaction: $\eta_{A\times B}^2 = \frac{SS_{A\times B}}{SS_T}$.

- A second, more conservative measure is omega-squared:

  Factor A: $\omega_A^2 = \frac{SS_A - df_A(MS_E)}{SS_T + MS_E}$,

  Factor B: $\omega_B^2 = \frac{SS_B - df_B(MS_E)}{SS_T + MS_E}$,

A × B interaction:

$$\omega_{A\times B}^2 = \frac{SS_{A\times B} - df_{A\times B}(MS_E)}{SS_T + MS_E}.$$

LO 8:   **Summarize the results of the two-way between-subjects ANOVA in APA format.**

- To summarize any type of two-way ANOVA, we report the test statistic, the degrees of freedom, and the p value for each significant main effect and interaction. Effect size should also be reported for each significant hypothesis test and for the simple main effect tests. To report the results of a post hoc test, identify the name of the post hoc test used and the p value for the test. Means and standard errors or standard deviations measured in a study can be summarized in a figure or a table, or in the main text.

LO 9:   **Compute the two-way between-subjects ANOVA using SPSS.**

- SPSS can be used to compute the two-way between-subjects ANOVA using the Analyze, General Linear Model, and Univariate options in the menu bar. These actions will display a dialog box that allows you to identify the variables, choose an appropriate post hoc test for the main effects, and run the analysis. SPSS does not perform simple main effect tests by default. If a significant interaction is obtained, then you must reorganize the data and conduct these tests separately (for more details, see Section 12.7).

• • • KEY TERMS

between-subjects factor
cell
complete factorial design
factorial design

interaction
main effect
simple main effect tests
two-way ANOVA

two-way between-subjects
  ANOVA
within-subjects factor

••• END-OF-CHAPTER PROBLEMS

Factual Problems

1. What is the difference between a one-way ANOVA and a two-way ANOVA?

2. A 3×2 ANOVA includes how many factors?

3. Define the following key terms: (a) *cell*, (b) *main effect*, and (c) *interaction*.

4. Suppose you construct a table with cells, rows, and columns to summarize each factor in a two-way ANOVA.

    (a) Where are the main effects located in the table?

    (b) Where is the interaction located in the table?

5. A researcher conducts a 3×3 between-subjects ANOVA with 15 participants assigned to each cell or group.

    (a) What is the total sample size in this study?

    (b) How many cells or groups are in this study?

6. When looking at a graph of an $A \times B$ interaction, describe the pattern that indicates that an interaction is possible.

7. State four assumptions for the two-way between-subjects ANOVA.

8. Which source of variation is placed in the denominator of the test statistic for each hypothesis test for the two-way between-subjects ANOVA?

9. Explain why the critical value can be different for each hypothesis test computed using the two-way between-subjects ANOVA.

10. A researcher obtains a significant interaction and a significant main effect. Which significant effect should the researcher typically analyze first? Explain.

11. Which effect (main effect or interaction) is unique to the factorial design, compared to the one-way ANOVA designs?

12. Which measure, eta-squared or omega-squared, is a more conservative estimate of proportion of variance?

Concept and Application Problems

13. State the total number of groups for each of the following examples of a two-way between-subjects ANOVA test.

    (a) An industrial organizational psychologist records the initial evaluation reports for new employees from 2-year and 4-year colleges (Factor A: type of college) with low, medium, or high leadership potential (Factor B: leadership potential).

    (b) A psychologist administers a small, medium, or large dose of a drug to a sample of mice (Factor A: drug dose) and measures reward-seeking behavior in three experimental trials (Factor B: trials).

14. A social scientist asks a sample of male and female students to read a vignette describing an immoral act for reasons of preservation, protection, or self-gain. She measures moral reasoning among those sampled. Identify each factor and the levels of each factor in this example.

15. An educator evaluates the effects of small, medium, and large class sizes on academic performance among male and female students. Identify each factor and the levels of each factor in this example.

16. The following table summarizes the cell, column, and row means for a 2×2 ANOVA.

		Factor A		Row Means
		A_1	A_2	
Factor B	B_1	2	6	4
	B_2	4	8	6
Column Means		3	7	

(a) Which means reflect a main effect for Factor A?

(b) Which means reflect a main effect for Factor B?

(c) Which means reflect the interaction between Factors A and B?

17. State the decision to retain or reject the null hypothesis for each of the following ANOVA tests at a .05 level of significance.

(a) $F(3, 24) = 3.29$

(b) $F(2, 40) = 3.00$

(c) $F(1, 120) = 4.00$

(d) $F(2, 60) = 3.10$

18. A researcher reports a significant two-way between-subjects ANOVA, $F(3, 40) = 2.96$. State the decision to retain or reject the null hypothesis for this test.

19. If the value of the mean square for Factor A increases, will the value of the test statistic for Factor A increase or decrease?

20. If the value of mean square error increases, will the value of the test statistic increase or decrease?

21. For each of the following, state whether $F = 0$ for a main effect, the A × B interaction, or both.

(a) Cell means are equal.

(b) Row totals are equal.

(c) Column totals are equal.

22. To better understand eating patterns that might contribute to obesity, a researcher measures the average number of calories (per meal) consumed by shift workers (morning, afternoon, night) during two seasons (summer and winter). The hypothetical results are given in the following table.

		Shift		
		Morning	Afternoon	Night
Season	Summer	450	500	480
		500	490	660
		550	550	570
		650	700	510
	Winter	700	700	710
		550	500	630
		750	750	600
		500	600	650

(a) Complete the *F* table and make a decision to retain or reject the null hypothesis for each hypothesis test.

(b) Explain why post hoc tests are not necessary.

23. Seasonal affective disorder (SAD) is a type of depression during seasons with less daylight (e.g., winter months). One therapy for SAD is phototherapy, which is increased exposure to light used to improve mood. A researcher tests this therapy by exposing a sample of patients with SAD to different intensities of light (low, medium, high) in a light box, either in the morning or at night (these are the times thought to be most effective for light therapy). All participants rated their mood following this therapy on a scale from 1 (*poor mood*) to 9 (*improved mood*). The hypothetical results are given in the following table.

		Light Intensity		
		Low	Medium	High
Time of Day	Morning	5	5	7
		6	6	8
		4	4	6
		7	7	9
		5	9	5
		6	8	8
	Night	5	6	9
		8	8	7
		6	7	6
		7	5	8
		4	9	7
		3	8	6

(a) Complete the *F* table and make a decision to retain or reject the null hypothesis for each hypothesis test.

(b) Compute Tukey's HSD to analyze the significant main effect. Summarize the results for this test using APA format.

24. Students (freshmen, sophomores, juniors, and seniors) at a local college who were in the same statistics class were given one of three tests (recall, recognition, or a mix of both). Test grades for each participant ($n = 10$) were recorded. Complete the *F* table for this study.

Source of Variation	SS	df	MS	F
Exam		2	95	
Student Class	60			
Exam × Student Class	540			
Error				
Total	2,410			

25. In an effort to promote a new product, a marketing firm asks participants to rate the effectiveness of ads that varied by length (short, long) and by type of technology (static, interactive). Higher ratings indicated greater effectiveness.

Source of Variation	SS	df	MS	F
Length	15			
Technology				
Length × Technology	144			
Error	570	114		
Total	849			

(a) Complete the *F* table and make a decision to retain or reject the null hypothesis for each hypothesis test.

(b) Based on the results you obtained, what is the next step?

26. A developmental psychologist placed children in a social situation in which they were either rewarded or punished (Factor A: consequence) by a parent, sibling, or stranger (Factor B: type of adult). Following this social situation, children were placed back in the same social situation, and the time it took them (in seconds) to engage in the punished or rewarded behavior was recorded. The hypothetical results are given in the following table.

		Consequences	
		Reward	Punishment
Type of Adult	Parent	15 16 14 13	45 43 46 50
Type of Adult	Sibling	22 16 19 14	41 38 49 52
Type of Adult	Stranger	14 15 18 23	25 29 32 39

(a) Complete the *F* table and make a decision to retain or reject the null hypothesis for each hypothesis test.

(b) Compute simple main effect tests for the type of adult factor at each level of the consequences factor. Use Tukey's HSD to analyze the significant simple main effects. State your conclusions using APA format.

27. Evidence suggests that those with an optimistic worldview tend to be happier than those with a pessimistic worldview. One potential explanation for this is that optimists tend to ignore negative events and outcomes more so than pessimists. To test this explanation, participants were assessed and categorized into groups based on whether they were optimistic and pessimistic and whether they had reported more positive or negative life events in the previous week. All participants were then asked to rate their overall life happiness (i.e., the dependent variable). The results from this hypothetical study are given in the table.

		Worldview	
		Optimistic	**Pessimistic**
Life Events Mostly Recalled	**Positive**	9 8 12 9 10 7 9 8	7 9 8 10 11 7 5 9
Life Events Mostly Recalled	**Negative**	9 10 9 11 8 9 8 7	4 6 8 7 4 5 6 5

(a) Complete the *F* table and make a decision to retain or reject the null hypothesis for each hypothesis test.

(b) Compute simple main effect tests for the Life Events factor at each level of the Worldview factor. State your conclusions using APA format.

28. Among other benefits, pets are thought to be great companions that increase satisfaction among pet owners, especially those who would otherwise live alone. A psychologist decides to test this notion. Participants who live with others or alone (Factor A: living status) and own pets or do not (Factor B: pet owner status) were asked to indicate how satisfied they were with their living arrangements. It was expected that pet owners would report greater overall satisfaction than those who did not have pets. The hypothetical results are given in the following table.

		Pet Owner	
		Yes	**No**
Live Alone	**Yes**	7 6 7 6	3 4 5 5
	No	6 6 7 5	4 2 5 7

(a) Complete the *F* table and make a decision to retain or reject the null hypothesis for each hypothesis test.

(b) Are post hoc tests necessary? Explain.

Problems in Research

29. **The null hypothesis and test statistic for an ANOVA.** The null hypothesis for an ANOVA states that the group means are not different. In terms of the population means, van Rossum, van de Schoot, and Hoijtink (2013) stated the following null hypothesis for an ANOVA with four group means: $H_0: \mu_1 = \mu_2 = \mu_3 = \mu_4$.

(a) If a researcher was computing a two-way ANOVA, then how many levels of each factor must have been observed in this example with four group means?

(b) According to this text, and B. H. Cohen (2002), "the denominator of all three *F* ratios [for the two-way ANOVA] is the same" (p. 196). What is the denominator of the test statistic for each test with the two-way between-subjects ANOVA?

30. **Rodent species and sociality.** Freitas, El-Hani, and da Rocha (2008) tested the hypothesis that rodent species (four different species) and sex (male, female) influence the level of affiliation acquired through social behavior. They measured the number of social behaviors exhibited by each rodent during a social encounter. As part of their study, they reported the following:

Hypothesis test was performed by means of a [factorial] two-way ANOVA. The test was able to detect significant differences only among species, not among sexes. (Freitas et al., 2008, p. 389)

(a) Is a significant main effect or interaction evident in this study and, if so, for which factor?

(b) What is the appropriate next step?

31. **Touching while you shop.** Otterbring (2016) tested individuals' intuitions regarding how restricting versus encouraging touching a product during an in-store product demonstration should influence the number of products purchased and the amount of money spent. A summary for one finding reported in Otterbring's study is graphically presented in the figure below. Is a main effect, interaction, or both depicted in the graph? Explain.

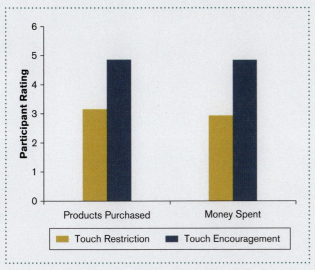

32. **Emoticons (facial feedback) with e-learning.** Tung and Deng (2007) studied how emoticons (computerized facial expressions) and sex influenced intrinsic motivation to complete a computer task. Emoticons were used as feedback for responses during the task. These faces were either static (presented still for the duration of feedback) or dynamic (presented as a neutral face and changed to the expression corresponding to the feedback). The researchers conducted a 2 × 2 between-subjects ANOVA, with emoticon style (static, dynamic) and sex (male, female) as the factors. The F table gives the data reported in the study.

Source of Variation	SS	df	MS	F
Emoticon Style	13.65	1	13.65	8.93
Sex	1.52	1	1.52	0.99
Emoticon Style × Sex	3.84	1	3.84	2.51
Error	258.57	169	1.53	
Total	277.58	172		

(a) Is a significant main effect or interaction evident in this study and, if so, for which factor?

(b) Are post hoc tests required? Explain.

Answers for even numbers are in Appendix D.

Sharpen your skills with **SAGE edge at edge.sagepub.com/priviteraess2e**

SAGE edge for Students provides a personalized approach to help you accomplish your coursework goals in an easy-to-use learning environment.

©iStockphoto.com/vvmich

Part V

Making Inferences About Patterns, Prediction, and Nonparametric Tests

©iStockphoto.com/Rawpixel Ltd

13 Correlation and Linear Regression

• • • Learning Objectives

After reading this chapter, you should be able to:

1. Identify the direction and strength of a linear correlation between two factors.

2. Compute and interpret the Pearson correlation coefficient and the coefficient of determination, and test for significance.

3. Identify and explain three assumptions and three limitations for evaluating a correlation coefficient.

4. Delineate the use of the Spearman, point-biserial, and phi correlation coefficients.

5. Distinguish between a predictor variable and a criterion variable.

6. Compute and interpret the method of least squares.

7. Identify each source of variation in an analysis of regression, and compute an analysis of regression and interpret the results.

8. Compute and interpret the standard error of estimate.

9. Summarize the results of a correlation coefficient and linear regression in APA format.

10. Compute the Pearson, Spearman, point-biserial, and phi correlation coefficients using SPSS.

11. Compute an analysis of regression using SPSS.

Testing relationships between variables can be quite informative and is a natural type of association to evaluate. We can identify, for example, how constructs such as love, attachment, personality, motivation, and cognition are related to other factors or behaviors such as tendencies toward depression, emotional well-being, and physical health. In everyday situations, you may notice relationships between exercise and health (e.g., people who are healthier tend to exercise more often) or between education and income (e.g., people who are more educated tend to earn a higher income). We can even ask questions about prediction, or the extent to which the relationships we observe can lead to a better understanding of what could happen in the future (i.e., our ability to predict behavior).

In hypothesis testing, there are often cases where we want to evaluate the relationship between two variables, or the extent to which we can predict behavior. In the basic structure of such a study, we measure two variables to test if they change in a related or in an independent fashion or to test if values of one factor can predict changes in another. For example, suppose we record the SAT scores and the freshman grade point average (GPA) in a sample of college students. We can evaluate how they are related (i.e., in this example, we may observe that higher SAT scores are related to higher GPA). Many colleges, however, may want to know if higher GPA scores among college applicants will predict higher GPA scores when the students enter college. Hence, in this example, understanding the relationship between these scores (correlation) and the ability of SAT scores to predict college freshman GPA (regression) is informative.

In this chapter, we explore the nature of hypothesis testing to evaluate the relationship between two variables and to evaluate predictive relationships. We further assess how to compute and interpret observed effects, and we explore other ways of adding information about the nature of observed effects and how to appropriately interpret them.

Master the content.

edge.sagepub.com/priviteraess2e

13.1 THE STRUCTURE OF DATA USED FOR IDENTIFYING PATTERNS AND MAKING PREDICTIONS

For hypothesis testing, beginning in Chapter 7, we described a variety of ways to compare group means. For each hypothesis test, we observed the levels of one factor, and in Chapter 12, we observed the combination of levels for two factors. Each level or combination of levels was a group, and in each group, we measured a dependent variable and analyzed mean differences between groups. Using this approach, significance indicated that two or more groups were different. Another approach to testing for mean differences is to compare two dependent variables to determine the extent to which changes in values for each variable are related, or change in an identifiable pattern. This type of approach is called a **correlation** and is most often used to identify the linear pattern or relationship between two variables.

Furthermore, we can use the information provided by a correlation to predict values of one factor, given known values of a second factor. A correlation reflects how closely two variables are related. In this chapter, we also evaluate the statistical procedure called **linear regression**, in which we use the value of a correlation to compute the equation of a regression line and then use this equation to predict values of one factor, given known values of a second factor in a population.

Throughout this chapter, data for correlations and regression are plotted in a graph called a **scatter plot**, which is used to illustrate the relationship between two variables, denoted (x, y). The x variable is plotted along the x-axis of the graph, and the y variable is plotted along the y-axis. Pairs of values for x and y are called **data points**. The data points are plotted along the x- and y-axis of a graph to see if a pattern emerges. The pattern that emerges can be described by the value of a correlation and by the equation of a regression line, as described in this chapter.

13.2 FUNDAMENTALS OF THE CORRELATION

Using a correlation, we compare two dependent variables to determine the extent to which changes in values for two variables are related, or change in an identifiable pattern. While the general structure of this analysis is much different than when we compared mean differences between groups, it is also comparable. To illustrate, suppose we observe students texting or not texting in class and compare differences in class performance (as an exam grade out of 100 points). In this example, illustrated in Figure 13.1a, the factor is texting (yes, no), and the dependent variable is class performance (an exam grade). This type of analysis will require the use of the two-independent-sample t test because we are comparing mean difference in exam scores between groups of students who did and did not text during class.

An alternative method using a correlation is to treat each factor like a dependent variable and measure the relationship between each pair of variables. For example, we could measure texting during class (number

A **correlation** is a statistical procedure used to describe the strength and direction of the linear relationship between two factors.

Linear regression, also called **regression**, is a statistical procedure used to determine the equation of a regression line to a set of data points and to determine the extent to which the regression equation can be used to predict values of one factor, given known values of a second factor in a population.

A **scatter plot**, also called a **scatter gram**, is a graphical display of discrete data points (x, y) used to summarize the relationship between two variables.

Data points are the x- and y-coordinates for each plot in a scatter plot.

FIGURE 13.1   Comparing Groups Means Versus the Correlational Method

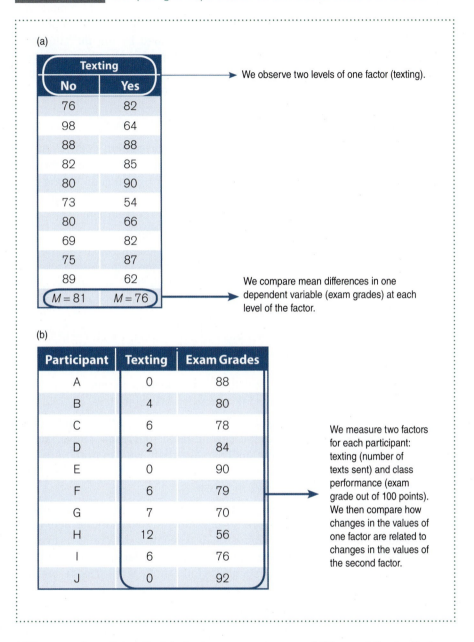

(a)

Texting	
No	**Yes**
76	82
98	64
88	88
82	85
80	90
73	54
80	66
69	82
75	87
89	62
$M = 81$	$M = 76$

We observe two levels of one factor (texting).

We compare mean differences in one dependent variable (exam grades) at each level of the factor.

(b)

Participant	Texting	Exam Grades
A	0	88
B	4	80
C	6	78
D	2	84
E	0	90
F	6	79
G	7	70
H	12	56
I	6	76
J	0	92

We measure two factors for each participant: texting (number of texts sent) and class performance (exam grade out of 100 points). We then compare how changes in the values of one factor are related to changes in the values of the second factor.

(a) The approach used in hypothesis testing to compare group means. (b) The correlational method. Instead of comparing mean differences for one dependent variable between groups, the correlational method examines the extent to which two measured factors are related.

of texts sent) and class performance (an exam grade out of 100 points) for each student in a class. We could then test to see if there is a relationship between the pairs of scores for each participant. In this example, illustrated in Figure 13.1b, if the scores are related, then we would expect exam scores to decrease as the number of texts sent increases.

A correlation can be used to (1) describe the pattern of data points for the values of two factors and (2) determine whether the pattern observed in a sample is also present in the population from which the sample was selected. The pattern of data points is described by the direction and strength of the relationship between two factors. In behavioral research, we mostly describe the linear (or straight-line) relationship between two factors. For this reason, this chapter focuses on linear relationships.

The Direction of a Correlation

FYI

The sign of a correlation coefficient indicates the direction of the relationship between two measured factors: + indicates that two factors change in the same direction; − indicates that two factors change in opposite directions.

The value of a correlation, measured by the **correlation coefficient (r)**, ranges from −1.0 to +1.0. Values closer to ±1.0 indicate stronger correlations, meaning that a correlation coefficient of $r = -1.0$ is as strong as a correlation coefficient of $r = +1.0$. The sign of the correlation coefficient (− or +) indicates only the direction or slope of the correlation.

A **positive correlation** ($0 < r \leq +1.0$) means that as the values of one factor increase, the values of the second factor also increase; as the values of one factor decrease, the values of the second factor also decrease. If two factors have values that change in the same direction, we can graph the correlation using a straight line. Figure 13.2 shows that values on the y-axis increase as values on the x-axis increase.

Figure 13.2a shows a *perfect* positive correlation, which occurs when each data point falls exactly on a straight line, although this is rare. More commonly, as shown in Figure 13.2b, a positive correlation is greater than 0 but less than +1.0, where the values of two factors change in the same direction but not all data points fall exactly on a straight line.

A **negative correlation** ($-1.0 \leq r < 0$) means that as the values of one factor increase, the values of the second factor decrease. If two factors have values that change in the opposite direction, we can graph the correlation using a straight line. Figure 13.3 shows that values on the y-axis decrease as values on the x-axis increase.

Figure 13.3a shows a *perfect* negative correlation, which occurs when each data point falls exactly on a straight line, although this is also rare. More commonly, as shown in Figure 13.3b, a negative correlation is greater than −1.0 but less than 0, where the values of two factors change in the opposite direction but not all data points fall exactly on a straight line.

The **correlation coefficient (r)** is used to measure the strength and direction of the linear relationship, or correlation, between two factors. The value of r ranges from −1.0 to +1.0.

A **positive correlation** ($0 < r \leq +1.0$) is a positive value of r that indicates that the values of two factors change in the same direction: As the values of one factor increase, the values of the second factor also increase; as the values of one factor decrease, the values of the second factor also decrease.

A **negative correlation** ($-1.0 \leq r < 0$) is a negative value of r that indicates that the values of two factors change in different directions, meaning that as the values of one factor increase, the values of the second factor decrease.

A **regression line** is the best-fitting straight line to a set of data points. A best-fitting line is the line that minimizes the distance of all data points that fall from it.

The Strength of a Correlation

A zero correlation ($r = 0$) means that there is no linear pattern or relationship between two factors. This outcome is rare because usually by mere chance, at least some values of one factor, X, will show some pattern or relationship with values of a second factor, Y. The closer a correlation coefficient is to $r = 0$, the weaker the correlation and the less likely that two factors are related; the closer a correlation coefficient is to $r = \pm1.0$, the stronger the correlation and the more likely that two factors are related.

The strength of a correlation reflects how consistently scores for each factor change. When plotted in a scatter plot, scores are more consistent the closer they fall to a **regression line**, or the straight line that best

FIGURE 13.2 A Perfect Positive (a) and a Positive (b) Linear Correlation

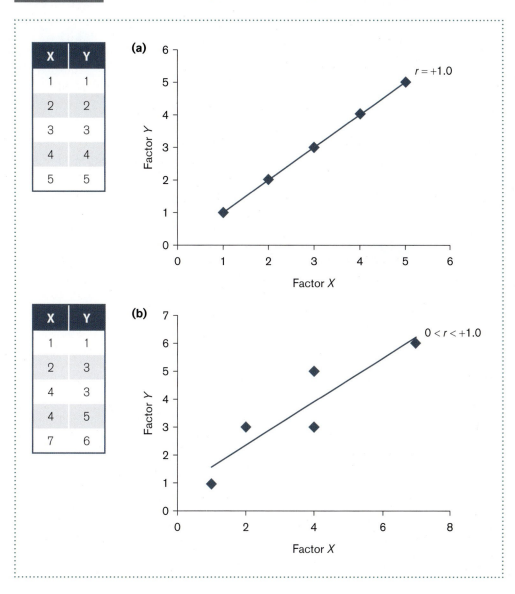

X	Y
1	1
2	2
3	3
4	4
5	5

(a) $r = +1.0$

X	Y
1	1
2	3
4	3
4	5
7	6

(b) $0 < r < +1.0$

Both the table and the scatter plot show the same data for (a) and (b).

fits a set of data points. The best-fitting straight line minimizes the total distance of all data points that fall from it. Figure 13.4 shows two positive correlations between exercise (Factor X) and body image satisfaction (Factor Y), and Figure 13.5 shows two negative correlations between number of class absences (Factor X) and grade on a quiz (Factor Y). In both figures, the closer a set of data points falls to the regression line, the stronger the correlation; hence, the closer a correlation coefficient is to $r = \pm 1.0$.

FYI

The closer a set of data points falls to a regression line, the stronger the correlation (the closer a correlation is to r = ±1.0).

FIGURE 13.3   A Perfect Negative (a) and a Negative (b) Linear Correlation

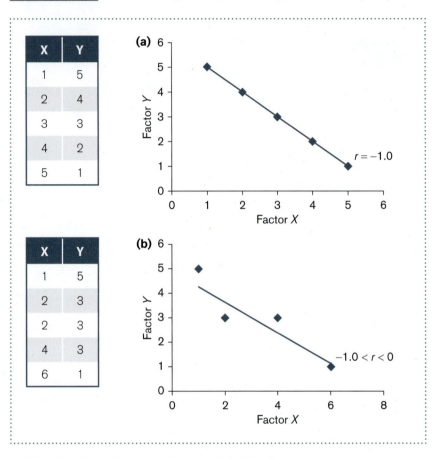

Both the table and the scatter plot show the same data for (a) and (b).

LEARNING CHECK 1

1. A researcher reports that the farther college students are from their parents, the more often they communicate with their parents (either by phone or by e-mail). Is this an example of a positive correlation or a negative correlation?

2. An instructor reports that as the number of student interruptions during class decreases, student scores on in-class quizzes increase. Is this an example of a positive correlation or a negative correlation?

3. Which of the following indicates the strongest correlation?

    (a) $r = -.57$ (b) $r = +.78$ (c) $r = -.90$ (d) $r = +.88$

4. What happens to the value of r the closer that data points fall to the regression line?

Answers: 1. A positive correlation; 2. A negative correlation; 3. (c); 4. The correlation coefficient increases closer to $r = \pm 1.0$.

FIGURE 13.4   The Consistency of Scores for a Positive Correlation

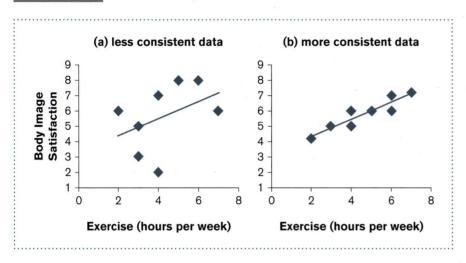

Both figures show approximately the same regression line, but the data points in (b) are more consistent, and thus show a stronger correlation, because they fall closer to the regression line than those in (a).

FIGURE 13.5   The Consistency of Scores for a Negative Correlation

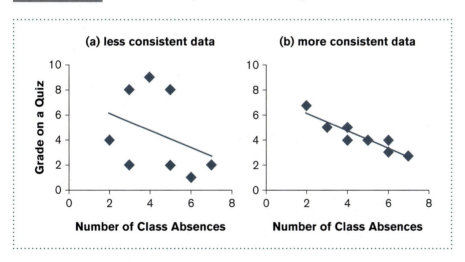

Both figures show approximately the same regression line, but the data points in (b) are more consistent, and thus show a stronger correlation, because they fall closer to the regression line than those in (a).

13.3 THE PEARSON CORRELATION COEFFICIENT

The most commonly used formula for computing r is the **Pearson correlation coefficient**, also called the **Pearson product-moment correlation coefficient**. The Pearson correlation coefficient is used to determine the strength and direction of the relationship between two factors on an interval or ratio scale of measurement. Recall from Chapter 5 that we located z scores by computing a z transformation on a set of data. In the same way,

The **Pearson correlation coefficient (r)**, also called the **Pearson product-moment correlation coefficient**, is a measure of the direction and strength of the linear relationship of two factors in which the data for both factors are measured on an interval or ratio scale of measurement.

FYI

The Pearson correlation coefficient is a popular correlation measure in the behavioral sciences.

FYI

The correlation coefficient measures the variance or distance that data points fall from the regression line.

we can locate a sample of data points by converting them to z scores and computing the following formula:

$$r = \frac{\sum(z_X z_Y)}{n-1}$$

Notice that the general formula for the Pearson correlation coefficient is similar to that for computing variance. This formula has the drawback of requiring that each score be transformed into a z score, and consequently, an equivalent formula that uses raw scores is used more often to calculate the Pearson correlation coefficient. Writing this formula in terms of the sum of the squares gives us the following correlation coefficient:

$$r = \frac{SS_{XY}}{\sqrt{SS_X SS_Y}}.$$

The value in the numerator of the Pearson correlation coefficient reflects the extent to which values on the x-axis (X) and y-axis (Y) vary together. The extent to which the values of two factors vary together is called **covariance**. The extent to which values of X and Y vary independently, or separately, is placed in the denominator. The formula for r can be stated as follows:

$$r = \frac{\text{covariance of } X \text{ and } Y}{\text{variance of } X \text{ and } Y \text{ separately}}.$$

The correlation coefficient, r, measures the variance of X and the variance of Y, which constitutes the total variance that can be measured. The total variance is placed in the denominator of the formula for r. The covariance in the numerator is the amount or proportion of the total variance that is shared by X and Y. The larger the covariance, the closer data points will fall to the regression line. When all data points for X and Y fall exactly on a regression line, the covariance equals the total variance, making the formula for r equal to +1.0 or −1.0, depending on the direction of the relationship. The farther that data points fall from the regression line, the smaller the covariance will be compared to the total variance in the denominator, resulting in a value of r closer to 0.

Covariance is the extent to which the values of two factors (X and Y) vary together. The closer data points fall to the regression line, the more the values of two factors vary together.

MAKING SENSE UNDERSTANDING COVARIANCE

If we conceptualize covariance as circles, as illustrated in Figure 13.6, then the variance of each factor (X and Y) is contained within each circle. The two circles, then, contain the total measured variance. The covariance of X and Y reflects the extent to which the total variance or the two circles overlap. In terms of computing r, the overlap or covariance is placed in the numerator; the total variance contained within each circle is placed in the denominator. The more the two circles overlap, the more the covariance (in the numerator) will equal the independent variances contained within each circle (in the denominator)—and the closer r will be to ±1.0.

FIGURE 13.6   Each Circle Represents the Variance of a Factor

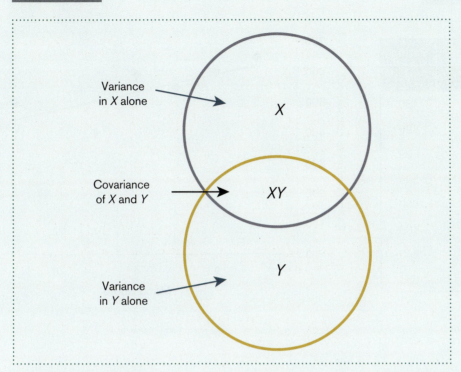

Two factors covary inasmuch as the two circles overlap. The more overlap or shared variance of two factors, the more the two factors are related.

In Example 13.1, we compute the Pearson correlation coefficient for data measured on an interval or ratio scale of measurement, following these steps:

Step 1: Compute preliminary calculations.

Step 2: Compute the Pearson correlation coefficient (r).

Example 13.1

An area of research of particular interest is the relationship between mood and appetite (Baxter, 2016; Hammen & Keenan-Miller, 2013; Sander, DeBoth, & Ollendick, 2016). As an example of one such study from this area of research, suppose a health psychologist tests if mood and eating are related by recording data for each variable in a sample of 8 participants. She measures mood using a 9-point rating scale in which higher ratings indicate better mood. She measures eating as the average number of daily calories that each participant consumed in the previous week. The results for this study are listed in Figure 13.7. We will compute the Pearson correlation coefficient using these data.

Step 1: Compute preliminary calculations. We begin by making the preliminary calculations listed in Table 13.1. The signs (+ and −) of the values we measure for each factor are essential to making accurate computations. The goal is to find the sum of squares needed to complete the formula for r.

FIGURE 13.7 A Table and Scatter Plot Showing Data for the Relationship Between Mood and Eating ($n = 8$)

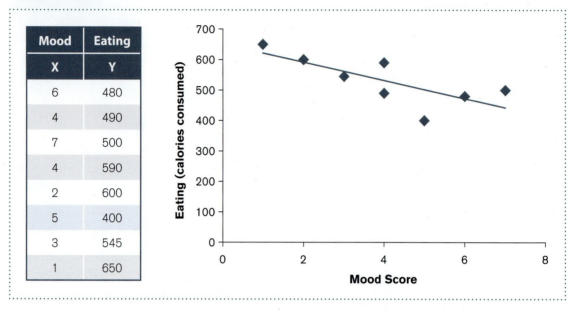

The regression line is given in the scatter plot. Both the table and the scatter plot show the same data.

TABLE 13.1 Preliminary Calculations in Step 1 of Example 13.1

Mood	Eating	Deviation Scores		Sum of Squares		
X	Y	$X - M_X$	$Y - M_Y$	$(X - M_X)(Y - M_Y)$	$(X - M_X)^2$	$(Y - M_Y)^2$
6	480	2	−52	−104	4	2,704
4	490	0	−42	0	0	1,764
7	500	3	−32	−96	9	1,024
4	590	0	58	0	0	3,364
2	600	−2	68	−136	4	4,624
5	400	1	−132	−132	1	17,424
3	545	−1	13	−13	1	169
1	650	−3	118	−354	9	13,924
$M_X = 4$	$M_Y = 532$			$SS_{XY} = -835$	$SS_X = 28$	$SS_Y = 44,997$

The sum of the products of deviations for X and Y   The sum of squares for X   The sum of squares for Y

The key values that are substituted into the formula for the Pearson correlation coefficient are circled.

1. Compute the average X and Y score. In Table 13.1, each column of X and Y scores was summed and then averaged. The result is that $M_X = 4$ and $M_Y = 532$.

2. Subtract each score from its respective mean. In the third column, each X score is subtracted from the mean for X (M_X); in the fourth column, each Y score is subtracted from the mean for Y (M_Y). Recall from Chapter 3 that the sum of each column should be equal to 0. This is a way to check your work.

3. Multiply and sum the deviation scores for X and Y. Multiply across the rows in the third and fourth columns. The sum of these scores is the sum of squares for XY, also called the **sum of products (SP)**:

$$SS_{XY} = -835.$$

The sum of products can be a negative value because positive and negative deviation values of X are multiplied by positive and negative deviation values of Y. Therefore, the sum of products determines whether a correlation coefficient is positive or negative.

4. Multiply and sum the deviation scores for X. Multiply the deviation scores of each X value in the third column by itself. The sum of these scores is the sum of squares of X:

$$SS_X = 28.$$

5. Multiply and sum the deviation scores for Y. Multiply the deviation scores for each Y value in the fourth column by itself. The sum of these scores is the sum of squares for Y:

$$SS_Y = 44,997.$$

Step 2: Compute the Pearson correlation coefficient (r). We computed each required computation in the formula. We now substitute these values into the formula to compute the Pearson correlation coefficient:

$$r = \frac{SS_{XY}}{\sqrt{SS_X SS_Y}} = \frac{-835}{\sqrt{28 \times 44,997}} = -.744.$$

The Pearson correlation coefficient is $r = -.744$. The sign of the correlation (–) indicates the direction of the relationship between mood and eating; the strength of the correlation is indicated by the value (.744), with values closer to −1.0 and +1.0 indicating that mood and eating are more closely related.

Effect Size: The Coefficient of Determination

A correlation coefficient ranges from −1 to +1, so it can be negative. To compute proportion of variance as an estimate of effect size, we square the correlation coefficient r. The value of r^2 or R^2 is called the **coefficient of determination**. The result of this calculation is a value between 0 and +1 that is mathematically equivalent to the value of eta-squared (η^2), which we computed for the t tests and analyses of variance (ANOVAs).

In Example 13.1, we want to measure the proportion of variance in calories consumed (eating) that can be explained by ratings of mood. The coefficient of determination for the data in Example 13.1 is

$$r^2 = -(.744)^2 = .553.$$

FYI

The sum of products is an estimate of the sum of squares of XY. The value of SP determines whether the direction of a correlation is positive or negative.

FYI

The coefficient of determination (r^2 or R^2) is mathematically equivalent to eta-squared (η^2).

The **sum of products (SP)** is the sum of squares for two factors, X and Y, which are also represented as SS_{XY}. SP is the numerator for the Pearson correlation formula. To compute SP, we multiply the deviation of each X value by the deviation of each Y value.

The **coefficient of determination (r^2 or R^2)** is a formula that is mathematically equivalent to eta-squared and is used to measure the proportion of variance of one factor (Y) that can be explained by known values of a second factor (X).

In terms of proportion of variance, we conclude that about 55% of the variability in calories consumed can be explained by participants' ratings of their mood.

Hypothesis Testing: Testing for Significance

We can also follow the steps to hypothesis testing to test for significance. By doing so, we can determine whether the correlation observed in a sample is present in the population from which the sample was selected. Using the data from Example 13.1, we will conduct a hypothesis test to test for significance.

Step 1: State the hypotheses. To test for the significance of a correlation, the null hypothesis is that there is no relationship between two factors (a zero correlation) in the population. The alternative hypothesis is that there is a relationship between two factors (a positive or negative correlation) in the population. For a population, the correlation coefficient is symbolized by the Greek letter rho, ρ. We can therefore state the hypotheses for Example 13.1 as follows:

H_0: $\rho = 0$ (Mood is not related to eating in the population.)

H_1: $\rho \neq 0$ (Mood is related to eating in the population.)

Step 2: Set the criteria for a decision. We will compute a two-tailed test at a .05 level of significance. The degrees of freedom are the number of scores that are free to vary for X and for Y. All X scores except one are free to vary, and all Y scores except one are free to vary. Hence, the degrees of freedom for a correlation are $n - 2$. In Example 13.1, $n = 8$; therefore, the degrees of freedom for this test are $8 - 2 = 6$.

To locate the critical values for this test, look in Table C.5 in Appendix C. Table 13.2 shows a portion of this table. The alpha levels for one-tailed and two-tailed tests are given in each column and the degrees of freedom in the rows in Table C.5 in Appendix C. At a .05 level of significance, the critical values for this test are ±.707. The probability is less than 5% that we will obtain a correlation stronger than $r = \pm.707$ when $n = 8$. If r is stronger than or exceeds ±.707, then we reject the null hypothesis; otherwise, we retain the null hypothesis.

Step 3: Compute the test statistic. The correlation coefficient r is the test statistic for the hypothesis test. We already measured this: $r = -.744$.

Step 4: Make a decision. To decide whether to retain or reject the null hypothesis, we compare the value of the test statistic to the critical values. Because $r = -.744$ exceeds the lower critical value, we reject the null hypothesis. We conclude that the correlation observed between mood and eating reflects a relationship between mood and eating in the population. If we were to report this result in a research journal, it would look something like this:

Using the Pearson correlation coefficient, a significant relationship between mood and eating was evident, $r = -.744$, $p < .05$.

FYI

A hypothesis test is used to determine whether an observed correlation in a sample is present in a population of interest.

TABLE 13.2	A Portion of the Pearson Correlation Table in Table C.5 in Appendix C

	Level of Significance for Two-Tailed Test			
$df = n - 2$	.10	.05	.02	.01
1	.988	.997	.9995	.9999
2	.900	.950	.980	.990
3	.805	.878	.934	.959
4	.729	.811	.882	.917
5	.669	.754	.833	.874
6	.622	.707	.789	.834
7	.582	.666	.750	.798
8	.549	.632	.716	.765
9	.521	.602	.685	.735
10	.497	.576	.658	.708

Source: Table VI of Fisher, R. A., & Yates, F. (1974). *Statistical tables for biological, agricultural and medical research* (6th ed.). London, England: Longman Group Ltd. (previously published by Oliver and Boyd Ltd., Edinburgh). Adapted and reprinted with permission of Addison Wesley Longman.

13.4 SPSS in Focus:
Pearson Correlation Coefficient

In Example 13.1, we concluded that mood and eating were significantly correlated, $r = -.744$, $p < .05$, using the Pearson correlation coefficient. Let us confirm this conclusion using SPSS.

1. Click on the Variable View tab and enter *mood* in the Name column; enter *eating* in the Name column below it. Reduce the value to 0 in the Decimals column for both rows.

2. Click on the Data View tab. Enter the data for mood in the first column; enter the corresponding data for eating in the second column.

3. Go to the menu bar and click Analyze, then Correlate and Bivariate, to display a dialog box.

4. Using the arrows, move both variables into the Variables: box.

5. Select OK, or select Paste and click the Run command.

(Continued)

(Continued)

The SPSS output table, shown in Table 13.3, gives the results of a two-tailed test at a .05 level of significance. The SPSS output is set up in a matrix with mood and eating listed in the rows and columns. Each cell in the matrix gives the direction and strength of the correlation ($r = -.744$ for mood and eating; this value is shown with an asterisk for significant correlations), the significance ($p = .034$), and the sample size ($N = 8$). To find the coefficient of determination, square the correlation coefficient.

TABLE 13.3 SPSS Output Table for Example 13.1

Correlations

		mood	eating
mood	Pearson Correlation	1	-.744*
	Sig. (2-tailed)		.034
	N	8	8
eating	Pearson Correlation	-.744*	1
	Sig. (2-tailed)	.034	
	N	8	8

*. Correlation is significant at the 0.05 level (2-tailed).

LEARNING CHECK 2

1. Name the correlation coefficient used to measure the strength and direction of the linear relationship of two factors on an interval or ratio scale of measurement.

2. Compute the Pearson correlation coefficient given the following data.

   (a) $SS_{XY} = -53$, $SS_X = 58$, $SS_Y = 255.20$

   (b) $SS_{XY} = 3.8$, $SS_X = 5.2$, $SS_Y = 5.2$

3. State the coefficient of determination for (a) and (b) in Question 2.

4. State whether each of the following is significant for a study with a sample of 12 participants. Use a .05 level of significance and conduct a two-tailed test.

   (a) $r = -.55$ (b) $r = +.78$ (c) $r = -.60$ (d) $r = +.48$

Answers: 1. Pearson correlation coefficient. 2. (a) $r = -.436$, (b) $r = +.731$; 3. (a) $r^2 = (-.436)^2 = .190$, (b) $r^2 = (.731)^2 = .534$; 4. (a) Not significant, (b) Significant, (c) Significant, (d) Not significant.

13.5 ASSUMPTIONS AND LIMITATIONS FOR LINEAR CORRELATIONS

We make many assumptions to test for the significance of a linear correlation. These assumptions apply to any type of linear correlation and not just the Pearson correlation coefficient. Three key assumptions described in this section are homoscedasticity, linearity, and normality.

Homoscedasticity

Homoscedasticity (pronounced "ho-mo-skee-das-ti-ci-ty") is the assumption of constant variance among data points. We assume that there is an equal ("homo") variance or scatter ("scedasticity") of data points dispersed along the regression line. Figure 13.8 shows an example in which this assumption is violated—in the figure, the variance of scores in Group B is obviously different from that in Group A. When the variance of data points from the regression line is not equal, the Pearson correlation coefficient (r) tends to underestimate the strength of a correlation.

FIGURE 13.8   Violation of Homoscedasticity

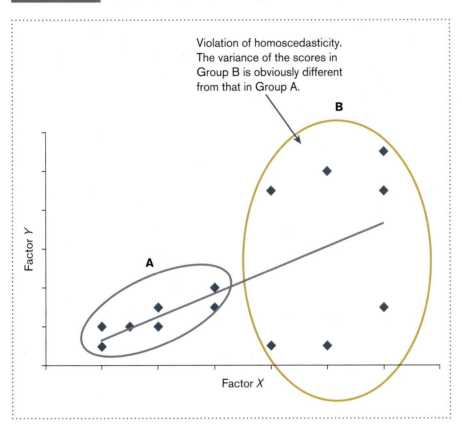

Violation of homoscedasticity. The variance of the scores in Group B is obviously different from that in Group A.

B

A

Factor Y

Factor X

This population of scores shows a scatter of data points with unequal variances.

Linearity

Linearity is the assumption that the best way to describe a pattern of data is using a straight line. In truth, we could fit just about any set of data points to a best-fitting straight line, but the data may actually conform better to other shapes, such as curvilinear shapes. Figure 13.9 shows an example where the data are curvilinear. In this situation, a linear correlation should not be used to describe the data because the assumption of linearity is violated.

Homoscedasticity is the assumption that there is an equal ("homo") variance or scatter ("scedasticity") of data points dispersed along the regression line.

Linearity is the assumption that the best way to describe a pattern of data is using a straight line.

FIGURE 13.9   Violation of Linearity

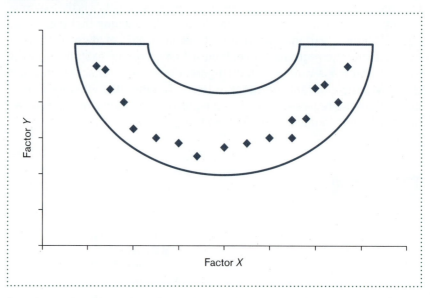

A population with a nonlinear relationship, which violates the assumption of linearity. In this example, the pattern is curvilinear.

Normality

To test for linear correlations, we must assume that the data points are normally distributed. This assumption is more complex than the assumptions of normality for the *t* tests and ANOVA tests. For a linear correlation between two factors, the assumption of normality requires that a population of *X* and *Y* scores for two factors forms a bivariate (two-variable) normal distribution, such that

1. the population of *X* scores (mood in Example 13.1) is normally distributed;

2. the population of *Y* scores (eating in Example 13.1) is normally distributed;

3. for each *X* score (mood in Example 13.1), the distribution of *Y* scores (eating in Example 13.1) is normal; and

4. for each *Y* score (eating in Example 13.1), the distribution of *X* scores (mood in Example 13.1) is normal.

We assume that *X* and *Y* are normally distributed both in general (1 and 2 in the list) and at each point along the distribution of the other variable (3 and 4 in the list). To see the importance of this assumption, we can look at an extreme violation of it. Suppose we select a sample of six people and ask them how many fingers they have on their right and left hands. We record the data displayed in Figure 13.10.

FIGURE 13.10 Violation of Normality

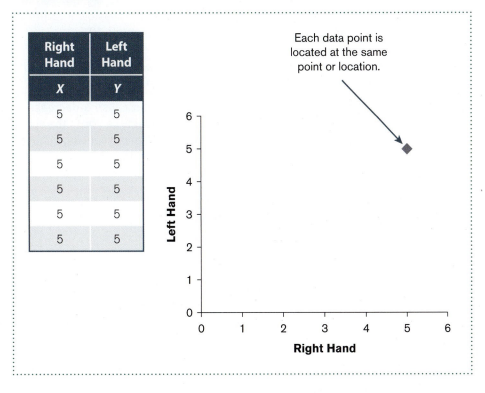

Right Hand	Left Hand
X	Y
5	5
5	5
5	5
5	5
5	5
5	5

Each data point is located at the same point or location.

The table and the scatter plot showing the relationship between the number of fingers on the right and left hands of six people. In this example, the data points do not vary, which violates the assumption of normality. Both the table and the scatter plot show the same data.

Notice that individuals with five fingers on their right hand also have five fingers on their left hand. The number of fingers on each hand is certainly related. However, in the scatter plot, only one data point is plotted because the data point for each person is the same (5, 5). As a result, the correlation coefficient will be a zero correlation: $r = 0$. This anomaly arises because of an extreme violation of the assumption of normality: All scores are the same and therefore are not normally distributed. In fact, these scores have no variance. Violating the assumption of normality can distort or bias the value of the correlation coefficient.

In addition, fundamental limitations using a correlation require that a significant correlation be interpreted with caution. Among the many considerations for interpreting a significant correlation, in this section we consider causality, outliers, and restriction of range.

Causality

Using a correlational design, we do not manipulate an independent variable, and we certainly do not overtly control for other possible factors that may covary with the two variables we measured. For this reason, a significant correlation does not show that one factor causes changes in a second

FYI

To compute a correlation, we assume that the data points have equal variance (homoscedasticity), are best fit to a straight line (linearity), and are normally distributed (normality).

FYI

Significant correlations show that two factors are related and not that one factor causes changes in a second factor.

FYI

Reverse causality occurs when the direction of causality for two factors, A and B, cannot be determined. Hence, changes in Factor A could cause changes in Factor B, or changes in Factor B could cause changes in Factor A.

factor (causality). Instead, a significant correlation shows the direction and the strength of the relationship between two factors. To highlight limitations of causality for a correlation, let us look at four possible interpretations for the significant correlation measured in Example 13.1.

1. Decreases in how we feel (mood) can cause an increase in the amount we eat (eating). This possibility cannot be ruled out.

2. Increases in the amount we eat (eating) can cause a decrease in how we feel (mood). So the direction of causality can be in the opposite direction. Hence, instead of changes in mood causing changes in eating, maybe changes in eating cause changes in mood. This possibility, called **reverse causality**, cannot be ruled out either.

FIGURE 13.11   Four Potential Explanations for a Significant Correlation

1. Changes in mood cause changes in eating:

Mood ————————————→ Eating

2. Changes in eating cause changes in mood (reverse causality):

Mood ←———————————— Eating

3. The two variables work together (systematically) to cause an effect:

Mood   Eating

4. Changes in both factors are caused by a third confound variable:

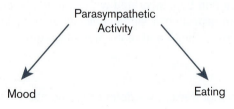

Parasympathetic
Activity

Mood   Eating

Because factors are measured, but not manipulated, using the correlational method, any one of these possibilities could explain a significant correlation.

Reverse causality is a problem that arises when the causality between two factors can be in either direction.

3. The two factors could be systematic, meaning that they work together to cause a change. If two factors are systematic, then Conclusions 1 and 2 could be correct. The worse we feel, the more we eat, and the more we eat, the worse we feel. This possibility, that each factor causes the other, cannot be ruled out either.

4. Changes in both factors may be caused by a third unanticipated factor, called a **confound variable**. Perhaps biological factors, such as increased parasympathetic activity, make people feel worse and increase how much they want to eat. So, it is increased parasympathetic activity that could be causing changes in both mood and eating. This confound variable and any number of additional confound variables could be causing changes in mood and eating and cannot be ruled out either.

Figure 13.11 summarizes each possible explanation for an observed correlation between mood and eating. The correlational design cannot distinguish between these four possible explanations. Instead, a significant correlation shows that two factors are related. It does not provide an explanation for how or why they are related.

Outliers

In addition, outliers can obscure the relationship between two factors by altering the direction and the strength of an observed correlation. An outlier is a score that falls substantially above or below most other scores in a data set. Figure 13.12a shows data for the relationship between income and education without an outlier in the data. Figure 13.12b shows how

FYI

Outliers can change the strength and direction of a correlation coefficient.

A **confound variable**, or **third variable**, is an unanticipated variable not accounted for in a research study that could be causing or associated with observed changes in one or more measured variables.

FIGURE 13.12 The Effects of an Outlier

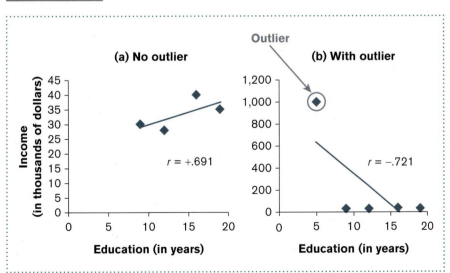

(a) displays a typical correlation between income and education, with more education being associated with higher income. (b) shows the same data with an additional outlier of a child movie star who earns $1 million. The inclusion of this outlier changed both the direction and the strength of the correlation.

an outlier, such as the income earned by a child movie star, changes the relationship between two factors. Notice in Figure 13.12 that the outlier changed both the direction and the strength of the correlation.

Restriction of Range

When interpreting a correlation, it is also important to avoid making conclusions about relationships that fall beyond the range of data measured. The **restriction of range** problem occurs when the range of data measured in a sample is restricted or smaller than the range of data in the general population.

Figure 13.13 shows how the range of data measured in a sample can lead to erroneous conclusions about the relationship between two factors in a given population. In the figure, a positive correlation for a hypothetical

FYI

Do not describe a correlation beyond the range of data observed to avoid the problem of restriction of range.

FIGURE 13.13   The Effects of Restriction of Range

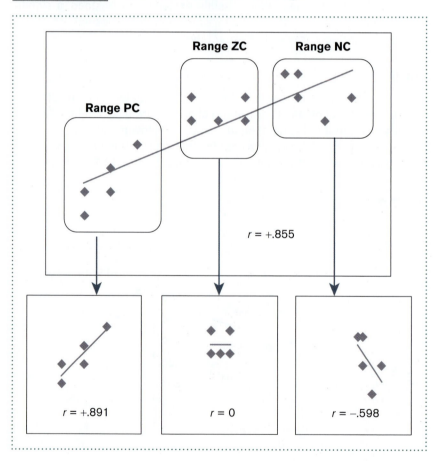

Restriction of range is a problem that arises when the range of data for one or both correlated factors in a sample is limited or restricted, compared to the range of data in the population from which the sample was selected.

In this population, shown in the top graph, there is a positive correlation between two factors ($r = +.855$). Also depicted are three possible samples we could select from this population. Range PC shows a positive correlation ($r = +.891$), Range ZC shows a zero correlation ($r = 0$), and Range NC shows a negative correlation ($r = -.598$)—all within the same population. Because different ranges of data within the same population can show very different patterns, correlations should never be interpreted beyond the range of data measured in a sample.

population (top graph) and the correlations in three possible samples we could select from this population (smaller graphs at bottom) are shown. Notice that, depending on the range of data measured, we could identify a positive, a negative, or zero correlation from the same population, although the data in the population are actually positively correlated. To avoid the problem of restriction of range, the direction and the strength of a significant correlation should only be generalized to a population within the limited range of measurements observed in the sample.

LEARNING CHECK 3

1. State three assumptions of tests for linear correlations.

2. A researcher reports a significant positive correlation and concludes that spending more time writing a research paper will cause a better grade on the paper. Is this conclusion appropriate? Explain.

3. How can an outlier alter the relationship between two factors?

4. The range of data for one or both factors in a sample is limited, compared to the range of data in the population from which the sample was selected. What is this problem called?

Answers: 1. Homoscedasticity, linearity, and normality; 2. No, because a correlation does not demonstrate cause; 3. An outlier can change the direction and strength of a correlation; 4. Restriction of range.

13.6 ALTERNATIVES TO PEARSON: SPEARMAN, POINT-BISERIAL, AND PHI

The Pearson correlation coefficient is used to describe the relationship between two factors on an interval or ratio scale. To analyze the correlation between factors on different scales of measurement requires new formulas. Each of these new formulas was derived from the Pearson correlation coefficient, and therefore, the Pearson formula can be used to conduct each of the additional tests introduced in this chapter. For this reason, we only briefly introduce each of these alternative correlation coefficients in this section. The following alternative tests are introduced in this section:

- Spearman correlation coefficient
- Point-biserial correlation coefficient
- Phi correlation coefficient

The Spearman Correlation Coefficient

In certain research situations, we want to determine the relationship between two ranked factors (ranks are an ordinal scale measurement). For example, we may want to identify the relationship between different polls in ranking college sports teams, or we may want to see how the order of completing a task is related from the first to the second trial. To measure the relationship between two ranked factors, we use the

Spearman rank-order correlation coefficient (r_s), or **Spearman's rho**. The formula for the Spearman rank-order correlation coefficient is

$$r_s = 1 - \frac{6\sum D^2}{n(n^2-1)}.$$

In this formula, D is the difference between the ranks of Factor X and Factor Y, and n is the number of pairs of ranks. The Spearman formula produces a value between −1.0 and +1.0, same as for any correlation coefficient. We use the Spearman formula when we measure two ranked factors. If scores for one or both factors are not ranked, then they must be transformed to ranks to fit this formula. Also, if one or more ranks are tied, or the same, then you must average the tied ranks before computing the Spearman formula.

To identify significance using the Spearman correlation coefficient, we can refer to Table C.6 in Appendix C to find the critical values for a Spearman correlation coefficient. A portion of this table is shown in Table 13.4. Table C.6 is similar to the table for Pearson except that n (not df) is listed in the rows. To illustrate, suppose we rank the order of 8 participants in two trials of a cognitive learning task. The critical value at a .05 level of significance with 8 participants is .738. We can then compute the Spearman formula to compare the correlation we observed to the critical value we identified in the table. When the correlation we computed is larger than the critical value, we decide to reject the null hypothesis that there is no relationship between ranks in the population; thus, we conclude that the correlation is significant. Otherwise, we retain the null hypothesis.

| **TABLE 13.4** | A Portion of the Spearman Correlation Table in Table C.6 in Appendix C |

Level of Significance for Two-Tailed Test				
N	.10	.05	.02	.01
4	1.000			
5	.900	1.000	1.000	
6	.829	.886	.943	1.000
7	.714	.786	.893	.929
8	.643	.738	.833	.881
9	.600	.700	.783	.833
10	.564	.648	.745	.794

The **Spearman rank-order correlation coefficient (r_s)**, or **Spearman's rho**, is a measure of the direction and strength of the linear relationship of two ranked factors on an ordinal scale of measurement.

Source: Reprinted with permission from the *Journal of the American Statistical Association.* Copyright 1972 by the American Statistical Association. All rights reserved.

The Point-Biserial Correlation Coefficient

In certain research situations, we can measure one factor that is continuous (on an interval or ratio scale of measurement) and a second factor that is dichotomous (on a nominal scale of measurement). A dichotomous factor has only two values or categories, such as sex (male, female) or pet owner (yes, no). For example, we may want to identify the relationship between sex (male, female) and job satisfaction, or between perceptions of happiness and pet ownership (yes, no). To measure the direction and strength of the linear relationship between one factor that is continuous and one factor that is dichotomous, we use the **point-biserial correlation coefficient**. The formula for the point-biserial correlation coefficient is

$$r_{pb} = \left(\frac{M_{Y_1} - M_{Y_2}}{s_Y} \right) \left(\sqrt{pq} \right), \text{ where } s_Y = \sqrt{\frac{SS_Y}{n}}.$$

In the point-biserial formula, p and q are the proportion of scores at each level of the dichotomous factor, s_Y is the standard deviation of Y scores (for the continuous factor), and n is the number of pairs of scores measured. Note that this new formula was derived from the Pearson formula—the two formulas are mathematically equivalent. Note also that the direction of a point-biserial correlation coefficient is not meaningful because it makes no sense to say that the levels of a dichotomous variable increase or decrease. Sex (male, female), for example, does not increase or decrease as, say, job satisfaction increases. If the correlation is significant, then we look back at the data to see which level of the dichotomous variable had a larger mean value. For example, if the correlation between sex and job satisfaction was significant, then we would look to see if men or women had higher job satisfaction scores. If men had higher scores, then we would conclude that sex and job satisfaction are related, with men having higher job satisfaction than women.

You may have noticed that the structure of the point-biserial test is quite similar to the two-independent-sample t test. For example, referring back to the example with sex and job satisfaction, the structure for a t test would be to make sex the groups (male, female) and job satisfaction the dependent variable that is measured in each group. To test for significance, we therefore convert the correlation coefficient, r, to a t value, then use the value of t to make a decision using the t table given in Table C.2 in Appendix C, same as for the two-independent-sample t test in Chapter 9. We can convert the value of r to a t statistic using the following equation:

$$t^2 = \frac{r^2}{(1-r^2)/df}.$$

The t test and point-biserial test are related in that their measures of effect size (r^2 and η^2) are mathematically the same, which allows the t test to be used as a test for the significance of a point-biserial correlation. To demonstrate how to compute this conversion, suppose we found that

The **point-biserial correlation coefficient (r_{pb})** is a measure of the direction and strength of the linear relationship of one factor that is continuous (on an interval or ratio scale of measurement) and a second factor that is dichotomous (on a nominal scale of measurement).

FYI

The direction (+ or −) of the correlation coefficient is meaningless for a point-biserial correlation because the dichotomous variable can only take on two values.

FYI

The t test and point-biserial test are related in that their measures of effect size (r² and η²) are mathematically the same, which allows the t test to be used as a test for the significance of a point-biserial correlation.

$r_{pb} = .163$ in a sample of 12 participants. In the equation, df are the degrees of freedom for the two-independent-sample t test, or $N - 2$: $df = 12 - 2 = 10$. We can substitute r and df into the formula:

$$t^2 = \frac{(.163)^2}{(1-(.163)^2)/10} = 0.272.$$

The square root of this solution is the t statistic:

$$t = \sqrt{t^2} = \sqrt{0.272} = 0.522.$$

Also, recall that r^2 equals η^2. To demonstrate this equivalence using the same example, we can compute eta-squared for the t test introduced in Chapter 9:

$$\text{Eta-squared: } \eta^2 = \frac{t^2}{t^2 + df} = \frac{(0.522)^2}{(0.522)^2 + 10} = .027.$$

$$\text{Coefficient of determination: } r^2 = (.163)^2 = .027.$$

Both formulas give the same value of effect size. The proportion of variance for the two-independent-sample t test (η^2) and the coefficient of determination (r^2) for the point-biserial correlation coefficient are thus equivalent.

The Phi Correlation Coefficient

In certain research situations, we can measure two dichotomous factors. Dichotomous factors, which can only take on two values, are typically categorical and are therefore measured on a nominal scale of measurement. To measure the direction and strength of the linear relationship between two dichotomous factors, we use the **phi correlation coefficient (r_φ)**. The notation used for the phi correlation coefficient is taken from the outcomes in a 2×2 matrix, which is shown in Table 13.5. The formula for the phi correlation coefficient using this notation is

$$r_\phi = \frac{ad-bc}{\sqrt{ABCD}}.$$

The **phi correlation coefficient (r_φ)** is a measure of the direction and strength of the linear relationship of two dichotomous factors on a nominal scale of measurement.

A positive correlation occurs when the values in cells a and d are larger than the values in cells b and c. A negative correlation occurs when the values in cells b and c are larger than the values in cells a and d. The denominator for this test is a mathematical adjustment used to ensure that the phi correlation coefficient always varies between −1.0 and +1.0. Note that this new formula was derived from the Pearson formula—again, the two formulas are mathematically equivalent. Note also that the direction of a phi correlation coefficient is not meaningful because it makes no sense to say that the levels of a dichotomous variable increase or decrease.

TABLE 13.5	A Matrix Displaying the Notation Used for the Phi Correlation Coefficient

| | | Variable X | | |
		X_1	X_2	
Variable Y	Y_1	a	b	A
	Y_2	c	d	B
		C	D	

The general structure of the phi correlation test is quite similar to a chi-square test for independence, which is introduced in the next chapter. To determine the significance of the phi correlation, we thus convert the phi coefficient, r, to a chi-square (χ^2) value using the following equation:

$$\chi^2 = r_\phi^2 N.$$

For this equation, N is the total number of participants in the study, and r_ϕ is the phi coefficient. For example, suppose we measure a phi coefficient equal to .40 in a sample of 40 participants. Using this example, we can substitute these values into the equation:

$$\chi^2 = (.40)^2 \times 40 = 6.40.$$

To locate the critical value for this test, we look in Table C.7 in Appendix C. A portion of this table is shown in Table 13.6. The levels of significance are listed in each column, and the degrees of freedom are listed in each row in the table. For this test, the degrees of freedom are always equal to 1.

TABLE 13.6	A Portion of the Chi-Square Table in Table C.7 in Appendix C

	Level of Significance	
df	.05	.01
1	3.84	6.64
2	5.99	9.21
3	7.81	11.34
4	9.49	13.28
5	11.07	15.09
6	12.59	16.81
7	14.07	18.48

(Continued)

TABLE 13.6	(Continued)	

Level of Significance		
df	.05	.01
8	15.51	20.09
9	16.92	21.67
10	18.31	23.21

Source: From Table IV of Fisher, R. A., & Yates, F. (1974). *Statistical tables for biological, agricultural and medical research* (6th ed.). London, England: Longman Group Ltd. Reprinted with permission of Addison Wesley Longman.

FYI

The phi correlation coefficient is derived from the Pearson correlation coefficient for measuring the correlation between two dichotomous factors.

If we compute a two-tailed test at a .05 level of significance, then the critical value with one degree of freedom is 3.84. Because the chi-square statistic ($\chi^2 = 6.40$) exceeds the critical value, we reject the null hypothesis.

Table 13.7 summarizes when it is appropriate to use each correlation coefficient introduced in this chapter based on the scales of measurement of the data.

TABLE 13.7	The Scales of Measurement for Factors Tested Using the Pearson, Spearman, Point-Biserial, and Phi Correlation Coefficients

Correlation Coefficient	Scale of Measurement for Correlated Variables
Pearson	Both factors are interval or ratio data.
Spearman	Both factors are ranked or ordinal data.
Point-Biserial	One factor is dichotomous (nominal data), and the other factor is continuous (interval or ratio data).
Phi	Both factors are dichotomous (nominal data).

13.7 SPSS in Focus:
Computing the Alternatives to Pearson

Using SPSS, the Spearman correlation coefficient can be computed by unchecking the Pearson box and checking the Spearman box in the Correlation Coefficients portion of the dialog box in Step 4 of the directions given for computing the Pearson correlation coefficient in SPSS. However, there is no command in SPSS to compute a point-biserial or a phi correlation coefficient. To compute either coefficient using SPSS, first code the dichotomous factor(s), then for the phi coefficient weight each variable using the Weight Cases . . . option in the menu bar, and finally compute a Pearson correlation coefficient. Because both correlation coefficients are derived mathematically from the Pearson correlation coefficient, the correlation value obtained using SPSS will be identical to that obtained for either correlation coefficient.

The SPSS output tables for these correlation coefficients will show the value of the correlation coefficient (r), the p value, and the total number of participants observed (N) for a test. As long as you code and weight the dichotomous factors, SPSS can be used to compute each of these alternatives to Pearson. To compute the coefficient of determination, square the correlation coefficient given in the SPSS output tables.

LEARNING CHECK 4

1. Name the correlation coefficient used to determine the relationship between two ranked or ordinal factors.

2. Name the correlation coefficient used to determine the direction and strength of the linear relationship between one factor that is continuous (on an interval or ratio scale of measurement) and another factor that is dichotomous (on a nominal scale of measurement).

3. The _____ is a measure of the direction and strength of the linear relationship of two dichotomous factors on a nominal scale of measurement.

Answers: 1. Spearman correlation coefficient; 2. Point-biserial correlation coefficient; 3. Phi correlation coefficient.

13.8 FUNDAMENTALS OF LINEAR REGRESSION

Linear regression, like analysis of variance, can be used to analyze any number of factors. In this chapter, however, we use regression to describe the linear relationship between two factors (X and Y) because many of the behaviors measured by researchers are related in a linear or straight-line pattern.

To use linear regression, we identify two types of variables: the predictor variable and the criterion variable. The **predictor variable (X)** is the variable with values that are known and can be used to predict values of the criterion variable; the predictor variable is plotted on the x-axis of a graph. The **criterion variable (Y)** is the variable with unknown values that we are trying to predict, given known values of the predictor variable; the criterion variable is plotted on the y-axis of a graph.

We can use linear regression to answer the following questions about the pattern of data points and the significance of a linear equation:

1. Is a linear pattern evident in a set of data points?

2. Which equation of a straight line can best describe this pattern?

3. Are the predictions made from this equation significant?

FYI

Linear regression is used to predict values of Y (the criterion variable), given values of X (the predictor variable).

The **predictor variable** or **known variable (X)** is the variable with values that are known and can be used to predict values of another variable.

The **criterion variable** or **to-be-predicted variable (Y)** is the variable with unknown values that can be predicted or estimated, given known values of the predictor variable.

The Regression Line

Once we have determined that there is a linear pattern in a set of data points, we want to find the regression line, or the straight line that has the best fit. The criterion we use to determine the equation of a regression line is the sum of squares (SS), or the sum of the squared distances of data points from a straight line. The line associated with the smallest total value for SS is the best-fitting straight line, which we call the regression line. The method of least squares is the statistical procedure used to square the distance that each data point falls from the regression line and to sum the squared distances.

To illustrate why each deviation is squared before summing, suppose we measure two factors, one predictor variable plotted on the *x*-axis and one criterion variable plotted on the *y*-axis. Figure 13.14 shows hypothetical data for these two factors.

The distance of each data point from the regression line is shown in the figure. Notice that data points A and D fall on the regression line. The distance of these data points from the regression line is 0. However, data points B and C in the scatter plot fall two units from the regression line. Data point B falls two units below the regression line (−2 units), and data point C falls two units above the regression line (+2 units). The sum of the distances of each data point from the regression line is $0 + 0 + 2 - 2 = 0$.

FIGURE 13.14   A Table and Scatter Plot of Four Hypothetical Data Points

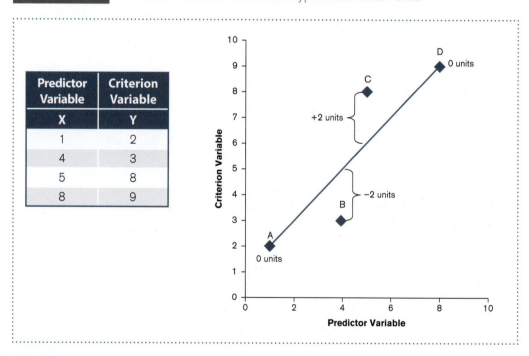

The regression line and the distances, in units, between the data points and the regression line are shown. Both the table and the scatter plot show the same data.

FIGURE 13.15 A Scatter Plot of the Same Data in Figure 13.14

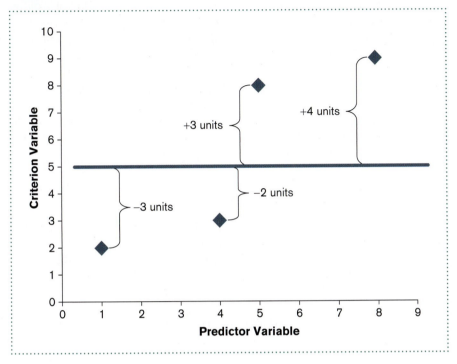

In this graph, a horizontal line is fit to the data, and the data points are now a farther total distance from the line compared to the best-fitting straight line for these data points, which is shown in Figure 13.14.

A zero solution will always occur when we sum the distances of data points from a regression line—same as the outcome observed when we sum the deviations of scores from the mean (see Chapter 3, p. 86).

To avoid a solution of 0, we compute SS by squaring the distance of each data point from the regression line, then summing—same as the solution used to find the variance of scores from the mean (see Chapter 4, p. 110). When we square the distance of each data point and then sum, we obtain $SS = 0^2 + 0^2 + 2^2 + (-2)^2 = 8$. This is the smallest possible solution for SS. The method of least squares, then, is the method of determining the line associated with the least squares, or the smallest possible value of the sum of squares (SS).

Any line other than the regression line shown in Figure 13.14 will produce a value of SS that is larger than 8 in this example. To illustrate, we fit another straight line to the same data in Figure 13.15. The distance of each data point from this line is +3 units and +4 units above the line and −2 units and −3 units below the line. If we compute the SS for these distances, we obtain $SS = 3^2 + 4^2 + (-2)^2 + (-3)^2 = 38$. This result is much larger than $SS = 8$, which is the value we obtained for the least squares regression line. Different lines have different values of SS. The regression line, or line of best fit, is the line with the smallest or least value of the SS.

FYI

The regression line is the line that makes the value of SS the smallest.

The Equation of the Regression Line

If we know the equation of the regression line, we can predict values of the criterion variable, Y, so long as we know values of the predictor variable, X. To make use of this equation, we need to know the equation of a straight line. The equation of a straight line is

$$Y = bX + a.$$

In this equation, Y is a value we plot for the criterion variable, X is a value we plot for the predictor variable, b is the slope of a straight line, and a is the y-intercept (where the line crosses the y-axis). To make use of this equation, we need to know the values of a and b in the equation. In this section, we explain what a and b measure, and in Section 13.9, we use the method of least squares to find the values of a and b.

The **slope**, represented as b, is a measure of how much a regression line rises or declines along the y-axis as values on the x-axis increase. The slope indicates the direction of a relationship between two factors, X and Y. When values of Y increase as values of X increase, the slope is positive. When the values of Y decrease as values of X increase, the slope is negative.

Thus, the slope of a straight line is used to measure the change in Y relative to the change in X:

$$\text{slope } (b) = \frac{\text{change in } Y}{\text{change in } X}.$$

The **y-intercept**, represented as a, is where a straight line crosses the y-axis on a graph. More specifically, the y-intercept is the value of Y when $X = 0$. The y-intercept is the value of the criterion variable (Y) when the predictor variable (X) is absent or equal to 0.

FYI

The equation of a straight line is Y = bX + a. In this equation, the slope (b) measures how Y changes as X increases, and the y-intercept (a) is the value of Y when X = 0.

The **slope (b)** of a straight line is used to measure the change in Y relative to the change in X. When X and Y change in the same direction, the slope is positive. When X and Y change in opposite directions, the slope is negative.

The **y-intercept (a)** of a straight line is the value of the criterion variable (Y) when the predictor variable (X) equals 0.

LEARNING CHECK 5

1. The regression line, or best-fitting straight line to a set of data points, is the line associated with the smallest possible value of _____.

2. The values of one factor increase as the values of a second factor decrease. Does this sentence describe a line with a positive slope or a negative slope?

3. The y-intercept is the value of Y when X equals _____.

Answers: 1. The sum of squares (SS); 2. A negative slope; 3. Zero ($X = 0$).

13.9 USING THE METHOD OF LEAST SQUARES TO FIND THE REGRESSION LINE

We use the **method of least squares** to find the equation of the regression line, which is the best-fitting straight line to a set of data points. Using this method in Example 13.2, we measure SS for Factor X and Factor Y and then use these values to compute the slope (b) and y-intercept (a) of the regression line. To use the method of least squares, we complete three steps:

Step 1: Compute preliminary calculations.

Step 2: Calculate the slope (b).

Step 3: Calculate the y-intercept (a).

The **method of least squares** is a statistical procedure used to compute the slope (b) and y-intercept (a) of the best-fitting straight line to a set of data points.

Example 13.2

Factors that can predict the effectiveness of behavioral therapies are of interest to clinicians and researchers (Cuijpers, Cristea, Weitz, Gentili, & Berking, 2016; Hans & Hiller, 2013). As an example of research for this area of study, suppose a psychologist wants to predict the effectiveness of a behavioral therapy (measured as the number of symptoms patients express) given the number of sessions a patient attends. She selects a sample of eight patients who expressed the same number of symptoms at the start of treatment. She then records the number of sessions attended (X) and the number of symptoms expressed (Y) by each patient. Figure 13.16 shows the data for this study.

FIGURE 13.16 A Table and a Scatter Plot Showing the Number of Sessions Eight Patients ($n = 8$) Attended and the Number of Symptoms They Expressed

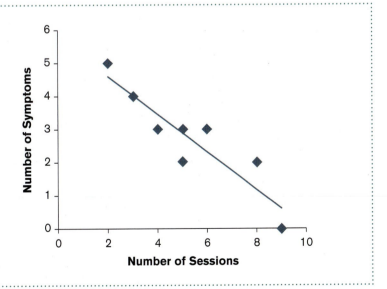

Number of Sessions	Number of Symptoms
X	Y
9	0
5	3
8	2
2	5
6	3
3	4
5	2
4	3

The regression line for these hypothetical data is shown in the scatter plot. Both the table and the scatter plot show the same data.

Step 1: Compute preliminary calculations. We begin by making preliminary calculations, which are shown in Table 13.8. The signs (+ and −) of the values we measure for each factor are essential to making accurate computations. The goal of this step is to compute the sum of squares needed to calculate the slope and y-intercept. We will describe each calculation in Table 13.8 from left to right.

TABLE 13.8   Preliminary Calculations in Step 1 for Example 13.2

X	Y	$X - M_X$ The deviation of each score (X) from the mean (M_X)	$Y - M_Y$ The deviation of each score (Y) from the mean (M_Y)	$(X - M_X)(Y - M_Y)$ The product of deviation scores for X and Y	$(X - M_X)^2$ The product of deviation scores for X
9	0	3.75	−2.75	−10.31	14.06
5	3	−0.25	0.25	−0.06	0.06
8	2	2.75	−0.75	−2.06	7.56
2	5	−3.25	2.25	−7.31	10.56
6	3	0.75	0.25	0.19	0.56
3	4	−2.25	1.25	−2.81	5.06
5	2	−0.25	−0.75	0.19	0.06
4	3	−1.25	0.25	−0.31	1.56
$M_X = 5.25$	$M_Y = 2.75$			$SS_{XY} = -22.50$	$SS_X = 39.50$

Mean number of sessions (X)   Mean number of symptoms (Y)   The sum of products for X and Y The sum of squares for X

Preliminary calculations in Step 1 for Example 13.2.

1. Compute the average X and Y score. In this example, the number of sessions attended is the predictor variable, X, and the number of symptoms expressed is the criterion variable, Y. In Table 13.8, each column of values for X and Y was summed and then averaged:

$$M_X = 5.25.$$
$$M_Y = 2.75.$$

2. Subtract each score from its respective mean. In the third column, each X score is subtracted from M_X; in the fourth column, each Y score is subtracted from M_Y. Remember from Chapter 3 that the sum of each column—the sum of the differences of scores from their mean—is equal to 0.

3. Multiply and sum the deviation scores for *X* and *Y*. We computed deviation scores by subtracting each score from its mean. Now multiply across the rows in the third and fourth columns. The sum of these scores is the sum of squares for *XY*, also called the sum of products (SP):

$$SP = SS_{XY} = -22.50.$$

4. Multiply and sum the deviation scores for *X*. Multiply the deviation score of each *X* value by itself. The sum of these scores is the sum of squares for *X*:

$$SS_X = 39.50.$$

MAKING SENSE SP, SS,
AND THE SLOPE OF A REGRESSION LINE

Recall from Chapter 4 that the formula for the sum of squares is

$$SS_X = \Sigma(X - M)^2.$$

A mathematically equivalent way to write this formula that gives us the same value of *SS* is

$$SS_X = \Sigma(X - M)(X - M).$$

To compute the sum of products (or the sum of squares for *XY*), we multiply the deviation of each *X* value by the deviation of each *Y* value:

$$SP = SS_{XY} = \Sigma(X - M_X)(Y - M_Y).$$

The structure of the formula for SP, then, is the same as the second formula we stated for SS_X. When we compute SS_X, we multiply each deviation by itself, which makes the solution positive: $SS_X \geq 0$. However, to compute SP, we multiply deviations of *X* by deviations of *Y*, so it is possible to obtain negative values of SP. For this reason, the value of SP will determine whether the slope is positive or negative.

Step 2: Calculate the slope (*b*). The slope of a straight line indicates the change in *Y* relative to the change in *X*. Because the value of SP can be negative or positive, this value indicates the direction that *Y* changes as *X* increases. We will use SP, which is the same as SS_{XY}, to estimate changes in *Y*, and we will use SS_X to estimate changes in *X*. The formula for computing the slope (*b*) is

$$b = \frac{\text{change in } Y}{\text{change in } X} = \frac{SS_{XY}}{SS_X} \text{ or } \frac{SP}{SS_X}.$$

We already computed $SS_{XY} = -22.50$ and $SS_X = 39.50$. The slope of the best-fitting straight line is

$$b = \frac{-22.50}{39.50} = -0.57.$$

Step 3: Calculate the *y*-intercept (*a*). The *y*-intercept is the value of *Y* when *X* = 0. To find this value, we need to know the mean of *Y* (M_Y), the mean of *X* (M_X), and the slope we just computed. The formula for determining the *y*-intercept (*a*) is

$$a = M_Y - bM_X.$$

FYI

SS$_{xy}$, which is the sum of products (SP), determines whether the slope of a straight line is positive or negative.

FYI

Once we compute the slope and y-intercept, we can substitute known values of X and solve for $\hat{Y}$, or the predicted value of Y for each known value of X.

We already computed $M_Y = 2.75$, $M_X = 5.25$, and $b = -0.57$. The y-intercept of the regression line is

$$a = 2.75 - [(-0.57)(5.25)] = 5.74.$$

Because we computed the slope, $b = -0.57$, and the y-intercept, $a = 5.74$, we can now state the equation of the least squares regression line as

$$\hat{Y} = -0.57X + 5.74.$$

In this equation, $\hat{Y}$ is the predicted value of Y, given values of X. For example, suppose we want to make a prediction. If one patient has attended four therapy sessions ($X = 4$), we can substitute 4 into the equation to solve for $\hat{Y}$:

$$\hat{Y} = -0.57(4) + 5.74.$$

$$\hat{Y} = 3.46.$$

In this example, we expect or predict that a patient will express 3.46, or between 3 and 4, symptoms following four therapy sessions. In this way, we use the equation to show how many symptoms we expect a patient to exhibit after a particular number of therapy sessions.

LEARNING CHECK 6

1. Assuming these data points have a linear pattern, make the following calculations to find the best-fitting line:

X	Y
1	3
2	2
3	1

(a) Compute the slope.

(b) Compute the y-intercept.

(c) Write the equation of the regression line.

Answers: 1. (a) $b = -\dfrac{2}{2} = -1.0$, (b) $a = 2.0 - [(-1.0)(2.0)] = 4.0$, (c) $\hat{Y} = -1X + 4.0$.

13.10 USING ANALYSIS OF REGRESSION TO DETERMINE SIGNIFICANCE

Analysis of regression, or **regression analysis**, is a statistical procedure used to test hypotheses for one or more predictor variables to determine whether the regression equation for a sample of data points can be used to predict values of the criterion variable (Y) given values of the predictor variable (X) in the population.

In Example 13.2, we used the method of least squares to determine the equation of the regression line for a sample of data. However, we did not determine the significance of this regression line. In other words, we did not determine whether this equation could be used to predict values of Y (criterion variable), given values of X (predictor variable) in the population.

To determine whether the regression equation for a sample of data can be used to make predictions of Y in the population, we use **analysis of regression**. An analysis of regression is similar to an ANOVA. In an analysis of regression, we measure the variation in Y and split the variation into two sources, similar to how we had two sources of variation using the one-way between-subjects ANOVA in Chapter 11. In this section, we follow the four steps to hypothesis testing to perform an analysis of regression using the data in Example 13.2.

Step 1: State the hypotheses. The null hypothesis is that the variance in Y is not related to changes in X. The alternative hypothesis is that the variance in Y is related to changes in X. The hypotheses in Example 13.2 are as follows:

H_0: The variance in the number of symptoms expressed (Y) is not related to changes in the number of therapy sessions attended (X).

H_1: The variance in the number of symptoms expressed (Y) is related to changes in the number of therapy sessions attended (X).

To evaluate these hypotheses, we measure the variance in Y that is and is not related to changes in X. The variance in Y that is related to changes in X is called **regression variation**. The closer that data points fall to the regression line, the larger the regression variation will be. The variance in Y that is not related to changes in X is called **residual variation**. This is the variance in Y that is residual, left over, or remaining. The farther data points fall from the regression line, the larger the residual variation will be.

An analysis of regression measures only the variance in Y, the criterion variable, because it is the value we want to predict. The total variance measured, then, equals the variance in Y. As shown in Figure 13.17, we attribute some of the variance in Y to changes in X (regression variation); the remaining variance in Y is not attributed to changes in X (residual variation). The more variance in Y that we attribute to changes in X (regression variation), the more likely we are to decide to reject the null hypothesis and conclude that values of X significantly predict values of Y.

FIGURE 13.17   An Analysis of Regression Measures the Variance in Y

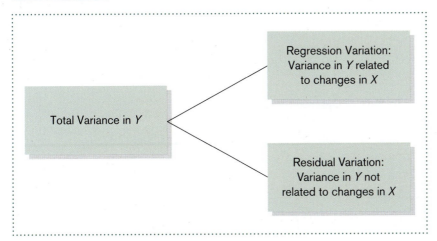

Some of the variance is attributed to changes in X; the remaining variance is not attributed to changes in X.

Regression variation is the variance in Y that is related to or associated with changes in X. The closer data points fall to the regression line, the larger the value of regression variation.

Residual variation is the variance in Y that is not related to changes in X. This is the variance in Y that is left over or remaining. The farther data points fall from the regression line, the larger the value of residual variation.

Step 2: Set the criteria for a decision. We will use a .05 level of significance, as we have for all hypothesis tests. We compute degrees of freedom (df) for each source of variation. The degrees of freedom for regression variation, or degrees of freedom numerator, are equal to the number of predictor variables. Because we have one predictor variable (X) in Example 13.2, df for regression variation is 1.

The degrees of freedom for residual variation, or degrees of freedom denominator, are equal to the sample size minus 2. We subtract 2 from n because we plot two scores for each data point (one X score and one Y score). In Example 13.2, $n = 8$, so df for residual variation is $(8 - 2) = 6$.

The critical value for this test is listed in Table C.3 in Appendix C. The critical value for a test with 1 (df numerator) and 6 (df denominator) degrees of freedom at a .05 level of significance is 5.99.

Step 3: Compute the test statistic. To compute the test statistic, we measure variance as a mean square, same as we did using the ANOVA tests. We place the variance or mean square (MS) attributed to regression variation in the numerator and the variance or mean square attributed to residual variation in the denominator:

$$F_{obt} = \frac{\text{variance of } Y \text{ related to changes in } X}{\text{variance of } Y \text{ not related to changes in } X} = \frac{MS_{regression}}{MS_{residual}}.$$

In our computations of the test statistic, we first compute the SS for each source of variation and then complete the F table.

To compute the sum of squares for the regression variation, we multiply the sum of squares of Y by the *coefficient of determination* or r^2:

$$SS_{regression} = r^2 SS_Y, \text{ where } r = \frac{SP_{XY}}{\sqrt{SS_X SS_Y}}.$$

Multiplying the coefficient of determination by the variability in Y (SS_y) will give us the proportion of variance in Y (number of symptoms) that is predicted by or related to changes in X (the number of sessions attended). Using the data given in Table 13.9, we can calculate the value of r:

$$r = \frac{-22.50}{\sqrt{39.50 \times 15.50}} = -.91.$$

The sum of squares regression is

$$SS_{regression} = r^2 SS_Y = (-.91)^2 \times 15.50 = 12.83.$$

The total variability of Y is 15.50 ($SS_y = 15.50$), of which we attribute 12.83 units of variability to changes in X. The remaining sum of squares, or sum of squares residual, is computed by multiplying SS_y by the remaining proportion of variance $(1 - r^2)$:

$$SS_{residual} = (1 - r^2) SS_Y.$$

TABLE 13.9 The Calculations for SS_Y Using the Data in Example 13.2

X	Y	$X - M_X$	$Y - M_Y$	$(X - M_X)(Y - M_Y)$	$(X - M_X)^2$	$(X - M_Y)^2$
9	0	3.75	−2.75	−10.31	14.06	7.56
5	3	−0.25	0.25	−0.06	0.06	0.06
8	2	2.75	−0.75	−2.06	7.56	0.56
2	5	−3.25	2.25	−7.31	10.56	5.06
6	3	0.75	0.25	0.19	0.56	0.06
3	4	−2.25	1.25	−2.81	5.06	1.56
5	2	−0.25	−0.75	0.19	0.06	0.56
4	3	−1.25	0.25	−0.31	1.56	0.06
				$SS_{XY} = -22.50$	$SS_X = 39.50$	$SS_Y = 15.50$
				The sum of products for X and Y	The sum of squares for X	The sum of squares for Y

The first six columns are taken from Table 13.8.

The residual variation formula will give us the proportion of variance in Y (number of symptoms) that is not predicted by or related to changes in X (the number of sessions attended). If we substitute the values of r and SS_Y, we obtain the remaining variation in Y measured as the sum of squares residual:

$$SS_{residual} = (1 - (-.91)^2) \times 15.50 = 2.67.$$

When we add the values for $SS_{regression}$ and $SS_{residual}$, this will sum to the total variability in Y:

$$SS_Y = SS_{regression} + SS_{residual} = 12.83 + 2.67 = 15.50.$$

To compute the test statistic, we need to complete the F table, which is set up just as it was for the ANOVA tests. The formulas needed to complete the F table and the solutions for Example 13.2 are given in Table 13.10. To compute variance or mean square, we divide SS by df for each source of variation, just as we did for the ANOVA tests. The value of the test statistic in Example 13.2 is

$$F_{obt} = \frac{12.83}{0.445} = 28.83.$$

Step 4: Make a decision. To decide whether to retain or reject the null hypothesis, we compare the value of the test statistic to the critical value. Because $F_{obt} = 28.83$ exceeds the critical value (5.99), we reject the null hypothesis. We conclude that the number of symptoms expressed (Y) is related to changes in the number of therapy sessions attended (X). That is, we can predict values of Y, given values of X in the population, using the equation we computed using the method of least squares: $\hat{Y} = -0.57X + 5.74$. If we were to report this result in a research journal, it would look something like this:

> An analysis of regression showed that the number of therapy sessions attended can significantly predict the number of symptoms expressed, $F(1, 6) = 28.83, p < .05, R^2 = .83$, using the following equation: $\hat{Y} = -0.57X + 5.74$.

In Example 13.2, we concluded that the equation $\hat{Y} = -0.57X + 5.74$ can predict values of Y given values of X in the population. Of course, not all the data points in our sample fell exactly on this line. Many data points fell some distance from the regression line. Whenever even a single data point fails to fall exactly on the regression line, there is error in how accurately the line will predict an outcome. This error can be measured using the **standard error of estimate (s_e)**.

TABLE 13.10   The *F* Table for an Analysis of Regression

Formulas for Completing the Analysis of Regression				
Source of Variation	SS	df	MS	F_{obt}
Regression	$r^2 SS_Y$	1	$\dfrac{SS_{regression}}{df_{regression}}$	$\dfrac{MS_{regression}}{MS_{residual}}$
Residual (error)	$(1 - r^2)SS_Y$	$n - 2$	$\dfrac{SS_{residual}}{df_{residual}}$	
Total	$SS_{regression} + SS_{residual}$	$n - 1$		
Solution to Example 13.2				
Source of Variation	SS	df	MS	F_{obt}
Regression	12.83	1	12.83	28.83*
Residual (error)	2.67	6	0.445	
Total	15.50	7		

The **standard error of estimate (s_e)** is an estimate of the standard deviation or distance that a set of data points falls from the regression line. The standard error of estimate equals the square root of the mean square residual.

An asterisk indicates significance at $p < .05$.

The standard error of estimate, s_e, measures the standard deviation or distance that data points in a sample fall from the regression line. It is computed as the square root of the mean square residual:

$$s_e = \sqrt{MS_{residual}}.$$

In Example 13.2, the mean square residual was 0.445 (given in Table 13.10). Hence, the standard error of estimate is

$$s_e = \sqrt{0.445} = 0.67.$$

The standard error of estimate indicates the accuracy of predictions made using the equation of a regression line, with smaller values of s_e associated with better or more accurate predictions. The standard error of estimate is quite literally a standard deviation (or the square root of the variance) for the residual variation. So it is a measure of the error or deviation of data points from the regression line.

FYI

Analysis of regression measures two sources of variation in Y: One source of variation is related to changes in X (regression variation), and the other is not (residual variation).

LEARNING CHECK 7

1. Name the statistical procedure used to determine whether the equation of a straight line can be used to make predictions in a population.

2. When we sum the value of $SS_{regression}$ and $SS_{residual}$, what value do we obtain?

3. A college administrator measures the SAT scores and high school GPAs of 12 college applicants and computes an analysis of regression. Complete the F table for this analysis and state whether the decision is to retain or reject the null hypothesis.

Source of Variation	SS	df	MS	F
Regression	140			
Residual				
Total	600			

Answers: 1. Analysis of regression; 2. The value of SS_Y; 3. $SS_{residual} = 460$, $df_{regression} = 1$, $df_{residual} = 10$, $df_{total} = 11$, $MS_{regression} = 140$, $MS_{residual} = 46$, $F = 3.04$. Decision: Retain the null hypothesis.

13.11 SPSS in Focus:
Analysis of Regression

To illustrate how all of our calculations are completed in SPSS, let us compute the data in Example 13.2 in SPSS. The data for Example 13.2 are reproduced in Table 13.11 from data originally given in Figure 13.16. We will compare how our analysis computed by hand matches the analysis computed using SPSS.

(Continued)

(Continued)

| TABLE 13.11 | A Table Showing the Number of Sessions Eight Patients ($n = 8$) Attended and the Number of Symptoms They Expressed |

Number of Sessions	Number of Symptoms
X	Y
9	0
5	3
8	2
2	5
6	3
3	4
5	2
4	3

These data are reproduced from data originally given in Figure 13.16.

1. Click on the Variable View tab and enter X in the Name column; enter Y in the Name column below it. In the Decimals column, reduce the value to 0 in both rows.

2. Click on the Data View tab. Enter the data for Example 13.2 in the columns for X and Y. Enter the data for number of sessions in the column labeled X; enter the data for number of symptoms in the column labeled Y.

3. Go to the menu bar and click Analyze, then Regression and Linear, to display the dialog box shown in Figure 13.18.

4. Using the arrows, move X into the box labeled Independent(s); move Y into the box labeled Dependent.

5. Select OK, or select Paste and click the Run command.

FIGURE 13.18   Dialog Box for Steps 3 to 5

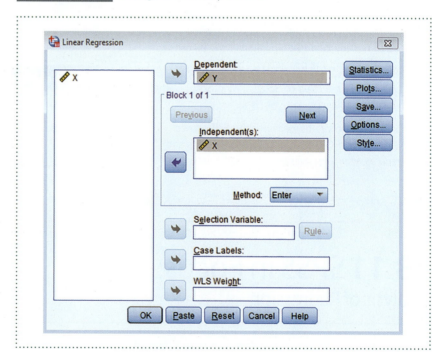

FYI

$SS_{residual}$ measures the proportion of variance in Y that is not related to changes in X.

FYI

$SS_{regression}$ measures the proportion of variance in Y that is related to changes in X.

FYI

The standard error of estimate (s_e) is the square root of the mean square residual. This measure gives an estimate of the accuracy in predictions of Y by estimating how far data points fall or deviate from the regression line.

The SPSS output, shown in Table 13.12, gives the value of the correlation coefficient, the coefficient of determination, and the values in the F table, which are the same as those we computed by hand, give or take rounding. The decision for this test is to reject the null hypothesis, same as the decision we made for this test. The SPSS output also gives the *standard error of estimate*, which is described in the next section.

TABLE 13.12 SPSS Output Table for the Analysis of Regression in Example 13.2

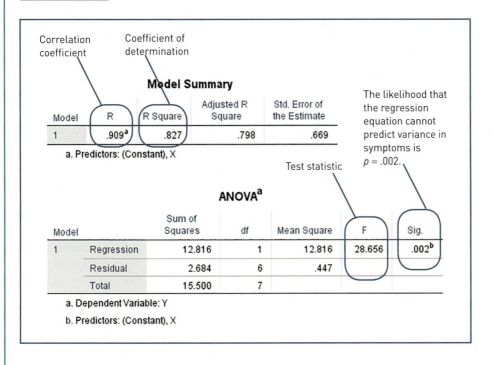

Correlation coefficient

Coefficient of determination

Model Summary

Model	R	R Square	Adjusted R Square	Std. Error of the Estimate
1	.909[a]	.827	.798	.669

a. Predictors: (Constant), X

The likelihood that the regression equation cannot predict variance in symptoms is $p = .002$.

Test statistic

ANOVA[a]

Model		Sum of Squares	df	Mean Square	F	Sig.
1	Regression	12.816	1	12.816	28.656	.002[b]
	Residual	2.684	6	.447		
	Total	15.500	7			

a. Dependent Variable: Y

b. Predictors: (Constant), X

13.12 A LOOK AHEAD TO MULTIPLE REGRESSION

In this chapter, we described research situations in which we use one variable (the predictor variable) to predict another variable (the criterion variable). While a single variable can be used to make accurate predictions, many behaviors are often too complex to be represented by a simple linear equation. That is, often, the changes in a single predictor variable do not allow us to accurately predict changes in a criterion variable.

We find that our predictions of many behaviors improve when we consider more information—specifically, when we consider more predictor variables. When we use multiple predictor variables to predict changes in a criterion variable, we use an analysis called **multiple regression**. In Example 13.2, for example, we could include other factors besides the number of sessions attended to better predict the effectiveness of a therapy. Examples of possible added predictor variables include how often the patient arrived on time for a therapy session, the level of support the patient received from others, and the age of the patient. Including any of these additional factors may improve our predictions regarding the effectiveness of a therapy.

Multiple regression is a statistical procedure that includes two or more predictor variables in the equation of a regression line to predict changes in a criterion variable.

To accommodate more predictor variables in the equation of a regression line, we add the slope, b, and the predictor variable, X, for each additional variable. To illustrate, the linear equations for one, two, and three variables are as follows:

[1] $\hat{Y} = bX + a$ (one predictor variable)

[2] $\hat{Y} = b_1 X_1 + b_2 X_2 + a$ (two predictor variables)

[3] $\hat{Y} = b_1 X_1 + b_2 X_2 + b_3 X_3 + a$ (three predictor variables)

Notice that we add another bX to the regression equation for each predictor variable we add. One advantage of including multiple predictors in the regression equation is that we can detect the extent to which two or more predictor variables interact. To illustrate what this means conceptually, let us examine an example from a published research study.

Harrell and Jackson (2008) conducted a study in which they measured the extent to which restrained eating and ruminative coping could predict changes in mood—specifically, depression—using a sample of female college students. When people are depressed, they can change their mood in several ways. Harrell and Jackson focused on two possible predictor variables related to changes in mood: restrained eating and ruminative coping. A *restrained eater* is someone who spends an inordinate amount of time thinking, planning, and obsessing over food choices and the consequences of those choices. *Ruminative coping* occurs when a person focuses repetitively on the meaning, causes, and consequences of his or her mood. In a depressed state, this focus tends to be negative, thereby making mood or depression worse.

The researchers first tested restrained eating as the only predictor variable of changes in depression using equation [1] from the list above. The results showed that restrained eating was a significant predictor of changes in depression. They then added ruminative coping into the linear equation. Because they were now testing two predictor variables (restrained eating and ruminative coping), they used equation [2] from the list above. With two predictor variables, they concluded that ruminative coping, and not restrained eating, significantly predicted changes in depression. While restrained eating did predict changes in depression using equation [1], this factor no longer predicted changes in depression when ruminative coping was added as a factor using the regression equation [2]. How can these two equations lead to such different conclusions?

To answer these questions, think of stealing cookies from a cookie jar. If cookies are stolen 10 times and your brother was near the cookie jar 8 of the 10 times, then there is a predictive relationship between your brother and the stolen cookies. However, if you add your friend who was near the cookie jar 10 out of 10 times the cookies were stolen, then now you can fully predict the stolen cookies based on this new factor (your friend). In the observation using two factors, the significance of your brother being near the cookie jar is smaller. Similarly, restrained eating predicted symptoms of depression when considered alone but was no longer a significant predictor when ruminative coping was added as a factor. Using multiple regression in this study allowed the researchers to detect the extent to which these two predictor variables interacted, in a way that would not be possible unless they were both included in the same regression equation.

FYI

Multiple regression is used to predict changes in a criterion variable with two or more predictor variables.

LEARNING CHECK 8

1. What statistical method includes two or more predictor variables in the equation of a regression line to predict changes in a criterion variable?

2. What two values are added to the regression equation when a new predictor variable is added to the regression equation?

Answers: 1. Multiple regression; 2. b and X are added to the regression equation for each additional predictor variable.

13.13 APA IN FOCUS: REPORTING CORRELATIONS AND LINEAR REGRESSION

To summarize correlations, we report the strength, the direction, and the p value for each correlation coefficient. The sample size and effect size should also be reported. The means and standard error or standard deviations measured in a study can be summarized in a figure or table or in the main text. When we compute many correlations in a single study, we often report each correlation coefficient in a table called a *correlation matrix*. For example, Lienemann and Stopp (2013) reported a Pearson correlation for many social factors involving the media in a sample of 218 participants. To report multiple correlations, we can report this in the text:

Using the Pearson correlation coefficient, a significant correlation was evident between general media exposure (GME) to film and importance of pop culture, $r = .19$, $p < .01$, GME to television and importance of pop culture, $r = .28$, $p < .001$, and GME to film and GME to television, $r = .28$, $p < .001$.

In this study, the authors actually reported the significance for a few dozen correlations and reported each correlation in a correlation matrix, as shown in Table 13.13 for the three correlations described here. A correlation matrix provides an informative and concise summary of each correlation measured in a study and is particularly useful when many correlations are reported at one time.

TABLE 13.13 A Correlation Matrix Displaying a Portion of the Results From a Study Authored by Lienemann and Stopp (2013)

Variable	1	2	3
1. GME: Film			
2. GME: Television	.28**		
3. Importance of Pop Culture	.19*	.28**	

* Correlation significant at $p < .01$, ** Correlation significant at $p < .001$. GME = general media exposure.

For a simple linear regression with one predictor variable, we report the test statistic, degrees of freedom, and p value for the regression analysis. The data points for pairs of scores are often summarized in a scatter plot or a figure displaying the regression line, as shown in Figure 13.16 for the linear regression analysis in Example 13.2. To illustrate, the following is an appropriate summary for the results we obtained in Example 13.2 (the p value is taken from the SPSS output table for Example 13.2 in Table 13.12):

An analysis of regression showed that the number of therapy sessions attended can significantly predict the number of symptoms expressed, $F(1, 6) = 28.83$, $p = .002$, $R^2 = .83$, using the following equation, $\hat{Y} = -0.57X + 5.74$.

• • • CHAPTER SUMMARY ORGANIZED BY LEARNING OBJECTIVE

LO 1: Identify the direction and strength of a linear correlation between two factors.

- A correlation is a statistical procedure used to describe the strength and direction of the linear relationship between two factors.

- The value of the correlation coefficient (r) is used to measure the strength and direction of the linear relationship between two factors. The value of r ranges from −1.0 to +1.0.

  (a) The direction of a correlation is indicated by the sign (+ or −) of r. When a correlation is positive (+), two factors change in the same direction; when a correlation is negative (−), two factors change in opposite directions.

  (b) The strength of the correlation is indicated by the value of r, with values closer to ±1.0 indicating stronger correlations and values closer to 0 indicating weaker correlations. The closer that data points fall to the regression line, the stronger the correlation.

LO 2: Compute and interpret the Pearson correlation coefficient and the coefficient of determination, and test for significance.

- The Pearson correlation coefficient (r) is a measure of the direction and strength of the linear relationship between two factors in which the data for both factors are measured on an interval or ratio scale of measurement. The Pearson correlation coefficient is

$$r = \frac{SP_{XY}}{\sqrt{SS_X SS_Y}}.$$

- The coefficient of determination (r^2 or R^2) measures the extent to which changes in one factor (Y) can be explained by changes in a second factor (X).

- To test for the significance of a Pearson correlation coefficient, follow the four steps to hypothesis testing and use r as the test statistic. The critical values for the test are given in Table C.5 in Appendix C.

LO 3: Identify and explain three assumptions and three limitations for evaluating a correlation coefficient.

- Three assumptions for interpreting a significant correlation coefficient are homoscedasticity, linearity, and normality. Homoscedasticity is the assumption that the variance of data points dispersed along the regression line is equal. Linearity is the assumption that the best way to describe the pattern of data is using a straight line. Normality is the assumption that data points are normally distributed.

- Three additional considerations, or limitations, for interpreting a correlation coefficient are that (1) correlations do not demonstrate cause, (2) outliers can change the direction and the strength of a correlation, and (3) never generalize the direction and the strength of a correlation beyond the range of data measured (restriction of range).

LO 4: Delineate the use of the Spearman, point-biserial, and phi correlation coefficients.

- The Spearman rank-order correlation coefficient (r_s) is a measure of the direction and strength of the linear relationship between two ranked factors. To test for significance, find the critical values for a Spearman correlation coefficient located in Table C.6 in Appendix C.

- The point-biserial correlation coefficient (r_{pb}) is a measure of the direction and strength of the linear relationship of one factor that is continuous (on an interval or ratio scale of measurement) and a second factor that is dichotomous (on a nominal scale of measurement). To test for significance, convert a point-biserial correlation coefficient to a t statistic and locate critical values in the t table given in Table C.2 in Appendix C.

- Equation to convert the value of r to a t statistic: $t^2 = \dfrac{r^2}{(1-r^2)/df}$.

- The phi correlation coefficient (r_φ) is a measure of the direction and strength of the linear relationship between two dichotomous factors. To test for significance, convert a phi correlation coefficient to a chi-square (χ^2) statistic and locate critical values in the chi-square table given in Table C.7 in Appendix C.

- Equation to convert the value of r to a χ^2 statistic: $\chi^2 = r_\varphi^{\,2} N$.

LO 5: **Distinguish between a predictor variable and a criterion variable.**

- To use linear regression, we identity two types of variables: The predictor variable (X) is the variable with values that are known and can be used to predict values of the criterion variable; the criterion variable (Y) is the variable with unknown values that we are trying to predict, given known values of the predictor variable.

LO 6: **Compute and interpret the method of least squares.**

- The method of least squares is a statistical procedure used to compute the slope (b) and y-intercept (a) of the best-fitting straight line to a set of data points, called the regression line.

- The equation of a straight line is $Y = bX + a$.

  o The slope (b) of a straight line is a measure of the change in Y relative to the change in X. When X and Y change in the same direction,

the slope is positive. When X and Y change in opposite directions, the slope is negative. The formula for the slope is

$$b = \frac{\text{change in } Y}{\text{change in } X} = \frac{SS_{XY}}{SS_X}.$$

  o The y-intercept (a) of a straight line indicates the value of Y when X equals 0. The formula for the y-intercept is

$$a = M_Y - bM_X.$$

LO 7: **Identify each source of variation in an analysis of regression, and compute an analysis of regression and interpret the results.**

- An analysis of regression is a statistical procedure used to test hypotheses for one or more predictor variables to determine whether the regression equation for a sample of data points can be used to predict values of the criterion variable (Y) given values of the predictor variable (X) in the population.

- An analysis of regression for one predictor variable includes two sources of variation:

1. Regression variation is a measure of the variance in Y that is related to changes in X. The closer that data points fall to the regression line, the larger the value of regression variation. The formula for regression variation is

$$SS_{\text{regression}} = r^2 SS_Y.$$

2. Residual variation is a measure of the variance in Y that is not related to changes in X. This is the variance in Y that is residual, left over, or remaining. The farther that data points fall from the regression line, the larger the value of residual variation. The formula for regression variation is

$$SS_{\text{residual}} = (1 - r^2) SS_Y.$$

- To make a decision, we compare the F statistic value to the critical value. When the F statistic is larger than the critical value, we reject the null hypothesis; otherwise, we retain the null hypothesis.

LO 8:   Compute and interpret the standard error of estimate.

- The standard error of estimate (s_e) is an estimate of the standard deviation or distance that a set of data points falls from the regression line. The standard error of estimate is equal to the square root of the mean square residual.

- The standard error of estimate uses the standard deviation of data points as an estimate of the error in predictions made by a regression line. The smaller the standard error of estimate, the closer values of Y will be to their predicted values, $\hat{Y}$, on the regression line and the more accurate the predictions of Y will be using known values of X.

LO 9:   Summarize the results of a correlation coefficient and linear regression in APA format.

- To summarize correlations, report the strength and direction of each correlation coefficient and the p value for each correlation. The sample size and the effect size should also be reported. The means and the standard error or standard deviations measured in a study can be summarized in a figure or table or in the main text. To report many correlations in a single study, use a correlation matrix.

- To summarize an analysis of regression involving a single predictor variable, we report the test statistic, the degrees of freedom, and the p value for the regression analysis. The data points for each pair of scores are often summarized in a scatter plot or figure displaying the regression line. The regression equation can be stated in the scatter plot.

LO 10:   Compute the Pearson, Spearman, point-biserial, and phi correlation coefficients using SPSS.

- SPSS can be used to compute the Pearson correlation coefficient using the Analyze, Correlate, and Bivariate options in the menu bar. These actions will display a dialog box that allows you to identify the variables and to run the correlation (for more details, see Section 13.4).

- SPSS can be used to compute the Spearman correlation coefficient by selecting the option to compute a Spearman correlation, then running the correlation. To compute the point-biserial correlation coefficient using SPSS, first code the dichotomous factor, and then follow the directions for computing a Pearson correlation coefficient. To compute a phi correlation coefficient using SPSS, first code each dichotomous factor, then weight each variable using the Weight Cases . . . option in the menu bar, and finally follow the directions for computing a Pearson correlation coefficient (for more details, see Section 13.7).

LO 11:   Compute an analysis of regression using SPSS.

- SPSS can be used to compute an analysis of regression using the Analyze, Regression, and Linear options in the menu bar. These actions will display a dialog box that allows you to identify the variables and run the analysis (for more details, see Section 13.11).

• • • Key Terms

analysis of regression
coefficient of determination

confound variable
correlation

correlation coefficient (r)
covariance

criterion variable (Y)
data points
homoscedasticity
known variable (X)
linear regression
linearity
method of least squares
multiple regression
negative correlation
Pearson correlation coefficient (r)
Pearson product-moment
  correlation coefficient

phi correlation coefficient (r_φ)
point-biserial correlation
  coefficient (r_{pb})
positive correlation
predictor variable (X)
regression
regression analysis
regression line
regression variation
residual variation
restriction of range
reverse causality

scatter gram
scatter plot
slope (b)
Spearman rank-order correlation
  coefficient (r_s)
Spearman's rho
standard error of estimate
sum of products (SP)
third variable
to-be-predicted variable (Y)
y-intercept (a)

• • • END-OF-CHAPTER PROBLEMS

Factual Problems

1. What is a correlation?

2. What information does the strength of a correlation coefficient convey?

3. What information does the direction of a correlation coefficient convey?

4. Describe what each of the following statistical terms measures:

   (a) SS_{XY}

   (b) $\sqrt{SS_X SS_Y}$

5. What is the coefficient of determination?

6. State three assumptions for computing linear correlations.

7. What method is used to determine the equation of the regression line for a set of data points?

8. Distinguish between the predictor variable and the criterion variable.

9. Describe regression variation in terms of variation in Y.

10. Describe residual variation in terms of variation in Y.

Concept and Application Problems

11. State which correlation coefficient (Pearson, Spearman, point-biserial, or phi) should be used given the following information.

    (a) Both factors are interval or ratio scale.

    (b) Both factors are dichotomous.

    (c) One factor is dichotomous, and the other factor is continuous.

    (d) Both factors are ranked.

12. State which correlation coefficient (Pearson, Spearman, point-biserial, or phi) should be used to study each of the following factors:

    (a) Activity (active, inactive) and depression (depressed, not depressed)

    (b) Time spent at school and time spent studying in hours per week

    (c) Veteran (yes, no) and level of patriotism indicated on a rating scale

    (d) The hierarchical ranking of a litter of mice for play and social behavior

13. State whether each of the following is an example of a positive correlation or a negative correlation.

    (a) Higher education level is associated with a larger annual income.

    (b) Increased testosterone is associated with increased aggression.

    (c) The smaller the class size, the more students believe they are receiving a quality education.

    (d) Rising prices of apples are associated with the sale of fewer apples.

14. For each example, state whether one correlation is stronger than the other. If one is stronger, then state which is the stronger correlation.

    (a) $r = +.04, r = -.40$
    (b) $r = +.50, r = +.23$
    (c) $r = +.36, r = -.36$
    (d) $r = -.67, r = -.76$

15. The graphs display the data points for a linear correlation. Based on the information provided in these graphs, answer the following questions.

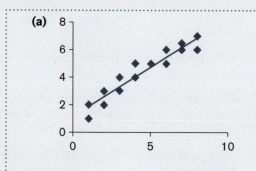

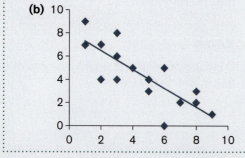

    (a) Which graph displays the negative correlation? Explain.

    (b) Which graph displays the stronger correlation? Explain.

16. A researcher working with socioeconomic data showed a significant positive correlation between the number of local hospitals and the life expectancy of local residents $(r = .19)$. Which of the following conclusions is appropriate? Explain why the other is not appropriate.

    (a) Of the variance in life expectancy, 3.61% can be explained by the number of local hospitals.

    (b) Increasing the number of local hospitals will cause life expectancy for local residents to increase.

17. A medical study found a negative relationship between exercise (in minutes per week) and stress-related health problems $(r = -.26)$. Which of the following conclusions is appropriate? Explain why the other is not appropriate.

    (a) Of the variance in stress-related health problems, 6.76% can be explained by the amount of weekly exercise.

    (b) Increasing the amount of exercise per week will cause stress-related health problems to decrease.

18. A social scientist measures the relationship between computer use (in hours per day) and daily exercise (in minutes per week). Answer the following questions based on the results provided.

Computer Use	Daily Exercise
3	80
2	60
5	95
4	75

    (a) Compute the Pearson correlation coefficient.

    (b) Add 2 hours to each measurement of computer use and recalculate the correlation coefficient.

    (c) Subtract 10 minutes from each measurement of daily exercise and recalculate the correlation coefficient.

    (d) True or false: Adding and subtracting a constant to one set of scores (X or Y) does not change the correlation coefficient. *Note:* Use your answers in (a) to (c) to answer true or false.

19. A researcher measures the relationship between the number of interruptions in class and time spent on task (in minutes). Answer the following questions based on the results provided.

Number of Interruptions	Time Spent on Task
8	18
3	40
6	20
2	32

(a) Compute the Pearson correlation coefficient.

(b) Multiply each measurement of interruptions by 3 and recalculate the correlation coefficient.

(c) Divide each measurement in half for time on task and recalculate the correlation coefficient.

(d) True or false: Multiplying or dividing a positive constant by one set of scores (X or Y) does not change the correlation coefficient. *Note:* Use your answers in (a) to (c) to answer true or false.

20. A researcher measures the relationship between education (in years) and investment gains (in thousands of dollars). Answer the following questions based on the results provided.

Education	Investment Gains
14	8
12	11
9	10
18	14

(a) Compute the Pearson correlation coefficient.

(b) Multiply each investment gain by −1 (so that it represents investment losses instead of gains). Recalculate the correlation coefficient.

(c) True or false: Multiplying or dividing a negative constant by one set of scores (X or Y) changes the sign of the correlation only, while the strength of the correlation coefficient remains unchanged. *Note:* Use your answers in (a) and (b) to answer true or false.

21. A researcher reports the following regression equation for the relationship between two variables: $\hat{Y} = 1.3X + 2$. Find the predicted value of Y, given that $X = 0$, 2, 4, and 8.

22. An animal trainer tests whether the number of hours of obedience training can predict where a dog places in a breed show. The hypothetical data are given below.

Hours of Training	Place in Breed Show
X	Y
18	1
4	6
10	2
7	4

In terms of the method of least squares, which of the following regression lines is the best fit for these data?

(a) $\hat{Y} = -0.338X + 6.545$ (b) $\hat{Y} = 0.338X - 6.545$

(c) $\hat{Y} = -1.3X + 5.25$ (d) $\hat{Y} = 1.3X - 5.25$

23. Forest bathing, also called *Shinrin-yoku*, is the practice of taking short, leisurely walks in a forest to enhance positive health. To test if forest bathing and mood are related, a clinical psychologist records the time spent forest bathing in minutes (X) and the corresponding change in mood using a standard self-report affect grid (Y) among 8 patients with a history of depression. The data are given in the following table.

Time Spent Forest Bathing (in minutes)	Change in Mood
X	Y
32	+24
24	+20
28	+25
17	+22
12	+16

(a) Compute the method of least squares to find the equation of the regression line.

(b) Use the regression equation computed in part (a) to determine the predicted change in mood of a person who spends 20 minutes forest bathing.

24. A community researcher measured the correlation between the average cost of housing and the crime rate in eight local communities. The results of this hypothetical study are listed in the following table.

Average Cost of Housing (in thousands of dollars)	Crime Rate (per 100,000 population)
X	Y
20	96
80	65
220	22
120	31
180	34
90	70
110	30
300	16

(a) Compute the Pearson correlation coefficient.

(b) Compute the coefficient of determination.

(c) Using a two-tailed test at a .05 level of significance, state the decision to retain or reject the null hypothesis.

25. Using the Pearson correlation coefficient, a study on addiction found a positive correlation between time of cravings and time of relapse ($r = .51$) in a sample of 20 people with a drug addiction. Using a two-tailed test at a .05 level of significance, state the decision to retain or reject the null hypothesis.

26. Using the Pearson correlation coefficient, researchers studying the dangers of cell phone use while driving found a positive correlation between cell phone use while driving and car

accidents ($r = .24$) in a sample of 52 participants. Using a two-tailed test at a .05 level of significance, state the decision to retain or reject the null hypothesis.

27. A researcher tested whether time of day could predict mood in a sample of 14 college students. If $SS_{residual} = 108$, then what is the standard error of estimate in this sample?

28. A team of clinical psychologists tested the extent to which levels of cognitive functioning were related to the number of symptoms for some disorder expressed in 15 patients. The researchers recorded the following values: $SS_{XY} = 48.60$, $SS_X = 355.73$, and $SS_Y = 96.40$.

(a) What is the proportion of variance, r^2, in symptoms (Y) that can be explained by levels of cognitive functioning (X)?

(b) If the total variation in Y is 96.40 ($SS_Y = 96.40$), then what is the $SS_{regression}$, or the amount of variation that is predicted by X?

(c) What is the $SS_{residual}$, or the amount of variation in Y that is remaining?

29. An instructor measured quiz scores and the number of hours studying among a sample of 20 college students. If $SS_{XY} = 43$, $SS_X = 99$, $M_Y = 6$, and $M_X = 5$, then what is the regression equation for this sample?

30. A health psychologist hypothesizes that students who study more also exercise less because they spend so much time studying. She measures whether the number of hours studying (per week) can predict the number of hours exercising in a sample of 62 students. Complete the following regression table for this hypothetical study and make a decision to retain or reject the null hypothesis.

Source of Variation	SS	df	MS	F_{obt}
Regression			80	
Residual (error)				
Total	1,440			

31. A psychologist noted that people have more difficulty sleeping in a bright room than in a dark room. She measured whether the intensity of the light could predict the time it took a sample of four participants to fall asleep. The data for this hypothetical study are listed in the following table. Compute an analysis of regression for this hypothetical study and make a decision to retain or reject the null hypothesis.

Intensity of Light (in watts)	Time It Took to Sleep (in minutes)
X	Y
5	10
10	18
20	30
40	35

Problems in Research

32. **Self-evaluation of verbal and math ability.** Möller and Marsh (2013) evaluated the relationship between the verbal and math ability of students (achievement) and their self-belief of their ability (self-concept). In their report, they identified a significant correlation between math achievement and math self-concept, $r = .61$, and a significant correlation between verbal achievement and verbal self-concept, $r = .49$.

    (a) Describe in words the relationship between math achievement and math self-concept.

    (b) Describe in words the relationship between verbal achievement and verbal self-concept.

33. **Brain volume and neurocognitive deficits.** Bonilha and colleagues (2008) measured brain volume reduction in a region of the prefrontal cortex called Brodmann Area 9 (BA9) in a sample of 14 adult patients with schizophrenia. Participants completed a cognitive performance test called the Wisconsin Card Sorting Test (WCST). The relationship between brain volume reduction and the number of errors on the WCST was measured. The following scatter plot shows the approximate standardized values the researchers measured.

    (a) Is the slope positive or negative?

    (b) Describe the relationship between prefrontal brain volume in BA9 and cognitive performance on the WCST.

34. **Mindfulness through the semester.** Danitz, Suvak, and Orsillo (2016) examined the association between change in acceptance, mindfulness practice, and academic values with other outcomes in a first-year undergraduate experience course that integrated an acceptance-based behavioral program. The researchers reported,

    > An examination of correlation indicated that changes in acceptance were negatively associated with changes in depression, $r(n = 213) = -.33, p < .001$. (p. 494)

    (a) What was the sample size in this study?

    (b) What was the value of the correlation coefficient? Was the correlation significant at a .05 level of significance? Explain.

35. **Skin conductance and toddler aggression.** Baker, Shelton, Baibazarova, Hay, and van Goozen (2013) studied the extent to which skin conductance activity (SCA) in toddlers could predict aggression in the toddlers two years later. In their study, they reported that the correlation between SCA and aggressive antisocial behavior at a baseline stage was $r = -.34$,

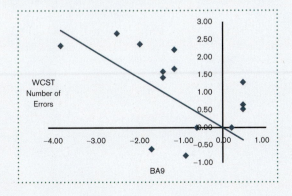

$p = .005$. Given that only one predictor variable was tested, what must the value of the standardized beta coefficient (β) be equal to for this result?

36. **Validity of a scale to measure daily intake of fat.** Privitera and Freeman (2012) constructed a scale to measure or estimate the daily fat intake of participants; the scale was called the estimated daily intake scale for fat (EDIS-F). To validate the assertion that the EDIS-F could indeed estimate daily intake of fat, the researchers tested the extent to which scores on the scale could predict liking for a high-fat food (as would be expected if the scale were measuring daily fat intake). Liking was recorded such that higher scores indicated greater liking for the food. The researchers found that liking for the high-fat food (Y) could be predicted by scores on the EDIS-F (X) using the following regression equation: $\hat{Y} = 1.01X + 4.71$. Using this regression equation:

(a) Is the *correlation* positive or negative? Explain.

(b) If a participant scores 40 on the EDIS-F, then what is the expected liking rating for the high-fat food?

Answers for even numbers are in Appendix D.

Sharpen your skills with **SAGE edge** at **edge.sagepub.com/priviteraess2e**

SAGE edge for Students provides a personalized approach to help you accomplish your coursework goals in an easy-to-use learning environment.

$SAGE edge™

©iStockphoto.com/Rawpixel Ltd

©iStockphoto.com/diane39

14 Chi-Square Tests
Goodness of Fit and the Test for Independence

• • • Learning Objectives

After reading this chapter, you should be able to:

1. Distinguish between nonparametric and parametric tests.

2. Explain how the test statistic is computed for a chi-square test.

3. Calculate the degrees of freedom for the chi-square goodness-of-fit test and locate critical values in the chi-square table.

4. Compute the chi-square goodness-of-fit test and interpret the results.

5. Identify the assumption and the restriction of expected frequency size for the chi-square test.

6. Calculate the degrees of freedom for the chi-square test for independence and locate critical values in the chi-square table.

7. Compute the chi-square test for independence and interpret the results.

8. Compute and interpret effect size for the chi-square test for independence.

9. Summarize the results of a chi-square test in APA format.

10. Compute the chi-square goodness-of-fit test and the chi-square test for independence using SPSS.

Counting is a common mathematical tool. Indeed, we often use counting anytime we use the phrase "Let's put it to a vote." We vote or count for many things, such as which movie is our favorite, which contestant on a show deserves to win, which team is most likely to "win it all," or what topic in a statistics class is the most difficult. In each case, we are "putting it to a vote" by counting the number of people who voted in each category (e.g., movies, contestants, teams, or topics), then comparing the counts recorded to identify how the voting was different in each category.

In hypothesis testing, we likewise have many cases in which we aim to evaluate the number of people counted in each of a finite set of categories. In the basic structure of such a study, we count the number of people in each category, then compare how the counts differed. For example, during an election, pollsters record the number of people who voted for each of two candidates; in business, marketers count the number of customers who prefer one brand or another; in public health, clinicians may count the number of people who fall into various categories for health. In each example, the number of people in each category (candidates, brands, or health) are counted and compared. In this type of test, the categories are the groups; the number of people counted in each category is the dependent variable. The null hypothesis for such a test is that the counts in each category are proportional; the alternative hypothesis states that the counts in each category are not proportional.

In this chapter, we explore the nature of hypothesis testing when evaluating the number of people counted in each of a finite set of categories, how to compute and interpret observed effects, and the informativeness of hypothesis testing for making such comparisons. We further explore other ways of adding information about the nature of observed effects and how to appropriately interpret them.

Master the content.

edge.sagepub.com/priviteraess2e

• • • Chapter Outline

14.1 DISTINGUISHING PARAMETRIC AND NONPARAMETRIC TESTS

Most statistical tests are computed on data that are on an interval or ratio scale of measurement; or are computed for data that are normally distributed, as is characteristic of many of the behaviors and events that behavioral scientists study. Each of the hypothesis tests taught in this book has so far assumed that data are interval or ratio and that the population distribution is normal. These hypothesis tests, such as the *t* tests, analysis of variance (ANOVA), correlations, and regression analysis, are collectively called **parametric tests** because these tests are used to test hypotheses about parameters in a population in which the data are normally distributed and measured on an interval or ratio scale of measurement.

However, data can also be nominal or ordinal, and often the distribution of data is nonnormal. When data are measured on an interval or ratio scale of measurement, the test statistic used for each hypothesis test measures variance in the formula (i.e., standard error). However, the variance can only meaningfully convey differences when data are measured on a scale in which the distance that scores deviate from their mean is meaningful. While data on an interval or ratio scale do meaningfully convey distance, data on a nominal or ordinal scale do not. Hence, when we measure data on a nominal or ordinal scale, we require hypothesis tests that use test statistics that do not analyze the variance of the data. In this chapter, we introduce two such hypothesis tests for nominal data. Collectively, these tests are part of a family of tests referred to as **nonparametric tests**, which are hypothesis tests for data that are not normally distributed and for data that are measured on a nominal or ordinal scale of measurement. In all, a nonparametric test has the following three key characteristics that distinguish it from a parametric test:

1. Nonparametric tests can be used even when we do not make inferences about parameters in a population, although they can be used to test hypothesized relationships in a population.

2. Nonparametric tests do not require that the data in the population be normally distributed. Because the data can have any type of distribution, nonparametric tests are often called distribution-free tests.

3. Nonparametric tests can be used to analyze data on a nominal or ordinal scale of measurement.

In this chapter, we introduce the following two nonparametric tests for nominal data:

- Chi-square goodness-of-fit test
- Chi-square test for independence

14.2 THE CHI-SQUARE GOODNESS-OF-FIT TEST

One type of test is commonly used to analyze the significance of counts recorded at each level of a categorical variable. To illustrate, suppose a marketing team asks a group of children which of two products they prefer (one with or one without a picture of a cartoon character). Table 14.1

Parametric tests are hypothesis tests that are used to test hypotheses about parameters in a population in which the data are normally distributed and measured on an interval or ratio scale of measurement.

Nonparametric tests are hypothesis tests that are used (1) to test hypotheses that do not make inferences about parameters in a population, (2) to test hypotheses about data that can have any type of distribution, and (3) to analyze data on a nominal or ordinal scale of measurement.

shows that 20 children chose the product with the cartoon character and 10 children chose the other product. In this example, we only recorded counts or frequencies—specifically, the number of children choosing one of two products. We do not record a dependent variable for each participant; instead, we record a single count in each category. It is meaningless to measure the variance of a single measure or count in each group or category. For this reason, the **chi-square (χ^2) test** (pronounced "kie-square") was developed to analyze data using such a method, without the need for computing variance. Instead, a chi-square test evaluates the discrepancy at each level of one or two categorical variables.

When we evaluate the discrepancy at each level of one categorical variable, we use the chi-square goodness-of-fit test. This test specifically evaluates how well a set of observed frequencies fits with what was expected. The structure for this type of test is illustrated in Table 14.1.

FYI

A chi-square goodness-of-fit test indicates how well a set of observed frequencies fits with what was expected.

FYI

The chi-square test is a nonparametric test that evaluates the discrepancy of counts or frequencies at each level of one or two categorical variables.

TABLE 14.1 The Count or Frequency of 30 Children Choosing One of Two Products

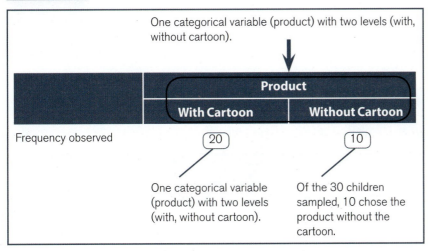

A single count or frequency is recorded in each category.

The **chi-square (χ^2) test** is a statistical procedure used to test hypotheses about the discrepancy between the observed and expected frequencies for the levels of a single categorical variable or two categorical variables observed together.

The **chi-square (χ^2) goodness-of-fit test** is a statistical procedure used to determine whether observed frequencies at each level of one categorical variable are similar to or different from the frequencies we expected at each level of the categorical variable.

LEARNING CHECK 1

1. The chi-square test is used to make tests about data on what scale of measurement?

2. Why is the chi-square called a goodness-of-fit test?

3. If the frequency of participants recorded in each of three groups was 7, 10, and 8, then what is the total number of participants observed in this study?

Answers: 1. Nominal scale; 2. A chi-square goodness-of-fit test indicates how well a set of observed frequencies fits with what was expected; 3. 25 participants.

We compute a chi-square goodness-of-fit test in Example 14.1.

Example 14.1

©iStockphoto.com/fmajor

The frequency of dreaming and the ability of people to recall their dreams are of particular interest to many researchers in the behavioral and neurological sciences (Aspy, 2016; Bachner, Raffetseder, Walz, & Schredl, 2012; Schredl & Göritz, 2015; Schredl, Stumbrys, & Erlacher, 2016). Suppose a team of researchers conducted a study with this area of focus by observing 80 participants as they slept overnight in a laboratory. As part of the study, the researchers woke each participant during rapid eye movement (REM) sleep, the stage of sleep in which people dream, and they asked participants whether or not they were dreaming. Table 14.2 is a frequency table showing the number of participants who did recall a dream, did not recall a dream, or were unsure if they were dreaming. On the basis of previous studies, the researchers expected 80% of participants to recall their dream, 10% to not recall, and 10% to be unsure. We will compute a chi-square goodness-of-fit test at a .05 level of significance.

Table 14.2 displays two rows of frequencies. The top row lists the **frequency observed (f_o)** in each category. This is the number of participants we observed in the study who said that they did recall a dream, did not recall a dream, or were unsure if they dreamed. In this study, 80 participants ($N = 80$) were observed, of whom 58 did recall a dream, 12 did not, and 10 were unsure.

| TABLE 14.2 | The Observed Frequency of Dreams Recalled and the Expected Frequency Based on Proportions in Each Category That Were Reported in Previous Studies |

	Dream Recall			
	Did Recall	**Did Not Recall**	**Unsure**	
f_o	58	12	10	
f_e	80(.80) = 64	80(.10) = 8	80(.10) = 8	
				$N = 80$

The **frequency observed (f_o)** is the count or frequency of participants recorded in each category or at each level of the categorical variable.

The **frequency expected (f_e)** is the count or frequency of participants in each category, or at each level of the categorical variable, as determined by the proportion expected in each category.

The bottom row in Table 14.2 lists the **frequency expected (f_e)** in each category. This value is computed based on the proportions expected in each category. In this example, 80 participants were observed, of whom we expected 80% to recall their dream, 10% to not recall, and 10% to be unsure. We can multiply the total number of participants (N) by the proportion expected in each category (p) to find the frequency expected in each category:

$$f_e = Np.$$

Table 14.2 shows the calculation of the frequency expected in each category. In a sample of 80 participants, we expected 64 to recall their dream, 8 to not recall, and 8 to be unsure. The chi-square goodness-of-fit test statistic will determine how well the observed frequencies fit with the expected frequencies.

The test statistic for the chi-square goodness-of-fit test is 0 when the observed and expected frequencies are equal and gets larger (more positive) as the discrepancies (or differences) get larger. The larger the discrepancies, the more likely we are to reject the null hypothesis. The test statistic for the chi-square goodness-of-fit test is

$$\chi^2_{obt} = \sum \frac{(f_o - f_e)^2}{f_e}.$$

FYI

The chi-square test statistic measures the size of the discrepancy between the observed and expected frequencies at each level of a categorical variable.

The difference between the observed and expected frequencies at each level of the categorical variable is squared in the numerator of the test statistic to eliminate negative values. The value in the numerator is divided by the expected frequency to determine the relative size of the discrepancy. To illustrate, suppose we observe a discrepancy of 10 in two studies. In Study 1, the expected frequency was 100 and we observed 110, and in Study 2, the expected frequency was 10 and we observed 20. The discrepancy in the second study is much larger in this example because 20 is twice as large as 10, whereas 110 is not nearly that different from 100.

MAKING SENSE THE RELATIVE SIZE OF A DISCREPANCY

The test statistic measures the relative size of the discrepancy in each category or at each level of the categorical variable. To further illustrate what a relative discrepancy is, suppose we observe 10 people ($f_o = 10$) in a category for which we expected to observe 5 people ($f_e = 5$). The discrepancy between the observed and expected frequencies is 5 ($10 - 5 = 5$). If we substitute these values into the formula, we find

$$\chi^2_{obt} = \frac{(10-5)^2}{5} = 5.00.$$

Now suppose we observe 30 people ($f_o = 30$) in a category for which we expected to observe 25 people ($f_e = 25$). In this category, the discrepancy between the observed and expected frequencies is again 5 ($30 - 25 = 5$). However, if we substitute these values into the formula, we find

$$\chi^2_{obt} = \frac{(30-25)^2}{25} = 1.00.$$

Notice that the value of χ^2_{obt} is smaller in the second example, even though the discrepancy is 5 in both. The reason is that, relatively speaking, 10 is twice as large as 5, whereas 30 is not nearly that different from 25. The difference may be more easily appreciated using an analogy to weight lifting. Lift 5 pounds, then 10 pounds, and you will likely notice the difference. Lift 45 pounds, then 50 pounds, and you will likely not notice the difference as much. As you lift heavier weights, a 5-pound difference becomes less and less noticeable. In a similar way, the denominator of the chi-square test statistic accounts for the relative size of a discrepancy.

We follow the four steps of hypothesis testing to determine how well the observed frequencies fit with the frequencies expected at each level of the categorical variable (dream recall) in Example 14.1.

Step 1: State the hypotheses. The null hypothesis for the chi-square goodness-of-fit test is that the expected frequencies are correct. The alternative hypothesis is that the expected frequencies are not correct. In other words, the null hypothesis states that the proportions (p) expected in each category are correct. The alternative hypothesis states that the proportions identified in the null hypothesis are not correct:

H_0: The distribution of proportions (8:1:1) is the same as expected.

$$p_{\text{did recall}} = .80.$$

$$p_{\text{did not recall}} = .10.$$

$$p_{\text{unsure}} = .10.$$

H_1: Not H_0. The distribution of proportions differs from that stated in the null hypothesis.

Step 2: Set the criteria for a decision. For this test, we compare the value of the test statistic to the critical value in a positively skewed **chi-square distribution**. The chi-square distribution is a set of chi-square test statistic values for all possible samples when the null hypothesis is true. Figure 14.1 shows the general shape of a chi-square distribution. There is an entire family of chi-square distributions, with each distribution having specified degrees of freedom. The degrees of freedom for each chi-square distribution are equal to the number of levels of the categorical variable (k) minus 1:

$$df = k - 1.$$

For Example 14.1, the level of significance is .05. With $k = 3$ levels of dream recall, $df = 3 - 1 = 2$. To locate the critical value for this test, find the intersection of the row for 2 degrees of freedom and the column for a .05 level of significance in Table C.7 in Appendix C. The critical value is 5.99. Figure 14.2 shows the chi-square distribution, with the rejection region beyond the critical value given. Because the chi-square distribution is positively skewed, the rejection region is always placed in the upper tail.

FIGURE 14.1   The General Shape of a Chi-Square Distribution

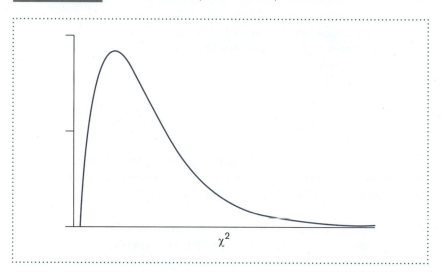

$$\chi^2$$

The **chi-square distribution** is a positively skewed distribution of chi-square test statistic values for all possible samples when the null hypothesis is true.

| **FIGURE 14.2** | The Rejection Region for a Chi-Square With 2 Degrees of Freedom |

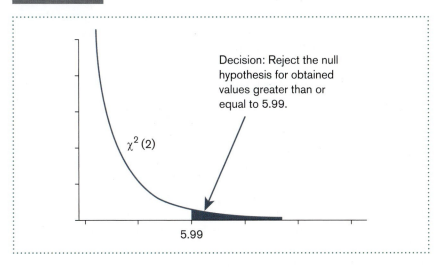

Decision: Reject the null hypothesis for obtained values greater than or equal to 5.99.

$\chi^2 (2)$

5.99

The critical value is 5.99.

Step 3: Compute the test statistic. The test statistic for the chi-square goodness-of-fit test is 0 when the observed and expected frequencies are equal and gets larger (more positive) as the discrepancies (or differences) get larger. The larger the discrepancies, the more likely we are to reject the null hypothesis. The test statistic for the chi-square goodness-of-fit test is

$$\chi^2_{obt} = \Sigma \frac{(f_o - f_e)^2}{f_e}.$$

To compute the test statistic for Example 14.1, we substitute the frequencies recorded in Table 14.2 into the test statistic formula and sum the discrepancy between the observed and expected frequencies one column at a time:

$$\chi^2_{obt} = \frac{(58 - 64)^2}{64} + \frac{(12 - 8)^2}{8} + \frac{(10 - 8)^2}{8}$$
$$= 0.56 + 2.00 + 0.50$$
$$= 3.06.$$

Step 4: Make a decision. We compare the value of the test statistic with the critical value. If the test statistic falls beyond the critical value, which is 5.99, then we reject the null hypothesis. In this example, $\chi^2_{obt} = 3.06$, and it fails to exceed the critical value of 5.99. We therefore retain the null hypothesis. If we were to report this result in a research journal, it would look something like this:

A chi-square goodness-of-fit test showed that the frequency of dream recall during REM sleep was similar to what was expected, $\chi^2(2) = 3.06$, $p > .05$.

FYI

The rejection region is always placed in the upper tail of the positively skewed chi-square distribution.

FYI

The chi-square test statistic measures the size of the discrepancy between the observed and expected frequencies at each level of a categorical variable.

Notice that our decision to retain the null hypothesis was the expected outcome. Interestingly, unlike parametric tests, the chi-square goodness-of-fit test is one of the few hypothesis tests used to confirm that a null hypothesis is correct. In Example 14.1, we found that the proportion of participants recalling dreams was consistent with what we would expect. This was the outcome we were testing—we had no reason to think this would not be the case.

Other examples of studies testing to show support for a null hypothesis are not hard to find. A researcher may want to demonstrate that roads in a local community are not more dangerous than "normal" by showing that the local community has traffic accident rates that are similar to those in the general population, or a human resources firm may want to demonstrate that its hiring practices are not discriminatory by showing that the distribution of the race of its employees is proportionate to that in the general community population. In each situation, the researcher or firm tests a hypothesis to show that the observed frequencies are similar to the expected frequencies. So a decision to retain the null hypothesis is actually the aim of the hypothesis test. The chi-square goodness-of-fit test is a rare example of a test that can be used for this purpose.

FYI

The chi-square goodness-of-fit test is a rare example of a test used to show that a null hypothesis is correct.

14.3 SPSS in Focus:
The Chi-Square Goodness-of-Fit Test

In Example 14.1, we concluded from the chi-square goodness-of-fit test that the frequency of dream recall during REM sleep was similar to what was expected, $\chi^2(2) = 3.06$, $p > .05$. Let us confirm this result using SPSS.

1. Click on the Variable View tab and enter *dream* in the Name column; enter *frequency* in the Name column below it. Go to the Decimals column and reduce the value to 0 for both rows.

2. To code the *dream* variable, click on the small gray box with three dots in the Values column. In the dialog box, enter *1* in the value cell and *did recall* in the label cell, and then click Add. Then enter *2* in the value cell and *did not recall* in the label cell, and then click Add. Then enter *3* in the value cell and *unsure* in the label cell, and then click Add. Select OK.

3. Click on the Data View tab. In the *dream* column, enter *1* in the first cell, *2* in the next cell, and *3* in the next cell. In the *frequency* column, enter the corresponding observed frequencies: *58*, *12*, and *10*, respectively.

4. Go to the menu bar and click Data, then Weight cases by, to display the dialog box shown in Figure 14.3. Select Weight cases by and move *frequency* into the Frequency Variable: cell, and then click OK.

5. Go to the menu bar and click Analyze, then Nonparametric tests and Chi-square, to display the dialog box shown in Figure 14.4.

6. Using the arrows, move *dream* into the Test Variable List: box. In the Expected Values box, notice that we have two options: assume all categories (or expected frequencies) are equal or enter the expected frequencies in the cell provided. Because the expected frequencies were not equal, we enter the expected frequencies one at a time and click Add to move them into the cell, same as shown in Figure 14.4.

7. Select OK, or select Paste and click the Run command.

The SPSS output displays two tables, which are both shown in Table 14.3. The top table displays the observed and expected frequencies. The bottom table lists the value of the test statistic, the degrees of freedom (*df*), and the *p* value (Asymp. Sig.) for the test. These data match the values we computed for Example 14.1.

FIGURE 14.3 SPSS Dialog Box for Step 4

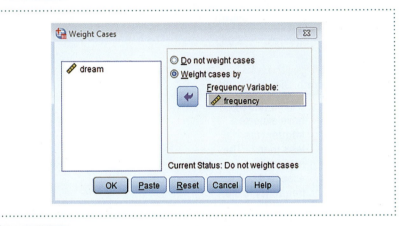

FIGURE 14.4 SPSS Dialog Box for Steps 5 and 6

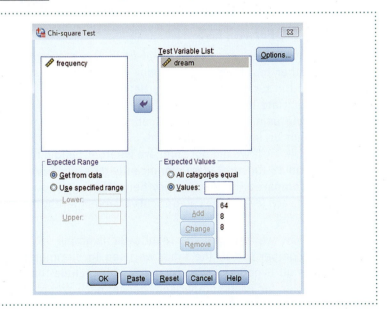

(Continued)

(Continued)

TABLE 14.3   The SPSS Output for the Chi-Square Goodness-of-Fit Test

dream

	Observed N	Expected N	Residual
did recall	58	64.0	-6.0
did not recall	12	8.0	4.0
unsure	10	8.0	2.0
Total	80		

Test Statistics

	dream
Chi-Square	3.063[a]
df	2
Asymp. Sig.	.216

a. 0 cells (0.0%) have expected frequencies less than 5. The minimum expected cell frequency is 8.0.

14.4 INTERPRETING THE CHI-SQUARE GOODNESS-OF-FIT TEST

Interpreting the chi-square goodness-of-fit test is different from interpreting any other test taught in this book in that the chi-square test is not interpreted in terms of differences between categories. Specifically, it is not appropriate to make comparisons *across the levels* of the categorical variable using a chi-square goodness-of-fit test, meaning that this test cannot be interpreted in terms of differences between categories. In Example 14.1, we did not compare whether 58 (did recall), 12 (did not recall), and 10 (unsure) were significantly different from each other. Instead, we compared the discrepancy between observed and expected frequencies *at each level* of the categorical variable, thereby making a total of *k* comparisons.

To show how we interpret the results for Example 14.1, Table 14.4 shows each comparison in the table we used to summarize the data. Because the null hypothesis was retained, we conclude that there were no discrepancies for each comparison; hence, each comparison was as expected.

TABLE 14.4 The Three Comparisons for the Categorical Variable in Example 14.1

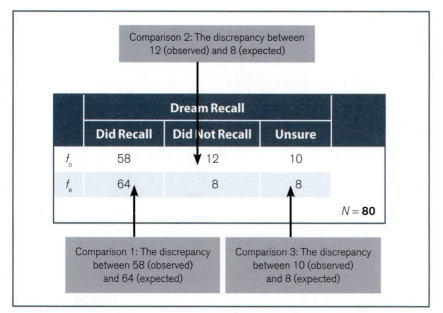

Because we retained the null hypothesis, no comparisons are significant.

FYI

To interpret a significant chi-square goodness-of-fit test, we compare observed and expected frequencies at each level of the categorical variable.

Comparisons are made at each level of the categorical variable because this is how the test statistic measures the discrepancies. The test statistic adds the discrepancy at each level of the categorical variable. Because the test statistic does not compare differences between the discrepancies, there is no statistical basis for identifying which discrepancies are actually significant. When a chi-square goodness-of-fit test is significant, we mostly speculate as to which observed frequencies were significantly different from the expected frequencies (i.e., which observed frequencies were unexpected). The more discrepancies we add (the larger k is), the more difficult it becomes to identify which observed frequencies were significantly different from the expected frequencies. One strategy is to identify the most obvious or largest discrepancies. Using this strategy, the largest discrepancies tend to be the focus of a significant result, with smaller discrepancies tending to be ignored.

Another consideration that should be made is the key assumption for the chi-square test that the observed frequencies are recorded independently, meaning that each observed frequency must come from different and unrelated participants. You cannot count the same person twice. In addition, we would violate this assumption if we compared preferences for a certain product among identical twins because these participants are related. Likewise, this assumption would be violated if we compared preferences over a series of trials because the same participants would be counted more than once.

Additionally, one restriction on using a chi-square test is that the size of an expected frequency should never be smaller than 5 in a given category.

For Example 14.1, this means that the expected frequency should have been at least 5 for each category of dream recall, and this was the case. To illustrate further, suppose we have two situations:

$$\text{Situation A: } f_o = 2, f_e = 1 \longrightarrow \chi_{obt}^2 = \frac{(2-1)^2}{1} = 1.00$$

$$\text{Situation B: } f_o = 21, f_e = 20 \longrightarrow \chi_{obt}^2 = \frac{(21-20)^2}{20} = 0.05$$

In both situations, the difference between the observed and expected frequencies is 1. Yet, if you compute χ^2 for each situation, you obtain very different values. In Situation A, you divide by an expected frequency of 1, whereas you divide by 20 in Situation B. The result is that smaller expected frequencies, those less than 5, tend to overstate the size of a discrepancy. There are two ways to overcome this limitation:

1.   Increase the sample size so that it is five times larger than the number of levels of the categorical variable. With three levels, we would need at least 15 participants ($3 \times 5 = 15$); with five levels, we would need at least 25 participants ($5 \times 5 = 25$); and so on.

2.   Increase the number of levels of the categorical variable. The more levels, or the larger k is, the larger the critical value for the hypothesis test. As a general rule, when k is greater than 4, having one expected frequency less than 5 is not as problematic.

LEARNING CHECK 2

1.   The following table summarizes the results of a study of preferences for one of four types of milk.

	Milk Products			
	1%	**2%**	**Whole**	**Skim**
f_o	35	40	10	15
f_e	30	30	20	20

   (a) How many participants were observed in this study (N)?

   (b) What are the degrees of freedom for this test?

   (c) Compute the test statistic and decide whether to retain or reject the null hypothesis.

2.   Two studies find a 6-point discrepancy between the observed and expected frequencies. If the discrepancy in Study A is 17 (observed) compared to 11 (expected), and the discrepancy in Study B is 82 (observed) compared to 76 (expected), which study will produce a larger chi-square test statistic value?

3.   When observed frequencies are a "good fit" with expected frequencies, do we reject or retain the null hypothesis?

4.   How is a chi-square goodness-of-fit test interpreted?

5.   What is the key assumption for the chi-square test?

14.5 THE CHI-SQUARE TEST FOR INDEPENDENCE

The chi-square test can also be used to test for independence. Specifically, when we record frequencies for two categorical variables, we can determine the extent to which the two variables are related, using an analysis similar to a correlation. This hypothesis test is called the **chi-square test for independence**.

The chi-square test for independence is used when we record observations across the levels of two categorical variables with any number of levels. Table 14.5 shows two examples of a chi-square test for independence. It helps to organize the data for such studies into tables, as shown. We describe these tables just as we did for the two-way ANOVA tests. That is, we refer to this test by referencing the levels of each categorical variable, as shown in Table 14.5. Each cell in the table represents a group or category where we record frequencies. We can determine the number of cells or groups in a table by multiplying the levels of each categorical variable. That is, the first table has a health status variable with two levels (healthy, overweight) and a physical examination variable with two levels (pass, fail), so this study has four cells or groups ($2 \times 2 = 4$ groups) represented in the table.

The chi-square test for independence is interpreted similar to a correlation. If two categorical variables are independent, they are not related or correlated. And conversely, if two categorical variables are dependent, they are related or correlated. To illustrate how to identify independent and dependent relationships in a frequency table, refer to Table 14.6. Table 14.6a shows that depression and serotonin (a brain chemical) have a dependent relationship. Thus, the frequency of people with depression is related to whether they have low or high levels of serotonin. Table 14.6b shows that depression and preferences for Coke or Pepsi have an independent relationship. Thus, the frequency of people with depression is not related to their preference for Coke or Pepsi. The table shows that the more frequencies vary across the table, the less independent, and therefore the more related, the two variables are.

FYI

A chi-square test for independence can be used to identify the relationship between two categorical variables with any number of levels.

TABLE 14.5	Two Examples of Two-Way Chi-Square Tests for Independence, as Organized in a Table

2×2 chi-square:

		Health Status	
		Healthy	Overweight
Physical Examination	Pass	1	2
	Fail	3	4

(Continued)

The **chi-square test for independence** is a statistical procedure used to determine whether frequencies observed at the combination of levels of two categorical variables are similar to frequencies expected.

TABLE 14.5 (Continued)

2 × 3 chi-square:

		Trimester		
		First	**Second**	**Third**
Stress Levels	**Low**	1	2	3
	High	4	5	6

The cells in each table represent a group or category where we record frequencies. To find the number of cells, multiply the levels of each categorical variable. A 2 × 2 chi-square has 2 × 2 = 4 cells. A 2 × 3 chi-square has 2 × 3 = 6 cells. The cells represent the groups and are numbered in each example.

TABLE 14.6   A Dependent (a) and an Independent (b) Relationship Between Two Categorical Variables

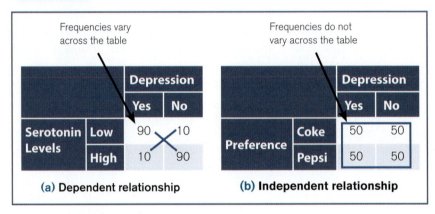

A dependent relationship indicates that two categorical variables are related and is evident when frequencies vary across the table.

In Example 14.2, we demonstrate how to compute a chi-square test for independence.

Example 14.2

©iStockphoto.com/asiseeit

Many studies look at the effectiveness of family and individual counseling in a variety of settings (Gelso, Nutt Williams, & Fretz, 2014; Guo & Slesnick, 2013; Kivlighan & Kivlighan, 2016). As an example of one such study in this area of research, suppose we hypothesize that more patients will complete counseling when the family is included in the counseling compared to individual-only counseling. To test this hypothesis, we measure the relationship between the type of counseling (family vs. individual) and the counseling outcome (completion vs. premature termination). Table 14.7 shows the results of this study. We will compute a chi-square test for independence using a .05 level of significance.

The categorical variables in Example 14.2 are type of counseling (2 levels) and outcome (2 levels). Each cell in the table represents a group where we can record frequencies. In

Table 14.7, we find there are $2 \times 2 = 4$ groups, and a frequency observed is listed in each group. The row totals show that 34 patients participated in family counseling and 76 in individual counseling. The column totals show that 53 patients completed counseling, and 57 ended counseling prematurely. The total number of patients observed is 110 patients.

TABLE 14.7 Observed Frequency

Frequency Observed (f_o)		Outcome		
		Completion	Premature Termination	
Type of Counseling	Family	22	12	34
	Individual	31	45	76
		53	57	$N = 110$

The observed frequency at each combination of levels of two categorical variables: type of counseling and outcome. In this study, 110 patients were observed. Row and column totals are also given.

Table 14.7 lists only the observed frequencies. To determine the expected frequencies, we need to know the number of participants observed in each group. To do this, we refer to the row and column totals in the table. When the row and column totals are equal, the expected frequencies in each cell will also be equal. In this case, we would divide the total number of participants observed (N) by the number of cells to find the expected frequency in each cell.

However, in Table 14.7, the row and the column totals are not equal. The number of patients in family and individual counseling is different; the number of patients completing and prematurely terminating counseling is different. To find the expected frequencies in this case, we must ask how many patients we expect to observe in each cell, given the number of patients who were observed. The size of the expected frequency in a given cell, then, is directly related to the number of patients observed. To determine expected frequencies:

1. Identify the row and column totals for each cell.

2. Compute the following formula for each cell:

$$f_e = \frac{\text{row total} \times \text{column total}}{N}.$$

Each calculation is shown in Table 14.8. The sum of the expected frequencies will equal N. The expected frequencies in each cell are the frequencies we expect to observe when the categorical variables are independent or not related. Table 14.8 shows the expected frequencies for Example 14.2.

We can now follow the four steps to hypothesis testing to evaluate the relationship between type of counseling (family, individual) and counseling

FYI

The size of the expected frequency in a given cell is directly related to the number of participants observed.

TABLE 14.8   Expected Frequency

Frequency Expected (f_e)		Outcome		
		Completion	Premature Termination	
Type of Counseling	Family	(34 × 53)/110 = 16.38	(34 × 57)/110 = 17.62	34
	Individual	(76 × 53)/110 = 36.62	(76 × 57)/110 = 39.38	76
		53	57	$N = 110$

The expected frequencies for type of counseling and counseling outcome. Calculations are given in each cell.

outcome (completion, premature termination) in Example 14.2. For simplicity, Table 14.9 lists the observed and expected frequencies (given in parentheses) for Example 14.2 in the same table. Using the values in Table 14.9, we will apply the four steps to hypothesis testing to compute a chi-square test for independence at a .05 level of significance.

TABLE 14.9   The Observed Frequencies and the Expected Frequencies for Example 14.2

		Outcome		
		Completion	Premature Termination	
Type of Counseling	Family	22 (16.38)	12 (17.62)	34
	Individual	31 (36.62)	45 (39.38)	76
		53	57	$N = 110$

The expected frequencies are given in parentheses.

Step 1: State the hypotheses. The null hypothesis states that the two categorical variables are independent or not related. The alternative hypothesis states that the two variables are dependent or related.

H_0:   The type of counseling and outcome of counseling are independent or not related. The observed frequencies will be equal to the expected frequencies in each cell.

H_1:   The type of counseling and outcome of counseling are dependent or related. The observed frequencies will not be equal to the expected frequencies in each cell.

Step 2: Set the criteria for a decision. To compute the degrees of freedom for a chi-square test for independence, we multiply the degrees of freedom for each categorical variable. Each categorical variable is associated with $k - 1$ degrees of freedom. The chi-square test for independence, then, is found by multiplying the degrees of freedom for each factor:

$$df = (k_1 - 1)(k_2 - 1).$$

Solving for the degrees of freedom in Example 14.2, we get

$$df = (2 - 1)(2 - 1) = 1.$$

As with the chi-square goodness-of-fit test, the degrees of freedom reflect the number of cells that are free to vary in a frequency table. To illustrate, Table 14.10 shows the expected frequency for one cell in Example 14.2. Because we know the row and column totals, we only need to compute the expected frequency for one cell; the remaining cells are not free to vary—the values in the remaining cells must make the cells sum to the row and column totals. Hence, $df = 1$ in Example 14.2.

TABLE 14.10   The Degrees of Freedom

Frequency Expected (f_e)		Outcome		
		Completion	Premature Termination	
Type of Counseling	Family	16.38	–	34
	Individual	–	–	76
		53	57	$N = 110$

The degrees of freedom are the number of cells that are free to vary. In a 2×2 chi-square, once we compute the expected frequency of one cell, the remaining cells are not free to vary—they must sum to the row and column totals. Hence, $df = 1$ for a 2×2 chi-square.

The level of significance for this test is .05, and the degrees of freedom are $df = 1$. To locate the critical value for this test, find the intersection of the row at one degree of freedom and the column at a .05 level of significance in Table C.7 in Appendix C. The critical value is 3.84. Figure 14.5 shows the chi-square distribution and the rejection region beyond the critical value.

FYI

Always place the rejection region in the upper tail of the positively skewed chi-square distribution.

Step 3: Compute the test statistic. The test statistic for the chi-square test for independence determines how similar the expected frequencies are to the observed frequencies. The computation of the test statistic does not change from that used with a chi-square goodness-of-fit test. For the chi-square test for independence, the formula will measure the discrepancy between the observed and expected frequency in each cell. Larger discrepancies make the value of the test statistic larger and increase the likelihood that we will reject the null hypothesis. A decision to reject the

| FIGURE 14.5 | The Rejection Region for a Chi-Square With 1 Degree of Freedom |

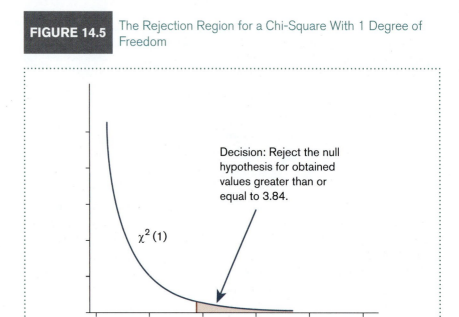

Decision: Reject the null hypothesis for obtained values greater than or equal to 3.84.

$\chi^2(1)$

3.84

The critical value is 3.84.

FYI

The test statistic for a chi-square goodness-of-fit test and a chi-square test for independence is the same.

null hypothesis indicates that the levels of two categorical variables are dependent or related. The formula for the test statistic is

$$\chi^2_{obt} = \sum \frac{(f_o - f_e)^2}{f_e}.$$

To compute the test statistic for Example 14.2, we substitute the observed frequencies and expected frequencies, given in Table 14.9, into the test statistic formula. Using the values in the table, sum the discrepancy between observed and expected frequencies one cell at a time:

$$\chi^2_{obt} = \frac{(22-16.38)^2}{16.38} + \frac{(12-17.62)^2}{17.62} + \frac{(31-36.62)^2}{36.62} + \frac{(45-39.38)^2}{39.38}$$

$$= 1.928 + 1.793 + 0.863 + 0.802$$

$$= 5.386.$$

Step 4: Make a decision. To make a decision, we compare the value of the test statistic to the critical value. If the test statistic falls beyond the critical value of 3.84, then we reject the null hypothesis; otherwise, we retain the null hypothesis. Because $\chi^2_{obt} = 5.386$ exceeds the critical value of 3.84, we reject the null hypothesis. If we were to report this result in a research journal, it would look something like this:

A chi-square test for independence showed a significant relationship between the type of counseling and outcome, $\chi^2(1) = 5.386$, $p < .05$. The data indicate that family involvement in counseling is associated with a greater proportion of patients completing counseling.

LEARNING CHECK 3

1. A researcher conducts a 2 × 3 chi-square test for independence.

   (a) How many cells are in this study?

   (b) What are the degrees of freedom for this hypothesis test?

2. What is the null hypothesis for a chi-square test for independence?

3. The following table summarizes the results of a study concerning the relationship between use of tanning beds and sex.

		Use Tanning Beds		
		Yes	No	Totals
Sex	Male	10	12	22
	Female	14	8	22
	Totals	24	20	

   (a) How many total participants were in this study?

   (b) What is the critical value for this test at a .05 level of significance?

   (c) Compute the test statistic and decide whether to retain or reject the null hypothesis.

Answers: 1. (a) 6 cells, (b) $df = (2-1)(3-1) = 2$; 2. The null hypothesis states that two categorical variables are independent or unrelated, or that each observed frequency will be equal to each expected frequency; 3. (a) $N = 44$, (b) 3.84, (c) $\chi^2_{obt} = \frac{(10-12)^2}{12} + \frac{(12-10)^2}{10} + \frac{(14-12)^2}{12} + \frac{(8-10)^2}{10} = 1.47$. Decision: Retain the null hypothesis.

14.6 MEASURES OF EFFECT SIZE FOR THE CHI-SQUARE TEST FOR INDEPENDENCE

Two common measures of effect size for the chi-square test for independence are the phi coefficient and Cramer's V. Both measures can be used to estimate effect size for the chi-square test for independence. Each measure of effect size is described in this section.

Effect Size Using the Phi Coefficient: $\Phi = \frac{\chi^2}{N}$

The square root of the proportion of variance can also be reported as an estimate of effect size. The square root of the proportion of variance is the phi coefficient, which is a type of correlation coefficient for the relationship between two categorical variables. Note that although phi is the square root of the proportion of *variance*, computing variance is not required to calculate phi in the formula. Using the phi coefficient to estimate effect size in Example 14.2, we take the square root of the chi-square statistic value (χ^2) divided by the total number of participants observed (N):

$$\phi^2 = \sqrt{\frac{5.386}{110}} = \sqrt{.05} = .224.$$

This value, $\phi = .224$, is the value of the phi coefficient when the chi-square test statistic is 5.386.

Effect Size Using Cramer's V: $\sqrt{\dfrac{\chi^2}{N \times df_{smaller}}}$

The phi coefficient can only be used for a 2×2 chi-square test for independence. When the levels of one or more categorical variables are greater than two, we use **Cramer's V** or **Cramer's phi** to estimate effect size.

In the formula, the term $df_{smaller}$ is the smaller of the two sets of degrees of freedom. For a 2×2 chi-square, both degrees of freedom equal 1, so the smaller degree of freedom is 1. If we compute this formula, we will reproduce the effect size that we already obtained using the phi coefficient:

$$V = \sqrt{\frac{5.386}{110 \times 1}} = \sqrt{.05} = .224.$$

Table 14.11 shows the effect size conventions for interpreting Cramer's V, as proposed by J. Cohen (1988). These conventions are guidelines, not cutoffs, for effect size. They are meant to help identify the importance of a result. Referring to Table 14.11, the discrepancy we observed in Example 14.2 was near a medium effect size.

TABLE 14.11	Effect Size Conventions for Cramer's V as Proposed by J. Cohen (1988)

| $df_{smaller}$ | Effect Size | | |
	Small	Medium	Large
1	.10	.30	.50
2	.07	.21	.35
3	.06	.17	.29

14.7 SPSS in Focus:
The Chi-Square Test for Independence

Cramer's V, also called **Cramer's phi (ϕ)**, is an estimate of effect size for the chi-square test for independence for two categorical variables with any number of levels.

In Example 14.2, a 2×2 chi-square test for independence showed a significant relationship between type of counseling and outcome of counseling, $p < .05$. Let us confirm this conclusion using SPSS.

1. Click on the Variable View tab and enter *row* in the Name column; enter *column* in the Name column below it; enter *frequency* in the

Name column below that. Go to the Decimals column and reduce the value to 0 for all rows.

2. To code the *row* variable, click on the small gray box with three dots in the Values column for *row*. In the dialog box, enter *1* in the value cell and *family* in the label cell, and then click Add. Then enter *2* in the value cell and *individual* in the label cell, and then click Add. To code the *column* variable, click on the small gray box with three dots in the Values column for *column*. In the dialog box, enter *1* in the value cell and *completion* in the label cell, and then click Add. Then enter *2* in the value cell and *premature termination* in the label cell, and then click Add. Select OK.

3. Click on the Data View tab. In the *row* column, enter *1*, *1*, *2*, and *2* in the first four cells. For the column labeled *column*, enter *1*, *2*, *1*, and *2* in each cell, respectively. Enter the corresponding observed frequencies in the *frequency* column: *22*, *12*, *31*, and *45*, respectively.

4. Go to the menu bar and click Data, then Weight cases, to display a dialog box. In the dialog box, click Weight cases by, move *frequency* into the Frequency Variable cell, and then click OK.

5. Go to the menu bar and click Analyze, then Descriptive statistics and Crosstabs, to display a new dialog box.

6. Using the arrows, move *row* into the Row(s) box and *column* into the Column(s) box. Click Statistics . . . to display another dialog box.

7. Select Chi-square. To compute effect size, select Phi and Cramer's *V* in the box labeled Nominal, as shown in Figure 14.6, and then click Continue.

8. Select OK, or select Paste and click the Run command.

FIGURE 14.6   SPSS Dialog Box for Steps 6 and 7

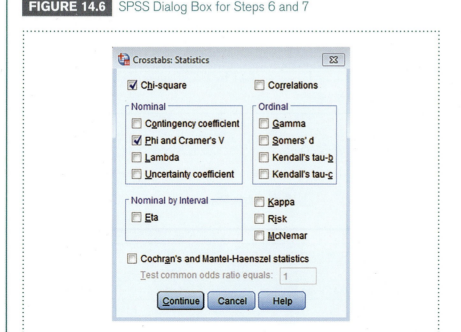

(Continued)

(Continued)

Table 14.12 shows the SPSS output for the chi-square test for independence. The frequency table (top table) shows the observed and expected frequencies. The first row of the bottom table lists the value of the chi-square test statistic, the degrees of freedom (df), and the p value (Asymp. Sig.) for the test. Read only the top row in the bottom table. Table 14.13 displays the results of the effect size estimate. The values in the SPSS output tables are the same as those we computed by hand, give or take rounding, for Example 14.2.

TABLE 14.12	SPSS Output for the Chi-Square Frequency Table (top) and for the Chi-Square Test for Independence (bottom)

row * column Crosstabulation

Count

		column		
		completion	premature termination	Total
row	family	22	12	34
	individual	31	45	76
Total		53	57	110

Chi-Square Tests

	Value	df	Asymptotic Significance (2-sided)	Exact Sig. (2-sided)	Exact Sig. (1-sided)
Pearson Chi-Square	5.382[a]	1	.020		
Continuity Correction[b]	4.466	1	.035		
Likelihood Ratio	5.433	1	.020		
Fisher's Exact Test				.024	.017
Linear-by-Linear Association	5.333	1	.021		
N of Valid Cases	110				

a. 0 cells (0.0%) have expected count less than 5. The minimum expected count is 16.38.

b. Computed only for a 2x2 table

TABLE 14.13	SPSS Output for Effect Size Using Phi and Cramer's *V*

Symmetric Measures

		Value	Approximate Significance
Nominal by Nominal	Phi	.221	.020
	Cramer's V	.221	.020
N of Valid Cases		110	

LEARNING CHECK 4

1. True or false: The phi coefficient can be converted to a chi-square and vice versa.

2. Which effect size measure or measures can be used with a 3 × 3 chi-square test for independence?

3. State the effect size using Cramer's *V* for each of the following tests:

a. 2 × 3 chi-square, $N = 60$, $\chi^2 = 8.12$

b. 4 × 3 chi-square, $N = 80$, $\chi^2 = 9.76$

c. 2 × 2 chi-square, $N = 100$, $\chi^2 = 3.88$

Answers: 1. True; 2. Cramer's *V* only; 3. (a) $\sqrt{\dfrac{8.12}{60 \times 1}} = .368$, (b) $\sqrt{\dfrac{9.76}{80 \times 2}} = .247$, (c) $\sqrt{\dfrac{3.88}{100 \times 1}} = .197$.

APA IN FOCUS: REPORTING THE CHI-SQUARE TESTS

To summarize the chi-square goodness-of-fit test, we report the test statistic, the degrees of freedom, and the *p* value. The observed frequencies can be summarized in a figure or a table or in the main text. For example, here is a summary of the results for the dream recall study in Example 14.1:

A chi-square goodness-of-fit test showed that the frequency of dream recall during REM sleep was similar to what was expected, $\chi^2(2) = 3.06$, $p > .05$.

To summarize the chi-square test for independence, we report effect size in addition to the test statistic, the degrees of freedom, and the *p* value. For example, here is a summary of the results for Example 14.2 using Cramer's *V* as the measure of effect size:

A chi-square test for independence showed a significant relationship between the type of counseling and outcome, $\chi^2(1) = 5.386$, $p < .05$ ($V = .224$). The data indicate that family involvement in counseling is associated with a greater proportion of patients completing counseling.

••• CHAPTER SUMMARY ORGANIZED BY LEARNING OBJECTIVE

LO 1: Distinguish between nonparametric and parametric tests.

- Parametric tests are used to test hypotheses about parameters in a population in which the data are normally distributed and measured on an interval or ratio scale of measurement.

- Nonparametric tests are used (1) to test hypotheses that do not make inferences about parameters in a population, (2) to test hypotheses about data that can have any type of distribution, and (3) to analyze data on a nominal or ordinal scale of measurement.

LO 2:   **Explain how the test statistic is computed for a chi-square test.**

- The test statistic for a chi-square test is

$$\chi_{obt}^2 = \sum \frac{(f_o - f_e)^2}{f_e}.$$

- The test statistic compares the discrepancy between the observed and expected frequencies stated in a null hypothesis. The larger the discrepancy between observed and expected frequencies, the larger the value of the test statistic.

LO 3–4:   **Calculate the degrees of freedom for the chi-square goodness-of-fit test and locate critical values in the chi-square table; compute the chi-square goodness-of-fit test and interpret the results.**

- The chi-square goodness-of-fit test is a statistical procedure used to determine whether observed frequencies at each level of one categorical variable are similar to or different from the frequencies we expected at each level of the categorical variable. The degrees of freedom for this test are $k - 1$.

- There is no statistical basis for interpreting which discrepancies are significant. The more discrepancies we add, or the larger k is, the more difficult it is to interpret a significant test. One strategy is to identify the largest discrepancies, which tend to be the focus of a significant result, with smaller discrepancies tending to be ignored.

LO 5:   **Identify the assumption and the restriction of expected frequency size for the chi-square test.**

- An assumption for the chi-square test is that observed frequencies are independently recorded in each category. A restriction of this test is that expected frequencies should be greater than 5 in each category. This restriction can be overcome when we increase the sample size such that it is five times larger than the number of levels of the categorical variable or increase the number of levels of the categorical variable.

LO 6–7:   **Calculate the degrees of freedom for the chi-square test for independence and locate critical values in the chi-square table; compute the chi-square test for independence and interpret the results.**

- The chi-square test for independence is a statistical procedure used to determine whether frequencies observed at the combination of levels of two categorical variables are similar to expected frequencies.

- To find the expected frequency in each cell of a frequency table for a chi-square test for independence, first find the row and column totals for each cell, then calculate the following formula for each cell:

$$f_e = \frac{\text{row total} \times \text{column total}}{N}.$$

- The test statistic is the same as that for the chi-square goodness-of-fit test. The degrees of freedom are $(k_1 - 1)(k_2 - 1)$. A significant outcome indicates that two categorical variables are related or dependent.

LO 8:   **Compute and interpret effect size for the chi-square test for independence.**

- Effect size for a chi-square test for independence measures the size of an observed effect. Two measures of effect size are as follows:

Effect size using the phi coefficient:

$$\phi = \sqrt{\frac{\chi^2}{N}}.$$

Effect size using Cramer's V:

$$V = \sqrt{\frac{\chi^2}{N \times df_{smaller}}}.$$

LO 9:   **Summarize the results of a chi-square test in APA format.**

- To summarize the chi-square goodness-of-fit test, report the test statistic, the degrees of freedom, and the p value. The observed frequencies can be summarized in a figure or table or in the main text. For the chi-square test for independence, an estimate for effect size should also be reported.

LO 10:   **Compute the chi-square goodness-of-fit test and the chi-square test for independence using SPSS.**

- The chi-square goodness-of-fit test is computed using the Analyze, Nonparametric tests, and Chi-square options in the menu bar. These actions will display a dialog box that allows you to identify the groups and run the test. A Weight cases option must also be selected from the menu bar (for more details, see Section 14.3).

- The chi-square test for independence is computed using the Analyze, Descriptive statistics, and Crosstabs options in the menu bar. These actions will display a dialog box that allows you to identify the groups and run the test. A Weight cases option must also be selected from the menu bar (for more details, see Section 14.7).

• • • KEY TERMS

chi-square distribution
chi-square goodness-of-fit
  test
chi-square (χ^2) test

chi-square test for independence
Cramer's phi (ϕ)
Cramer's V
frequency expected (f_e)

frequency observed (f_o)
nonparametric tests
parametric tests

• • • END-OF-CHAPTER PROBLEMS

Factual Problems

1. State three ways that nonparametric tests differ from parametric tests.

2. A chi-square test is used when we compare frequencies for data on what scale of measurement?

3. How many factors are observed using a chi-square goodness-of-fit test?

4. Define the following terms:

   (a) Frequency observed (f_o)

   (b) Frequency expected (f_e)

5. What is the decision likely to be for values of χ^2_{obt} close to 0?

6. Write the formula for finding the expected frequency for a chi-square goodness-of-fit test.

7. How are the degrees of freedom computed for each test listed below?

   (a) A chi-square goodness-of-fit test

   (b) A chi-square test for independence

8. What is the shape of the chi-square distribution?

9. Name one assumption and one restriction for the chi-square test.

10. Write the formula for the frequency expected for a chi-square test for independence.

11. Write the formula for each of the following effect size measures for the chi-square test for independence:

    (a) Phi coefficient

    (b) Cramer's V

12. When is Cramer's V the only measure of effect size that can be used with the chi-square test for independence?

Concept and Application Problems

13. Based on the scale of measurement for the data, which of the following tests are parametric? Which are nonparametric?

    (a) A researcher measures the proportion of schizophrenic patients born in each season.

    (b) A researcher measures the average age that schizophrenia is diagnosed among male and female patients.

    (c) A researcher tests whether frequency of Internet use and social interaction are independent.

    (d) A researcher measures the amount of time (in seconds) that a group of teenagers uses the Internet for school-related and non-school-related purposes.

14. For each of the following examples, state whether the chi-square goodness-of-fit test or the chi-square test for independence is appropriate.

    (a) A study concerning the number of individuals who prefer one of four career options

    (b) A study concerning the frequency of aberrant behavior among high school freshmen, sophomores, juniors, and seniors

    (c) A study testing the relationship between the frequency of intimacy (low, high) and personality type (extrovert, introvert)

15. For each of the following examples, state whether the chi-square goodness-of-fit test or the chi-square test for independence is appropriate, and state the degrees of freedom (*df*) for the test.

    (a) An instructor tests whether class attendance (low, high) and grade point average (low, average, high) are independent.

    (b) An educator tests whether the teacher's speaking style (monotone, dynamic) and student interest (low, high) are independent.

    (c) A sports psychologist compares the number of athletes with Type A or Type B personality traits.

(d) A public health employee evaluates the proportion of lean, healthy, overweight, and obese students at a local college.

16. A chi-square goodness-of-fit test has the following expected frequencies: 12, 4, and 8. Should a chi-square goodness-of-fit test be used to analyze these data? Explain.

17. Students are asked to rate their preference for one of four video games. The following table lists the observed preferences in a sample of 120 students. State whether to reject or retain the null hypothesis for a chi-square goodness-of-fit test given the following expected frequencies.

	Video Games			
	McStats	**Tic-Tac Stats**	**Silly Stats**	**Super Stats**
Frequency Observed	30	30	30	30

    (a) Expected frequencies: 25%, 25%, 25%, 25%, respectively

    (b) Expected frequencies: 70%, 10%, 10%, 10%, respectively

18. The Better Business Bureau (BBB) wants to determine whether a certain business is engaging in fair hiring practices. The BBB finds that a local business employs 66 men and 34 women. The general population of workers in this industry is 60% men and 40% women. Using a chi-square goodness-of-fit test, decide to retain or reject the null hypothesis that the distribution of men and women in the local business is consistent with, or proportional to, that in the general population of workers. Use a .05 level of significance.

19. A local brewery produces three premium lagers named Half Pint, XXX, and Dark Night. Of its premium lagers, the brewery bottles 40% Half Pint, 40% XXX, and 20% Dark Night. In a marketing test of a sample of consumers, 26 preferred the Half Pint lager, 42 preferred the XXX lager, and 12 preferred the Dark Night lager. Using a chi-square goodness-of-fit test,

decide to retain or reject the null hypothesis that production of the premium lagers matches these consumer preferences using a .05 level of significance.

20. A behavioral therapist records the number of children who are spanked and not spanked by their parents as a form of punishment in a sample of parents who were spanked by their parents as children. The following table shows the results of a chi-square goodness-of-fit test. If we expect to observe equal frequencies, then compute a chi-square goodness-of-fit test using a .05 level of significance and decide to retain or reject the null hypothesis.

Child Is Not Spanked	Child Is Spanked
28	46

21. A psychologist studying addiction tests whether cravings for cocaine and relapse are independent or related. The following table lists the observed frequencies in the small sample of people who use drugs.

Obs. Freq.		Relapse Yes	No	
Cravings	Yes	20	10	30
	No	8	17	25
		28	27	$N = 55$

(a) Conduct a chi-square test for independence at a .05 level of significance. Decide whether to retain or reject the null hypothesis.

(b) Compute effect size using φ and Cramer's V. *Hint:* Both should give the same estimate of effect size.

22. A researcher tests whether home ownership (own, rent/other) is related to or independent of participants' positive or negative views of the economy. The researcher records whether or not 105 participants own a home and whether their economic viewpoint is positive or negative. The following table lists the observed frequencies for this study. Conduct a

chi-square test for independence at a .05 level of significance. Decide whether to retain or reject the null hypothesis.

Obs. Freq.		View of the Economy Positive	Negative	
Home Ownership	Own	35	32	67
	Rent/Other	20	18	38
		55	50	$N = 105$

23. A professor tests whether the loudness of noise during an exam (low, medium, high) is independent of exam grades (pass, fail). The following table shows the observed frequencies for this test.

		Noise Level Low	Medium	High	
Exam	Pass	20	18	8	46
	Fail	8	6	10	24
		28	24	18	$N = 70$

(a) Conduct a chi-square test for independence at a .05 level of significance. Decide whether to retain or reject the null hypothesis.

(b) Compute effect size using Cramer's V.

24. What is the proportion of variance (ϕ^2) for each of the following values in a 2 × 2 chi-square test for independence?

(a) $\chi^2 = 3.96, N = 50$

(b) $\chi^2 = 5.23, N = 75$

(c) $\chi^2 = 12.00, N = 100$

25. What is Cramer's V for each of the following values for the chi-square test for independence?

(a) $\chi^2 = 11.54, N = 150, df_{smaller} = 3$

(b) $\chi^2 = 8.12, N = 120, df_{smaller} = 2$

(c) $\chi^2 = 4.36, N = 80, df_{smaller} = 1$

26. Based on Cohen's effect size conventions, what is the size of the effect for each of the following values of Cramer's V?

(a) $V = .08, df_{smaller} = 1$

(b) $V = .24, df_{smaller} = 2$

(c) $V = .30, df_{smaller} = 3$

Problems in Research

27. **Issues, priorities, and politics in an election year.** In March 2016, a Gallup poll asked a sample of Americans to reply to the following question: "How much do you personally worry about pollution of drinking water?" The following table lists the responses recorded in a sample of 1,019 adults worldwide. Compute a chi-square goodness-of-fit test at a .05 level of significance for these data with a null hypothesis that the promotion in each category (from left to right) is 60:30:10. State the value of the chi-square test statistic, and decide whether to retain or reject the null hypothesis.

A Great Deal	A Fair Amount/ Only a Little	Not at All
622	326	71

Source: http://pollingreport.com/enviro.htm

28. **Undercover officers and marital stress.** Love, Vinson, Tolsma, and Kaufmann (2008) studied the psychological effects of being an undercover officer, including the stress it places on a marriage. The researchers recorded the number of officers reporting symptoms of marital stress, as listed in the following table. If we expect to observe equal frequencies, then compute a chi-square goodness-of-fit test at a .05 level of significance. Decide whether to retain or reject the null hypothesis.

Marital Stress for Former Undercover Officers	
Yes	No
145	94

29. **Sex differences for people with an intellectual disability.** Yen, Lin, and Chiu (2013) compared the number of male and female people with an intelligence disability (ID) to the proportion of males and females in the general population. In their study, they reported that the number of males with an ID was 49,451 and the number of females with an ID was 45,935. The researchers identified that the proportion of males and females in the general population was 50.8% males and 49.2% females. Using these proportions to compute expected frequencies, conduct a chi-square goodness-of-fit test and decide whether to retain or reject the null hypothesis.

30. **Choosing effect size.** Volker (2006) analyzed methods and approaches for reporting effect size in psychological research. In his assessment of estimates for effect size using the chi-square test, he wrote,

> Given that Cramer's V is an extension of the coefficient, the values of effect size ϕ and Cramer's V will be identical when a 2 × 2 [chi-square] is analyzed. (Volker, 2006, p. 666)

(a) Which coefficient is Volker (2006) referring to?

(b) Why are the two values of effect size identical when analyzing a 2 × 2 chi-square?

31. **Sex and depression.** Altamura, Dell'Osso, Vismara, and Mundo (2008) measured the relationship between sex and duration of untreated illness (DUI) among a sample of those suffering from major depressive disorder (MDD). The following table lists the observed frequencies from this study. Compute a chi-square test for independence at a .05 level of significance. Decide whether to retain or reject the null hypothesis.

	Duration of Untreated Illness		
	DUI ≤ 12 Months	DUI > 12 Months	
Sex — Male	20	5	25
Sex — Female	55	33	88
	75	38	$N = 113$

32. **Sex discrimination among the elderly.** Keskinoglu and colleagues (2007) studied sex discrimination among the elderly. As part of their study, they recorded whether participants were involved in or made decisions concerning personal income and earnings (personal income) and whether they were exposed to negative sex discrimination. The following table lists the observed frequencies from this study. Compute a chi-square test for independence at a .05 level of significance. Decide whether to retain or reject the null hypothesis.

	Negative Sex Discrimination		
	Yes	No	
Personal Income — Yes	32	71	103
Personal Income — No	26	19	45
	58	90	$N = 148$

Answers for even numbers are in Appendix D.

Sharpen your skills with **SAGE edge at edge.sagepub.com/priviteraess2e**

SAGE edge for Students provides a personalized approach to help you accomplish your coursework goals in an easy-to-use learning environment.

©iStockphoto.com/diane39

••• Afterword

A Final Thought on the Role of Statistics in Research Methods

One of the goals for this book has been to introduce statistics in the context of the types of research problems that behavioral scientists study. This goal is important because many of you will take a research methods course at some point at the college level. To understand research methods, you will need to bring knowledge of statistics with you to your research methods course. To give you a sense of how statistics fits in research, Figure 15.1 provides a general overview of the process researchers engage in to study behavior.

I. The research process begins with exploration. In this phase, researchers review, among other things, published literature and the statistical conclusions reported in them; conduct pilot studies (small, inexpensive studies) to determine the power or likelihood of showing an effect, if such an effect exists; and collaborate or work together with other researchers to share ideas.

II. The next phase is used to generate hypotheses. In this book, hypotheses have been primarily given to you. But hypotheses do not simply appear. Instead, they are explored and extensively developed before ever being tested. Researchers use statistics to gauge the significance of a result and the power of detecting an effect. These types of analyses play a central role in determining which hypotheses are eventually tested and which are not.

III. Once hypotheses are generated, they are tested using hypothesis testing. Choosing an appropriate hypothesis test is determined by a variety of factors, including, but not limited to, the number of participants and groups being tested, how often participants are observed, the design of the study (can the study show cause?), the types of hypotheses being tested (parametric or nonparametric), and the scales of measurement of the data being measured (nominal, ordinal, interval, or ratio). Many of these factors have been reviewed in this book.

IV. The hypothesis tests then require interpretation. You are already aware of the fact that interpretation can be tricky. For example, conclusions concerning different scales of measurement require different interpretations. Conclusions for tests that show cause (experimental design) are different from those that show relationships (quasi-experimental and correlational designs). It follows that once an effect is shown or not shown, researchers must go back and reconsider whether they should make changes to existing hypotheses or begin testing new hypotheses. Correctly interpreting an effect and making the appropriate changes requires statistical know-how, much of which you have already attained by reading this book.

The general phases of the research process are cyclic—researchers continue to work through each phase to explore and test new ideas and stronger hypotheses. Statistics plays a large role in each phase of the research process from the development of hypotheses to the testing of hypotheses. It is an important tool in the process of conducting research in the behavioral sciences. Therefore, rest assured that the knowledge you have gained by studying statistics in this book will prove invaluable as you continue to develop as a critical consumer of knowledge and to explore methods of discovery in your own pursuits.

FIGURE 15.1   A General Overview of Conducting Research: Statistics Plays a Role in Each Phase of the Research Process

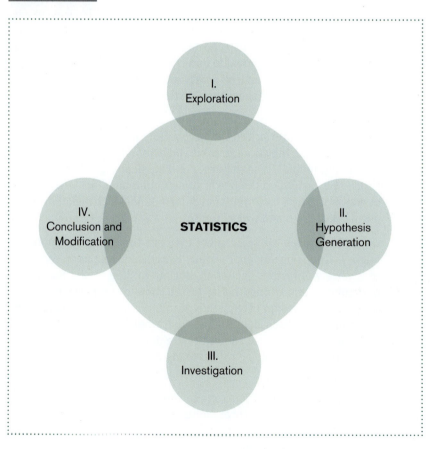

••• Appendix A

Basic Math Review and Summation Notation

A.1 POSITIVE AND NEGATIVE NUMBERS

While an understanding of mathematics becomes more important as you advance in your use of statistics, you need only a basic level of mathematics to do well in an introductory statistics course. The fundamentals of statistics are based largely on basic addition, subtraction, multiplication, division, and problem solving. That being said, we begin this appendix with an introduction to positive and negative numbers.

- Theoretically, numbers can range from $-\infty$ to $+\infty$ (negative infinity to positive infinity), with the average value of all numbers that could possibly exist being equal to 0. Anything less than 0 is negative, and anything greater than 0 is positive. For every positive value, there is a negative counterpart. If we think of numbers as units away from 0, then +5 and −5 would each be 5 units away from 0: One is 5 units above 0 (+5), and one is 5 units below 0 (−5). As shown in Figure A.1, each number is the same distance from 0 but in the opposite direction.

A positive number is not necessarily one with a positive outlook on life—a "glass half full" kind of number—although you may have seen smiling numbers like that on *Sesame Street* or *Blue's Clues* as a kid. It means, of course, that the value of the number is greater than 0. Zero (0) is not

FIGURE A.1 Positive and Negative Signs Indicate Units Above and Below 0 (respectively)

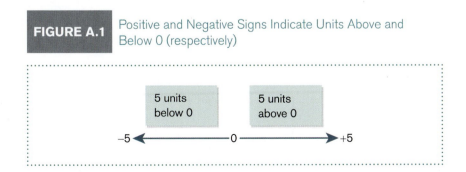

positive, and it is not negative; it is considered a neutral number. We can define positive and negative numbers using the following rules.

[1]   A constant written without a sign is positive (+).

$$+2 = 2 \qquad + x = x, \text{ where } x \neq 0$$

[2]   A constant preceded by a negative sign (−) is negative.

$$-2 \neq 2 \qquad - x \neq x, \text{ where } x \neq 0$$

These rules apply mostly to constants (as opposed to variables). A **variable** is a characteristic or property that can take on different values at different times. In contrast, a **constant** is a characteristic or property that can take on only a single value. Variables are typically expressed alphabetically.

For example, x and y are variables that are commonly used to represent numbers. The value of one of these variables can be anything you define it to be. You could even assign a negative number for x, making $+x$ a negative number and thus violating Rule [1]. You could similarly violate Rule [2], which is why these rules apply mostly to constants. Constants are represented as numbers. You will be introduced to many constants and variables in statistics.

A.2 Addition

Addition is arguably the most basic mathematical function. Both positive and negative numbers can be added. The following rules apply to adding positive and negative numbers.

[3]   When adding numbers with the same sign, add them and keep the sign of the individual numbers the same.

$$+2 + (+4) = +6 \qquad 2 + 4 = 6 \qquad -2 + (-4) = -6$$

Notice that Rule [3] applies to both positive and negative numbers. So long as the individual numbers have the same sign, all you do is add them and not change the sign. Adding positive numbers yields a solution of greater magnitude or value; adding negative numbers yields a solution of lesser magnitude or value.

[4]   When adding numbers with different signs, either add the numbers in the order they are listed or reorganize them so that all positive numbers precede all negative numbers.

$$(+8) + (-3) + (+2) + (-4) = +3$$

A **variable** is a characteristic or property that can take on different values at different times.

A **constant** is a characteristic or property that can take on only a single value.

Consider the problem given above. One way to approach it, particularly for students who are good at these kinds of problems, is to just do the math in order. The thought process would be something like this: $8 + (-3) = 5$,

5 + 2 equals 7, and 7 + (−4) equals 3. Thus, the answer is +3. A second approach for those not as comfortable with math would be to reorganize the problem by the sign of the numbers as follows:

$$(+8) + (+2) + (−3) + (−4) = +3$$

Notice that all the positive values precede the negative values. This makes it easier to do the problem because you separated the positive and negative values. The thought process for this approach would be something like this: $8 + 2 = 10$, $10 + (−3) = 7$, and $7 + (−4) = 3$. Thus, the answer is +3. This becomes particularly useful when the string of numbers in the problem is longer, as in the one below. In this case, reorganizing the problem may be very helpful. Try it yourself and see whether you find it easier to do the problem this way.

$$(+9) + (−3) + (−7) + (+2) + (−4) + (+5) + (+6) + (−1) + (+8) = +15$$

Also, note that whenever there are two ways to approach a problem, you can check your work by doing it both ways, particularly on an exam. You can lose a lot of points because of simple math errors that can be avoided by checking your work. On multiple-choice exams, simple math errors can cost you the entire value of the problem because partial credit is not an option in most cases. If you have time to go through a problem two ways, then why not check your work? It can only help you redeem points that you otherwise would have lost.

A.3 SUBTRACTION

Subtraction and addition are opposites: Addition increases the value of the number, and subtraction decreases the value. Two rules can be stated for positive and negative numbers.

[5]   A positive sign preceding a negative sign makes a negative, and vice versa.

$$5 + (−3) = 5 − 3 = 2$$
$$12 − (+7) = 12 − 7 = 5$$
$$−6 + (−6) = −6 − 6 = −12$$

Whether we add a negative number or subtract a positive number, the sign between the two numbers will be negative. In a sense, adding a negative number and subtracting a positive number are two ways of describing the same thing.

[6]   A negative sign preceding a negative sign makes a positive.

$$5 − (−5) = 5 + 5 = 10$$
$$(−4) − (−4) = −4 + 4 = 0$$
$$0 − (−5) = 0 + 5 = 5$$

Note that two negatives make a positive. It may be easier to think of negative values in terms of debt, which is something often too familiar to college students. Suppose you are in debt 4 dollars (represented numerically as −$4.00). If your friend subtracts or takes away 4 dollars of your debt, then he takes away the amount of your debt: −$4.00 − (−$4.00) = $0; he erases your debt. Hence, when you subtract a negative number, you are actually adding.

LEARNING CHECK 1

1. A _____ is defined as a characteristic or property that can take on different values at different times.

2. True or false: Zero (0) is neither a positive nor a negative number.

3. Compute the following problems: (a) 7 + (−3) + 6 = ?; (b) 7 − 3 + 6 = ?

4. Compute the following problems: (a) 7 − (−3) − 6 = ?; (b) −7 − 3 − 6 = ?

Answers: 1. Variable; 2. True; 3. (a) 10, (b) 10; 4. (a) +4, (b) −16.

A.4 MULTIPLICATION

Multiplication is really a simplified way to add a lot of numbers together. For example, suppose you have six 5-dollar bills. You could add them all up to get the total amount of money: $5.00 + $5.00 + $5.00 + $5.00 + $5.00 + $5.00 = $30.00. However, an easier calculation is to multiply the $5.00 by the number of bills you have (6). Thus, $5.00 × 6 bills = $30.00.

There are four ways to indicate or symbolize multiplication: a × sign, a center dot (·), parentheses with no operational sign between the numbers, and an asterisk (*). Each symbol means the same thing: Multiply the numbers between them. Below is an example of each:

$$6 \times 4 = 24 \qquad 6 \cdot 4 = 24 \qquad 6(4) = 24 \qquad 6 * 4 = 24$$

As for addition and subtraction, you can multiply negative and positive numbers. There are a few rules to follow when multiplying numbers.

[7] When multiplying two numbers with the same sign, the answer is always *positive*.

Whether we multiply two positive numbers or two negative numbers, the result is the same: It produces a positive solution. To illustrate, the following is an example in which the solution to each example is the same (+63).

$$9 \times 7 = +63$$
$$-9 \times -7 = +63$$

[8]   When multiplying two numbers with different signs, the answer is always *negative*.

When multiplying one positive and one negative number, the solution will always be negative. To illustrate, the following is an example in which the solution to each equation is the same (−63).

$$-9 \times 7 = -63$$
$$9 \times -7 = -63$$

Whether the 9 or the 7 is the negative number, the result is the same—the solution is always negative (−63). In this way, multiplication can be used as a shortcut for adding because it does not violate the general rules of addition.

A.5 DIVISION

There are three ways to indicate division: a ÷ sign, a fraction, and a √ sign. Each of these signs means the same thing: Divide the numbers among them. The following is an example of each:

$$6 \div 2 = 3$$
$$\frac{6}{2} = 3$$
$$2\sqrt{6} = 3$$

You can think of division as the opposite of multiplication. If we multiply 7 by 3, then we obtain 21. But we can do the opposite: We can divide 21 by 7 to obtain 3, or we can divide 21 by 3 to obtain 7. Hence, we can multiply two numbers to obtain 21, or we can divide those numbers to get 3 and 7. Because these two operations are similar in this way, so too are the rules.

[9]   When dividing two numbers with the same sign, the answer is always *positive*.

$$-9 \div -3 = 3$$
$$9 \div 3 = 3$$

It is sometimes easier to make sense of this by looking at the process in a different way. The first problem is actually asking how many −3s we must add to get −9. The answer is 3 (−3 + −3 + −3 = −9). Hence, we must add (−3) three times to get −9. The answer is positive. The second problem would be calculated likewise (3 + 3 + 3 = 9). In this case, +3 would be added three times to get +9.

[10]   When more than two numbers are multiplied or divided, the answer will be positive if the number of negative values is even; the answer will be negative if the number of negative values is odd.

$$-9 \div 3 = -3$$

$$9 \div -3 = -3$$

For this rule, same signs mean positive values; different signs mean negative values. However, this rule is true only when two numbers are calculated. For instances in which more than two numbers are multiplied or divided, the following rule applies.

[11]   When more than two numbers are multiplied or divided, if there are an even number of negative values, the answer will be positive; if there are an odd number of negative values, the answer will be negative.

$$2 \times -4 \times 2 \times -4 = +64$$

$$2 \times -4 \times 2 \times 4 = -64$$

Let us work through each of these problems, two numbers at a time. For the first example, $2 \times -4 = -8$, because numbers with different signs yield a negative result. Next, $-8 \times 2 = -16$, because the signs again are different for each number. Finally, $-16 \times -4 = +64$. The sign changed because now both numbers have the same sign—both numbers are negative (-16 and -4).

The second problem starts out the same way: $2 \times -4 = -8$, because numbers with different signs yield a negative result. For the same reason, the next solution is again negative: $-8 \times 2 = -16$. The last calculation is where the solution changes, $-16 \times 4 = -64$. Because the signs for this last calculation are different, the answer becomes negative. Hence, an even number of negative values will produce a positive solution (such as two negative values in the first problem), and an odd number of negative values will produce a negative solution (such as one negative value in the second problem).

LEARNING CHECK 2

1. True or false: When multiplying two numbers with the same sign, the answer is always *negative*.

2. Compute: (a) $6 \times 8 = ?$ (b) $9 \times -5 = ?$

3. True or false: When dividing two numbers with different signs, the answer is always *negative*.

4. Compute: (a) $20 \div 4 = ?$ (b) $\frac{16}{4} = ?$ (c) $2\sqrt{6} = ?$

Answers: 1. False. The answer is always positive; 2. (a) 48, (b) −45; 3. True; 4. (a) 5, (b) 4, (c) 3.

A.6 FRACTIONS

Fractions represent a division operation. A fraction is the division of the numerator (the top expression) by the denominator (the bottom expression). Fractions are used more often to represent values to the right of the decimal point than values to the left. For example, because $\frac{6}{2}$ is 3, it makes more sense to represent that value as the whole number 3. Yet if the expression reads $\frac{2}{6}$, then the division would produce a value less than 1. In this case, leaving the expression as a fraction might be easier to read.

Fractions are important in statistics because many statistical formulas include them. In many cases, you will probably find it easier to leave a solution as a fraction. The following rules are used for fractions.

[12]   Dividing 0 into any number is undefined.

$$\frac{0}{100} = 0$$

$$\frac{100}{0} = \text{undefined}$$

The term *undefined* is used because it does not make sense to say that 0 goes into anything except itself. Statistical theorists recognize this rule and take care not to allow undefined problems. Therefore, if your answer to a problem in statistics is "undefined," it is likely an arithmetic mistake, and you should probably do the problem again.

[13]   Whole numbers are also fractions, with the whole number in the numerator and a 1 in the denominator.

$$5 = \frac{5}{1}$$

$$10 = \frac{10}{1}$$

$$1{,}000 = \frac{1{,}000}{1}$$

Making any whole number a fraction is as simple as placing the whole number over 1. This rule will be especially useful when you need to add, subtract, multiply, or divide fractions using whole numbers.

[14]   To add or subtract fractions, you must find the *least common denominator* and then add the numerators together.

$$\frac{2}{5} + \frac{3}{10} = \frac{(2 \times 2)}{(5 \times 2)} + \frac{(3 \times 1)}{(10 \times 1)} = \frac{4}{10} + \frac{3}{10} = \frac{7}{10}$$

$$\frac{2}{5} - \frac{3}{10} = \frac{(2 \times 2)}{(5 \times 2)} - \frac{(3 \times 1)}{(10 \times 1)} = \frac{4}{10} - \frac{3}{10} = \frac{1}{10}$$

The *least common denominator* is a fancy way of saying that only fractions with the same denominator can be added and subtracted. Each example above shows how this works. Note that multiplying the numerator and denominator by the same number does not change the value of a fraction. For example, $\frac{2}{4}$ is the same as $\frac{4}{8}$. If we multiply both the numerator and the denominator by 2, the fraction becomes $\frac{4}{8}$. Both values are equal. Therefore, in the above example, we determine that 10 is the least common denominator—it is the lowest multiple that makes the denominators equal. This is because $5 \times 2 = 10$, and $10 \times 1 = 10$. This will make both denominators 10, but whatever we do to the denominator, we must also do to the numerator. This gives us a new, but equal, problem: $\frac{4}{10} + \frac{3}{10}$. Now that the denominators are the same, we add the numerators together and leave the denominator alone. We do the same for subtraction, except that we subtract the numerators.

[15]   To multiply fractions, multiply the numerators together and multiply the denominators together.

$$\frac{2}{3} \times \frac{4}{5} = \frac{8}{15}$$

$$\frac{1}{5} \times 3 = \frac{1}{5} \times \frac{3}{1} = \frac{3}{5}$$

$$\frac{3}{4} \times \frac{2}{3} = \frac{6}{12} = \frac{1}{2}$$

When multiplying fractions, multiply across the numerator and denominator. It is also worth remembering that fractions are a way of representing a division operation. Therefore, you are allowed to simplify or reduce values before multiplying across. You can reduce any value in the numerator with any value in the denominator. Consider the following example:

$$\frac{4}{12} \times \frac{6}{8} = \frac{1}{4}$$

Here we could reduce $\frac{4}{12}$ to $\frac{1}{3}$ by dividing the numerator and denominator by 4, and we could reduce $\frac{6}{8}$ to $\frac{3}{4}$ by dividing each by 2. It follows that $\frac{1}{3} \times \frac{3}{4} = \frac{3}{12}$, which could be further reduced to $\frac{1}{4}$ by dividing each by 3. We could also reduce across the multiplication sign. For example, the 4 and 8 are divisible by 2 (i.e., 4 reduces to 1 and 8 to 2), and the 6 and 12 are divisible by 2 as well (i.e., 6 reduces to 1 and 12 to 2). It follows that $\frac{1}{2} \times \frac{1}{2} = \frac{1}{4}$. Both methods result in the same answer, and many times it is easier to reduce the fractions before you multiply.

[16]   To divide fractions, invert the second fraction and multiply.

$$\frac{3}{5} \div \frac{2}{3} = \frac{3}{5} \times \frac{3}{2} = \frac{9}{10}$$

When dividing fractions, invert the fraction that is doing the dividing (the divisor) and multiply it into the fraction you were going to divide (the dividend). You never actually perform the division operation.

In statistics, it is also common to see this problem written as

$$\frac{\frac{3}{5}}{\frac{2}{3}}$$

To solve this problem, move the bottom fraction to the right, and follow Rule [16]:

$$\frac{3}{5} \div \frac{2}{3} = \frac{3}{5} \times \frac{3}{2} = \frac{9}{10}$$

LEARNING CHECK 3

1. The _____ is the lowest multiple that makes the denominators of more than one fraction equal.

2. Compute: (a) $\frac{15}{21} + \frac{2}{7} = ?$ (b) $\frac{3}{4} - \frac{3}{12} = ?$

3. Compute: (a) $\frac{3}{4} - \frac{3}{12} = ?$ (b) $\frac{\frac{4}{5}}{\frac{3}{3}} = ?$

Answers: 1. Least common denominator; 2. (a) $\frac{15}{21} + \frac{6}{21} = \frac{21}{21} = 1.0$, (b) $\frac{9}{12} - \frac{3}{12} = \frac{6}{12} = \frac{1}{2}$; 3. (a) $\frac{5}{4} \div \frac{3}{3} = \frac{4}{5} \times \frac{3}{3} = \frac{3}{5}$, (b) $\frac{4}{5} \div \frac{3}{3} = \frac{4}{5} \times \frac{3}{3} = \frac{3}{5}$.

A.7 DECIMALS AND PERCENTS

Because decimals are another way to express fractions, you can write decimals as fractions and fractions as decimals.

[17]   The decimal is a fraction with 10, 100, 1,000, and so on as the denominator.

$$2.6 = 2\frac{6}{10}$$

$$4.35 = 4\frac{35}{100}$$

$$5.004 = 5\frac{4}{1,000}$$

If the decimal is to the tenths place, then put the decimal over 10 when making it a fraction; if to the hundredths place, then place it over 100; if to the thousandths place, then place it over 1,000; and so on. When converting decimals to fractions, remember that you can leave any whole numbers alone; simply change the decimal to a fraction.

[18]   To combine whole numbers with fractions, multiply the denominator by the whole number, then add that result to the numerator.

$$2\frac{6}{10} = \frac{26}{10} \qquad 3\frac{2}{3} = \frac{11}{3}$$

In the first problem, you first multiply the denominator by the whole number: $10 \times 2 = 20$, then add the result to the numerator: $20 + 6 = 26$. This makes the new numerator 26; the denominator does not change. Similarly, in the second problem, $3 \times 3 = 9$, and $9 + 2 = 11$. This makes the new numerator 11; the denominator does not change.

[19]   Percentages are fractions to the hundredths place.

$$25\% = \frac{25}{100} = .25$$

$$3\% = \frac{3}{100} = .03$$

$$4.7\% = \frac{4.7}{100} = .047$$

Decimal places go from tenths (one place), to hundredths (two places), to thousandths (three places), and so on. A percentage is two places to the right of the decimal and ranges between 0% and 100%.

A.8 EXPONENTS AND ROOTS

[20]   An exponent tells how many times a number or expression is multiplied by itself.

$$2^4 = 2 \times 2 \times 2 \times 2 = 16$$

$$4^2 = 4 \times 4 = 16$$

$$3^3 = 3 \times 3 \times 3 = 27$$

The exponent is placed to the upper right of a number. In the three examples above, the exponents are (from the top) 4, 2, and 3. It is common to see numbers squared (x^2) in statistics because this gets rid of negative values; remember, *any negative number multiplied by itself will be positive.*

[21]   Roots are the reverse of exponents: A root represents a value that, when multiplied by itself, equals that number.

$$\sqrt[4]{16} = 2$$

$$\sqrt{16} = 4$$

$$\sqrt[3]{27} = 3$$

Roots are expressed using radical signs: $\sqrt{}$. You take the root of everything under the radical. Consider the examples given above. The fourth root of 16 is 2, the square root of 16 is 4, and the third root (cube root) of 27 is 3. This means 2 must be multiplied four times to equal 16 (i.e., $2 \times 2 \times 2 \times 2 = 16$), 4 must be multiplied twice to equal 16 (i.e., $4 \times 4 = 16$), and 3 must be multiplied three times to equal 27 (i.e., $3 \times 3 \times 3 = 27$). The number on the "tail" of the radical represents the root.

$$\sqrt[2]{4} = \sqrt{4} = 2$$

No number needs to "sit on the radical" for square roots—it is assumed that you are taking the square root of the number under the radical unless otherwise indicated. This is important because we will rarely deal with anything beyond square roots in statistics.

LEARNING CHECK 4

1. True or false: A fraction can be stated as a decimal.

2. State each of the following as a fraction.
   (a) 0.08   (b) 2.45   (c) −0.952   (d) 13%

3. True or false: Roots are the reverse of exponents.

4. Perform the following computations:
   (a) $\sqrt{25}$ = ?   (b) $\sqrt{81}$ = ?   (c) 7^2 = ?   (d) 15^2 = ?

Answers: 1. True; 2. (a) $\frac{8}{100}$, (b) $2\frac{45}{100}$ or $\frac{245}{100}$, (c) $-\frac{952}{1000}$, (d) $\frac{13}{100}$; 3. True; 4. (a) 5, (b) 9, (c) 49, (d) 225.

A.9 ORDER OF COMPUTATION

Statistics include calculations of addition, subtraction, division, multiplication, parentheses, exponents, and roots, and sometimes all in the same problem. "Doing the math" often becomes confusing, even with a calculator. It truly is "math errors" that needlessly cost many students points on exams. The following rules will make it easier to work your way through many problems in this book.

[22]   Always perform mathematical operations in the parentheses first.

To begin, you should treat whatever is inside parentheses as a single number. For example, $5(4 + 6) = 5(10) = 50$. In this example, first add 4 and 6, then multiply that result by 5. It is a good idea to start with the parentheses before you perform any other calculations. The following are additional examples with parentheses.

$$7 + (4 - 2) = 7 + 2 = 9$$
$$4\left(\sqrt{4}\right) = 4(2) = 8$$

$$32 - (4^2) = 32 - 16 = 16$$
$$\frac{(3+2)}{\sqrt{25}} = \frac{5}{\sqrt{25}} = 1$$

[23]   When parentheses are nested, start working from the inside out.

Nested parentheses are those located inside other parentheses. In this case, you should begin doing mathematical operations for all parentheses inside other ones. Keep working your way out until you have calculated operations in every pair of parentheses. Below are a few examples of how this works.

$$2\left(\left(\sqrt{9} - \sqrt{4}\right) - (3 + 4)\right) = 2((3 - 2) - 7)$$

$$= 2(1 - 7) = 2 \times (-6) = -12$$

$$4 + \left(\left(5 - 4\right) + \left(3 \times \frac{1}{3}\right)\right) = 4 + \left(1 + 1\right) = 4 + 2 = 6$$

$$\frac{8}{((3 + 3) - (\sqrt{4} - 0))} = \frac{8}{(6 - 2)} = \frac{8}{4} = 2$$

$$\frac{((5 + 2) \times (7 - 4))}{((5 + 2) - (7 - 7))} = \frac{(7 \times 3)}{(7 - 0)} = \frac{21}{7} = 3$$

[24]   In problems without parentheses, calculate square roots and exponents first (they are treated as single numbers). Then do all multiplication and division before any addition or subtraction.

This rule can be memorized by using the acronym: Please Roughly Excuse My Dear Aunt Sally, which stands for Parentheses, Roots, Exponents, Multiplication, Division, Addition, and Subtraction. Make sure to follow all the previous rules when performing the order of computation. Below is an example to help guide you through each of the steps.

$$= 4 - 20 + (16 - 8)\ 2^2 \div \sqrt{64}\ (\textit{parentheses})$$

$$= 4 - 20 + 8 \times 2^2 \div \sqrt{49}\ (\textit{roots})$$

$$= 4 - 20 + 8 \times 2^2 \div 8\ (\textit{exponents})$$

$$= 4 - 20 + 8 \times 4 \div 8\ (\textit{multiplication})$$

$$= 4 - 20 + 32 \div 8\ (\textit{division})$$

$$= 4 - 20 + 4\ (\textit{addition})$$

$$= 4 - 16\ (\textit{subtraction})$$

$$= -12$$

LEARNING CHECK 5

1. True or false: The correct order of computation is parentheses, roots, exponents, multiplication, division, addition, and subtraction.

2. True or false: When parentheses are nested, start working from the inside out.

3. Perform the following computations:

   (a) $8^2 - \sqrt{9}$ (b) $8^2 - \sqrt{9} + (4 \times 2^2)^2$ (c) $\frac{8^2 - \sqrt{9} + (4 \times 2^2)^2}{\sqrt{144} - \sqrt{4}}$

Answers: 1. True; 2. True; 3. (a) 61, (b) 317, (c) 31.7.

A.10 EQUATIONS: SOLVING FOR *x*

An equation is two expressions joined by an equals sign. The values on each side of the equals sign must be equal—otherwise they would be unequal. Because both sides are equal, anything you do to one side of the equation, you must also do to the other. You can perform almost any mathematical operation on an equation, so long as both sides of the equation remain equal. This is why you must treat both sides the same—so that they remain equal.

[25]   Adding and subtracting from both sides of the equation is allowed.

$6 + 2 = 8$ $5 + 7 + 3 = 20 - 5$ $30 - 4 + 14 = 50 - 10$

$8 = 8$ $15 = 15$ $40 = 40$

$55 + 2 = 33 + 24$ $2 - 1 + 3 = 8 - 4$ $7 + 21 - 3 = 25$

$57 = 57$ $4 = 4$ $25 = 25$

[26]   Multiplying and dividing from both sides of the equation is allowed.

$6 + 4 = 100 \div 10$ $10 + 11 = 7 \times 3$ $5 + 3 \times 2 = 7 \times 5 - 5$

$10 = 10$ $21 = 21$ $30 = 30$

$21 \div \sqrt{49} = 3$ $6 \times 4 \div 2 = 12^2 \div 12$ $4^2 = 8 \times 2$

$3 = 3$ $12 = 12$ $16 = 16$

[27]   When solving for *x*, you must follow Rules [25] and [26] until *x* is alone on one side of the equation.

When given an equation with undefined variables (such as *x*), we can often solve for *x*. In other words, we can apply Rules [25] and [26] to find the value for x. Also, it is worth noting that an x alone is assumed to have a 1 in front of it (i.e., $x = 1x$). Consider the following example:

$$x - 3 + 9 = 2x$$

$$-3 + 9 = x \text{ (subtract } 1x \text{ from each side of the equation)}$$

$$6 = x \text{ (add } -3 + 9 \text{ to solve for } x)$$

In this example, the first step we made was to subtract $1x$ from each side of the equation. Ultimately, we want to get x alone on one side of the equation. By subtracting $1x$ from each side, we got rid of x on the left side ($1x - 1x = 0x$). Because zero multiplied by anything is zero, then $0x$ must equal 0 ($0x = 0$). Subtracting $1x$ on the right side resulted in x being alone on that side ($2x - 1x = 1x$ or x). Here is another example with x in the numerator of a fraction:

$$\frac{x-5}{5} = 4$$

$$5(4) = 1(x - 5) \text{ (cross multiply)}$$

$$20 = x - 5 \text{ (do the multiplication on each side of the equation)}$$

$$25 = x \text{ (add 5 to each side of the equation to solve for } x)$$

You will need to solve for x in certain cases, such as for problems in Chapter 6. In that chapter, we work with problems where we need to find scores and percentages. To illustrate, suppose your professor says he or she will give the top 15% of students an A in the class. For this problem, we will solve for x to find the cutoff score (x) for an A grade. In this way, being familiar with solving equations is going to help you with some of the topics covered in this book.

LEARNING CHECK 6

1. True or false: Adding, subtracting, multiplying, and dividing from both sides of an equation is allowed.

2. Solve for x:

    (a) $x + 4 = 9$ (b) $2x - 6 = 8$ (c) $-x + 6 = -12$

    (d) $8 = \frac{x}{2}$ (e) $\frac{2}{3} = \frac{x}{6}$ (f) $5 = \frac{x-2}{6}$

Answers: 1. True; 2. (a) $x = 5$, (b) $x = -1$, (c) $x = 18$, (d) $x = 16$, (e) $x = 4$, (f) $x = 32$.

A.11 SUMMATION NOTATION

A summation sign looks like an M on its side: Σ. This symbol is referred to as *sigma,* and it is used throughout statistics. A summation sign that precedes some value is telling you to sum everything that comes next.

For example, suppose you are asked to sum three values: $x_1 = 2$, $x_2 = 3$, $x_3 = 4$. To make this calculation, sum the values.

$$\Sigma x = x_1 + x_2 + x_3$$

$$= 2 + 3 + 4$$

$$= 9$$

The sigma notation can be a bit more complicated than this. For example, suppose you are given the three values above but asked instead to add only x_2 and x_3. To use summation notation, we have to identify where to begin and where to stop adding. To do this, we use the following notation: $\sum_{i=2}^{i=3} x_i$. The i represents different values of x, such that each x (i.e., x_1, x_2, and x_3) is represented as x_i. This notation reads "sum of x from x_2 to x_3." The notation underneath sigma tells you where to start adding; the notation above sigma tells you where to stop adding. This notation system works only when *adding in order*. The solution to this problem is given below.

$$\sum_{i=2}^{i=3} x = x_2 + x_3$$

$$= 3 + 4$$

$$= 7$$

For the formulas used in statistics, you will rarely be asked to sum a limited number of scores or values. Instead, when you see a sigma sign in a statistical formula, you will be asked to sum all scores. In situations where you are asked to add all numbers in a data set, the i notation is not necessary. If nothing is above or below the sigma, then add all values.

[28] $\Sigma x = \sum_{i=1}^{i=n} x$, where n represents the subscript of x where we stop adding.

Certain types of summation will appear often in statistics. Using the formulas in this book, summation requires summing all the given scores. In this section, we will focus on the types of summation commonly used in statistics.

In some cases, a summation sign is located inside parentheses, and it is squared: $(\Sigma x)^2$. Using the mnemonic Please Roughly Excuse My Dear Aunt Sally, we compute the summation in the parentheses first. Then we square the total; this notation reads "sum of x, quantity squared." Using the same x values given previously ($x_1 = 2$, $x_2 = 3$, $x_3 = 4$), we will solve the following problem.

$$(\Sigma x)^2 = (x_1 + x_2 + x_3)^2$$

$$= (2 + 3 + 4)^2$$

$$= 9^2$$

$$= 81$$

In another case, we use a similar notation, except without the parentheses: $\sum x^2$. In this case, you must square each individual score, and then add. Using the mnemonic Please Roughly Excuse My Dear Aunt Sally, we know that exponents are calculated first (there are no parentheses or roots here, so we skip the P [Please] and the R [Roughly] in the mnemonic and start with the E [Excuse]), then add. Using the same x values given previously ($x_1 = 2$, $x_2 = 3$, $x_3 = 4$), we can solve this problem.

$$\sum x^2 = x_1^2 + x_2^2 + x_3^2$$

$$= 2^2 + 3^2 + 4^2$$

$$= 4 + 9 + 16$$

$$= 29$$

A few problems using summation also involve two or more variables. In this section, we will limit the discussion to the summation of two variables. Suppose we have three rectangles with the following lengths and widths given in Table A.1:

TABLE A.1   The Length and Width of Three Rectangles

Length	Width
8	3
10	12
20	2

To find the area of a rectangle, we use the following formula: Area = Length × Width ($A = l \times w$). Therefore, if we were asked to sum the areas of these rectangles, we could represent that as $\sum(l \times w)$, where $l_1 = 8$, $l_2 = 10$, $l_3 = 20$, $w_1 = 3$, $w_2 = 12$, and $w_3 = 2$. The following is the solution for summing the areas of these rectangles:

$$\sum(l \times w) = (l_1 \times w_1) + (l_2 \times w_2) + (l_3 \times w_3)$$

$$= (8 \times 3) + (10 \times 12) + (20 \times 2)$$

$$= 24 + 120 + 40 = 184$$

Now suppose we are interested in knowing the squared sum of the areas. To do this, we represent the summation notation as $\sum(l \times w)^2$.

$$\sum(l \times w)^2 = (l_1 \times w_1)^2 + (l_2 \times w_2)^2 + (l_3 \times w_3)^2$$

$$= (8 \times 3)^2 + (10 \times 12)^2 + (20 \times 2)^2$$

$$= 576 + 14{,}400 + 1{,}600$$

$$= 16{,}576$$

Finally, suppose we are interested in knowing the sum of the areas, quantity squared. To do this, we represent the summation notation as $\sum(l \times w)^2$.

$$(\sum l \times w)^2 = ((l_1 \times w_1) + (l_2 \times w_2) + (l_3 \times w_3))^2$$

$$= ((8 \times 3) + (10 \times 12) + (20 \times 2))^2$$

$$= (24 + 120 + 40)^2$$

$$= (184)^2$$

$$= 33,856$$

In all, the math covered in this appendix is as much math as you need to do well in this course topic. Sure, there is a lot of math in statistics, but this is as hard as the math will get. You can calculate any statistic by applying the basic principles discussed in this appendix.

LEARNING CHECK 7

1. True or false: The summation problem $(\sum x)^2$ reads "sum of x, quantity squared."

2. Perform the following computations for two scores, where $x_1 = 5$ and $x_2 = 4$:
    (a) $\sum x$ (b) $\sum x^2$ (c) $(\sum x)^2$

3. Perform the following computations with the same values of x given in Question 2:
    (a) $\sqrt{\sum x}$ (b) $\sum x^2$ (c) $\left(\sqrt{\sum x}\right)^2$

Answers: 1. True; 2. (a) $5 + 4 = 9$, (b) $5^2 + 4^2 = 41$, (c) $(5 + 4)^2 = 9^2$; 3. (a) $\left(\sqrt{5+4}\right) = \left(\sqrt{9}\right) = 3$, (b) $\sqrt{5^2 + 4^2} = \sqrt{41} = 6.4$, (c) $\left(\sqrt{5+4}\right)^2 = \left(\sqrt{9}\right)^2 = 3^2 = 9$.

KEY TERMS

constant   variable

REVIEW PROBLEMS

SECTION A.1—Positive and Negative Numbers

Identify whether the following are negative, positive, or neither.

1. 2.8

2. −36

3. 10

4. −5.99

5. +20

6. 700

7. 0

8. *x*

9. −*y*

10. *y*

Identify whether the following are constants or variables.

11. 8

12. −5

13. −*x*

14. *y*

15. 0

16. *xy*

SECTIONS A.2–A.3—Addition and Subtraction

1. $1 + 5 = ?$

2. $(+2) + (+8) = ?$

3. $(-3) + 3 = ?$

4. $3 + (-8) = ?$

5. $(-3) + (-6) = ?$

6. $3 + 10 + 6 = ?$

7. $(-7) + 3 + (-4) = ?$

8. $9 - (-9) = ?$

9. $10 - 4 + 6 = ?$

10. $(-3) - (-3) = ?$

SECTIONS A.4–A.5—Multiplication and Division

Compute the following:

1. $6 \times 5 = ?$

2. $8(4) = ?$

3. $-7 \times -3 = ?$

4. $12 \times 5 = ?$

5. $8 \times 4 \times -1 = ?$

6. $7(2)(-3)(-2) = ?$

7. $-4 \times 4 = ?$

8. $-8 \div 8 = ?$

9. $12 \div 12 = ?$

10. $5\overline{)15} = ?$

11. $\frac{18}{2} = ?$

12. $-\frac{3}{6} = ?$

13. $-18 \div -9 = ?$

14. $10 \div (-2) = ?$

15. $-20\overline{)5} = ?$

16. $9(2)(-3) = ?$

State whether the following statements are true or false:

17. $\frac{1}{2} = 0.50$

18. $2\sqrt{3} = \frac{3}{2}$

19. $6 \times 5 = 5 \times 6$

20. $2\sqrt{3} = \frac{3}{2}$

SECTIONS A.6–A.7—Fractions, Decimals, and Percents

Identify whether the following are equal to 0 or undefined.

1. $\dfrac{2}{0}$

2. $\dfrac{0}{10}$

3. $\dfrac{0}{81}$

4. $\dfrac{16}{0}$

Convert the following mixed fractions into a single fraction:

5. $2\dfrac{5}{8}$

6. $1\dfrac{1}{2}$

7. $-5\dfrac{2}{7}$

8. $-12\dfrac{2}{3}$

Convert the following decimals into fractions:

9. 0.20

10. −0.35

11. 0.002

12. 0.0052

13. −0.8

14. 1.25

Convert the following decimals into percents:

15. .1000

16. .0250

17. .0500

18. .5000

Compute the following:

19. $\dfrac{2}{3} \times \dfrac{4}{5} = ?$

20. $\dfrac{5}{8} + \dfrac{3}{2} = ?$

21. $\dfrac{1}{3} + \dfrac{1}{5} + \dfrac{2}{3} = ?$

22. $-\dfrac{2}{7} \times \dfrac{1}{2} \times \dfrac{4}{5} = ?$

23. $\dfrac{2}{3} \div \dfrac{4}{5} = ?$

24. $\dfrac{2}{3} - \dfrac{3}{7} = ?$

25. $\dfrac{5}{6} - \dfrac{11}{12} = ?$

26. $-\dfrac{5}{3} \div \dfrac{10}{6} = ?$

SECTIONS A.8–A.9—Exponents, Roots, and Order of Computation

1. $4^1 = ?$

2. $\sqrt{81} = ?$

3. $\sqrt[3]{8} = ?$

4. $12^2 = ?$

5. $5^3 = ?$

6. $\sqrt{2+7} = ?$

7. $\sqrt{16^2} = ?$

8. $(\sqrt{16})^2 = ?$

9. $8 \times 4 + 3 = ?$

10. $3 + 8 \div 4 = ?$

11. $1 + 2 \times 3 \div 5 = ?$

12. $(3 + 2 \times 4) \div 5 = ?$

13. $(6 \div 11) \times 1 \div 12 = ?$

14. $\dfrac{\frac{1}{2} + \frac{2}{4}}{\frac{1}{2}} = ?$

SECTIONS A.10–A.11—Equations and Summation Notation

Solve for x.

1. $x + 3 = 12$

2. $\dfrac{x}{2} = 4$

3. $6x = 18$

4. $5x + 10 = 20$

5. $\dfrac{x+3}{2} = 1.96$

6. $\dfrac{x-15}{7} = -1.96$

7. $\dfrac{x+9}{3} = 1.645$

8. $\dfrac{x+4}{8} = -1.645$

Use the following values of x and y to compute the following problems:

$x_1 = 2,\ x_2 = 4,\ x_3 = 6$

$y_1 = 3,\ y_2 = 5,\ y_3 = 7$

9. $\left(\sum x\right)^2 = ?$

10. $\sum y^2 = ?$

11. $\sum x + \sum y = ?$

12. $\sum xy = ?$

13. $\sqrt{\sum x^2} = ?$

14. $\sqrt{\sum xy} = ?$

15. $\sum (x + y)^2 = ?$

16. $\sum \left(x^2 + y^2\right) = ?$

••• Appendix B

SPSS General Instructions Guide

The General Instruction Guidebook (GIG) for using SPSS provides standardized instructions for using SPSS to enter and analyze data. The instructions provided in the GIG are also given with an example in each chapter in the SPSS in Focus sections. For each section, we include the page number for where you can find that SPSS in Focus section in the book. Each chapter, except Chapter 7, gives at least one step-by-step SPSS in Focus section. These sections provide step-by-step instructions for using SPSS to enter data and compute the statistics taught in each chapter. On the other hand, this guide provides general instructions without the context of a specific example. You can use these instructions to complete each exercise and refer to the SPSS examples in each chapter to clear up any points of confusion.

The instructions here are organized by exercise in this guide to make it easier for you to find the appropriate instructions to complete each SPSS exercise. The instructions for each exercise are given with a reference for which SPSS in Focus section provides an example for following the steps. Note that the term *factor* will be used in this guide to describe an independent variable and a quasi-independent variable. This guidebook will not distinguish between each type of variable because both can be entered and analyzed using SPSS.

1.1: ENTERING AND DEFINING VARIABLES

These commands are illustrated in **Chapter 1, Section 1.7** (p. 24).

Enter data by column:

1. Open the **Variable View** tab. In the **Name column**, enter each variable name (one variable per row).

2. Go to the **Decimals column** and reduce that value to the degree of accuracy of the data.

3. Open the **Data View** tab. You will see that each variable is now the title for each column. Enter the data for each variable in the appropriate column.

Enter data by row (this requires *coding* the grouped data):

1. Open the **Variable View** tab. Enter the variable name in the first row and a name of the dependent variable in the second row.

2. Go to the **Decimals column** and reduce that value to 0 for the first row because values in this column will be coded using whole numbers. Reduce the decimal column in the second row to the degree of accuracy of the data.

3. Go to the **Values column** in the first row and click on the small gray box with three dots. In the dialog box, enter a number in the **Value cell** and the name of each level of the factor in the **Label cell**. After each entry, select **Add**. Repeat these steps for each level of the factor, and then select **OK**. The data are now coded as numbers.

4. Open the **Data View** tab. In the first column, enter each code *n* times. For example, if you measure five scores at each level of the factor, then you will enter each number (or code) five times in the first column. In the second column, enter the values of the dependent variable. These values should match up with the levels of the factor you coded.

2.1: FREQUENCY DISTRIBUTIONS FOR QUANTITATIVE DATA

These commands are illustrated in **Chapter 2, Section 2.4** (p. 47).

1. Click on the **Variable View** tab and enter the variable name in the first row of the **Name column**. Reduce the **Decimals column** value in the first row to the degree of accuracy of the data.

2. Click on the **Data View** tab and enter the values of the variable in the first column. Enter the data in any order you wish, but make sure all the data are entered correctly.

3. Go to the **menu bar** and click **Analyze**, then **Descriptive Statistics** and **Frequencies**, to display a dialog box.

4. In the dialog box, select the variable name and click the arrow in the center to move the variable into the **Variable(s):** box to the right. Make sure the option to "Display frequency tables" is selected.

5. Select **OK**, or select **Paste** and click the **Run** command.

2.2: FREQUENCY DISTRIBUTIONS FOR CATEGORICAL DATA

These commands are illustrated in **Chapter 2, Section 2.7** (p. 52).

1. Click on the **Variable View** tab and enter the variable name in the first row of the **Name column**. In the second row, enter *frequencies*. In the **Decimals column**, reduce that value to 0 in the first row and reduce it to the degree of accuracy of the data in the second row.

2. Code the data for the variable listed in the first row (refer to the instructions given in the directions for 1.1 in this SPSS guide, p. 513).

3. Click on the **Data View** tab and enter each numeric code one time in the first column. In the second column, enter the frequency across from the appropriate numeric code.

4. Go to **Data,** then **Weight cases . . .** to display a dialog box. Select **Weight cases by** and move *frequencies* into the **Frequency Variable:** box. Now each frequency is linked to each level of the variable.

5. Go to the **menu bar** and click **Analyze**, then **Descriptive Statistics** and **Frequencies**, to display a dialog box.

6. In the dialog box, select the variable and click the arrow in the center to move it into the box labeled **Variable(s):** to the right. Make sure the option to "Display frequency tables" is selected.

7. Select **OK**, or select **Paste** and click the **Run** command.

2.3: HISTOGRAMS, BAR CHARTS, AND PIE CHARTS

These commands are illustrated in **Chapter 2, Section 2.11** (p. 62).

1. Click on the **Variable View** tab and enter the variable name in the **Name column**. In the **Decimals column**, reduce the value to the degree of accuracy of the data.

2. Click on the **Data View** tab and enter the values for the variable in the first column. Enter the data in any order you wish, but make sure all the data are entered correctly.

3. Go to the **menu bar** and click **Analyze**, then **Descriptive Statistics** and **Frequencies**, to display a dialog box.

4. In the dialog box, select the variable name and click the arrow in the center to move it into the box labeled **Variable(s):** to the right. Because we only want the graphs and charts in this example, make sure the option to "Display frequency tables" is not selected.

5. Click on the **Charts** option in the dialog box. Here you have the option to select **bar charts**, **pie charts**, or **histograms**. You can select only one at a time. Once you select a graph, select **Continue**.

6. Select **OK**, or select **Paste** and click the **Run** command.

3.1: MEAN, MEDIAN, AND MODE

These commands are illustrated in **Chapter 3, Section 3.6** (p. 94).

1. Click on the **Variable View** tab and enter the variable name in the **Name column**. In the **Decimals column**, reduce the value to the degree of accuracy of the data.

2. Click on the **Data View** tab and enter the values for the variable in the first column.

3. Go to the **menu bar** and click **Analyze**, then **Descriptive Statistics** and **Frequencies**, to display a dialog box.

4. In the dialog box, select the variable name and click the arrow in the center, which will move it into the box labeled **Variable(s):** to the right. Make sure the option to "Display frequency tables" is not selected, and then select **Statistics** to display another dialog box.

5. In this dialog box, select **Mean**, **Median**, and **Mode** to the right; then select **Continue**.

6. Select **OK**, or select **Paste** and click the **Run** command.

4.1: RANGE, VARIANCE, AND STANDARD DEVIATION

These commands are illustrated in **Chapter 4, Section 4.10** (p. 124).

1. Click on the **Variable View** tab and enter the variable name in the **Name column**. In the **Decimals column**, reduce the value to the degree of accuracy of the data.

2. Click on the **Data View** tab and enter the values for the variable in the first column.

3. Go to the **menu bar** and click **Analyze**, then **Descriptive Statistics** and **Frequencies**, to display a dialog box.

4. In the dialog box, select the variable name and click the arrow in the center, which will move it into the box labeled **Variable(s):** to the right. Make sure the option to "Display frequency tables" is not selected, and then select **Statistics** to display another dialog box.

5. In this dialog box, select **Std. deviation**, **Variance**, and **Range**; then select **Continue.**

6. Select **OK**, or select **Paste** and click the **Run** command.

5.1: CONVERTING RAW SCORES TO STANDARD z SCORES

These commands are illustrated in **Chapter 5, Section 5.10** (p. 155).

1. Click on the **Variable View** tab and enter the variable name in the **Name column**. In the **Decimals column**, reduce the value to the degree of accuracy of the data.

2. Click on the **Data View** tab and enter the values for the variable in the first column.

3. Go to the **menu bar** and click **Analyze**, then **Descriptive Statistics** and **Descriptives**, to display a dialog box.

4. In the dialog box, select the variable name and click the arrow to move it into the **Variable(s)** box. Select the "Save standardized values as variables" box.

5. Select **OK**, or select **Paste** and click the **Run** command.

6.1: ESTIMATING THE STANDARD ERROR OF THE MEAN

These commands are illustrated in **Chapter 6, Section 6.6** (p. 178).

1. Click on the **Variable View** tab and enter the variable name in the **Name column**. In the **decimals column**, reduce the value to the degree of accuracy of the data.

2. Click on the **Data View** tab and enter the values for the variable in the first column.

3. Go to the **menu bar** and click **Analyze**, then **Descriptive Statistics** and **Descriptives**, to display a dialog box.

4. In the dialog box, select the variable name and click the arrow to move it into the box labeled **Variable(s):** to the right. Click the **Options . . .** tab to display a new dialog box.

5. In the new dialog box, select **S.E. mean** in the Dispersion box and click **Continue**.

6. Select **OK**, or select **Paste** and click the **Run** command.

8.1: ONE-SAMPLE *t* TEST

These commands are illustrated in **Chapter 8, Section 8.8** (p. 244).

1. Click on the **Variable View** tab and enter the variable name in the **Name column**. In the **Decimals column**, reduce the value to the degree of accuracy of the data.

2. Click on the **Data View** tab and enter the values for the variable in the first column.

3. Go to the **menu bar** and click **Analyze**, then **Compare Means** and **One-Sample T Test**, to display a dialog box.

4. In the dialog box, select the variable name and click the arrow in the middle to move it to the **Test Variable(s):** box.

5. Enter the value stated in the null hypothesis in the **Test Value:** box. The value in SPSS is 0 by default. To check confidence intervals, select **Options . . .** in the dialog box. By default, the level of confidence is set at 95%.

6. Select **OK**, or select **Paste** and click the **Run** command.

9.1: TWO-INDEPENDENT-SAMPLE *t* TEST

These commands are illustrated in **Chapter 9, Section 9.8** (p. 270).

1. Click on the **Variable View** tab and enter the factor in the **Name column**. In the second row, enter the name of the dependent variable in the Name column. Reduce the value to 0 in the **Decimals column** in the first row and to the degree of accuracy of the data in the second row.

2. In the **Values** column, code the levels of the factor listed in the first row (refer to the instructions given in the directions for 1.1 in this SPSS guide, p. 513).

3. In the **Data View** tab, enter each code *n* times in the first column. For example, if you measure five scores in each group (or at each level of the factor), then enter each numeric code five times in the first column. In the second column, enter the values for the dependent variable so that they correspond with the code for each group.

4. Go to the **menu bar** and click **Analyze**, then **Compare Means** and **Independent-Samples T Test**, to display a dialog box.

5. Using the arrows to move the variables, select the dependent variable and place it in the **Test Variable(s):** box; select the factor and move it into the **Grouping Variable:** box. Two question marks will appear in the Grouping Variable box. To check confidence intervals, select **Options . . .** in the dialog box. By default, the level of confidence is set at 95%.

6. Click **Define Groups . . .** to display a new dialog box. Place the numeric code for each group in the spaces provided and then click **Continue**. The numeric codes should now appear in the Grouping Variable: box (instead of question marks).

7. Select **OK**, or select **Paste** and click the **Run** command.

10.1: THE RELATED-SAMPLES *t* TEST

These commands are illustrated in **Chapter 10, Section 10.7** (p. 298).

1. Click on the **Variable View** tab and enter the name of the first group in the **Name column** in the first row; enter the name of the second group in the second row. Reduce the **Decimals column** value in both rows to the degree of accuracy of the data.

2. Click on the **Data View** tab. Enter the data for each group. Each pair of scores should line up in each row.

3. Go to the **menu bar** and click **Analyze**, then **Compare Means** and **Paired-Samples T Test**, to display a dialog box.

4. In the dialog box, select each group in the left box and move it to the right box using the arrow in the middle. The groups should be side

by side in the box to the right. To check confidence intervals, select **Options . . .** in the dialog box. By default, the level of confidence is set at 95%.

5. Select **OK**, or select **Paste** and click the **Run** command.

11.1: THE ONE-WAY BETWEEN-SUBJECTS ANOVA

These commands are illustrated in **Chapter 11, Section 11.5** (p. 332).

1. Click on the **Variable View** tab and enter the name of the factor in the **Name column**. Go to the **Decimals column** for this row and reduce the value to 0 (because this variable will be coded). In the second row, enter the name of the dependent variable in the name column. Reduce the **Decimals column** value in the second row to the degree of accuracy of the data.

2. In the **Values** column, code the levels of the factor listed in the first row (refer to the instructions given in the directions for 1.1 in this SPSS guide, p. 513).

3. In the **Data View** tab, enter each code *n* times in the first column. For example, if you measure five scores in each group (or level), then enter each numeric code five times in the first column. In the second column, enter the values for the dependent variable so that they correspond with the codes for each group.

4. Go to the **menu bar** and click **Analyze**, then **Compare Means** and **One-Way ANOVA**, to display a dialog box.

5. Use the appropriate arrows to move the factor into the **Factor:** box. Move the dependent variable into the **Dependent List:** box.

6. Click the **Post Hoc** option to display a new dialog box. Select an appropriate post hoc test and click **Continue**.

7. Select **OK**, or select **Paste** and click the **Run** command.

11.2: THE ONE-WAY WITHIN-SUBJECTS ANOVA

These commands are illustrated in **Chapter 11, Section 11.9** (p. 348).

1. Click on the **Variable View** tab and enter the name of each group (or level of the factor) in the **Name column**. One group should be entered in each row. Go to the **Decimals column** and reduce the value to the degree of accuracy of the data for each row.

2. Click on the **Data View** tab. Each group is now listed in each column. Enter the data for each respective column.

3. Go to the **menu bar** and click **Analyze**, then **General Linear Model** and **Repeated Measures**, to display a dialog box.

4. In the **Within-Subject Factor Name** box, enter a name for the repeated measures factor. In the **Number of Levels** box, SPSS is asking for the number of levels of the factor (or the number of groups). Enter the number and the **Add** option will illuminate. Click **Add** and the factor (with the number of levels in parentheses) will appear in the box below. Click **Define** to display a new dialog box.

5. In the dialog box, use the appropriate arrows to move each column into the **Within-Subjects Variables (cues)** box.

6. Then select **Options** to display a new dialog box. To compute effect size, use the arrow to move the factor into the **Display Means for:** box. Then check the **Compare main effects** option. Use the drop-down arrow under the **Confidence interval adjustment** heading to select an appropriate post hoc test. Then select **Continue.**

7. Select **OK**, or select **Paste** and click the **Run** command.

12.1: THE TWO-WAY BETWEEN-SUBJECTS ANOVA

These commands are illustrated in **Chapter 12, Section 12.7** (p. 393).

1. Click on the **Variable View** tab and enter the name of each factor (one in each row) in the **Name column**; in the third row, enter a name of the dependent variable in the Name column. Reduce the value to 0 in the **Decimals column** for the first two rows (for both factors). Reduce the value to the degree of accuracy of the data in the third row.

2. In the **Values** column, code the levels of both factors listed in the first two rows (refer to the instructions given in the directions for 1.1 in this SPSS guide, p. 513).

3. In the **Data View** tab, enter each code for the first factor n times in the first column. Enter each code for the second factor n times and in the second column. The two columns create the cells. In the second column, enter the values for the dependent variable such that the data in each cell are listed across from the corresponding codes for each cell.

4. Go to the **menu bar** and click **Analyze**, then **General Linear Model** and **Univariate**, to display a dialog box.

5. Use the appropriate arrows to move the factors into the **Fixed Factor(s):** box. Move the dependent variable into the **Dependent Variable:** box.

6. Finally, click **Options** to display a new dialog box. In the **Factor(s) and Factor Interactions** box, move the main effects and interaction

into the **Display Means for** box by using the arrow. Then click **Continue**.

7. Select **Post Hoc . . .** to display another dialog box. Use the arrow to bring both main effects from the **Factor(s)** box into the **Post Hoc Tests for** box. Select an appropriate pairwise comparison for the main effects and select **Continue**. (*Note:* SPSS does not perform simple effect tests. If you get a significant interaction, you will have to conduct these tests separately.)

8. Select **OK**, or select **Paste** and click the **Run** command.

13.1: PEARSON CORRELATION COEFFICIENT

These commands are illustrated in **Chapter 13, Section 13.4** (p. 419).

1. Click on the **Variable View** tab and enter the first variable name in the **Name column**; enter the second variable name in the Name column below it. Go to the **Decimals column** and reduce the value to the degree of accuracy of the data for each row.

2. Click on the **Data View** tab. Enter the data for each variable in the appropriate columns.

3. Go to the **menu bar** and click **Analyze**, then **Correlate** and **Bivariate**, to display a dialog box.

4. Use the arrows to move both variables into the **Variables** box.

5. Select **OK**, or select **Paste** and click the **Run** command.

13.2: SPEARMAN CORRELATION COEFFICIENT

These commands are described in **Chapter 13, Section 13.7** (p. 432).

1. Click on the **Variable View** tab and enter the first variable name in the **Name column**; enter the second variable name in the Name column below it. Go to the **Decimals column** and reduce the value to the degree of accuracy of the data for each row.

2. Click on the **Data View** tab. Enter the original scores or ranks (including tied ranks) for each variable in the appropriate columns.

3. Go to the **menu bar** and click **Analyze**, then **Correlate** and **Bivariate**, to display a dialog box.

4. Use the arrows to move both variables into the **Variables** box. Uncheck the Pearson box and check the Spearman box in the **Correlation Coefficients** portion of the dialog box.

5. Select **OK**, or select **Paste** and click the **Run** command.

13.3: POINT-BISERIAL CORRELATION COEFFICIENT

These commands are described in **Chapter 13, Section 13.7** (p. 432).

1. Click on the **Variable View** tab and enter the name of the dichotomous factor in the **Name column**; enter the name of the continuous factor in the Name column below it. Go to the **Decimals column** and reduce the value to 0 for the dichotomous factor and to the degree of accuracy of the data for the continuous factor.

2. In the **Values** column, code the levels of the dichotomous factor listed in the first row (refer to the instructions given in the directions for 1.1 in this SPSS guide, p. 513).

3. Click on the **Data View** tab. In the first column, enter each code *n* times such that the number of codes entered for each level of the dichotomous factor is equal to the number of scores at each level of the dichotomous factor. In the second column, enter the values of the continuous factor as they correspond with the levels of the dichotomous variable.

4. Go to the **menu bar** and click **Analyze**, then **Correlate** and **Bivariate**, to display a dialog box.

5. Use the arrows to move both factors into the **Variables** box.

6. Select **OK**, or select **Paste** and click the **Run** command.

13.4: PHI CORRELATION COEFFICIENT

These commands are described in **Chapter 13, Section 13.7** (p. 432).

1. Click on the **Variable View** tab and enter the name of the first dichotomous factor in the **Name column**. Below that enter the name of the second dichotomous factor in the same column. Because these factors will be coded, go to the **Decimals column** and reduce the value to 0 for both rows. In the third row, enter *frequencies* in the name column and reduce the **Decimals column** value to 0.

2. In the **Values** column, code the levels of the dichotomous factors listed in the first two rows (refer to the instructions given in the directions for 1.1 in this SPSS guide, p. 513).

3. Go to the Data View tab and enter the numeric codes in the first and second columns. For a phi correlation coefficient, always enter 1, 1, 2, and 2 in the first column and 1, 2, 1, and 2 in the second column. In the third column, enter the corresponding frequencies for each coded cell.

4. Go to the menu bar and click **Data**, then **Weight Cases . . .** , to display a new dialog box. Select **Weight cases by** and move the *frequencies* column into the **Frequency Variable** box, and then select **OK**.

5. Again, go to the **menu bar** and click **Analyze**, then **Correlate** and **Bivariate**, to display a dialog box. Use the arrows to move both dichotomous factors into the **Variables** box.

6. Select **OK**, or select **Paste** and click the **Run** command.

13.5: ANALYSIS OF REGRESSION

These commands are illustrated in **Chapter 13, Section 13.11** (p. 445).

1. Click on the **Variable View** tab and enter the predictor variable name in the **Name column**; enter the criterion variable name in the Name column below it. Go to the **Decimals column** and reduce the value in both rows to the degree of accuracy for the data.

2. Click on the **Data View** tab. Enter the data for the predictor variable (X) in the first column. Enter the data for the criterion variable (Y) in the second column.

3. Go to the **menu bar** and click **Analyze**, then **Regression** and **Linear**, to display a dialog box.

4. Use the arrows to move the predictor variable into the **Independent(s)** box; move the criterion variable into the **Dependent** box.

5. Select **OK**, or select **Paste** and click the **Run** command.

14.1: THE CHI-SQUARE GOODNESS-OF-FIT TEST

These commands are illustrated in **Chapter 14, Section 14.3** (p. 468).

1. Click on the **Variable View** tab and enter the nominal variable name in the **Name column** in the first row; enter *frequencies* in the Name column below it. Go to the **Decimals column** and reduce the value to 0 for both rows.

2. In the **Values** column, code the levels of the nominal variable listed in the first row (refer to the instructions given in the directions for 1.1 in this SPSS guide, p. 513).

3. Click on the **Data View** tab. In the first column, enter each coded value one time. In the second column, enter the observed frequencies that correspond to each coded value.

4. Go to the menu bar and click **Data**, then **Weight Cases . . .** , to display a dialog box. In the new dialog box, click **Weight cases by** and move *frequencies* into the **Frequency Variable** cell. Select **OK**.

5. Go to the **menu bar** and click **Analyze**, **Nonparametric Tests**, then **Legacy Dialogs**, and **Chi-square** to display a new dialog box.

6. Use the arrows to move the nominal variable into the **Test Variables List:** box. In the **Expected Values** box, notice that we have two options: We can assume that all expected frequencies are equal, or we can enter the frequencies for each cell. If the expected

frequencies are equal, then leave this alone; if they are not equal, then enter the expected frequencies one at a time and click **Add** to move them into the cell.

7. Select **OK**, or select **Paste** and click the **Run** command.

14.2: THE CHI-SQUARE
TEST FOR INDEPENDENCE

These commands are illustrated in **Chapter 14, Section 14.7** (p. 480).

1. To organize the data, write out the contingency table on a separate piece of paper such that one variable is listed in the row and a second variable is listed in the column. Click on the **Variable View** tab, and in the **Name column**, enter the name of the *row* variable in the first row and the name of the *column* variable in the second row. In the third row, enter *frequencies* in the name column. Reduce the value to 0 in each row in the **Decimals column**.

2. In the **Values** column, code the levels of both nominal variables listed in the first two rows (refer to the instructions given in the directions for 1.1 in this SPSS guide, p. 513).

3. In the **Data View** tab, set up the cells by row and column. Enter the codes for the row and column variable in the appropriately labeled column. For example, if the *row* variable has two levels and the *column* variable has three levels, then enter 1, 1, 1, 2, 2, and 2 in the first column of the Data View. Set up the cells in the second column by entering the levels in numeric order across from each level of the *row* variable. Using the same example, enter 1, 2, 3, 1, 2, and 3 in the second column. The two columns create the cells. Enter the corresponding observed frequencies for each cell in the third column.

4. Go to the menu bar and click **Data**, then **Weight Cases . . .**, to display a dialog box. In the new dialog box, click **Weight cases by** and move *frequencies* into the **Frequency Variable:** cell. This tells SPSS that the frequencies you enter are those for each row–column combination. Select **OK**.

5. Go to the **menu bar** and click **Analyze**, then **Descriptive Statistics** and **Crosstabs**, to display a dialog box.

6. Use the arrows to move the *row* variable into the **Row(s)** box and move the *column* variable into the **Column(s)** box. Click **Statistics . . .** to open a new dialog box.

7. Select **Chi-square** in the top left. To compute effect size, select **Phi and Cramer's *V*** in the box labeled **Nominal**. Click **Continue**.

8. Select **OK**, or select **Paste** and click the **Run** command.

··· Appendix C

Statistical Tables

TABLE C.1 The Unit Normal Table

Column (A) lists *z*-score values. Column (B) lists the proportion of the area between the mean and the *z*-score value. Column (C) lists the proportion of the area beyond the *z* score in the tail of the distribution. (*Note:* Because the normal distribution is symmetrical, areas for negative *z* scores are the same as those for positive *z* scores.)

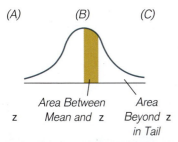 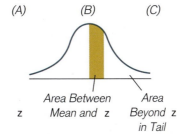 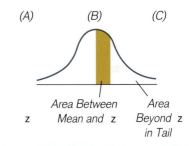

(A) z	(B) Area Between Mean and z	(C) Area Beyond z in Tail	(A) z	(B) Area Between Mean and z	(C) Area Beyond z in Tail	(A) z	(B) Area Between Mean and z	(C) Area Beyond z in Tail
0.00	.0000	.5000	0.15	.0596	.4404	0.30	.1179	.3821
0.01	.0040	.4960	0.16	.0636	.4364	0.31	.1217	.3783
0.02	.0080	.4920	0.17	.0675	.4325	0.32	.1255	.3745
0.03	.0120	.4880	0.18	.0714	.4286	0.33	.1293	.3707
0.04	.0160	.4840	0.19	.0753	.4247	0.34	.1331	.3669
0.05	.0199	.4801	0.20	.0793	.4207	0.35	.1368	.3632
0.06	.0239	.4761	0.21	.0832	.4168	0.36	.1406	.3594
0.07	.0279	.4721	0.22	.0871	.4129	0.37	.1443	.3557
0.08	.0319	.4681	0.23	.0910	.4090	0.38	.1480	.3520
0.09	.0359	.4641	0.24	.0948	.4052	0.39	.1517	.3483
0.10	.0398	.4602	0.25	.0987	.4013	0.40	.1554	.3446
0.11	.0438	.4562	0.26	.1026	.3974	0.41	.1591	.3409
0.12	.0478	.4522	0.27	.1064	.3936	0.42	.1628	.3372
0.13	.0517	.4483	0.28	.1103	.3897	0.43	.1664	.3336
0.14	.0557	.4443	0.29	.1141	.3859	0.44	.1700	.3300

(Continued)

TABLE C.1 (Continued)

(A) z	(B) Area Between Mean and z	(C) Area Beyond z in Tail	(A) z	(B) Area Between Mean and z	(C) Area Beyond z in Tail	(A) z	(B) Area Between Mean and z	(C) Area Beyond z in Tail
0.45	.1736	.3264	0.78	.2823	.2177	1.11	.3665	.1335
0.46	.1772	.3228	0.79	.2852	.2148	1.12	.3686	.1314
0.47	.1808	.3192	0.80	.2881	.2119	1.13	.3708	.1292
0.48	.1844	.3156	0.81	.2910	.2090	1.14	.3729	.1271
0.49	.1879	.3121	0.82	.2939	.2061	1.15	.3749	.1251
0.50	.1915	.3085	0.83	.2967	.2033	1.16	.3770	.1230
0.51	.1950	.3050	0.84	.2995	.2005	1.17	.3790	.1210
0.52	.1985	.3015	0.85	.3023	.1977	1.18	.3810	.1190
0.53	.2019	.2981	0.86	.3051	.1949	1.19	.3830	.1170
0.54	.2054	.2946	0.87	.3078	.1922	1.20	.3849	.1151
0.55	.2088	.2912	0.88	.3106	.1894	1.21	.3869	.1131
0.56	.2123	.2877	0.89	.3133	.1867	1.22	.3888	.1112
0.57	.2157	.2843	0.90	.3159	.1841	1.23	.3907	.1093
0.58	.2190	.2810	0.91	.3186	.1814	1.24	.3925	.1075
0.59	.2224	.2776	0.92	.3212	.1788	1.25	.3944	.1056
0.60	.2257	.2743	0.93	.3238	.1762	1.26	.3962	.1038
0.61	.2391	.2709	0.94	.3264	.1736	1.27	.3980	.1020
0.62	.2324	.2676	0.95	.3289	.17 11	1.28	.3997	.1003
0.63	.2357	.2643	0.96	.3315	.1685	1.29	.4015	.0985
0.64	.2389	.2611	0.97	.3340	.1660	1.30	.4032	.0968
0.65	.2422	.2578	0.98	.3365	.1635	1.31	.4049	.0951
0.66	.2454	.2546	0.99	.3389	.1611	1.32	.4066	.0934
0.67	.2486	.2514	1.00	.3413	.1587	1.33	.4082	.0918
0.68	.2517	.2483	1.01	.3438	.1562	1.34	.4099	.0901
0.69	.2549	.2451	1.02	.3461	.1539	1.35	.4115	.0885
0.70	.2580	.2420	1.03	.3485	.1515	1.36	.4131	.0869
0.71	.2611	.2389	1.04	.3508	.1492	1.37	.4147	.0853
0.72	.2642	.2358	1.05	.3531	.1469	1.38	.4162	.0838
0.73	.2673	.2327	1.06	.3554	.1446	1.39	.4177	.0823
0.74	.2704	.2296	1.07	.3577	.1423	1.40	.4192	.0808
0.75	.2734	.2266	1.08	.3599	.1401	1.41	.4207	.0793
0.76	.2764	.2236	1.09	.3621	.1379	1.42	.4222	.0778
0.77	.2794	.2206	1.10	.3643	.1357	1.43	.4236	.0764

(A) z	(B) Area Between Mean and z	(C) Area Beyond z in Tail	(A) z	(B) Area Between Mean and z	(C) Area Beyond z in Tail	(A) z	(B) Area Between Mean and z	(C) Area Beyond z in Tail
1.44	.4251	.0749	1.77	.4616	.0384	2.10	.4821	.0179
1.45	.4265	.0735	1.78	.4625	.0375	2.11	.4826	.0174
1.46	.4279	.0721	1.79	.4633	.0367	2.12	.4830	.0170
1.47	.4292	.0708	1.80	.4641	.0359	2.13	.4834	.0166
1.48	.4306	.0694	1.81	.4649	.0351	2.14	.4838	.0162
1.49	.4319	.0681	1.82	.4656	.0344	2.15	.4842	.0158
1.50	.4332	.0668	1.83	.4664	.0336	2.16	.4846	.0154
1.51	.4345	.0655	1.84	.4671	.0329	2.17	.4850	.0150
1.52	.4357	.0643	1.85	.4678	.0322	2.18	.4854	.0146
1.53	.4370	.0630	1.86	.4686	.0314	2.19	.4857	.0143
1.54	.4382	.0618	1.87	.4693	.0307	2.20	.4861	.0139
1.55	.4394	.0606	1.88	.4699	.0301	2.21	.4864	.0136
1.56	.4406	.0594	1.89	.4706	.0294	2.22	.4868	.0132
1.57	.4418	.0582	1.90	.4713	.0287	2.23	.4871	.0129
1.58	.4429	.0571	1.91	.4719	.0281	2.24	.4875	.0125
1.59	.4441	.0559	1.92	.4726	.0274	2.25	.4878	.0122
1.60	.4452	.0548	1.93	.4732	.0268	2.26	.4881	.0119
1.61	.4463	.0537	1.94	.4738	.0262	2.27	.4884	.0116
1.62	.4474	.0526	1.95	.4744	.0256	2.28	.4887	.0113
1.63	.4484	.0516	1.96	.4750	.0250	2.29	.4890	.0110
1.64	.4495	.0505	1.97	.4756	.0244	2.30	.4893	.0107
1.65	.4505	.0495	1.98	.4761	.0239	2.31	.4896	.0104
1.66	.4515	.0485	1.99	.4767	.0233	2.32	.4898	.0102
1.67	.4525	.0475	2.00	.4772	.0228	2.33	.4901	.0099
1.68	.4535	.0465	2.01	.4778	.0222	2.34	.4904	.0096
1.69	.4545	.0455	2.02	.4783	.0217	2.35	.4906	.0094
1.70	.4554	.0446	2.03	.4788	.0212	2.36	.4909	.0091
1.71	.4564	.0436	2.04	.4793	.0207	2.37	.4911	.0089
1.72	.4573	.0427	2.05	.4798	.0202	2.38	.4913	.0087
1.73	.4582	.0418	2.06	.4803	.0197	2.39	.4916	.0084
1.74	.4591	.0409	2.07	.4808	.0192	2.40	.4918	.0082
1.75	.4599	.0401	2.08	.4812	.0188	2.41	.4920	.0080
1.76	.4608	.0392	2.09	.4817	.0183	2.42	.4922	.0078

(Continued)

TABLE C.1 (Continued)

(A) z	(B) Area Between Mean and z	(C) Area Beyond z in Tail	(A) z	(B) Area Between Mean and z	(C) Area Beyond z in Tail	(A) z	(B) Area Between Mean and z	(C) Area Beyond z in Tail
2.43	.4925	.0075	2.74	.4969	.0031	3.05	.4989	.0011
2.44	.4927	.0073	2.75	.4970	.0030	3.06	.4989	.0011
2.45	.4929	.0071	2.76	.4971	.0029	3.07	.4989	.0011
2.46	.4931	.0069	2.77	.4972	.0028	3.08	.4990	.0010
2.47	.4932	.0068	2.78	.4973	.0027	3.09	.4990	.0010
2.48	.4934	.0066	2.79	.4974	.0026	3.10	.4990	.0010
2.49	.4936	.0064	2.80	.4974	.0026	3.11	.4991	.0009
2.50	.4938	.0062	2.81	.4975	.0025	3.12	.4991	.0009
2.51	.4940	.0060	2.82	.4976	.0024	3.13	.4991	.0009
2.52	.4941	.0059	2.83	.4977	.0023	3.14	.4992	.0008
2.53	.4943	.0057	2.84	.4977	.0023	3.15	.4992	.0008
2.54	.4945	.0055	2.85	.4978	.0022	3.16	.4992	.0008
2.55	.4946	.0054	2.86	.4979	.0021	3.17	.4992	.0008
2.56	.4948	.0052	2.87	.4979	.0021	3.18	.4993	.0007
2.57	.4949	.0051	2.88	.4980	.0020	3.19	.4993	.0007
2.58	.4951	.0049	2.89	.4981	.0019	3.20	.4993	.0007
2.59	.4952	.0048	2.90	.4981	.0019	3.21	.4993	.0007
2.60	.4953	.0047	2.91	.4982	.0018	3.22	.4994	.0006
2.61	.4955	.0045	2.92	.4982	.0018	3.23	.4994	.0006
2.62	.4956	.0044	2.93	.4983	.0017	3.24	.4994	.0006
2.63	.4957	.0043	2.94	.4984	.0016	3.25	.4994	.0006
2.64	.4959	.0041	2.95	.4984	.0016	3.30	.4995	.0005
2.65	.4960	.0040	2.96	.4985	.0015	3.35	.4996	.0004
2.66	.4961	.0039	2.97	.4985	.0015	3.40	.4997	.0003
2.67	.4962	.0038	2.98	.4986	.0014	3.45	.4997	.0003
2.68	.4963	.0037	2.99	.4986	.0014	3.50	.4998	.0002
2.69	.4964	.0036	3.00	.4987	.0013	3.60	.4998	.0002
2.70	.4965	.0035	3.01	.4987	.0013	3.70	.4999	.0001
2.71	.4966	.0034	3.02	.4987	.0013	3.80	.4999	.0001
2.72	.4967	.0033	3.03	.4988	.0012	3.90	.49995	.00005
2.73	.4968	.0032	3.04	.4988	.0012	4.00	.49997	.00003

Source: Based on Freund, J. E. (2004) *Modern elementary statistics* (11th ed.). Upper Saddle River, NJ: Pearson Prentice Hall.

TABLE C.2   Critical Values for the *t* Distribution

Table entries are values of *t* corresponding to proportions in one tail or in two tails combined.

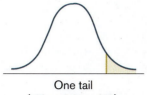 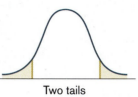

One tail
(either right or left)

Two tails
combined

	Proportion in One Tail					
	.25	.10	.05	.025	.01	.005
	Proportion in Two Tails Combined					
df	.50	.20	.10	.05	.02	.01
1	1.000	3.078	6.314	12.706	31.821	63.657
2	0.816	1.886	2.920	4.303	6.965	9.925
3	0.765	1.638	2.353	3.182	4.541	5.841
4	0.741	1.533	2.132	2.776	3.747	4.604
5	0.727	1.476	2.015	2.571	3.365	4.032
6	0.718	1.440	1.943	2.447	3.143	3.707
7	0.711	1.415	1.895	2.365	2.998	3.499
8	0.706	1.397	1.860	2.306	2.896	3.355
9	0.703	1.383	1.833	2.282	2.821	3.250
10	0.700	1.372	1.812	2.228	2.764	3.169
11	0.697	1.363	1.796	2.201	2.718	3.106
12	0.695	1.356	1.782	2.179	2.681	3.055
13	0.694	1.350	1.771	2.160	2.650	3.012
14	0.692	1.345	1.761	2.145	2.624	2.977
15	0.691	1.341	1.753	2.131	2.602	2.947
16	0.690	1.337	1.746	2.120	2.583	2.921
17	0.689	1.333	1.740	2.110	2.567	2.898
18	0.688	1.330	1.734	2.101	2.552	2.878
19	0.688	1.328	1.729	2.093	2.539	2.861
20	0.687	1.325	1.725	2.086	2.528	2.845

(Continued)

TABLE C.2 (Continued)

df	Proportion in One Tail					
	.25	.10	.05	.025	.01	.005
	Proportion in Two Tails Combined					
	.50	.20	.10	.05	.02	.01
21	0.686	1.323	1.721	2.080	2.518	2.831
22	0.686	1.321	1.717	2.074	2.508	2.819
23	0.685	1.319	1.714	2.069	2.500	2.807
24	0.685	1.318	1.711	2.064	2.492	2.797
25	0.684	1.316	1.708	2.060	2.485	2.787
26	0.684	1.315	1.706	2.056	2.479	2.779
27	0.684	1.314	1.703	2.052	2.473	2.771
28	0.683	1.313	1.701	2.048	2.467	2.763
29	0.683	1.311	1.699	2.045	2.462	2.756
30	0.683	1.310	1.697	2.042	2.457	2.750
40	0.681	1.303	1.684	2.021	2.423	2.704
60	0.679	1.296	1.671	2.000	2.390	2.660
120	0.677	1.289	1.658	1.980	2.358	2.617
∞	0.674	1.282	1.645	1.960	2.326	2.576

Source: Table III of Fisher, R. A., & Yates, F. (1974). *Statistical tables for biological, agricultural and medical research* (6th ed.). London, England: Longman Group Ltd. (previously published by Oliver and Boyd Ltd., Edinburgh). Adapted and reprinted with permission of Addison Wesley Longman.

TABLE C.3   Critical Values for the *F* Distribution

Critical values at a .05 level of significance are given in lightface type.
Critical values at a .01 level of significance are given in boldface type.

<table>
<tr><th colspan="13">Degrees of Freedom Numerator</th></tr>
<tr><th></th><th>1</th><th>2</th><th>3</th><th>4</th><th>5</th><th>6</th><th>7</th><th>8</th><th>9</th><th>10</th><th>20</th><th>∞</th></tr>
<tr><td>1</td><td>161
4052</td><td>200
5000</td><td>216
5403</td><td>225
5625</td><td>230
5764</td><td>234
5859</td><td>237
5928</td><td>239
5928</td><td>241
6023</td><td>242
6056</td><td>248
6209</td><td>254
6366</td></tr>
<tr><td>2</td><td>18.51
98.49</td><td>19.00
99.00</td><td>19.16
99.17</td><td>19.25
99.25</td><td>19.30
99.30</td><td>19.33
99.33</td><td>19.36
99.34</td><td>19.37
99.36</td><td>19.38
99.38</td><td>19.39
99.40</td><td>19.44
99.45</td><td>19.5
99.5</td></tr>
<tr><td>3</td><td>10.13
34.12</td><td>9.55
30.92</td><td>9.28
29.46</td><td>9.12
28.71</td><td>9.01
28.24</td><td>8.94
27.91</td><td>8.88
27.67</td><td>8.84
27.49</td><td>8.81
27.34</td><td>8.78
27.23</td><td>8.66
26.69</td><td>8.5
26.1</td></tr>
<tr><td>4</td><td>7.71
21.20</td><td>6.94
18.00</td><td>6.59
16.69</td><td>6.39
15.98</td><td>6.26
15.52</td><td>6.16
15.21</td><td>6.09
14.98</td><td>6.04
14.80</td><td>6.00
14.66</td><td>5.96
14.54</td><td>5.80
14.02</td><td>5.6
13.5</td></tr>
<tr><td>5</td><td>6.61
16.26</td><td>5.79
13.27</td><td>5.41
12.06</td><td>5.19
11.39</td><td>5.05
10.97</td><td>4.95
10.67</td><td>4.88
10.45</td><td>4.82
10.27</td><td>4.78
10.15</td><td>4.74
10.05</td><td>4.56
9.55</td><td>4.37
9.02</td></tr>
<tr><td>6</td><td>5.99
13.74</td><td>5.14
10.92</td><td>4.76
9.78</td><td>4.53
9.15</td><td>4.39
8.75</td><td>4.28
8.47</td><td>4.21
8.26</td><td>4.15
8.10</td><td>4.10
7.98</td><td>4.06
7.87</td><td>3.87
7.39</td><td>3.67
6.88</td></tr>
<tr><td>7</td><td>5.59
13.74</td><td>4.74
9.55</td><td>4.35
8.45</td><td>4.12
7.85</td><td>3.97
7.46</td><td>3.87
7.19</td><td>3.79
7.00</td><td>3.73
6.84</td><td>3.68
6.71</td><td>3.63
6.62</td><td>3.44
6.15</td><td>3.23
5.65</td></tr>
<tr><td>8</td><td>5.32
11.26</td><td>4.46
8.65</td><td>4.07
7.59</td><td>3.84
7.01</td><td>3.69
6.63</td><td>3.58
6.37</td><td>3.50
6.19</td><td>3.44
6.03</td><td>3.39
5.91</td><td>3.34
5.82</td><td>3.15
5.36</td><td>2.93
4.86</td></tr>
<tr><td>9</td><td>5.12
10.56</td><td>4.26
8.02</td><td>3.86
6.99</td><td>3.63
6.42</td><td>3.48
6.06</td><td>3.37
5.80</td><td>3.29
5.62</td><td>3.23
5.47</td><td>3.18
5.35</td><td>3.13
5.26</td><td>2.93
4.80</td><td>2.71
4.31</td></tr>
<tr><td>10</td><td>4.96
10.04</td><td>4.10
7.56</td><td>3.71
6.55</td><td>3.48
5.99</td><td>3.33
5.64</td><td>3.22
5.39</td><td>3.14
5.21</td><td>3.07
5.06</td><td>3.02
4.95</td><td>2.97
4.85</td><td>2.77
4.41</td><td>2.54
3.91</td></tr>
<tr><td>11</td><td>4.84
9.65</td><td>3.98
7.20</td><td>3.59
6.22</td><td>3.36
5.67</td><td>3.20
5.32</td><td>3.09
5.07</td><td>3.01
4.88</td><td>2.95
4.74</td><td>2.90
4.63</td><td>2.86
4.54</td><td>2.65
4.10</td><td>2.40
3.60</td></tr>
<tr><td>12</td><td>4.75
9.33</td><td>3.89
6.93</td><td>3.49
5.95</td><td>3.26
5.41</td><td>3.11
5.06</td><td>3.00
4.82</td><td>2.92
4.65</td><td>2.85
4.50</td><td>2.80
4.39</td><td>2.76
4.30</td><td>2.54
3.86</td><td>2.30
3.36</td></tr>
<tr><td>13</td><td>4.67
9.07</td><td>3.80
6.70</td><td>3.41
5.74</td><td>3.18
5.20</td><td>3.02
4.86</td><td>2.92
4.62</td><td>2.84
4.44</td><td>2.77
4.30</td><td>2.72
4.19</td><td>2.67
4.10</td><td>2.46
3.67</td><td>2.21
3.17</td></tr>
<tr><td>14</td><td>4.60
8.86</td><td>3.74
6.51</td><td>3.34
5.56</td><td>3.11
5.03</td><td>2.96
4.69</td><td>2.85
4.46</td><td>2.77
4.28</td><td>2.70
4.14</td><td>2.65
4.03</td><td>2.60
3.94</td><td>2.39
3.51</td><td>2.13
3.00</td></tr>
<tr><td>15</td><td>4.54
8.68</td><td>3.68
6.36</td><td>3.29
5.42</td><td>3.06
4.89</td><td>2.90
4.56</td><td>2.79
4.32</td><td>2.70
4.14</td><td>2.64
4.00</td><td>2.59
3.89</td><td>2.55
3.80</td><td>2.33
3.36</td><td>2.07
2.87</td></tr>
</table>

Degrees of Freedom Denominator

(Continued)

TABLE C.3 (Continued)

		1	2	3	4	5	6	7	8	9	10	20	∞
		Degrees of Freedom Numerator											
Degrees of Freedom Denominator	16	4.49 **8.53**	3.63 **6.23**	3.24 **5.29**	3.01 **4.77**	2.85 **4.44**	2.74 **4.20**	2.66 **4.03**	2.59 **3.89**	2.54 **3.78**	2.49 **3.69**	2.28 **3.25**	2.01 **2.75**
	17	4.45 **8.40**	3.59 **6.11**	3.20 **5.18**	2.96 **4.67**	2.81 **4.34**	2.70 **4.10**	2.62 **3.93**	2.55 **3.79**	2.50 **3.68**	2.45 **3.59**	2.23 **3.16**	1.96 **2.65**
	18	4.41 **8.28**	3.55 **6.01**	3.16 **5.09**	2.93 **4.58**	2.77 **4.25**	2.66 **4.01**	2.58 **3.85**	2.51 **3.71**	2.46 **3.60**	2.41 **3.51**	2.19 **3.07**	1.92 **2.57**
	19	4.38 **8.18**	3.52 **5.93**	3.13 **5.01**	2.90 **4.50**	2.74 **4.17**	2.63 **3.94**	2.55 **3.77**	2.48 **3.63**	2.43 **3.52**	2.38 **3.43**	2.15 **3.00**	1.88 **2.49**
	20	4.35 **8.10**	3.49 **5.85**	3.10 **4.94**	2.87 **4.43**	2.71 **4.10**	2.60 **3.87**	2.52 **3.71**	2.45 **3.56**	2.40 **3.45**	2.35 **3.37**	2.12 **2.94**	1.84 **2.42**
	21	4.32 **8.02**	3.47 **5.78**	3.07 **4.87**	2.84 **4.37**	2.68 **4.04**	2.57 **3.81**	2.49 **3.65**	2.42 **3.51**	2.37 **3.40**	2.32 **3.31**	2.09 **2.88**	1.81 **2.36**
	22	4.30 **7.94**	3.44 **5.72**	3.05 **4.82**	2.82 **4.31**	2.66 **3.99**	2.55 **3.76**	2.47 **3.59**	2.40 **3.45**	2.35 **3.35**	2.30 **3.26**	2.07 **2.83**	1.78 **2.31**
	23	4.28 **7.88**	3.42 **5.66**	3.03 **4.76**	2.80 **4.26**	2.64 **3.94**	2.53 **3.71**	2.45 **3.54**	2.38 **3.41**	2.32 **3.30**	2.28 **3.21**	2.04 **2.78**	1.76 **2.26**
	24	4.26 **7.82**	3.40 **5.61**	3.01 **4.72**	2.78 **4.22**	2.62 **3.90**	2.51 **3.67**	2.43 **3.50**	2.36 **3.36**	2.30 **3.25**	2.26 **3.17**	2.02 **2.74**	1.73 **2.21**
	25	4.24 **7.77**	3.38 **5.57**	2.99 **4.68**	2.76 **4.18**	2.60 **3.86**	2.49 **3.63**	2.41 **3.46**	2.34 **3.32**	2.28 **3.21**	2.24 **3.13**	2.00 **2.70**	1.71 **2.17**
	26	4.22 **7.72**	3.37 **5.53**	2.98 **4.64**	2.74 **4.14**	2.59 **3.82**	2.47 **3.59**	2.39 **3.42**	2.32 **3.29**	2.27 **3.17**	2.22 **3.09**	1.99 **2.66**	1.69 **2.13**
	27	4.21 **7.68**	3.35 **5.49**	2.96 **4.60**	2.73 **4.11**	2.57 **3.79**	2.46 **3.56**	2.37 **3.39**	2.30 **3.26**	2.25 **3.14**	2.20 **3.06**	1.97 **2.63**	1.67 **2.10**
	28	4.20 **7.64**	3.34 **5.45**	2.95 **4.57**	2.71 **4.07**	2.56 **3.76**	2.44 **3.53**	2.36 **3.36**	2.29 **3.23**	2.24 **3.11**	2.19 **3.03**	1.96 **2.60**	1.65 **2.07**
	29	4.18 **7.60**	3.33 **5.42**	2.93 **4.54**	2.70 **4.04**	2.54 **3.73**	2.43 **3.50**	2.35 **3.33**	2.28 **3.20**	2.22 **3.08**	2.18 **3.00**	1.94 **2.57**	1.63 **2.04**
	30	4.17 **7.56**	3.32 **5.39**	2.92 **4.51**	2.69 **4.02**	2.53 **3.70**	2.42 **3.47**	2.34 **3.30**	2.27 **3.17**	2.21 **3.06**	2.16 **2.98**	1.93 **2.55**	1.61 **2.01**
	31	4.16 **7.53**	3.30 **5.36**	2.91 **4.48**	2.68 **3.99**	2.52 **3.67**	2.41 **3.45**	2.32 **3.28**	2.25 **3.15**	2.20 **3.04**	2.15 **2.96**	1.92 **2.53**	1.60 **1.89**
	32	4.15 **7.50**	3.29 **5.34**	2.90 **4.46**	2.67 **3.97**	2.51 **3.65**	2.40 **3.43**	2.31 **3.26**	2.24 **3.13**	2.19 **3.02**	2.14 **2.93**	1.91 **2.51**	1.59 **1.88**

		1	2	3	4	5	6	7	8	9	10	20	∞
		Degrees of Freedom Numerator											
Degrees of Freedom Denominator	33	4.14 **7.47**	3.28 **5.31**	2.89 **4.44**	2.66 **3.95**	2.50 **3.63**	2.39 **3.41**	2.30 **3.24**	2.23 **3.11**	2.18 **3.00**	2.13 **2.91**	1.90 **2.49**	1.58 **1.87**
	34	4.13 **7.44**	3.28 **5.29**	2.88 **4.42**	2.65 **3.93**	2.49 **3.61**	2.38 **3.39**	2.29 **3.22**	2.23 **3.09**	2.17 **2.98**	2.12 **2.89**	1.89 **2.47**	1.57 **1.86**
	35	4.12 **7.42**	3.27 **5.27**	2.87 **4.40**	2.64 **3.91**	2.49 **3.59**	2.37 **3.37**	2.29 **3.20**	2.22 **3.07**	2.16 **2.96**	2.11 **2.88**	1.88 **2.45**	1.56 **1.85**
	36	4.11 **7.40**	3.26 **5.25**	2.87 **4.38**	2.63 **3.89**	2.48 **3.57**	2.36 **3.35**	2.28 **3.18**	2.21 **3.05**	2.15 **2.95**	2.11 **2.86**	1.87 **2.43**	1.55 **1.84**
	37	4.11 **7.37**	3.25 **5.23**	2.86 **4.36**	2.63 **3.87**	2.47 **3.56**	2.36 **3.33**	2.27 **3.17**	2.20 **3.04**	2.14 **2.93**	2.10 **2.84**	1.86 **2.42**	1.54 **1.83**
	38	4.10 **7.35**	3.24 **5.21**	2.85 **4.34**	2.62 **3.86**	2.46 **3.54**	2.35 **3.32**	2.26 **3.15**	2.19 **3.02**	2.14 **2.92**	2.09 **2.83**	1.85 **2.40**	1.53 **1.82**
	39	4.09 **7.33**	3.24 **5.19**	2.85 **4.33**	2.61 **3.84**	2.46 **3.53**	2.34 **3.30**	2.26 **3.14**	2.19 **3.01**	2.13 **2.90**	2.08 **2.81**	1.84 **2.39**	1.52 **1.81**
	40	4.08 **7.31**	3.23 **5.18**	2.84 **4.31**	2.61 **3.83**	2.45 **3.51**	2.34 **3.29**	2.25 **3.12**	2.18 **2.99**	2.12 **2.88**	2.07 **2.80**	1.84 **2.37**	1.51 **1.80**
	42	4.07 **7.27**	3.22 **5.15**	2.83 **4.29**	2.59 **3.80**	2.44 **3.49**	2.32 **3.26**	2.24 **3.10**	2.17 **2.96**	2.11 **2.86**	2.06 **2.77**	1.82 **2.35**	1.50 **1.78**
	44	4.06 **7.24**	3.21 **5.12**	2.82 **4.26**	2.58 **3.78**	2.43 **3.46**	2.31 **3.24**	2.23 **3.07**	2.16 **2.94**	2.10 **2.84**	2.05 **2.75**	1.81 **2.32**	1.49 **1.76**
	60	4.00 **7.08**	3.15 **4.98**	2.76 **4.13**	2.53 **3.65**	2.37 **3.34**	2.25 **3.12**	2.17 **2.95**	2.10 **2.82**	2.04 **2.72**	1.99 **2.63**	1.75 **2.20**	1.39 **1.60**
	120	3.92 **6.85**	3.07 **4.79**	2.68 **3.95**	2.45 **3.48**	2.29 **3.17**	2.18 **2.96**	2.09 **2.79**	2.02 **2.66**	1.96 **2.56**	1.91 **2.47**	1.66 **2.03**	1.25 **1.38**
	∞	3.84 **6.63**	3.00 **4.61**	2.60 **3.78**	2.37 **3.32**	2.21 **3.02**	2.10 **2.80**	2.01 **2.64**	1.94 **2.51**	1.88 **2.41**	1.83 **2.32**	1.57 **1.88**	1.00 **1.00**

Source: The entries in this table were computed by the author.

TABLE C.4   The Studentized Range Statistic (q)

The critical values for q correspond to alpha = .05 (lightface type) and alpha = .01 (boldface type).

df_E	Range								
	2	3	4	5	6	7	8	9	10
6	3.46	4.34	4.90	5.30	5.63	5.91	6.13	6.32	6.50
	5.24	**6.32**	**7.02**	**7.55**	**7.98**	**8.33**	**8.62**	**8.87**	**9.10**
7	3.34	4.17	4.68	5.06	5.36	5.60	5.82	5.99	6.15
	4.95	**5.91**	**6.54**	**7.00**	**7.38**	**7.69**	**7.94**	**8.17**	**8.38**
8	3.26	4.05	4.53	4.89	5.17	5.41	5.60	5.78	5.93
	4.75	**5.64**	**6.21**	**6.63**	**6.97**	**7.26**	**7.47**	**7.70**	**7.89**
9	3.20	3.95	4.42	4.76	5.03	5.24	5.43	5.60	5.74
	4.60	**5.43**	**5.95**	**6.34**	**6.67**	**6.91**	**7.13**	**7.33**	**7.50**
10	3.15	3.88	4.33	4.66	4.92	5.12	5.30	5.46	5.60
	4.48	**5.27**	**5.77**	**6.14**	**6.43**	**6.67**	**6.89**	**7.06**	**7.22**
11	3.11	3.82	4.27	4.59	4.83	5.03	5.21	5.36	5.49
	4.38	**5.16**	**5.63**	**5.98**	**6.25**	**6.48**	**6.69**	**6.85**	**7.01**
12	3.08	3.78	4.20	4.51	4.75	4.96	5.12	5.26	5.39
	4.32	**5.05**	**5.50**	**5.84**	**6.10**	**6.32**	**6.52**	**6.67**	**6.82**
13	3.05	3.73	4.15	4.47	4.69	4.88	5.06	5.21	5.33
	4.26	**4.97**	**5.41**	**5.74**	**5.98**	**6.19**	**6.39**	**6.53**	**6.68**
14	3.03	3.70	4.11	4.41	4.64	4.83	4.99	5.13	5.25
	4.21	**4.90**	**5.33**	**5.64**	**5.88**	**6.10**	**6.28**	**6.41**	**6.56**
15	3.01	3.68	4.09	4.38	4.59	4.79	4.95	5.09	5.21
	4.17	**4.84**	**5.26**	**5.56**	**5.80**	**6.01**	**6.18**	**6.31**	**6.46**
16	2.99	3.65	4.05	4.33	4.56	4.74	4.89	5.03	5.15
	4.13	**4.79**	**5.19**	**5.50**	**5.72**	**5.94**	**6.10**	**6.23**	**6.37**
17	2.98	3.63	4.02	4.30	4.52	4.70	4.85	4.99	5.11
	4.10	**4.75**	**5.15**	**5.44**	**5.66**	**5.86**	**6.02**	**6.14**	**6.28**
18	2.97	3.62	4.01	4.29	4.49	4.68	4.84	4.97	5.08
	4.07	**4.71**	**5.10**	**5.39**	**5.60**	**5.80**	**5.95**	**6.08**	**6.21**
19	2.96	3.59	3.98	4.26	4.47	4.65	4.80	4.93	5.04
	4.05	**4.68**	**5.05**	**5.35**	**5.56**	**5.75**	**5.91**	**6.03**	**6.15**
20	2.95	3.58	3.96	4.24	4.45	4.63	4.78	4.91	5.01
	4.02	**4.64**	**5.02**	**5.31**	**5.51**	**5.71**	**5.86**	**5.98**	**6.09**
22	2.94	3.55	3.93	4.20	4.41	4.58	4.72	4.85	4.96
	3.99	**4.59**	**4.96**	**5.27**	**5.44**	**5.62**	**5.76**	**5.87**	**6.00**

df_E	Range								
	2	3	4	5	6	7	8	9	10
24	2.92 **3.96**	3.53 **4.55**	3.91 **4.92**	4.17 **5.17**	4.37 **5.37**	4.54 **5.55**	4.69 **5.70**	4.81 **5.81**	4.92 **5.93**
26	2.91 **3.94**	3.52 **4.51**	3.89 **4.87**	4.15 **5.13**	4.36 **5.33**	4.53 **5.49**	4.67 **5.63**	4.79 **5.74**	4.90 **5.86**
28	2.90 **3.91**	3.50 **4.48**	3.87 **4.83**	4.12 **5.09**	4.33 **5.28**	4.49 **5.45**	4.63 **5.58**	4.75 **5.69**	4.86 **5.81**
30	2.89 **3.89**	3.49 **4.45**	3.85 **4.80**	4.10 **5.05**	4.30 **5.24**	4.47 **5.40**	0.60 **5.54**	4.73 **5.64**	4.84 **5.76**
40	2.86 **3.82**	3.45 **4.37**	3.79 **4.70**	4.05 **4.93**	4.23 **5.11**	4.39 **5.26**	4.52 **5.39**	4.65 **5.49**	4.73 **5.60**
60	2.83 **3.76**	3.41 **4.28**	3.75 **4.60**	3.98 **4.82**	4.16 **4.99**	4.31 **5.13**	4.44 **5.25**	4.56 **5.36**	4.65 **5.45**
100	2.81 **3.72**	3.36 **4.22**	3.70 **4.52**	3.93 **4.74**	4.11 **4.90**	4.26 **5.04**	4.39 **5.15**	4.50 **5.23**	4.59 **5.34**
∞	2.77 **3.64**	3.31 **4.12**	3.63 **4.40**	3.86 **4.60**	4.03 **4.76**	4.17 **4.88**	4.28 **4.99**	4.39 **5.08**	4.47 **5.16**

Source: The entries in this table were computed by the author.

TABLE C.5 Critical Values for the Pearson Correlation*

*To be significant, the sample correlation, r, must be greater than or equal to the critical value in the table.

$df = n - 2$	Level of Significance for One-Tailed Test			
	.05	.025	.01	.005
	Level of Significance for Two-Tailed Test			
	.10	.05	.02	.01
1	.988	.997	.9995	.99999
2	.900	.950	.980	.990
3	.805	.878	.934	.959
4	.729	.811	.882	.917
5	.669	.754	.833	.874
6	.622	.707	.789	.834
7	.582	.666	.750	.798
8	.549	.632	.716	.765
9	.521	.602	.685	.735
10	.497	.576	.658	.708
11	.476	.553	.634	.684
12	.458	.532	.612	.661
13	.441	.514	.592	.641
14	.426	.497	.574	.623
15	.412	.482	.558	.606
16	.400	.468	.542	.590
17	.389	.456	.528	.575
18	.378	.444	.516	.561
19	.369	.433	.503	.549
20	.360	.423	.492	.537
21	.352	.413	.482	.526
22	.344	.404	.472	.515
23	.337	.396	.462	.505
24	.330	.388	.453	.496

df = n − 2	Level of Significance for One-Tailed Test			
	.05	.025	.01	.005
	Level of Significance for Two-Tailed Test			
	.10	.05	.02	.01
25	.323	.381	.445	.487
26	.317	.374	.437	.479
27	.311	.367	.430	.471
28	.306	.361	.423	.463
29	.301	.355	.416	.456
30	.296	.349	.409	.449
35	.275	.325	.381	.418
40	.257	.304	.358	.393
45	.243	.288	.338	.372
50	.231	.273	.322	.354
60	.211	.250	.295	.325
70	.195	.232	.274	.302
80	.183	.217	.256	.283
90	.173	.205	.242	.267
100	.164	.195	.230	.254

Source: Table VI of Fisher, R. A., & Yates, F. (1974). *Statistical tables for biological, agricultural and medical research* (6th ed.). London, England: Longman Group Ltd., 1974 (previously published by Oliver and Boyd Ltd., Edinburgh). Adapted and reprinted with permission of Addison Wesley Longman.

TABLE C.6   Critical Values for the Spearman Correlation*

*To be significant, the sample correlation, r, must be greater than or equal to the critical value in the table.

	Level of Significance for One-Tailed Test			
	.05	.025	.01	.005
	Level of Significance for Two-Tailed Test			
n	.10	.05	.02	.01
4	1.000			
5	.900	1.000	1.000	
6	.829	.886	.943	1.000
7	.714	.786	.893	.929
8	.643	.738	.833	.881
9	.600	.700	.783	.833
10	.564	.648	.745	.794
11	.536	.618	.709	.755
12	.503	.587	.671	.727
13	.484	.560	.648	.703
14	.464	.538	.622	.675
15	.443	.521	.604	.654
16	.429	.503	.582	.635
17	.414	.485	.566	.615
18	.401	.472	.550	.600
19	.391	.460	.535	.584
20	.380	.447	.520	.570
21	.370	.435	.508	.556
22	.361	.425	.496	.544
23	.353	.415	.486	.532
24	.344	.406	.476	.521
25	.337	.398	.466	.511
26	.331	.390	.457	.501
27	.324	.382	.448	.491

n	Level of Significance for One-Tailed Test			
	.05	**.025**	**.01**	**.005**
	Level of Significance for Two-Tailed Test			
	.10	**.05**	**.02**	**.01**
28	.317	.375	.440	.483
29	.312	.368	.433	.475
30	.306	.362	.425	.467
35	.283	.335	.394	.433
40	.264	.313	.368	.405
45	.248	.294	.347	.382
50	.235	.279	.329	.363
60	.214	.255	.300	.331
70	.190	.235	.278	.307
80	.185	.220	.260	.287
90	.174	.207	.245	.271
100	.165	.197	.233	.257

Source: Reprinted with permission from the *Journal of the American Statistical Association.* Copyright 1972 by the American Statistical Association. All rights reserved.

TABLE C.7   Critical Values for Chi-Square (χ^2)

df	Level of Significance .05	Level of Significance .01
1	3.84	6.64
2	5.99	9.21
3	7.81	11.34
4	9.49	13.28
5	11.07	15.09
6	12.59	16.81
7	14.07	18.48
8	15.51	20.09
9	16.92	21.67
10	18.31	23.21
11	19.68	24.72
12	21.03	26.22
13	22.36	27.69
14	23.68	29.14
15	25.00	30.58
16	26.30	32.00
17	27.59	33.41
18	28.87	34.80
19	30.14	36.19
20	31.41	37.47
21	32.67	38.93
22	33.92	40.29
23	35.17	41.64
24	36.42	42.98
25	37.65	44.31
26	38.88	45.64
27	40.11	46.96
28	41.34	48.28
29	42.56	49.59
30	43.77	50.89
40	55.76	63.69
50	67.50	76.15
60	79.08	88.38
70	90.53	100.42

Source: From Table IV of Fisher, R. A., & Yates, F. (1974). *Statistical tables for biological, agricultural and medical research* (6th ed.). London, England: Longman Group Ltd., 1974 (previously published by Oliver and Boyd Ltd., Edinburgh). Adapted and reprinted with permission of Addison Wesley Longman.

••• Appendix D

Solutions for Even-Numbered Problems

CHAPTER 1

2. Data describe a set of measurements (made up of raw scores); a raw score describes individual measurements.

4. Experimental, quasi-experimental, and correlational research methods.

6. The four scales of measurement are nominal, ordinal, interval, and ratio. Ratio scale measurements are the most informative.

8. Interval variables *do not* have a true zero, and ratio variables *do* have a true zero.

10. Continuous and discrete variables.

12. (a) False. (b) True. (c) True.

14. The statistics class has a *population* of 25 students enrolled, but a *sample* of only 23 students attended.

16. An experimental research method because the researcher claims to have demonstrated *cause*.

18. (a) Quasi-independent variable. (b) Quasi-independent variable. (c) Independent variable. (d) Independent variable. (e) Quasi-independent variable. (f) Independent variable.

20. (a) Mindfulness training. (b) Impulsive behavior.

22. Nominal, ordinal, interval, and ratio.

24. (a) Qualitative. (b) Quantitative. (c) Quantitative. (d) Qualitative.

26.

Variable	Continuous vs. Discrete	Quantitative vs. Qualitative	Scale of Measurement
Sex (male, female)	Discrete	Qualitative	Nominal
Seasons (spring, summer, fall, winter)	Discrete	Qualitative	Nominal
Time of day	Continuous	Quantitative	Ratio
Rating scale score	Discrete	Quantitative	Interval
Movie ratings (1 to 4 stars)	Discrete	Quantitative	Ordinal
Number of students in your class	Discrete	Quantitative	Ratio
Temperature (degrees Fahrenheit)	Continuous	Quantitative	Interval
Time (in minutes) to prepare dinner	Continuous	Quantitative	Ratio
Position standing in line	Discrete	Quantitative	Ordinal

28. An operational definition.

30. (a) Continuous. (b) Quantitative. (c) Ratio scale.

32. Rating scale data are often treated as interval scale data because the data have no true zero and it is assumed that data on these scales are equidistant.

CHAPTER 2

2. Grouped data are distributed in intervals; ungrouped data are not.

4. To ensure that a single score cannot be counted in more than one interval.

6. Ungrouped data sets with only a few different scores, and qualitative or categorical variables.

8. Midpoint; Upper boundary.

10. Discrete/categorical data.

12. (a)

Classes	$f(x)$
L	9
C	16
R	5

(b) Yes, the rat did press the center lever the most.

14. Three errors are (1) the intervals overlap, (2) the class width for each interval is not equal, and (3) the distribution includes an open interval.

16. The upper boundaries are 3, 6, 9, 12, 15, and 18.

18. The interval width for each interval is 3.

20. Sixty children qualify for the new cognitive behavioral therapy.

22. (a) Histogram. (b) Bar chart. (c) Histogram. (d) Bar chart.

24. (a) A = 78, B = 86, C = 68, D = 13. (b) Yes, this was a difficult test because half the class would fail.

26.

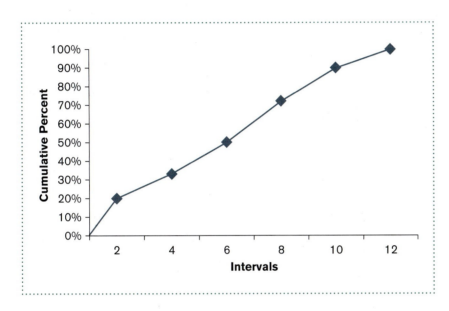

28.

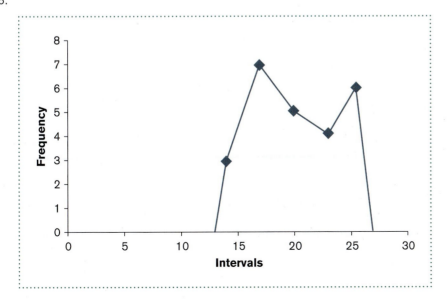

30. The percentile point for the 50th percentile is 74.5.

32. (a) While more men earned a bachelor's degree in psychology in 1970–1971, women earned more than three times the number of bachelor's degrees in psychology as of 2005–2006. (b) Ungrouped data, because years are not distributed consecutively.

34. (a) A relative percent distribution. (b) About 742 adults worldwide.

CHAPTER 3

2. Measures of central tendency are statistical measures used to locate a single score that is most representative or descriptive of all scores in a distribution.

4. A population mean is the mean for a set of scores in an entire population, whereas the sample mean is the mean for a sample, or subset of scores from a population.

6. The weighted mean equals the arithmetic mean when the sample sizes or "weights" for a set of scores are the same or equal.

8. Data that are skewed and ordinal data.

10. (a) Median. (b) Mean. (c) Mean.

12. (a) College students: mean = 25, median = 18, mode = 21. Parents: mean = 14, median = 18, mode = 21. (b) Because both distributions are skewed, the median would be the appropriate measure of central tendency. This might be misleading, though, because the median indicates that texting was the same between groups (the median was 18 in both samples), even though differences exist in regard to the mean.

14. The mean because the data are normally distributed, and the duration (in hours) is a ratio scale measure.

16. The median because the data are negatively skewed.

18. Bimodal distribution.

20. Weighted mean = 3.65.

22. (a) $M = 22$ points. (b) $M = 10$ points. (c) $M = 24$ points. (d) $M = 6$ points.

24. The sum of the differences of scores from the mean is 0.

26. The mean will increase.

28. The new mean weight is 190 pounds.

30. (a) Women. (b) Men. (c) Men.

32. Yes, participants consumed most of the food that was closest to them in each group.

CHAPTER 4

2. Two scores; the largest and smallest score in a distribution.

4. The variance is preferred because it includes all scores to estimate variability.

6. The variance of the sample will equal the variance of the population from which the sample was selected, on average.

8. The standard deviation measures the average distance that scores deviate from their mean.

10. The standard deviation is always positive; is used to describe quantitative variables, typically reported with the mean; and is affected by the value of every score in a distribution.

12. (a) Range = 98 − 77 = 21. (b) IQR = 96 − 85 = 11. (c) SIQR = 5.5. (d) $s^2 = 55.41$. (e) $SD = 7.44$.

14. (a) $df = 30$. (b) $s^2 = \frac{120}{30} = 4.0$, $SD = \sqrt{4} = 2$.

16. No. In both cases, the variance is the square of the standard deviation. So the population and sample variance will be $12^2 = 144$.

18. (a) Decrease. (b) Increase. (c) No effect.

20. (a) Increase. (b) No effect. (c) Decrease.

22. $s^2 = \frac{240}{60-1} = 4.07$; $SD = \sqrt{4.07} = 2.02$.

24. (a) $SD = 4$. (b) $SD = 8$.

26. $SS = 37.50$, $s^2 = 5.36$, $SD = 2.31$.

28. $SD = 0.5$.

30. (a) Yes. Husbands and wives show a similar distribution in their ratings of love.

    (b) The ratings of love data are negatively skewed for husbands and for wives. Thus, most husbands and most wives appear to give higher ratings of love, with a few giving much lower ratings.

32. (a) Life satisfaction. (b) Both participant variables show an approximately negatively skewed distribution because the mean for both variables is closer to the high end of the range, indicating that the skew is to the left.

CHAPTER 5

2. Two characteristics of probability: Probability varies between 0 and 1 and can never be negative.

4. The normal distribution.

6. The mean equals 0, and the standard deviation equals 1.

8. The standard normal transformation is the difference between a score and the mean, divided by the standard deviation.

10. Step 1: Locate the z score associated with a given proportion in the unit normal table. Step 2: Transform the z score into a raw score (x).

12. 3,000 mothers were not satisfied.

14. (a) .6915. (b) .0934. (c) .5000. (d) .0250. (e) .4602.

16. (a) The areas are equal. (b) The first area is bigger. (c) The first area is bigger. (d) The second area is bigger. (e) The second area is bigger.

18. (a) $z = 1.645$. (b) $z = -1.96$. (c) $z = -0.51$. (d) $z = 0$. (e) $z = 0$.

20. Students with a 3.56 GPA or higher will be offered a scholarship.

22. (a) The areas are equal. (b) The first area is bigger. (c) The second area is bigger. (d) The areas are equal. (e) The second area is bigger.

24. $SD = 1.50$.

26. $M = 136$.

28. Based on the empirical rule, it is informative to know whether a data set is normally distributed because the proportion or probability at each standard deviation from the mean is known and over 99% of data are accounted for within 3 SD of the mean.

30. (a) $p = .1587$. (b) $p = .0122$.

32. (a) Fast group. (b) Slow group.

CHAPTER 6

2. Sampling without replacement and conditional probabilities are related in that when we sample without replacement, the probability of each selection is conditional or dependent on the person or item that was selected in the previous selection.

4. When order matters, each time we select participants in a different order, it is counted as a different possible sample. When order does not matter, selecting participants in a different order is counted as the same sample.

6. The central limit theorem states that regardless of the distribution of scores in a population, the sampling distribution of sample means selected from that population will be approximately normal.

8. Yes, it can. The mean can be any value between positive infinity ($+\infty$) and negative infinity ($-\infty$).

10. To compute standard error, you need to know the population standard deviation and the sample size.

12. (a) The standard error would increase. (b) The standard error would decrease.

14. No, because each student is not selected at random, and each student's name is not replaced before selecting another student.

16. (a) 625 samples. (b) 4,096 samples. (c) 65,536 samples. (d) 6,250,000 samples.

18. (a) $\mu_M = 8$. (b) $\mu_M = 0$. (c) $\mu_M = -20$. (d) $\mu_M = \infty$. (e) $\mu_M = -\infty$. (f) $\mu_M = .03$.

20. (a) False. The central limit theorem explains that regardless of the distribution of scores in a population, the sampling distribution of sample means selected at random from that population will approach the shape of a normal distribution, as the number of samples in the sampling distribution increases. (b) True. (c) True.

22. (a) The shape of the sampling distribution is normally distributed. (b) 5. (c) A sample mean of 3.5 is less likely in Sample B, because as sample size increases, standard error decreases.

24. (a) $\mu_M = -30$. (b) $\sigma_M = \sigma_M = \dfrac{4}{\sqrt{16}} = 1.00$. (c) Sketch of sampling distribution with $M \pm 3\ SEM$:

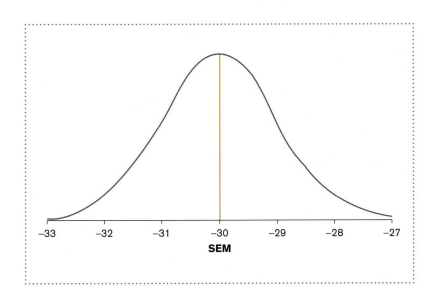

SEM

26. (a) Decreases. (b) Increases. (c) Decreases. (d) Increases.

28. (a) $5^3 = 125$ possible samples. (b) $\mu = \dfrac{9}{5} = 1.80$. The population mean is 1.80. (c) $= \sigma = \sqrt{\dfrac{28.80}{5}} = \sqrt{5.76} = 2.40$. The population standard deviation is 2.40.

30. $\sigma_M = \dfrac{2.40}{\sqrt{3}} = 1.39$.

32. A sampling distribution informs us of the likelihood of sample outcomes. Thus, we can infer (i.e., make a statistical inference) the likelihood of selecting any one sample, if we know the sampling distribution for the population from which the sample was selected.

CHAPTER 7

2. Reject the null hypothesis and retain the null hypothesis.

4. A Type II error is the probability of retaining a null hypothesis that is actually false. Researchers do not directly control for this type of error.

6. Critical values $= \pm 1.96$.

8. All four terms describe the same thing. The level of significance is represented by alpha, which defines the rejection region or the region associated with the probability of committing a Type I error.

10. Population standard deviation, beta error, and standard error.

12. In hypothesis testing, the significance of an effect determines whether or not an effect exists in some population. Effect size is used as a measure of how big the effect is in the population.

14. The population standard deviation is always larger than the standard error when $n > 1$ because the population standard deviation is divided by the square root of the sample size to calculate the standard error.

16. The sample size in the second sample was larger. Therefore, the second sample had more power to detect the effect, which is likely why the decisions were different.

18. (a) $\alpha = .05$. (b) $\alpha = .01$. (c) $\alpha = .001$.

20. (1a) Reject the null hypothesis. (1b) Reject the null hypothesis. (1c) Reject the null hypothesis. (1d) Retain the null hypothesis. (2a) Retain the null hypothesis. (2b) Retain the null hypothesis. (2c) Reject the null hypothesis. (2d) Reject the null hypothesis.

22. (a) $\sigma_M = \frac{7}{\sqrt{49}} = 1.0$; hence, $z_{obt} = \frac{74-72}{1} = 2.00$. The decision is to reject the null hypothesis. (b) $d = \frac{74-72}{7} = 0.29$. A medium effect size.

24. (a) $d = \frac{0.05}{0.4} = 0.125$. (b) $d = \frac{0.1}{0.4} = 0.25$ (c) $d = \frac{0.4}{0.4} = 1.00$.

26. (a) $d = \frac{1}{1} = 1.00$. Large effect size. (b) $d = \frac{1}{2} = 0.50$. Medium effect size.

    (c) $d = \frac{1}{4} = 0.25$. Medium effect size. (d) $d = \frac{1}{6} = 0.17$. Small effect size.

28. This will decrease standard error, thereby increasing power.

30. The point the authors are making is that it is possible with the same data to retain the null hypothesis for a two-tailed test and reject the null hypothesis for a one-tailed test.

32. (a) Two-tailed z test. (b) $\alpha = .05$.

34. Reject the null hypothesis.

CHAPTER 8

2. Because the sample variance is an unbiased estimator of the population variance—the sample variance will equal the value of the population variance on average.

4. The t distribution is a sampling distribution with a standard error that is computed using the sample variance to estimate the population variance. Hence, the degrees of freedom for sample variance $(n - 1)$ are also associated with each t distribution.

6. Estimated Cohen's d, eta-squared, and omega-squared.

8. Point estimation is a statistical procedure that involves the use of a sample statistic (e.g., a sample mean) to estimate a population parameter (e.g., a population mean). Interval estimation is a statistical procedure in which a sample of data is used to find the interval or range of possible values within which a population parameter is likely to be contained.

10. Step 1: Compute the sample mean and standard error. Step 2: Choose the level of confidence and find the critical values at that level of confidence. Step 3: Compute the estimation formula to find the confidence limits.

12. (1a) Reject the null hypothesis. (1b) Retain the null hypothesis. (1c) Reject the null hypothesis. (1d) Reject the null hypothesis. (2a) Retain the null hypothesis. (2b) Retain the null hypothesis. (2c) Reject the null hypothesis. (2d) Retain the null hypothesis.

14. (a) ±2.201. (b) −2.602. (c) ±2.779. (d) +1.699.

16. The decision would have been to retain the null hypothesis because the value of the null hypothesis, $\mu = 100$, is contained within the identified confidence interval.

18. (a) $t_{obt} = \frac{4.0 - 4.0}{0.474} = 0$. The decision is to retain the null hypothesis. (b) Estimated Cohen's $d = 0$ (no effect size).

20. (a) Yes. (b) $\eta^2 = .15$ (medium effect size).

22. (a) 90% CI = 66.39 to 73.61. (b) No. The new teaching strategy actually decreased grades compared to the population mean grade of 75 points.

24. (a) Large. (b) Medium. (c) Medium. (d) Small.

26. Yes, the researchers did observe a significant increase in mood because 0, the null hypothesis for this test, was not contained within the confidence interval.

28. (a) It is unknown because we do not know the population variance; instead, we use the sample variance to estimate the population variance. (b) The sample standard deviation is the denominator in the Cohen's d formula. Increasing sample size makes the sample standard deviation a better estimate of the population standard deviation,

thereby making estimated Cohen's *d* a better estimate of the actual size of an effect in a population.

30. The authors refer to the assumption of independence in that each observation in a sample is independent, meaning that one observation does not influence another.

32. Interval estimate.

CHAPTER 9

2. Different participants are observed in each group.

4. In terms of evaluating the difference between two groups, the less that scores in two groups overlap, the more likely we are to decide that two groups are different (i.e., a decision to reject the null hypothesis). The more that scores in two groups overlap, the more likely we are to attribute differences to random variation or error (i.e., a decision to retain the null hypothesis).

6. Estimated Cohen's *d*, eta-squared, and omega-squared.

8. The pooled sample standard deviation, which is the square root of the pooled sample variance.

10. Step 1: Compute the sample mean and standard error. Step 2: Choose the level of confidence and find the critical values at that level of confidence. Step 3: Compute the estimation formula to find the confidence limits.

12. (a) $df = 25$. (b) $df = 28$. (c) $df = 44$.

14. (a) Decrease. (b) Increase. (c) No effect.

16. (a) Increase. (b) No effect. (c) Decrease.

18. (a) The decision would have been to reject the null hypothesis because 0 is not contained within the confidence interval. (b) The point estimate is 2.0.

20. (a) $t_{obt} = \dfrac{(65.0 - 75.5) - 0}{4.413} = -1.926$. The decision is to reject the null hypothesis. (b) Estimated Cohen's *d*: $d = \dfrac{(65.0 - 75.5)}{9.842} = -0.86$ (large effect size).

22. The sample size is 20 at each school. The decision was to reject the null hypothesis ($p < .05$). The study showed a medium effect size.

24. (a) Medium. (b) Large. (c) Large.

26. (a) One-sample *t* test; two-independent-sample *t* test. (b) The smaller the degrees of freedom, the larger the value of the test statistic needed to reach a decision to reject the null hypothesis. Hence, for a given sample size, $N - 2$ will be associated with less power than $n - 1$ degrees of freedom.

28. The two-independent-sample *t* test, because the two groups being compared had different participants assigned (children who did and did not participate in sports).

30. The reason that researchers would remove outliers in a data set that are nonnormal is to satisfy the assumption for the two-independent-sample *t* test that the data are normally distributed. Removing outliers would make the data less skewed and thus presumably more normal in shape.

32. The assumption of normality, because if the data are skewed, this would directly violate this assumption.

CHAPTER 10

2. The repeated-measures design and the matched-pairs design.

4. Participants can be matched through experimental manipulation and natural occurrence.

6. The degrees of freedom for the related-samples *t* test are the number of difference scores minus 1.

8. Computing difference scores eliminates between-persons error.

10. No. Both research designs are associated with selecting related samples. The way that participants are selected is different, but not the computation of the test statistic for a related-samples *t* test.

12. Step 1: Compute the sample mean and standard error. Step 2: Choose the level of confidence and find the critical values at that level of confidence. Step 3: Compute the estimation formula to find the confidence limits.

14. (a) Matched-pairs design, $df = 19$. (b) Repeated-measures design, $df = 29$. (c) Matched-pairs design, $df = 24$. (d) Repeated-measures design, $df = 11$.

16. (a) $M_D = \frac{-4}{5} = -0.8$; $s_D = \sqrt{\frac{30.8}{5-1}} = 2.8$; $s_{MD} = \frac{2.8}{\sqrt{5}} = 1.3$.

(b)

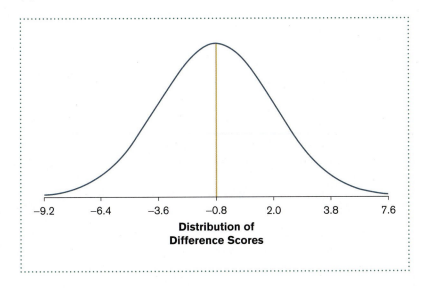

Distribution of Difference Scores

(c)

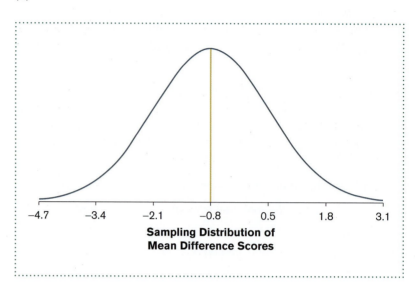

**Sampling Distribution of
Mean Difference Scores**

18. (a) $t_{obt} = \dfrac{4}{2} = 2.00$. (b) $t_{obt} = \dfrac{4}{8} = 0.5$. (c) $t_{obt} = \dfrac{8}{2} = 4.0$. (d) $t_{obt} = \dfrac{8}{16} = 0.5$.

20. (a) $t_{obt} = \dfrac{-5.5 - 0}{1.18} = -4.661$. The decision is to reject the null hypothesis.
    (b) Estimated Cohen's $d = \dfrac{-5.5}{3.338} = -1.65$ (large effect size).

22. (a) $t_{obt} = \dfrac{-195}{180.19} = -1.082$. The decision is to retain the null hypothesis.
    (b) Omega-squared: $\omega^2 = \dfrac{(-1.082)^2 - 1}{(-1.082)^2 + 9} = .02$ (small effect size). (c) The
    researcher did not find support for his hypothesis; the decision is that
    there is no mean difference in number of calories consumed between
    normal-weight and overweight siblings.

24. This was a repeated-measures design. The sample size was 120 par-
    ticipants. The decision was to reject the null hypothesis. This was a
    large effect size.

26. (a) Decrease. (b) No effect. (c) Increase.

28. (a) 95% CI = 7.03 to 16.97. (b) Yes. Children took between 7.03 and
    16.97 more bites of food wrapped in familiar packaging compared to
    plain packaging.

30. A within-subjects repeated-measures design means that the same
    participants are observed before and again after some treatment.

32. (a) $n = 102$. (b) Repeated-measures design. (c) $\eta^2 = \dfrac{(12.51)^2}{(12.51)^2 + 101} = .61$
    (large effect size).

34. Effect size.

CHAPTER 11

2. Study 1 because different participants were observed in each group.

4. Between-groups variation and within-groups variation.

6. (a) The sum of squares associated with the variability of scores between groups. (b) The sum of squares associated with the variability of scores within each group. (c) A measure of variance associated with differences between group means. It is the numerator for the test statistic. (d) A measure of variance associated with differences within each group. It is the denominator for the test statistic.

8. Compute post hoc tests.

10. When the same participants are observed in each group.

12. Omega-squared is the more conservative estimate.

14. (a) Within-subjects design. (b) Between-subjects design. (c) Between-subjects design. (d) Within-subjects design.

16. (a) No, because $k = 2$. (b) Yes, because $k > 2$ and the result is significant. (c) No, because the result is not significant.

18. $F = 0$. Because all group means are the same ($M = 6$), there is no variability between groups. The mean square between groups in the numerator is equal to 0, making the value of the test statistic equal to 0.

20. (a)

Source of Variation	SS	df	MS	F_{obt}
Between groups	30	2	15	11.72
Within groups (error)	50	39	1.28	
Total	80	41		

(b) $\eta^2 = \frac{30}{80}$ = .38. Large effect size. (c) Reject the null hypothesis.

22. (a) Decision: Reject the null hypothesis.

Source of Variation	SS	df	MS	F_{obt}
Between groups	76	2	38	7.13
Within groups (error)	80	15	5.33	
Total	156	17		

(b) A one-way ANOVA was significant, $F(2, 15) = 7.13$, $p < .05$, with recall being the greatest following no delay compared with a one-second delay (Tukey's HSD, $p < .05$). Otherwise, no significant differences were evident.

24. (a) Decision: Reject the null hypothesis.

Source of Variation	SS	df	MS	F_{obt}
Between groups	**396**	**2**	198	**5.50**
Between persons	234	**9**	**26**	
Within groups (error)	**648**	**18**	**36**	
Total	1,278	29		

(b) $\eta_p^2 \dfrac{396}{1{,}278-234} = .38.$

26. Decision: Reject the null hypothesis.

Source of Variation	SS	df	MS	F_{obt}
Between groups	77.46	3	25.82	17.77
Between persons	33.50	5	6.70	
Within groups (error)	21.79	15	1.45	
Total	132.75	23		

28. The four assumptions for the one-way between-subjects ANOVA are normality, random sampling, independence, and homogeneity of variance.

30. Eta-squared (η^2).

32. (a) 3 groups. (b) 123 total participants. Note: $df_E = N - k = 120$; $k = 3$; N must equal 123. (c) Yes. The decision was to reject the null hypothesis; the outcome was significant.

CHAPTER 12

2. Two factors: one with three levels and a second with two levels.

4. (a) Main effects are located in the row and column totals outside the table. (b) An interaction is located in the cells inside the table.

6. When two lines are not parallel, meaning that they touch or cross.

8. The within-groups or error source of variation.

10. The interaction because it is potentially most informative.

12. Omega-squared.

14. Factor A: Sex (two levels: male, female). Factor B: Reason for immoral act in the vignette (three levels: preservation, protection, self-gain).

16. (a) $M = 3$, $M = 7$ for the column totals. (b) $M = 4$, $M = 6$ for the row totals. (c) $M = 2$, $M = 6$, $M = 4$, $M = 8$ for each cell.

18. Reject the null hypothesis.

20. The value of the test statistic will decrease.

22. (a)

Source of Variation	SS	df	MS	F_{obt}
Season	44,204.17	1	44,204.17	5.139
Shift	1,900.00	2	950.00	0.110
Season × Shift	233.34	2	116.67	0.014
Error	154,825.00	18	8,601.39	
Total	201,162.51	23		

Decision: Reject the null hypothesis for the main effect of season. Retain the null hypothesis for the other main effect and the interaction.

(b) The main effect of season has only two levels. Multiple comparisons are not needed. Participants consumed more calories in winter compared to summer.

24.

Source of Variation	SS	df	MS	F_{obt}
Exam	**190**	2	95	**6.33**
Student Class	60	**3**	**20**	**1.33**
Exam × Student Class	540	**6**	**90**	**6.00**
Error	**1,620**	108	15	
Total	2,410	**119**		

26. (a)

Source of Variation	SS	df	MS	F_{obt}
Adult	226.08	2	113.04	5.79
Consequence	3,504.17	1	3504.17	179.45
Adult × Consequence	343.58	2	171.79	8.80
Error	351.50	18	19.53	
Total	4,425.33	23		

Decision: Reject the null hypothesis for both main effects and the interaction.

(b) Simple effect test for type of adult with rewarding consequence:

Source of Variation	SS	df	MS	F_{obt}
Adult	26.17	2	13.08	1.30
Within groups (error)	90.75	9	10.08	
Total	116.92	11		

Decision: Retain the null hypothesis—times did not vary by type of adult for a rewarding consequence.

Simple main effect test for type of adult with punishing consequence:

Source of Variation	SS	df	MS	F_{obt}
Adult	543.50	2	271.75	9.38
Within groups (error)	260.75	9	28.97	
Total	804.25	11		

Decision: Reject the null hypothesis—times did vary by type of adult for a punishing consequence.

Conclusion: A two-way ANOVA showed a significant Adult × Consequence interaction, $F(4, 27) = 4.45$, $p < .05$. Simple effect tests indicated that the three types of adults had similar influence in the reward condition ($p > .05$) but not in the punishment condition, $F(2, 9) = 9.38$, $p < .05$. Post hoc tests showed that parents and siblings had more influence in the punishment condition compared to strangers (Tukey's HSD, $p < .05$).

28. (a)

Source of Variation	SS	df	MS	F_{obt}
Living status	0.06	1	0.06	0.04
Pet owner status	14.06	1	14.06	9.00
Living × Owner	0.56	1	0.56	0.36
Error	18.75	12	1.56	
Total	33.43	15		

Decision: Reject the null hypothesis for the main effect of pet owner status. Retain the null hypothesis for the other main effect and the interaction.

(b) There is only a significant main effect of pet owner status. Because there are only two levels of this factor, post hoc tests are not necessary.

30. (a) Yes. This study found a significant main effect of species. (b) Conduct pairwise comparisons for the species factor.

32. (a) Yes. This study found a significant main effect of emoticon style. (b) Post hoc tests are not required because there are only two levels of emoticon style; the two levels of this factor must significantly differ.

CHAPTER 13

2. The strength of a correlation reflects how close data points fall to the regression line. The closer a correlation is to $r = \pm 1.0$, the stronger the correlation.

4. (a) SS_{XY} is used to measure the covariance in X and Y or the extent to which X and Y vary together. (b) $\sqrt{SS_X SS_Y}$ is used to measure the independent variance of X and Y.

6. Homoscedasticity, linearity, and normality.

8. The predictor variable (X) is a known value that is used to predict the value of a criterion variable. The criterion variable (Y) is the variable that is predicted by known values of the predictor variable.

10. Residual variation is a measure of the variance in Y that is unrelated to changes in X. This is the variance in Y that is left over or remaining. The farther that data points fall from the regression line, the larger the value of residual variation.

12. (a) Phi. (b) Pearson. (c) Point-biserial. (d) Spearman.

14. (a) $r = -.40$ is the stronger correlation. (b) $r = +.50$ is the stronger correlation. (c) These correlations are equal strength. (d) $r = -.76$ is the stronger correlation.

16. (a) is the appropriate conclusion. (b) is not appropriate because correlations do not demonstrate cause.

18. (a) $r = .894$. (b) $r = .894$. (c) $r = .894$. (d) True.

20. (a) $r = .574$. (b) $r = -.574$. (c) True.

22. Regression Equation (a).

24. (a) $r = -.843$. (b) $r^2 = (-.843)^2 = .711$. (c) Reject the null hypothesis.

26. Retain the null hypothesis.

28. (a) $r^2 = (.26)^2 = .07$. (b) $SS_{regression} = .07 \ (96.40) = 6.75$. (c) $SS_{residual} = (1 - .07)96.40 = 89.65$.

30.

Source of Variation	SS	df	MS	F_{obt}
Regression	80	1	80	3.53
Residual (error)	1,360	60	22.67	
Total	1,440	61		

The decision is to retain the null hypothesis.

32. (a) The more students believe in their ability to do well in math, the better their achievement in math. (b) The more students believe in their ability to do well in verbal, the better their achievement in verbal.

34. (a) 213 participants. (b) $r = -.33$; Yes. The result was significant; p was less than .05.

36. (a) The correlation is positive because the value of the slope is positive. (b) $\hat{Y} = 1.01(40) + 4.71 = 45.11$.

CHAPTER 14

2. Nominal scale of measurement.

4. (a) The frequency observed (f_o) is the count or frequency of participants recorded in each cell or category. (b) The frequency expected (f_e) is the count or frequency of participants in each cell or category, as determined by the proportion in each group or category stated by the null hypothesis.

6. The sample size multiplied by the proportion expected in a given cell: $f_e = np$.

8. Positively skewed.

10. The frequency expected in each cell is $f_e = \dfrac{\text{row total} \times \text{column total}}{N}$.

12. When the levels of one or more categorical variables are greater than two.

14. (a) Chi-square goodness-of-fit test. (b) Chi-square goodness-of-fit test. (c) Chi-square test for independence.

16. No, because at least one expected frequency is less than 5.

18. $\chi^2_{obt} = \dfrac{(66-60)^2}{60} + \dfrac{(34-40)^2}{40} = 1.50$.

The decision is to retain the null hypothesis. The distribution of men and women employed is "fair" or consistent with that in the general population for this industry.

20. $\chi^2_{obt} = \frac{(28-37)^2}{37} + \frac{(46-37)^2}{37} = 4.378.$

The decision is to reject the null hypothesis. Parents who were spanked by their parents as children more frequently spank their own children.

22. $\chi^2_{obt} = \frac{(35-35.1)^2}{35.1} + \frac{(32-31.9)^2}{31.9} + \frac{(20-19.9)^2}{19.9} + \frac{(18-18.1)^2}{18.1} = 0.001.$

The decision is to retain the null hypothesis. Whether or not a person owns a home is independent of his or her viewpoint of the economy.

24. (a) $\phi^2 = \frac{3.96}{50} = .079.$ (b) $\phi^2 = \frac{5.23}{75} = .070.$ (c) $\phi^2 = \frac{12.00}{100} = .120.$

26. (a) Small effect size. (b) Medium effect size. (c) Large effect size.

28. $\chi^2_{obt} = \frac{(145-119.5)^2}{119.5} + \frac{(94-119.5)^2}{119.5} = 10.884.$ The decision is to reject the null hypothesis.

30. (a) The phi coefficient. (b) The smallest degrees of freedom equal 1. This makes the solution to both formulas identical.

32. $\chi^2_{obt} = \frac{(32-40.4)^2}{40.4} + \frac{(71-62.6)^2}{62.6} + \frac{(26-17.6)^2}{17.6} + \frac{(19-27.4)^2}{27.4} = 9.375.$

The decision is to reject the null hypothesis.

APPENDIX A

SECTION A.1

2. Negative

4. Negative

6. Positive

8. Positive

10. Positive

12. Constant

14. Variable

16. Variable

SECTIONS A.2–A.3

2. 10

4. −5

6. 19

8. 18

10. 0

SECTIONS A.4–A.5

2. 32

4. 60

6. 84

8. −1

10. 3

12. $-\frac{1}{2} = 0.50$

14. −5

16. −54

18. False

20. False

SECTIONS A.6–A.7

2. 0

4. Undefined

6. $\dfrac{3}{2}$

8. $-\dfrac{38}{3}$

10. $-\dfrac{35}{100}$

12. $\dfrac{52}{10,000}$

14. $\dfrac{125}{100}$

16. 2.5%

18. 50%

20. $\dfrac{17}{8}$

22. $-\dfrac{8}{70}$

24. $\dfrac{5}{21}$

26. $-\dfrac{2}{2} = -1.00$

SECTIONS A.8–A.9

2. 9

4. 144

6. $\sqrt{9} = 3$

8. 16

10. 5

12. 2.2

14. 2

SECTIONS A.10–A.11

2. $x = 8$

4. $x = 2$

6. $x = 1.28$

8. $x = -17.16$

10. 83

12. 68

14. $\sqrt{68} = 8.25$

16. 139

···Glossary

This glossary includes all terms and symbols that are boxed and defined in each chapter. The number in parentheses following each definition states the chapter(s) where the term is boxed and defined.

Alpha level (α) the level of significance or criterion for a hypothesis test. It is the largest probability of committing a Type I error that researchers will allow and still decide to reject the null hypothesis (7).

Alternative hypothesis (H_1) a statement that directly contradicts a null hypothesis by stating that the actual value of a population parameter, such as the mean, is less than, greater than, or not equal to the value stated in the null hypothesis (7).

Analysis of regression a statistical procedure used to test hypotheses for one or more predictor variables to determine whether the regression equation for a sample of data points can be used to predict values of the criterion variable (Y) given values of the predictor variable (X) in the population; also called *regression analysis* (13).

Analysis of variance (ANOVA) a statistical procedure used to test hypotheses for one or more factors concerning the variance among two or more group means ($k \geq 2$), where the variance in one or more populations is unknown (11).

Arithmetic mean see *mean* (3).

Average see *mean* (3).

Bar chart a graphical display used to summarize the frequency of discrete and categorical data that are distributed in whole units or classes; also called a *bar graph* (2).

Bar graph see *bar chart* (2).

Bell-shaped distribution see *normal distribution* (3, 5).

Beta (β) error see *Type II error* (7).

Between-groups variation the variation attributed to mean differences between groups (11).

Between-persons variation the variance attributed to differences between person means averaged across groups. Because the same participants are observed across groups using a within-subjects design, this source of variation is removed or omitted from the error term in the denominator of the test statistic for within-subjects designs (11).

Between-subjects design a research design in which we select independent samples, meaning that different participants are observed at each level of one factor, or in each group created by combining the levels of two factors (9).

Between-subjects factor a type of factor in which different participants are observed at each level of the factor (12).

Biased estimator any sample statistic, such as a sample variance when we divide SS by n, obtained from a randomly selected sample that does not equal the value of its respective population parameter, such as a population mean, on average (4).

Bimodal distribution a distribution of scores in which two scores occur most often or most frequently. A bimodal distribution has two modes (3).

Cell the combination of one level from each factor, as represented in a cross tabulation. Each cell is a group in a research study (12).

Central limit theorem a theorem that explains that regardless of the distribution of scores in a population, the sampling distribution of sample means selected at random from that population will approach the shape of a normal distribution, as the number of samples in the sampling distribution increases (6).

Central tendency statistical measures for locating a single score that is most representative or descriptive of all scores in a distribution. Examples include the mean, the median, and the mode (3).

Chebyshev's theorem defines the percent of data from *any* distribution that will be contained within any number of standard deviations from the mean, where $SD > 1$ (4).

Chi-square distribution a positively skewed distribution of chi-square test statistic values for all possible samples when the null hypothesis is true (14).

Chi-square goodness-of-fit test a statistical procedure used to determine whether observed frequencies at each level of one categorical variable are similar to or different from the frequencies we expected at each level of the categorical variable (14).

Chi-square (χ^2) test a statistical procedure used to test hypotheses about the discrepancy between the observed and expected frequencies for the levels of a single categorical variable or two categorical variables observed together (14).

Chi-square test for independence a statistical procedure used to determine whether frequencies observed at the combination of levels of two categorical variables are similar to frequencies expected (14).

Class width see *interval width* (2).

Coding the procedure of converting a nominal or categorical variable to a numeric value (1).

Coefficient of determination (r^2 or R^2) is a formula that is mathematically equivalent to eta-squared and is used to measure the proportion of variance of one factor (Y) that can be explained by known values of a second factor (X) (13).

Cohen's *d* a measure for effect size in terms of the number of standard deviations that mean scores have shifted above or below the population mean stated by the null hypothesis. The larger the value for *d*, the larger the effect in the population (7).

Cohen's effect size conventions standard rules for identifying small, medium, and large effects based on typical findings in behavioral research (7).

Complete factorial design a research design in which each level of one factor is combined or crossed with each level of the other factor, with participants observed in each cell or combination of levels (12).

Computational formula for variance a way to calculate the population variance and the sample variance without needing to sum the squared differences of scores from their mean to compute the *SS* in the numerator; also called the *raw scores method* (4).

Confidence interval (CI) the interval or range of possible values within which an unknown population parameter is likely to be contained (8).

Confound variable an unanticipated variable not accounted for in a research study that could be causing or associated with observed changes in one or more measured variables; also called a *third variable* (13).

Constant a characteristic or property that can take on only a single value (A).

Continuous variable a variable measured along a continuum at any place beyond the decimal point. A continuous variable can thus be measured in fractional units (1).

Correlation a statistical procedure used to describe the strength and

direction of the linear relationship between two factors (13).

Correlation coefficient (*r*) used to measure the strength and direction of the linear relationship, or correlation, between two factors. The value of *r* ranges from −1.0 to +1.0 (13).

Covariance a measure for the extent to which the values of two factors (X and Y) vary together. The closer data points fall to the regression line, the more that the values of two factors vary together (13).

Cramer's phi (φ) see *Cramer's V* (14).

Cramer's *V* an estimate of effect size for the chi-square test for independence for two categorical variables with any number of levels; also called *Cramer's phi* (14).

Criterion variable (*Y*) the variable with unknown values that can be predicted or estimated, given known values of the predictor variable; also called the *to-be-predicted variable* (13).

Critical value a cutoff value that defines the boundaries beyond which 5% or less of sample means can be obtained if the null hypothesis is true. Sample means obtained beyond a critical value result in a decision to reject the null hypothesis (7).

Cumulative frequency distribution a summary display that distributes the sum of frequencies across a series of intervals (2).

Cumulative percent distribution a summary display that distributes the sum of relative percents across a series of intervals (2).

Cumulative relative frequency distribution a summary display that distributes the sum of relative frequencies across a series of intervals. Relative frequencies can be added or cumulated from the bottom up or the top down in a frequency distribution (2).

Data (plural) a set of scores, measurements, or observations that are typically numeric (1).

Data points the *x*- and *y*-coordinates for each plot in a scatter plot (13).

Datum (singular) a single measurement or observation, usually referred to as a *score* or *raw score* (1).

Definitional formula for variance a way to calculate the population variance and sample variance that requires summing the squared differences of scores from their mean to compute the *SS* in the numerator (4).

Degrees of freedom (*df*) for a *t* distribution are equal to the degrees of freedom for sample variance for a given sample: $n - 1$. Each *t* distribution is associated with specified degrees of freedom; as sample size increases, the degrees of freedom also increase (8).

Degrees of freedom between groups (df_{BG}) the degrees of freedom associated with the variance for the group means in the numerator of the test statistic. They are equal to the number of groups (k) minus 1; also called *degrees of freedom numerator* (11).

Degrees of freedom between persons (df_{BP}) the degrees of freedom associated with the variance of person means averaged across groups. They are equal to the number of participants (n) minus 1 (11).

Degrees of freedom denominator (df_{den}) see *degrees of freedom error* (11).

Degrees of freedom error (df_E) the degrees of freedom associated with the error variance in the denominator. They are equal to the total sample size (N) minus the number of groups (k); also called *degrees of freedom denominator* or *degrees of freedom within groups* (11).

Degrees of freedom (*df*) for sample variance the number of scores in a sample that are free to vary. All scores except one are free to vary in a sample: $n - 1$ (4).

Degrees of freedom numerator (df_{num}) see *degrees of freedom between groups* (11).

Degrees of freedom within groups see *degrees of freedom error* (11).

Dependent sample see *related sample* (10).

Dependent variable (DV) the variable that is measured in each group of a study and is believed to change in the presence of the independent variable. It is the "presumed effect," so to speak (1).

Descriptive statistics procedures used to summarize, organize, and make sense of a set of scores called *data*. Descriptive statistics are typically presented graphically, in tabular form (in tables), or as summary statistics (single values) (1).

Deviation the difference of each score from its mean. Denoted $(x - \mu)$ for a population and denoted $(x - M)$ for a sample (4).

Difference score a score or value obtained by subtracting one score from another (10).

Directional tests hypothesis tests where the alternative hypothesis is stated as "greater than" (>) or "less than" (<) a value stated in the null hypothesis. Hence, the researcher is interested in a specific alternative to the null hypothesis; also called *one-tailed tests* (7).

Discrete variable measured in whole units or categories that are not distributed along a continuum (1).

Effect the difference between a sample mean and the population mean stated in the null hypothesis. In hypothesis testing, an effect is not significant when we retain the null hypothesis; an effect is significant when we reject the null hypothesis (7).

Effect size a statistical measure of the size of an observed effect in a population, which allows researchers to describe how far scores shifted in the population, or the percentage of variance that can be explained by a given variable (7).

Empirical rule a rule that states that for data that are normally distributed, at least 99.7% of data lie within 3 *SD* of the mean, at least 95% of data lie within 2 *SD* of the mean, and at least 68% of data lie within 1 *SD* of the mean (4).

Equidistant scales a set of numbers distributed in equal units (1).

Error any unexplained difference that cannot be attributed to, or caused by, having different treatments. The standard error of the mean is used to measure the error or unexplained differences in a statistical design (10).

Estimated Cohen's *d* a measure of effect size in terms of the number of standard deviations that mean scores shift above or below the population mean stated by the null hypothesis. The larger the value of estimated Cohen's *d*, the larger the effect is in the population (8).

Estimated standard error (s_M) an estimate of the standard deviation of a sampling distribution of sample means selected from a population with an unknown variance. It is an estimate of the standard error or the standard distance that sample means can be expected to deviate from the value of the population mean stated in the null hypothesis (8).

Estimated standard error for difference scores (s_{MD}) an estimate of the standard deviation of a sampling distribution of mean difference scores. It is an estimate of the standard error or standard distance that the mean difference scores deviate from the mean difference score stated in a null hypothesis (10).

Estimated standard error for the difference ($S_{M1 - M2}$) an estimate of the standard deviation of a sampling distribution of mean differences between two sample means. It is an estimate of the standard error or the standard distance that mean differences can be expected to deviate from the mean difference stated in the null hypothesis (9).

Estimation a statistical procedure in which a sample statistic is used to estimate the value of an unknown population parameter. Two types of estimation are point estimation and interval estimation (8).

Experiment the use of methods and procedures to make observations in which the researcher fully controls the conditions and experiences of participants by applying three required elements of control (manipulation, randomization, and comparison/control) to isolate cause-and-effect relationships between variables (1).

Experimentwise alpha the aggregated alpha level, or probability of committing a Type I error for all tests, when multiple tests are conducted on the same data (11).

F distribution a positively skewed distribution derived from a sampling distribution of *F* ratios (11).

F obtained see F *statistic* (11).

F statistic (F_{obt}) the test statistic for an ANOVA. It is computed as the mean square (or variance) between groups divided by the mean square (or variance) within groups; also called F *obtained* (11).

Factorial design a research design in which participants are observed across the combination of levels of two or more factors (12).

Fixed event any event in which the outcome observed is always the same (5).

Frequency the number of times or how often a category, score, or range of scores occurs (2).

Frequency distribution a summary display for a distribution of data organized or summarized in terms of how often a category, score, or range of scores occurs (2).

Frequency expected (f_e) the count or frequency of participants in each category, or at each level of the categorical variable, as determined by the proportion expected in each category (14).

Frequency observed (f_o) the count or frequency of participants recorded in each category or at each level of the categorical variable (14).

Frequency polygon a dot-and-line graph used to summarize the frequency of continuous data at the midpoint of each interval (2).

Gaussian distribution see *normal distribution* (3, 5).

Grouped data a set of scores distributed into intervals, where the frequency of each score can fall into any given interval (2).

Histogram a graphical display used to summarize the frequency of continuous data that are distributed in numeric intervals (2).

Homoscedasticity the assumption that there is an equal ("homo") variance or scatter ("scedasticity") of data points dispersed along the regression line (13).

Hypothesis a statement or proposed explanation for an observation, a phenomenon, or a scientific problem that can be tested using the research method. A hypothesis is often a statement about the value for a parameter in a population (7).

Hypothesis testing a method for testing a claim or hypothesis about a parameter in a population, using data measured in a sample. In this method, we test a hypothesis by determining the likelihood that a sample statistic would be selected if the hypothesis regarding the population parameter were true. Also called *significance testing* (7).

Independent sample the selection of participants to each group or sample, where the participants are unrelated in that they are observed once in only one sample. To observe independent samples, participants are selected from two or more populations or selected from a single population and randomly assigned to different groups (9).

Independent variable (IV) the variable that is manipulated in an experiment. This variable remains unchanged (or "independent") between conditions being observed in an experiment. It is the "presumed cause," so to speak (1).

Inferential statistics procedures used that allow researchers to infer or generalize observations made with samples to the larger population from

which they were selected. Examples include *z* tests, *t* tests, and *F* tests (1).

Interaction a source of variation associated with the variance of group means across the combination of levels of two factors. It is a measure of how cell means at each level of one factor change across the levels of a second factor (12).

Interquartile range (IQR) the range of values between the upper (Q_3) and lower (Q_1) quartiles of a data set (4).

Interval a discrete range of values within which the frequency of a subset of scores is contained (2).

Interval boundaries the upper and lower limits for each interval in a grouped frequency distribution (2).

Interval estimate a statistical procedure in which a sample of data is used to find the interval or range of possible values within which a population parameter is likely to be contained (8).

Interval scales measurements that have no true zero and are distributed in equal units. Examples include Likert scores, temperature, latitude, and longitude (1).

Interval width the range of values contained in each interval of a grouped frequency distribution; also called *class width* (2).

Known variable (X) see *predictor variable* (13).

Law of large numbers a theorem or a rule that increasing the number of observations or the sample size in a study will decrease the standard error. The smaller the standard error, the closer a distribution of the sample means will be to the population mean (6).

Level of confidence the probability or likelihood that an interval estimate will contain an unknown population parameter (8).

Level of significance refers to criterion of judgment upon which a decision is made regarding the value stated in a null hypothesis. The criterion

is based on the probability of obtaining a statistic measured in a sample if the value stated in the null hypothesis were true. Also called *significance level* (7).

Levels of the factor (k) the number of groups or different ways in which an independent or quasi-independent variable is observed; also called the *levels of the independent variable* for groups in experimental research designs (11).

Levels of the independent variable specific conditions of the independent variable; also called the *levels of the factor* for groups in quasi-experiments and correlational research designs (1).

Linear regression a statistical procedure used to determine the equation of a regression line to a set of data points and the extent to which the regression equation can be used to predict values of one factor, given known values of a second factor in a population; also called *regression* (13).

Linearity the assumption that the best way to describe a pattern of data is using a straight line (13).

Lower boundary the smallest value in each interval of a grouped frequency distribution (2).

Main effect a source of variation associated with mean differences across the levels of a single factor (12).

Matched-pairs design a research design in which pairs of participants are selected and then matched, either experimentally or naturally, based on common characteristics or traits; also called a *matched-samples design* or a *matched-subjects design* (10).

Matched-samples design see *matched-pairs design* (10).

Matched-subjects design see *matched-pairs design* (10).

Mean the sum of a set of scores in a distribution, divided by the total number of scores summed; also called an *arithmetic mean* or *average* (3).

Mean square between groups (MS_{BG}) the variance attributed to differences between group means. It is the numerator of the test statistic for an ANOVA (11).

Mean square between persons (MS_{BP}) the variance attributed to mean differences in scores between persons (11).

Mean square error (MS_E) the variance attributed to differences within each group. It is the denominator of the test statistic for an ANOVA; also called *mean square within groups* (11).

Mean square within groups see *mean square error* (11).

Median the middle value in a distribution of data listed in numeric order (3).

Method of least squares a statistical procedure used to compute the slope (*b*) and *y*-intercept (*a*) of the best-fitting straight line to a set of data points (13).

Modal distribution a distribution of scores in which one or more scores occur most often or most frequently (3).

Mode the value in a data set that occurs most often or most frequently (3).

Multimodal distribution a distribution of scores in which more than two scores occur most often or most frequently. A multimodal distribution has more than two modes (3).

Multiple regression a statistical procedure that includes two or more predictor variables in the equation of a regression line to predict changes in a criterion variable (13).

Negative correlation ($-1.0 \leq r < 0$) a negative value for *r*, which indicates that the values of two factors change in different directions, meaning that as the values of one factor increase, the values of the second factor decrease (13).

Negatively skewed a distribution of scores that includes one or a few scores that are substantially smaller (toward the left tail in a graph) than most other scores (3).

Nominal scales measurements in which a number is assigned to represent something or someone. Nominal variables are typically categorical variables that have been coded (1).

Nondirectional tests hypothesis tests in which the alternative hypothesis is stated as *not equal to* ($\neq$) a value stated in the null hypothesis. Hence, the researcher is interested in any alternative to the null hypothesis; also called *two-tailed tests* (7).

Nonmodal distribution a distribution of scores with no mode; hence, all scores occur at the same frequency; also called a *rectangular distribution* (3).

Nonparametric tests hypothesis tests that are used (1) to test hypotheses that do not make inferences about parameters in a population, (2) to test hypotheses about data that can have any type of distribution, and (3) to analyze data on a nominal or ordinal scale of measurement (14).

Normal distribution a theoretical distribution with data that are symmetrically distributed around the mean, median, and mode; also called a *symmetrical*, *Gaussian*, or *bell-shaped distribution* (3, 5).

Null hypothesis (H_o) a statement about a population parameter, such as the population mean, that is assumed to be true; a hypothesis test is structured to decide whether or not to reject this assumption (7).

Observed power a type of post hoc or retrospective power analysis that is used to estimate the likelihood of detecting a population effect, assuming that the observed results in a study reflect a true effect in the population (11).

Obtained value the value of a test statistic. This value is compared to the critical value(s) of a hypothesis test to make a decision. When the obtained value exceeds a critical value, we decide to reject the null hypothesis; otherwise, we retain the null hypothesis (7).

Ogive a dot-and-line graph used to summarize the cumulative percent of continuous data at the upper boundary of each interval (2).

One-sample *t* test a statistical procedure used to compare a mean value measured in a sample to a known value in the population. It is specifically used to test hypotheses concerning the mean in a single population with an unknown variance (8).

One-sample *z* test a statistical procedure used to test hypotheses concerning the mean in a single population with a known variance (7).

One-tailed tests see *directional tests* (7).

One-way between-subjects ANOVA a statistical procedure used to test hypotheses for one factor with two or more levels concerning the variance among the group means. This test is used when different participants are observed at each level of a factor and the variance in any one population is unknown (11).

One-way repeated-measures ANOVA see *one-way within-subjects ANOVA* (11).

One-way within-subjects ANOVA a statistical procedure used to test hypotheses for one factor with two or more levels concerning the variance among the group means. This test is used when the same participants are observed at each level of a factor and the variance in any one population is unknown (11).

Open class see *open interval* (2).

Open interval an interval with no defined upper or lower boundary; also called an *open class* (2).

Operational definition a description of some observable event in terms of the specific process or manner by which it was observed or measured (1).

Ordinal scales measurements where values convey order or rank alone (1).

Outliers extreme scores that fall substantially above or below most of the scores in a particular data set (2).

p value the probability of obtaining a sample outcome, given that the value stated in the null hypothesis is true. The p value for obtaining a sample outcome is compared to the level of significance or criterion for making a decision (7).

Pairwise comparison a statistical comparison for the difference between two group means. A post hoc test evaluates all possible pairwise comparisons for an ANOVA with any number of groups (11).

Parametric tests hypothesis tests that are used to test hypotheses about parameters in a population in which the data are normally distributed and measured on an interval or ratio scale of measurement (14).

Pearson correlation coefficient (r) a measure of the direction and strength of the linear relationship of two factors in which the data for both factors are measured on an interval or ratio scale of measurement; also called the *Pearson product-moment correlation coefficient* (13).

Pearson product-moment correlation coefficient see *Pearson correlation coefficient (r)* (13).

Percentile point the value of a score on a measurement scale below which a specified percentage of scores in a distribution fall (2).

Percentile rank the percentage of scores with values that fall below a specified score in a distribution (2).

Phi correlation coefficient (r_i) a measure of the direction and strength of the linear relationship of two dichotomous factors on a nominal scale of measurement (13).

Pie chart a graphical display in the shape of a circle that is used to summarize the relative percent of discrete and categorical data into sectors (2).

Point-biserial correlation coefficient (r_{pb}) a measure of the direction and strength of the linear relationship of one factor that is continuous (on an interval or ratio scale of measurement) and a second factor that is dichotomous (on a nominal scale of measurement) (13).

Point estimate a statistical procedure that involves the use of a sample statistic to estimate a population parameter (8).

Pooled sample standard deviation $\left(\sqrt{s_p^2} \right)$ the combined sample standard deviation of two samples. It is computed by taking the square root of the pooled sample variance. This measure estimates the standard deviation for the difference between two population means (9).

Pooled sample variance (s_p^2) the combined sample variance of two samples. When the sample size is unequal, the variance in each group or sample is weighted by its respective degrees of freedom (9).

Population a set of *all* individuals, items, or data of interest. This is the group about which scientists will generalize (1).

Population mean (μ) the sum of a set of scores in a population, divided by the total number of scores summed (3).

Population parameter a characteristic (usually numeric, such as the mean or variance) that describes a population. The population characteristic typically of greatest interest to a researcher is the mean score (1).

Population size (N) the number of individuals that constitute an entire group or population (3).

Population standard deviation (σ) a measure of variability for the average distance that scores in a population deviate from their mean. It is calculated by taking the square root of the population variance (4).

Population variance (s^2) a measure of variability for the average squared distance that scores in a population deviate from the mean. It is computed only when all scores in a given population are known (4).

Positive correlation ($0 < r \leq +1.0$) a positive value of r that indicates that the values of two factors change in the same direction: As the values of one factor increase, the values of the second factor also increase; as the values of one factor decrease, the values of the second factor also decrease (13).

Positively skewed a distribution of scores that includes one or a few scores that are substantially larger (toward the right tail in a graph) than most other scores (3).

Post hoc test a statistical procedure computed following a significant ANOVA to determine which pair or pairs of group means significantly differ. These tests are necessary when $k > 2$ because multiple comparisons are needed. When $k = 2$, only one comparison is made because only one pair of group means can be compared (11).

Power the probability of rejecting a false null hypothesis. Specifically, it is the probability that a randomly selected sample will show that the null hypothesis is false when the null hypothesis is in fact false (7).

Predictor variable (X) the variable with values that are known and can be used to predict values of another variable; also called the *known variable* (13).

Pre-post design a type of repeated-measures design in which researchers measure a dependent variable for participants before (pre) and after (post) a treatment (10).

Probability (p) the frequency of times an outcome occurs divided by the total number of possible outcomes (5).

Proportion a part or portion of all measured data. The sum of all proportions for a distribution of data is 1.0 (2).

Proportion of variance (η^2, ω^2) is a measure of effect size in terms of the proportion or percentage of variability in a dependent variable that can be explained or accounted for by a treatment (8).

Qualitative variable varies by class. This is often represented as a label and describes nonnumeric aspects of phenomena (1).

Quantitative variable varies by amount. This is measured numerically and is often collected by measuring or counting (1).

Quartiles divide data evenly into four equal parts (4).

Quasi-independent variable a preexisting variable that is often a characteristic inherent to an individual, which differentiates the groups or conditions being compared in a research study (1).

Random assignment a random procedure used to ensure that participants in a study have an equal chance of being assigned to a particular group or condition (1).

Random event any event in which the outcomes observed can vary (5).

Range the difference between the largest (L) and the smallest value (S) in a data set (4).

Ratio scales measurements that have a true zero and are distributed in equal units (1).

Raw score see *datum* (1).

Raw scores method for variance see *computational formula for variance* (4).

Real range one more than the difference between the largest and smallest values in a data set (2).

Rectangular distribution see *nonmodal distribution* (3).

Regression see *linear regression* (13).

Regression analysis see *analysis of regression* (13).

Regression line the best-fitting straight line to a set of data points. A best-fitting line is the line that minimizes the distance that all data points fall from it (13).

Regression variation the variance in Y that is related to or associated with changes in X. The closer that data points fall to the regression line, the larger the value of regression variation (13).

Rejection region the region beyond a critical value in a hypothesis test. When the value of a test statistic is in the rejection region, we decide to reject the

null hypothesis; otherwise, we retain the null hypothesis (7).

Related sample a group or sample in which the participants are related. Participants can be related in one of two ways: They are observed in more than one group (a repeated-measures design), or they are matched, experimentally or naturally, based on common characteristics or traits (a matched-pairs design); also called a *dependent sample* (10).

Related-samples *t* test an inferential statistic used to test hypotheses concerning two related samples selected from populations in which the variance in one or both populations is unknown (10).

Relative frequency distribution a summary display that distributes the proportion of scores occurring in each interval of a frequency distribution. It is computed as the frequency in each interval divided by the total number of frequencies recorded (2).

Relative percent distribution a summary display that distributes the percentage of scores occurring in each class interval relative to all scores distributed (2).

Repeated-measures design a research design in which the same participants are observed in each group or treatment. Two types of repeated-measures designs are called the pre-post design and the within-subjects design (10).

Research method a set of systematic techniques used to acquire, modify, and integrate knowledge concerning observable and measurable phenomena; also called *scientific method* (1).

Residual variation the variance in Y that is not related to changes in X. This is the variance in Y that is left over or remaining. The farther that data points fall from the regression line, the larger the value of residual variation (13).

Restriction of range a problem that arises when the range of data for one or both correlated factors in a sample is limited or restricted, compared to the

range of data in the population from which the sample was selected (13).

Reverse causality a problem that arises when the direction of causality between two factors can be in either direction (13).

Root mean square deviation see *standard deviation* (4).

Sample a set of individuals, items, or data selected from a population of interest (1).

Sample design a specific plan or protocol for how individuals will be selected or sampled from a population of interest (6).

Sample mean (M or $\bar{X}$) the sum of a set of scores in a sample, divided by the total number of scores summed (3).

Sample size (n) the number of individuals that constitute a subset of those selected from a larger population (3).

Sample space the total number of possible outcomes that can occur in a given random event; also called *outcome space* (5).

Sample standard deviation (s or SD) a measure of variability for the average distance that scores in a sample deviate from their mean. It is calculated by taking the square root of the sample variance (4).

Sample statistic a characteristic (usually numeric, such as the mean or variance) that describes a sample (1).

Sample variance (s^2 or SD^2) a measure of variability for the average squared distance that scores in a sample deviate from the mean. It is computed when only a portion or sample of data is measured in a population (4).

Sampling distribution for the mean, it is a distribution of all sample means that could be obtained in samples of a given size from the same population (6).

Sampling error the extent to which sample means selected from the same population differ from one another. This difference, which occurs by chance, is measured by the standard error of the mean (6).

Sampling with replacement a method of sampling in which each participant or item selected is replaced before the next selection. This method of sampling is used in the development of statistical theory (6).

Sampling without replacement a method of sampling in which each participant or item selected is not replaced before the next selection. This method of sampling is the most common method used in behavioral research (6).

Scales of measurement identify how the properties of numbers can change with different uses. Four scales of measurement are nominal, ordinal, interval, and ratio (1).

Scatter gram see *scatter plot* (13).

Scatter plot a graphical display of discrete data points (x, y) used to summarize the relationship between two variables; also called a *scatter gram* (13).

Science the study of phenomena, such as behavior, through strict observation, evaluation, interpretation, and theoretical explanation (1).

Scientific method see *research method* (1).

Score see *datum* (1).

Sector the particular portion of a pie chart that represents the relative percentage of a particular class or category. To find the central angle for each sector, multiply each relative percent by 3.6 (2).

Semi-interquartile range (SIQR) a measure of half the distance between the upper quartile (Q_3) and lower quartile (Q_1) of a data set, computed by dividing the IQR in half; also called a *quartile deviation* (4).

Significance a decision made concerning a value stated in the null hypothesis. When the null hypothesis is rejected, we reach significance. When the null hypothesis is retained, we fail to reach significance. Also called *statistical significance* (7).

Significance level see *level of significance* (7).

Significance testing see *hypothesis testing* (7).

Simple frequency distribution a summary display for (1) the frequency of each individual score or category (ungrouped data) in a distribution or (2) the frequency of scores falling within defined groups or intervals (grouped data) in a distribution (2).

Simple main effect tests hypothesis tests used to analyze a significant interaction by comparing the mean differences or simple main effects of one factor at each level of a second factor (12).

Skewed distribution a distribution of scores that includes outliers or scores that fall substantially above or below most other scores in a data set (3).

Slope (*b*) a measure of the change in Y relative to the change in X. When X and Y change in the same direction, the slope is positive. When X and Y change in opposite directions, the slope is negative (13).

Source of variation any variation that can be measured in a study (11).

Spearman rank-order correlation coefficient (r_s) a measure of the direction and strength of the linear relationship of two ranked factors on an ordinal scale of measurement; also called *Spearman's rho* (13).

Spearman's rho see *Spearman rank-order correlation coefficient* (13).

Standard deviation a measure of variability for the average distance that scores deviate from their mean. It is calculated by taking the square root of the variance; also called the *root mean square deviation* (4).

Standard error see *standard error of the mean* (6).

Standard error of estimate (s_e) an estimate of the standard deviation or distance that a set of data points falls from the regression line. The standard error of estimate equals the square root of the mean square residual (13).

Standard error of the mean (σ_M) the standard deviation of a sampling distribution of sample means. It is the standard error or distance that sample mean values deviate from the value of the population mean; also stated as *standard error* (6).

Standard normal distribution a normal distribution with a mean equal to 0 and a standard deviation equal to 1. It is distributed in z score units along the *x*-axis; also called a z *distribution* (5).

Standard normal transformation a formula used to convert any normal distribution with any mean and any variance to a standard normal distribution with a mean equal to 0 and a standard deviation equal to 1; also called a z *transformation* (5).

Statistical significance see *significance* (7).

Statistics a branch of mathematics used to summarize, analyze, and interpret a group of numbers or observations (1).

Studentized range statistic (*q*) a statistic used to determine critical values for comparing pairs of means at a given range. This statistic is used in the formula to find the critical value for Tukey's honestly significant difference (HSD) post hoc test (11).

Student's *t* see t *distribution* (8).

Sum of products (SP) the sum of squares for two factors, X and Y, which are also represented as SS_{XY}. SP is the numerator for the Pearson correlation formula. To compute SP, multiply the deviation of each X value by the deviation of each Y value (13).

Sum of squares (SS) the sum of the squared deviations of scores from their mean. *SS* is the numerator in the variance formula (4).

Sum of squares between groups (SS_{BG}) the sum of squares attributed to variability between groups (11).

Sum of squares between persons (SS_{BP}) the sum of squares attributed to variability in participant scores across groups (11).

Sum of squares error (SS_E) the sum of squares attributed to variability within each group; also called *sum of squares within groups* (11).

Sum of squares total (SS_T) the overall sum of squares across all groups (11).

Sum of squares within groups (SS$_{WG}$) see *sum of squares error* (11).

Symmetrical distribution see *normal distribution* (3, 5).

***t* distribution** a normal-like distribution with greater variability in the tails than a normal distribution because the sample variance is substituted for the population variance to estimate the standard error in this distribution (8).

***t* observed** see t *statistic* (8).

***t* obtained** see t *statistic* (8).

***t* statistic** an inferential statistic used to determine the number of standard deviations in a *t* distribution that a sample mean deviates from the mean value or mean difference stated in the null hypothesis. Also referred to as t *observed* or t *obtained* (8).

Test statistic a mathematical formula that identifies how far or how many standard deviations a sample outcome is from the value stated in a null hypothesis. It allows researchers to determine the likelihood or probability of obtaining sample outcomes if the null hypothesis were true. The value of the test statistic is used to make a decision regarding a null hypothesis (7).

Testwise alpha the alpha level, or probability of committing a Type I error, for each test or pairwise comparison made on the same data (11).

Third variable see *confound variable* (13).

To-be-predicted variable (Y) see *criterion variable* (13).

Treatment any unique characteristic of a sample or any unique way that a researcher treats a sample in hypothesis testing (8).

True zero the value 0 truly indicates nothing or the absence of the phenomena being measured on a scale of measurement (1).

Two-independent-sample *t* test a statistical procedure used to compare the mean difference between two independent groups. This test is specifically used to test hypotheses concerning the difference between two population means, where the variance in one or both populations is unknown (9).

Two-tailed tests see *nondirectional tests* (7).

Two-way ANOVA a statistical procedure used to test hypotheses concerning the variance of groups created by combining the levels of two factors. This test is used when the variance in any one population is unknown (12).

Two-way between-subjects ANOVA a statistical procedure used to test hypotheses concerning the combination of levels of two factors using the 2-between or between-subjects design (12).

Type I error the probability of rejecting a null hypothesis that is actually true. Researchers directly control for the probability of committing this type of error by stating an alpha level (7).

Type II error the probability of retaining a null hypothesis that is actually false. Also called *beta* (β) *error* (7).

Type III error a type of error possible with one-tailed tests in which a decision would have been to reject the null hypothesis, but the researcher decides to retain the null hypothesis because the rejection region was located in the wrong tail (7).

Unbiased estimator any sample statistic obtained from a randomly selected sample that equals the value of its respective population parameter on average (4).

Ungrouped data a set of scores or categories distributed individually, where the frequency for each individual score or category is counted (2).

Unimodal distribution a distribution of scores, where one score occurs most often or most frequently. A unimodal distribution has one mode (3).

Unit normal table a type of probability distribution table displaying a list of *z* scores and the corresponding probabilities (or proportions of area) associated with each *z* score listed; also refer to as z *table* (5).

Upper boundary the largest value in each interval of a grouped frequency distribution (2).

Variability a measure of the dispersion or spread of scores in a distribution. It ranges from 0 to +∞. Examples include the range, the variance, and the standard deviation (4).

Variable a characteristic or property that can take on different values at different times (A).

Variance a measure of variability for the average squared distance that scores deviate from their mean (4).

Weighted mean (M$_W$) the combined mean of two or more groups of scores, where the number of scores in each group is disproportionate or unequal (3).

Within-groups variation the variation attributed to mean differences within each group. This source of variation cannot be attributed to or caused by having different groups and is therefore called error variation (11).

Within-subjects design a type of repeated-measures design in which researchers observe the same participants across many treatments but not necessarily before and after a treatment (10).

Within-subjects factor a type of factor in which the same participants are observed across the levels of the factor (12).

y-intercept (a) the value of the criterion variable (Y) when the predictor variable (X) equals 0 (13).

***z* distribution** see *standard normal distribution* (5).

***z* score** a value on the *x*-axis of a standard normal distribution; the numerical value of a *z* score specifies the distance or the number of standard deviations that a value is above or below the mean (5).

***z* statistic** an inferential statistic used to determine the number of standard deviations in a standard normal distribution that a sample mean deviates from the population mean stated in the null hypothesis (7).

***z* table** see *unit normal table* (5).

***z* transformation** see *standard normal transformation* (5).

... References

Aillaud, M., & Piolat, A. (2012). Influence of gender on judgment of dark and nondark humor. *Individual Differences Research, 10*, 211–222.

Albert, U., Salvi, V., Saracco, P., Bogetto, P., & Maina, G. (2007). Health-related quality of life among first-degree relatives of patients with obsessive-compulsive disorder in Italy. *Psychiatric Services, 58*, 970–976.

Altamura, A. C., Dell'Osso, B., Vismara, S., & Mundo, E. (2008). May duration of untreated illness influence the long-term course of major depressive disorder? *European Psychiatry, 23*, 92–96.

American Psychological Association. (2010). *Publication manual of the American Psychological Association* (6th ed.). Washington, DC: Author.

Andrade, A. M., Kresge, D. L., Teixeira, P. J., Baptista, F., & Melanson, K. J. (2012). Does eating slowly influence appetite and energy intake when water intake is controlled? *International Journal of Behavioral Nutrition and Physical Activity, 9*, 135. doi:10.1186/1479-5868-9-135

Ansari, A., & Crosnoe, R. (2016). Children's hyperactivity, television viewing, and the potential for child effects. *Children and Youth Services Review, 61*, 135–140. doi:10.1016/j.childyouth.2015.12.018

Apatu, E., Alperin, M., Miner, K. R., & Wiljer, D. (2013). A drive through web 2.0: An exploration of driving safety promotion on Facebook™. *Health Promotion Practice, 14*, 88–95. doi:10.1177/1524839911405845

Aspy, D. J. (2016). Is dream recall underestimated by retrospective measures and enhanced by keeping a logbook? An empirical investigation. *Consciousness and Cognition: An International Journal, 42*, 181–203. doi:10.1016/j.concog.2016.03.015

Azrin, N. H., Brooks, J., Kellen, M. J., Ehle, C., & Vinas, V. (2008). Speed of eating as a determinant of the bulimic desire to vomit. *Child & Family Behavior Therapy, 30*, 263–270. doi:10.1080/07317100802275728

Bachner, J., Raffetseder, P., Walz, B., & Schredl, M. (2012). The effects of dream socialization in childhood on dream recall frequency and the attitude towards dreams in adulthood: A retrospective study. *International Journal of Dream Research, 5*, 102–107. doi:10.11588/ijodr.2012.1.9307

Baker, E., Shelton, K. H., Baibazarova, E., Hay, D. F., & van Goozen, S. H. M. (2013). Low skin conductance activity in infancy predicts aggression in toddlers 2 years later. *Psychological Science, 24*, 1051–1056. doi:10.1177/0956797612465198

Bakker, M., & Wicherts, J. M. (2014). Outlier removal, sum scores, and the inflation of the Type I error rate in independent samples *t* tests: The power of alternatives and recommendations. *Psychological Methods.* Advance online publication. doi:10.1037/met0000014

Ballas, D., & Dorling, D. (2013). The geography of happiness. In S. A. David, I. Boniwell, & A. Conley Ayers (Eds.), *The Oxford handbook of happiness* (pp. 465–481). New York, NY: Oxford University Press.

Bar-eli, M., Azar, O. H., Ritov, I., Keidar-Levin, Y., & Schein, G. (2007). Action bias among elite soccer goalkeepers: The case of penalty kicks. *Journal of Economic Psychology, 28*, 606–621.

Bauer, M., Glenn, T., Rasgon, N., Marsh, W., Sagduyu, K., Munoz, R., . . . Whybrow, P. C. (2011). Association between median family income and self-reported mood symptoms in bipolar disorder. *Comprehensive Psychiatry, 52*, 17–25. doi:10.1016/j.comppsych.2010.04.005

Baxter, L. C. (2016). Appetite changes in depression. *The American Journal of Psychiatry, 173*, 317–318. doi:10.1176/appi.ajp.2016.16010010

Beck, A. T., Steer, R. A., & Brown, G. K. (1996). *Beck Depression Inventory–II manual.* San Antonio, TX: The Psychological Corporation.

Bell, K. E., & Limber, J. E. (2010). Reading skill, textbook marking, and course performance. *Literacy Research and Instruction, 49*, 56–67. doi:10.1080/19388070802695879

Bellou, V. (2007). Psychological contract assessment after a major organizational change: The case of mergers and acquisitions. *Employee Relations, 29*, 68–88.

Berndt, N., Bolman, C., Froelicher, E. S., Muddle, A., Candel, M., de Vries, H., & Lechner, L. (2013). Effectiveness of a telephone delivered and a face-to-face delivered counseling intervention for smoking cessation in patients with coronary heart disease: A 6-month follow-up. *Journal of Behavioral Medicine.* Advance online publication. doi:10.1007/s10865-013-9522-9

Bernstein, I. L. (1978). Learned taste aversions in children receiving chemotherapy. *Science, 200*, 1302–1303.

Bernstein, P. L. (1998). *Against the gods: The remarkable story of risk.* New York, NY: Wiley.

Bickel, W. K., Madden, G. J., & Petry, N. M. (1998). The price of change: The behavioral economics of drug dependence. *Behavior Therapy, 29*, 545–565. doi:10.1016/S0005-7894(98)80050-6

Black, D. W., Shaw, M., & Allen, J. (2016). Five-year follow-up of people diagnosed with compulsive shopping disorder. *Comprehensive Psychiatry, 68*, 97–102. doi:10.1016/j.comppsych.2016.03.004

Blokland, G. A. M., Mosing, M. A., Verweij, K. J. H., & Medland, S. E. (2013). Twin studies and behavioral genetics. In T. D. Little (Ed.), *The Oxford handbook of quantitative methods: Statistical analysis* (Vol. 2, pp. 198–218). New York, NY: Oxford University Press.

Bonilha, L., Molnar, C., Horner, M. D., Anderson, B., Forster, L., George, M. S., & Nahas, Z. (2008). Neurocognitive deficits and prefrontal cortical atrophy in patients with schizophrenia. *Schizophrenia Research, 101*, 142–151.

Botvinick, M. M., Niv, Y., & Barto, A. G. (2012). Hierarchically organised behaviour and its neural foundations: A reinforcement-learning perspective. In A. K. Seth, T. J. Prescott, & J. J. Bryson (Eds.), *Modelling natural action selection* (pp. 264–299). New York, NY: Cambridge University Press.

Brown, T., Mapleston, J., & Nairn, A. (2012). Can cognitive and perceptual standardized test scores predict functional performance in adults diagnosed with stroke? A pilot study. *Physical & Occupational Therapy in Geriatrics, 30*, 31–44. doi: 10.3109/02703181.2011.652348

Burt, C. B. (2015). *New employee safety: Risk factors and management strategies.* Cham, Switzerland: Springer International. doi:10.1007/978-3-319-18684-9

Capaldi, E. D., & Privitera, G. J. (2008). Decreasing dislike for sour and bitter in children and adults. *Appetite, 50*, 139–145. doi:10.1016/j.appet.2007.06.008

Centers for Disease Control and Prevention. (2009). Who marries and when? Age at first marriage in the United States: 2002. *NCHS Data Brief, 19*, 1–8.

Centers for Disease Control and Prevention. (2016). *Defining adult overweight and obesity.* Retrieved from https://www.cdc.gov/obesity/adult/defining.html

Chafouleas, S. M., Kehle, T. J., & Bray, M. A. (2012). Exploring the utility of self-modeling in decreasing disruptive behavior in students with intellectual disability. *Psychology in the Schools, 49*, 82–92. doi:10.1002/pits.20616

Cheatham, G. A., & Ostrosky, M. M. (2011). Whose expertise? An analysis of advice giving in early childhood parent-teacher conferences. *Journal of Research in Childhood Education, 25*, 24–44. doi:10.1080/02568543.2011.533116

Chen, X.-L., Dai, X.-Y., & Dong, Q. (2008). A research of Aitken Procrastination Inventory applied to Chinese college students. *Chinese Journal of Clinical Psychology, 16*, 22–23.

Cheng, R. W., & Lam, S. (2007). Self-construal and social comparison effects. *British Journal of Educational Psychology, 77*, 197–211.

Cho, H.-C., & Abe, S. (2013). Is two-tailed testing for directional research hypotheses tests legitimate? *Journal of Business Research, 66*, 1261–1266. doi:10.1016/j.jbusres.2012.02.023

Cohen, B. H. (2002). Calculating a factorial ANOVA from means and standard deviations. *Understanding Statistics, 1*, 191–203.

Cohen, J. (1988). *Statistical power analysis for the behavioral sciences.* Hillsdale, NJ: Erlbaum.

Collins, M. W., & Morris, S. B. (2008). Testing for adverse impact when sample size is small. *Journal of Applied Psychology, 93*, 463–471.

Cozolino, L. (2014). *The neuroscience of human relationships: Attachment and the developing social brain* (2nd ed.). New York, NY: Norton.

Cribbie, R. A., Fiksenbaum, L., Keselman, H. J., & Wilcox, R. R. (2012). Effect of non-normality on test statistics for one-way independent groups designs. *British Journal of Mathematical and Statistical Psychology, 65*, 56–73. doi:10.1111/j.2044-8317.2011.02014.x

Crosnoe, R., Benner, A. D., & Davis-Kean, P. (2016). *Preschool enrollment, classroom instruction, elementary school context, and the reading achievement of children from low-income families.* Bingley, UK: Emerald Group. doi:10.1108/S1479-353920150000019003

Cuijpers, P., Cristea, I. A., Weitz, E., Gentili, C., & Berking, M. (2016). The effects of cognitive and behavioural therapies for anxiety disorders on depression: A meta-analysis. *Psychological Medicine, 46*(16), 3451–3462. doi:10.1017/S0033291716002348

Dai, X., Wertenbroch, K., & Brendl, C. M. (2008). The value heuristic in judgments of relative frequency. *Psychological Science, 19*, 18–19.

Danitz, S. B., Suvak, M. K., & Orsillo, S. M. (2016). The mindful way through the semester: Evaluating the impact of integrating an acceptance-based behavioral program into a first-year experience course for undergraduates. *Behavioral Therapy, 47*, 487–499. doi:10.1016/j.beth.2016.03.002

Davis, R. E., & Loprinzi, P. D. (2016). Examination of accelerometer reactivity among a population sample of children, adolescents, and adults. *Journal of Physical Activity & Health, 13*(12), 1325–1332.

De Moivre, A. (1733, November 12). *Approximatio ad summam terminorum binomii $(a+b)^n$ in seriem expansi.* Self-published pamphlet, 7 pages.

DeTienne, K. B., Agle, B. R., Phillips, J. C., & Ingerson, M.-C. (2012). The impact of moral stress compared to other stressors on employee fatigue, job satisfaction, and turnover: An empirical investigation. *Journal of Business Ethics, 110*, 377–391. doi:10.1007/s10551-011-1197-y

DeVoe, S. E., & House, J. (2012). Time, money, and happiness: How does putting a price on time affect our ability to smell the roses? *Journal of Experimental Social Psychology, 48*, 466–474. doi:10.1016/j.jesp.2011.11.012

Di Lorenzo, P. M., & Youngentob, S. L. (2013). Taste and olfaction. In R. J. Nelson, S. J. Y. Mizumori, & I. B. Weiner (Eds.), *Handbook of psychology: Behavioral neuroscience* (Vol. 3, 2nd ed., pp. 272–305). New York, NY: Wiley.

Diemand-Yauman, C., Oppenheimer, D. M., & Vaughan, E. B. (2011). Fortune favors the bold (and the italicized): Effects of disfluency on educational outcomes. *Cognition, 118*, 114–118. doi:10.1016/j.cognition.2010.09.012

Doherty, A. M., & Kelly, B. D. (2010). Social and psychological correlates of happiness in 17 European countries. *Irish Journal of Psychological Medicine, 27*, 130–134.

Drakou, A., Kambitsis, C., Charachousou, Y., & Tzetzis, G. (2006). Exploring life satisfaction of sport coaches in Greece. *European Sport Management Quarterly, 6*, 239–252.

Dubovsky, S. L., Antonius, D., Ellis, D. G., Ceusters, W., Sugarman, R. C., Roberts, R., & . . . Braen, G. R. (2017). A preliminary study of a novel emergency department nursing triage simulation for research applications. *BMC Research Notes, 10*, 1–12. doi:10.1186/s13104-016-2337-3

Dyke, K. R. (2014). Academic achievement of elementary students: A comparison study of student athletes versus nonathletes. *Dissertation Abstracts International, 74*(9-A)(E).

Educational Testing Service. (2017). *Concordance tables: Verbal reasoning and quantitative reasoning*. Retrieved from http://www.ets.org/s/gre/pdf/concordance_information.pdf

El-Sheikh, M., Arsiwalla, D. D., Staton, L., Dyer, J., & Vaughn, B. E. (2013). Associations between preschoolers' daytime and nighttime sleep patterns. *Behavioral Sleep Medicine, 11*, 91–104. doi:10.1080/15402002.2011.625460

Elias, S. M. (2007). Influence in the ivory tower: Examining the appropriate use of social power in the university classroom. *Journal of Applied Social Psychology, 37*, 2532–2548.

Elshout, R., Scherp, E., & van der Feltz-Cornelis, C. M. (2013). Understanding the link between leadership style, employee satisfaction, and absenteeism: A mixed methods design study in a mental health care institution.

Neuropsychiatric Disease and Treatment, 9, 823–837. doi:10.2147/NDT.S43755

Eskesen, S. T., Eskesen, F. N., & Ruvinsky, A. (2004). Natural selection affects frequencies of AG and GT dinucleotides at the 5¢ and 3¢ ends of exons. *Genetics, 167*, 543–550.

Faber, R. J., & Vohs, K. D. (2011). Self-regulation and spending: Evidence from impulsive and compulsive buying. In K. D. Vohs & R. F. Baumeister (Eds.), *Handbook of self-regulation: Research, theory, and applications* (pp. 537–550). New York, NY: Guilford Press.

Faith, M. A., Fiala, S. E., Cavell, T. A., & Hughes, J. N. (2011). Mentoring highly aggressive children: Pre-post changes in mentors' attitudes, personality, and attachment tendencies. *Journal of Primary Prevention, 32*, 253–270. doi:10.1007/s10935-011-0254-8

Farrelly, M. C., Duke, J. C., Davis, K. C., Nonnemaker, J. M., Kamyab, K., Willett, J. G., & Juster, H. R. (2012). Promotion of smoking cessation with emotional and/or graphic antismoking advertising. *American Journal of Preventative Medicine, 43*, 475–482. doi:10.1016/j.amepre.2012.07.023

Feist, G. J., Reiter-Palmon, R., & Kaufman, J. C. (2017). *The Cambridge handbook of creativity and personality research*. New York, NY: Cambridge University Press.

Fornell, C., Rust, R. T., & Dekimpe, M. G. (2010). The effect of customer satisfaction on consumer spending growth. *Journal of Marketing Research, 47*, 28–35. doi:10.1509/jmkr.47.1.28

Freitas, J. N. S., El-Hani, C. N., & da Rocha, P. L. B. (2008). Affiliation in four echimyid rodent species based on intrasexual dyadic encounters: Evolutionary implications. *Ethology, 114*, 389–397.

Furnham, A., Stumm, S., & Fenton-O'Creevy, M. (2015). Sex differences in money pathology in the general population. *Social Indicators Research, 123*(3), 701–711.

Garcia, J., Kimeldorf, D. J., & Koelling, R. A. (1955). A conditioned aversion

towards saccharin resulting from exposure to gamma radiation. *Science, 122*, 157–158.

Gelso, C. J., Nutt Williams, E., & Fretz, B. R. (2014). Beyond the individual: Group, couple, and family therapy. In C. J. Gelso, E. Nutt Williams, & B. R. Fretz (Eds.), *Counseling psychology* (3rd ed., pp. 447–493). Washington, DC: American Psychological Association. doi:10.1037/14378-016

Germanic, O. (2013). Leading the way: Young people cocreating a safe driving culture. In R. V. Roholt, M. Baizerman, & R. W. Hildreth (Eds.), *Civic youth work: Cocreating democratic youth spaces* (pp. 103–111). Chicago, IL: Lyceum Books.

Gibson, D. M., & Myers, J. E. (2006). Perceived stress, wellness, and mattering: A profile of first-year Citadel cadets. *Journal of College Student Development, 47*, 647–660.

Gilman, R., Huebner, E. S., Tian, L., Park, N., O'Byrne, J., Schiff, M., . . . Langknecht, H. (2008). Cross-national adolescent multidimensional life satisfaction reports: Analyses of mean scores and response style differences. *Journal of Youth Adolescents, 37*, 142–154.

Godsil, B. P., & Fanselow, M. S. (2013). Motivation. In A. F. Healy, R. W. Proctor, & I. B. Weiner (Eds.), *Handbook of psychology: Experimental psychology* (Vol. 4, 2nd ed., pp. 32–60). Hoboken, NJ: Wiley.

Goldberg, S. (2012). Psychology's contribution to military training. In J. H. Laurence & M. D. Matthews (Eds.), *The Oxford handbook of military psychology* (pp. 241–261). New York, NY: Oxford University Press.

Good, P. I., & Hardin, J. W. (2003). *Common errors in statistics (and how to avoid them)*. New York, NY: Wiley.

Grafström, A., & Schelin, L. (2014). How to select representative samples. *Scandinavian Journal of Statistics, 41*, 277–290. doi:10.1111/sjos.12016

Gulledge, A. K., Stahmann, R. F., & Wilson, C. M. (2004). Seven types of nonsexual romantic physical affection among Brigham Young University students. *Psychological Reports, 95*, 609–614.

Guo, X., & Slesnick, N. (2013). Family versus individual therapy: Impact on discrepancies between parents' and adolescents' perceptions over time. *Journal of Marital and Family Therapy, 39*, 182–194. doi:10.1111/j.1752-0606.2012.00301.x

Hafer, R. W. (2017). New estimates on the relationship between IQ, economic growth and welfare. *Intelligence, 61*, 92–101. doi:10.1016/j.intell.2017.01.009

Hahn, E. J. (2017). Lung cancer worry and home screening for radon and secondhand smoke in renters. *Journal of Environmental Health, 79*(6), 8–13.

Hammen, C., & Keenan-Miller, D. (2013). Mood disorders. In G. Stricker, T. A. Widiger, & I. B. Irving (Eds.), *Handbook of psychology: Clinical psychology* (Vol. 8, 2nd ed., pp. 121–146). Hoboken, NJ: Wiley.

Hans, E., & Hiller, W. (2013). Effectiveness of and dropout from outpatient cognitive behavioral therapy for adult unipolar disorder: A meta-analysis of nonrandomized effectiveness studies. *Journal of Consulting and Clinical Psychology, 81*, 75–88. doi:10.1037/a0031080

Harrell, Z. A., & Jackson, B. (2008). Thinking fat and feeling blue: Eating behaviors, ruminative coping, and depressive symptoms in college women. *Sex Roles, 58*, 658–665.

Harrell, Z. A., & Karim, N. M. (2008). Is gender relevant only for problem alcohol behaviors? An examination of correlates of alcohol use among college students. *Addictive Behaviors, 33*, 359–365.

Hilari, K., & Northcott, S. (2006). Social support in people with chronic aphasia. *Aphasiology, 20*, 17–36.

Hoekstra, R., Johnson, A., & Kiers, H. A. (2012). Confidence intervals make a difference: Effects of showing confidence intervals on inferential reasoning. *Educational and Psychological Measurement, 72*, 1039–1052. doi:10.1177/0013164412450297

Hoenig, J. M., & Heisey, D. M. (2001). The abuse of power: The pervasive fallacy of power calculations in data analysis. *The American Statistician, 55*, 19–24.

Hollands, J. G., & Spence, I. (1992). Judgments of change and proportion in graphical perception. *Human Factors, 34*, 313–334.

Hollands, J. G., & Spence, I. (1998). Judging proportions with graphs: The summation model. *Applied Cognitive Psychology, 12*, 173–190.

Holmes, V. M., Malone, A. M., & Redenbach, H. (2008). Orthographic processing and visual sequential memory in unexpectedly poor spellers. *Journal of Research in Reading, 31*, 136–156.

Huttunen-Lenz, M., Song, F., & Poland, F. (2010). Are psychoeducational smoking cessation interventions for coronary heart disease patients effective? Meta-analysis of interventions. *British Journal of Health Psychology, 15*, 749–777. doi:10.1348/135910709X480436

Institute of Medicine (IOM). (2015). *Public health implications of raising the minimum age of legal access to tobacco products.* Washington, DC: National Academies Press.

Jamieson, P. E., & Romer, D. (2008). Unrealistic fatalism in U.S. youth ages 14 to 22: Prevalence and characteristics. *Journal of Adolescent Health, 42*, 154–160.

Jirout, J., & Klahr, D. (2012). Children's scientific curiosity: In search of an operational definition of an elusive concept. *Developmental Review, 32*, 125–160. doi:10.1016/j.dr.2012.04.002

Johnston, C. A., Tyler, C., Stansberry, S. A., Moreno, J. P., & Foreyt, J. P. (2012). Brief report: Gum chewing affects standardized math scores in adolescents. *Journal of Adolescence, 35*, 455–459. doi:10.1016/j.adolescence.2011.04.003

Jones, N., Blackey, H., Fitzgibbon, K., & Chew, E. (2010). Get out of MySpace! *Computers & Education, 54*, 776–782.

Kaiser, H. F. (1960). Directional statistical decisions. *Psychological Review, 67*, 160–167.

Katz-Navon, T., Unger-Aviram, E., & Block, C. (2016). Examining the cross-level influence of dispositional and team goal orientations on employee self-regulation and performance in a complex task environment. *Journal of Applied Behavioral Science, 52*, 396–421. doi:10.1177/0021886316665460

Kent, S. C., Wanzek, J., & Al Otaiba, S. (2012). Print reading in general education kindergarten classrooms: What does it look like for students at-risk for reading difficulties? *Learning Disabilities Research & Practice, 27*, 56–65. doi:10.1111/j.1540-5826.2012.00351.x

Keskinoglu, P., Ucuncu, T., Yildirim, I., Gurbuz, T., Ur, I., & Ergor, G. (2007). Gender discrimination in the elderly and its impact on the elderly health. *Archives of Gerontology and Geriatrics, 45*, 295–306.

Kiernan, R. J., Mueller, J., & Langston, J. W. (1987). *Neurobehavioral Cognitive Status Examination (Cognistat).* Fairfax, CA: Northern California Neurobehavioral Group.

Kirkpatrick, K., & Hall, G. (2005). Learning and memory. In J. J. Bolhuis, L. Giraldeau, J. J. Bolhuis, & L. Giraldeau (Eds.), *The behavior of animals: Mechanisms, function, and evolution* (pp. 146–169). Malden, MA: Blackwell.

Kivlighan, D. I., & Kivlighan, D. J. (2016). Treatment modalities: Comparing treatment outcomes and therapeutic processes in individual, family, and group counseling and psychotherapy. In S. Maltzman & S. Maltzman (Eds.), *The Oxford handbook of treatment processes and outcomes in psychology: A multidisciplinary, biopsychosocial approach* (pp. 498–514). New York, NY: Oxford University Press.

Kleisen, L. M. B. (2013). A positive view on road safety: Can "car karma" contribute to safe driving styles? *Accident Analysis and Prevention, 50*, 705–712. doi:10.1016/j.aap.2012.06.022

Knaster, P., Estlander A.-M., Karlsson, H., Kaprio, J., & Kalso, E (2016). Diagnosing depression in chronic pain patients: *DSM-IV* major depressive disorder vs. Beck

Depression Inventory (BDI). *PLoS ONE, 11*(3), e0151982. doi:10.1371/journal. pone.0151982

Knechtle, B., Rüst, C. A., Rosemann, T., Knechtle, P., & Bescos, R. (2012). Estimation bias: Body mass index and body height in endurance athletes. *Perceptual & Motor Skills: Physical Development & Measurement, 115*, 833–844. doi:11.2466/03.27.PMS.115 .6.833-844

Kohn, N., Kellermann, T., Gur, R. C., Schneider, F., & Habel, U. (2011). Gender differences in the neural correlates of humor processing: Implications for different processing modes. *Neuropsychologia, 49*, 888–897. doi:10.1016/ j.neuropsychologia.2011.02.010

Krans, E. E., Davis, M. M., & Palladino, C. L. (2013). Disparate patterns of prenatal care utilization stratified by medical and psychosocial risk. *Maternal and Child Health Journal, 17*, 639–645. doi:10.1007/ s10995-012-1040-9

Kreinovich, V., & Servin, C. (2015). How to test hypotheses when exact values are replaced by intervals to protect privacy: Case of *t*-tests. *International Journal of Intelligent Technologies & Applied Statistics, 8*, 93–102. doi:10.6148/ IJITAS.2015.0802.01

Kruger, J., & Savitsky, K. (2006). *The persuasiveness of one- vs. two-tailed tests of significance: When weak results are preferred over strong* [Abstract]. Retrieved from http:// ssrn.com/abstract=946199

Kylesten, B. (2013). Dynamic decision-making on an operational level: A model including preconditions and working method. *Cognition, Technology & Work, 15*, 197–205. doi:10.1007/s10111-012-0221-z

Lambdin, C. (2012). Significance tests as sorcery: Science is empirical—significance tests are not. *Theory & Psychology, 22*, 67–90. doi:10.1177/0959354311429854

Laming, D. (2006). Predicting free recalls. *Journal of Experimental Psychology: Learning, Memory, and Cognition, 32*, 1146–1163.

Landry, V. L. (2015). How should very large Likert datasets be analyzed?

The International Journal of Sciences and Humanities Invention, 2, 1327–1349.

Lantz, B. (2013). The impact of sample non-normality on ANOVA and alternative methods. *British Journal of Mathematical and Statistical Psychology, 66*, 224–244. doi:10.1111/j.2044-8317.2012.02047.x

Lattal, K. A., St. Peter, C., & Escobar, R. (2013). Operant extinction: Elimination and generation of behavior. In G. J. Madden, W. V. Dube, T. D. Hackenberg, G. P. Hanley, K. A. Lattal, G. J. Madden, . . . K. A. Lattal (Eds.), *APA handbook of behavior analysis* (Vol. 2, pp. 77–107). Washington, DC: American Psychological Association. doi:10.1037/13938-004

Lau, W. W. F. (2017). Effects of social media usage and social media multitasking on the academic performance of university students. *Computers and Human Behavior, 68*, 286–291. doi:10.1016/ j.chb.2016.11.043

Leary, T. G., Green, R., Denson, K., Schoenfeld, G., Henley, T., & Langford, H. (2013). The relationship among dysfunctional leadership dispositions, employee engagement, job satisfaction, and burnout. *The Psychologist-Manager Journal, 16*, 112–130. doi:10.1037/ h0094961

Lee, S., Cappella, J. N., Lerman, C., & Strasser, A. A. (2013). Effects of smoking cues and argument strength of antismoking advertisements on former smokers' self-efficacy, attitude, and intention to refrain from smoking. *Nicotine & Tobacco Research, 15*, 527–533. doi:10.1093/ntr/nts171

Levitt, J. T., Malta, L. S., Martin, A., Davis, L., & Cloitre, M. (2007). The flexible applications of a manualized treatment for PTSD symptoms and functional impairment related to the 9/11 World Trade Center attack. *Behaviour Research and Therapy, 45*, 1419–1433.

Lienemann, B. A., & Stopp, H. T. (2013). The association between media exposure of interracial relationships and attitudes toward interracial

relationships. *Journal of Applied Social Psychology, 43*, E398–E415. doi:10.1111/jasp.12037

Lin, H. J., & Yusoff, M. S. B. (2013). Psychological distress, sources of stress and coping strategy in high school students. *International Medical Journal, 20*, 672–676.

Lo, J. C., Dijk, D.-J., & Groger, J. A. (2014). Comparing the effects of nocturnal sleep and daytime napping on declarative memory consolidation. *PLOS One, 9*, e108100. doi:10.1371/journal. pone.0108100

Lopez, M. N., Pierce, R. S., Gardner, R. D., & Hanson, R. W. (2013). Standardized Beck Depression Inventory–II scores for male veterans coping with chronic pain. *Psychological Services, 10*, 257–263. doi:10.1037/a0027920

Love, K. G., Vinson, J., Tolsma, J., & Kaufmann, G. (2008). Symptoms of undercover police officers: A comparison of officers currently, formerly, and without undercover experience. *International Journal of Stress Management, 15*, 136–152.

Machulda, M. M., Hagen, C. E., Wiste, H. J., Mielke, M. M., Knopman, D. S., Roberts, R. O., . . . Petersen, R. C. (2017). Practice effects and longitudinal cognitive change in clinically normal older adults differ by Alzheimer imaging biomarker status. *The Clinical Neuropsychologist, 31*, 99–117. doi:10.1080/13854046.2016.12 41303

Marjanovic, Z., Holden, R. R., Struthers, W., Cribbie, R. A., & Greenglass, E. (2014). The inter-item standard deviation (ISD): An index that discriminates between conscientious and random responders. *Personality and Individual Differences*. Retrieved from https://www.researchgate.net/ publication/277026085

Marjanovic, Z., Struthers, C. W., Cribbie, R. A., & Greenglass, E. R. (2014). The conscientious responders scale: A new tool for discriminating between conscientious and random responders. *SAGE Open, 4*, 1–10. doi:10.1177/2158 244014545964

Martins, S., Paiva, J. A., Simões, M. R., & Fernandes, L. (2017). Delirium in elderly patients: Association with educational attainment. *Acta Neuropsychiatrica, 29,* 95–101. doi:10.1017/neu.2016.40

Matthews, E. M., & Wagner, D. R. (2008). Prevalence of overweight and obesity in collegiate American football players, by position. *Journal of American College Health, 57,* 33–37. doi:10.3200/JACH.57.1.33-38

McCroskey, J. (2007). *Introversion scale.* Retrieved from http://www.jamescmccroskey.com/measures/introversion.htm

McNeil, J. A., & Morgan, C. A., III (2010). Cognition and decision making in extreme environments. In C. H. Kennedy & J. L. Moore (Eds.), *Military neuropsychology* (pp. 361–382). New York, NY: Springer.

Mediakix. (2016). *How much time do we spend on social media?* Retrieved from http://mediakix.com/2016/12/how-much-time-is-spent-on-social-media-lifetime/#gs.pjnonr4

Mennella, J. A., & Bobowski, N. K. (2015). The sweetness and bitterness of childhood: Insights from basic research on taste preferences. *Physiology & Behavior, 152*(Part B), 502–507. doi:10.1016/j.physbeh.2015.05.015

Mickes, L., Walker, D. E., Parris, J. L., Mankoff, R., & Christenfeld, N. J. S. (2012). Who's funny: Gender stereotypes, humor prediction, and memory bias. *Psychonomic Bulletin & Review, 19,* 108–112. doi:10.3758/s13423-011-0161-2

Möller, J., & Marsh, H. W. (2013). Dimensional comparison theory. *Psychological Review, 120,* 544–560. doi:10.1037/a0032459

Montoya, R. M. (2007). Gender similarities and differences in preferences for specific body parts. *Current Research in Social Psychology, 13,* 133–144.

Morrell, K. (2016). Understanding and measuring employee turnover. In G. Saridakis & C. L. Cooper (Eds.), *Research handbook on employee turnover* (pp. 26–58). Northampton, MA: Edward Elgar.

Mosing, M. A., Medland, S. E., McRae, A., Landers, J. G., Wright, M. J., & Martin, N. G. (2012). Genetic influences on lifespan and its relationship to personality: A 16-year follow-up study of a sample of aging twins. *Psychosomatic Medicine, 74,* 16–22. doi:10.1097/PSY.0b013e3182385784

Mullen, J., Kelloway, E. K., & Teed, M. (2017). Employer safety obligations, transformational leadership and their interactive effects on employee safety performance. *Safety Science, 91,* 405–412. doi:10.1016/j.ssci.2016.09.007

Naglieri, J. A. (2015). Hundred years of intelligence testing: Moving from traditional IQ to second-generation intelligence tests. In S. Goldstein, D. Princiotta, & J. A. Naglieri (Eds.), *Handbook of intelligence: Evolutionary theory, historical perspective, and current concepts* (pp. 295–316). New York, NY: Springer Science + Business Media. doi:10.1007/978-1-4939-1562-0_20

Netemeyer, R. G., Heilman, C. M., & Maxham, J. G., III. (2012). Identification with the retail organization and customer-perceived employee similarity: Effects on customer spending. *Journal of Applied Psychology, 97,* 1049–1058. doi:10.1037/a0028792

Neupane, S., & Doku, D. T. (2012). Determinants of time of start of prenatal care and number of prenatal care visits during pregnancy among Nepalese women. *Journal of Community Health, 37,* 865–873. doi:10.1007/s10900-011-9521-0

Nevill, A. M., Winter, E. M., Ingham, S., Watts, A., Metsios, G. S., & Stewart, A. D. (2010). Adjusting athletes' body mass index to better reflect adiposity in epidemiological research. *Journal of Sports Sciences, 28,* 1009–1016. doi:10.1080/02640414.2010.487071

Nobre, P. J., & Pinto-Gouveia, J. (2008). Cognitions, emotions, and sexual response: Analysis of the relationship among automatic thoughts, emotional responses, and sexual arousal. *Archives of Sexual Behavior, 37,* 652–661.

Olesen, S. C., Butterworth, P., Leach, L. S., Kelaher, M., & Pirkis, J. (2013). Mental health affects future employment as job loss affects mental health: Findings from a longitudinal study. *BMC Psychiatry, 13,* 144. doi:10.1186/1471-244X-13-144

Oosterveer, D. M., Mishre, R. R., van Oort, A., Bodde, K., & Aerden, L. M. (2017). Depression is an independent determinant of life satisfaction early after stroke. *Journal of Rehabilitation Medicine, 49,* 223–227. doi:10.2340/16501977-2199

Orathinkal, J., Vansteenwegen, A., & Burggraeve, R. (2008). Forgiveness: A perception and motivation study among married adults. *Scandinavian Journal of Psychology, 49,* 155–160.

O'Sullivan, M. (2007). Unicorns or Tiger Woods: Are lie detection experts myths or rarities? A response to *On Lie Detection "Wizards"* by Bond and Uysal. *Law and Human Behavior, 31,* 117–123.

Ottenbacher, K. J. (1993). The interpretation of averages in health professions research. *Evaluation & the Health Professions, 16,* 333–341.

Otterbring, T. (2016). Touch forbidden, consumption allowed: Counter-intuitive effects of touch restrictions on customers' purchase behavior. *Food Quality and Preference, 50,* 1–506. doi:10.1016/j.foodqual.2015.12.011

Özdemir, A. F. (2013). Comparing two independent groups: A test based on a one-step *M*-estimator and bootstrap-*t. British Journal of Mathematical and Statistical Psychology, 66,* 322–337. doi:10.1111/j.2044-8317.2012.02053.x

Palesh, O., Butler, L. D., Koopman, C., Giese-Davis, J., Carlson, R., & Spiegel, D. (2007). Stress history and breast cancer recurrence. *Journal of Psychosomatic Research, 63,* 233–239.

Pastizzo, M. J., & Carbone, R. F., Jr. (2007). Spoken word frequency counts based on 1.6 million words in American English. *Behavior Research Methods, 39*, 1025–1028.

Patten, C. A., Brockman, T. A., Ames, S. C., Ebbert, J. O., Stevens, S. R., Thomas, J. L., . . . Carlson, J. M. (2008). Differences among Black and White young adults on prior attempts and motivation to help a smoker quit. *Addictive Behaviors, 33*, 496–502.

Pearson, K. (1924). Historical note on the origin of the normal curve of errors. *Biometrika, 16*(3–4), 402–404. doi:10.1093/biomet/16.3-4.402

Peng, C. J., & Chen, L. (2014). Beyond Cohen's *d*: Alternative effect size measures for between-subject designs. *Journal of Experimental Education, 82*, 22–50. doi:10.1080/00220973.2012.745471

Pérez Escoda, N., & Alegre, A. (2016). Does emotional intelligence moderate the relationship between satisfaction in specific domains and life satisfaction? *International Journal of Psychology & Psychological Therapy, 16*(2), 131–140.

Phillips, L., Norris, S., Hayward, D., & Lovell, M. (2017). Unique contributions of maternal reading proficiency to predicting children's preschool receptive vocabulary and reading proficiency. *Early Childhood Education Journal, 45*, 111–119. doi:10.1007/s10643-014-0632-y

Piffer, D. (2012). Can creativity be measured? An attempt to clarify the notion of creativity and general directions for future research. *Thinking Skills and Creativity, 7*, 258–264. doi:10.1016/j.tsc.2012.04.009

Pisacreta, J., Tincani, M., Connell, J. E., & Axelrod, S. (2011). Increasing teachers' use of a 1:1 praise-to-behavior correction ratio to decrease student disruption in general education classrooms. *Behavioral Interventions, 26*, 243–260. doi:10.1002/bin.341

Pope, D. (2010). Decibel levels and noise generators on four medical/surgical nursing units. *Journal of Clinical Nursing, 19*, 2463–2470. doi:10.1111/j.1365-2702.2010.03263.x

Poulin, F., Nadeau, K., & Scaramella, L. V. (2012). The role of parents in young adolescents' competence with peers: An observational study of advice giving and intrusiveness. *Merrill-Palmer Quarterly, 58*, 437–462.

Price, J., McElroy, K., & Martin, N. J. (2016). The role of font size and font style in younger and older adults' predicted and actual recall performance. *Aging, Neuropsychology, and Cognition, 23*, 366–388.

Privitera, G. J. (2016). Health psychology. In C. McCarthy, M. DeLisi, A. Getzfeld, G. J. Privitera, C. Spence, J. Walker, . . . C. Youssef (Eds.), *Introduction to applied behavioral science* (pp. 32–54). San Diego, CA: Bridgepoint Education.

Privitera, G. J. (2017). *Research methods for the behavioral sciences* (2nd ed.). Thousand Oaks, CA: Sage.

Privitera, G. J. (2018). *Statistics for the behavioral science*s (3rd ed.). Thousand Oaks, CA: Sage.

Privitera, G. J., Antonelli, D. E., & Creary, H. E. (2013). The effect of food images on mood and arousal depends on dietary histories and the fat and sugar content of foods depicted. *Journal of Behavioral and Brain Science, 3*, 1–6. doi:10.4236/jbbs.2013.31001

Privitera, G. J., Cooper, K. C., & Cosco, A. R. (2012). The influence of eating rate on satiety and intake among participants exhibiting high dietary restraint. *Food & Nutrition Research, 56*, 10202. doi:10.3402/fnr.v56i0.10202

Privitera, G. J., Diaz, M., & Haas, M. C. (2014). Enhanced auditory arousal increases intake of less palatable and healthier foods. *Global Journal of Health Science, 6*, 1–8. doi:10.5539/gjhs.v6n3p1

Privitera, G. J., & Freeman, C. S. (2012). Validity and reliability of an estimated daily intake scale for fat. *Global Journal of Health Science, 4*, 36–41. doi:10.5539/gjhs.v4n2p36

Privitera, G. J., Mulcahey, C. P., & Orlowski, C. M. (2012). Human sensory preconditioning in a flavor preference paradigm. *Appetite, 59*,

414–418. doi:10.1016/j.appet.2012.06.005

Privitera, G. J., & Wallace, M. (2011). An assessment of liking for sugars using the estimated daily intake scale. *Appetite, 56*, 713–718. doi:10.1016/j.appet.2011.02.008

Privitera, G. J., & Zuraikat, F. M. (2014). Proximity of foods in a competitive food environment influences consumption of a low calorie and a high calorie food. *Appetite, 76*, 175–179. doi:10.1016/j.appet.2014.02.004

Reese, E. (2015). What good is a picturebook? Developing children's oral language and literacy through shared picturebook reading. In B. Kümmerling-Meibauer, J. Meibauer, K. Nachtigäller, K. J. Rohlfing, B. Kümmerling-Meibauer, J. Meibauer, . . . K. J. Rohlfing (Eds.), *Learning from picturebooks: Perspectives from child development and literacy studies* (pp. 194–208). New York, NY: Routledge/Taylor & Francis Group.

Rietveld, T., & van Hout, R. (2015). The *t* test and beyond: Recommendations for testing the central tendencies of two independent samples in research on speech, language and hearing pathology. *Journal of Communication Disorders, 58*, 158–168. doi:10.1016/j.jcomdis.2015.08.002

Rochon, J., & Kieser, M. (2011). A closer look at the effect of preliminary goodness-of-fit testing for normality for the one-sample *t*-test. *British Journal of Mathematical and Statistical Psychology, 64*, 410–426. doi:10.1348/0007-1102.002003

Rojas, N. L., Sherrit, L., Harris, S., & Knight, J. R. (2008). The role of parental consent in adolescent substance use research. *Journal of Adolescent Health, 42*, 192–197.

Rouder, J. N., Morey, R. D., Verhagen, J., Swagman, A. R., & Wagenmakers, E. (2016). Bayesian analysis of factorial designs. *Psychological Methods*. Advance online publication. doi:10.1037/met0000057

Ruxton, G. D., Wilkinson, D. M., & Neuhäuser, M. (2015). Advice on testing the null hypothesis that a sample is drawn from a normal distribution. *Animal Behaviour, 107*, 249–252. doi:10.1016/j.anbehav.2015.07.006

Ryan, R. S. (2006). Hands-on exercise improves understanding of the standard error of the mean. *Teaching of Psychology, 33*, 180–183.

Sanchez-Meca, J., & Marin-Martinez, F. (2008). Confidence intervals for the overall effect size in random-effects meta-analysis. *Psychological Methods, 13*, 31–48.

Sander, J. B., DeBoth, K., & Ollendick, T. H. (2016). Internalizing behaviors. In M. K. Holt & A. E. Grills (Eds.), *Critical issues in school-based mental health: Evidence-based research, practice, and interventions* (pp. 18–28). New York, NY: Routledge/Taylor & Francis Group.

Saridakis, G., & Cooper, C. L. (2016). *Research handbook on employee turnover.* Northampton, MA: Edward Elgar. doi:10.4337/978-1-78471-115-3

Schoenfeld, E. A., Bredow, C. A., & Huston, T. L. (2012). Do men and women show love differently in marriage? *Personality and Social Psychology Bulletin, 38*, 1396–1409. doi:10.1177/0146167212450739

Schredl, M., & Göritz, A. S. (2015). Changes in dream recall frequency, nightmare frequency, and lucid dream frequency over a 3-year period. *Dreaming, 25*, 81-87. doi:10.1037/a0039165

Schredl, M., Stumbrys, T., & Erlacher, D. (2016). Dream recall, nightmare frequency, and spirituality. *Dreaming, 26*(1), 1–9. doi:10.1037/drm0000015

Segovia, D. A., Strange, D., & Takarangi, M. T. (2017). Trauma memories on trial: Is cross-examination a safeguard against distorted analogue traumatic memories? *Memory, 25*, 95–106. doi:10.1080/09658211.2015.1126608

Serlin, R. C., & Harwell, M. R. (2004). More powerful tests of predictor subsets in regression analysis under nonnormality. *Psychological Methods, 9*, 492–509.

Silvers, V. L., & Kreiner, D. S. (1997). The effects of pre-existing inappropriate highlighting on reading comprehension. *Reading Research and Instruction, 36*, 217–223. doi:10.1080/19388079709558240

Sinacore, J. M., Chang, R. W., & Falconer, J. (1992). Seeing the forest despite the trees: The benefit of exploratory data analysis to program evaluation research. *Evaluation & the Health Professions, 15*, 131–146.

Son, J. T., & Lee, E. (2015). Effects of the amount of rice in meals on postprandial blood pressure in older people with postprandial hypotension: A within-subjects design. *Journal of Clinical Nursing, 24*, 2277–2285. doi:10.1111/jocn.12864

Sormanen, N., Lauk, E., & Uskali, T. (2017). Facebook's ad hoc groups: A potential source of communicative power of networked citizens. *Communication & Society, 30*(2), 77–95. doi:10.15581/003.30.2.77-95

Stevens, S. S. (1946). On the theory of scales of measurement. *Science, 103*, 677–680.

Stillman, T. F., Baumeister, R. F., & DeWall, C. N. (2007). What's so funny about not having money? The effects of power on laughter. *Personality and Social Psychology Bulletin, 33*, 1547–1558.

Student. (1908). The probable error of a mean. *Biometrika, 6*, 1–25.

Taber-Thomas, B. C., & Tranel, D. (2012). Social and moral functioning: A cognitive neuroscience perspective. In V. Anderson & M. H. Beauchamp (Eds.), *Developmental social neuroscience and childhood brain insult: Theory and practice* (pp. 65–90). New York, NY: Guilford Press.

Tekinarslan, E. (2008). Computer anxiety: A cross-cultural comparative study of Dutch and Turkish university students. *Computers in Human Behavior, 24*, 1572–1584.

Theorell-Haglöw, J., Berglund, L., Berne, C., & Lindberg, E. (2014). Both habitual short sleepers and long sleepers are at greater risk of obesity: A population-based 10-year follow-up in women. *Sleep Medicine, 15*, 1204–1211. doi:10.1016/j.sleep.2014.02.014

Thomas, D. R., & Zumbo, B. D. (2012). Difference scores from the point of view of reliability and repeated-measures ANOVA: In defense of difference scores for data analysis. *Educational and Psychological Measurement, 72*, 37–43. doi:10.1177/0013164411409929

Thompson, B. (2007). Effect sizes, confidence intervals, and confidence intervals for effect sizes. *Psychology in the Schools, 44*, 423–432.

Thorburn, S., & De Marco, M. (2010). Insurance-based discrimination during prenatal care, labor, and delivery: Perceptions of Oregon mothers. *Maternal and Child Health Journal, 14*, 875–885. doi:10.1007/s10995-009-0533-7

Thorndike, E. L. (1898). Animal intelligence: An experimental study of the associate processes in animals. *Psychological Review Monograph Supplement, 2*, 1–8.

Timperio, A., Crawford, D., Ball, K., & Salmon, J. (2017). Typologies of neighbourhood environments and children's physical activity, sedentary time and television viewing. *Health and Place, 43*, 121–127. doi:10.1016/j.healthplace.2016.10.004

Toll, S. W. M., Kroesbergen, E. H., & Van Luit, J. E. H. (2016). Visual working memory and number sense: Testing the double deficit hypothesis in mathematics. *British Journal of Educational Psychology, 86*, 429–445. doi:10.1111/bjep.12116

Tucha, L., & Simpson, W. (2011). The role of time on task performance in modifying the effects of gum chewing on attention. *Appetite, 56*, 299–301. doi:10.1016/j.appet.2010.12.021

Tung, F.-W., & Deng, Y.-S. (2007). Increasing social presence of social actors in e-learning environments: Effects of dynamic and static emoticons on children. *Displays, 28*, 174–180.

Tunney, R. J. (2006). Preference reversals are diminished when gambles are presented as relative frequencies. *Quarterly Journal of Experimental Psychology, 59,* 1516–1523.

Turner, S., & Dabney, A. R. (2015). A story-based simulation for teaching sampling distributions. *Teaching Statistics Trust, 37*(1), 23–25.

van der Velden, P. G., van Loon, P., Benight, C. C., & Eckhardt, T. (2012). Mental health problems among search and rescue workers deployed in the Haïti earthquake 2010: A pre-post comparison. *Psychiatric Research, 198,* 100–105. doi:10.1016/j.psychres.2012.02.017

van Rossum, M., van de Schoot, R., & Hoijtink, H. (2013). "Is the hypothesis correct" or "Is it not": Bayesian evaluation of one information hypothesis for ANOVA. *Methodology, 9,* 13–22. doi:10.1027/1614-2241/a000050

Vejrup, K., Lien, N., Klepp, K.-I., & Bere, E. (2008). Consumption of vegetables at dinner in a cohort of Norwegian adolescents. *Appetite, 51,* 90–96.

Volker, M. A. (2006). Reporting effect size estimates in school psychology research. *Psychology in the Schools, 43,* 653–672.

Wagner, L. G. (2013). College students' attention behaviors during independent study and course level academic performance. *Dissertation Abstracts International Section A: Humanities and Social Sciences, 73,* 12(E).

Wainwright, P. E., Leatherdale, S. T., & Dublin, J. A. (2007). Advantages of mixed models over traditional ANOVA models in developmental studies: A worked example in a mouse model of fetal alcohol syndrome. *Developmental Psychobiology, 49,* 664–674.

Wall Emerson, R. (2017). ANOVA and *t* tests. *Journal of Visual Impairment & Blindness, 111*(2), 193–196.

Weiten, W., Halpern, D. F., & Bernstein, D. A. (2012). A textbook case of textbook ethics. In E. R. Landrum & M. A. McCarthy (Eds.), *Teaching ethically: Challenges and opportunities* (pp. 43–54). Washington, DC: American Psychological Association.

White, S., Chen, J., & Forsyth, B. (2010). Reading-related literacy activities of American adults: Time spent, task types, and cognitive skills used. *Journal of Literacy Research, 42,* 276–307. doi:10.1080/1086296X.2010.503552

Wilens, T. E., Biederman, J., Adamson, J. J., Henin, A., Sgambati, S., Gignac, M., . . . Monteaux, M. C. (2008). Further evidence of an association between adolescent bipolar disorder with smoking and substance abuse disorders: A controlled study. *Drug and Alcohol Dependence, 95,* 188–198.

Wilfley, D. E., Crow, S. J., Hudson, J. I., Mitchell, J. E., Berkowitz, R. I., Blakesley, V., . . . Walsh, B. T. (2008). Efficacy of sibutramine for the treatment of binge-eating disorder: A randomized multicenter placebo-controlled double-blind study. *American Journal of Psychiatry, 165,* 51–58.

Williams, D. M., Dunsiger, S., Jennings, E. G., & Marcus, B. H. (2012). Does affective valence during and immediately following a 10-min walk predict concurrent and future physical activity? *Annals of Behavioral Medicine, 44,* 43–51. doi:10.1007/s12160-012-9362-9

Williams, E., Stewart-Knox, B., Helander, A., McConville, C., Bradbury, I., & Rowland, I. (2006). Associations between whole-blood serotonin and subjective mood in healthy male volunteers. *Biological Psychology, 71,* 171–174.

Wilson, M. A., Bennett, W., Jr., Gibson, S. G., & Alliger, G. M. (2012). *The handbook of work analysis: Methods, systems, applications, and science of work measurement in organizations.* New York, NY: Routledge/Taylor & Francis Group.

Witt, P. L., & Schrodt, P. (2006). The influence of instructional technology use and teacher immediacy on student affect for teacher and course. *Communication Reports, 19,* 1–15.

Yang, C.-C., & Chiou, W.-B. (2010). Substitution of healthy for unhealthy beverages among college students: A health-concerns and behavioral-economics perspective. *Appetite, 54,* 512–516. doi:10.1016/j.appet.2010.02.004

Yang, Y., & Montgomery, D. (2013). Gaps or bridges in multicultural teacher education: A Q study of attitudes toward student diversity. *Teaching and Teacher Education, 30,* 27–37. doi:10.1016/j.tate.2012.10.003

Yen, C.-F., Lin, J.-D., & Chiu, T.-Y. (2013). Comparison of population pyramid and demographic characteristics between people with an intelligence disability and the general population. *Research in Developmental Disabilities, 34,* 910–915. doi:10.1016/j.ridd.2012.11.019

Yip, J. J., & Kelly, A. E. (2013). Upward and downward social comparisons can decrease prosocial behavior. *Journal of Applied Social Psychology, 43,* 591–602. doi:10.1111/j.1559-1816.2013.01039.x

Yu, T., Washington, P. M., & Kernie, S. G. (2016). Injury-induced neurogenesis: Mechanisms and relevance. *The Neuroscientist, 22,* 61–71. doi:10.1177/1073858414563616

Yuan, K., & Maxwell, S. (2005). On the post hoc power in testing mean differences. *Journal of Educational and Behavioral Statistics, 30,* 141–167.

Zimmerman, D. W. (2012). Correcting two-sample *z* and *t* tests for correlation: An alternative to one-sample tests on difference scores. *Psicológica, 33,* 391–418.

Zou, G. Y. (2007). Toward using confidence intervals to compare correlations. *Psychological Methods, 12,* 399–413.

Zwick, R., & Sklar, J. C. (2005). Predicting college grades and degree completion using high school grades and SAT scores: The role of student ethnicity and first language. *American Educational Research Journal, 42,* 439–464.

... Index

DECISION TREES

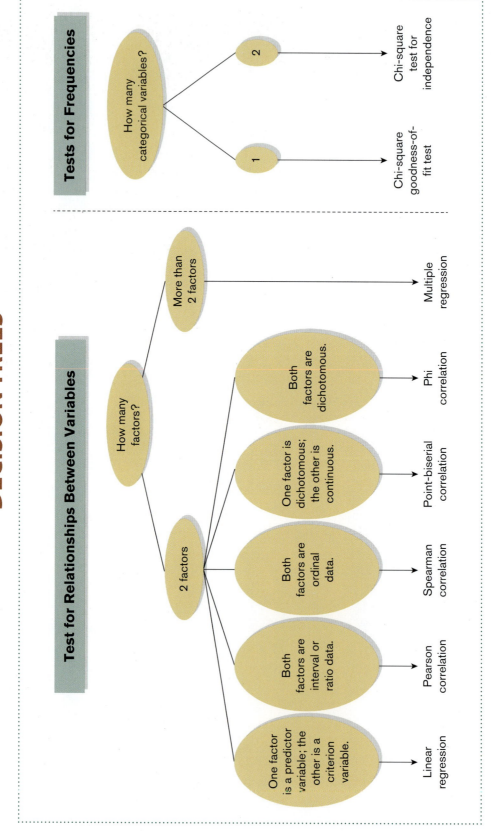

Tests for Frequencies

How many categorical variables?

1 → Chi-square goodness-of-fit test

2 → Chi-square test for independence

Test for Relationships Between Variables

How many factors?

More than 2 factors → Multiple regression

2 factors →

One factor is a predictor variable; the other is a criterion variable. → Linear regression

Both factors are interval or ratio data. → Pearson correlation

Both factors are ordinal data. → Spearman correlation

One factor is dichotomous; the other is continuous. → Point-biserial correlation

Both factors are dichotomous. → Phi correlation